Jesus and His Promised Second Coming

Jesus *and* His Promised Second Coming

Jewish Eschatology and Christian Origins

—

Tucker S. Ferda

William B. Eerdmans Publishing Company
Grand Rapids, Michigan

Wm. B. Eerdmans Publishing Co.
4035 Park East Court SE, Grand Rapids, Michigan 49546
www.eerdmans.com

Published 2024

Book design by Lydia Hall

Printed in the United States of America

30 29 28 27 26 25 24 1 2 3 4 5 6 7

ISBN 978-0-8028-7990-5

Library of Congress Cataloging-in-Publication Data

Names: Ferda, Tucker S., author.
Title: Jesus and his promised Second Coming : Jewish eschatology and Christian origins / Tucker S. Ferda.
Description: Grand Rapids, Michigan : William B. Eerdmans Publishing Company, 2024. | Includes bibliographical references and index. | Summary: "An examination and rebuttal of the critical consensus that Jesus of Nazareth did not predict or anticipate his post-death return"—Provided by publisher.
Identifiers: LCCN 2024002440 | ISBN 9780802879905 | ISBN 9781467463614 (epub)
Subjects: LCSH: Eschatology. | Eschatology, Jewish. | Christianity and other religions—Judaism. | Judaism—Relations—Christianity. | Bible—Criticism, interpretation, etc. | BISAC: RELIGION / Biblical Studies / New Testament / Jesus, the Gospels & Acts | RELIGION / Christian Theology / History
Classification: LCC BT821.3 .F45 2024 | DDC 232.9/06—dc23/eng/20240513
LC record available at https://lccn.loc.gov/2024002440

For David Hultberg

Behold, already it has eluded mortals to know everything from the days of old and the secret of the day of death and the secret of the day when King Messiah will come. Who will find out by one's wisdom?

—*Targum Qoheleth* 7:24

Contents

Foreword

Tucker Ferda's *Jesus and His Promised Second Coming* not only fills a huge hole in recent research on Jesus of Nazareth: it also contributes significantly to understanding the history of our discipline. Beyond those two key virtues, the book is impressively learned, well-written, carefully argued, and refreshingly independent in its judgments. It is a book with which to reckon.

Although the main question Ferda sets out to answer—How did the expectation of Jesus's future return emerge?—seems simple, it is not. For several centuries now, various answers have been offered. No less significantly, many scholars, even when writing about Jesus's eschatological expectations, have largely passed over the issue, paying it little heed. But Ferda, putting the topic front and center, shows just how prevalent and early the expectation was, and he forcefully argues that the best explanation is not that some Christ followers concocted it from the Jewish Scriptures or inferred it from belief in Jesus's resurrection, or that an influential prophet's ecstatic speech produced something brand new. Rather, the doctrine had its roots in Jesus's own speech, in his own eschatological scenario.

One of Ferda's signal contributions is to trace the larger cultural and theological contexts for what one might imagine to have been and to be a purely historical question. He does this by bringing to light a detailed, fascinating genealogy for the view that the so-called second coming derives not from Jesus but from post-Easter Christ followers. As it turns out, in this respect Hermann Samuel Reimarus (1694–1768), who in so much secondary literature is the point of origin for the critical study of Jesus, was a latecomer. He inherited from the deists the view that it was the disciples, not Jesus, who came up with the idea—so implausible to so many from the eighteenth century on—of a return on the clouds of heaven. Already before Reimarus was born, Charles Blount urged that, after Easter, the apostles reverted to the Jewish notion of a "temporal Messias," from which notion Jesus had distanced himself. This differentiation between what Jesus hoped for and the fallacious dreams of his followers is, Ferda demonstrates, rather common in deistic and Enlightenment literature. Among others, Anthony Collins, Thomas Woolston, Matthew Tindal, Thomas Morgan, Peter Annet, and Baron d'Holbach endorsed it or took it for granted.

In doing so, these thinkers betrayed not only their animus against the eschatological "enthusiasts" of their own day but exhibited their anti-Judaism, for they attributed the disciples' "odd" (Morgan), "vulgar" (Collins), and "grossly mistaken" (Tindal) expectations to their Jewish heritage, to (in Hegel's words) "the vain nationalistic hopes of the Jews." The same line of thought thereafter appears in Schleiermacher and Ferdinand C. Baur, whose impact upon nineteenth-century German theological scholars was immense; and Ferda has no problem drawing lines of connection between those two German luminaries and subsequent scholarship.

The upshot is that what so many take to be a sure historical-critical conclusion was born long ago of ideological assumptions, including a prejudice against Judaism—a prejudice that, as Ferda shows, stands in continuity with the old *Adversus Judaeos* literature and with Christian thinkers of various times who denigrated Jewish messianic expectations as "carnal," "earthly," "nationalistic," "worldly," and so on. He writes: "the attempt of medieval and early modern Christians to defend orthodoxy and connect the tradition of the church to the biblical witness ended up creating the very categories that later critics would use for the deconstruction of the same." Ferda further documents, in illuminating and convincing fashion, how opinions about the doctrine of the second coming have been, in recent centuries, and not just earlier times, leveraged to make statements about what Christian identity should and should not be.

All this, which offers much that will be new to everybody, is worth the price of the book. But there follow Ferda's own exegesis and provocative historical reconstruction, which are of equal value. Jesus, according to Ferda, identified himself with the "one like a son of man" in Daniel 7 and furthermore expected to suffer and die in the eschatological crisis and thereafter rise (not by himself but) at the general resurrection of the dead. If, then, he did not expect his death to coincide with the consummation, it follows that he almost certainly contemplated some sort of interim period, a space between his death and the end. "The expectation would be that, should Jesus perish in the great tribulation, he would, nonetheless, be revealed as the son of man in the near future at a specific time known only to God" (p. 339).

Ferda is not simply drawing an inference from the sources and imagining what Jesus might have thought. He rather directs our attention to materials—such as calls to watchfulness and several parables—that thematize the prospect of an interim, and he gives reasons for believing that they do not misrepresent Jesus. On his view, Jesus anticipated death, a brief period of absence, and a "return" after the general resurrection or even a "coming from heaven." With this result, Ferda is justified in contemplating, with due modesty, an almost wholly unexplored albeit fascinating topic—namely, how Jesus might have thought about himself during an interim period. Here his discussion helpfully calls attention to Jewish texts in which the righteous dead enter the heavenly realm at death as well as to traditions about certain well-known individuals, such as Moses and Elijah, who were thought of as being now in heaven but destined to return to earth. As a possible, partial parallel, Ferda observes that Paul could believe in the nearness of the end and yet, in 2 Corinthians and Philippians, still hope that, at death and before the general resurrection, he would find himself in heaven.

There is much more to be said, but Ferda should do the saying. It is enough for me to observe that this volume is a brilliant model of what the critical study of Jesus should involve—careful exegesis, methodological savvy, provocative suggestions, sober judgment, historical imagination, mastery of the secondary literature, plus knowledge of the history of the discipline and its place within larger cultural developments. *Jesus and His Promised Second Coming* is, without question, one of the best and most important books on Jesus in the last quarter century.

Dale C. Allison Jr.
Princeton Seminary

Preface

In the opening scene of the book of Acts, the disciples of Jesus stand on the Mount of Olives and watch Jesus disappear in a cloud. Two angels then interrupt their gazing: "Men of Galilee, why do you stand looking up toward heaven? This Jesus, who has been taken up from you into heaven, will come in the same way as you saw him go into heaven" (Acts 1:11). This artful composition by the Third Evangelist recalls Jesus's own teaching about his future coming in the Gospel of Luke at the same time that it gives meaning to the subsequent activity of the disciples in Acts before Jesus's return. On a literary level, it is clear for this text that the expectation for Jesus's second advent—to adopt the language of later tradition—stands both behind and before the disciples and makes intelligible the time in between.

How did this expectation for Jesus's future coming, for his second advent, emerge? That is the question at the heart of this book. As I will discuss in due course, the working assumption of most modern critical scholars has been that this expectation originated only after the death of Jesus as a product of early Christian theologizing. In other words, it was not something that Jesus himself had talked about but instead something that early Christians had made him talk about after the fact when they wrote the Gospels. What is unusual about this working assumption is that, despite the very crowded study of the New Testament and Christian origins, there have been few critical discussions the past sixty years of the emergence of the second-coming hope and how it might relate to teachings of Jesus. The default view of a later origin in the post-Easter period, then, has not been produced and sustained in recent years by robust discussion. During the past four decades, debates concerning the eschatological nature of Jesus's message about the kingdom have raged on, but those who have defended a modified version of Albert Schweitzer's eschatological Jesus have not done so by arguing that Jesus had indeed spoken of his own imminent coming. The common view has been, instead, that Jesus spoke about the imminent coming of the kingdom, and his early followers made the leap to include Jesus in that future coming as well.

In the following pages, I offer a counterargument. My argument remains within, and yet also modifies and hopefully clarifies, an eschatological portrait of Jesus defended by many others today. My contention is that the most plausible reconstruction we can offer is one in which the hope for Jesus's imminent coming stems from his own teaching before his death, and that when we get this right, it helps to resolve a number of other historical dilemmas in the study of Christian origins.

My study also contributes to recent discussion in ways that go beyond my specific reconstruction of Jesus. In part 2, I aim to deepen our understanding of the reception history of the Bible and the history of Christian anti-Judaism, specifically the origin and impact of the construction of "Jewish messianism" in Christian biblical exegesis. I will argue that the second-coming hope was already easily detached from Jesus by the time of the nineteenth-century quest because of the ways in which Christian exegetes and theologians had for centuries defined "Jewish messianism" and sought to distance Jesus from it. As I will show, this had happened in precritical exegetical and polemical literature "against the Jews," as well as other works, whose impact on early New Testament criticism has been overlooked in histories of scholarship. As my argument is informed by recent work on messianism and Second Temple Judaism since the discovery of the Dead Sea Scrolls, I hope that a more nuanced understanding of Second Temple Judaism on its own terms clears the way for a fresh reconstruction of the origin of the second-coming hope.

As I will further explain in part 1, I also take an approach to the task of historical reconstruction different from what has been typical in the earlier seminal works on this topic. I will work *backward* from the claims of the early Christians to Jesus (rather than forward from Jesus to the early church), and I will work *downward* from the broad to the detailed in terms of tradition (rather than start with the particulars and build up). A significant emphasis in my argument is that we must attend more carefully to how our sources understand the traditions that they contain (and/or invent) and what *claims* they make with these traditions, rather than focus at first on the authenticity of individual sayings (so an atomistic approach) or immediately group material thematically and synchronically (so an increasingly popular holistic approach that prioritizes recurrent attestation).

In sum, then, I hope to contribute to the discussion of the second-coming hope in three key ways: by providing a reception history of this expectation that exposes certain anti-Jewish tendencies in early biblical scholarship, by working backward (in terms of time) and downward (in terms of tradition), and by reconstructing Jesus in such a way that accounts for larger tendencies and assumptions in the early Christian movement. This also justifies the layout of the book and its progression from parts 1 to 4: critical evaluation of extant scholarship (part 1), reception history (part 2), reconstructing the claims of early Christians about Jesus (part 3), reconstructing Jesus (part 4). For organizational purposes, each of these parts is further divided into smaller chapters of varied lengths, with concluding thoughts at the end of each part. Given the size of the topic and the number of historical and interpretive questions involved, I do not provide much background material in this book about the history of the quest for the historical Jesus or even introductory matters about the Gospels and first-century Judaism. I am assuming that my readers have at least some general knowledge of Jesus research and New Testament studies.

As should be evident here, my interests in this book are historical in nature, and I have no intention of making any kind of theological statement about the second-coming hope for contemporary Christianity. While the nature of my discussion in the pages that follow should make such a disclaimer unnecessary, I did feel it was important to state my intentions clearly in fear of being misunderstood. Given the current state of the field, and due to the fraught reception history of this topic that I will explore in due course, it is hard to say anything about the second coming without being heard in a theological key. Moreover, others have expressed concern—and somewhat justifiably, given the history of Protestant biblical exegesis—that interest in origins is actually a rhetorical ploy to invest one's conclusions with theological power. While I have a hard time seeing how my conclusions about eschatology in Christian origins could be construed as theologically advantageous, I at least wanted to be open about my goals, and state upfront that my interest in Christian origins is historical and not theological in nature.

I have been working on this book on and off for seven years. It actually began with an exploratory article on the origin of the second-coming hope that I wrote before I defended my dissertation in 2016, presented portions of in various forums,[1] but never published. I was intrigued and somewhat perplexed by the ways

1. I presented "The Origin of the Second Advent Reconsidered" at the Annual Meeting of the Eastern Great Lakes Biblical Society (New Testament section) in Perrysville, OH, March 12, 2015, as well as "The Enlightenment, Deism, and the 'Painful Thorn' of the Parousia Expectation," at the Annual Meeting of the Society of Biblical Literature (History of Interpretation section), Atlanta, November 21, 2015. I am grateful to the participants in both of these sections for the lively discussion. I also appreciate feedback received from Dale Allison and Daniel Frayer-Griggs on both of these studies.

in which proponents of an eschatological Jesus had not really grappled—in my view—with what the prospect of Jesus's death had meant for his expectations about the future. I had also, in dissertation research, stumbled upon a number of nineteenth-century biographies of Jesus that argued that Jesus did, in fact, predict his future coming but only after he had been rejected (the so-called Galilean crisis, the subject of my first book). I found the entire topic intriguing, of clear historical importance, and oddly missing from recent discussion of the historical Jesus (the reasons for which further research would clarify). Since then, the project only continued to grow, if sometimes slowly in light of unexpected challenges. The book nearly halted during the first two years of the COVID-19 pandemic. Now I am grateful to be finished, but I also expect some sadness in letting go of something so compelling that would teach, challenge, and inspire me at every turn.

I owe a number of people my sincere thanks. I am grateful first for my students at Pittsburgh Theological Seminary who have shared with me their love of learning; for my wonderful colleagues who have sharpened my scholarship and broadened my horizons; for the leadership of our dean, Angela Dienhart Hancock, and president, Asa J. Lee, who have encouraged and supported my research; for my brilliant colleagues at Barbour Library (especially Mark Russell and Tisha Woo), who shared their expertise in numerous ways; for the Pittsburgh Seminary Board of Directors who approved a spring 2022 sabbatical leave during which I was able to finish this project; for my wise and careful research assistant, Brian Devereaux, and my friend Trent Hancock, who helped me with the indexes. My colleague Daniel Frayer-Griggs read the entire manuscript and offered invaluable feedback, and another good friend and colleague, Kenneth Woo, did the same for part 2. I am grateful for the entire Eerdmans team, especially Trevor Thompson and Laurel Draper, and for Justin Howell, who improved this book in more ways than can be named here.

Finally, I must thank my family: my daughters Lucy and Junia, whom I adore; my wife, Liberty, who is better than I deserve; and my extended family on both sides far away, who have taught me many things and been a constant source of encouragement. I dedicate this book to my father-in-law and friend, David Hultberg, who has modeled a life of simplicity, charity, and service.

Abbreviations

All abbreviations follow the *SBL Handbook of Style*, 2nd ed. At times, in the footnotes I include an original publication date for later translations and editions when such knowledge is important for the discussion at hand. Translations of primary and secondary sources are my own unless otherwise indicated.

1 Apol.	Justin, *First Apology*
1 Clem.	1 Clement
1 En.	1 Enoch
1Q33	M
1QH	Hodayot
1QM	Milḥamah
1QpHab	Pesher Habakkuk
1QS	Rule of the Community
1QS^b	Rule of the Blessings
2 Bar.	2 Baruch
2 Clem.	2 Clement
2 En.	2 Enoch
3 En.	3 Enoch
4Q161	pIsa^a
4Q171	pPs^a
4Q174	Florilegium
4Q215a	Time of Righteousness (*olim* part of TNaph)

4Q246	Apocryphon of Daniel
4Q252	Commentary on Genesis A
4Q285	Sefer ha-Milḥamah (*olim* Serekh ha-Milḥamah)
4Q379	apocrJosh[b] (*olim* Psalms of Joshua[b])
4Q401	ShirShabb[b]
4Q471b	Self-Glorification Hymn
4Q521	Messianic Apocalypse
4Q522	Prophecy of Joshua (apocrJosh[c]?) (*olim* Work with Place Names)
4Q530	EnGiants[b] ar
4Q558	papVision[b] ar
4QMMT[d]	Miqṣat Maʿaśê ha-Torah[d]
11Q13	Melchizedek
11Q19	Temple Scroll
AB	Anchor Bible
ABD	*Anchor Bible Dictionary*. Edited by David Noel Freedman. 6 vols. New York Doubleday, 1992
ʾAbot R. Nat.	ʾAbot de Rabbi Nathan
ABR	*Australian Biblical Review*
ABRL	Anchor Bible Reference Library
AcOr	*Acta Orientalia*
Adv. Jud.	Augustine, *Treatise against the Jews*
Ag. Ap.	Josephus, *Against Apion*
AGJU	Arbeiten zur Geschichte des antiken Judentums und des Urchristentums
An.	Tertullian, *The Soul*
ANF	*The Ante-Nicene Fathers: Translations of the Writings of the Fathers Down to A.D. 325*. Edited by Alexander Roberts and James Donaldson. 10 vols. 1885–1887. Repr., Peabody, MA: Hendrickson, 1994
ANRW	*Aufstieg und Niedergang der römischen Welt: Geschichte und Kultur Roms im Spiegel der neueren Forschung*. Part 2, *Principat*. Edited by Hildegard Temporini and Wolfgang Haase. Berlin: de Gruyter, 1972–
Ant.	Josephus, *Jewish Antiquities*
Antichr.	Hippolytus, *On the Antichrist*
ANTJ	Arbeiten zum Neuen Testament und Judentum
Apoc. Ab.	Apocalypse of Abraham
Apoc. Adam	Apocalypse of Adam
Apoc. Dan.	Apocalypse of Daniel
Apoc. El.	Apocalypse of Elijah
Apoc. El. (C)	Coptic Apocalypse of Elijah

Apoc. Sedr.	Apocalypse of Sedrach
Apol.	Tertullian, *Apology*
Apos. Con.	Apostolic Constitutions and Canons
ArBib	*The Aramaic Bible: The Targums*. 19 vols. Edited by Martin J. McNamara et al. Wilmington, DE: Glazier, 1987–1994
b.	Babylonian Talmud
Barn.	Epistle of Barnabas
B. Bat.	Baba Batra
BBR	*Bulletin for Biblical Research*
BECNT	Baker Exegetical Commentary on the New Testament
Ber.	Berakot
BETL	Bibliotheca Ephemeridum Theologicarum Lovaniensium
Bib	*Biblica*
BibInt	Biblical Interpretation Series
BibInt	*Biblical Interpretation*
Bibl. hist.	Diodorus Siculus, *Bibliotheca historica*
BJRL	*Bulletin of the John Rylands University Library of Manchester*
BK	*Bibel und Kirche*
BRLJ	Brill Reference Library of Judaism
BSac	*Bibliotheca Sacra*
BTS	Biblical Tools and Studies
BWANT	Beiträge zur Wissenschaft vom Alten und Neuen Testament
BZ	*Biblische Zeitschrift*
BZAW	Beihefte zur Zeitschrift für die alttestamentliche Wissenschaft
BZNW	Beihefte zur Zeitschrift für die neutestamentliche Wissenschaft
C. Ar.	Athanasius, *Orations against the Arians*
Cat.	Cyril of Jerusalem, *Catechetical Lectures*
CBQ	*Catholic Biblical Quarterly*
CD	Cairo Genizah copy of the Damascus Document
CEJL	Commentaries on Early Jewish Literature
Cels.	Origen, *Against Celsus*
CH	*Church History*
ChrCent	*Christian Century*
Civ.	Augustine, *The City of God*
Comm. Ap.	Victorinus of Pettau, *Commentary on the Apocalypse*
Comm. Dan.	*Commentary on Daniel*
Comm. Harm. Ev.	Calvin, *Commentary on the Harmony of the Evangelists*
Comm. Isa.	Jerome, *Commentary on Isaiah*
Comm. Jo.	*Commentary on the Gospel of John*

Comm. Luc.	Theophylact, *Commentary on Luke*
Comm. Matt.	*Commentary on Matthew*
Comm. ser. Matt.	Origen, *Series Commentary on Matthew*
Conf.	Philo, *On the Confusion of Tongues*
CurBR	*Currents in Biblical Research*
Dem.	Aphrahat, *Demonstrations*
Deut. Rab.	Deuteronomy Rabbah
Dial.	Justin, *Dialogue with Trypho*
Did.	Didache
DSD	*Dead Sea Discoveries*
EB	Echter Bibel
EBib	Etudes Bibliques
EC	*Early Christianity*
ECL	Early Christianity and Its Literature
EdF	Erträge der Forschung
EJL	Early Judaism and Its Literature
EKKNT	Evangelisch-katholischer Kommentar zum Neuen Testament
Enarrat. Ps.	Augustine, *Enarrations on the Psalms*
Enc	*Encounter*
Ep.	Augustine, *Epistles*
Ep. Apos.	Epistle to the Apostles
ETL	*Ephemerides Theologicae Lovanienses*
ETR	*Etudes théologiques et religieuses*
EvQ	*Evangelical Quarterly*
Exod. Rab.	Exodus Rabbah
Exp. Luc.	Ambrose, *Exposition of the Gospel according to Luke*
ExpTim	*Expository Times*
Ezek. Trag.	Ezekiel the Tragedian
FC	Fathers of the Church
Frg. Tg.	Fragmentary Targum
FRLANT	Forschungen zur Religion und Literatur des Alten und Neuen Testaments
FZPhTh	*Freiburger Zeitschrift für Philosophie und Theologie*
GCS	Die griechischen christlichen Schriftsteller der ersten [drei] Jahrhunderte
Gen. Rab.	Genesis Rabbah
Gloss. Ord.	Glossa Ordinaria
Gos. Mary	Gospel of Mary
Gos. Phil.	Gospel of Philip

Haer.	Irenaeus, *Refutation of All Heresies*
Ḥag.	Ḥagigah
Her.	Philo, *Who Is the Heir?*
Herm. Sim.	Shepherd of Hermas, Similitude(s)
HibJ	*Hibbert Journal*
Hist.	Tacitus, *Histories*
Hist. eccl.	*Ecclesiastical History*
Hist. Rech.	History of the Rechabites
Hom. 1 Thess.	John Chrysostom, *Homilies on 1 Thessalonians*
Hom. Act.	John Chrysostom, *Homilies on the Acts of the Apostles*
Hom. Ev.	Bede, *Homilies on the Gospels*
Hom. Jo.	John Chrysostom, *Homilies on John*
Hom. Matt.	John Chrysostom, *Homilies on Matthew*
HTR	*Harvard Theological Review*
HTS	Harvard Theological Studies
HvTSt	*Hervormde Teologiese Studies* (*HTS Teologiese Studies/HTS Theological Studies*)
IAHI	International Archives of the History of Ideas
ICC	International Critical Commentary
IDS	*In die Skriflig*
IJT	*Indian Journal of Theology*
Il.	Homer, *Iliad*
Inc.	Athanasius, *De incarnatione*
Int	*Interpretation*
ITQ	*Irish Theological Quarterly*
JAJ	*Journal of Ancient Judaism*
JBL	*Journal of Biblical Literature*
JECS	*Journal of Early Christian Studies*
JETS	*Journal of the Evangelical Theological Society*
JPSR	*Jewish Political Studies Review*
JQR	*Jewish Quarterly Review*
JR	*Journal of Religion*
JSHJ	*Journal for the Study of the Historical Jesus*
JSJSup	Supplements to the Journal for the Study of Judaism
JSNT	*Journal for the Study of the New Testament*
JSNTSup	Journal for the Study of the New Testament Supplement Series
JSOTSup	Journal for the Study of the Old Testament Supplement Series
JSP	*Journal for the Study of the Pseudepigrapha*
JSPL	*Journal for the Study of Paul and His Letters*

JSPSup	Journal for the Study of the Pseudepigrapha Supplement Series
JSS	*Journal of Semitic Studies*
JTS	*Journal of Theological Studies*
Jub.	Jubilees
J.W.	Josephus, *Jewish War*
KBANT	Kommentare und Beiträge zum Alten und Neuen Testament
KD	*Kerygma und Dogma*
KJV	King James Version
LAB	Liber antiquitatum biblicarum (Pseudo-Philo)
LAE	Life of Adam and Eve
LCL	Loeb Classical Library
Lev. Rab.	Leviticus Rabbah
LNTS	The Library of New Testament Studies
LW	Luther's Works
LXX	Septuagint
m.	Mishnah
Marc.	Tertullian, *Against Marcion*
Mart. Ascen. Isa.	Martyrdom and Ascension of Isaiah
Mart. Pol.	Martyrdom of Polycarp
Mek.	Mekilta
Metam.	Ovid, *Metamorphoses*
Midr. Ps.	Midrash Psalms
Mos.	Philo, *On the Life of Moses*
MT	Masoretic Text
NASB	New American Standard Bible
NCBC	New Cambridge Bible Commentary
NETS	New English Translation of the Septuagint
NIB	*The New Interpreter's Bible*. Edited by Leander E. Keck. 12 vols. Nashville: Abingdon, 1994–2004
NICNT	New International Commentary on the New Testament
NIGTC	New International Greek Testament Commentary
NovT	*Novum Testamentum*
NovTSup	Supplements to Novum Testamentum
NPNF	*A Select Library of Nicene and Post-Nicene Fathers of the Christian Church*. Edited by Philip Schaff and Henry Wace. 28 vols. in 2 series. 1886–1889. Repr., Peabody, MA: Hendrickson, 1994
NRSV	New Revised Standard Version
NSBT	New Studies in Biblical Theology
NTL	New Testament Library

NTOA	Novum Testamentum et Orbis Antiquus
NTS	*New Testament Studies*
Num. Rab.	Numbers Rabbah
ÖBS	Österreichische biblische Studien
Od.	Homer, *Odyssey*
Odes Sol.	Odes of Solomon
OECT	Oxford Early Christian Texts
Orig. World	On the Origin of the World
OTP	*Old Testament Pseudepigrapha*. Edited by James H. Charlesworth. 2 vols. New York: Doubleday, 1983, 1985
Pesiq. Rab.	Pesiqta Rabbati
Praem.	Philo, *On Rewards and Punishments*
Princ.	Origen, *First Principles*
Ps.-Clem. Rec.	Pseudo-Clementines, *Recognitions*
Ps. Rab.	Psalms Rabbah
Pss. Sol.	Psalms of Solomon
PSTJ	*Perkins (School of Theology) Journal*
PTS	Patristische Texte und Studien
QD	Quaestiones Disputatae
QG	Philo, *Questions and Answers on Genesis*
Qidd.	Qiddušin
Qoh. Rab.	Qoheleth Rabbah
RB	*Revue biblique*
RBS	Resources for Biblical Study
RCT	*Revista catalana de teología*
RelS	*Religious Studies*
ResQ	*Restoration Quarterly*
RevScRel	*Revue des sciences religieuses*
RSECW	Routledge Studies in the Early Christian World
RSR	*Recherches de science religieuse*
RTR	*Reformed Theological Review*
Šabb.	Šabbat
Sacr.	Philo, *On the Sacrifices of Cain and Abel*
Sanh.	Sanhedrin
SANt	Studia Aarhusiana Neotestamentica
SBLDS	Society of Biblical Literature Dissertation Series
SBLMS	Society of Biblical Literature Monograph Series
SBLSP	Society of Biblical Literature Seminar Papers
SBLSymS	Society of Biblical Literature Symposium Series

SBS	Stuttgarter Bibelstudien
SBT	Studies in Biblical Theology
SemeiaSt	Semeia Studies
SHCT	Studies in the History of Christian Traditions
SHR	Studies in the History of Religions
SHT	Studies in Historical Theology
Sib. Or.	Sibylline Oracles
SJHC	Studies in Jewish History and Culture
SJT	*Scottish Journal of Theology*
SNT	Studien zum Neuen Testament
SNTSMS	Society for New Testament Studies Monograph Series
SNTU	*Studien zum Neuen Testament und seiner Umwelt*
SNTW	Studies of the New Testament and Its World
SP	Sacra Pagina
ST	*Studia Theologica*
StBibLit	Studies in Biblical Literature
STDJ	Studies on the Texts of the Desert of Judah
SVTP	Studia in Veteris Testamenti Pseudepigrapha
Ta'an.	Ta'anit
T. Ab.	Testament of Abraham
TB	Theologische Bücherei: Neudrucke und Berichte aus dem 20. Jahrhundert
TBei	*Theologische Beiträge*
T. Benj.	Testament of Benjamin
TBN	Themes in Biblical Narrative
T. Dan	Testament of Dan
TDNT	*Theological Dictionary of the New Testament*. Edited by Gerhard Kittel and Gerhard Friedrich. Translated by Geoffrey W. Bromiley. 10 vols. Grand Rapids: Eerdmans, 1964–1976
TENTS	Texts and Editions for New Testament Study
TF	Theologische Forschung
Tg. 1 Sam.	Targum 1 Samuel
Tg. Cant.	Targum Canticles
Tg. Chr.	Targum 1 Chronicles
Tg. Eccl.	Targum Ecclesiastes
Tg. Isa.	Targum Isaiah
Tg. Jer.	Targum Jeremiah
Tg. Lam.	Targum Lamentations
Tg. Mic.	Targum Micah

Tg. Neof.	Targum Neofiti
Tg. Num.	Targum Numbers
Tg. Obad.	Targum Obadiah
Tg. Onq.	Targum Onqelos
Tg. Ps.	Targum Psalms
Tg. Ps.-J.	Targum Pseudo-Jonathan
Tg. Yer.	Targum Yerušalmi
Tg. Zech.	Targum Zechariah
Them	*Themelios*
THKNT	Theologischer Handkommentar zum Neuen Testament
ThViat	*Theologia Viatorum*
T. Isaac	Testament of Isaac
T. Iss.	Testament of Issachar
TJ	*Trinity Journal*
T. Jud.	Testament of Judah
T. Levi	Testament of Levi
T. Mos.	Testament of Moses
TQ	*Theologische Quartalschrift*
Tract. Ev. Jo.	Augustine, *Tractates on the Gospel of John*
Treat. Res.	Treatise on the Resurrection
TRu	*Theologische Rundschau*
TS	*Theological Studies*
TSAJ	Texte und Studien zum antiken Judentum
T. Sim.	Testament of Simeon
TTZ	*Trierer theologische Zeitschrift*
TUGAL	Texte und Untersuchungen zur Geschichte der altchristlichen Literatur
TynBul	*Tyndale Bulletin*
TZ	*Theologische Zeitschrift*
T. Zeb.	Testament of Zebulun
USQR	*Union Seminary Quarterly Review*
VC	*Vigiliae Christianae*
Vesp.	Suetonius, *Vespasian*
WBC	Word Biblical Commentary
WD	*Wort und Dienst*
WMANT	Wissenschaftliche Monographien zum Alten und Neuen Testament
WUNT	Wissenschaftliche Untersuchungen zum Neuen Testament
y.	Jerusalem Talmud

ZAC	*Journal of Ancient Christianity/Zeitschrift für Antikes Christentum*
ZAW	*Zeitschrift für die alttestamentliche Wissenschaft*
ZNT	*Zeitschrift für Neues Testament*
ZNW	*Zeitschrift für die neutestamentliche Wissenschaft und die Kunde der älteren Kirche*
ZRGG	*Zeitschrift für Religions- und Geistesgeschichte*
ZTK	*Zeitschrift für Theologie und Kirche*
ZWT	*Zeitschrift für wissenschaftliche Theologie*

PART ONE

Reading the Future of Jesus Backward

A FRESH APPROACH

> Intellectual progress usually occurs through sheer abandonment of questions together with both of the alternatives they assume—an abandonment that results from their decreasing vitality and a change of urgent interest. We do not solve them: we get over them. Old questions are solved by disappearing, evaporating, while new questions corresponding to the changed attitude of endeavor and preference take their place.
>
> —John Dewey[1]

In a large lecture hall for an undergraduate class on the origins of Christianity, a student in the front row raised her hand. The topic of the day was the eschatological teaching of Jesus. "But professor," the student asked, "Jesus said all the time that he was going to come back again. So why do people think he was disappointed about the failure of the kingdom to come in his lifetime?" The teacher replied, "Well, scholars are in agreement that Jesus didn't actually say those things. Those passages reflect only the hopes of the early church."

I witnessed this exchange many years ago as a preceptor for this course. The moment passed about as quickly as it takes to read it, and the discussion moved on to other things. But I have kept thinking about it. I see in this exchange, now

1. John Dewey, *How We Think* (Boston: Heath, 1910), 19.

years later, a microcosm of the state of New Testament studies when it comes to the question of the second coming. An honest question is met not with argument but with an appeal to the consensus of the guild. To be fair, had I been the one lecturing and receiving the question, I would not have had anything better to say. I did not have a good argument on hand to respond to this student's question, nor was I aware of a single recent study that took that question about the second coming seriously as it pertains to the teaching of the historical Jesus. My entire training as a New Testament scholar had essentially told me, not by "explicit" argument, but by the "implicit" and the "null" of scholarship,[2] as it were, that this was a settled issue. The origin of the second advent hope, whatever it was, was not the Jesus of history.

It turns out that the professor's comment about a consensus on the matter is both right and wrong. And the rightness and the wrongness of that comment illustrate a paradox in the history of scholarship that has not received the attention that it should. On the one hand, it is true that very few of the most significant historical Jesus studies in the past decades have contended that Jesus predicted a coming again after death. We will discuss these studies in due course. So one may rightly speak of some consensus on the matter. On the other hand, this scholarly agreement has not been produced by substantial study and robust discussion; it is rather a consensus of silence. One searches in vain in most recent historical Jesus studies not just for the contention that the second-coming hope originated with Jesus but for much discussion of the second advent at all. Of course, study of the second-coming hope in other New Testament texts, especially the epistles of Paul, abounds.[3] But the last major, monograph-length studies on the question

2. These terms are borrowed from the influential study on pedagogy by Elliott Eisner, *The Educational Imagination: On the Design and Evaluation of School Programs* (New York: Macmillan, 1979).

3. Some important studies include Oscar Cullmann, "Die Hoffnung der Kirche auf die Wiederkunft Christi nach dem Neuen Testament" (1944), in *Vorträge und Aufsätze 1925–1962*, ed. K. Fröhlich (Tübingen: Mohr Siebeck, 1966), 378–402; Wilfried Joest, "Die Kirche und die Parusie Jesu Christi," in *Gott in Welt: Festgabe für Karl Rahner*, ed. Johannes Baptist Metz et al. (Freiburg: Herder, 1964), 1:536–50; Arthur L. Moore, *The Parousia in the New Testament*, NovTSup 13 (Leiden: Brill, 1966); Ulrich Luz, *Das Geschichtsverständnis des Paulus* (München: Kaiser, 1968); Hans Grass, "Zur Frage der Wiederkunft Christi," in *Altes Testament und christliche Verkündigung: Festschrift für Antonius H. J. Gunneweg zum 65. Geburtstag*, ed. Antonius H. J. Gunneweg, Manfred Oeming, and Axel Graupner (Köln: Kohlhammer, 1987), 136–47; Harold E. Fagal, "The Advent Hope in the New Testament," in *The Advent Hope in Scripture and History*, ed. V. Norskon Olsen (Washington, DC: Review & Herald, 1987), 46–64; Nicholas H. Taylor, "Early Christian Expectations concerning the Return of Jesus," *JTSA* 104 (1999): 32–43; John T. Carroll et al., *The Return of Jesus in Early Christianity* (Peabody, MA: Hendrickson, 2000); Osvaldo D. Vena, *The Parousia and Its Rereadings: The*

of origins and the historical Jesus are more than sixty years old: Francis Glasson's *The Second Advent* in 1945 and John A. T. Robinson's *Jesus and His Coming* in 1957. Both studies argue, on slightly different grounds, that the second advent hope is an invention of the early church as it grappled with new, post-Easter realities. These works are still cited authoritatively, while not engaged substantively. Since then, there has been a remarkable dearth of literature on the topic. It is telling in this respect that, among the multitude of topics covered in the four-volume *Handbook for the Study of the Historical Jesus* (2010), there is not a single article devoted to the question of the future coming of Jesus.[4]

The impression of widespread agreement, then, is as much a product of what scholars are *not* talking about as what they are talking about. Discussion of the second advent has historically fallen under the study of early Christianity, not the historical Jesus, and current research has not challenged that modus operandi.[5]

Development of the Eschatological Consciousness in the Writings of the New Testament, SBT 27 (New York: Lang, 2001); Joseph Plevnik, *Paul and the Parousia: An Exegetical and Theological Investigation* (Eugene, OR: Wipf & Stock, 2014); J. Andrew Doole, "Did Paul Really Think He Wasn't Going to Die? Paul, the Parousia, and the First Person Plural in 1 Thess 4:13–18," *NovT* 62 (2020): 44–59.

4. Tom Holmén and Stanley Porter, eds., *Handbook for the Study of the Historical Jesus*, 4 vols. (Leiden: Brill, 2010).

5. Even then, there is a similar oversight in two important recent works that are concerned with not the historical Jesus but the exegesis of the New Testament, and this illuminates the trend. First, it is striking that Simon Gathercole's excellent study, *The Gospel and the Gospels* (Grand Rapids: Eerdmans, 2022), pays such scant attention to the future coming of Jesus. Gathercole wishes to argue that there are "substantial differences in theological content between Matthew, Mark, Luke, and John, on the one hand . . . and most 'noncanonical' early Christian Gospels, on the other" (1). He focuses in particular on four features he thinks were distinctive of the apostolic proclamation ("the gospel") that have made an impact on each of the canonical gospels: the messiahship of Jesus, vicarious death, his resurrection, and the fulfillment of Scripture. Why not include the parousia among these four? It may be for the simple reason that Gathercole summarizes "the gospel with the four elements" (49) by looking at 1 Cor 15:1–11 (49–54), which does not mention the future coming of Jesus. But it is odd to have the tradition rehearsed in 1 Cor 15—recalled here, of course, only to address a particular question about the resurrection in the Corinthian context—delineate the content of the gospel in such a fashion. We know from 1 Thess 1:9–10 that the proclamation of Jesus's return was crucial in Paul's earlier preaching, and from 4:15 that it was for him tradition. All of this will, of course, receive a full treatment in later chapters. In addition, I would mention Joshua W. Jipp's *The Messianic Theology of the New Testament* (Grand Rapids: Eerdmans, 2020), which contends that the messianic identity of Jesus is the presupposition for and primary content of New Testament theology (3). This book has almost nothing to say about the hope for Jesus's future coming in the Gospels. Jipp's rich and compelling exegesis and his focus on the use of Scripture in the Gospels are, in my view, beholden to an overrealized eschatology by virtue of what is not discussed (rather than any explicit claims by Jipp himself). We will discuss this more in due course.

The first task of this book is to explain how this perplexing situation came about. How could it be that, in a field as well trod as New Testament studies and Christian origins, where there is "such enduring discord among the experts" on every imaginable topic,[6] there exists some concord on this particular issue, and concord largely in the absence of robust discussion? One might opine that the evidence is so obvious as to render critical debate null. But this is quite far from the truth. The primary answer, this book aims to show, lies in reception history. I will make a case that the historical study of the second coming (including the conspicuous lack thereof) has been shaped by social and cultural forces that stem from well before the beginnings of the so-called quest for the historical Jesus. This approach broadens the lens of our investigation to consider not just history but the history of the historians themselves.[7] This sort of reception-historical work has not been done on the second advent in New Testament scholarship.

The second task of this book is to fill the notable gap in recent Christian origins research and offer a reconstruction of the genesis of the second-coming expectation that is sensitive to its fraught reception history. I will agree with Glasson and Robinson in two key respects. The second advent hope was indeed convenient for a sect that claimed the messiah had come but could offer little tangible evidence of a changed social, political, and spiritual world in the aftermath. As such, the hope grew and changed as one might expect, and this is reflected in the New Testament itself. Moreover, I greet with equal suspicion a popular view in second-century Christianity that the messiah was expected in the Scriptures to come twice after all: first in humility (so Isa 53) and second in power and glory (so Dan 7).[8] Nevertheless, I will argue against Glasson and Robinson that there is a more probable reconstruction of Christian origins in which the consistent portrait of Jesus in the Synoptic Gospels—a Jesus who speaks of postmortem activity as Dan 7's son of man—is much nearer the historical truth than they and much subsequent scholarship have realized.

Part 1 aims to accomplish three things. First, I articulate my approach and the intended results of the reception history, which occupies part 2. Second, I detail

6. For this line, see Dale C. Allison Jr., *The Historical Christ and the Theological Jesus* (Grand Rapids: Eerdmans, 2009), 8.

7. For a similar phrase, see David Dugan, "Albert Schweitzer's Disillusionment with the Historical Reconstructions of the Life of Jesus," *PSTJ* 29 (1976): 30.

8. Cf. Justin Martyr, *Dial.* 31; Hippolytus, *Antichr.* 44; Tertullian, *Marc.* 3.7; Cyril of Jerusalem, *Cat.* 15.1; etc. This interpretation may already undergird 1 Pet 1:11–12. Cf. Craig A. Evans, "Isaiah 53 in the Letters of Peter, Paul, Hebrews, and John," in *The Gospel according to Isaiah 53*, ed. Darrell L. Bock and Mitch Glaser (Grand Rapids: Kregel, 2012), 145–70.

the arguments of a few seminal contributions on the question of the origin of the second coming to set forth the logic of my alternative approach in the chapters that follow. And third, I engage some more recent work on the eschatology of Jesus to raise important questions in need of further discussion. This part, then, is about offering critiques, staking claims, and understanding why both are important.

1

Reception History and Expanding the Conversation

It is by now conventional wisdom that the traditional threefold division of the quest for Jesus—the "old," "new," and "third," as some have described it[1]—is flawed.[2] Much of the criticism has focused on how selectively that typology maps the great sea of literature that stems from Reimarus and the Wolfenbüttel fragments controversy to the present day. It is also common to hear that the periodization itself is inaccurate and that there are better ways to chart the development of scholarship.

1. See, e.g., N. T. Wright, "Jesus, Quest for the Historical," *ABD* 3:796–802.

2. See Clive Marsh, "Quests of the Historical Jesus in New Historicist Perspective," *BibInt* 5 (1997): 403–37; Dale C. Allison Jr., "Secularizing Jesus," in *Resurrecting Jesus: The Earliest Christian Tradition and Its Interpreters* (London: T&T Clark, 2005), 2 (the threefold division "in its simplicity . . . is simplistic: it obscures far more than it illumines"); Halvor Moxnes, "From Unique Personality to Charismatic Movement: 100 Years of Shifting Paradigms in Historical Jesus Research," in *Religion in Late Modernity: Essays in Honor of Pål Repstad*, ed. Inger Furseth and Paul Leer-Salvesen (Trondheim: Tapir, 2007), 187–200; Fernando Bermejo Rubio, "The Fiction of the 'Three Quests': An Argument for Dismantling a Dubious Historiographical Paradigm," *JSHJ* 7 (2009): 211–53; Helen K. Bond, "The Quest for the Historical Jesus: An Appraisal," in *The Blackwell Companion to Jesus*, ed. Delbert Burkett (Malden, MA: Blackwell, 2011), 337–54; Anthony Le Donne, "The Quest for the Historical Jesus: A Revisionist History through the Lens of Jewish-Christian Relations," *JSHJ* 10 (2012): 63–86; Le Donne, "Remapping Schweitzer's Quest through Jewish-Christian Polemic, Apology, and Dialogue," in *Soundings in the Religion of Jesus: Perspectives and Methods in Jewish and Christian Scholarship*, ed. Bruce Chilton, Anthony Le Donne, and Jacob Neusner (Minneapolis: Fortress, 2012), 111–28.

Both of those criticisms are justified. But there is a third problem, sometimes observed but far less extensively researched, that will occupy the attention of part 2 of our study: the "quest for the historical Jesus" did not begin with Reimarus in 1778.[3] Albert Schweitzer was responsible for making Reimarus the fountainhead of subsequent critical research in his survey, *Von Reimarus zu Wrede*, but this was an inaccurate and, frankly, self-serving starting point.[4] Schweitzer admired Reimarus's iconoclastic posture and thought that his attempt to situate Jesus in first-century Jewish eschatological thought was on target, even if Reimarus misunderstood its nature. In both respects, Schweitzer's book implies, Reimarus was a prototype of Schweitzer himself. Schweitzer wrote that "there had been nothing to prepare the world for a work of such power as that of Reimarus."[5] This comment frames Reimarus as the great stone that smashed the statue of the theological Jesus fashioned by so-called precritical Christianity. Schweitzer intended his work to do the same to nineteenth-century liberalism. Schweitzer's affinity for Reimarus also stems from his nationalistic academic culture, captured by the opening words of *Von Reimarus zu Wrede*: "When, at some future day, our period of civilization shall lie, closed and completed, before the eyes of later generations, German theology will stand out as a great, a unique phenomenon in the mental and spiritual life of our time."[6]

3. A few important studies on the topic include August C. Lundsteen, *Hermann Samuel Reimarus und die Anfänge der Leben-Jesu Forschung* (Copenhagen: Olsen, 1939), 108–33; Harvey K. McArthur, *The Quest through the Centuries: The Search for the Historical Jesus* (Philadelphia: Fortress, 1966), 1–102; Henning Graf Reventlow, "Das Arsenal der Bibelkritik des Reimarus: Die Auslegung der Bibel, insbesondere des Alten Testaments, bei den englischen Deisten," in *Hermann Samuel Reimarus (1694–1768): Ein "bekannter Unbekannter" der Aufklärung in Hamburg* (Göttingen: Vandenhoeck & Ruprecht, 1973), 44–65; Colin Brown, *Jesus in European Protestant Thought, 1778–1860*, SHT 1 (Durham: Labyrinth, 1985), 29–55; William Baird, *From Deism to Tübingen*, vol. 1 of *History of New Testament Research* (Minneapolis: Fortress, 1992), 3–57; James Carleton Paget, "Quests for the Historical Jesus," in *The Cambridge Companion to Jesus*, ed. Markus Bockmuehl (Cambridge: Cambridge University Press, 2001), 140–41; Jonathan C. P. Birch, "The Road to Reimarus: Origins of the Quest of the Historical Jesus," in *Holy Land as Homeland?*, ed. Keith W. Whitelam, SWBA 7 (Sheffield: Sheffield Phoenix, 2011), 19–47; Jonathan C. P. Birch, "Reimarus and the Religious Enlightenment: His Apologetic Project," *ExpTim* 129 (2018): 245–53; Jonathan C. P. Birch, "Revolutionary Contexts for the Quest: Jesus in the Rhetoric and Methods of Early Modern Intellectual History," *JSHJ* 17 (2019): 35–80; Tucker S. Ferda, *Jesus, the Gospels, and the Galilean Crisis*, LNTS 601 (London: Bloomsbury T&T Clark, 2019), 15–62.

4. For some critical reflections, see Simon J. Gathercole, "The Critical and Dogmatic Agenda of Albert Schweitzer's *The Quest of the Historical Jesus*," *TynBul* 51 (2000): 261–83; Michael J. Thate, *Remembrance of Things Past? Albert Schweitzer, the Anxiety of Influence, and the Untidy Jesus of Markan Memory*, WUNT 2/351 (Tübingen: Mohr Siebeck, 2013), 95–124.

5. Albert Schweitzer, *The Quest of the Historical Jesus*, trans. William Montgomery (New York: Macmillan, 1955), 14. This version is based on Schweitzer's first German edition in 1906.

6. Schweitzer, *Quest of the Historical Jesus*, 1. Cf. Andrew M. Mbuvi, *African Biblical Studies:*

The reality, though, is that Reimarus was far less original than Schweitzer makes him out to be.[7] By the late eighteenth century, conversation was already well underway about the political nature of the kingdom of God in the first century, the relationship of Jesus to first-century Judaism, and the way in which Jesus's ethical teaching compared to the beliefs of his first followers. In fact, many of Reimarus's most distinctive and memorable views on Jesus can be found in earlier writings. For instance, John Toland had already argued that Jesus did not reject Judaism to found a new religion.[8] Thomas Woolston had already made the case that the disciples stole the body of Jesus and feigned his resurrection.[9] And a good number of critics had put forth the idea that the disciples (and early Christian leaders generally) sought power and wealth and spread newly invented Christian doctrines for self-serving interests.[10] Thus the most accurate way to understand Reimarus in historical context—and not only him but the rest of the late eighteenth and early nineteenth-century quest for Jesus—is not to set him apart from earlier research as the harbinger of a new and distinct period of scholarship (though there were developments, of course). It is rather to say that Reimarus and his contemporaries reframed and recast older interpretive traditions in a new historical context and with more sophisticated historical tools.[11]

These Enlightenment rationalists and deists were not historical critics in the manner of Reimarus and others in the nineteenth century, to be sure. The former were content with isolated studies of certain topics of interest, whereas Reimarus and his progeny tried to offer more robust and comprehensive historical accounts of Christian origins. Nevertheless, the indebtedness of the so-called old quest for

---

Unmasking Embedded Racism and Colonialism in Biblical Studies (London: Bloomsbury T&T Clark, 2023), 31–57.

7. Cf. Fernando Bermejo Rubio, "Was 'Von dem Zwecke Jesu und seiner Jünger' an Innovative Contribution? On Reimarus' Significance in the History of Jesus Research," in *From Jesus to Christian Origins: Second Annual Meeting of Bertinoro (1–4 October, 2015)*, ed. Adriana Destro and Mauro Pesce (Brepols: Turnhout, 2019), 261–83. See also Colin Brown with Craig A. Evans, *A History of the Quests for the Historical Jesus* (Grand Rapids: Zondervan Academic, 2022), 1:121–235.

8. Cf. John Toland, *Nazarenus, or, Jewish, Gentile, and Mahometan Christianity* (London: Brown, Roberts, Brotherson, 1718), vi ("Jesus did not take away or cancel the Jewish law in any sense whatsoever"). For discussion and other sources, see Matti Myllykoski, "'Christian Jews' and 'Jewish Christians': The Jewish Origins of Christianity in English Literature from Elizabeth I to Toland's *Nazarenus*," in *The Rediscovery of Jewish Christianity: From Toland to Baur*, ed. F. Stanley Jones, SBLHBS 5 (Atlanta: Society of Biblical Literature, 2012), 30–36.

9. Cf. Thomas Woolston, discussed in Brown, *Jesus in European Protestant Thought*, 41.

10. Cf. the response already in Hugo Grotius's 1627 *The Truth of the Christian Religion, with Jean Le Clerc's Notes and Additions*, trans. John Clarke, ed. Maria Rosa Antognazza (Indianapolis: Liberty Fund, 2012), 103.

11. See Ferda, *Jesus, the Gospels, and the Galilean Crisis*, 65.

Jesus to earlier biblical exegesis, historical investigation, and theological polemic has been overlooked by New Testament scholars for far too long. This is a symptom of a larger problem that N. T. Wright noted in his 2018 Gifford Lectures: New Testament critics have tended to understand the development of scholarship "with minimal reference to the larger cultural scene."[12] This lack of perspective is particularly troublesome in our case because already by the time of Reimarus, the question of the second advent of Christ, considered both doctrinally and historically, carried tremendous ideological baggage. This baggage, as part of the horizon of modern critical exegesis,[13] has invariably shaped the way that critics have approached the topic.[14] In subsequent years, the second advent has only been further problematized as a flashpoint in theological culture wars and as a point of embarrassment for some seeking to square a modern understanding of the world with first-century cosmologies.[15] Framing New Testament scholarship on the second advent within this wider cultural and theological history is much needed for a proper thick description of the *status quaestionis*.[16] I will argue, among other things, that such a widening of the lens explains the origin of the assumption that this topic belongs in studies of the early church, rather than in studies of the life of Jesus, as well as why there has been such a conspicuous lack of attention given to the question in recent years.

Habits of Reading

What is the procedure for this reception history? To use one phrase, it is to consider the subtle yet impactful formation of what Brenda Schildgen has called

12. N. T. Wright, *History and Eschatology: Jesus and the Promise of Natural Theology* (Waco, TX: Baylor University Press, 2019), 16.

13. For this language, see Hans-Georg Gadamer, *Truth and Method*, 2nd ed. (New York: Crossroad, 1989), 301–5.

14. A number of recent studies have aimed to look more closely at the situatedness of New Testament research in its larger social, cultural, and political contexts. See, e.g., Dieter Georgi, "The Interest in Life of Jesus Theology as a Paradigm for the Social History of Biblical Criticism," *HTR* 85 (1992): 51–83; Brian K. Blount, *Cultural Interpretation: Reorienting New Testament Criticism* (Minneapolis: Fortress, 1995); William Arnal, *The Symbolic Jesus: Historical Scholarship, Judaism, and the Construction of Contemporary Identity* (London: Equinox, 2005); Halvor Moxnes, Ward Blanton, and James Crossley, eds., *Jesus beyond Nationalism: Constructing the Historical Jesus in a Period of Cultural Complexity* (London: Equinox, 2010); James Crossley, *Jesus in an Age of Neoliberalism: Scholarship, Intellectuals and Ideology* (London: Equinox, 2012).

15. Cf. A. C. Thiselton, "The Parousia in Modern Theology: Some Questions and Comments," *TynBul* 27 (1976): 27–53. I will develop this point in detail later.

16. So Clifford Geertz, *The Interpretation of Cultures* (New York: Basic, 1973).

"habits of reading."[17] This helpful expression assumes the basic theoretical point that readers of texts are not individual, autonomous selves who discover textual meaning alone in personal study (which is not to deny that originality exists in biblical interpretation). Rather, as readers read in and from particular social contexts, the meaning-making that occurs in textual interpretation is inevitably shaped by the perspectives and preoccupations operative in those contexts. Hence Schildgen contends that readers are formed by certain habits of reading in their social contexts and, in a way, trained to read texts in certain ways.[18] This habituation happens both consciously and unconsciously via the readers' adoption of the particular reading practices of their "interpretive communities."[19]

The upshot of Schildgen's relatively uncontroversial hermeneutic is that the reception history of the Bible should not be about merely the identification of which readings and interpretations are shared and passed down over time, or even recovering forgotten readings (although both are very important tasks).[20] Reception history must also be concerned with identifying "what interests in the historical context shape particular renderings."[21] In our case, this means identifying which interests in various historical contexts have shaped particular renderings of the second-coming idea, its relationship to first-century Judaism, and its theological profile in early Christianity. To be sure, there is great need for reception histories of the Bible that go beyond literary media produced by intellectuals and exegetes, and some promising work has begun to emerge on this front.[22] But my study, with its concentration on the development of modern biblical studies, will require that I focus on the contributions of those who have been the most influential in shaping scholarly discourse.

17. Brenda Schildgen, *Power and Prejudice: The Reception of the Gospel of Mark* (Detroit: Wayne State University Press, 1999).

18. Schildgen, *Power and Prejudice*, 17: "The history of how the Bible has been read emphasizes more forcefully than the history of any other text how tentative and yet how powerful reading-interpretive habits are."

19. The phrase originated in the work of Stanley Fish, *Is There a Text in This Class? The Authority of Interpretive Communities* (Cambridge: Harvard University Press, 1980). For the related idea of "textual community," developed in religious studies more specifically, see Brian Stock, *The Implications of Literacy: Written Language and Models of Interpretation in the Eleventh and Twelfth Centuries* (Princeton: Princeton University Press, 1983).

20. See here Nancy Klancher, "A Genealogy for Reception History," *BibInt* 21 (2013): 99–129.

21. Schildgen, *Power and Prejudice*, 20.

22. See, e.g., James Crossley, "Chartism and Forgotten Quests," in *The Next Quest for the Historical Jesus*, ed. James Crossley and Chris Keith (Grand Rapids: Eerdmans, 2024), 201–21; Brandon Massey, "The Radical Historical Jesus in Chicago: History from Below and New Directions in the History of the Quest" (paper presented at the Annual Meeting of the Society of Biblical Literature [Historical Jesus section], San Antonio, November 21, 2023).

The importance of this approach to reception history is apparent in light of the fact that each new generation of New Testament critics does not enter the world of scholarship on their own terms; they rather find a field that exists within certain boundaries and rules of engagement: scholarly preoccupations are already set, debates are already framed, and certain interpretive models and conclusions are dominant.[23] To state this reality is not to dramatize and exaggerate it. But it is essential that we investigate how such boundaries, preoccupations, and interpretive models were formed and maintained over time. Such investigation does not require one to assume an overarching hermeneutical metatheory that mitigates or even eliminates the agency of texts in their reception. It merely acknowledges that, for certain issues and questions, the formation and maintenance of certain interpretive models and conclusions—their "social construction," to adopt a loaded term—may be more acute.[24] Investigation here could presumably open up genuinely new avenues for rediscovering the claims of New Testament literature and better understanding the world that produced them.

Christian Anti-Judaism

We have seen the opening of such avenues before in New Testament studies, to be sure, particularly when the topic at hand involves hypotheses about the nature of first-century Judaism. The history of the field, and of Christian biblical interpretation in general, is a history where anti-Jewish caricature has too often passed as genuine historical reconstruction.[25] The exposure and criticism of such caricatures have led to serious advances in New Testament scholarship. One need look no further than E. P. Sanders's *Paul and Palestinian Judaism*.[26] Sanders shows that Christian exegesis of Paul since the Reformation has read Paul alongside a

23. Helpful here is Laudan's notion of "research traditions." See Larry Laudan, *Progress and Its Problems: Towards a Theory of Scientific Growth* (Berkeley: University of California Press, 1977). Lauden contends that structural and intergenerational "research traditions" can decide what needs and does not need defending, what questions should be pursued, and even what heuristics might be followed.

24. See Anne-Marie Pelletier, *D'âge en âge, les Écritures: La Bible et l'herméneutique contemporaine* (Brussels: Lessius, 2004).

25. Amy-Jill Levine, *The Misunderstood Jew: The Church and the Scandal of the Jewish Jesus* (San Francisco: HarperSanFrancisco, 2006), 120: "today a number of stereotypes of Judaism, based ever so tentatively on historical investigation, substitute for rigorous historical inquiry." See also the famous study by George Foot Moore, "Christian Writers on Judaism," *HTR* 14 (1921): 197–254, as well as Marcel Simon, *Verus Israel: Étude sur les relations entre chrétiens et juifs dans l'empire romain (135–425)* (Paris: Boccard, 1964). These studies and others will be engaged in part 2.

26. E. P. Sanders, *Paul and Palestinian Judaism* (Minneapolis: Fortress, 1977).

phantom interlocutor—a legalistic religion called "Judaism" defined by "works righteousness"—to which Paul's theology was regarded as intellectually and morally superior. Sanders believed that this understanding of Judaism was more or less presupposed and advanced without argument; to use Schildgen's language, it had become a "habit of reading." Even if Sanders merely approximates the truth of the matter, and there is room for much debate on the details, the theology of Paul needs to be seriously reconsidered.[27] Is there a better way to summarize what has happened in Pauline studies since 1977?

The reception of the second coming, too, is deeply intertwined with Christian caricatures about Judaism and specifically the nature of Jewish messianism, though this has gone largely undiscussed by New Testament critics. One of the main objectives of this book is to argue that there is a dynamic at play in the history of interpretation of the second advent that is very similar to what Sanders observed in the study of Paul. We may summarize its most brazen form in this way: some critics denied the second advent hope to the historical Jesus because it was far too carnal, unspiritual, and, in their words, "Jewish," to be harmonized with his superior ethical teachings. My contention is that, like many post-Reformation readings of Paul, approaches to the second advent in Christian origins have been shaped by a particular construction, or caricature, of Judaism.

In the end, it is fair to say that the search for "habits of reading" is really a search for the production and maintenance of assumptions in scholarship. As Sanders's own work attests, reception history, so conceived and defined, is hardly novel. In fact, I would argue that the most significant advances in the history of New Testament studies have been due not to new readings or innovative historical reconstructions but rather to the way in which prior scholarship is shown beholden to certain unjustified assumptions (which makes possible new readings). I am compelled to return here to Albert Schweitzer. Schweitzer's periodization of the quest may be off, and his own reconstruction of Jesus idiosyncratic. But Schweitzer detailed, in page after page, the ways in which the nineteenth-century quest for the historical Jesus had been a drawn-out project of liberal Protestant eisegesis. Some histories of scholarship credit Schweitzer with the discovery of eschatology and the construction of a new portrait of Jesus.[28] But that is not true. Moreover, as brilliant and important as Schweitzer's thoroughgoing eschatology

27. Cf. Timo Eskola, "Paul et le Judaïsme du Second Temple: La sotériologie de Paul avant et après E. P. Sanders," *RSR* 90 (2002): 377–98.

28. See, e.g., James M. Robinson, "The Legacy of Albert Schweitzer's Quest of the Historical Jesus," in *Reverence for Life: The Ethics of Albert Schweitzer for the Twenty-First Century*, ed. Marvin Meyer and Kurt Bergel (Syracuse: Syracuse University Press, 2002), 246–55; N. T. Wright, *Who Was Jesus?* (Grand Rapids: Eerdmans, 1992), 1–6.

was, he was wrong in the details, and few if any follow him today in toto. It is his critique that endures.

At the same time, caution is necessary here. While I am not compelled by Robert Miller's reconstruction of the historical Jesus, I am sympathetic to this reflection on the legacy of Schweitzer's criticism of others before him:

> The greatest benefit of Schweitzer's analysis has been the inculcation of a healthy circumspection about and steady refinement of historical method. Its most baneful effect is that it has armed scholars with a rhetorical weapon of mass destruction. To accuse an opponent of coming up with a Jesus after his or her own image is singularly satisfying. Not only does it let you discredit your opponent's position without having to engage any of his or her arguments; it is also impossible to refute.[29]

That is fair.[30] It is indeed possible for reception history to focus so much on a systemic level of analysis that it never gets around to attend to a scholar's actual arguments. It is also possible—and this is perhaps one of the great ironies of contemporary trends in hermeneutical discussion—for a critic to stress the ambiguity and inherent subjectivity of texts while claiming to know the motives of readers with a kind of moral certainty. It would surely be a mistake to dismantle the old objectivist paradigm for textual interpretation only to shift that objectivism onto the readers. But there is a better way, and it is nothing flashy or unique: pairing larger sociocultural analysis with careful engagement of various reconstructions of Jesus. That is what I hope to do in what follows, as my objective is not merely to expose the cultural and ideological embeddedness of the historical conversation about the second coming but ultimately to offer a more compelling reconstruction of the past. Moreover, it seems to me that both the macroscopic and the microscopic are required if we are to follow the historiographical golden rule and treat others the way we wish to be treated. I imagine most cherish the hope that, should future generations consult our work at all, they not only attend to our various social positions and cultural backgrounds, as they should, but they also read what we have to say.

29. Robert J. Miller, "Theological Stakes in the Apocalyptic Jesus Debate," in *Apocalypticism, Anti-Semitism and the Historical Jesus: Subtexts in Criticism*, ed. John S. Kloppenborg with John W. Marshall (London: T&T Clark International, 2006), 112.

30. For another appraisal of Schweitzer, see Alexander J. M. Wedderburn, *Jesus and the Historians*, WUNT 269 (Tübingen: Mohr Siebeck, 2010), 58–66.

2

Two Seminal Contributions

We turn now to look at what some others have had to say (or failed to say) about the origin of the second-coming hope. While discussion of "the larger cultural scene" occupies part 2, the details of historical argument and exegesis show clearly enough that a reconsideration of the second advent in New Testament studies is overdue. I begin with summary and critique of the seminal contributions of Glasson and Robinson from over a half century ago. The next chapter will consider more recent work on the eschatology of Jesus and raise important questions that require further investigation.

T. Francis Glasson's *The Second Advent: The Origin of the New Testament Doctrine* appeared first, in 1945,[1] and Robinson's *Jesus and His Coming: The Emergence of a Doctrine* a decade later (1957).[2] While Robinson's work differs from Glasson's in a few key areas, it essentially develops the central tenets of Glasson's thesis, and so both studies can be summarized together. The logic of their historical arguments emerges from the very structure of their books. In essence, both critics work *forward* from the historical Jesus to the early church. In terms of sources, this means that they consider the Gospels first in order to reconstruct Jesus, and then they discuss other

1. T. Francis Glasson, *The Second Advent: The Origin of the New Testament Doctrine*, 3rd ed. (Eugene, OR: Wipf & Stock, 2009). In what follows, I work with the third edition, noting that its chapters and content are exactly the same as the first edition. It was merely in the notes and at the end of each chapter that he made modifications. His later defense, "The Second Advent—25 Years Later," *ExpTim* 82 (1971): 307–9, simply restates his position.

2. John A. T. Robinson, *Jesus and His Coming: The Emergence of a Doctrine* (New York: Abingdon, 1957).

New Testament sources, especially Paul's epistles. By the time they consider Paul's letters, then, both critics have already reconstructed their historical Jesus, which they rely on in various ways to evaluate the state of the tradition in Paul's time.

Glasson does make one move prior to reconstructing Jesus: he attempts to contextualize his study in the context of first-century Judaism. In fact, he brackets his larger investigation of Jesus and the early Christians with discussion of pre- and post-Christian Jewish literature, respectively.[3] Discussing the pre-Christian texts first, he claims to find nothing therein that would lead one to anticipate the second coming of the messiah. As his next move is to reconstruct the historical Jesus, he is already suspicious of any claims in the Gospels about the parousia, since he believes the notion is foreign to Jewish messianism. At the end of his study, Glasson finds some potentially interesting parallels to claims found in the New Testament about Jesus's return in post-Christian Jewish literature. But he dismisses anything found in the Similitudes of Enoch, 4 Ezra, 2 Baruch, the Sibylline Oracles, and rabbinic writings as irrelevant to the study of Christian origins, because he dates these sources to a later period after the writing of the New Testament.[4] Emerging from his survey of non-Christian sources is a clear conclusion: the second-coming hope has no *Vorlage* in Jewish messianism. The expectation for the messiah to return from heaven is, evidently, a Christian invention. Unlike Glasson, Robinson does not investigate putative Jewish parallels to the second advent hope in any detail, but he does reassert at various points Glasson's conclusion: the hope of early Christ followers has no parallel in "the traditional Jewish scheme." The belief is "absent . . . from Judaism."[5]

Of course, the oddness of early Christian belief raises another historical question from which both critics, to their credit, do not shy away: from where, then, does the new idea come? For both Glasson and Robinson, the answer to that question is not found in the teaching of the historical Jesus. It is important to trace the means by which they arrive at that conclusion in some detail.

Approach

In general, both critics take an atomistic approach to reconstructing Jesus.[6] Such was standard fare in the 1940s and 1950s when New Testament criticism was still

3. Glasson, *Second Advent*, 1–53.

4. Moreover, Glasson, *Second Advent*, 230, notes that, were we to find in Jewish apocalyptic texts "traces of a similar conception" to the Christian idea of the second coming, we should think it due to Christian influence.

5. Robinson, *Jesus and His Coming*, 22, 24.

6. On atomization, see William R. Telford, "Major Trends and Interpretive Issues in the Study

deeply influenced by the work of early twentieth-century form criticism.[7] To describe their approach as atomistic means that they look at individual sayings of Jesus and clusters of sayings, pulled from their narrative contexts and the interpretive frames of the evangelists; they deem these individual sayings either authentic or inauthentic; and they group authentic sayings together with other authentic sayings to reconstruct the teaching of Jesus. The teaching of Jesus, then, is pieced together, bit by bit, leaving behind the inauthentic pieces, the origin of which neither critic finds pressing to explain. As these books are focused studies on the second coming, neither has time to reconstruct the teaching of Jesus in toto. So both approach the Gospels in a necessarily selective manner, choosing individual sayings and clusters of sayings that, historically, have been thought to refer to the second advent. In general, both critics treat this material in one of two ways. Either they argue that the saying does in fact refer to the future coming of Jesus but does not go back to Jesus (such sayings are thus regarded as inventions of the early church). Or they argue that the saying does go back to Jesus but originally had nothing to do with a future return. The evangelists themselves, or later exegetical tradition, have twisted authentic words of Jesus to mean something he did not.[8]

A good example of the second approach appears in a very important passage for both Glasson and Robinson: the reply of Jesus to Caiaphas (Mark 14:62 and parr.). They both offer a nearly identical reading. They assume that this exchange took place, but Jesus's allusion to his own coming as Dan 7's son of man had nothing to do with a return from heaven. Glasson paraphrases Jesus's point: "al-

---

of Jesus," in *Studying the Historical Jesus: Evaluations of the State of Current Research*, ed. Bruce Chilton and Craig A. Evans (Leiden: Brill, 1994), 49–50.

7. This is not to link the authenticity criteria with form criticism, per se, as argued by Chris Keith, "The Indebtedness of the Criteria Approach to Form Criticism and Recent Attempts to Rehabilitate the Search for an Authentic Jesus," in *Jesus, Criteria, and the Demise of Authenticity*, ed. Chris Keith and Anthony Le Donne (London: T&T Clark, 2012), 25–48; Keith, "The Narratives of the Gospels and the Historical Jesus: Current Debates, Prior Debates and the Goal of Historical Jesus Research," *JSNT* 38 (2016): 426–55. Cf. Tom Holmén, "Seven Theses on the So-Called Criteria of Authenticity of Historical Jesus Research," *Revista Catalana de Teología* 33 (2008): 343–76; Tobias Hägerland, "The Future of Criteria in Historical Jesus Research," *JSHJ* 13 (2015): 4, 7–11.

8. A very similar strategy is adopted by Thomas Kazen in his essay, "The Coming Son of Man Revisited," *JSHJ* 5 (2007): 155–74, where he argues that Jesus had used Dan 7 but in a collective sense to refer to the vindication of Jesus's kingdom community and their current praxis. According to Kazen's scenario, then, the evangelists distorted the true meaning of Jesus in almost every extant saying by introducing the new ideas of Jesus individually being the son of man and of his future return, but they nevertheless have left enough crumbs for us to see he really meant something different.

though He was about to be put to a shameful death He was really entering upon His reign."[9] The language of the onlookers "seeing," the throne, and the clouds are all metaphorical ways of expressing Jesus's confidence that God will exalt and vindicate him. Both critics contend that the addition of the phrase "from now on" by Matthew and Luke to the utterance of Jesus in Mark 14:62 (hence: "you will see from now on . . .") not only communicates Jesus's real intention more clearly than Mark's wording does; it is likely what Mark's Gospel originally contained, and it may even be what Jesus himself actually said.[10] Jesus was talking about the inauguration of his reign, despite death, rather than the consummation of his reign at some future time. Robinson takes this approach to numerous other sayings of Jesus: logia about "rising again," "being perfected," "sitting at the right hand," "entering" the kingdom, and having "glory" are all ways of describing the "vindication" of Jesus in general.[11] He treats such terminologies essentially as synonyms and urges that they must not be read literally.

Glasson and Robinson contend that many passages in the Gospels are like Mark 14:62: Jesus had indeed said what the Gospels claim, but he has been misunderstood. Both critics think that this misunderstanding occurred particularly in sayings where Jesus was originally predicting the destruction of Jerusalem or was trying to convince his hearers to take seriously the "crisis" of his appearance at the present hour. For instance, Glasson believes this has happened with the so-called Lukan apocalypse in Luke 17:22–37. The description of the "days of the son of man," the allusion to Noah and the ark, Lot and Sodom, and the taking of one and the leaving of another were all originally about "the doom of His own nation." The Third Evangelist, Glasson believes, is partly responsible for muddling the true meaning of Jesus, because he has inserted here two lines of "dubious" (in his words) authenticity—v. 24 ("as the lightning . . . so will the son of man be") and v. 30 ("on the day that the son of man is revealed")—which he admits clearly refer to the future return of Christ.[12] But these can be skimmed off the top, he thinks, leaving behind an otherwise authentic speech of Jesus. Robinson differs only slightly here in terms of exegesis, but he arrives at nearly the same place: this Lukan material was originally about the need to heed the seriousness of the present hour and respond to Jesus's message in faith.[13] Description of the

9. Glasson, *Second Advent*, 55; see also 56–60 and literature cited. Robinson, *Jesus and His Coming*, 45, paraphrases thus: "out of suffering and death he is about to be brought in triumph to the throne of God, in a crowning act of vindication which they themselves will witness."

10. Glasson, *Second Advent*, 56, 59; Robinson, *Jesus and His Coming*, 47–49.

11. Robinson, *Jesus and His Coming*, 36–58.

12. Glasson, *Second Advent*, 77, 80, 81.

13. Robinson, *Jesus and His Coming*, 59–82.

significance of his present advent has been misunderstood as a prediction of a second, and with that the consummation of history.

Both critics treat a number of isolated (as they see them) sayings of Jesus, as well as the parables, in the same manner.[14] Glasson acknowledges that many parables appear, on the surface, to anticipate Jesus leaving for some time and then returning after an interval. But this is a misinterpretation due again to the misleading presentation of the evangelists. As with Luke 17, the evangelists have added to these parables "appended explanations" that more clearly reference the parousia of Christ.[15] Originally these parables were attempts to call his hearers to decision in the present; they were not about Jesus's future absence and return but about his ministry then and there. Such is the case, for example, with the parable of the pounds (Luke 19:11–27 and parr.), the parable of the virgins (Matt 25:1–13), the parable of the wedding feast (Matt 22:1–14 and par.), and the parable of the householder (Mark 13:32–37 and parr.). Robinson makes the same case, drawing heavily on Joachim Jeremias's influential proposal regarding "crisis parables."[16]

Glasson and Robinson do believe that there are other texts in the Gospels that cannot be read in any other way than to say they predict a future return. But, they argue, none of these sayings are historical.[17] For instance, Glasson regards the entirety of Mark 13 and parallels a foreign interpolation from the early church and sets it aside from his discussion of the historical Jesus. He draws on Timothee Colani's view that the chapter originated as a "fly-sheet" that "formerly had a separate existence."[18] Robinson has a slightly more complex approach to Mark 13, but he ends in the same place. The Markan text as it stands is a composite speech: the earlier sections (vv. 1–23) contain dominical material,[19] while the predictions of the

14. For instance, Glasson, *Second Advent*, 93–94, argues that Mark 13:32 ("no one knows the day or the hour") is "almost certainly a genuine saying of Jesus," yet the context provided in Mark 13 is artificial. This independent saying was not, originally, about the parousia. Glasson makes the same case concerning Matt 23:37–39 (*Second Advent*, 94–98).

15. Glasson, *Second Advent*, 86–87.

16. Robinson, *Jesus and His Coming*, 64–82. Cf. Joachim Jeremias, *The Parables of Jesus*, trans. S. H. Hooke, 2nd ed. (New York: Scribner's Sons, 1972). Also important here was C. H. Dodd's earlier work, *The Parables of the Kingdom*, rev. ed. (New York: Scribner's Sons, 1961), 122–39.

17. Both critics regard Matt 10:23 in this manner. See Glasson, *Second Advent*, 100; Robinson, *Jesus and His Coming*, 80 (the saying can be "more easily fitted into a situation after the death of Jesus than into anything we know of the Ministry itself").

18. Glasson, *Second Advent*, 71. Glasson writes, "[Mark 13] must be reserved for Part Three, where it will take its place in a discussion of the teaching of the early Church . . . [it] cannot be used with confidence if we are making a serious inquiry into Jesus' teaching on the subject of His return" (75). Colani's work and its impact will be discussed in detail below.

19. Robinson, *Jesus and His Coming*, 119 (though even here he sees "secondary features and editorial touches").

parousia of the son of man in vv. 24–27 are not historical in any sense.[20] In his view, vv. 24–27 are much later, secondary, even, to the original Gospel of Mark. Robinson even believes that the earliest copy of Mark ended not on a note of future anticipation but with something like the realized eschatology in Matt 28:18: "all authority in heaven and earth has been given to me." He makes the astounding claim that Mark's original gospel contained no hope for the parousia, but it was expanded and glossed in light of new eschatological and apocalyptic expectations that were foreign not just to the teaching of Jesus but even to Mark's story itself.[21]

If we step back to consider these arguments as a whole, we see that both critics practice historical criticism as a process of selective negation. That is to say, they take up materials traditionally read in one way and argue that Jesus was in fact *not* like this or did *not* mean that. This approach to history may be compared to a sculptor's theoretical approach to a new block of marble: the historian/artist does not produce the figure as much as releases or frees it from the inside by chipping away at the exterior. When Glasson and Robinson set down their tools, then, one finds a resultant image of Jesus, though it is not really one that they have presumed to argue *for*. For both critics, the Jesus who survives the chisel is a Jesus who spoke most of all about something happening now in his ministry and message; he was not a predictive prophet but spoke only of his confidence that God would vindicate him; he had no imminent eschatology to speak of, and he would not have been disappointed by the historical developments that occurred after his ministry and death. Glasson's Jesus "looked forward to a long period in which the Kingdom of God would spread through the world until at last the old prophecies would come to pass and the knowledge of the Lord would cover the earth."[22] As such, Glasson argues that Jesus transformed popular, nationalistic views of the kingdom of God in Judaism into "the conquest of evil in men's lives,"[23] and he thought that the kingdom would come "germinally."[24] Robinson is left with much the same Jesus, albeit described with different terminology:

20. Robinson, *Jesus and His Coming*, 56, 118–39.

21. Robinson, *Jesus and His Coming*, 128–39.

22. Glasson, *Second Advent*, 152. Glasson argues that Jesus did not anticipate any cataclysmic end of history, or even speak much of the final judgment. See *Second Advent*, 129–36. He relies on von Dobschütz to argue that Jesus had a "transmuted eschatology": rather than expect external change in a new messianic era, Jesus transferred what was to come to inward, personal change (138). See Ernst von Dobschütz, *The Eschatology of the Gospels* (London: Hodder & Stoughton, 1910).

23. Glasson, *Second Advent*, 105, 111 ("Jesus re-interpreted the Kingdom, and announced its presence").

24. Glasson, *Second Advent*, 105, 110 (Glasson argues "some great development . . . [would] result from His death"), 152 (Jesus "looked forward to a long period in which the Kingdom of

Jesus announced God's "visitation" and his own "vindication."[25] God was now, in Jesus, visiting Israel to redeem and to save, and the cause of Jesus would, despite opposition and death, continue.

For both critics, therefore, not only does the second-coming hope have no genesis in the authentic teaching of Jesus; it is, in many respects, theologically opposed to his teaching. Glasson believes that the second advent is an ideological relative of John the Baptist's hope for "catastrophic intervention," whereas Jesus's "method and programme did not consist in force and domination, but in joyous and redemptive ministry."[26] Robinson cites approvingly Vincent Taylor's famous line that it is necessary to "detach from his [Jesus's] shoulders the glittering apocalyptic robe with which primitive Christianity clothed him, and with which he is still draped in popular Christian expectation." Robinson believes the realized or inaugurated eschatology of the Gospel of John is "in all essentially identical with that of . . . Jesus himself,"[27] just as Paul's later theology (believing that Paul developed from an apocalyptic eschatological outlook to a nonapocalyptic one) is "more faithful to the original tradition."[28]

Explaining Origins

At this point, of course, neither critic has offered a constructive historical hypothesis about the origin of the expectation. This they eventually do, though in different ways. Robinson's solution is conceptual and theological; Glasson's is exegetical. Robinson proposes that the second advent hope was created as a theodicy of sorts, an answer to "whether or not the messianic event had yet taken place, whether the Christ had come or not."[29] In other words, at some point, Christians started to ask themselves, Could this be it? And they developed the parousia hope as their collective answer: No, there must be more to come.[30] Glasson's *Ursprung* is not

God would spread through the world until at last the old prophecies would come to pass and the knowledge of the Lord would cover the earth").

25. Robinson, *Jesus and His Coming*, 36–40.

26. Glasson, *Second Advent*, 123. He wrote at 139, "apart from the fact that Jesus spoke of the Kingdom of God as already initiated, His whole attitude and the spirit of His teaching is inconsistent with the view that He expected a world catastrophe to arrive at any moment."

27. Robinson, *Jesus and His Coming*, 97, 162.

28. Robinson, *Jesus and His Coming*, 161 n. 1. He develops authenticity of the Johannine portrait in chapter 8 (160–85), arguing that in John, as with the historical Jesus, there is "an essential unity between the 'now' and the 'not yet'" (169).

29. Robinson, *Jesus and His Coming*, 142.

30. Robinson, *Jesus and His Coming*, 88: "In the course of transmission his teaching became

christological tension but early Christian exegesis of the Old Testament. He recognizes that descriptions of Christ's return in New Testament texts interact with Old Testament passages that speak of *God's* coming or appearance, contending that it was possible for early Christians to make this connection between Jesus and God's appearance only when they believed Jesus was not only "Messiah" but "Lord" (κύριος).[31] Thus, he concludes, the notion of the future coming of Jesus is a product of a later, and higher, Christology.[32] With the origin of the hope thus pinned by both critics on theological developments in early Christianity, it is not surprising to find that neither thinks the "original Gospel" of the apostles (as preserved in the speeches of Acts, they think) contained the hope of the parousia.[33]

---

focused not upon the present event whose urgency he was proclaiming but upon another event whose imminence he was predicting."

31. Glasson, *Second Advent*, 176.

32. This particular argument of Glasson has been very popular, refracted in various ways. See further his later study, T. Francis Glasson, "Theophany and Parousia," *NTS* 34 (1988): 259–70. I will engage this argument in detail in part 4.

33. Glasson, *Second Advent*, 154–59; Robinson, *Jesus and His Coming*, 28–29 ("we are left with the surprising conclusion that no evidence is to be found that the Parousia expectation formed part of the earliest strata of Apostolic Christianity"), 136–37, 144–59. Both contend that speeches in Acts, which they think preserve early material, consistently "end" with mention of "witnessing" to Christ's death and resurrection in the now; predictions of his return in the future are conspicuously absent. I will offer another explanation for this phenomenon in subsequent chapters.

3

Critique

I begin with a detailed discussion of Glasson and Robinson not merely for the sake of introduction but because I wish to frame my own approach in conversation with—and often in contrast to—these seminal works. This is not a matter of quibbling over minor details here and there. I have rather three rather significant criticisms that fall under these areas: method and approach, exegesis, and the question of historical explanation. The discussion of these points in sequence will provide an opportunity to explain the rationale of my argument to come, as well as to show what I believe the new contributions of this project to be for New Testament studies.

One of the positive contributions of both Glasson's and Robinson's works is that they show just what is at stake historically and exegetically for the investigation of the second coming in Christian origins. There are, indeed, a number of moving pieces here: the Judaism of the New Testament period, the reconstruction of Jesus as a figure in history, the relationship between Jesus and the "Jesus-loyalists" that came after him,[1] and the interpretation of so-called eschatological or apocalyptic passages in the Gospels. But with so many potential topics and issues on the table, there is the risk that where one begins, and what one chooses to prioritize, will go a long way in determining where one ends up. So, where to begin? How does one start the process of reconstructing Jesus and Christian ori-

1. For this term, see Richard Horsley, *You Shall Not Bow Down and Serve Them: The Political Economic Projects of Jesus and Paul* (Eugene, OR: Cascade, 2021), 114, 130.

gins when it comes to this topic? It is here, I think, that both Glasson and Robinson get off on the wrong foot.

As mentioned above, both critics essentially work *forward* in time from the historical Jesus to the early church. On its face, this appears logical: Jesus, of course, lived before Paul and other Christians, so the historical approach follows the actual sequence of events in the past. But this is problematic in terms of method, because while Jesus was indeed first and the church second, for historians, considering our source material, it is the church first and Jesus second. Historical time may move forward, but historians must work backward:[2]

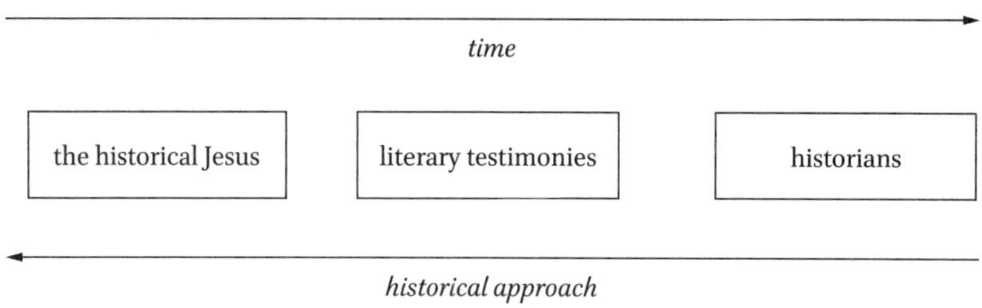

The point is basic but overlooked by Glasson, Robinson, and many others when it comes to our topic: Jesus is not accessible to the historian apart from the fragmentary literary sources that have been preserved about his activity. There is no way to get around these sources to evaluate them by means of some other objective medium.[3] Thus, anything that we conclude about Jesus must come from, in this order, *interpretation* of the sources and *inference* about the past on the basis of that interpretation.[4] Historical Jesus research is essentially a process of interpreting "texts" (conceived broadly) and positing various hypothetical scenarios about

2. Paula Fredriksen, *Jesus of Nazareth, King of the Jews: A Jewish Life and the Emergence of Christianity* (New York: Knopf, 1999), 40, put this memorably while rewriting Kierkegaard: "though history is always done backward, life is only lived forward."

3. In stating this, however, I agree with F. Gerald Downing, "Feasible Researches in Historical Jesus Tradition: A Critical Response to Chris Keith," *JSNT* 40 (2017): 57: "Whatever encompassing hypothesis seems promising to any one of us, she or he has to 'go behind' the text to argue its particular historicity," and "there is no possible avoidance of going 'behind' or 'under' our available texts for any history, whether of Jesus or of the early churches and their traditions."

4. For a similar distillation of historical criticism with different language ("interpretation" and "explanation"), see Ben F. Meyer, *The Aims of Jesus* (London: SCM, 1979), 76–81. Also helpful here is Tom Holmén, "An Introduction to the Continuum Approach," in *Jesus from Judaism to Christianity: Continuum Approaches to the Historical Jesus*, ed. Tom Holmén, LNTS 352 (London: Bloomsbury T&T Clark, 2007), 12, when he writes, "the Christian *Wirkungsgeschichte* should be dealt with on its own *before* turning to a consideration of Jesus."

the past to make sense of those "texts."[5] So Jens Schröter, using spatial imagery that resembles the diagram above, writes,

> historical-critical Jesus research moves within a certain "fuzzy sphere," since it deals as a historical endeavor with sources that do not mediate an unambiguous picture of the past. Therefore, its goal cannot be to reach the *one* Jesus *behind* the texts but to reach a conception grounded on the weighing of plausibilities, which as an abstraction from the sources always moves *in front of* the sources.[6]

I would contend that Glasson and Robinson and many others have failed to acknowledge seriously their position "in front of" the sources, as well as the fact that they can only reconstruct what Jesus said of the future by facing the past, backward (so Schröter: "an abstraction from the sources"). What both of them do, instead, is quickly pass over the large bulk of our literary testimony about Jesus, atomistically selecting individual passages from individual gospels that they believe represent the beliefs of the Jesus of history. They then read this constructed historical Jesus *forward* and largely against the grain of the rest of our literary testimony.

For example, after Glasson's opening five chapters in part 1, "The Parousia in Jewish Literature Extant in the Time of Jesus," he turns in chapter 6 to reconstruct Jesus's teaching by going immediately for Mark 14:62: the reply to Caiaphas. As noted above, he argues that Jesus here speaks not of his second coming but "entering upon his reign." Glasson then opens chapter 7 with these words:

> One consideration to be borne in mind in discussing the eschatological sayings reported in the Gospels is that the original words of Jesus may have been coloured by the beliefs of the early Church.[7]

5. Cf. Beth M. Sheppard, *The Craft of History and the Study of the New Testament* (Atlanta: Society of Biblical Literature, 2012), 15: the historian's task "can be boiled down to one word: 'interpretation.'" See also Rafael Rodríguez, *Structuring Early Christian Memory: Jesus in Tradition, Performance, and Text*, LNTS 407 (London: T&T Clark, 2010), 39–80.

6. Jens Schröter, *Jesus of Nazareth: Jew from Galilee, Savior of the World*, trans. Wayne Coppins and S. Brian Pounds (Waco, TX: Baylor University Press, 2014), 17. See also the interesting formulation by Bruce Chilton, "Implications and Prospects of Jewish Jesus Research: A Review Essay," *JSHJ* 16 (2018): 76: "the kind of 'history' that 'the historical Jesus' involves has changed. No longer what really happened (as in the 'First Quest'), nor what ultimately must be presupposed (as in the 'Second'), history emerges from inferences of what lies behind all the available evidence, literary and not."

7. T. Francis Glasson, *The Second Advent: The Origin of the New Testament Doctrine*, 3rd ed. (Eugene, OR: Wipf & Stock, 2009), 69.

That is a truism. But notice what Glasson has done here: after focusing on a single (albeit climactic and important) utterance, Glasson believes that he has, *in nuce*, the authentic eschatological outlook of Jesus, such that he can read with a critical eye anything in the Gospels that (he believes) does not cohere with what he found there. Later in chapter 7, Glasson will set aside the entirety of Mark 13 on the grounds that its contents "seem alien to his message."[8] But one might well ask, How does Glasson know, at this point, the contours of Jesus's message, such that he can already identify what is alien to it? Glasson comes close here to begging the very question under consideration. Even if Glasson is correct in what he affirms about Mark 14:62, he has more or less presupposed that this interpretation captures the eschatological vision of Jesus and, moreover, captures that vision with sufficient clarity that we can identify anything resembling the parousia hope as a clear contrast to it. To return to the sculptor analogy above, the artist, like our historians, may have *theorized* that her work was merely releasing or freeing what was inside by chipping away at the outside. But the artist was, indeed, positively constructing that image, regardless of whether her approach acknowledged it. Herein we see the necessity of engaging how "habits of reading" are formed by means of reception history, which will occupy part 2. If Glasson's approach does not acknowledge what in fact he is doing—that the Jesus he is left with is in fact a Jesus constructed by someone, even if *he* did not spend much time constructing it—it only forces the question: Where did this Jesus come from? What reception history has created the assumptions that make it possible for such a Jesus to be advanced by an author without much positive argument at all?

It should be clear that this first critique is not about the poor execution of an argument. The criticism concerns how the argument is set up to begin with; it is about how one conceives of the task of historical Jesus research. Glasson and Robinson generally regard the interpretive postures of the evangelists and other sources as barriers to be overcome, not as historical facts to be explained. They engage the Gospels atomistically with little to no interest in what our sources—particularly the Gospels—*claim* because they are immediately and solely after what Jesus himself actually taught. They thus give meager attention to the way in which sayings of Jesus were understood by the very sources that contain them,[9] and they do not feel a pressing need to explain where these interpretive frames

8. Glasson, *Second Advent*, 73.

9. There are exceptions to this. Glasson, *Second Advent*, 65, writes of certain sayings that "an apocalyptic element has crept into them." He thinks this happened with special frequency in Matthew's Gospel: e.g., he claims, Matt 16:28 rewrites Mark 9:1 and "introduces" the parousia (66); Matt 24:3 adds a new eschatological dimension to the disciples' question in Mark 13:4 (66); Matthew has most of the material concerning gehenna and the final judgment (67).

came from. Moreover, they never grapple with the upshot of their own argument: that our main literary sources for the life of Jesus have catastrophically misunderstood his teaching about the future. This reality creates no crisis of confidence in their ability to reconstruct the past.

A Different Way Back

The atomistic and forward-working approach of Glasson and Robinson is shared by many others who have, in article-length studies or excurses in larger projects, taken up the question at hand (and which we will discuss in due course). This book takes a different approach. Rather than start with small details and move forward in time, we will start with broader tendencies and move backward in time. That is to say, we will begin with the claims and impressions of our sources, primarily Paul's epistles and the Gospels of Mark, Matthew, Luke, and John.[10] Our first task is not to probe for historically authentic material as Glasson and Robinson did but to seek to understand what these sources explicitly *claim* and implicitly *presuppose* about Jesus.[11] Unlike Glasson and Robinson, this approach will not lead us to the rather bizarre situation of arriving at our earliest written source from Christian origins—1 Thessalonians—having already decided where the second-coming hope came from. Discussion of these diverse literary witnesses from the New Testament will also provide opportunity to compare and contrast early Christian eschatologies and better understand the theological and redactional *Tendenzen*

10. Canonical bias in New Testament studies needs to be challenged, of course. See Francis Watson, *Gospel Writing: A Canonical Perspective* (Grand Rapids: Eerdmans, 2013), 3–5. However, and as most critics agree, it is still true that when it comes to reconstructing the historical Jesus, the most important literary sources we have also happen to be the later-canonized gospels, especially the Synoptics (John is more debated, and I will say more about this later). For discussion see Per Bilde, *The Originality of Jesus: A Critical Discussion and a Comparative Attempt*, SANt 1 (Göttingen: Vandenhoeck & Ruprecht, 2013), 28–31; Jens Schröter and Christine Jacobi, eds., *The Jesus Handbook*, trans. Robert L. Brawley (Grand Rapids: Eerdmans, 2022), 125–55. I have been persuaded by Simon Gathercole, *The Composition of the Gospel of Thomas: Original Language and Influences*, SNTSMS 151 (Cambridge: Cambridge University Press, 2012), and Mark Goodacre, *Thomas and the Gospels: The Case for Thomas's Familiarity with the Synoptics* (Grand Rapids: Eerdmans, 2012), that the Gospel of Thomas is a second-century text that is of little use for reconstructing the teaching of Jesus.

11. Note here C. K. Barrett, *Jesus and the Gospel Tradition* (London: SPCK, 1967), 68–69, who offers this wisdom: "We must begin by considering the gospels as they stand; when we have done this we shall be able to consider how faithfully they represent, and how far they pervert, the teaching of Jesus in this matter."

of early Christian traditions. Only after this significant interpretive task (part 3) will we turn to wager hypotheses about the Jesus of history: *inference* drawn from, and seeking to make sense of, *interpretation* (part 4). Our task, as Chris Keith has helpfully remarked about historical Jesus research in general, is to "posit a historical Jesus . . . on the basis of the interpretations of the early Christians . . . as part of a larger process of accounting for how and why early Christians came to view Jesus in the ways that they did."[12]

In such a task, the discussion of Second Temple Jewish messianism and eschatological expectations occupies a different place in the overall historical reconstruction. Glasson started with this, suggesting that Christian claims about Jesus's return were anomalous and thereby (he suggests) historically suspect. But there are multiple problems with this approach and conclusion.[13] Aside from the question of interpretation (which we will deal with later), our evidence for such topics is highly fragmentary—much has survived only by accident.[14] Dating is also very difficult. Glasson's dismissal of anything found in the Similitudes of Enoch, 4 Ezra, the Sibylline Oracles, 2 Baruch, and rabbinic writings is cavalier; and even if his dating of these sources is correct, he fails even to entertain the possibility that they contain earlier tradition. In all, arguments from silence must be carefully posited and qualified, which Glasson does not. Moreover, if we can say anything positively about such hopes, it is that there was no single messianic expectation or a singular eschatological scenario in Second Temple Judaism. There are repeated motifs, to be sure, and, one might say, a "grammar" of messianism can be identified.[15] But

12. Chris Keith, "The Narratives of the Gospels and the Historical Jesus: Current Debates, Prior Debates and the Goal of Historical Jesus Research," *JSNT* 38 (2016): 426. Fredriksen, *Jesus of Nazareth*, 77, also speaks of working backward by charting various trajectories in Paul and the Gospels.

13. One of which is that Glasson himself is not consistent here. The interpretation of Isa 53 to refer to the suffering and death of the messiah cannot be found in pre-Christian Judaism (much like what Glasson says of the second advent idea), and yet Glasson argues that this is how the historical Jesus read the passage. See *Second Advent*, 119–26. He also argues throughout that Jesus's understanding of the kingdom was "radically different from the popular one" (105). One might say that, for Glasson, "radically different" also means "radically superior." He writes at 209 that Jesus had "re-interpreted both the Kingdom and the Messiah, finding the secret of His kingship not in material splendor or coercion, but in service and love, and regarding the Cross as the true way of victory."

14. Amy-Jill Levine, introduction to *The Historical Jesus in Context*, ed. Amy-Jill Levine, Dale C. Allison Jr., and John Dominic Crossan (Princeton: Princeton University Press, 2006), 10: "our knowledge of first-century Galilean and Judean Jewish thought and practice [is] incomplete, such that what may seem 'dissimilar' is an accident of what was preserved and what was lost."

15. Matthew V. Novenson, *The Grammar of Messianism: An Ancient Jewish Political Idiom and Its Users* (Oxford: Oxford University Press, 2017).

one of the most significant achievements of work on Second Temple Judaism in the years following Glasson and Robinson is a greater appreciation of the diversity of opinion on messianism and eschatology in this period, even though this can be overstated. The once-common attempt to frame New Testament exegesis with "Jewish background," and specifically a monolithic "messianic idea," required absurd oversimplifications, some of which will be the subject of the following chapter.[16] In fact, the publication history of Glasson's own book testifies to this development: the initial publication date of 1945 was too soon to learn from the new findings at Khirbet Qumran (he had finished writing in 1943), but the third edition, published in 1947, included an admission that the Dead Sea Scrolls show "there was a wider variety of Jewish beliefs concerning Messianic and eschatological matters than was often allowed for a few years ago."[17] This discovery did not, however, impact Glasson's argument from the first edition at all.

The point is this: given the spotty nature of our knowledge of Second Temple Jewish messianism, troubles with dating the sources, and the general diversity of opinion that appears to have been common fare, it is dubious *to start* one's reconstruction of Jesus by allowing such literature to frame the possibilities of Jesus's eschatological teaching. So we will not do that. Our approach, again, is to work backward, starting not with a reconstructed pre-Christian idea about messiah or kingdom but with our earliest sources written by people who believed Jesus was the messiah and expected him to appear again. To start here is to start with the acknowledgment that claiming that Jesus was going to return made sense to a great number of people, and they drew on so-called messianic texts and interpretive traditions to do so. The historical task, then, becomes contextualizing that claim and explaining how it came to be. This is part and parcel with that task of "accounting for how and why early Christians came to view Jesus in the ways that they did." Unlike Glasson, we will not have a separate part or chapter engaging "Jewish background" to the second advent idea but will engage relevant literature at the same time as we make historical inferences about the past and seek to position Jesus as a "believable figure in first-century Palestine."[18]

One significant consequence of the approach of this volume as sketched thus far is that it leads us to inquiries different from those prioritized by Glasson and Robinson. It also makes possible surer results. If one starts with Paul and the

16. Cf. Amy-Jill Levine, "Bearing False Witness: Common Errors Made about Early Judaism," in *The Jewish Annotated New Testament*, ed. Amy-Jill Levine and Marc Z. Brettler, 2nd ed. (Oxford: Oxford University Press, 2017), 759–62.

17. Glasson, *Second Advent*, vi.

18. E. P. Sanders, *Jesus and Judaism* (Philadelphia: Fortress, 1985), 166–67.

Gospels and works backward, the pressing historical question becomes not, Is this or that saying historical? but rather, What historical Jesus need we hypothesize to make sense of the early Jesus movement that appears in our sources? Our goal is to have a proposal whose merit does not ultimately depend on the historicity of this or that saying in the Gospels, or on the particular interpretation of a single saying (like Mark 14:62) or a select few sayings of Jesus, but rather the relative probability of a proposed historical scenario in comparison to other scenarios. This approach coheres with recent developments in method in Jesus studies that have shifted focus away from judging the historicity of individual logia in order to begin with wider themes in the tradition.[19] To my mind, not all recent criticisms of the criteria of authenticity are of equal force, and the logic of some of the criteria seems essential and more or less inevitable for any historical research about the ancient world. I have written about this elsewhere.[20] But I do find compelling the criticism of the use of the criteria to deliver sure results about small, individual pieces of the tradition. As Dale Allison memorably put it in his initial chapter on method in *Constructing Jesus*, "We should trust first, if we are to trust at all, what is most likely to be trustworthy."[21]

It is important to stress here that focus on "what is most likely to be trustworthy" does not mean that it is in fact trustworthy. Some have urged that those who dispense with the criteria of authenticity in favor of a "memory" or "gist" approach merely assume at the outset that the Gospels are historically dependable.[22] The critique may be justified for some recent studies. But our approach of

19. Cf. Helen K. Bond, *The Historical Jesus: A Guide for the Perplexed* (London: Bloomsbury T&T Clark, 2012), 21: "most have abandoned the process of sifting through the sayings of Jesus in favor of constructing a *larger picture* which incorporates most of the data." See also Rebekah Eklund, "Jesus of Nazareth," in *The State of New Testament Studies: A Survey of Recent Research*, ed. Scot McKnight and Nijay K. Gupta (Grand Rapids: Baker Books, 2019), 140–46.

20. For further reflections, see Tucker S. Ferda, *Jesus, the Gospels, and the Galilean Crisis*, LNTS 601 (London: Bloomsbury T&T Clark, 2019), 10–14. See also Gerd Theissen and Dagmar Winter, *Die Kriterienfrage in der Jesusforschung: Vom Differenzkriterium zum Plausibilitätskriterium* (Göttingen: Vandenhoeck & Ruprecht, 1997), which lists problems but also seeks rehabilitation.

21. Dale C. Allison Jr., *Constructing Jesus: Memory, Imagination, and History* (Grand Rapids: Baker Books, 2010), 16.

22. On "gist," see Allison, *Constructing Jesus*, 1–30, and also 14 n. 73 for others who have taken a similar approach. See the criticism in Michael J. Thate, *Remembrance of Things Past? Albert Schweitzer, the Anxiety of Influence, and the Untidy Jesus of Markan Memory*, WUNT 2/351 (Tübingen: Mohr Siebeck, 2013), 215 ("In the end, memory seems to serve as a rather fiduciary approach in taking the Gospel sources as reliable memories of his previous constructions of the historical Jesus"). See also Paul Foster, "Memory, Orality, and the Fourth Gospel: Three Dead-Ends in Historical Jesus Research," *JSHJ* 10 (2012): 191–227 (though he is more appreciative of Allison's work on memory). And Paula Fredriksen, *When Christians Were Jews* (New Haven: Yale University

working backward from interpretation to inference presupposes nothing at the outset about the reliability of the Gospels. In fact, the approach offered here actually stems from a skepticism that exceeds what one finds in the works of Glasson, Robinson, and many others. For in going immediately after the historical Jesus, and individual utterances of Jesus at that, Glasson and Robinson claim to know much more than we can reasonably know. Did Jesus utter Mark 14:62? This book will not venture an argument one way or another. Who could know?[23] Origen acknowledged centuries ago that "the endeavour to show, with regard to almost any history, however true, that it actually occurred, and to produce an intelligent conception regarding it, is one of the most difficult undertakings that can be attempted, and is in some instances an impossibility" (*Cels.* 1.42 [*ANF* 4:414]). Certainty is, of course, impossible, but in many cases, like this one, it is not apparent how one could ever move the arrow beyond "it is possible." Such skepticism stems not just from the "wrongness" of our historical tools but from the most basic insight of modern biblical criticism on the Gospels:[24] we know, in general, that the new realities of the post-Easter period had a creative impact on the Jesus tradition. Sayings, stories, and themes developed in accord with changing circumstances—a fact we can trace with a synopsis—and theology created history. In light of that basic fact, the fact that sayings *were* placed on the lips of Jesus, how do we decide when it happened and when it did not? I do not think that we often can. The exegesis of part 3 will substantiate this claim.

Nevertheless, that skepticism, which I believe is necessary, is not cause for abandoning historical Jesus research. There may be a better way. If we are unable to say whether Jesus did, on a certain occasion before Caiaphas, utter the Aramaic equivalent of Mark 14:62, may we still, given where we end up with early Christian memory

Press, 2018), 214 n. 17: "I am leery of the current vogue in 'memory studies' in recent work on the historical Jesus. A 'memory' implies the existence of something that indeed happened in the past, which is then passed on ('remembered'). Memory studies and borrowing from cognitive science seem a slippery way of sanctioning with an aura of (questionable) historicity some bit of tradition whose originary context most likely falls well after circa 30 C.E." For important discussions of memory studies and Jesus research, see *EC* 6 (2015), which collected essays from several scholars on the topic, as well as Alan Kirk and Tom Thatcher, eds., *Memory, Tradition, and Text: Uses of the Past in Early Christianity*, SemeiaSt 52 (Atlanta: Society of Biblical Literature, 2005), and Loren T. Stuckenbruck, Stephen C. Barton, and Benjamin G. Wold, eds., *Memory in the Bible and Antiquity*, WUNT 212 (Tübingen: Mohr Siebeck, 2007).

23. Note here Martin Dibelius, *Jesus* (Philadelphia: Westminster, 1949), 28: "Discussion as to whether a particular saying is 'genuine' is often idle because on neither side are the arguments decisive. In general the historian will do well to look at the tradition as a whole, and not build too much upon an individual saying if it is at variance with the rest of the tradition."

24. See Morna D. Hooker, "On Using the Wrong Tool," *Theology* 75 (1972): 570–81.

about Jesus and the impressions of our sources about him, conclude it is plausible, if not probable, that Jesus said things like Mark 14:62?[25] The resultant image may be fuzzier (to recall Schröter) than what one finds in the work of Glasson and Robinson, but it is still an image. The historian and philosopher of history Johann Droysen wrote, "The outcome of criticism is not 'the exact historical fact.' It is the placing of the material in such a condition as renders possible a relatively safe and correct view."[26] That is what this study aims to provide: not "the exact historical fact"—as that is unattainable—but "a relatively safe and correct view" that stems from, and circles back to explain, the tendencies of early Christian memories about Jesus.

Exegesis

That is the first criticism, and with it a sketch of an alternative way forward. The second, which can be treated more briefly, is closely related and concerns the exegesis of the Gospels. To make a general point to start, I disagree with the way in which Glasson and Robinson routinely deliteralize the eschatological and apocalyptic utterances of Jesus and take them as mere symbolic or metaphoric descriptions of the existential challenge of his present activity or the imminent destruction of the temple. By noting a lingering ambiguity in both Glasson's and Robinson's studies, we highlight the importance of the issue: both critics argue that Mark 14:62 has nothing to do with the parousia, but Mark 13:24–27—arguably the climax of Mark's apocalyptic discourse—does.[27] Both thus regard Mark 13:24–27 an invention of the early church, whereas Mark 14:62 gets us into Jesus's head. But

25. Helpful here is Brant Pitre's interest in the *substantia verba Jesu*—the substance of the words of Jesus—rather than in the *ipsissima verba Jesu*—the exact words of Jesus. He writes, "I am claiming that the basic substance or content of the teaching or action can be reasonably concluded as having originated with him. That is what I mean by historical—no more, and no less." See *Jesus and the Last Supper* (Grand Rapids: Eerdmans, 2015), 47. This is similar to David E. Aune, "Oral Tradition and the Aphorisms of Jesus," in *Jesus, the Gospel Tradition and Paul in the Context of Jewish and Greco-Roman Antiquity*, WUNT 303 (Tübingen: Mohr Siebeck, 2013), 283 (where he concludes that "authentic" means we have the *ipsissima structura* of Jesus's aphorisms, not the *ipsissima verba*). See also Nils Alstrup Dahl, "The Problem of the Historical Jesus," in *Jesus the Christ: The Historical Origins of Christological Doctrine*, ed. Donald A. Juel (Minneapolis: Fortress, 1991), 95, who argues that we should be after "what was typical and . . . a total picture in which there appears something that is characteristic of Jesus. Whether the historicity of individual words or episodes remains uncertain is consequently of less importance."

26. Johann Gustav Droysen, *Outline of the Principles of History*, trans. E. Benjamin Andrews (New York: Fertig, 1893), 25–26.

27. Glasson, *Second Advent*, 72; John A. T. Robinson, *Jesus and His Coming: The Emergence of a Doctrine* (New York: Abingdon, 1957), 57.

why read the very similar language of both passages—featuring, respectively, "the son of man," "coming," "with/on the clouds of heaven"—so differently? I leave it to part 3 to work out the specifics, wishing here only to highlight the question. The proper interpretation of such language is of course hotly debated in current New Testament scholarship, and so engaging this issue will expand our conversation partners to those whose interests go beyond the second advent per se, including, not least, C. H. Dodd, George Caird, N. T. Wright, and Richard Horsley (all of whom have supported interpretations similar to those of Glasson and Robinson).[28]

Apart from the exegesis of individual passages, however, there is a more substantial problem with the way in which both critics—and many others who have taken up the question—conceive of the nature of the Gospels. At issue here is not the results of their exegesis (as above) but assumptions about the sources that make such exegesis possible. Glasson and Robinson appear to regard the Gospels as having a twofold nature. On the one hand, they tell us a lot about the historical Jesus, which means they contain lots of authentic material that can essentially be taken on its face: Jesus actually said Mark 14:62; Jesus delivered many of the so-called parables of delay; Jesus issued something much like Luke 17:22–37; and so on (although they urge that one must appreciate the metaphorical nature of the language, as noted above). These passages provide essentially unfiltered access to the past. But on the other hand, the Gospels are interpretations of this authentic teaching that get him quite wrong. Such misinterpretations are due to a superficial shaping that, they think, once recognized and removed, essentially leaves intact the authentic teaching of Jesus. The evangelists (mis)shape the teaching of Jesus by adding small, explanatory comments to the endings of parables,[29] by inserting short, isolated sayings (which Jesus did not say),[30] and by introducing larger blocks of teaching that grind later eschatological axes (like, for Glasson, Mark 13 as a whole).[31]

The underlying assumption that the Gospels consist of this neatly divisible twofold or binary nature is surely mistaken. Nonetheless, if it were true, it should obviously be the result or upshot of an argument, and not the presumed basis or premise for others. As it is, however, both Glasson and Robinson presume and leverage this view of the Gospels in various ways to the great benefit of their the-

28. E.g., George Caird, *The Language and Imagery of the Bible* (Worcester: Duckworth, 1980); N. T. Wright, *The New Testament and the People of God* (Minneapolis: Fortress, 1992), 280–338, and more recently "Hope Deferred? Against the Dogma of Delay," *EC* 9 (2018): 37–82; Richard Horsley, *The Prophet Jesus and the Renewal of Israel: Moving beyond a Divisionary Debate* (Grand Rapids: Eerdmans, 2012).

29. Glasson, *Second Advent*, 85, 86 ("we must . . . be on the look-out for any additions made to the parables"), 87–92; Robinson, *Jesus and His Coming*, 66–72.

30. Glasson, *Second Advent*, 65–69, 81, 100–101; Robinson, *Jesus and His Coming*, 52–57, 79–81.

31. Glasson, *Second Advent*, 71–74; Robinson, *Jesus and His Coming*, 99–100.

ses. In particular, the presumption of this twofold nature permits them to discuss individual passages in a gospel without ever considering how other, clearly related texts in the same source may affect interpretation. This is hugely problematic. If we acknowledge the interpretive debate surrounding Jesus's reply to Caiaphas, for instance, surely the meaning of its near relative—Mark 13:24–27—should be a relevant consideration. Yet Glasson and Robinson never permit the larger gospel narratives to help answer questions that smaller sayings might raise. They thus conclude that certain passages in the Gospels—often the crucial ones that get to the heart of Jesus's eschatological message, like Mark 14:62—are unaffected by the larger outlook of the source as a whole. This exegetical approach allows these critics to posit the existence of significant discontinuities or tensions in our sources without sufficient argument, or rather any argument at all. It may well be, of course, that the evangelists have misunderstood Jesus's message as drastically as Glasson and Robison have posited. But if that were true, a more honest conclusion would avail itself: the historical Jesus has been buried so deeply beneath the beliefs of his followers that we can now know little to nothing about him. The success of Glasson's and Robinson's projects requires an unrealistically high estimation of the capabilities of modern historians.[32]

A better way is to consider the Gospels as wholes and seek at first to situate individual passages, like Mark 14:62, in the larger scope of that source's eschatological outlook. This coincides with the different approach of this book: working backward in terms of time and downward in terms of tradition. In part 3, my initial interest in Mark 14:62 is not what Jesus meant by it but what Mark meant by it, presuming that one cannot arrive at a probable understanding of Mark's claim if one sets aside the rest of Mark's story. This is not to imply that the Gospels are systematic theologies by any means. As the Gospels stem from earlier tradition and have undergone change, redaction, and expansion before we see them, naturally there are thematic and ideological tensions to be found (and will be, in this study). But it should be uncontroversial to note that the Gospels exhibit some literary and theological intentionality, which means that their authors wrote what they wrote for a reason. It is fair to assume that the evangelists, in selecting what to write, had some idea about what Jesus meant, even if they were wrong. Thus, if we want to know what they claimed Jesus meant, we should not ignore the rest of what they selected (and even invented) to write. This is essential work because, as noted above, the accurate description of what our sources *claim* about Jesus should be the first step for and basis of any further inferences made about the past. (And

32. For a similar criticism of nonapocalyptic reconstructions of Jesus in general, see Dale C. Allison Jr., "A Plea for Thoroughgoing Eschatology," *JBL* 113 (1994): 652.

again, the careful descriptions of such claims do not presuppose anything about the reliability or unreliability of our sources.)

Historical Explanation

I move now to the third and final criticism that concerns historical explanation, and with it another proposed alternative. An atomistic, forward-working approach has not challenged critics like Glasson and Robinson to grapple with the larger historical consequences of their proposals as they should.[33] These studies, like many others we will engage later, too easily pick and choose which logia or themes they think are authentic, referring the rest to the creative processes of post-Easter theology in the church. But this move, which became common among the early twentieth-century form critics, is a sleight of hand. It provides a pseudoconfidence in having solved a historical question, but this confidence is born from ignoring the question altogether. As mentioned already, the best we can do with this material, given the nature of our sources, is to develop hypothetical historical scenarios to make sense of the fragmentary witnesses that have been preserved. To that end, we must measure the relative probability of these proposed scenarios by the degree to which they explain the contours of early Christian memorial culture in the setting of first-century Judaism. While it may appear possible in the minutiae to suggest that certain utterances of Jesus have been supplemented with an imminent eschatological outlook, a critic is not thereby excused from offering an argument about where such supplemental frameworks came from. Our hypotheses about the past, like any in historical Jesus research, must attend to the macro as well as the micro. They must succeed in offering a compelling explanation of historical change and development.

We see the problem clearly when Robinson finally turns to address directly the question of origin on page 140 of his 185-page study. By this point, he has argued that there is "a gulf fixed" between the actual teaching of Jesus, on the one hand,

33. We need "eine sachliche Verhältnisbestimmung Jesu zu seinem Kontext und zu seiner Wirkungsgeschichte," so Theissen and Winter, *Die Kriterienfrage in der Jesusforschung*, 176; see also 175–93, 212–14 (on "Wirkungsplausibilität" and "Gesamtplausibilität"). See also Ernst Baasland, "Fourth Quest? What Did Jesus Really Want?," in *Handbook for the Study of the Historical Jesus*, ed. Tom Holmén and Stanley Porter (Leiden: Brill, 2010), 1:31–56, on what he calls the "criterion of consequence." See also Holmén, "Introduction to the Continuum Approach," 4: "A Jesus who can be placed within early Judaism but who cannot be understood in relation to early Christianity is no more historically plausible than a Jesus who can be combined with nascent Christianity while remaining an enigma to a Jew of his time."

and the beliefs of the early church, on the other. So how did we get from point A to point B? It turns out that Robinson is not quite sure. He appeals to "an unresolved crisis in the Christology of the primitive Church" to explain the change, as summarized above, but then qualifies his proposal: "It cannot be more than a hypothesis. And even if it is not wholly adequate, the facts of the problem remain until some better hypothesis is forthcoming."[34] Robinson's humility would be admirable if the gulf between Jesus and the church were a self-evident fact that all must explain. But it is not. The gulf has been fixed by Robinson's own construction; it is the result of his own atomistic procedure of combing through the Gospels and deciding what is authentic and what is not. Robinson's inability to leap the gulf that he himself has created, then, is not inconsequential; it throws into jeopardy his larger historical reconstruction. This is not just a lingering question at the end; it is the question at the center of the whole endeavor.

We can be more concrete still. Glasson's and Robinson's studies posit all kinds of significant historical changes and developments between Jesus and the church that they fail to defend adequately, or even try to explain. The most significant of these discontinuities pertain to eschatology. I can put this bluntly, as a series of questions. Are we really to believe that, when early Christians peered into the future, they expected, without significant exception, the resurrection of the dead, the final judgment, and the return of Jesus, but when Jesus peered into the future, he saw no supernatural intervention of God but merely the gradual takeover of the world by a "new spiritual order"?[35] Are we really to believe that, on either side of Jesus with John the Baptist and the apostle Paul, we find an imminent expectation for God to act in a powerful and decisive way, but Jesus, the middle term, used eschatological language only symbolically?[36] Are we to regard it probable that,

34. Robinson, *Jesus and His Coming*, 83, 142–43.

35. Glasson, *Second Advent*, 117. The language here is drawn from a line by Sir Edwyn Hoskyns, cited approvingly by Glasson, which is worth quoting in full:

> Our Lord's eschatological language, as indeed all His teaching and actions, was mainly symbolical. To speak humanly, He felt Himself standing on the brink of a new spiritual order, an order which was to come into being as a direct result of His life and death, and which was to be the fulfillment of the longings of the greatest of the Jewish prophets. To express this Gospel He used the traditional language of Jewish expectation of the End, since it provided Him with a vehicle to express the significance of His life and death.

Hoskyns implies that Jesus imbued "the traditional language of Jewish expectations" with nontraditional meaning.

36. See Glasson, *Second Advent*, 131. Glasson appears to grant that exegesis of the Old Testament theophany tradition would not itself produce the "note of imminence" in early Christian eschatology, so to explain that he claims the imminence was (1) borrowed from the antichrist tradition and (2) spurred by messianic expectations operative in Judaism (many were looking "for

in our earliest recorded evidence for Christian origins, 1 Thessalonians, we have Paul responding to a crisis that people have died before God's end-time transformation of history, and yet the founder of this new sect had merely expected his own passion, resurrection, and the fall of the temple?[37]

Eschatological development, as well as variation, disagreement, and outright contradiction in expectation, is to be expected in early Christianity.[38] But it does not bode well for the overall plausibility of a historical hypothesis if it requires us to conclude that Jesus was so roundly misunderstood by those who came after him.[39] We know that Jesus followers disagreed about lots of important things, yet it appears that there was some widespread agreement about the general contours of end-time events. (I will defend this claim in more detail in part 3.) If Jesus himself had no hand in this, how do we explain that (so part 4)? It is surely improbable to believe that different Christian groups living in different places in the ancient Mediterranean world stumbled upon the same exegetical inferences (so Glasson) or offered the same theological solutions to certain christological conundrums (so Robinson). Moreover, there would be insufficient motive. If Jesus was who Glasson and Robinson say he was—if he anticipated only his impending death and resurrection and the birth of the church—there was no apparent reason for early Christians to change him into something else. Indeed, if Glasson and Robinson are right, what Jesus predicted would happen (death, resurrection, church) is precisely what happened. So why were early Christians so collectively unsatisfied? Why take a biblical passage like Dan 7, which should have been regarded as *fulfilled* by his life, death, and enthronement—given the way in which their Jesuses used it—and transform it to generate a new, outstanding, and crisis-inducing expectation about the future that was unparalleled to date in Second Temple Judaism (as they believe)?

The asking of big-picture questions like these concerning historical causation and change can help expose blind spots. Yet care is necessary. Joseph Klausner was

---

the speedy arrival of the Messianic Age," he says) (204–5). Robinson's eschatology collapses into a kind of existentialism that sounds a lot like Rudolf Bultmann's. See, e.g., *Jesus and His Coming*, 173.

37. Robinson, *Jesus and His Coming*, 88, argues that the "spirit of expectation" came from John the Baptist. He further contends at 105, "the more apocalyptic the passage, the remoter is its connexion with anything in the Gospel tradition which may claim to be primitive or provide evidence for the teaching of Jesus."

38. Cf. Patrick Mitchel, "New Testament Eschatologies," in McKnight and Gupta, *State of New Testament Studies*, 224–52; Benjamin E. Reynolds and Loren T. Stuckenbruck, eds., *The Jewish Apocalyptic Tradition and the Shaping of New Testament Thought* (Minneapolis: Fortress, 2017).

39. So also Lewis A. Muirhead, *The Eschatology of Jesus, or, The Kingdom Come and Coming: A Brief Study of Our Lord's Apocalyptic Language in the Synoptic Gospels* (London: Melrose, 1904), 35: "They [Jesus's followers] misunderstood, in particular, His way of thinking and speaking about its consummation."

right to remind his reader repeatedly that *ex nihilo nihil fit*,[40] and yet we may not in each circumstance be able, from our position, to run the clock backward.[41] To switch metaphors, we should heed Henry Cadbury's warning in his learned book on Jesus that we must be careful in thinking that we can easily follow smoke to fire. Sometimes, he presses, the location of the smoke and the location of the fire do not exactly correspond.[42] So it is important to reemphasize what was said above: it all comes down to the relative probability of one's historical scenario in comparison with other scenarios. I find Glasson's and Robinson's attempts to pin the entirety of the second-coming hope on the early church improbable not because of the collective weight of second-coming tropes and themes in early Christian reflection on Jesus (in terms of the quantity and/or frequency of attestation, that is) but because their proposals result in a very improbable historical scenario concerning development and change in Christian origins. And here I should be clear: I find equally improbable a maximalist view that regards everything the Four Gospels presume as natural and necessary—particularly with respect to a mission to the gentiles, Jesus's own suffering and death in the manner of the servant from Isa 53, and Jesus's individual resurrection from the dead—to be identical to the expectation of the historical Jesus. All three items have a noticeable mass in our sources, but to infer all three impressions are historical would result in quite improbable historical scenarios. To take a single issue with final example to illustrate: far from anticipating Jesus's individual resurrection from the dead after three days, the disciples do not appear to be expecting anything. A probable scenario must account for these facts, as much as explain how our sources remember Jesus in the ways they do. That is what I hope to offer in parts 3 and 4 for the genesis of second-coming hope.

40. The phrase appears frequently in this learned book. See, e.g., Joseph Klausner, *Jesus of Nazareth: His Life, Times and Teaching*, trans. Herbert Danby (New York: Macmillan, 1925), 246, 255, etc.

41. Anthony Le Donne, *The Historiographical Jesus: Memory, Typology, and the Son of David* (Waco, TX: Baylor University Press, 2009), 13, claims that "the multiple (and sometimes contradictory) interpretations of Jesus found in the Gospels allow the historian to chart trajectories of memory refraction that have been propelled forward by the initial perception of Jesus by his contemporaries." That memory was "refracted" in multiple and sometimes contradictory ways is true, but on the difficulties of charting them, see reflections in Zeba A. Crook, "Collective Memory Distortion and the Quest for the Historical Jesus," *JSHJ* 11 (2013): 53–76.

42. Henry J. Cadbury, *The Peril of Modernizing Jesus* (London: SPCK, 1937), 40.

4

Complexifying the Eschatological Jesus

The above engagement with Glasson and Robinson serves to introduce the many issues involved in any historical reconstruction as well as to frame the approach of this volume. But for anyone who knows anything about the history of the quest, it is clear that many of their arguments would be rejected by those who trace their scholarly lineage to Albert Schweitzer and advocate for a similarly eschatological Jesus. So one may ask, How have defenders of a more eschatological Jesus engaged the topic of the second coming, and how do such approaches relate to the arguments of this study? This is the final issue to be addressed in part 1.

I make an initial point to provide some perspective. For heuristic purposes, one can envision three streams of scholarship on Jesus and eschatology flowing through the twentieth and the twenty-first century to the present.[1] One includes Albert Schweitzer, and downstream scholars such as E. P. Sanders, Paula Fredriksen, and Dale Allison. These critics all believe the eschatological and apocalyptic

1. For some broader discussions, see Shirley Jackson Case, "The Life of Jesus During the Last Quarter-Century," *JR* 5 (1925): 561–75; Walter P. Weaver, *The Historical Jesus in the Twentieth Century: 1900–50* (Harrisburg, PA: Trinity International, 1999); Adela Yarbro Collins, "Apocalypticism and New Testament Theology," in *The Nature of New Testament Theology*, ed. Christopher Rowland and Christopher Tuckett (Malden, MA: Blackwell, 2006), 31–50; Benedict T. Viviano, "Eschatology in the Quest for the Historical Jesus," in *The Oxford Handbook of Eschatology*, ed. Jerry L. Walls (Oxford: Oxford University Press, 2008), 73–90; Jörg Frey, "New Testament Eschatology—an Introduction: Classical Issues, Disputed Themes, and Current Perspectives," in *Eschatology of the New Testament and Some Related Documents*, ed. Jan G. van der Watt, WUNT 2/315 (Tübingen: Mohr Siebeck, 2011), 3–34.

language in the Gospels describes supernatural, transcendent events that were expected to occur in the immediate future.[2] A second stream buoys the likes of C. H. Dodd and, nearer our time, N. T. Wright. These critics do not deny such eschatological and apocalyptic imagery to the historical Jesus, but they read that imagery metaphorically or symbolically—Jesus adopted such potent language to describe the impact of his present activity, his vindication, or historical events soon to occur (like the destruction of the temple).[3] And a final stream includes the first opponents and critics of Schweitzer who advocated what we might call a non-eschatological Jesus; nearer our time, one would find here John Dominic Crossan, Marcus Borg, Stephen Patterson, and the Jesus Seminar.[4] Their argument is that the kind of eschatological enthusiasm Schweitzer believed characteristic of Jesus

2. On Schweitzer's impact, see Gregory Dawes, *The Historical Jesus Question: The Challenge of History to Religious Authority* (Louisville: Westminster John Knox, 2001), 122–58; Francis Watson, "Eschatology and the Twentieth Century," in *Eschatologie—Eschatology: The Sixth Durham-Tübingen Research Symposium; Eschatology in Old Testament, Ancient Judaism and Early Christianity*, ed. Hans-Joachim Eckstein, Christof Landmesser, and Hermann Lichtenberger, WUNT 272 (Tübingen: Mohr Siebeck, 2011), 331–47. An interesting defense of a Schweitzerian reading of the Gospels, against his former *Doktorvater* (Georg Kümmel), is Erich Grässer, *Das Problem der Parusieverzögerung in den synoptischen Evangelien und in der Apostelgeschichte*, 3rd ed. (Berlin: de Gruyter, 1977). For Grässer, anything that does not adhere to *konsequente Eschatologie* is historically suspect.

3. See C. H. Dodd, *The Parables of the Kingdom*, rev. ed. (New York: Scribner's Sons, 1961), 60–84; Dodd, *The Apostolic Preaching and Its Developments* (New York: Harper, 1960), 31: "within a very few years the perspective of the kerygma must have altered [from Jesus's own view], namely, in respect of the relation conceived to exist between the death, resurrection, and exaltation of Christ on the one hand, and His second advent on the other." An antecedent of this view may be found in J. Stuart Russell, *The Parousia: A Critical Inquiry into the New Testament Doctrine of Our Lord's Second Coming* (Grand Rapids: Baker Books, 1982 [orig. 1887]). Cf. N. T. Wright, *The New Testament and the People of God* (Minneapolis: Fortress, 1992), 284–85, 333, 459–64; Wright, "Hope Deferred? Against the Dogma of Delay," *EC* 9 (2018): 76–78; and also Scot McKnight, *A New Vision for Israel: The Teachings of Jesus in National Context* (Grand Rapids: Eerdmans, 1999), 134–37, 142 (the "coming of the son of man" refers to Jesus's future vindication and the destruction of Jerusalem). For a similar view wherein Jesus merely "expected the vindication of the son of man after suffering," see Vincent Taylor, *Life and Ministry of Jesus* (New York: Abingdon, 1955), 179–80.

4. John Dominic Crossan, *The Historical Jesus: The Life of a Mediterranean Jewish Peasant* (New York: HarperCollins, 1991); Robert Funk, Roy W. Hoover, and the Jesus Seminar, *The Five Gospels: The Search for the Authentic Words of Jesus* (New York: Macmillan, 1993); Marcus Borg, *Conflict, Holiness and Politics in the Teachings of Jesus*, 2nd ed. (Harrisburg, PA: Trinity International, 1998); Stephen J. Patterson, *The God of Jesus: The Historical Jesus and the Search for Meaning* (Harrisburg, PA: Trinity International, 1998). See also Robert Funk, *Honest to Jesus: Jesus for a New Millennium* (San Francisco: HarperSanFrancisco, 1996).

was actually distinctive of the early church, which remade Jesus in their image. Of course, many studies of Jesus cannot be neatly categorized into one of these three streams, and Glasson and Robinson may themselves be good examples of that. (I would contend they have feet in both of the second and third streams.)

This rough sketch of scholarship helps explain why so few have found the topic of the second coming worthy of serious reconsideration in over sixty years. Given the way in which most in the second or third streams characterize the nature of Jesus's message in general, it does not surprise that few of them believe that Jesus predicted his own return in the near future. So even if such critics disagree with some or many of Glasson's and Robinson's arguments along the way, there is a natural affinity in streams two and three for their final conclusion: the hope for Christ's return finds its origin in the theology of the early church (however one might explain that).

The influence of Rudolf Bultmann is also crucial to mention here. Bultmann himself may have belonged in the first stream; he never wavered in his view that the portrait of Jesus found in Johannes Weiss—his teacher—was near the truth, and it was precisely the eschatological nature of the early Jesus movement that motivated the need for demythologization.[5] But Bultmann did not think Jesus anticipated his own return. Bultmann argued that Jesus, when he did speak of the future coming of "the son of man," was talking about someone else.[6] Moreover, while Bultmann's Jesus was eschatological through and through, he argued that eschatology often made its impact in a noneschatological way: eschatology functioned to intensify his ethical demand.[7] Thus, it was possible for Bultmann's immense shadow to fall on subsequent scholarship in two very different directions—one emphasizing the eschatological, and the other the noneschatological or existential demand in the present—and in neither case is the second-coming hope linked to Jesus in any notable way.[8] One sees precisely this twofold legacy in the work of Bultmann's students—especially Ernst Käsemann, Hans Conzel-

5. See Rudolf Bultmann, *Jesus and the Word*, trans. Louise Pettibone Smith and Erminie Huntress Lantero (New York: Scribner's Sons, 1934), 38–39; Bultmann, *Jesus Christ and Mythology* (New York: Scribner's Sons, 1958), 13 ("if the conception of the Kingdom of God is an eschatological one, then it is impossible to make use of this conception in dogmatics").

6. Rudolf Bultmann, *History of the Synoptic Tradition*, trans. John Marsh, 5th ed. (Peabody, MA: Hendrickson, 1963), 122; Bultmann, *The Theology of the New Testament*, trans. Kendrick Grobel (New York: Scribner's Sons, 1955), 1:29–32.

7. See Bultmann, *Jesus and the Word*, 35–37.

8. For a brilliant argument about this legacy, see Stephen Patterson, "Bultmann's Jesus in America," in *"To Recover What Has Been Lost": Essays on Eschatology, Intertextuality, and Reception History in Honor of Dale C. Allison Jr.*, ed. Tucker S. Ferda, Daniel Frayer-Griggs, and Nathan C. Johnson, NovTSup 183 (Leiden: Brill, 2021), 405–28.

mann, Günther Bornkamm, and Helmut Koester[9]—whose collective impact on New Testament studies is hard to quantify.[10]

Different Eschatological Jesuses

What, then, of the second-coming hope for scholars in the first Schweitzerian stream, a stream of tradition in which this book itself belongs? This makes for a more interesting tale. One might expect that, if anyone is going to suggest that "the hope of the early Church"—to borrow Brian Daley's phrase—goes back to Jesus himself, it would be these critics making the case.[11] But the surprising reality is that very few have argued as much, including the influential critics mentioned above: E. P. Sanders, Paula Fredriksen, and Dale Allison. Current New Testament scholarship—in *all* three streams—is either characterized by a strange silence on this topic or has given it very little attention. One does not find robust arguments for or against but rather the general absence of much argument at all.

This volume does more, however, than simply provide attention where attention is needed. I contend that the collective demurral among the heirs of Schweitzer's Jesus to grapple with the origin of the second advent complexifies some widespread and oft-cited conclusions about the so-called eschatological Jesus. In other words, this project is not just about filling gaps in a common portrait of Jesus; it is also about contesting some research about Jesus and eschatology. To make this point, I engage Sanders, Fredriksen, and Allison not only because of their unquestionable

9. See, e.g., Ernst Käsemann, "Das Problem des Historischen Jesus," *ZTK* 51 (1954): 125–53; Käsemann, "Die Anfänge christlicher Theologie," *ZTK* 57 (1960): 162–85; Hans Conzelmann, *Jesus*, ed. John Reumann, trans. J. Raymond Lord (Philadelphia: Fortress, 1973), 77 (Jesus's kingdom proclamation left "no room for another interim figure between the present time and the in-breaking of the kingdom . . . [and] neither is there time for his own preceding removal and 'parousia'" [46]); Günther Bornkamm, *Jesus of Nazareth*, trans. Irene and Fraser McLuskey, with James M. Robinson (New York: Harper, 1960), 90–95, 175–78; Helmut Koester, "GNOMAI DIAPHOROI: The Origin and Nature of Diversification in the History of Early Christianity," in *Trajectories through Early Christianity*, ed. Helmut Koester and James Robinson (Eugene, OR: Wipf & Stock, 2006), 114–57.

10. Cf. James M. Robinson, *A New Quest of the Historical Jesus and Other Essays* (Philadelphia: Fortress, 1983); Irvin W. Batdorf, "Interpreting Jesus since Bultmann: Selected Paradigms and Their Hermeneutic Matrix," in *Society of Biblical Literature 1984 Seminar Papers*, ed. Kent Harold Richards, SBLSP 23 (Chico, CA: Scholars Press, 1985), 187–215; Warren S. Kissinger, *The Lives of Jesus: A History and Bibliography* (New York: Garland, 1985), 85–92; William Baird, *From C. H. Dodd to Hans Dieter Betz*, vol. 3 of *History of New Testament Research* (Minneapolis: Fortress, 2013), 129–94.

11. Brian E. Daley, *The Hope of the Early Church: A Handbook of Patristic Eschatology* (Cambridge: Cambridge University Press, 1991).

influence on New Testament studies but because their positions serve to map a spectrum of possible historical scenarios about the second coming in this eschatological stream of tradition. To be sure, these critics may have broadly similar approaches to and conclusions about the eschatological or apocalyptic Jesus, but beneath the surface, there are rather significant disagreements among them when one considers what their reconstructions state, or imply, about the origin of the second advent hope in particular. To my knowledge, these deeper disagreements have not been sufficiently named or explored,[12] and we can outline them here briefly.

Sanders provides perhaps the least explicit reflection on the question, which is not wholly surprising given his skepticism about making much of the sayings tradition.[13] Yet Sanders clearly does not believe that the expectation for Christ's return in 1 Thess 4:13–18 and elsewhere goes back to the historical Jesus. Sanders's Jesus was an eschatological prophet who may well have spoken about a coming "son of man" with imagery that resembles 1 Thess 4 and the apocalyptic discourses in the Synoptics.[14] But for Sanders, like Bultmann before him, there has been an important shift in perspective in these texts: Jesus, if he said such things, was talking about some other person. Sanders writes, "The early teachers and apostles changed the expectation of the son of man coming with his angels to the return of the Lord, just as in the synoptic tradition they identified the son of man with Jesus."[15] Sanders ties the second-coming hope to other developments in early Christian theology, including the belief that Jesus was a transcendent being.[16] He devotes no time to exploring how the expectation came about, suggesting in passing that it "seems intrinsically likely" that the belief "depend(s) very heavily on the resurrection appearances."[17]

12. Note, e.g., the survey by Albert Hogeterp, *Expectations of the End*, STDJ 83 (Leiden: Brill, 2009), 7–15, which is helpful in what it affirms but still refers generally to "eschatological" and "non-eschatological" positions.

13. E. P. Sanders, *Jesus and Judaism* (Philadelphia: Fortress, 1985), 2, 5, 13, etc.

14. Sanders, *Jesus and Judaism*, 144: "the general theme of a heavenly figure who comes with angels is very early and quite possibly goes back to Jesus."

15. Sanders, *Jesus and Judaism*, 145 (yet noting that "the general expectation probably goes back to Jesus"), 229, 233 ("We can understand better how the disciples could so readily shift their hopes to awaiting the return of the Lord from heaven. If they had always expected an eschatological miracle, it is easy to understand the role of the resurrection appearances in the creation of Christian belief in a heavenly kingdom"). See also E. P. Sanders, *The Historical Figure of Jesus* (London: Penguin Books, 1993), 182, 247–48.

16. Sanders, *Jesus and Judaism*, 21 ("the early church came to believe that Jesus was a transcendent being, that God sent him to save the world, that he would soon return in glory, and that all who believed in him would be saved").

17. Sanders, *Jesus and Judaism*, 21. See also Sanders, *Historical Figure of Jesus*, 182, 247–48. In

Sanders provides little reflection on two other related questions. While Sanders's Jesus expected the restoration of Israel and the advent of the son of man "imminently," Sanders is not very clear about how imminent "imminently" is. Moreover, Sanders believes that, while Jesus did not go up to Jerusalem in pursuit of death (as Schweitzer's did), he did not shy away from this fate when its likelihood became apparent.[18] Thus, Sanders makes two intriguing proposals: Jesus expected the kingdom "imminently," and he also expected, at some point, to die. Sanders nowhere attempts to connect Jesus's impending death with his larger eschatological scenario.[19] This is partly due to the fact that Sanders, self-admittedly, does not give much space in *Jesus and Judaism* to the question of Jesus's understanding of his death.

Paula Fredriksen goes another way here and offers a bit more explicit reflection on questions that Sanders does not.[20] While Sanders left the question of when Jesus expected the end somewhat ambiguous, Fredriksen is clear: Jesus expected the Passover festival on which he died to be the last Passover in history.[21] Fredriksen's Jesus, in other words, had expected the kingdom to come "imminently" in the sense of within his own lifetime. In this, she is perhaps nearer to Schweitzer than Sanders is. In fact, she believes that Jesus had predicted that the kingdom would come on this particular Passover, which is part of the reason why the nameless crowd, not Jesus's own followers, decided to name him the messiah (a title Jesus did not claim for himself, in her view). Fredriksen claims that Jesus "lost control of his audience" in Jerusalem, but he was at least partly to blame for stirring up the eschatological waters.[22] Fredriksen suggests that the flight of the disciples at his arrest demonstrates that they did not expect anything like this on the horizon.

Jesus and Judaism, 37, he asserts that those who identify Jesus with the son of man are guilty of "a retrojection of Christian theology back into the mind of Jesus."

18. Sanders, *Jesus and Judaism*, 324. Sanders does not spend much time discussing this question either—a fact he acknowledges ("The reader may well be surprised to find that I have said so little about two important topics: titles and how Jesus thought of his death")—and he points with approval to the important study by C. K. Barrett, *Jesus and the Gospel Tradition* (London: SPCK, 1967), 35–67.

19. Sanders, *Jesus and Judaism*, 332, suggests it is possible, given Mark 14:25, "that even that late he hoped for the divine intervention which would establish the kingdom before he died."

20. Fredriksen's fullest account appears in *Jesus of Nazareth, King of the Jews: A Jewish Life and the Emergence of Christianity* (New York: Knopf, 1999).

21. Fredriksen, *Jesus of Nazareth*, 244–45, 251, 257. Fredriksen defends the same in her more recent *When Christians Were Jews* (New Haven: Yale University Press, 2018), 67–73, 74, 90. For a similar view, see Gerd Theissen and Annette Merz, *The Historical Jesus: A Comprehensive Guide*, trans. John Bowden (Minneapolis: Fortress, 1998), 552–53 (Jesus expected his parousia as the son of man in his lifetime but was disappointed in Jerusalem).

22. Fredriksen, *Jesus of Nazareth*, 247, 257 (see also 245).

From where, then, did the second-coming hope arise? Fredriksen argues it was a combination of the resurrection experiences and the creative impulses of Jewish restoration eschatology. The resurrection appearances, she contends, had a generative influence: they convinced the disciples that Jesus was, in fact, the messiah of Israel, yet as they began to cease, they also highlighted the failure of the kingdom to arrive in full.[23] Moreover, as Jesus's teaching and deeds were themselves intelligible within Jewish restoration eschatology, the disciples continued to play out various, widely held hopes for the end, such as the expectation for the gentiles to turn to God. As the disciples were therefore convinced that Jesus is the messiah, and that the end-time events predicted by the prophets were underway, they inferred that he would come again on the clouds as a warrior:

> The pressures of more traditional Jewish messianic thought are precisely what prompt the early Christian revisions of it, expressed in the expectation of Jesus' Second Coming. . . . Leading armies of angels, descending to the sounding of trumpets, gathering in the elect: Jesus of Nazareth, in life the least military of figures, transforms in traditions of his own Second Coming into a recognizably—thus traditional—messianic figure, whose advent will establish the Kingdom of his Father.[24]

23. Fredriksen, *When Christians Were Jews*, 113: "the Kingdom's persistent (and baffling) nonarrival, coupled with the falling away of the resurrection appearances, rendered Jesus' *second* coming a necessity." See also at 122–23.

24. Fredriksen, *Jesus of Nazareth*, 246. Later she describes the second advent as "Christianity's singular contribution to the variety of messianic expectations in late Second Temple Judaism," yet she concedes it "resonates precisely with the Davidic paradigm" (264). Concerning Paul, she writes, "It is in Paul's descriptions of Jesus' Second Coming that we see, finally, the strength of traditional Jewish expectations about the role and function of the Davidic Messiah. Jesus' first appearance had not been messianic, and Paul knew it. He even emphasized it: Paul preached 'Christ crucified, a stumbling block to Jews and folly to the Gentiles'" (135). And again, "When Christ came again, said Paul, he would come the way the royal Messiah was supposed to come: in power" (135). See also *From Jesus to Christ: The Origins of the New Testament Images of Christ*, 2nd ed. (New Haven: Yale University Press, 2000), 168, where she calls the parousia a "classically messianic performance . . . to offset his untraditional earthly ministry." See also Fredriksen, *When Christians Were Jews*, 99–107. For a similar view, see David Flusser, "Jewish Messianism Reflected in the Early Church," in *Sages and Literature*, vol. 2 of *Judaism of the Second Temple Period*, ed. David Flusser and Azzan Yadin (Grand Rapids: Eerdmans, 2009), 276. See also Amy-Jill Levine, *The Misunderstood Jew: The Church and the Scandal of the Jewish Jesus* (San Francisco: HarperSanFrancisco, 2006), 56–62; Matthew V. Novenson, *The Grammar of Messianism: An Ancient Jewish Political Idiom and Its Users* (Oxford: Oxford University Press, 2017), 208 ("The predominant early Christian mechanism for maintaining biblical messiah traditions in the face of the suboptimal circumstances of Jesus's life is the belief in the Parousia of Jesus").

For Fredriksen, then, we have a clear development in the second-coming hope that is both continuous and discontinuous with the teaching of Jesus. There is continuity in terms of general eschatological expectation, but discontinuity in terms of the specific content of the expectation. "To the sound of trumpets, leading angelic hosts, defeating the powers of evil, the Risen Christ would return as a warrior."[25] The way in which Fredriksen depicts the militancy of the second coming, and thus contrasts it with the teaching of Jesus, resembles what we found in Glasson and Robinson above.[26]

Dale Allison has provided a slightly different portrait still, one that in some respects stands as a middle term between Sanders and Fredriksen. All three agree that Jesus was wrong about the end. But *in what sense* was Jesus wrong? On the one hand, Allison argues, like Sanders, that Jesus expected to die.[27] So Allison would disagree with Fredriksen's argument that Jesus was wrong because the kingdom failed to come in his own lifetime, even though Allison is not always clear in his various works what exactly "imminent" means (here he also resembles Sanders).[28] On the other hand, Allison argues, contra Sanders, that Jesus believed *he* had the "starring role in the eschatological drama"[29]—Jesus never spoke of some other "son of man."[30] Nevertheless, in *Constructing Jesus*—Allison's most comprehen-

25. Fredriksen, *Jesus of Nazareth*, 264.

26. Fredriksen, *When Christians Were Jews*, 114 ("Jesus' military messianic future, when he returned, in a sense would compensate for his irenic, non-Davidic earthly mission").

27. Dale C. Allison Jr., *Constructing Jesus: Memory, Imagination, and History* (Grand Rapids: Baker Books, 2010), 387–434, at 433 ("to entertain the suggestion that Jesus did not go to his death willingly requires positing either a widespread conscious cover-up or a catastrophic memory failure in the early Christian sources").

28. Allison does, however, write that, if Mark 14:25 is historical, "we might wonder whether he hoped that the end would come in the next few days." See *Constructing Jesus*, 146 n. 518.

29. Allison, *Constructing Jesus*, 231. This assertion appears in Allison's chapter on "the Christology of Jesus" (221–304), but it could be found just as well in his chapter on "the eschatology of Jesus"; if it were, then he would surely have to confront the second advent idea more head-on. I will return to this later.

30. Allison, *Constructing Jesus*, 241. Though this should be nuanced a bit. Allison suggests as a possibility ("I do not pretend to know," 303) that Jesus may have referred to the "son of man" as his heavenly twin or celestial doppelgänger (296–303), believing that, in the future, he "would become one" with him (300). Allison cites Klaus Koch and David Catchpole as others who had written briefly about this (300 n. 331). To that list could be added Rudolf Otto, *The Kingdom of God and the Son of Man: A Study in the History of Religion*, trans. Floyd V. Filson and Bertram Lee Woolf (Grand Rapids: Zondervan, 1938), 162–243, who draws heavily on the Enochic literature for this argument. In his earlier work, *Jesus of Nazareth: Millenarian Prophet* (Philadelphia: Fortress, 1998), 65, Allison argues, concerning Jesus's use of the phrase, "son of man," that "the two most likely options" (n. 242) are (1) Jesus was speaking of someone else, or (2) he was talking about

sive discussion of eschatology in the Jesus tradition—he does not argue that Jesus predicted his own future return as the son of man after an interim period. In *The End of the Ages Has Come*, Allison's first book, he flatly asserted that the notion of the second coming "cannot be found in the authentic words of Jesus,"[31] and he took a position that closely resembles where Jeremias ended up: "In the eyes of Jesus," he wrote, "resurrection and Parousia were functionally equivalent: both referred to the coming vindication of the saints after tribulation."[32] The resurrection of Jesus fulfilled only half of that vindication, so what was for Jesus an original unity became Easter (present/past) and parousia (pushed to the future).

Upon close inspection, then, it turns out that these three hailed proponents of the eschatological Jesus actually disagree about important matters when it comes to eschatology. If eschatology includes, if nothing else, beliefs about things that will happen in the future, these three critics disagree about *what* some of the consequential things are, and *when* in the future Jesus expected them to occur.

A Fresh Look

The need for this study should thus be clear. The issue is not just that scholars have failed to give the second coming the attention it deserves; the issue is that their reconstructions actually carry (if they do not raise the point explicitly otherwise) certain historical implications about the genesis of the second advent that are not acknowledged or adequately defended.[33] Moreover, it is not clear how certain historical claims hold together: both Allison and Sanders, for instance, maintain that Jesus expected to die, but they also claim that Jesus expected the kingdom to come "imminently." How do these two claims relate to each other? If one concludes that Jesus thought he might die—which I will in this volume—what are the implications for the eschatology of Jesus in general, and the origin of the second advent hope in particular? I think it is fair to say that this question is

---

the suffering and vindication of the saints (a collectivist reading he links to the work of T. W. Manson and others).

31. Dale C. Allison Jr., *The End of the Ages Has Come: An Early Interpretation of the Passion and Resurrection of Jesus* (Philadelphia: Fortress, 1985), 160.

32. Allison, *End of the Ages*, 160. Recently, Allison has reasserted the position; see *The Resurrection of Jesus: Apologetics, Criticism, History* (New York: Bloomsbury T&T Clark, 2021), 200–201 (where he cites approvingly C. H. Dodd).

33. Fredriksen may avoid this critique, given she does indeed acknowledge the question of origin and even offers an argument. I just respectfully disagree with her position, as I will discuss in following chapters.

crucial for my own reconstruction of Jesus in the following pages, as I explained in the prologue to this study.

I suspect that this oversight has much to do with the form and scope of so much recent work on Jesus. Few critics anymore write lives of Jesus, and Sanders and Allison, for their part, have contributed to Jesus research with focused studies on particular topics. To be sure, the focus and reserve of both critics is one reason why their works remain among, in my opinion, some of the best studies of Jesus ever written. Sanders's *Jesus and Judaism*, and even more, *The Historical Figure of Jesus*, is nearer a life of Jesus than Allison's numerous contributions, perhaps, and yet it still attends only to particular questions pertaining to eschatology and the place of Jesus in Christian origins. Allison's *Constructing Jesus* and *Resurrecting Jesus* are really collections of essays on different topics. In *Constructing Jesus*, Allison has one chapter on eschatology, and another chapter on the death of Jesus, but there is no point in the book where the results of these two studies converse with each other in a robust way. It is interesting in this respect to observe that Paula Fredriksen's more forthright attempt to integrate the death of Jesus with his eschatological hopes is related to her more *Leben*-like study in *Jesus of Nazareth*. It is the form of her project, if nothing else, that demanded that.

It also needs to be recognized that much of the formative work on eschatology in the Schweitzerian stream of tradition has been forged in times of contestation. The 1980s to the early 2000s was a period of intense debate between critics who reconstructed near completely different Jesuses: an eschatological Jesus of Sanders and others, and a Jesus who had essentially no eschatology to speak of.[34] In 1996, the interlocutors of Allison's important *Journal of Biblical Literature* article, "A Plea for Thoroughgoing Eschatology," were not people convinced that eschatology was the key to Christian origins but happened to hold some disagreements about the particulars;[35] the interlocutors in that piece, as well as in *Jesus of Nazareth: Millenarian Prophet* and even the lengthy chapter on eschatology in *Constructing Jesus*, were critics like Crossan and Borg, and more recently Robert Miller and Stephen Patterson, who believed that Jesus had very little interest in apocalyptic eschatology

34. A debate that is by no means settled, of course. Cf. Ralph Hochschild, "Eschatologischer Prophet oder 'Non-Eschatological Jesus'? Wissenschaftssoziologische Überlegungen zur Rezeption von Johannes Weiß: 'Die Predigt Jesu vom Reiche Gottes,'" in *Jesus—Gestalt und Gestaltungen: Rezeptionen des Galiläers in Wissenschaft, Kirke und Gesellschaft; Festschrift für Gerd Theißen zum 70. Geburtstag*, ed. Petra von Gemünden, David G. Horrell, and Max Küchler, NTOA 100 (Göttingen: Vandenhoeck & Ruprecht, 2013), 411–28.

35. Dale C. Allison Jr., "A Plea for Thoroughgoing Eschatology," *JBL* 113 (1994): 651–68. In *Constructing Jesus*, 145, he writes that he "regret[s] my earlier endorsement of Schweitzer's phrase 'thoroughgoing eschatology.'"

at all.[36] In a similar way, Allison and Fredriksen in particular have also engaged in debate with critics like N. T. Wright and others who read the eschatological material in the Gospels as theological commentary on sociopolitical realities.[37] Given the nature of this disagreement, it is understandable why this discussion, too, has remained on a more global level concerning matters of definition, genre, and worldview. But if, as I believe, this Schweitzerian stream of tradition has won the debate against other noneschatological and symbolically eschatological reconstructions of Jesus—a claim I will defend in subsequent pages—it is now time for a more in-house discussion, as it were, about the eschatology of Jesus. Indeed, this book is a quest for clarity and nuance within the Schweitzerian stream of tradition.

This quest for clarity leads me to pursue a slightly different historical approach to the question. Sanders, Fredriksen, and Allison have all championed reconstructions of Jesus that place little weight on the historicity of individual logia of Jesus.[38] No doubt this kind of careful reticence is one reason their works have endured and will continue to endure.[39] It has also shaped my own approach. But in basing one's reconstructions on large tendencies in the tradition, the payoff will necessarily be more limited in terms of what we actually learn about the historical Jesus.[40] For instance, in his most extensive defense of the eschatological Jesus, Allison claims to identify a "global pattern" in the gospel tradition that leaves us with a clear choice "between an apocalyptic Jesus and no Jesus at all." It is hard to see how Allison loses this either-or debate. But *what* apocalyptic scenario did Jesus anticipate? Allison understands "apocalyptic eschatology" as

36. Allison, *Jesus of Nazareth*, 95–128. So also Robert J. Miller, ed., *The Apocalyptic Jesus: A Debate* (Santa Rosa, CA: Polebridge, 2001) (where Allison's conversation partners are Borg, Crossan, and Patterson).

37. Paula Fredriksen, "*Al Tirah* ('Fear Not!'): Jewish Apocalyptic Eschatology, from Schweitzer to Allison, and After," in Ferda, Frayer-Griggs, and Johnson, *"To Recover What Has Been Lost"*, 15–38. See also Dale C. Allison Jr., "Jesus and the Victory of Apocalyptic," in *Jesus and the Restoration of Israel: A Critical Assessment of N. T. Wright's* Jesus and the Victory of God, ed. Carey C. Newman (Downers Grove, IL: InterVarsity Press, 1999), 126–41.

38. There are exceptions to this, especially in the case of Sanders, *Jesus and Judaism*, 98–102, 256–59, who places tremendous weight on the thrones saying (Matt 19:28 and parr.) and the prohibition of divorce (Mark 10:2–12 and parr.; Matt 5:31–32; Luke 16:18), among a few others.

39. As noted also by Brant Pitre, *Jesus and the Last Supper* (Grand Rapids: Eerdmans, 2015), 31–36, 46–50, when affirming what he calls Sanders's "triple-context approach."

40. Cf. Tom Holmén, "Authenticity Criteria," in *Encyclopedia of the Historical Jesus*, ed. Craig A. Evans (New York: Routledge, 2008), 47: "the recurrently attested motifs tend to be rather general ones. Consequently, the knowledge yielded by the criterion will usually remain on quite a general level. The composite picture of Jesus based solely on such knowledge, again, will turn out nonspecific and cursory."

> convenient shorthand for a cluster of themes well attested in Jewish literature, themes that were prominent in a then-popular account of the world that ran, in brief, as follows. Although God created a good world, evil spirits have filled it with wickedness, so that it is in disarray and full of injustice. A day is coming, however, when God will repair the broken creation and restore scattered Israel. Before that time, the struggle between good and evil will come to a climax, and a period of great tribulation and unmatched woe will descend upon the world. After that period, God will, perhaps through one or more messianic figures, reward the just and requite the unjust, both living and dead, and then establish divine rule forever.[41]

Allison convincingly shows that the historical Jesus was beholden to this "cluster of themes," and, of course, he makes many arguments about many more specific matters. But there are very different reconstructions of the historical Jesus possible within this larger typology.[42]

It may well be that the best we can do with the sources we have is deal with broad themes like this that produce, necessarily, fairly general results about Jesus.[43] But there is another problem here. Sometimes the generalizations do not, on close inspection, actually do justice to the specifics. In *Constructing Jesus*, Allison starts his argument that Jesus "publicly promoted some version" of the apocalyptic story cited above by providing an impressive catalogue of thirty-two units from the Gospels—ranging from individual sayings to narrative events. Again, to be fair to Allison, his main interlocutors here are critics who dispute the general portrait of Jesus as an eschatological prophet. Yet it seems to me that Allison does not adequately discuss the fact that, from the perspective of the evangelists, several of these units are patently about the future coming of Jesus. The first item in Allison's catalogue is Mark 9:1, Mark 13:30, and Matt 10:23, to which he provides this summative commentary: "Two logia from Mark and one from Matthew, all three of which may be variants of the same original, openly declare that the sands of ordinary time have just about run out."[44] That is true. But there is a lot more going

41. Allison, *Constructing Jesus*, 32, 46–47.

42. Tobias Hägerland, "The Future of Criteria in Historical Jesus Research," *JSHJ* 13 (2015), makes a similar critique here. He notes that, "however detailed this representation of Jesus' past is made [Allison's, that is], it necessarily remains somewhat static and one-dimensional, inasmuch it misses those singular, unrepeatable major events in Jesus' life which by definition cannot be recurrently attested, yet were crucial to the shaping and outcome of his career" (54).

43. Allison, *Constructing Jesus*, 263 (stressing that his interest is "more in the general than in the particular"); see also 19.

44. Allison, *Constructing Jesus*, 33. See a similar move in Allison, "Plea for Thoroughgoing Eschatology," 656; Allison, *Jesus of Nazareth*, 147–50.

on in these passages than the general idea of eschatological imminence. They are all about Jesus. Mark surely understands 9:1 to refer to the return of Jesus (8:38: "when the son of man comes in the glory of his Father"), as well as 13:30 (the "these things" which have taken place includes the coming of the son of man in vv. 24–27), and Matt 10:23 predicts what will occur "before the son of man comes."[45]

Sanders and Fredriksen frequently make a similar move.[46] Fredriksen, for example, offers an intriguing reflection on Paul's "word of the Lord" about the parousia of Christ in 1 Thess 4:13–18 that is worth quoting at length:

> Might not some version of this teaching go back through those who were apostles before Paul to the teaching of Jesus himself? Jesus' messianic, triumphant appearance as the vindicated, militant Son most easily coheres, it is true, with post-Crucifixion developments. It compensates for the disappointment of Jesus' crucifixion and clearly stands as a specifically Christian embellishment on earlier Jewish traditions of Messiah and Kingdom. . . . But the Kingdom itself, the belief that it is coming, that it will particularly manifest in Jerusalem, that it will involve the restored nation of Israel as well as Gentiles who have renounced their idolatry—all these beliefs predate Jesus' death by centuries and are also found variously in other Jewish writings roughly contemporary with him. . . . Predicting his own Second Coming may indeed be historically implausible. Predicting the good news of the coming Kingdom of God, not at all.[47]

The argument is that the "word of the Lord" in 1 Thess 4 correctly informs us about Jesus's expectation of the soon-to-arrive kingdom of God, but the saying misleads as to what it actually claims about the return of Jesus from heaven. The

45. Also telling is the way in which Allison summarizes the eschatology chapter as a whole in *Constructing Jesus*, 157, highlighting only "a resurrection of the dead, a universal divine judgment, and a new, idyllic world with evil undone, all coming soon," while his earlier catalogues of material spoke of much more than that.

46. Sanders, *Jesus and Judaism*, 118, cites approvingly the argument of Barry Crawford, "Near Expectation in the Sayings of Jesus," *JBL* 101 (1982): 225–44, that we can be confident the expectation for the soon arrival of the kingdom can be regarded as authentic even if the specific sayings pointing to that fact are not historical. See also *Jesus and Judaism*, 145–46. Helen K. Bond, *The Historical Jesus: A Guide for the Perplexed* (London: Bloomsbury T&T Clark, 2012), 146, wrote that the Last Supper had been overlain with later concerns, e.g., "the clear hope of Jesus' imminent return—Jesus preached the coming of God, rather than his own return." Note also James Crossley, *Jesus and the Chaos of History: Redirecting the Life of the Historical Jesus* (Oxford: Oxford University Press, 2015), 66, where he summarizes an impressive list of sources, arguing for continuity between Paul and John the Baptist, with a general assertion: "Paul would continue to believe that end times were imminent."

47. Fredriksen, *Jesus of Nazareth*, 97.

assumption is that we can strip the passage of its specific content—which is considered unhistorical—but regard its general eschatological notions of arrival and imminence to be reliable.[48]

A similar move is made in the common and oft-cited argument popularized by E. P. Sanders: because John the Baptist and the early church sandwich the historical Jesus, and because both the before and the after expected an imminent consummation, we should expect that Jesus did, too.[49] This argument is true on the level of form (imminence) but somewhat misleading on the level of content. It does not appear that early Christians expected the imminent consummation of history in general; they had a very particular hope that their messiah would reappear for the impending consummation (something I will demonstrate in part 3). So Sanders's wording of this argument, which is really an argument about historical continuity, actually disguises an underlying discontinuity in his reconstruction of Christian origins.

Is the gleaning of the general from the particular in these various ways a justified move? It may be, but that has not been demonstrated. As with the historical arguments of Glasson and Robinson considered above, one wonders whether the effort to reconstruct the Jesus of history has again not sufficiently attended to what our sources *claim* about Jesus. With Sanders, Fredriksen, and Allison, we are on far surer footing than the older atomistic approach to the tradition. Yet at times, we remain on similar terrain. On the one hand, there is the reality that, in selecting particular motifs and eschatological topoi from the Gospels, certain things get left out. I believe that all three of these critics, and many others in the Schweitzerian tradition, spend far too little time in the parables of Jesus.[50] On the other hand, while these critics do not often seek to demonstrate the authen-

48. Note Fredriksen, *Jesus of Nazareth*, 79: Paul and his communities had a "lively apocalyptic expectation." A similar move can be identified in the summary provided in Fredriksen, *When Christians Were Jews*, 1–2.

49. Sanders, *Jesus and Judaism*, 91–94.

50. Cf. Allison's less than two-page treatment in *Constructing Jesus*, 116–18, where he makes two negative arguments: (1) the parables do not *exclude* an apocalyptic worldview, and (2) they can be read very differently depending on context and thus need to be handled with caution. Robert J. Miller, "Theological Stakes in the Apocalyptic Jesus Debate," in *Apocalypticism, Anti-Semitism and the Historical Jesus: Subtexts in Criticism*, ed. John S. Kloppenborg with John W. Marshall (London: T&T Clark International, 2006), 121, has issued a similar criticism in an otherwise problematic article (and his own reading of the parables as modern existential riddles is an inadequate substitute). He wrote, "it cannot be a coincidence that scholarly reconstructions of the apocalyptic Jesus give such short shrift to the parables," and he actually singles out Sanders ("virtually absent"), Fredriksen ("seems to make no use of them at all"), and Allison ("seems to relegate parables to the footnotes, where they serve only to document themes Jesus taught more

ticity of individual items of material, they sometimes glean particular motifs and themes from the gospel tradition with little regard for the placement of these items in the larger gospel narratives in which they are found. This is true for some of Allison's impressive catalogues of material. For example, the first item in the eschatological catalogue, as mentioned above, does not sufficiently attend to what sense Mark and Matthew made of the sayings in Mark 9:1, 13:30, and Matt 10:23. If he did, it would be impossible to avoid addressing the second-coming tradition more directly here. This, I think, is one of the potential pitfalls of a "gist" approach that is necessary to keep in mind, its important benefits notwithstanding. It is not the case that "gist" assumes reliability (at least Allison does not conceive of it that way),[51] but we must ensure that our identification of the "gist," as but a first step in making a historical argument about the past, is true to the specifics and nuances of what the texts claim.

---

clearly elsewhere"). Miller also criticizes John Meier, but this was before Meier published *Probing the Authenticity of the Parables*, vol. 5 of *A Marginal Jew* (New Haven: Yale University Press, 2016).

51. As noted by Michael Patrick Barber, "Did Jesus Anticipate Suffering a Violent Death? The Implications of Memory Research and Dale C. Allison's Methodology," *JSHJ* 18 (2020): 203–8, who appears to represent fairly Allison's position on the matter.

CONCLUDING THOUGHTS ON PART 1

This book not only takes up a neglected question in Christian origins research, but it also takes an approach different from the earlier major studies by Glasson and Robinson. Moreover, as much as my approach and conclusions have been shaped by more recent historical Jesus scholarship in the Schweitzerian stream of tradition, I will seek to clarify and build upon some unresolved tensions and overlooked problems in the discussion of the eschatology of Jesus.

To summarize the procedure, the first task is to contextualize the current *status quaestionis* and the "consensus of silence" (on this phrase, see p. 2 above) with a proposal regarding the fraught reception history of the second coming (part 2). I will then proceed with an in-depth discussion of our key sources, particularly Paul's letters and the Gospels, in an attempt to first understand what these sources claim, and assume, about Jesus and the future (part 3). The final move, then, will be to make probabilistic inferences about the past with the hope of accounting for the interpretive postures of our sources and reconstruct Jesus as a "believable figure in first-century Palestine" (part 4).[1] My approach will not resolve all questions about this complex and fascinating topic. But I believe I can demonstrate the probability of the thesis that the earliest Christians hoped that their messiah would return at the end because Jesus himself had provided the impetus for that belief. Majority views on the origin of the second coming have more to do with the legacy of the theological doctrine than anything in the historical record of Christian origins. It is to that legacy and its impact that we now turn.

1. E. P. Sanders, *Jesus and Judaism* (Philadelphia: Fortress, 1985), 166–67.

PART TWO

The "Painful Thorn" of the Parousia

THE RECEPTION OF THE SECOND COMING IN BIBLICAL STUDIES

> What a pity, that so hard on the heels of Christ come the Christians. There is no breather. The disciples turn into the early Christians between one rushed verse and another. What a dismaying pity, that here come the Christians already, flawed to the core, full of wild ideas and hurried self-importance. They are already blocking, with linked arms, the howling gap in the weft of things that their man's coming and going tore.
>
> —Annie Dillard[1]

Annie Dillard is one of my favorite writers. But since she is not a historian of Christian origins who has spent years of research in Second Temple Judaism and early Christianity, I wonder where her confidence in this quotation comes from. How can she pronounce so clearly and matter-of-factly this contrast between the historical Jesus and his messed-up early followers? I think the answer is fairly simple. The confidence stems from a "habit of reading," passed down for so many centuries as to seem now commonsensical.[2] It is the same habit

1. Annie Dillard, "The Book of Luke," in *The Annie Dillard Reader* (New York: HarperCollins, 1994), 276–77.

2. On "habit of reading," borrowed from Brenda Schildgen, *Power and Prejudice: The*

that produced this memorable line from John Lennon: "Jesus was all right, but his disciples were thick and ordinary. It's them twisting it that ruins it for me."[3]

There is a reason that this distinction between Jesus and his followers continues to be made again and again. As with any other religious movement, embodied engagement with Christianity in a given context is never an all or nothing deal; there are practices and beliefs people find valuable and others that they do not. What has happened in this case is that "Jesus" has been identified with what is valuable about Christianity, and "the disciples" are left to bear the weight of whatever blunders are left. How these decisions are made will inevitably differ depending on context and interest, and in the case of Dillard and Lennon, it is not hard to spy in both statements the value systems that undergird their judgments. Dillard distances Jesus from "wild ideas," that is, much of the speculative and the supernatural in Christian theology. By contrast, Jesus leaves a "howling gap in the weft of things," just like great art and literature (according to Dillard's own descriptions).[4] And for Lennon, it is a sin to be "thick and ordinary," which sounds like something a celebrity from the 1960s would say.

I write these opening comments lightheartedly, but there is an important historical question here that is directly related to the reception history of the New Testament. It is possible that Jesus and his disciples were as different as the wheat and the chaff. The trouble for historians is that the views of Jesus and the views of his followers are all mixed up in our sources. So any attempt to differentiate them is an otherwise contestable historical claim that requires demonstration. Unfortunately, since at least the Enlightenment period, these kinds of bifurcations have been assumed—that is, replaced argument—and to similar rhetorical effect as above. "Jesus" and "the disciples" have been placeholders for readers to construct the boundaries of modern religious identities.[5]

Part 2 aims to show that, due to some very significant developments in the history of Christianity, the hope for the return of Jesus has been variously problematized and, conveniently, distanced from his authentic teaching. It became

Reception of the Gospel of Mark (Detroit: Wayne State University Press, 1999), see discussion at pp. 10–11 above.

3. John Lennon, interview by Maureen Cleves, "How Does a Beatle Live?," *London Evening Standard*, March 4, 1966.

4. For Dillard's reflections on these matters, see her brilliant collection of essays, *Living by Fiction* (New York: Harper & Row, 1988).

5. For important studies along similar lines of inquiry, see William Arnal, *The Symbolic Jesus: Historical Scholarship, Judaism, and the Construction of Contemporary Identity* (London: Equinox, 2005); Halvor Moxnes, Ward Blanton, and James Crossley, eds., *Jesus beyond Nationalism: Constructing the Historical Jesus in a Period of Cultural Complexity* (London: Equinox, 2010).

one of those "wild ideas" introduced only after he left the scene. While I discussed in part 1 the emergence of the consensus of silence on the origin question, my objective now is to explain the creation of the "plausibility structure" that undergirded that (initially, at least).[6] (Part 2 will therefore focus mostly on literature *prior to* the twentieth- to twenty-first-century work discussed in part 1.) I will suggest that the construction of this plausibility structure was underway long before the supposed beginnings of the quest of the historical Jesus with Hermann Samuel Reimarus in 1778.

The particular argument of part 2 is twofold. First, I will show that early historical criticism of the New Testament sits squarely within a larger theological conversation in Christianity that had problematized eschatology in general and the second advent hope in particular. Moreover, this problematization was not just about ideas; it arose from very concrete social and political realities as Christians contested the markers and boundaries of religious identity. Second, I uncover how a centuries-long exegetical attempt by Christians to contrast Jesus to Judaism—thereby elevating him above it—had served to define Jewish messianism as inherently violent, political, carnal, and nationalistic (to use common descriptors). Similar adjectives also came to characterize the second-coming hope in some disputes about Christian eschatology. Thus, for persons already troubled by the hope for Christ's return, and who wished to distinguish Jesus from Judaism, an expedient historical reconstruction became prominent: the historical Jesus did not speak of a return from heaven; his followers did, after his death, having reverted back to older "Jewish ideas."[7]

6. The term stems from the work of Peter Berger, *The Sacred Canopy: Elements of a Sociological Theory of Religion* (New York: Anchor, 1991), and has been developed extensively since then in various fields. In religious and theological studies, it refers to the notion that religious ideas are typically regarded as true or real to the degree that they are sustained by the social institutions, processes, and conventions of the day (called "base" structures).

7. My arguments in part 2 are aware of and informed by a number of important studies that have problematized the ways in which the Jewishness of Jesus has been leveraged in service of various Christian theological interests. See especially Arnal, *Symbolic Jesus*, 29, further at 20–37; Halvor Moxnes, "Jesus in Discourses of Dichotomies: Alternative Paradigms for the Historical Jesus," *JSHJ* 11 (2013): 144–45; James G. Crossley, "A 'Very Jewish' Jesus: Perpetuating the Myth of Superiority," *JSHJ* 11 (2013): 109–29. I have written about this myself as well: Tucker S. Ferda, "The Messiah of That Most Mischievous Superstition: Jesus and the Parting of the Ways in the Study of Christian Origins," *EC* 14 (2023): 13–15. Since no serious scholar today disputes the Jewishness of Jesus, critiquing the non-Jewish nature of some reconstructions, while praising the "very Jewish" nature of others, can function as a way for critics to support reconstructions that they prefer and denigrate those that they do not. As Crossley has shown, in Christian contexts, the highly praised very Jewish Jesuses tend also to be those that are most theologically agreeable for the

Part 2 therefore contributes to the reception history of the Bible more widely, situating the early quest for Jesus within a number of influential historical, cultural, and theological trends in the early modern period. As part of a larger methodological trend in the reception history of the Bible, this effort regards the unspoken aspects of debate, the types of questions that readers pose of texts, the sets of expectations that readers have about their source documents, not as givens but rather contingent facts that themselves require historical explanation. My interests reach beyond the claims of authors to the production and maintenance of the assumptions and presuppositions that make their claims possible in a certain time and place.

By way of transition, I return to Glasson and Robinson, whose arguments the last chapters scrutinized in detail. My critiques there concerned more granular matters in their historical and exegetical proposals, but I have one more. It is hard to read their work without getting the impression that both have deep theological stakes in the matter. Glasson's study opens with a quotation from T. H. Huxley: "If [Jesus] believed and taught that [his second coming was near], then assuredly he was under an illusion, and he is responsible for that which the mere effluxion of time has demonstrated to be a prodigious error." But Glasson's book, as a lengthy response to this quotation, assures that one need not worry. He writes at one point,

> The bearing of Jesus is not that of a distraught, wild-eyed apocalyptist shrieking out the vain message that millions now living will never die; it is rather that of the patient farmer who has perfect confidence that the harvest is sure, that one stage of development will inevitably follow another, that small and unpretentious beginnings will have great results.[8]

We have here two religious types, "the patient farmer" versus the "wild-eyed apocalyptist," and it is no mystery which Glasson (and, he assumes, his reader) prefers. Glasson's study is riddled with theological value judgments and typological antinomies like this. He distances Jesus from the "crude literalism of the millena-

---

critic in question, while Jesuses less serviceable to Christian theological interests are vilified as non-Jewish. Assertions about the Jewishness of Jesus, then, carries the potential for misuse and lacks explanatory power in helping us weigh specific proposals about Jesus's behavior in light of the diversity of Second Temple Judaism. In any case, in part 2 we are not trying to reconstruct Jesus but rather engage critically much earlier research and chart its clear anti-Jewish tendencies and their import for one particular topic.

8. T. Francis Glasson, *The Second Advent: The Origin of the New Testament Doctrine*, 3rd ed. (Eugene, OR: Wipf & Stock, 2009), xiii, 139.

rians," asserts that Jesus was about "joyous and redemptive ministry" not "force and domination," "service and love" not "material splendor or coercion," "love and attraction" not "miracle and coercion."[9] He calls Jesus's stress on realized or inaugurated eschatology a "nobler view," and notes that Paul's eager expectation for Christ's return in his early career was an "imperfect message."[10] Glasson characterizes Jesus's message as superior to his Jewish context—"radically different from the popular" Jewish view.[11] And, as noted in a prior chapter, he makes Jesus's disciples responsible for the misunderstanding, since they had been conditioned in Judaism to "look for the speedy arrival of the Messianic Age" in a cataclysmic manner.[12]

Robinson's volume is not so on the nose, but he also opens with explicitly theological reflections. The opening paragraph states that the new cosmology and scientific worldview of modernity throw into question the validity of the second-coming hope as formulated in Christian tradition.[13] Yet his book, like Glasson's, will ultimately quell such concerns by distancing the expectation from Jesus. It was "the early Church," he states, that "translated" Jesus's message into "the thought-form of apocalyptic." For Robinson, recovering the truth of the matter is not a mere antiquarian concern: "much distortion and not a little sheer fantasy has resulted from a one-sided Adventism. We owe it to the Church and to ourselves to try to recover the wholeness of the Christian hope."[14] As noted in part 1, this "wholeness" he claims to find in the Gospel of John, where he argues for a "unity" of the "now" and the "not-yet."[15] John did not expect "a second supernatural event" in the future, he claims, and neither did the historical Jesus.[16]

It would be unfair to characterize and dismiss the works of Glasson and Robinson as theological projects disguised as history. That is why my fundamental issues with their studies are historical and exegetical in nature, as explained in part 1. But our discussion of their work would be incomplete if we failed to note that they arrive at conclusions that are very much at home in a modern, liberal,

9. Glasson, *Second Advent*, 123, 209, 215; see also 65 on fundamentalists and the millennium.

10. Glasson, *Second Advent*, 206, 220.

11. Glasson, *Second Advent*, 105, 111 (Jesus "re-interpreted the Kingdom, and announced its presence"), 117 (Jesus "used the traditional language of Jewish expectation of the End" as a "vehicle" for his own view).

12. Glasson, *Second Advent*, 205. See also Glasson's critique of Schweitzer in "Schweitzer's Influence: Blessing or Bane?," *JTS* 28 (1977): 289–302.

13. John A. T. Robinson, *Jesus and His Coming: The Emergence of a Doctrine* (New York: Abingdon, 1957), 9.

14. Robinson, *Jesus and His Coming*, 98, 159.

15. Robinson, *Jesus and His Coming*, 169. Robinson makes a similar existential move in *In the End, God: A Study of the Christian Doctrine of the Last Things* (London: Clarke, 1950), 64.

16. Robinson, *Jesus and His Coming*, 173.

Protestant milieu. The Jesus they recover is the Jesus they theologically prefer, and the disciples, who confused his message, closely parallel the misguided, eschatologically enthused Christians of their own day (Robinson even names the closest parallel: "the modern Fundamentalist").[17] We also find sweeping generalizations that do a good deal of legwork in their arguments: "Jews" in Jesus's day expected a certain kind of kingdom and end to history, while Jesus's opinions on such matters stand out as unique (e.g., superior); "the early Church," as though it were a single character on a single stage, acted in new, decisive, unified ways in the post-Easter period; the ideas of religious people can be understood as uniform and typological, such that a "patient farmer" does not think like a "wild-eyed apocalyptist," and vice versa.[18]

T. W. Manson once remarked, "by their Lives of Jesus ye shall know them."[19] That is surely true, to some degree at least, for anyone who writes about the historical Jesus. But as Manson himself knew, "by their Lives of Jesus" we learn about more than individual scholars; we learn about the ideological and cultural situatedness of modern biblical criticism. For the theological preoccupations evident in Glasson's and Robinson's work are hardly unique to them. Their disdain for certain literalist forms of eschatology and specifically for millenarianism is almost a cliché in elite circles of academic theology in the West. They did not invent their descriptions of first-century Judaism, or Jewish messianism. And the character of "the early Church" in their reconstructions is easily recognizable, having danced a nearly identical routine in so many earlier performances.

How did we get here?

---

17. Robinson, *Jesus and His Coming*, 9. This appears in the second paragraph of the book.

18. See, e.g., Glasson, *Second Advent*, 139: "His whole attitude and the spirit of His teaching is inconsistent with the view that He expected a world catastrophe to arrive at any moment."

19. Cited in John Reumann, "'Lives of Jesus' during the Great Quest of the Historical Jesus," *IJT* 23 (1974): 33.

5

Charting Christian Eschatology over the Centuries

Albert Schweitzer's *Von Reimarus zu Wrede* was intentionally unappealing to the sensibilities of the nineteenth-century theological elite, and the reception of his work tells us something important about the context of the nineteenth-century and early twentieth-century quests when it comes to eschatology.[1] Schweitzer himself did not think that Jesus expected the parousia, traditionally conceived. His Jesus expected to be revealed as the son of man during his own lifetime—twice, in fact. But there is an irony in the reception of Schweitzer's position that has been overlooked in histories of scholarship. Schweitzer is sometimes characterized as the great rebel and heterodox historian whose work sought to dismantle orthodoxy. But the truth is that, concerning eschatology at least, Schweitzer's Jesus shares a closer family resemblance to traditional portraits of Jesus over the vast majority of Christian

1. On the "shared traffic" between Schweitzer's rehearsal/critique of the history of Jesus scholarship in the nineteenth century and his larger philosophical critique of modernity, see the insightful study by Ward Blanton, "Albert Schweitzer's Apocalyptic Jesus and the End of Modernity," in *Jesus beyond Nationalism: Constructing the Historical Jesus in a Period of Cultural Complexity*, ed. Halvor Moxnes, Ward Blanton, and James Crossley (London: Equinox, 2010), 57–78 ("shared traffic" at 76). At the same time, we should note that other aspects of Schweitzer's work, especially concerning his missionary activity in Lambaréné, are quite at home in nineteenth-century European culture, as highlighted by Andrew M. Mbuvi, *African Biblical Studies: Unmasking Embedded Racism and Colonialism in Biblical Studies* (London: Bloomsbury T&T Clark, 2023), 31–57.

history than to what most historians in the nineteenth century were churning out. Schweitzer's Jesus expected to be revealed in glory and power. His coming would transform the world in undeniable ways—much like what many Christians before had expected at the parousia. Schweitzer just did not think that Jesus expected an interim period before that happened. The more radical and theologically innovative view, it seems to me, is that of the developmental and progressively expanding kingdom of God one finds in the work of Albrecht Ritschl and so many other liberal Protestant historians whose work dominated this period of research.

I must therefore address and challenge another narrative about the situation of modern biblical criticism in the larger sweep of Christian views of eschatology. In his 2018 Gifford Lectures, N. T. Wright argues that Schweitzer, and others like him who contend that Jesus expected "the end of the world," are the true innovators in Christian tradition (of course, Wright is no sympathizer with the developmental eschatology of the nineteenth-century quest, but that is not his focus here).[2] Wright makes the argument that the expectation for "the end of the world" only makes sense in a decidedly modern intellectual context where God had been shunned from the normal operations of world history—a context he describes as "the triumph of Epicureanism."[3] This distinctly modern worldview (Wright contends) is the prerequisite for any suggestion that God must invade human affairs at some future point of time and bring history to a close.[4] He asserts, "The idea of the literal and imminent 'end of the world' as a central belief of first-century Jews, including Jesus and his early followers, is a modern myth."[5] "The modern mistake emerged," he claims, "by a typical projection of contemporary concerns onto a fictitious historical screen."[6]

There are two interrelated problems with this claim. One is that Wright obfuscates the terms "end" and "transformation," thereby turning Schweitzer's escha-

2. N. T. Wright, *History and Eschatology: Jesus and the Promise of Natural Theology* (Waco, TX: Baylor University Press, 2019).

3. Wright, *History and Eschatology*, 3–40. Wright highlights the special import of the Lisbon earthquake in 1755, though in his view, the process was already underway.

4. Wright, *History and Eschatology*, 31: "*the same cultural presuppositions which have shaped Enlightenment thought as a whole have also shaped the practice of history itself, and with it the historical study of Jesus.*" See again at 36: "the resurgence of Epicureanism in the modern West has been the major contextualizing factor, culturally as well as philosophically, within which the great questions have been posed and answers given."

5. Wright, *History and Eschatology*, 47; see also 59. Wright even makes the particular suggestion that Schweitzer's portrait reflects his musical tastes: "He was a Wagner fan" (53). He continues, "Wagner's great epic, coupled of course with Nietzsche's philosophy, gave Schweitzer the clue he needed: the idea of a culture and its horizon headed for disaster" (55).

6. Wright, *History and Eschatology*, 152.

tology into a straw man. For Wright, the original Christian hope was "for a great transformation, not for the end of the world of space, time and matter." Wright further defines this "transformation" as "the *end of the present state of affairs*."[7] But where exactly does Schweitzer assert that Jesus expected the end of space, time, and matter? It seems to me that "the *end of the present state of affairs*" is an excellent summary of what Schweitzer thought Jesus meant by the kingdom of God. Schweitzer just believed that Jesus expected "transformation" in the sense of real, undeniable change in the normal operations of history.[8] It is miraculous.[9] Thus, everything turns on what exactly we mean by "transformation." Pitting "the end of space, time, and matter" over and against "transformation" is tendentious; the question is how we understand "transformation."[10]

This leads to the second problem, which is that Wright's more symbolic understanding of "transformation," rather than Schweitzer's more literal one, is likely the true innovation in Christian eschatology and, I would argue, a product of the modern Western world. The inconvenient fact about Wright's linkage of Schweitzerian eschatology to modern Epicureanism is that it requires him to skip over much of the prior history of Christianity to make his case. To state this is not to downplay or overlook crucial discontinuities between Schweitzer's project and those before him. Nor is it to deny that Wright's arguments about modern Epicureanism are completely unfounded. It is only to say that, for the vast majority of Christian history, eschatological hope, specifically for the parousia of Christ, has been hope for a real change of scenery. (And here I importantly step over the New Testament literature, leaving it to later chapters to challenge Wrightian and Cairdian readings of its eschatological language.) The striking thing about our modern context, contra Wright, is the degree to which the second advent of Christ has been increasingly problematized, increasingly avoided, and increasingly denied among Christians themselves. Indeed, it is precisely this reception history of the second advent that has made possible the creation of new, modern

7. Wright, *History and Eschatology*, 57.

8. The contention of Wright, *History and Eschatology*, 58, that the kingdom's advent issues "*a new state of affairs on earth*" may well have come from Schweitzer's own hand.

9. John Dominic Crossan, *The Historical Jesus: The Life of a Mediterranean Jewish Peasant* (New York: HarperCollins, 1991), 238, offers a helpful clarification here: "by end of the world I mean that the apocalypticist expected a divine intervention so transcendentally obvious that one's adversaries or enemies, oppressors or persecutors would be forced to acknowledge it and to accept conversion or concede defeat."

10. I would note that in Dale C. Allison Jr., "A Plea for Thoroughgoing Eschatology," *JBL* 113 (1994): 651 n. 1, Allison actually prefers to speak of "transformation" rather than the "end" of the world.

eschatologies—a category in which I would include Wright's own. I will defend this alternative historical account in the chapters that follow, as well as articulate social, political, and intellectual factors that led to it.

"And He Will Come Again with Glory"

Historians disagree about the degree to which the homousian Christology of the Nicene Creed represents popular-level Christianity at the time, particularly with respect to the Arian controversy. But there is another line in the creed that does not appear to have been that controversial: "and he will come again with glory to judge the living and the dead" (καὶ πάλιν ἐρχόμενον μετὰ δόξης κρῖναι ζῶντας καὶ νεκρούς). In Brian Daley's magisterial study of Christian eschatology up through the sixth century, he identifies what he calls a "common doctrine," which includes the hope for Jesus to "come again as judge of history."[11] While there are obviously exceptions,[12] Daley stresses the ubiquity and "realism" of this hope, by which he means it would herald concrete, undeniable change "within history." In fact, it is that very assumption that makes it possible for theologians and exegetes to compare and contrast Jesus's first and second "comings" as they frequently do: both the former and latter are (or are expected to be) undeniable historical events, different only in character and effects. The dominant assumption—not argued for as much as assumed as the basis for other arguments—is that the ministry of Jesus includes two distinct advents, and that Jesus accomplishes tasks particular to both.[13] As such, the work of Christ is really thought incomplete without the second advent when he will come with glory to execute the final judgment.[14] As

11. Brian E. Daley, *The Hope of the Early Church: A Handbook of Patristic Eschatology* (Cambridge: Cambridge University Press, 1991), 217. He also notes here "Christ is always the heart and goal of Christian hope, and as such, its source of unity," and "the expectations of early Christians for the future formed, on the whole, a remarkably consistent picture, despite serious areas of unresolved disagreement" (223). Cf. Paul J. Landa, "The Advent Hope in Early Christianity," in *The Advent Hope in Scripture and History*, ed. V. Norskon Olsen (Washington, DC: Review & Herald, 1987), 65–95, esp. 73. See also Jeffrey S. Striker, "The Parousia of Jesus in Second- and Third-Century Christianity," in *The Return of Jesus in Early Christianity* (Peabody, MA: Hendrickson, 2000), 147–68; Charles E. Hill, *Regnum Caelorum: Patterns of Millennial Thought in Early Christianity*, 2nd ed. (Grand Rapids: Eerdmans, 2001).

12. More on this below.

13. See, e.g., Justin Martyr, *Dial.* 121; Athanasius, *Inc.* 56.

14. By already the mid-second century, it had seemed commonsensical to Justin Martyr that if Jesus's first coming "was without honor and comeliness," and yet he was known "in every nation on earth," how much more would his "glorious advent" reshape human history. See

far as I can tell, theological opinion does not change noticeably until after the Protestant Reformation.[15] This is a remarkable thing in light of the disagreement, polemic, and theological diversity that constitute the history of Christianity.[16]

Of course, there was vigorous debate about *when* the parousia would occur, as well as *what* its precise nature and effects would be. Some believed the return was imminent, others that world history would last six thousand years (or more) before it happened (hence a good deal of time beyond their present generation).[17] Some believed that Jesus would rule on earth and establish a new kingdom in Jerusalem (the view known as chiliasm, held by Papias, Justin Martyr, Irenaeus, and many others in the first centuries of Christianity), while others thought that his return would lead to a purely spiritual or heavenly rule.[18] In any case, even those theologians most frequently credited with challenging chiliastic readings of the New Testament and encouraging a more symbolic understanding of escha-

1 Apol. 40 and discussion in L. W. Barnard, "Justin Martyr's Eschatology," *VC* 19 (1965): 86–98. See also Irenaeus, *Haer.* 1.10.1 and discussion in John Lawson, *The Biblical Theology of St. Irenaeus* (London: Epworth, 1948), 288–90; A. Skevington Wood, "The Eschatology of Irenaeus," *EvQ* 40 (1968): 30–41; John Behr, *Identifying Christianity* (Oxford: Oxford University Press, 2013), 180–85.

15. On the traditional or creedal eschatological expectations of the Reformers themselves, see Bryan W. Ball, *A Great Expectation: Eschatological Thought in English Protestantism to 1660*, SHCT 12 (Leiden: Brill, 1975), 15–16; V. Norskov Olsen, "The Christian Hope in the Reformation of the Sixteenth Century," in Olsen, *Advent Hope in Scripture and History*, 115–31.

16. For some key texts, see Did. 10.6; 16.1–3; 1 Clem. 23.2–5; 42.3; 50.3; 2 Clem. 16.3; 17.4; Barn. 15.5; Justin Martyr, *1 Apol.* 51, 52; *2 Apol.* 7; *Dial.* 31, 85; Mart. Ascen. Isa. 4.13; Ep. Apos. 16–17; Sib. Or. 2.241; 8.244; Herm. Sim. 9.27.3; 9.25.2; Herm. Vis. 2.2.7; Irenaeus, *Haer.* 4.33.1; 5.27.1; Tertullian, *Apol.* 21; Eusebius, *Hist. eccl.* 3.20.4; Ambrose, *Exp. Luc.* 10.7–43. On ideological diversity in early Christianity, see Bradley J. Bitner, "Unity and Diversity in Emergent Christianity," in *Into All the World: Emergent Christianity in Its Jewish and Greco-Roman Context*, ed. Mark Harding and Alanna Nobbs (Grand Rapids: Eerdmans, 2017), 74–104.

17. So the important work of Hippolytus, *Comm. Dan.* 4.23–24, rejects the notion of an imminent parousia in favor of the idea that history will last six thousand years before the eschatological rest at the return of Christ. He believed Christ first appeared at the year five thousand five hundred, and hence his parousia would be five hundred years later (well beyond Hippolytus's time). For discussion, see David Dunbar, "The Delay of the Parousia in Hippolytus," *VC* 37 (1983): 313–27; Thomas C. Schmidt and Nick Nicholas, *Hippolytus of Rome: Commentary on Daniel and "Chronicon,"* GSECP 67 (Piscataway, NJ: Gorgias, 2017).

18. On this debate, see Hill, *Regnum Caelorum*, for texts and discussion. See also Jean Daniélou, *The Theology of Jewish Christianity* (London: Darton, Longman & Todd, 1964), 377–404; John M. Court, *Approaching the Apocalypse: A Short History of Christian Millenarianism* (London: Tauris, 2008), 51–60. It is interesting to note how Eusebius deals with this tradition. He basically tries to blame it all on Papias. He says that anyone (naming Irenaeus explicitly) who continued to think this way afterward was inspired by Papias and his misunderstanding of the "figurative" writings of the apostles (cf. *Hist. eccl.* 3.39.11–13).

tological language, still very much believed that the return of Christ would be a historical event in the future, and that this expectation stems from the teaching of Jesus himself. In other words, when a theological problematizing of the return of Christ appears, it concerns largely the *when* and the *how*, not the *that*.

Origen and Augustine

Origen is one of the most difficult to pin down here, and some have suggested that his expectation for the gradual spiritual perfection of souls—an "individual eschatology," one might say—leaves no room for the return of Christ.[19] In his fascinating reading of the Olivet Discourse in his commentary on Matthew, however, he expressly asserts that his "spiritual reading" "is not . . . to reject as spurious the simpler understood second coming of the Son of God,"[20] acknowledging that "the catholic church seems to have received the tradition that the second advent of Christ will be in glory, along with other traditions about this advent."[21] As typical for Origen, he offers his spiritual reading not as a replacement of the literal but as a deepening for those who want "solid food" and not "milk."[22] So, Origen claims that Christ's predictions of "famines" (Matt 24:7) are about spiritual hunger, "persecutions" (24:9–14) are the false teachings of heretics, "the abomination of desolation" (24:15) is any unfaithful interpretation of Scripture, the "clouds" under the feet of the son of man (24:30) are the writings of the apostles, and the "angels" (24:31) represent the words of the prophets. The second coming of Christ can be understood as "the coming of the Word into the soul," "in perfect people," who are able to perceive the splendor of his beauty.[23]

Similar in approach, though certainly more impactful, was Augustine. Augustine's position with respect to the return of Christ is also clearer than Origen's, as he professes "that which the whole Church of the true God holds and professes

19. Landa, "Advent Hope in Early Christianity," 77. See the larger discussion in Daley, *Hope of the Early Church*, 47–59; Anders-Christian Jacobsen, "Eschatology in Origen from Alexandria," in *Eschatology in Antiquity: Forms and Functions*, ed. Hilary Marlow, Karla Pollmann, and Helen Van Noorden (London: Routledge, 2021), 435–46.

20. Origen, *Comm. Matt.* 12.30 in *The Commentary of Origen on the Gospel of Matthew*, trans. Ronald E. Heine, OECT (Oxford: Oxford University Press, 2018), 1:114.

21. Origen, *Comm. ser. Matt.* 50 (trans. Heine, 2:624). It is also worth noting Origen's reply to Celsus's critique that Jesus was a poor general who could not maintain the loyalty of his followers. Origen opines that, at Christ's return, he would have all the power and glory that critics claim he lacked in life. Cf. *Cels.* 2.29.

22. Origen, *Comm. Matt.* 12.31 (trans. Heine, 1:114). On Origen's spiritual reading and eschatology, see Robert M. Grant, *The Earliest Lives of Jesus* (London: SPCK, 1961), 107.

23. Origen, *Comm. ser. Matt.* 32 (trans. Heine, 2:588).

as its creed: that Christ shall come from heaven to judge the quick and the dead, this we call the last day, or last time, of the divine judgment."[24] Augustine had issue instead with millenarian readings of Revelation (in particular) and with eschatological enthusiasts in his day who sought to predict the time of Christ's return. He famously spiritualized the thousand-year reign of Christ in Rev 20 by identifying it with the present era of the church, offering a symbolic reading that resembles Origen's own in the Olivet Discourse and elsewhere.[25] And he issued a plea for agnosticism concerning the date of Christ's return, as well as any attempt to connect current events to particular biblical prophecies.[26] He wrote: "To all those who make such calculations on this subject comes the command, 'Relax your fingers, and give them a rest.'"[27] Augustine's position stemmed from a clear pastoral concern, as he believed those disappointed by failed predictions ultimately doubt his coming at all.[28] He identified the ideal posture in this way:

> The person who longs for his coming, then, is not the person who claims that the coming of the Lord is drawing near or the person who claims that it is not drawing near. It is, rather, the person who awaits his coming, whether it is near or far off, with the sincerity of faith, the firmness of hope, and the ardor of love.[29]

As evident here, for Augustine there was indeed a theological problem with the second-coming hope, but it stemmed from the ways in which later Christians understood and made use of it. Augustine believed that his own mediating view was in step with the teachings of Jesus and the apostles. For while Jesus himself

24. Augustine, *Civ.* 20.1 (*NPNF* 1/2:421). See also *Enarrat. Ps.* 96.14. Augustine spoke of what he called the three advents of Christ: creation, incarnation, and second coming. See Richard K. Emmerson, "The Advent Hope in the Middle Ages," in Olsen, *Advent Hope in Scripture and History*, 103.

25. See discussion in Johannes van Oort, "The End Is Now: Augustine on History and Eschatology," *HvTSt* 68 (2012): 1–7.

26. Augustine writes in *Ep.* 199.6 that if Christ said that it was not for his apostles to know the day or the hour, it would certainly be presumptuous on our part to try. See also *Ep.* 199.13. Centuries later, Maimonides would take a similar position when writing about the messiah's advent: it would happen, but its time cannot be calculated. See discussion in Raphael Patai, *The Messiah Texts* (Detroit: Wayne State University Press, 1979), xxix; Kenneth Seeskin, "Maimonides and the Idea of a Deflationary Messiah," in *Rethinking the Messianic Idea in Judaism*, ed. Michael L. Morgan and Steven Weitzman (Bloomington: Indiana University Press, 2015), 93–107. Rabbi Yehudah HeHasid, the main author of *Sefer Hasidim*, equated messianic calculations with witchcraft. See again Patai, *Messiah Texts*, 157.

27. Cited by Emmerson, "Advent Hope in the Middle Ages," 98.

28. See Augustine, *Ep.* 199.53, where he discusses the "grave harm" caused by such predictions.

29. Augustine, *Ep.* 199.15 (FC 30:367).

clearly predicted the final judgment and his own return from heaven,[30] Augustine thought, a number of his sayings about the future are "ambiguous," possibly referring to the coming of Jesus "continually" in the church or even the destruction of Jerusalem.[31] Jesus wanted his disciples to live in eager expectation of his return but not seek to predict it.[32] Augustine intimates that the ambiguities of Jesus's teaching about the future are themselves clues about this intended result. He could have been clearer but was not by choice.[33]

It is hard to overstate the impact of the way in which Augustine held together an affirmation of the literal return of Christ with a general reticence about speculative exegesis and eschatological enthusiasm. Paula Fredriksen notes that Augustine's eschatology "virtually defined the content of all later Catholic commentaries."[34] This is certainly true up through the thirteenth century, after which we would find, if anything, *more* speculative eschatological interest, not less.[35]

30. See Augustine, *Civ.* 20.24. He argues here that at Christ's second coming, he will not "keep silent"—so the servant from Isa 53. It was common to contrast Isa 53 with the triumphant return of Christ. More on this below.

31. Augustine, *Civ.* 20.5 (*NPNF* 1/2:424): "For when he speaks of this [the destruction of Jerusalem], he often uses language which is applicable to the end of the world and that last and great day of judgment, so that these two events cannot be distinguished."

32. See Augustine, *Ep.* 199.1 (Christians should be "constantly aflame" in longing for him), 7, 9 (ready at all times).

33. Augustine, *Civ.* 20.5, 30. In a discussion of 2 Thess 2, Augustine argues that the apostle Paul took the same strategy (*Ep.* 199.2 [FC 30:365]): "he obviously did not want them to believe those who thought the coming of the Lord was already at hand. Neither, moreover, did he want them to be like the wicked servant and say, 'my lord will not be coming for a long time . . .' Thus, Paul's desire that they should not listen to false rumors about the imminent approach of the last day was consistent with his wish that they should await the coming of their Lord fully prepared and ready for the journey with lamps burning." This became a very common interpretive move, as discussed below. Cf. Tertullian, *An.* 33 (*ANF* 3:215): faith "awaits in trembling expectation, keeping her gaze ever fixed on that day, in her perpetual ignorance of when it will arrive, daily trembling at that for which she yet daily hopes"; Athanasius, *C. Ar.* 3.49 (*NPNF* 2/4:420): the timing of the last day, like a person's own death, "is uncertain and always in prospect, [so that] we may advance day by day as if summoned, reaching forward to the things before us and forgetting the things behind"; John Chrysostom, *Hom. Matt.* 77.2 (*NPNF* 1/10:464): "if ordinary persons knew when they were going to die, they would surely be striving earnestly at that hour. In order therefore that they may strive, not at that hour only, he does not tell them the hour of the day. He wants to keep them on their toes looking for it, that they might always be striving." See also Hilary of Poitiers, *Comm. Matt.* 26.6; Ambrose, *Exp. Luc.* 8.33–39; Leo the Great, *Hom.* 32.

34. Paula Fredriksen, "Apocalypse and Redemption in Early Christianity: From John of Patmos to Augustine of Hippo," *VC* 45 (1991): 166. See also Landa, "Advent Hope in Early Christianity," 88; Walter Klassen, *Living at the End of the Ages: Apocalyptic Expectation in the Radical Reformation* (Lanham, MD: University Press of America, 1992), 4–5.

35. For discussion, see Bernard McGinn, *Visions of the End: Apocalyptic Traditions in the*

Jesus and the Disciples

While the questions of the *when* and the *how* of the second coming (rather than the *that*) are variously problematized and debated by the likes of Origen, Augustine, and others, it is interesting to note how infrequently before the Reformation the disciples are leveraged against Jesus as being in some way responsible for later misunderstandings.[36] It is most often the case that the disciples, or the apostles more specifically, are grouped *with* Jesus as those who shared his eschatological outlook, even if they lacked perfect knowledge. This worked in both positive and negative ways. On the negative side, critics of Christianity rarely spare Jesus by sacrificing his followers. They went down together. So Porphyry, for example, in a fascinating passage that points out the failure of eschatological prediction in one of Paul's letters (1 Thess 4), does not distinguish Jesus from Paul or single out Paul as uniquely responsible for distorting the teaching of Jesus. He simply draws attention to this "astonishingly silly" teaching about the soon coming of Jesus on the clouds of heaven that he calls a "lie" that "reaches up to heaven." It is so absurd, he says, that it would even make animals "bellow or croak or quack" to hear of it.[37]

For self-avowed Christians, on the other hand, Jesus and the apostles were often held together in the sense that the apostles were regarded as models for the proper eschatological outlook of contemporary believers, rather than foils. This tendency developed in the work of various proto-orthodox theologians, perhaps most notably Irenaeus, who stressed the unity of the Christian message from Christ and the apostles from the beginning as a means of critiquing other Christian groups. According to his retelling, it was only fringe characters who came on the scene later, like Simon Magus and other gnostic leaders, who challenged and corrupted the publicly proclaimed gospel shared between Jesus and his imme-

---

Middle Ages (New York: Columbia, 1979); Emmerson, "Advent Hope in the Middle Ages," 108; Klassen, *Living at the End of the Ages*, 15.

36. Though note Irenaeus's claim in *Haer.* 1.26.2 that the Ebionites rejected Paul and thought he was an apostate from the law. See also Eusebius, *Hist. eccl.* 6.38 on the Elchasaites, and the Pseudo-Clementine literature. Criticism of Paul, though, should not be conflated with criticism of the followers/disciples of Jesus in general, which is the focus here. For other early critiques of Paul in particular, see Patrick Gray, *Paul as a Problem in History and Culture: The Apostle and His Critics through the Centuries* (Grand Rapids: Baker Books, 2016), 25–46.

37. From Macarius, *Apocrit.* 4.2. Translations here from R. Joseph Hoffmann, trans. and ed., *Porphyry's* Against the Christians*: The Literary Remains* (Amherst: Prometheus Books, 1994), 68. For pointed criticisms of Jesus, see *Porphyry's* Against the Christians, 30–31 (on Matt 17:15 and John 5:31), 40 (Matt 26:36, a saying he says is "both stupid and unclear"), 44–45 (on Matt 19:24), 77 (on Matt 13:31–33). A critique of Jesus for saying things that did not happen may be implied in Origen, *Cels.* 8.41.

diate followers (cf. *Haer.* 1.31.1; 3.11.9).[38] Aside from Irenaeus, the historical development of the canon only intensified the sacralization of the apostles and close disciples themselves, since these sacred writings were attributed to close followers of Jesus (or their associates). To critique the apostles would be to critique the New Testament itself.[39] The work of Marcion here may be an interesting exception that proves the rule. Marcion's attempts to privilege an edited version of Luke and an edited collection of Paul's epistles required that he disparage the "Jewish disciples" of Jesus who corrupted his message after his earthly ministry.[40] This move appears to be rare, and it is notable that it emerged relatively early—mid-second century—when the canonical status of various New Testament texts was still up for grabs. Others who wished to challenge the status of certain authoritative books did so *by* disputing their apostolicity.[41] The key point, though, is this: it became increasingly rare to polemicize the disciples of Jesus as the status of New Testament texts as sacred Scripture continued to develop and solidify.

This is not to say that that the disciples were completely idealized by any means. But their well-known failures, when highlighted, were not considered reason to doubt the veracity of their public proclamation in general and their eschatological message in particular. It becomes something of a trope in commentarial literature to periodize the experiences and outlook of the disciples around Pentecost—before, and after, the bestowal of the Spirit. Ignorance reigned only before the Spirit arrived to "lead into all truth" (John 16:13). The reception of the exchange between Jesus and his disciples at the beginning of Acts is a fascinating and relevant case in point. It appears on a straightforward reading that "the apostles" (1:2) still very much expect a terrestrial or political kingdom to be set up on earth: "Lord, is this the time when you will restore the kingdom to Israel?" (1:6).

38. See also Cyril of Jerusalem, *Cat.* 6.31 (on the "evil followers of Mani" and the production of the Gospel of Thomas).

39. On the general acceptance of the authorship of the Gospels as written, see Grant, *Earliest Lives of Jesus*, 2–4.

40. For a rich discussion, see Judith M. Lieu, *Marcion and the Making of a Heretic: God and Scripture in the Second Century* (Cambridge: Cambridge University Press, 2015).

41. So the third-century bishop Dionysius of Alexandria, in his book *On the Promises*, rejected the book of Revelation on the grounds that it was not written by the author of the Fourth Gospel and the epistles—and hence was not apostolic. For discussion see Werner Georg Kümmel, *The New Testament: The History of the Investigation of Its Problems*, trans. S. McLean Gilmour and Howard C. Kee (Nashville: Abingdon, 1972), 15–16. Similarly, the third-century Roman bishop Gaius, in his dispute with certain gnostic-Montanist Christians, rejected both the Fourth Gospel and the Apocalypse by disputing its traditional connection to John the son of Zebedee. See Ernst Haenchen, *A Commentary on the Gospel of John: Chapters 1–6*, Hermeneia, trans. Robert W. Funk (Philadelphia: Fortress, 1984), 23.

How could they ask such a misguided (from a proto-orthodox or orthodox perspective) question? John Chrysostom speaks for a great cloud of witnesses: "it appears to me that they had not any clear notion of the nature of that kingdom, for the Spirit had not yet instructed them."[42] When the Spirit was given (Acts 2:1–4), the same Spirit that inspired the writings of the New Testament, such errors were dispelled, well before they started writing the rest of the Bible.

A similar interpretation dominates the reception of numerous other passages in the Gospels.[43] Concerning James and John's request to sit at Christ's right and left hand "in glory" (Mark 10:35–45), the compendium of Byzantine exegesis in the *Catena in Marcum* asserts the following:

> But let no one lay charge against the apostles, if they had this rather imperfect state of mind. For there was now no Cross, and there was as yet no grace of the Spirit. This is why he reveals their deficiencies, in order that later they might realize what kind of persons they had become by grace.[44]

Here the eschatological mistake of James and John is only temporary and actually functions positively to highlight the transformative nature of God's grace.[45]

42. John Chrysostom, *Hom. Act.* 2 (*NPNF* 1/11:11). In *Hom. 1 Thess.* (*NPNF* 1/13:360), he stresses that the disciples had asked Jesus misguided questions both before the passion and after (so Acts 1:6), but not "when they had been vouchsafed the Holy Ghost. Not only do they not themselves inquire, nor complain of this ignorance, but they repress those who labor under this unseasonable curiosity." He continues later, "You see how many advantages there are, and yet there are more than these that arise from not knowing the time of the end. . . . On this account he so comes as a thief in the night, that we might not abandon ourselves to wickedness, nor to sloth." Bede would write that, at the point of Acts 1, the disciples were "still materially minded." See *The Venerable Bede: Commentary on the Acts of the Apostles*, trans. Lawrence T. Martin (Kalamazoo, MI: Cistercian, 1989), 11.

43. It was common to think that when Jesus admitted to speaking "in figures of speech" but promised to later "no longer speak in figures, but will tell you plainly of the Father" (16:25), he was not talking about the end of days but about the forty-day period after his resurrection when he was with the disciples "speaking about the kingdom of God" (Acts 1:3)—an interesting harmonization of John and Acts here. So Cornelius à Lapide, vol. 6 of *The Great Commentary*, trans. Thomas W. Mossman, 4th ed. (Edinburgh: Grant, 1908 [orig. 1681]), 180, who also makes reference to Augustine, Bede, Maldonatus, "and others." See also John Chrysostom, *Hom. Jo.* 79.2.

44. See William R. S. Lamb, ed. and trans., *The* Catena in Marcum*: A Byzantine Anthology of Early Commentary on Mark* (Leiden: Brill, 2012), 367. See also Origen, *Comm. Matt.* 16.4 (trans. Heine, 1:235), on the request of James and John's mother that her sons sit at Jesus's right and left in glory: "grant that the two apostles as well, as men who were still imperfect and did not think anything very profound about the kingdom of Christ, had the same assumptions about sitting with Jesus."

45. For a similar reading, see Theophylact, *Comm. Matt.* on 20:24–28.

Commentators will at other times suggest that such misunderstandings provide opportunities for Jesus to clarify the nature of Christian eschatological hope, assuming that these teachings were ultimately—while perhaps not immediately—successful in changing the disciples' expectations. We should note that such readings function as thinly veiled criticisms of later Christian groups in these interpreters' own day, as the teaching of Christ, representing true Christian belief, responds to and corrects misguided eschatological (or christological) thought in Jesus's time *as well as* in the interpreters' own. In this fusion of horizons, the criticism of the disciples of Jesus does not extend to the apostolic witness as a whole. Such a targeted critique is possible precisely because the misunderstanding among Jesus's immediate followers is thought to stem from a temporary, pre-Pentecost stage of Christian history.

Imminence and Ethics

Of course, there are many other passages in the New Testament where a sense of eschatological imminence appears positively affirmed, rather than implicitly criticized by the text itself (as in the question of the apostles in Acts 1:6, etc.). It was not a modern discovery that the apostle Paul seems to speak as though the return of Christ is very near, or that the writings of close followers of Jesus like Peter and John (as it was thought) urge their readers to expect the parousia at any moment. Were such disciples wrong in writing such things, thereby corrupting the original teaching of Jesus? As noted above, once the scriptural status of New Testament texts was widely affirmed, and the apostolic authorship of these texts assumed, to admit as much would be to assert that the Sacred Writ teaches theological falsehood.[46] Understandably, then, precritical exegesis of the New Testament only rarely intimates that the followers of Jesus themselves were so gravely mistaken about the future.[47] There develops, instead, a fairly uniform interpretive approach to such texts: their point is not exact prediction about the future but exacting a righteous life in the present. Why might it be that John the Baptist said that the

46. On the assumed truth of the Scriptures, see Vasile Milhoc, "How Did the Church Fathers Understand the History of Jesus?," in *Gospel Images of Jesus Christ in Church Tradition and Biblical Scholarship*, ed. Christos Karakolis, Karl-Wilhelm Niebuhr, and Sviatoslav Rogalsky, WUNT 288 (Tübingen: Mohr Siebeck, 2012), 116–17.

47. Though see Porphyry on 1 Thess 4 in Hoffmann, *Porphyry's* Against the Christians, 69–70: "there is more to Paul's lying: He very clearly says, 'We who are alive.' For it is now three hundred years since he said this and nobody—not Paul and not anyone else—has been caught up in the air. It is high time to let Paul's confusions rest in peace!"

axe is "now laid" at the foot of the tree (Luke 3:9), given that the final judgment has not yet occurred? Pseudo-Chrysostom: "because these trees have reason and free power to do good, or leave undone; so that when they see the axe laid to their root, they may fear and bring forth fruit."[48] Why did John the apostle write that "it is the last hour" (1 John 2:18), even though Jesus said it was not for them to know "the times" (Acts 1:7)? Augustine: this was not an attempt to pinpoint the exact time ("the disciples of Jesus were as ignorant as we are," he says) but rather to urge the readers to be watchful and prepared.[49] (Augustine explicitly holds up the apostles as exemplars, encouraging Christians to "imitate the apostles in having our hearts ready.")[50] Why did Paul declare that "the night is far gone, and the day is near" (Rom 13:11–12), since history has long since continued? Chrysostom: "It was not unlikely that at the beginning of their early endeavors they would be most earnest, in that their desire was then at its full vigor, but that as time went on, their earnestness would wither down . . . [but] he says they ought to be doing the reverse, not to get relaxed as time went on but to be the more full of vigor."[51] Why did John write that "the time is near" at the beginning of Revelation (Rev 1:3)? Victorinus of Pettau: to highlight the fact that the blessing at the beginning (1:3) is pronounced "to him that reads and hears and keeps, that he who takes pains about the reading may thence learn to do works, and may keep the precepts."[52]

The basic idea here, so common as to preclude listing further examples, is that mention of eschatological imminence in the writings of the apostles functions to produce alertness in the present.[53] Readers misread if they focus on exact prediction, since the point is to urge more faithful discipleship now. On this point, most interpreters thought that the disciples were closely following the example of Jesus himself.[54] Whether ambiguous about future timing, or similarly expressing some hint of imminent arrival, Jesus's point is the same: "keep awake!" Why, for instance,

48. Cited by Thomas Aquinas, *Catena Aurea: Commentary on the Four Gospels Collected out of the Works of the Fathers*, trans. John Henry Newman (Southampton: Saint Austin, 1997), 1:101.

49. Augustine, *Ep.* 199.1, 3 (FC 30:357–59).

50. Augustine, *Ep.* 199.6 (FC 30:361–62).

51. John Chrysostom, *Hom. Rom.* 23 (*NPNF* 1/11:517).

52. Victorinus of Pettau, *Comm. Ap.* ad loc. (*ANF* 7:344).

53. See a helpful case study of Bede in Celia Chazelle, "Debating the End Times with Bede," *ITQ* 80 (2015): 212–32, which discusses his belief that imminent expectation undergirds the moral will.

54. Origen at one point connected the eschatological teaching of the apostles to Jesus not just in terms of proper temporal expectation but also spiritual description. Readers must receive the representations of Scripture about eschatological matters "according to the understanding of the apostles" and not, he contends, "in a Jewish sense." See *Princ.* 2.11.2–3 (SC 252:396–99). We will return to this caricature of Judaism below.

did Jesus say that there "are some standing here who will not taste death" before they see the kingdom (Matt 16:28)? Jerome explains that it was because Jesus had just delivered his radical call to cross-bearing discipleship (16:24–6), and the disciples might be afraid of this or flag in obedience, or both, while thinking that his return is far off. Jesus thus "compensates for their present fear with an immediate reward."[55] The apostles went forth after Pentecost and taught likewise.

We end this discussion confident in two general conclusions. First, as argued at the beginning of this chapter, the expectation for the parousia of Christ, like the final judgment that it ensues, is largely an unquestioned facet of Christian belief in precritical exegesis. Debate and disagreement about timing, nature, and effects all presuppose the conviction that "he will come again with glory" as the launchpad for further theologizing. Second, it became a "habit of reading" to connect and read together the message of Jesus and the message of his followers when it comes to eschatology—a view reinforced by convictions about the inspired nature of Scripture itself. Governing exegesis was something akin to what Richard Hays has described as a "hermeneutic of trust":[56] interpreters forgo at the outset the prospect that the continual march of history since the first century had disproven assertions about the future from the apostolic generation. So whatever the proper interpretation of these eschatological images and descriptions in the New Testament might be (and here there was serious disagreement), they are certainly not misrepresentative of the message of Jesus.[57] Accusations of misrepresentation fell on later interpreters of Scripture. The disciples, after all, once sat at the feet of the teacher himself, and were later led by the Holy Spirit.

55. Jerome, *Comm. Matt.* ad loc. (FC 117:197).

56. Richard B. Hays, "A Hermeneutic of Trust," in *The Conversion of the Imagination: Paul as Interpreter of Israel's Scripture* (Grand Rapids: Eerdmans, 2005), 190–201.

57. Of course, all this assumes that Jesus could not have been wrong. On the omniscience of Christ, see the excellent study by Kevin Magidan, "*Christus Nesciens*? Was Christ Ignorant of the Day of Judgment?," in *The Passions of Christ in High-Medieval Thought: An Essay on Christological Development* (Oxford: Oxford University Press, 2007), 39–50. See also Raymond Moloney, "Approaches to Christ's Knowledge in the Patristic Era," in *Studies in Patristic Christology*, ed. Thomas Finan and Vincent Twomey (Portland: Four Courts, 1998), 37–66. I discuss the impact of creedal understandings of Jesus's knowledge in *Jesus, the Gospels, and the Galilean Crisis*, LNTS 601 (London: Bloomsbury T&T Clark, 2019), 18–19.

6

The "Painful Thorn" of the Parousia

While it may be obvious, it needs to be stressed that these two widespread interpretive tendencies in the so-called precritical period appear not because Christians were reading Scripture individually and reaching the same conclusions on their own. These tendencies can be understood only in light of the prevalence of certain interpretive practices, shared hermeneutical commitments, and collective theological interests. That is, these widely shared interpretive conclusions about the future coming of Jesus and the teaching of the disciples require a certain "plausibility structure" that the interpretive context provides (and stating this in no way precludes the agency of texts in reception). But if we are to highlight the formation of "habits of reading" in the precritical period and note that certain creedal and institutional realities undergird interpretive convention, we ought to do the same for the formative context of modern biblical criticism. If we are to judge, we too must be judged.

What I wish to demonstrate in this chapter, then, is that the tendencies just outlined in precritical exegesis are all but reversed in modern biblical criticism, and that happened well before the works of Glasson, Robinson, and others discussed in part 1.[1] Indeed, if one takes the long view, it is apparent that Glasson's

1. For important background here and a broader perspective, see Michael C. Legapsi, *The Death of Scripture and the Rise of Biblical Studies* (Oxford: Oxford University Press, 2010). Legapsi points to the Reformation period as a significant watershed, after which the Bible "could no longer function unproblematically as Scripture," as the Bible became "a kind of textual proving ground for the legitimacy of extrascriptural theoretical understandings" (4). He further

and Robinson's studies, while certainly controversial in certain theological and exegetical contexts, were actually quite mainstream if not predictable given their intellectual milieu and the reception-historical forces that shaped them. The parousia of Jesus, traditionally conceived, had already been subjected to new theological scrutiny, problematized, and distanced from the historical Jesus, and the disciples had many times before become the purveyors of these new "wild ideas."

The Enlightened Jesus

In fact, these developments predate the work of Hermann Samuel Reimarus and the supposed beginnings of the quest for Jesus by over one hundred years. In 1678, the deist Charles Blount made the case that the second-coming expectation was a significant misrepresentation of the message of Jesus. He wrote,

> [after the disciples were assured of his resurrection] they resumed their hopes of a temporal Messias, and the last Interrogatory they propose unto him, is, *Lord, wilt thou at this time restore the Kingdom to* Israel? . . . [and after Pentecost], being possest with the desire and hopes of a Messiah, and being further ascertain'd by the Apostle *Peter, That Jesus* (whom *Pilate* had crucify'd) *was the Lord and Christ* . . . [they added many to their number and went] about, and ordaining likewise others to preach the glad tidings of a Messiah come; who (tho' dead) was risen again (according to the obscure Prediction of *David*) for the salvation of *Israel*: and whose second appearance would compleat the happiness of all Nations."[2]

In light of the discussion in the last chapter, it is interesting to observe a shift in the history of biblical exegesis concerning the treatment of the question from the apostles in Acts 1:6. Blount does not periodize this question before Pentecost but rather takes it as indicative of the mistaken apostolic proclamation as a whole (indeed, Blount reads *together* Acts 1:6 with a line from Peter's Pentecost speech [Acts 2:36] after the reception of the Spirit). Moreover, Blount argues that the hope for Christ's return is a reversion (they "resumed their hope") to Jewish messianic

highlights the impulse to "overcome confessional loyalties" (9) in biblical scholarship, which is crucial for the reception history of the second-coming hope.

2. Charles Blount, "*To the Right Honourable and Most Ingenious* Strephon, *Giving a Political Human Account of the Subversion of* Judaism, *Foundation of* Christianity, and *Origination of the* Millenaries," in *The Miscellaneous Works of Charles Blount* (London: s.n., 1695), 165–67.

expectation (described as the belief in a "temporal Messias")—an office that Jesus himself had rejected and redefined. Blount does not contend that the disciples intended to deceive; rather, the second-coming hope stems from misunderstanding the Scriptures and drawing false inferences about Jesus's resurrection in line with preexisting Jewish messianic expectation.

Blount was not a lone voice crying in the wilderness. This manner of distancing the second coming from Jesus was very common in Enlightenment Christianity and has been massively overlooked in histories of New Testament scholarship.[3] Here is a sampling from some of the leading and most influential thinkers in the eighteenth century:

- Anthony Collins (1724): "all the Primitive Christians were, for a considerable time after the ascension of Jesus, in the vulgar error of expecting him to come in the clouds and reign personally and triumphantly upon earth in *a kingdom that was at hand*."[4]
- Thomas Woolston (1725): "the Priesthood (for many Ages past) have been vending, and palming upon their Hearers, many gross Mistakes concerning God and the Devil, Heaven and Hell, Revelation and Prophecy, the Second Coming of Christ, the End of the World, the Resurrection of the Dead, and a Future Judgment."[5]
- Matthew Tindal (1730): "as to those Prophecies, if they may be so call'd, in the New Testament, relating to the *Second Coming of Christ*, and *the End of the World*, the best Interpreters and Commentators own, the Apostles themselves were grossly mistaken . . . they do not assert this as a mere Matter of Speculation, but build Motives and Arguments upon it, to excite People to the Practice of Piety."[6]

3. On defining "the Enlightenment," see Peter Gay, *The Enlightenment: An Interpretation* (London: Weidenfeld & Nicolson, 1967), 3–27; Jonathan I. Israel, *Radical Enlightenment: Philosophy and the Making of Modernity 1650–1750* (Oxford: Oxford University Press, 2001), 3–22; Albrecht Beutel, *Kirchengeschichte im Zeitalter der Aufklarung: Ein Kopendium* (Göttingen: Vandenhoeck & Ruprecht, 2009), 15–34.

4. Anthony Collins, *Discourse of the Grounds and Reasons of the Christian Religion* (London: Senex, 1724), 33.

5. Thomas Woolston, *A Second Supplement to the Moderator between an Infidel and an Apostate* (London: the author, 1725), 51.

6. Matthew Tindal, *Christianity as Old as the Creation, or, The Gospel, a Republication of the Religion of Nature* (London: s.n., 1730), 233. Cf. 232–36. Note also: "the Apostles first became Jesus' Disciples upon temporal Motives; and the Belief of Christ's temporal Kingdom was so firmly rooted in them, that Jesus neither during his Life, nor even after his Resurrection, was able to remove it" (42–43).

- Thomas Morgan (1737): "his Disciples and Followers soon fell into very odd Notions about him, and reported several Things of him, that were neither consistent with his Character and general Design, nor with the Religion which he had preach'd and propogated. . . . They made him prophesy of the End of the World, and of his second Coming to Judgment, as a Thing very shortly to happen during the present Generation. In a Word, they understood and reported every Thing that he said according to their own Prejudices and false Opinions concerning the Messias."[7]
- Peter Annet (1744): "I think it's plain, that because Jesus had not taken the Kingdom, before the Report of his Resurrection, and Ascension, the Apostles said, that before that Generation was Dead, he would come again, raise them that believed in him, reign over the Jews, and subdue the Gentiles."[8]
- Edmund Law (1745): "For some time the Apostles themselves were ignorant of *Christ's* true Office and the Nature of his Kingdom. They could not conceive that he was to suffer and die for the whole World, they expected nothing but a temporal prince, and thought that his Kingdom was to be confined to a remnant of the *Jews* . . . most of them concluded that *Christianity* and the World itself would speedily come to an end."[9]
- Baron d' Holbach (1770): "the principles of the new sect had powerful attractions. Its maxims, which tended to introduce equality and a community of goods, were calculated to entice persons despised. Its promises flattered miserable fanatics, to whom was announced the end of a perverse world, the approaching arrival of Jesus, and a kingdom wherein abundance and happiness would reign."[10]

Among these selections, there is some disagreement about the role of the disciples in the production of this "vulgar error" (so Collins)—that is, they were un-

7. Thomas Morgan, *The Moral Philosopher: In a Dialogue between Philalethes a Christian Deist, and Theophanes a Christian Jew* (London: s.n., 1737), 440.

8. Peter Annet, *The Resurrection of Jesus Considered: In Answer to the Tryal of the Witnesses* (London: the author, 1744), 16.

9. Edmund Law, *Considerations on the State of the World with Regard to the Theory of Religion* (Cambridge: Bentham, 1745), 165–66. His argument in this book is that human history is a giant education project, and religion is a key component. Thinkers in his day had progressed beyond the "Infant State of the World" (157).

10. Paul Tiry d'Holbach, *Ecce Homo! or, A Critical Inquiry into the History of Jesus Christ*, 2nd ed. (London: Eaton, 1813), 290. See also 297. Though d'Holbach, of course, was hardly an apologist for Christ: "he was a fanatic, who really thought himself inspired, favoured by Heaven, sent to his nation, and in short, the Messiah . . . he made no difficulty to employ frauds the best calculated to succeed" (281).

intentionally misinformed, or intentionally deceived others.[11] But that difference notwithstanding, we see here a very similar treatment of the origin of the second-coming hope in certain intellectual circles prior to the posthumous publication of Reimarus's work in 1778.[12] Jesus, spared from eschatological error, remains exemplary as an ethical teacher and in many ways the ideal enlightened man.[13] Christianity's blunders and absurdities—such as the idea of Christ returning "on aetherial Clouds, as on a Wool-sack"—stem from his followers.[14]

11. On the obfuscation of the teaching of Jesus in the early church, see, e.g., Toland, *Christianity Not Mysterious*, 71. Cf. Henning Graf Reventlow, *The Authority of the Bible and the Rise of the Modern World*, trans. John Bowden (Philadelphia: Fortress, 1985), 300–301. On the perceived simplicity of earliest Christianity, see David S. Katz, *God's Last Words: Reading the English Bible from the Reformation to Fundamentalism* (New Haven: Yale University Press, 2004), 136–37; Margaret C. Jacob, "The Enlightenment Critique of Christianity," in *Enlightenment, Reawakening and Revolution 1660–1815*, vol. 7 of *The Cambridge History of Christianity*, ed. Stewart J. Brown and Timothy Tackett (Cambridge: Cambridge University Press, 2006), 269. John Orr, *English Deism: Its Roots and Its Fruits* (Grand Rapids: Eerdmans, 1934), 31, generalizes: "[the deists] claimed Jesus to be of their party." The influence of anticlericalism for this reconstruction of Christian origins has been well documented. See S. J. Barnett, *Idol Temples and Crafty Priests: The Origins of Enlightenment Anticlericalism* (New York: St. Martin's, 1999).

12. Though some other perspectives are worthy of note. Lord Bolingbroke, and here in agreement with Hobbes, made much of the fact that Christ clearly declared his kingdom *would not* be inaugurated until his second coming—a point meant to challenge the presumed authority of the church in the present age that claimed the kingdom had come at his resurrection. See Henry Bolingbroke, *The Works of the Late Right Honourable Henry St. John, Lord Viscount Bolingbroke* (London: Mallet, 1754), 4:536–50. Others do not make much of the doctrine, as far as my research can discern: Toland (*Christianity Not Mysterious*, and *Nazarenus*), Bury (*Naked Gospel*). But this silence, too, is significant.

13. Cf., e.g., John Locke, *The Reasonableness of Christianity*, ed. I. T. Ramsey (London: Black, 1958 [orig. 1695]), 61–67 (though Locke believed in the second advent as part of the confession of Jesus's messiahship, see 71); Thomas Paine, *The Age of Reason, Being an Investigation of the True and Fabulous Theology* (Paris: s.n., 1794), 9–10, 12–13, 35. See Alister E. McGrath, *The Making of Modern German Christology: From the Enlightenment to Pannenberg* (Oxford: Blackwell, 1986), 13 ("Christ possessed to a greater degree what every man has latent within him"). Spinoza was influential here; see *Tractatus theologico-politicus*, trans. Samuel Shirley (Leiden; Brill, 1989 [orig. 1677]). He argued that Jesus was a profound moral teacher, a philosopher, in fact, who "did not want to correct external actions so much as the heart" (7.32; see also 5.71). Cf. Steven Frankel, "The Invention of Liberal Theology: Spinoza's Theological-Political Analysis of Moses and Jesus," *Review of Politics* 63 (2001): 287–315; Pierre Gire, "L'idée du Christ chez Spinoza," *Théophilyon* 18 (2013): 345–57. Though others did not spare Jesus, such as Voltaire. See *Mélanges* (Paris: Gallimard, 1961), 1061–62. Though Voltaire also called Jesus "Socrates of Galilee," cited by Albrecht Beutel in Jens Schröter and Christine Jacobi, eds., *The Jesus Handbook*, trans. Robert L. Brawley (Grand Rapids: Eerdmans, 2022), 30.

14. Cf. Thomas Woolston, *A Third Discourse on the Miracles of Our Saviour* (London: the au-

Two particular features of these excerpts should not escape notice. First, few of these critics feel the need to provide much of an argument in support of their suggestion. That is partly due to the theological and philosophical nature of some of these works (meaning, some lack much historical argumentation at all), but it is also because the above sentiment is a borrowed and recycled trope about Christian origins whose plausibility stems more from the cultural, social, and intellectual contexts of these authors than the actual arguments they offer in its favor (more on that in the next chapter below). In other words, it had already become, in this time as well, a "habit of reading" in certain circles to sidestep those features of the Gospels that Enlightenment Christianity had routinely problematized: in this case, miracles and motivating ethical behavior by fear of future punishment.[15] Second, and related to this, it is clear that pinning the invention of the second-coming hope on the disciples of Jesus functioned as a two-level drama of its own, not unlike the quotations from Annie Dillard and John Lennon that began part 2. To point out the mistaken theology of the disciples was to make a not-so-subtle criticism of contemporary Christianity and its misunderstanding of the true teaching of Jesus when it comes to eschatology.[16] This move was less common in precritical exegesis, as noted above, because it was assumed that many of these same people authored the sacred texts of the New Testament. But after the Reformation, and when the texts of Scripture themselves began to receive the same manner of criticism that Protestants leveled at church tradition, it is natural to find that the disciples of Jesus suffer the same. To put it a different way, it is not a coincidence that the higher criticism of Scripture itself emerges at about the same time that critics start critiquing the early followers of Jesus and blaming them for distorting his message. (In fact, even Luther and Calvin at some points distinguish between the eschatological views of Jesus and those of his followers in a way that deviates from the sources discussed above.)[17] Hence a conceptual

thor, 1728), 24–25: "As to that literal and common Pulpit-Story (with all its Appendages) of *Jesus's* second Coming on aetherial Clouds, as on a Wool-sack, in his human, tho' glorious and majestick Appearance . . . it is the most absurd, nonsensical and unphilosophical, (such groundless and worthless Stuff have the *Clergy* sold and preach'd to God's People!) that ever was told against Reason, against prophetic and evangelical Scripture, and against other ancient and good Authority."

15. For Spinoza's influential views on this matter, see *Tractatus theologico-politicus*, 4.14. See also my discussion in *Jesus, the Gospels, and the Galilean Crisis*, 53–54.

16. Though, of course, another strategy was simply to take down Jesus head-on, so d'Holbach, *Ecce Homo!*, 188, where Jesus says to the disciples, "Speak of the end of the world; this will intimidate women and poltroons."

17. See Calvin, *Comm. Harm. Ev.* at Matt 24:3, suggests that the seemingly awkward structure of the discourse, which could be seen as conflating the destruction of the temple and "the end of the world" (Calvin's words), is due to the wrong-headed question from the disciples to Jesus at

distinction between "Scripture" and "Tradition" in Protestantism,[18] and the privileging of the former over the latter, had developed in Enlightenment Christianity into a distinction between Jesus's own intentions and the "opinions" (as it was said) of those who came after him.[19] Here distaste for a traditional eschatological scenario as described in the past chapter produced a historical reconstruction of Christian origins that distanced from Jesus those items deemed problematic, thereby diminishing their theological significance.[20]

Downplaying Eschatology

Concerns about the parousia were not limited to those set on challenging church teaching or who were otherwise on a more progressive end of the theological spectrum.[21] The writings of more traditional Christian exegetes betray the influence of similar cultural trends. In seventeenth- and eighteenth-century paraphrases of the Gospels, sometimes themselves called lives of Jesus, one can find a muting or downplaying of the eschatological predictions of Jesus. In Jeremy Taylor's *Life* (1649), for instance, he skips entirely the apocalyptic discourse of Jesus in his

24:3 and parr. Thus, he argues, Jesus answers both questions, but they appear together because of *their* question, not because of his conflation of these two distinct realities.

18. I am not assuming that Protestants understood "Tradition" in a completely unique way, and of course within Protestantism there were different ways to articulate this relationship. See Heiko A. Oberman, *The Harvest of Medieval Theology* (Grand Rapids: Baker Books, 2000), 361–422.

19. Cf. Thomas Chubb, *The True Gospel of Jesus Christ Asserted* (London: Cox, 1738), 46: "the gospel of Jesus Christ is not any *particular private opinion* of any, or of all the writers of the history of his life and ministry; nor . . . of all those whom he sent out to publish his gospel to the world."

20. Cf. Kümmel, *New Testament*, 51–61; Alister E. McGrath, *Christian Theology: An Introduction*, 3rd ed. (Oxford: Blackwell, 2001), 561–62 (on "eschatology as superstition" in the Enlightenment period). Though the final judgment itself sometimes received more positive treatment, as many of the early deists believed that judgment was necessary to maintain a just ethical system. See, e.g., Herbert of Cherbury, the so-called father of English Deism, *De Veritate* (London: Routledge, 1992 [orig. 1624]).

21. In 1627, Hugo Grotius, *The Truth of the Christian Religion, with Jean Le Clerc's Notes and Additions*, trans. John Clarke, ed. Maria Rosa Antognazza (Indianapolis: Liberty Fund, 2012), admitted that the disciples "expected that the End of the whole World was just at hand, as is plain from their own Writings, and those of the Christians that came after them" (104). He also claimed that the Four Gospels agree in the main "Precepts, concerning the Life of Christ, his Death, and Return to Life again" (152), but he says little to nothing about the parousia with respect to the teaching of Jesus.

broad summary of the final week, and when describing the Jewish trial of Jesus, he claims that "[Jesus] openly affirmed he was Christ the Son of God, which when Caiaphas heard, he cried out blasphemy."[22] Here Taylor omits the mention of the coming of the son of man on the clouds of heaven in favor of a simple assertion about Jesus's identity.[23] There was also a vibrant debate about the "realism" of eschatological passages in the Gospels and the degree to which these images should be "spiritualized."[24] Some critics even appear to grant in their exegesis the possibility that the wording of a text paints a problematic or even erroneous picture about the future, but they are clear to rescue Jesus himself from any such error.[25] Matthew Henry's commentaries sometimes point out the "confusion" of the disciples on eschatological matters, suggesting that *they* (not Jesus) had believed in his near arrival or conflated the destruction of the temple with the parousia.[26] In

22. Jeremy Taylor, *The Life of Our Blessed Saviour Jesus Christ* (Somerset: Patton, 1818 [orig. 1649]), 117–19, 123.

23. Taylor maintains hope for the second coming in his own little prayer at the very end (*Life of Our Blessed Saviour Jesus Christ*, 140), but the whole is quite muted. Note also Claude Fleury, *An Historical Account of the Manners and Behaviour of the Christians*, 2nd ed. (London: Midwinter & Leigh, 1703 [orig. 1682]), who believed that Jesus used the "son of man" title as a humbling self-description (13), and in his summary of the ministry skips over the apocalyptic discourse. He claims that Jesus rightly predicted the destruction of Jerusalem in the lifetime of that generation (29), but not his own parousia in that time frame.

24. Cf. Gösta Lundström, *The Kingdom of God in the Teaching of Jesus: A History of Interpretation from the Last Decades of the Nineteenth Century to the Present Day*, trans. Joan Bulman (Richmond: John Knox, 1963), 27–28. Some pleaded agnosticism on the basis of the figurative language, so Thomas Ellwood, *Sacred History, or, The Historical Part of the Holy Scriptures of the New Testament: Gathered out from the Other Parts Thereof, and Digested (as Near as Well Could Be) into Due Method, with Respect to the Order of Time and Place*, 2nd ed. (London: Sowle, 1719 [orig. 1705]), 230 (on the apocalyptic discourse): "Divers other Things and Passages there are, in this deep Discourse, which our Saviour had, at that time, with his Disciples; some where of have been already touched, on other Occasions, in other parts of this History: and Others, being for the most part, Figurative Speeches, and of uncertain Signification (with respect to the Times to which they should be referred) have caused much Diversity of Opinion among Interpreters." See also Grotius, *Truth of the Christian Religion*, 217 (the supposedly unfulfilled predictions of the Gospels "are obscure" and "may have a different Signification").

25. See John Calvin, *Comm. Harm. Ev.* at Matt 24:1–31; Matthew Poole, *A Commentary on the Holy Bible* (McLean: MacDonald, 1962 [orig. 1700]), 3:572 ("the apostles ordinarily in their epistles speak of the world as nigh to an end in their age"). The English Baptist John Gill expressly denies in his commentary on 1 Thessalonians in *Gill's Commentary* (Grand Rapids: Baker Books, 1980 [orig. 1746–1748), 6:560, that Paul "thought that he and the saints then in the flesh should live and continue till the second coming of Christ." But he feels it necessary to assert the point strongly.

26. Cf. Matthew Henry, *Commentary on the Whole Bible*, ed. Leslie F. Church (Grand Rapids: Zondervan, 1960 [orig. 1708–1710]), 1235, 1485, 1637.

a clever exegetical treatment of the Olivet Discourse, Henry argues that Christ speaks first of the destruction of the temple, then of his own return, precisely because the disciples had wrongly joined those events in their question to him (see Mark 13:4).[27] Here Henry aims to take the very thing that still for some causes exegetical consternation—the appearance of some juxtaposition between the temple's destruction and the messiah's return—and turns it on its head:[28] he takes the sequence as evidence of separation rather than conjunction. Bengel offered another solution, which became even more influential: in a landscape painting, background and foreground may appear very close together, like Mark 13:23 and 13:24, but they are actually far apart in the mind of the artist.[29]

Removing the Thorn

If we are to understand what happens with eschatology and specifically the question of the origin of the second-coming expectation in the nineteenth-century quest for Jesus, we must appreciate how influential these intellectual and cultural trends proved to be.[30] The great historian Hans Hillerbrand wrote, "it hardly needs repeating that the English Christian Deists' notions, no matter how specious in their specifics and how controversial in their acceptance, have arguably been a most potent interpretation of the Christian faith ever since."[31] The most obvious indication is the continuation of the same general scenario for the development of eschatology in Christian origins. This is due in part to the well-known fact that many of the researchers engaged in the nineteenth-century quest were themselves liberal Protestants who shared a similar distaste for the eschatological and the supernatural in Christianity (there is more to this story, as the next chapter will detail) and felt pressure to square Christian theology with new developments in sci-

27. Henry, *Commentary on the Whole Bible*, 1397. Calvin had already made this move.

28. Cf. already Victorinus of Pettau, *Comm. Ap.* 7 (*ANF* 7:352): readers "must not unordinarily fix upon the chronology of what is said."

29. See Johann Albrecht Bengel (with J. C. F. Steudel), *Gnomon of the New Testament*, 3rd ed., trans. James Bandinel (Philadelphia: Smith, English, 1860), 1:417, 426.

30. As noted in part 1, Schweitzer greatly influenced subsequent histories of New Testament scholarship by distancing the work of Hermann Samuel Reimarus from any before him. But this sharp periodization cannot be maintained—as recent studies have increasingly recognized. For literature, see p. 7 above.

31. Hans J. Hillerbrand, "The Decline and Fall of the True Christian Church: The English Deist View," *ZRGG* 60 (2008): 110. See also William Baird, *From Deism to Tübingen*, vol. 1 of *History of New Testament Research* (Minneapolis: Fortress, 1992), 31–57.

ence.[32] In the wake of the Copernican revolution, what were modern Christians to make of Christ "ascending to heaven," and predictions of him some day "descending to earth," as though these were literal spaces in a vertical cosmology?[33] The assertion that Jesus did not actually make those predictions after all was shaped as much by the theological convenience of that position as by a new skepticism.[34]

So historical treatments of the second advent in Christian origins throughout the eighteenth-century and nineteenth-century quest continued to mirror the arguments of earlier thinkers—albeit with greater exegetical and historical sophistication. For many, the second-coming hope continued to be, in the words of one honest critic, a "painful thorn,"[35] yet removable from Jesus himself and hence true Christianity.[36] Below is a sampling of perspectives from critics who were not exactly marginal figures from this period:

32. Cf. here especially Jonathan Rowlands, *The Metaphysics of Historical Jesus Research: A Prolegomenon to a Future Quest for the Historical Jesus* (New York: Routledge, 2023), 117–32. See also Martin Werner, *The Formation of Christian Dogma: An Historical Study of Its Problem*, trans. S. G. F. Brandon (New York: Harper, 1957), 318–20; Claude Welch, *1799–1870*, vol. 1 of *Protestant Thought in the Nineteenth Century* (New Haven: Yale University Press, 1972), 30–41; Günter Gawlick, "Der Deismus als Grundzug der Religionsphilosophie der Aufklärung," in *Hermann Samuel Reimarus (1694–1768): Ein "bekannter Unbekannter" der Aufklärung in Hamburg* (Göttingen: Vandenhoeck & Ruprecht, 1973), 22–36; Richard H. Hiers, *Jesus and the Future: Unresolved Questions for Understanding and Faith* (Atlanta: John Knox, 1981), 88–90.

33. See here Walter Bundy, *Our Recovery of Jesus* (Indianapolis: Bobbs-Merrill, 1929), 178 (on how the coming of Jesus on the clouds is "quite out of harmony with the modern world-view").

34. On key factors that contributed to this development, see Gregory Dawes, *The Historical Jesus Question: The Challenge of History to Religious Authority* (Louisville: Westminster John Knox, 2001), 1–38. See also Rennie B. Schoepflin, "Apocalypticism in an Age of Science," in *Apocalypticism in the Modern Period and the Contemporary Age*, vol. 3 of *The Encyclopedia of Apocalypticism*, ed. Stephen J. Stein (New York: Continuum, 1998), 427–41.

35. Arthur Titius, *Lehre Jesu vom Reiche Gottes*, vol. 1 of *Die neutestamentliche Lehre von der Seligkeit und ihre Bedeutung für die Gegenwart* (Freiburg: Mohr, 1895), 183.

36. See Konstantin Wieland, *Hat Jesus geirrt? Ein Lösungsversuch zur Parusiefrage* (Dillingen: Keller, 1910), 63. A few other important studies have rightly emphasized the impact of theological concerns about eschatological imminence on historical reconstructions of Jesus. See Klaus Koch, *The Rediscovery of Apocalyptic: A Polemical Work on a Neglected Area of Biblical Studies and Its Damaging Effects on Theology and Philosophy* (Naperville, IL: Allenson, 1972), 57–97; Herbert Braun, *Jesus of Nazareth: The Man and His Time* (Philadelphia: Fortress, 1979), 36–43; Anthony E. Harvey, *Jesus and the Constraints of History* (Philadelphia: Westminster, 1982), 66–97; E. P. Sanders, *Jesus and Judaism* (Philadelphia: Fortress, 1985), 143, also 154; Dale C. Allison Jr., "Apocalyptic, Polemic, Apologetics," in *Resurrecting Jesus: The Earliest Christian Tradition and Its Interpreters* (London: T&T Clark, 2005), 111–48; Adela Yarbro Collins, "Apocalypticism and Christian Origins," in *The Oxford Handbook of Apocalyptic Literature*, ed. John J. Collins (Oxford: Oxford University Press, 2014), 326–39.

- G. W. F. Hegel wrote a short life of Jesus that contains a remarkable paraphrase of Jesus's apocalyptic discourse. Hegel's Jesus declares, "This expectation concerning a messiah will visit great tribulation on my countrymen, and, together with the rest of their prejudices and blind obstinacy, will set the stage for their total undoing. This chimerical hope will make them playthings in the hands of cunning betrayers and mindless enthusiasts." Moreover, in the place where the gospel text reads that "the gospel must be preached to all nations, and then the end will come," Hegel's Jesus says instead, "Only when reason and virtue instead of names and slogans are recognized and practiced all over the earth may you declare the divine plan to have been accomplished. It is unwavering loyalty to this hope for mankind, not to the vain nationalistic hopes of the Jews, that will keep you free of sectarian sentiment and keep you forever upright and courageous."[37]
- W. M. L. de Wette argued that for Jesus, the kingdom of God was "a state of things whereby men, through life and free duty (not through the compulsion of law), unify, away from the world, to make an inner community with God and bring his will on earth and worship him in spirit and in truth."[38] The belief in the "founding of a supernatural ideal reign on earth" in the immediate future stems from "the chiliastic-messianic beliefs of the apostles and the earliest church."[39]
- Friedrich Schleiermacher asserted in his famous lectures on the life of Jesus that the resurrection, ascension, and second-coming hope had no role in the teaching of the historical Jesus. They stem, rather, from the yearning of early Christians to be united with Christ.[40]

37. G. W. F. Hegel, *Three Essays, 1793–1795: The Tübingen Essay, Berne Fragments, the Life of Jesus*, ed. and trans. Peter Fuss and John Dobbins (Notre Dame: University of Notre Dame Press, 1984), 150–52. McGrath, *Making of Modern German Christology*, 33, aptly calls Jesus in Hegel's view "an itinerant Kantian." For Kant's own view, see *Religion within the Limits of Reason Alone*, trans. Theodore M. Greene and Hoyt H. Hudson (New York: Harper, 1960), 124–26 (on Luke 17:21–22).

38. W. M. L. de Wette, *Lehrbuch der christliche Dogmatik in ihrer historischen Entwicklung dargestellt* (Berlin: Realschulbuchhandlung, 1813), 243–44.

39. De Wette, *Lehrbuch der christliche Dogmatik*, 206. He expressly calls the second-coming hope "unbiblisch" (210). He also explains away some of Jesus's language as "accommodation" to the "sensual" hopes of his contemporaries. On accommodation theory and its underpinnings, see John W. Rogerson, *W. M. L. de Wette: Founder of Modern Biblical Criticism; An Intellectual Biography*, JSOTSup 126 (Sheffield: JSOT Press, 1992), 119.

40. Friedrich Schleiermacher, *The Life of Jesus*, ed. Jack C. Verheyden, trans. Maclean Gilmour (Philadelphia: Fortress, 1975 [orig. 1864]), 476 ("after Christ's ascension his discourses suggested to the apostles the idea of his return"). Cf. Eckhard Rau and Silke Petersen, *Perspektiven des*

- Ferdinand C. Baur believed that the Sermon on the Mount captures most clearly "the fundamental idea" of Jesus's message: the revolution of "the moral consciousness" in a social community. Jesus called for theocracy "in a spiritualized form"—he did not predict an imminent and supernatural interruption. A driving aim of his career was to redefine the dominant "political" understanding of the messiah around his spiritual message.[41]
- Albrecht Ritschl argued that for Jesus, talk about the kingdom of God was fundamentally talk about the establishment of a community ruled by God.[42] Jesus's "this-worldly, monistic, and ethical" kingdom would "grow" over time and as a result of human agency.[43] Jesus saw the growth of the mustard seed rather than the advent of the son of man on the clouds when he peered into the future.

As evident in these selections, it is not just that the second-coming idea is absent from the teaching of Jesus; the expectation is actually regarded as contrary to his central ethical message.[44] The hope for Christ's return from heaven was a longing for a divine, supernatural act, whereas Jesus's message about the kingdom was about human reformation by inner/ethical transformation. One critic wrote that

---

Lebens Jesu: Plädoyer für die Anknüpfung an eine schwierige Forschungstradition (Stuttgart: Kohlhammer, 2013), 116. On Schleiermacher's noted impact by a contemporary, see David Friedrich Strauss, *A New Life of Jesus*, trans. s.n. (London: Williams & Norgate, 1865), 1:26.

41. Ferdinand C. Baur, *The Church History of the First Three Centuries*, trans. Allan Menzies, 3rd ed. (London: Williams & Norgate, 1878 [orig. 1853]), 1:22–43, esp. 32–33. In his *Kritische Untersuchungen über die kanonischen Evangelien* (Tübingen: Dues, 1847), he argues that the apocalyptic discourse in Matt 24 actually dates to the time of the Bar Kokhba revolt and hence has nothing to do with the Jesus of history (and he assumed Matthean priority). On Baur's view of the son of man and the kingdom, see Chester Charlton McCown, *The Search for the Real Jesus: A Century of Historical Study* (New York: Scribner's Sons, 1940), 95–97. See also Annette Yoshiko Reed, "Messianism between Judaism and Christianity," in *Rethinking the Messianic Idea in Judaism*, ed. Michael L. Morgan and Steven Weitzman (Bloomington: Indiana University Press, 2015), 40–41.

42. Albrecht Ritschl, *Die christliche Lehre von der Rechtfertigung und Versöhnung*, 3 vols. (Hildescheim: Olms, 1978 [orig. 1870–74]).

43. See Lundström, *Kingdom of God in the Teaching of Jesus*, 3–9. Cf. Norman Perrin, *The Kingdom of God in the Teaching of Jesus* (Philadelphia: Westminster, 1963), 15–16; Claude Welch, *1870–1914*, vol. 2 of *Protestant Thought in the Nineteenth Century* (New Haven: Yale University Press, 1985), 17–25.

44. Hermann Weisse, *Die evangelische Geschichte, kritisch und philosophisch bearbeit* (Leipzig: Breitkopf & Hartel, 1838), 593–95, argues that the second-coming hope could no more come from Jesus than a vine could bear thorns or a fig tree thistles. See also Daniel Schenkel, *Das Charakterbild Jesu*, 3rd ed. (Wiesbaden: Kreidel, 1864), 280.

Jesus's program would happen "without using force . . . merely by the gentile influence of convincing instruction,"[45] and another that the kingdom would come by inner change not "falling stars."[46] It became very common among nineteenth-century historians (often Christian) to identify Jesus with Old Testament prophets who sought to reform Israel by urging for mass repentance and renewed ethical seriousness, rather than trust in a miraculous divine fix in the sacrificial system and temple cult (so the argument went).[47] There is an interesting parallel here. Apocalyptic eschatology became a casualty in a larger theological battle over divine and human agency in Christianity.[48] It was common in some circles to argue that the eschatological language of Jesus was largely, if not entirely, symbolic in nature, and what might seem like predictions of the end of the world were actually about the impact of the kingdom on subsequent human history.[49] In the exegesis of Mark 13, some who disagreed and argued that the apocalyptic language can be taken only literally were nevertheless assured that the most troublesome lines (especially vv. 24–27, 30) were inauthentic.[50] Even in more conservative scholarship, one finds a muting of eschatological elements in the teaching of Jesus to greater and lesser degrees.[51]

45. F. V. Reinhard, *Plan of the Founder of Christianity*, trans. Oliver A. Taylor from 5th German ed. (New York: Carvill, 1831 [orig. 1781]), 8. Also from this volume: "[Jesus] chose the gentlest means possible [to achieve his plan]. . . . Instruction . . . was the principal means of which he intended to avail himself in the accomplishment of his object" (112–13); "So thoroughly convinced, however, was he [Jesus], of the excellency of his view and of their agreement with the counsels of God, that he could assert with perfect confidence, that his cause would stand so long as the human race existed. This renders it clear, that the space of time which was to be occupied in the gradual execution of his plan, was the series of centuries that should constitute the duration of the human family" (199); "The plan which Jesus devised for the general good, has nothing in it chimerical, extravagant, or impracticable. It is constructed in every respect with reference to the character and wants of human nature and the course of human affairs" (221).

46. Edward Clodd, *Jesus of Nazareth: Embracing a Sketch of Jewish History to the Time of His Birth* (London: Paul, 1880), 255.

47. For discussion, see Ferda, *Jesus, the Gospels, and the Galilean Crisis*, 48–49.

48. Cf. Jean G. H. Hoffmann, *Les vies de Jésus et le Jésus de l'histoire: Étude de la valeur historique des vies de Jésus de langue française, non catholiques, d'Ernest Renan à Charles Guignebert* (Paris: Prostant apud Messageries Évangéliques, 1947), esp. 95–104; Lundström, *Kingdom of God in the Teaching of Jesus*, 27; Warren S. Kissinger, *The Lives of Jesus: A History and Bibliography* (New York: Garland, 1985), 28.

49. See, e.g., Schenkel, *Das Charakterbild Jesu*, 183–85.

50. See, e.g., the influential study of Hans Hinrich Wendt, *Der Inhalt der Lehre Jesu* (Göttingen: Vandenhoeck & Ruprecht, 1890), 113–29, 293–324.

51. Note, e.g., Alfred Edersheim, *The Life and Times of Jesus the Messiah*, 3rd ed., 2 vols. (Grand Rapids: Eerdmans, 1943 [orig. 1883]), believed that Jesus predicted both the destruction of the temple and his own second coming and "had placed an indefinite period between the

Some critical scholars attributed imminent eschatological hopes to Jesus, and some even the second-coming idea itself, but not in a way that was necessarily advantageous theologically. That is to say, some reconstructions maintained an evaluation of the parousia tradition that resembles the perspectives above but still dared to connect Jesus himself to those "wild ideas." Some of the biographies of Jesus that featured a "Galilean crisis" (a great moment or moments of rejection) originated the second-coming hope in the teaching of Jesus but linked its inception to Jesus's experience of failure as his response to recalcitrance. In other words, according to this view, the future parousia after an interim was never part of Jesus's original plan; such a notion developed as his response to new circumstances and specifically the rejection of his message.[52] Similar to the positions advanced above, this move identifies major development and change in eschatological thought in the formative period but contextualizes that development inside the contours of Jesus's ministry itself, whereas others pointed to the transition between the life of Jesus and the activity of the early church.[53] The influential works of Ernest Renan, Theodor Keim, Bernard Weiss, and many others saw this kind of development in Jesus's own ministry.[54]

---

two" (2:433), but the Gospels as written—being testimonies of the disciples and not the exact teaching of Jesus himself—introduce some confusion here. On Mark 13 and parr., Edersheim wrote that the evangelists themselves "may not have fully understood the meaning of what they recorded. This may account for the rapid and unconnected transitions from subject to subject" (2:450)—a move that essentially admits error but saves Jesus from it.

52. For a positive spin on a similar interpretive move, discussed in Ferda, *Jesus, the Gospels, and the Galilean Crisis*, 87–88, note that some nineteenth-century dispensationalists wrote a larger theology of history around this basic premise. It became popular to argue that Jesus had offered the kingdom of heaven (a terrestrial kingdom to be established in Jerusalem) to "Israel" (e.g., his Jewish contemporaries), but the realization of this offer was contingent on Israel's obedience. Because Jesus was rejected, then, a new "dispensation" or period of salvation history began that centered on the preaching of grace, a universal kingdom of God for all people, and the activity of the church. See John Nelson Darby himself: "Suppose for a moment that Christ had not been rejected, the kingdom would have been set up on earth." Cf. "Lectures on the Second Coming of Christ," in *The Collected Writings of J. N. Darby*, ed. William Kelly, 2nd ed. (London: Morrish, n.d.), 11:431.

53. I have elsewhere pointed out important parallels between lives of Jesus and larger theories about theological development in Christian origins. See Ferda, *Jesus, the Gospels, and the Galilean Crisis*, 68–93, 109–10, 125–33.

54. Ernest Renan, *The Life of Jesus*, trans. s.n. (New York: Modern Library, 1927 [orig. 1863]). Theodor Keim, *The History of Jesus of Nazara, Freely Investigated in Its Connection with the National Life of Israel, and Related in Detail*, trans. Arthur Ransom, 2nd ed., 6 vols. (London: Williams & Norgate, 1876–83). Keim argued that Jesus expected to die after the so-called Galilean storms, and it was not part of his original plan (4:275–78). So, too, he later hoped that he would return to earth after that death (4:285). Keim even contends that those who deny the second

Theological Culture Wars

Some notable exegetes were able to moderate the impact of critical biblical scholarship by returning to the old strategy we saw already in the early deists of blaming the disciples for any lingering errors in the predictive material of the Gospels.[55] But in other circles, the significant challenge posed by critical scholarship against a traditional or creedal eschatological scenario caused an equal and opposite reaction. We see in the eighteenth and nineteenth centuries not only the continuation of historical scenarios that distanced the historical Jesus from the second advent hope (or otherwise problematized it); we see, in response to that widespread move, the emergence of apologetical literature set on defending the historicity of the orthodox position. The Baptist exegete John Gill (1697–1771) identified 2 Peter's "scoffers" who deride "the promise of his coming" (3:3–4) with the liberal skeptics of his own time. "Most of all," he laments, "things to come are the object of their scorn and derision; as the second coming of Christ, the resurrection of the dead, a future judgment, the torments of hell, and the joys of heaven; all of which they represent as the tricks and juggles of designing men."[56]

There is an irony in that orthodox respondents claimed to recover and defend the historic teaching of the church, but it was actually the deconstructive efforts of Enlightenment Christianity that had created the conditions and terms for their own defensive reply.[57] The reception history of the second advent in biblical schol-

advent hope to Jesus wish to protect him from "phantasies and fanaticism" (4:289). He, too, however, finds comfort in the fact that Jesus's expectation to return after death was not in his original plan; it was only "a last resource" that shows him "the pure realist" (4:290). See also Bernard Weiss, *The Life of Christ*, trans. John Walter Hope, Clark's Foreign Theological Library 14–16 (Edinburgh: T&T Clark, 1883). On the second coming, see 3:84–85.

55. So, for instance, one of the greatest German exegetes of the nineteenth-century, H. A. W. Meyer. He argued that, while Jesus did indeed predict a literal future coming, he also predicted more immediate events: the giving of the Holy Spirit and the work of God in the aftermath of his exaltation to heaven. Jesus similarly predicted the destruction of Jerusalem. The disciples, unable to follow along, attributed imminence to the second-coming hope within the lifetime of that generation. Meyer was widely followed. See, e.g., his *Kritisch exegetisches Handbuch über das Evangelium des Matthäus* (Göttingen: Vandenhoeck & Ruprecht, 1864), 510–15.

56. Gill, *Gill's Commentary*, 6:869.

57. You see this already in the seventeenth-century. Cf. John Hull, *Saint Peters Prophesie of These Last Daies: Discovering the Iniquity of the Time, and Atheisme of the Age* (London: Paules, 1610), praef.: "Men are secure, scoffers increase, Epicures abound, Atheisme is ripe. The creation is accounted a figment: the deluge a fable: the worldes burning a tale: the Scriptures but humanity; and religion but policy: Christs comming is derided: the day of iudgement despised: the resurrection not beleeued." Some feel the need to make the argument that the second coming is doctrinally essential, so Christopher Love, *The Penitent Pardoned* (London: Rothwell, 1657), 115;

arship is a story of the creation of a theological culture war that partly explains, I believe, the contours of twentieth- and twenty-first-century discussion and the emergence of the consensus of silence as detailed in part 1. Both Reimarus and Strauss reflected on the way in which the topic of the second coming had become a theological lightning rod already in their own times. Reimarus accuses theologians of "passing nimbly over the matter because it is not beneficial to their purposes," or, due to embarrassment, "try[ing] to cultivate a very different object in the return of Christ in the clouds of heaven, from that which he and his apostles taught."[58] Reimarus even offers some personal reflection on his own research: at one time, he had hoped to find in the work of "the heroes of the faith" a way of dealing with the failure of eschatological expectation in the apostolic generation, but to no avail.[59] Strauss, as typical, attacks those on his left and on his right—both the supernaturalists who defend the literal scenario and the naturalists who explain it away.[60] Both, he reasons, are apologetics under different names.[61] It is not necessary for our purposes to discuss in detail the nature of the more conservative or orthodox responses to critical scholarship on the second coming and the teaching of Jesus. The arguments are predictable in light of the theological assumptions. But the brevity of our coverage here must not obscure the extent and breadth of these reactionary treatments. The literature is immense.[62]

Thomas Vincent, *Christ's Sudden and Certain Appearance to Judgment* (Morgan: Soli Deo Gloria, 1996 [orig. 1667]). Richard Sibbes, *The Bride's Longing* (London: Purslow, 1638), 15, 146, suggests that one can weed out true Christians from false based upon one's ethical life, because one's ethical life makes plain that one truly believes in the second coming of Christ or not. Some regarded departure from the historic teaching of the church itself as evidence of the imminence of the end. For a broader discussion, see Bryan W. Ball, *A Great Expectation: Eschatological Thought in English Protestantism to 1660*, SHCT 12 (Leiden: Brill, 1975), 103–7.

58. Hermann Samuel Reimarus, *Reimarus: Fragments*, ed. Charles H. Talbert, trans. Ralph S. Fraser (Chico, CA: Scholars Press, 1985 [orig. 1779]), 227.

59. Reimarus, *Fragments*, 229. He writes at 228, "the openly appointed time for the second coming of Jesus has long passed by" and "one of the mainstays of Christianity is shown to be utterly worthless."

60. David Friedrich Strauss, *The Life of Jesus Critically Examined*, trans. George Eliot, 4th ed. (London: Sonnenschein, 1902 [orig. 1835–1836]), 584–92. Though he admits that, should Jesus have said what Mark 13 has him say, it would "inflict a fatal wound on Christianity; hence it is natural that exegetists should endeavour by all means to obviate them" (584–85).

61. Strauss, *Life of Jesus*, 592: "The question is not: what will it satisfy the Christian consciousness of the present day to believe or not to believe concerning Christ? But, what stands written concerning Christ? And to this the above consciousness must accommodate itself as it best may."

62. See, e.g., Edmond de Pressense, *Jesus Christus: Seine Zeit, sein Leben und sein Werk* (Halle: Waisenhauses, 1866); *Second Coming of Christ: Premillennial Essays of the Prophetic Conference* (Chicago: Revell, 1879) (the opening "call for the conference" begins, "Dear brethren in Christ:

By the early to mid-twentieth century, then, the second-coming hope had become an ideologically loaded topic of contestation. We see this on display in the United States in *The Fundamentals*, which doubled down on the "personal, glorious, and imminent" nature of Christ's return as a central element of his original message.[63] At the same time, many Christian historians and theologians were exchanging the old literal rendering of the second coming for a metaphorical and existential meaning in the present.[64] In such circles, the use of the category "eschatology" undergoes a subtle shift: associated no longer with specific expectations about the future, eschatology becomes synonymous with "the ultimate" or "finality" in the exegesis of Rudolf Bultmann and Ernst Käsemann and many theologians, as well as in more popular-level Christian literature.[65] As Dieter Georgi

---

When from any cause some vital doctrine of God's Word has fallen into neglect or suffered contradiction and reproach, it becomes the serious duty of those who hold it, not only strongly and constantly to re-affirm it, but to seek by all means in their power to bring back the Lord's people to its apprehension and acceptance. The precious doctrine of Christ's second personal appearing has, we are constrained to believe, long lain under such neglect and misapprehension" [11]); William Hanna, *The Life of Christ* (New York: Carter, 1883); David Smith, *The Days of His Flesh: The Earthly Life of Our Lord and Saviour Jesus Christ* (London: Hodder & Stoughton, 1906); Louis Billot, *La Parousie* (Paris: Beauchesne, 1920), (at 9: "Il est un point dans l'Évangile sur lequel s'est particulièrement exercée la critique moderniste, qui a cru y trouver un argument décisive pour son oeuvre de démolition de la religion chrétienne, en tant que religion transcendante et révélée de Dieu. Ce point, c'est le point concernant le second avènement de Jésus-Christ").

63. See Charles R. Erdman, "The Coming of Christ," in vol. 11 of *The Fundamentals: A Testimony to the Truth* (Chicago: Testimony, 1910–1915), 87–99.

64. For helpful discussions, see Lundström, *Kingdom of God in the Teaching of Jesus*, 141–44; G. C. Berkouwer, *The Return of Christ*, Studies in Dogmatics (Grand Rapids: Eerdmans, 1972), 9–31 (at 26 observes that twentieth-century dialectical theology "called eschatological inquiry back from excessive emphasis on the future to a study of the present relevance of the future"); Anthony C. Thiselton, "The Parousia in Modern Theology: Some Questions and Comments," *TynBul* 27 (1976): 27–53; Hiers, *Jesus and the Future*, 96–110; Yvonne Sherwood, "'Not with a Bang but a Whimper': Shrunken Eschatologies of the Twentieth Century—and the Bible," in *Apocalyptic in History and Tradition*, ed. Christopher Rowland and John Barton, JSPSup 43 (Sheffield: Sheffield Academic, 2002), 94–116; Jerry L. Walls, introduction to *The Oxford Handbook of Eschatology*, ed. Jerry L. Walls (Oxford: Oxford University Press, 2007), 7; Markus Mühling, *T&T Clark Handbook of Christian Eschatology*, trans. Jennifer Adams-Maßmann and David Andrew Gilland (London: Bloomsbury, 2015), 22–25, 252–55; Judith Wolfe, "The Eschatological Turn in German Philosophy," *Modern Theology* 35 (2019): 55–70. Similar tendencies concerning eschatology and messianism can be found in Judaism in the modern era. See Ellis Rivkin, "The Meaning of the Messiah in Jewish Thought," *USQR* 26 (1971): 404–6.

65. Cf. Rudolf Bultmann, *Jesus and the Word*, trans. Louise Pettibone Smith and Erminie Huntress Lantero (New York: Scribner's Sons, 1934), 41 ("the ultimate Either-Or"); Ernst Käsemann, "Das Problem des Historischen Jesus," *ZTK* 51 (1954): 125–53. For a recent example of a popular-level treatment, cf. Barbara Brown Taylor, "Expecting the Second Coming: Don't Say

and John Kloppenborg have noted, what functioned for Schweitzer to distance Jesus from the modern world soon emphasized Jesus's unique demand and, ironically, his relevance for the modern world.[66] In addition, many theologians from the twentieth century to the present have problematized eschatological hopes like the second coming by claiming they encourage quietism and distract from the important work of social justice in the present. Miguel A. De La Torre captures the sentiment when he writes, "this present age has too much oppression to be distracted by visions of kingdoms not seen."[67] Thomas Kazen strikes a similar note: "ideas of a returning Jesus have led people to a passive and quietist withdrawal from social issues" and "ideas of cloud-riding individual redeemers rebooting the globe may sell Hollywood scripts but hardly make for crisis-consciousness or building community and network."[68] In one of his later works, Marcus Borg asks what to his mind is a rhetorical question:

> Was Jesus' message to his contemporaries "Don't worry, God's going to fix everything soon?" or was his message to the poor about empowerment and resistance? Was his inclusive meal practice with marginalized people primarily an affirmation that the kingdom, when it comes, will include these? Or was it an affirmation of a different vision of life now?[69]

Quite varied theological movements that might not otherwise have that much to agree about have at least shared a common distaste for imminent escha-

---

When," *ChrCent* 121 (2004): 34–35, 37–38, wherein Jesus's call for eschatological alertness becomes a call for existential mindfulness (at 38: "No matter where Jesus is, it is time to stop living in the past and in the future and to start living right now").

66. See Dieter Georgi, "Rudolf Bultmann's *Theology of the New Testament* Revisited," in *Bultmann, Retrospect and Prospect: The Centenary Symposium at Wellesley*, HTS 35 (Philadelphia: Fortress, 1985), 82; John S. Kloppenborg, "As One Unknown, without a Name? Co-opting the Apocalyptic Jesus," in *Apocalypticism, Anti-Semitism and the Historical Jesus: Subtexts in Criticism*, ed. John S. Kloppenborg with John W. Marshall (London: T&T Clark International, 2006), 1–23.

67. Miguel A. De La Torre, *Embracing Hopelessness* (Minneapolis: Fortress, 2017), 52. For a very different take that emphasizes Christ's return, see James Cone, *God of the Oppressed*, rev. ed. (Maryknoll, NY: Orbis Books, 1997), esp. 116–22. Cone writes, "the power of Christ's future coming and the vision that it bestows upon the people is the key to why the oppressed can 'keep on keepin' on' even when their fight seems fruitless" (120), and "the future reality of Jesus means that what is contradicts what ought to be" (121).

68. Thomas Kazen, "The Coming Son of Man Revisited," *JSHJ* 5 (2007): 174. Kazen goes on to argue that the historical Jesus had aimed to enact the kingdom "through various types of communal practices" (174).

69. Marcus Borg, *Jesus: Uncovering the Life, Teachings, and Relevance of a Religious Revolutionary* (New York: HarperOne, 2008), 257–58.

tological expectation in general and the hope for the second coming of Jesus in particular.[70]

There are of course legitimate questions we could pursue about how and in what way certain eschatological perspectives can lead to quietism. But for the purposes of this study, what I want to ask is this: how could this theological and cultural reality *not* impact the "pre-understanding" (Bultmann's term) of new generations of New Testament scholars?[71] Perhaps I may be permitted to end this chapter with a personal reflection. When I started working on this project in earnest, some of my New Testament colleagues raised their eyebrows. They had assumed that suggesting the second-coming hope had anything to do with the historical Jesus was something only a Christian apologist would do. That reaction tells us a great deal about our modern interpretive context. The organization of certain topics under the purview of serious historians, and others under the purview of tendentious ideologues—all prior to the consideration of the actual arguments and conclusions themselves—is a distinct product of this turbulent reception history. It is a learned "habit of reading." In fact, the very notion of considering "the second advent" as a topic distinct from other eschatological topics like the coming of the kingdom or the final judgment is beholden to the doctrinalization of "the second advent" in Christian discussion and the history of its creedal theological formulation. Indeed, the way we divvy up these "topics" in historical Jesus scholarship may tell us as much about ourselves as the primary sources.

The emergence of the consensus of silence as discussed in part 1 turns out to be not so mysterious after all, then. There are evident social and cultural explanations for why historical Jesus scholars from the twentieth century to today have decided to pursue other questions.

70. Cf. Søren Kierkegaard: "It is the believer who is nearest the eternal, while the apocalyptic visionary is furthest from the eternal." Cited in Anthony Rudd, *Kierkegaard and the Limits of the Ethical* (Oxford: Clarendon, 1993), 172.

71. See Rudolf Bultmann, "Is Exegesis without Presuppositions Possible?," in *Existence and Faith: Shorter Writings of Rudolf Bultmann* (New York: Meridian, 1960), 289–96.

7

Elitism and Anti-Judaism

The preceding chapters challenge, I believe, a key element of N. T. Wright's account of the reception and development of eschatology in the modern world. Wright focuses on the addition of new, contextually specific mindsets of the modern era, particularly what he calls "the triumph of Epicureanism," and highlights their distorting effects. As already noted, he has his finger on something important. But in making this case, it seems to me that Wright fails to offer a sufficiently broad (in its own cultural contexts) and deep (in the history of Christianity) description of eschatological thought by modern biblical criticism. For Wright has very little to say about what is surely the most remarkable development of all: what was once taken more or less for granted about the parousia—namely, that Christ will indeed return from heaven to consummate the kingdom, and that Jesus and his disciples were essentially unified in thought about this (chapter 5)—was theologically problematized and brought into question in new and influential ways (chapter 6). The underlying plausibility structure supporting the precritical consensus had been remade in certain circles.

I now turn attention to that new plausibility structure. I would like to go beyond *what* biblical critics said about the second advent (or not) to make a few suggestions about *why* it was believed to make so much sense by the nineteenth century. Many have written about changes in intellectual history that help explain certain developments in Enlightenment Christianity, and I have little to add to that conversation. I wish to focus instead on how the conversation about eschatology and messianism was embedded in and shaped by concrete social realities. My argument in this chapter is that many took issue with the second-coming hope because of what was at stake in this discussion for the markers and boundaries of religious identity. Critical biblical scholarship emerged in a largely Protestant milieu and among the social and academic elite. Debate about the second advent reflects that social location in two particular ways. The first is the existence of disparaging attitudes toward popular-level eschatologies—for example, the eschatological beliefs of common religious practitioners—manifest especially in millenarian and revolutionary movements. The second is the attempt to distance Jesus from "Jewish messianism," which was described as inherently violent, political, carnal, and nationalistic. As we shall see, this discussion goes beyond matters of individual bias or prejudice; this is about the creation and maintenance of certain habits of reading—habits produced and sustained by assumptions about the kind of person Jesus was and the kind of person Jesus was not.

Enthusiasm and Fanaticism

I begin with David Friedrich Strauss. Strauss wrote that if Jesus predicted his own second coming, "he is for us nothing but a fanatic (Schwärmer)."[1] He also stated why, in his estimation, many in his own day denied this conclusion: "it makes Jesus an enthusiast."[2] These are loaded terms. "Fanaticism" and "enthusiasm" are not merely pejorative descriptions of "wild ideas"; they stem from a certain social lexicon as pejorative descriptions of *the kind of people* who hold such wild ideas.[3] In the centuries prior to Strauss in France, Germany, and especially in Britain, "enthusiasm" describes a religiosity of strong emotion, interest in theological speculation and imagination, with confidence that God communicates directly to persons to clarify the divine will and predict the future.[4] "Fanaticism" has a similar range of

1. David Friedrich Strauss, *A New Life of Jesus*, trans. s.n. (London: Williams & Norgate, 1865), 1:322. For the German, see *Das Leben Jesu für das deutsche Volk bearbeitet* (Leipzig: Brockhaus, 1864), 236. Strauss is ultimately agnostic about whether this is true: "we cannot tell" if the hope comes from Jesus himself or his followers.

2. David Friedrich Strauss, *Das Leben Jesu kritisch bearbeitet* (Tübingen: Osiander, 1835–1836), 1:494: "Wer diese Ansicht von dem Hintergrunde des messianischen Planes Jesu blos deswegen scheut, weil er durch dieselbe Jesum zum Schwärmer zu Machen glaubt."

3. For a few examples, and denial of the second-coming hope to Jesus on these grounds, see Gustav Volkmar, *Jesus Nazarenus und die erste christliche Zeit* (Zurich: Schmidt, 1882), 155; Paul Schwartzkopff, *Die Weissagungen Jesu Christi von seinem Tode, seiner Auferstehung und Wiederkunft und ihre Erfüllung* (Göttingen: Vandenhoeck & Ruprecht, 1895), 193; Adalbert Merx, *Das Evangelium Matthäus* (Berlin: Reimer, 1902), 355; Julius Wellhausen, *Einleitung in die drei ersten Evangelien*, 2nd ed. (Berlin: Reimer, 1911), 96–97.

4. Cf. David Hume, "Of Superstition and Enthusiasm," in vol. 3 of *The Philosophical Works of*

use, if perhaps a sharper political edge; "fanatics" are often described as a threat to the social order. Christian millenarians, unsurprisingly, commonly suffer the brunt of such critiques. In Britain, "enthusiasm" and "fanaticism" would be linked to the English Civil War and its aftermath, as Oliver Cromwell and the Fifth Monarchists were inspired by Dan 7 and believed the fifth ruler would be the government of God and the saints (established by force, if necessary).[5]

We find the polemical use of such terms increase as millenarianism in Europe reached new heights in the seventeenth and eighteenth centuries.[6] John Locke, Robert Boyle, and Samuel Clarke all wrote critically of these contemporary eschatological movements.[7] One especially vocal opponent was Pierre Bayle, whose *Dictionnaire historique et critique* (1697) was a foundational text for the European Enlightenment. Bayle excoriated individual millenarians, and he wrote critically of those he called "visionaries," "fanatics," "fools," and "enthusiasts."[8] Many of the de-

---

David Hume, ed. T. H. Green and T. H. Grose (London: Longmans, Green, 1875), 145: "Hope, pride, presumption, a warm imagination, together with ignorance, are, therefore, the true sources of enthusiasm." Another important influence was Spinoza on prophets and prophecy. See discussion in Gregory Dawes, *The Historical Jesus Question: The Challenge of History to Religious Authority* (Louisville: Westminster John Knox, 2001), 43–49. Spinoza argued that God had communicated to the prophets via their imaginations, which thereby limited their message to their particular cultural milieu. Claims about the future arose from the prophet's experience of the external world and was hence fallible. Spinoza argued that the prophets are better resources for "uprightness and morality" than predicting the future.

5. Cf. Richard Kyle, *The Last Days Are Here Again: A History of the End Times* (Grand Rapids: Baker Books, 1998), 55–67; Patrick Gray, *Paul as a Problem in History and Culture: The Apostle and His Critics through the Centuries* (Grand Rapids: Baker Books, 2016), 56. See also Hillel Schwartz, *Knaves, Fools, Madmen, and That Subtle Effluvium: A Study of the Opposition to the French Prophets in England, 1706–1710* (Gainesville: University of Florida Press, 1978).

6. On widespread eschatological fervor in seventeenth-century Europe, see Jerome Friedman, "The Myth of Jewish Antiquity: New Christians and Christian-Hebraica in Early Modern Europe," in *Jewish Christians and Christian Jews: From the Renaissance to the Enlightenment*, ed. Richard H. Popkin and Gordon M. Weiner, IAHI 138 (Dordrecht: Kluwer, 1994), 57–58; Hillel Schwartz, "The Eschatology of Everyday Things," in *The Millenarian Turn: Millenarian Contexts of Science, Politics, and Everyday Anglo-American Life in the Seventeenth and Eighteenth Centuries*, vol. 3 of *Millenarianism and Messianism in Early Modern European Culture*, ed. James E. Force and Richard H. Popkin, IAHI 175 (Dordrecht: Kluwer, 2001), 171–80; Crawford Gribben, *Evangelical Millennialism in the Trans-Atlantic World, 1500–2000* (New York: Palgrave Macmillan, 2011), 37–70.

7. See Daniel J. Cook, "Leibniz on 'Prophets,' Prophecy, and Revelation," *RelS* 45 (2009): 269–87. See also discussion in Richard Popkin, "Three English Tellings of the Sabbatai Zevi Story," *Jewish History* 8 (1994): 43–54.

8. Cf. John Christian Laursen, "Bayle's Anti-millenarianism: The Dangers of Those Who Claim to Know the Future," in *Continental Millenarians: Protestants, Catholics, Heretics*, vol. 4 of

ists and freethinkers mentioned already in part 2 were of a similar mind. Frank E. Manuel wrote,

> While orthodox believers took comfort in the wisdom of the prophets who had foretold the coming of Christ and sometimes naively talked of the "sons of the prophets" as sorts of universities of ancient Judaea, those Deists who wanted neither Christ coming once or twice, nor a future Jewish Messiah, made the biblical prophets sound like the Protestant "prophets of London," those persecuted Huguenots from the Cevennes who were afflicted with glossolalia and held scandalous seances predicting doomsday.[9]

We might add to Manuel's keen description that it is not just "the biblical prophets" who appear like "the prophets of London" in the writings of some of these critics (to use but one example), but they depict the disciples of Christ in similar terms. These first followers of Jesus, like the millenarians of their own day, spread falsehoods about the imminent return of the Lord. Descriptions of the former and the latter share a family resemblance, and that is not a coincidence.

These kinds of connections persist across the Atlantic into the nineteenth century, captured in a particularly poignant way in the religious writings of Thomas Jefferson. In the early 1800s, Jefferson sought to separate what he called the "diamonds" from the "dunghills"—that is, the teaching of Jesus from the theology of his disciples. By sifting through the "dross of his biographers," Jefferson famously carved up the Gospels to produce what he thought was the essence of Jesus's philosophical and ethical teaching, on par, he thought, with that of Socrates and other luminaries.[10] How Jefferson regarded these disciples of Jesus socially, culturally, and intellectually leaves little to the imagination: Jesus's teachings were "beyond the powers of their feeble minds"; they wrote about him based on their own "vulgar ignorance"; and they corrupted his teaching on account of "the stupidity of some, and roguery of others."[11] Similar language games emerged in theological reflection in America after Jefferson's time as theologians responded to the

---

Millenarianism and Messianism in Early Modern European Culture, ed. John Christian Laursen and Richard H. Popkin, IAHI 176 (Dordrecht: Kluwer, 2001), 98–99.

9. Frank E. Manuel, "Israel and the Enlightenment," *Daedalus* 111 (1982): 43.

10. See Thomas Jefferson, *The Jefferson Bible: With the Annotated Commentaries on Religion of Thomas Jefferson*, ed. O. I. A. Roche (New York: Potter, 1964). The "dross" line is cited by Peter Manseau, *The Jefferson Bible: A Biography* (Princeton: Princeton University Press, 2020), 6. Jefferson also called the theological reflections of the disciples "rubbish" (cited at 58).

11. These lines from various writings by Jefferson are cited by Manseau, *Jefferson Bible*, 53, 65, 52, respectively.

Millerites and other mass eschatological movements, including the popular-level belief in the rapture.[12]

The Learned Jesus

It should be evident, then, that David Strauss's comments about Jesus possibly being an "enthusiast" or "fanatic" are biting for the nineteenth-century critic not merely because of what they indicate about Jesus's ideas, but because of what they imply about Jesus's social location. With which crowd does one associate Jesus? A good deal of the early, formative scholarship on the historical Jesus depicted him more at home among the intellectuals and academics of Enlightenment Christianity and certainly distant from street prophets announcing the speedy reversal of all things. The poet Percy Shelley was clear: Jesus's teachings are wholly unlike "the gross imaginations of the vulgar."[13] Many of the most controversial works on Jesus in the nineteenth-century quest were those that not merely challenged orthodox or creedal commitments; they were the studies that also distanced Jesus socially from nineteenth-century intelligentsia.[14] Ernst Renan's *Life of Jesus*, perhaps the most famous book on the historical Jesus ever written, is a paradoxical case in point (paradoxical given Renan's own embeddedness in the bourgeoisie of his time and his racist depiction of Jesus).[15] Renan's Jesus, whose theology changes

12. Cf. Paul Boyer, *When Time Shall Be No More: Prophecy Belief in Modern American Culture* (Cambridge: Harvard University Press, 1992); Bryan Wilson, "Millennialism and Sect Formation in the Nineteenth and Twentieth Centuries," in *Apocalyptic in History and Tradition*, ed. Christopher Rowland and John Barton, JSPSup 43 (Sheffield: Sheffield Academic, 2002), 212–32; Tina Pippin, "The Rapture in American Imagination," in *The Oxford Handbook of the Bible and American Popular Culture*, ed. Dan W. Clanton Jr. and Terry R. Clark (Oxford: Oxford University Press, 2021), 262–75. On the Millerites in particular and the association between their eschatological views and insanity, see Ronald L. Numbers and Janet S. Numbers, "Millerism and Madness: A Study of 'Religious Insanity' in Nineteenth-Century America," in *The Disappointed: Millerism and Millenarianism in the Nineteenth Century*, ed. Ronald L. Numbers and Jonathan M. Butler (Bloomington: Indiana University Press, 1987), 92–118.

13. Cited in Dale C. Allison Jr., "Percy Bysshe Shelley and the Historical Jesus," in *Resurrecting Jesus: The Earliest Christian Tradition and Its Interpreters* (London: T&T Clark, 2005), 106.

14. For a similar critique, see Dieter Georgi, "The Interest in Life of Jesus Theology as a Paradigm for the Social History of Biblical Criticism," *HTR* 85 (1992): 83: "I observe the main cause in the continuous social and historical situation of the whole quest for the historical Jesus, that is, its location within the evolution of bourgeois consciousness, not just as an ideal but as an expression of a socioeconomic and political momentum."

15. See Susannah Heschel, *The Aryan Jesus: Christian Theologians and the Bible in Nazi Germany* (Princeton: Princeton University Press, 2008), 33–38. On Renan's bourgeois culture of

over the course of his ministry in response to various challenges, ends up with "fanatical" tendencies: he predicts the coming wrath of God and anticipates his own supernatural vindication.[16] For Renan, the historical Jesus is responsible for the imminence of Mark 13:30, which history proved false. John Seeley's incredibly popular *Ecce Homo*, which was in many ways a response to Renan in Britain, offered a proper theological *and social* corrective.[17] In contrast to Renan's portrait, Seeley asserts of Jesus,

> No other career ever had so much unity; no other biography is so simple, or can so well afford to dispense with details. Men in general take up scheme after scheme, as circumstances suggest one or another. . . . But Christ formed one plan and executed it; no important change took place in his mode of thinking, speaking, or acting; at least the evidence before us does not enable us to trace any such change.[18]

It is no surprise that, unlike Renan's Jesus, Seeley's does not develop the idea of the second coming in response to rejection. In fact, Jesus does not hold to that expectation at all, according to Seeley. It has no place in his message.[19]

The rhetorical practice of leveraging the putative social resonance of certain eschatological perspectives as a means of critiquing or approving them has by no means ceased, nor did it begin in the seventeenth century, nor is it unique to Christianity.[20] In the early twentieth century, one significant attempt to re-

---

production, see Georgi, "Interest in Life of Jesus Theology," 78. On popular interest in Renan's life of Jesus, and its print history, see Robert D. Priest, "Reading, Writing, and Religion in Nineteenth-Century France: The Popular Reception of Renan's Life of Jesus," *Journal of Modern History* 86 (2014): 258–94.

16. Ernest Renan, *The Life of Jesus*, trans. s.n. (New York: Modern Library, 1927 [orig. 1863]), 235, 249, 260–67 (here qualifies that Jesus was not "only an enthusiast"—for if he were, we could not explain his impact). Renan writes at one point concerning Jesus's more radical teaching: "Sometimes one would have said that his reason was disturbed" (293), and "Jesus . . . aimed less at convincing his hearers than at exciting their enthusiasm" (293). Cf. Daniel L. Pals, *The Victorian "Lives" of Jesus* (San Antonio: Trinity University Press, 1982), 34.

17. See Pals, *Victorian "Lives" of Jesus*, 48.

18. John Seeley, *Ecce Homo: A Survey of the Life and Work of Jesus Christ* (Boston: Roberts Brothers, 1867), 24. For a similar view of Jesus's consistency that was also highly influential, see August Neander, *Das Leben Jesu Christi: In seinem geschichtlichen Zusammenhange und seiner geschichtlichen Entwickelung dargestellt* (Hamburg: Perthes, 1837).

19. It is telling that, while marching through the Gospels more or less chronologically, Seeley skips over Mark 13 and par. and moves directly to the Last Supper. On the (noneschatological) significance of that meal, see *Ecce Homo*, 188.

20. Jewish historian Abraham Geiger's work on Jesus is interesting in this respect. Geiger

spond to the crisis caused by the rediscovery of eschatology in early Christianity was penned by Maurice Blondel, who argued that the earliest Christian hope for an imminent parousia was a divine accommodation to "simple" people.[21] Part 2 began with very similar comments in the crucial mid-twentieth-century works of Glasson and Robinson—Glasson contrasting "the patient farmer" with "the wild-eyed apocalyptist," and Robinson expressly connecting imminent eschatology to "the modern fundamentalist." We could fill the entire chapter with lines to similar effect from the mid-twentieth century to the present day. In the earliest centuries of the church, chiliasm was routinely subject to ad hominem critiques in sociocultural code: Irenaeus wrote dismissively of Papias as a man "of very small intelligence";[22] Hippolytus's *Commentary on Daniel* tells of a misguided Christian in Pontus who "believed his own visions" as is typical of "simple men";[23] Origen asserted that Christians looking forward to "bodily pleasure and luxury" in the kingdom of God "refuse the labor of thinking";[24] Augustine attributed the expectations for physical blessings in the afterlife to "carnal sluggishness, or the slowness of an uneducated and undisciplined mind."[25]

I do not want to belabor this point, or create by means of it an unfair ad hominem critique of my own. The central and crucial point is simply this: the reception history of the second coming has been about much more than debating the logical and theological soundness of a doctrine. It has been a matter of crafting and negotiating Christian social identity—that is, what it *is* or *should be*, and what it *is not* or *should not be*—by means of it. The academic discussion of the second coming in biblical studies, and of eschatology in general, has been inseparable from the perceived social embodiment of eschatological perspectives in particular times and places. The plausibility structure undergirding the downplaying or outright

argues that Jesus was closely aligned with the Pharisees, but his message was successful in Galilee because the people who lived there had less education and were thereby prone to be led astray by apocalypticism. For larger discussion, see Susannah Heschel, *Abraham Geiger and the Jewish Jesus* (Chicago: University of Chicago Press, 1998).

21. Maurice Blondel, *"The Letter on Apologetics" and "History and Dogma,"* trans. Alexander Dru and Illtyd Trethowan (Grand Rapids: Eerdmans, 1994 [orig. 1904]), 249. Imminent eschatology, he argues, while mistaken, contained within it a greater truth about detachment from the world, attentiveness, and the realism of salvation. Blondel's main interlocutor in this piece was Alfred Loisy, interestingly enough.

22. Eusebius, *Hist. eccl.* 3.39.13.

23. Hippolytus, *Comm. Dan.* 4.19.1 (SC 14:183–84).

24. Origen, *Princ.* 2.11.2 (*ANF* 4:297).

25. Augustine, *Civ.* 20.21 (FC 24:307): "it is only a lazy and worldly person or one who is ignorant or uneducated who will rest content with the literal and superficial sense and refuse to penetrate the deeper meaning."

elimination of the second advent hope from the proclamation of Jesus in the early formative period of modern biblical criticism has a very real social form.

None of this would be news to Albert Schweitzer.[26] In his critique of the nineteenth-century liberal quest for Jesus, he wrote at one point,

> [Jesus's] ethical enthusiasm and the directness and power of his way of thinking remained inaccessible to them [modern scholars] because they knew nothing of this in their own thought and experience. So they continually endeavored to make of this "fanatic" (Schwärmer) a "modern man" and a theologian who served moderation and propriety in all things.[27]

Schweitzer, clearly in touch with the social dynamics at play with these terms, takes the feared label and turns it on its head. Not only have these historians made Jesus into their own image, Schweitzer contends that the religious characteristic they fear most ("fanaticism") is precisely what makes Jesus worthy of great honor. In fact, he argues that Jesus's fanaticism makes his theology superior to that of the nineteenth-century liberal project. He continues to claim that nineteenth-century liberalism, for all its theological brilliance, had a "willing and hoping and longing" that was "not inwardly tuned to the same pitch" as Jesus.[28] This is tendentious, too (even if I personally find it profound). But it shows that Schweitzer was already near the trail we are walking on here.[29]

26. And even before him, note H. J. Holtzmann, *Sammlung Theologischer Lehrbücher: Neutestamentliche Theologie* (Freiburg: Mohr, 1897), 325–32, who was of course Schweitzer's *Doktorvater.* Also noteworthy is the theologian Herman Bavinck's summary of Jesus research in his time in his 1908/1909 Stone Lectures at Princeton Seminary in *The Philosophy of Revelation* (New York: Longmans, Green, 1909). He suggests that, unlike the "humanitarian" figure of other prominent nineteenth-century critics (247), the eschatological Jesus of Baldensperger and Weiss was "a totally different kind of man. He was not a quiet, pious man, and not a philosophic teacher of virtue, but a prophet, an enthusiast, a fanatic, who lived under the impression of the speedy advent of the kingdom of God, and therefore exhorted his contemporaries to faith and conversion . . . he was not nearly so great as the liberal theology has presented him . . . he was . . . a limited and superstitious man" (248). The social resonance of these descriptors is patent, while stressing that was not Bavinck's intent here (he takes these Jesuses as different ways of relating Christianity to culture).

27. Cited in David Dungan, "Albert Schweitzer's Disillusionment with the Historical Reconstructions of the Life of Jesus," *PSTJ* 29 (1976): 42.

28. Cited in Dungan, "Albert Schweitzer's Disillusionment," 42.

29. Andrew M. Mbuvi, *African Biblical Studies: Unmasking Embedded Racism and Colonialism in Biblical Studies* (London: Bloomsbury T&T Clark, 2023), 45, rightly notes that "Schweitzer's reproach of the lack of self-awareness and self-critique by the preceding European biblical

Eschatology and Anti-Judaism

Not only did the second-coming hope carry some fraught social connotations in certain intellectual circles, to many the expectation sounded too similar to traditional Jewish messianic beliefs as characterized by Christian discourse. Thus, the reception of the second advent in biblical studies has been deeply impacted by another manner of religious identity construction: the attempt to define Jesus, and Christianity, by means of contrast to Judaism.[30] I would argue that these efforts have been just as enduring and impactful as the question of Jesus's social location on the creation of the consensus of silence so far described and the habits of reading that sustained it. I should also stress that the following discussion does not assume that genuine differences of opinion about messianism among Jewish and Christian groups may not exist; it is an overstatement to say that "'the Messiah' is an all but blank screen onto which a given community would project its concerns."[31] In any case, our interest, rather, is on the reification of categories and the crafting of definitions.[32]

For many in the nineteenth-century quest and well into the twentieth century, the supposedly Jewish nature of the second-coming hope was a significant problem because it was commonly thought that one of the central aims of Jesus's teaching ministry was to critique "Jewish messianism" and replace it with his own alternative vision.[33] To understand how this view emerged, we return initially to

scholars in their interpretation of the Bible . . . did not seem to translate into his perception of missionary work in Africa where he seemed completely blind to his own critique."

30. Few have been as insightful on the history and persistence of this rhetorical maneuver as Amy-Jill Levine. See, e.g., *The Misunderstood Jew: The Church and the Scandal of the Jewish Jesus* (San Francisco: HarperSanFrancisco, 2006), 118–66. On the question of messianism in particular, Levine challenges the view she calls "endemic in the Christian popular imagination" that "all Jews wanted a warrior messiah who would defeat Rome" (124). She further notes that "by speaking of Jews as warlike, Christians can ignore the warlike aspects of their own canonical tradition, including statements made by Jesus himself, and so claim for him the peaceful high ground" (125). See also 127–31. Cf. as well Anthony Le Donne, "The Quest of the Historical Jesus: A Revisionist History through the Lens of Jewish-Christian Relations," *JSHJ* 10 (2012): 63–86.

31. Jacob Neusner, *Messiah in Context: Israel's History and Destiny in Formative Judaism* (Minneapolis: Fortress, 1984), xi.

32. On debated questions of perception versus projection in the early period, see the thoughtful essay by James Carleton Padget, "Anti-Judaism and Early Christian Identity," *ZAC* (1997): 195–225. Also insightful here is William Horbury, *Jews and Christians: In Contact and Controversy* (Edinburgh: T&T Clark, 2006), 24–25 (on the "interplay between stereotypical views and more genuine perception").

33. Cf., e.g., F. V. Reinhard, *Plan of the Founder of Christianity*, trans. Oliver A. Taylor from the 5th German ed. (New York: Carvill, 1831 [orig. 1781]), 28–31; Johann Herder, *Vom Erlöser*

Hermann Samuel Reimarus. Reimarus's historical take on the second coming is completely unoriginal in the sense that he argued the disciples of Jesus made it up themselves after stealing Jesus's body and feigning his resurrection.[34] "If the apostles had not promised such a glorious return of Christ," he reasoned, "no man would have concerned himself about their Messiah, or have listened to their preachings."[35] Despite the obvious continuity here with earlier discussion (as should by now be clear), Reimarus's work is indeed significant in the history of Jesus research because it served to raise the theological stakes. Even though Reimarus did not trace the second-coming hope back to Jesus, he linked his memorable and controversial portrait of Jesus as a violent, military messiah very closely to the church's hope for the second coming. That is because, for Reimarus, traditional Jewish messianic beliefs stand behind both the earthly aims of the historical Jesus and the theological dreams of his earliest followers. Reimarus believed that Jews in the Second Temple period had a fairly well-defined expectation for what the messiah was to be and do: he would be a political ruler who, like his ancestor David, would be a "man of blood" and liberate Israel from the clutches of foreign oppression before setting up his own earthly kingdom in Jerusalem.[36] Reimarus

---

der Menschen nach unsern drei ersten Evangelien (Riga: Hartknoch, 1796), 93; Carl Weizsäcker, *Untersuchungen über die evangelische Geschichte: Ihre Quellen und den Gang ihrer Entwicklung*, 2nd ed. (Tübingen: Mohr, 1901 [orig. 1864]), 334; Willibald Beyschlag, *New Testament Theology, or, Historical Account of the Teaching of Jesus and of Primitive Christianity according to the New Testament Sources*, trans. Neil Buchanan (Edinburgh: T&T Clark, 1895 [orig. 1891–1892]), 1:59 (on the gulf between Jesus's idea of the messiah and "the popular idea"); Wilhelm Bousset, *Jesus*, trans. J. P. Trevelyan (London: Williams & Norgate, 1906), 86–89. On the lives of Jesus by Sabatier, Stapfer, Reville, and others, see Jean G. H. Hoffmann, *Les vies de Jésus et le Jésus de l'histoire: Étude de la valeur historique des vies de Jésus de langue française, non catholiques, d'Ernest Renan à Charles Guignebert* (Paris: Prostant apud Messageries Évangéliques, 1947), 78. On F. C. Baur, see Annette Yoshiko Reed, "Messianism between Judaism and Christianity," in *Rethinking the Messianic Idea in Judaism*, ed. Michael L. Morgan and Steven Weitzman (Bloomington: Indiana University Press, 2015), 41.

34. Hermann Samuel Reimarus, *Reimarus: Fragments*, ed. Charles H. Talbert, trans. Ralph S. Fraser (Chico, CA: Scholars Press, 1985 [orig. 1779]), 215 (he calls this a "new creed").

35. Reimarus, *Fragments*, 215. Reimarus believed that Judaism already had the notion of a twofold advent of the messiah that the disciples simply adopted. Jonathan C. P. Birch, "The Road to Reimarus: Origins of the Quest of the Historical Jesus," in *Holy Land as Homeland?*, ed. Keith W. Whitelam, SWBA 7 (Sheffield: Sheffield Phoenix, 2011), 40, notes that "almost everything Reimarus wrote about Christian origins after the death of Jesus flows from the imposture hypothesis."

36. See, e.g., Reimarus, *Fragments*, 126: "the prevailing idea of the Messiah and his kingdom was that he would be a great temporal king and would establish a powerful kingdom in Jerusalem, whereby he would free them of all servitude and make them masters over other peoples."

argued that the historical Jesus failed in this bid, but the disciples, in proclaiming the hope of his second coming, persisted with the same messianic profile. Jesus would complete after death what he failed to do in life. On Reimarus's reading, then, the disciples of Jesus developed the hope of the second coming by returning to the same pool of messianic expectations that had inspired Jesus himself.

It is essential to recognize both how impactful this depiction of Jewish messianism was for Reimarus's project and that he did not invent it. Histories of Jesus research have often followed Schweitzer's lead in presenting Reimarus as a radical and subversive thinker who bucked the theological trends of the time. That is partly true in terms of Reimarus's largely negative evaluation of Jesus himself (as many of the deists and other freethinkers were typically more sympathetic). But Reimarus's controversial portrait was actually fairly uncontroversial—indeed rather conventional—when it comes to its claims about Jewish messianism in the Second Temple period.[37] Reimarus's work as a historian was effectively this: he took a preexisting understanding of messianism and argued that the life of Jesus in the Gospels, if sliced and diced just so, can fit neatly inside it.[38] We see here the unfortunate consequence of standard periodizations of New Testament research that rarely look much before the nineteenth and late eighteenth century to identify any formative developments on the quest for Jesus and the study of Christian origins. That oversight results in exaggerations about the discontinuity between nineteenth- and late eighteenth-century scholarship and earlier work on Jesus and the Gospels.

Reimarus's depiction of Jewish messianism was not only extant in the time of the deists and others before him, but it also had deeply impacted narratives about Christian origins, not least those critical of tracing the second-coming hope

37. Note especially the work of Christian Heinrich Schoettgen, *Horae Hebraicae et Talmudicae, in quibus adnotationes criticae et exegeticae, in Sacram Scripturam, praecipue in Novum Testamentum, ex fontibus Hebraicis et Talmudicis desumptae, exhibentur* (Hamburg: Langenhemii, 1733), and a second volume published in 1742. Schoettgen observes that there were different views of the messiah within Judaism but stresses the political and military aspects and contrasts this with the collective witness of the New Testament. He argues that, against the dominant Jewish view, the Gospels and Paul collectively saw Jesus as a spiritual messiah whose kingdom was not political or nationalistic. On the influence of this work up through the nineteenth century, see William Horbury, "The New Testament and Rabbinic Study: An Historical Sketch," in *The New Testament and Rabbinic Literature*, ed. R. Bieringer (Leiden: Brill, 2010), 27 ("remained a standard resource").

38. Cf. Henning Graf Reventlow, "Das Arsenal der Bibelkritik des Reimarus: Die Auslegung der Bibel, insbesondere des Alten Testaments, bei den englischen Deisten," in *Hermann Samuel Reimarus (1694–1768): Ein "bekannter Unbekannter" der Aufklärung in Hamburg* (Göttingen: Vandenhoeck & Ruprecht, 1973), 57.

to Jesus. Thomas Morgan, in a quotation already cited in part 2, criticized the second advent idea by claiming the disciples "understood and reported every Thing that he said according to their own Prejudices and false Opinions concerning the Messias."[39] What he means is that the disciples of Jesus, *being Jews*, returned to "their own" *Jewish* "Prejudices and false Opinions" about messianism in developing the second-coming expectation.[40] The intended implication of his argument is that Christians in his own day who hold fast to the hope for Christ's literal return actually adhere to Jewish "Prejudices and false Opinions" and thus recapitulate the error of the apostolic generation, whereas Morgan and like-minded company had grasped the pure, unadulterated teaching of Jesus that stood above and apart from that Jewish milieu.[41] This manner of leveraging the ethnic identity of the disciples of Jesus to challenge whatever theological issue Morgan disapproves of was common in this period.[42] It was also aided by a peculiar seventeenth-century social reality: the rise and fall of the Jewish messianic claimant Sabbatai Zevi. The Smyrnian rabbi who told his followers that he was the long-awaited messiah eventually succeeded in garnering a large following—including the support of numerous influential rabbis—to lead one of the most widespread messianic movements in Jewish history. His close ally, Nathan of Gaza (who declared himself to be Elijah *redivivus*), predicted that the messianic age would begin in 1666 with the restoration of the twelve tribes in the land of Israel, which even led some

39. Morgan, *Moral Philosopher*, 440.

40. On Morgan's depiction of Judaism, see Anders Gerdmar, *Roots of Theological Anti-Semitism: German Biblical Interpretation and the Jews, from Herder and Semler to Kittel and Bultmann*, SJHC 20 (Leiden: Brill, 2009), 31–38. See also Thomas Chubb, *The Posthumous Works of Mr. Thomas Chubb* (London: Baldwin, 1748), 2:304: "as the apostles were bred Jews; so they were liable to be prejudiced in favour of those Jewish principles they had been educated in."

41. For some broader reflections on anti-Judaism in this period, see Jacob I. Dienstag, "Maimonides in English Christian Thought and Scholarship: An Alphabetical Survey," *Hebrew Studies* 26 (1985): 249; Adam Sutcliffe, *Judaism and Enlightenment* (New York: Cambridge University Press, 2003); Gerdmar, *Roots of Theological Anti-Semitism*, 23–38.

42. Cf. John Evelyn, *The History of the Three Late Famous Imposters* (London: Herringman, 1669), 42–43; John Bradley, *An Impartial View of the Truth of Christianity* (London: Clavel, 1699), 65 ("all must be Slaves to them [Jews] at the Coming of the Messias"); Voltaire, "Messie," in *Dictionnaire philosophique*, in vol. 41 of *Oeuvres complètes de Voltaire* (Paris: Werdet & Lequien, 1827 [orig. 1764]), 177–95. For discussion, see Richard Popkin, "Jewish-Christian Relations in the Sixteenth and Seventeenth Centuries: The Conception of the Messiah," *Jewish History* 6 (1992): 163–77; Hans J. Hillerbrand, "The Decline and Fall of the True Christian Church: The English Deist View," *ZRGG* 60 (2008): 104; Dagmar Winter, "The Dissimilar Jesus: Anti-Semitism, Protestantism, Hero-Worship, and Dialectical Theology," in *Soundings in the Religion of Jesus: Perspectives and Methods in Jewish and Christian Scholarship*, ed. Bruce Chilton, Anthony Le Donne, and Jacob Neusner (Minneapolis: Fortress, 2012), 129–30.

Jewish communities in Europe to prepare for travel. It is a remarkable historical moment. But as Zevi was eventually captured in Constantinople and converted to Islam,[43] the dissolution of his movement became a point of ridicule in the hands of Christians and Muslims alike. For Christians in particular, it was proof positive of the folly of "Jewish messianism" and its hopes for worldly restoration and political sovereignty. As Elisheva Carlebach observed, "Failed Jewish messianic movements played right into Christian literary and theological discourse on the Jewish endtime and provided historical confirmation for what would have otherwise seemed like an absurd polemical exaggeration."[44] Zevi frequently emerges in later discussion as a foil for Jesus's messianic mission and his ethical teaching.[45]

Back Further Still

One reason that Zevi's story was so serviceable to Christian messaging is that it was relatively easy to connect his legacy to stereotypical depictions of Jewish

43. This turn of events divided his followers. Some abandoned the movement; others pressed on with increased fervor, believing this was a messianic ruse. See the famous study by Gershom Scholem, *Sabbatai Sevi: The Mystical Messiah*, trans. R. J. Zwi Werblowsky (Princeton: Princeton University Press, 1973).

44. Elisheva Carlebach, "Jews, Christians, and the Endtime in Early Modern Germany," *Jewish History* 14 (2000): 339. See also Popkin, "Jewish-Christian Relations," 170 (after Zevi's downfall, "Christians could look at the whole episode as just a Jewish mistake"). It was also common to pit the character of Jesus against the character of Muhammad. The life of Muhammad came to embody the alternative messianism of violence, terrestrial politics, and personal aggrandizement that Jesus explicitly rejected. Cf., e.g., Charles Leslie, *A Short and Easy Method with the Jews: Wherein the Certainty of the Christian Religion Is Demonstrated*, rev. ed. (London: Goakman, 1812 [orig. 1689?]), 34 (even claims that "the Jews flocked to him [Muhammad], as their Messiah, to which character he at first pretended"). On Muhammad and "the sword," see 112. Martin Luther had also made a connection between Jewish messianism and Islam in *About the Jews and Their Lies, 1543*, in *Christian Life in the World*, vol. 5 of *The Annotated Luther*, ed. Hans J. Hillerbrand (Minneapolis: Fortress, 2017), 293.

45. This was encouraged by the reality of significant interplay between some Jewish messianic speculation and Christian millenarianism in the seventeenth century. Cf. Richard Popkin, "Jewish Messianism and Christian Millenarianism," in *Culture and Politics from Puritanism to the Enlightenment*, ed. Perez Zagorin (Berkeley: University of California Press, 1980), 67–90 (he notes at 86, "One last consequence from this interaction and intermixture is probably a skepticism about the claims of both the messianists and the millenarians"). See also Popkin, "Jewish-Christian Relations," 163–77, and especially his discussion of Rabbi Menasseh ben Israel, who argued in *Vindiciae Judaeorum* (1656) that the difference between Judaism and Christianity is nothing more than "a detail about what happened in the first-century" (so Popkin, 166).

messianism that had emerged from Christian *adversus Judaeos* literature, especially as it developed after Constantine. Indeed, the larger construction of Jewish messianism in Enlightenment discourse and its use as a foil for the teaching of Jesus stems ultimately from this *adversus* tradition as well, I would argue. I would like to linger for a moment on this important point before returning to Reimarus and the modern quest for Jesus.

Before Constantine, it was common for Christian intellectuals and apologists to criticize other Christian views and police orthodox belief (as understood by the author in question) by linking heterodox views to Jews or Judaism.[46] This rhetorical strategy has been extensively researched.[47] What I wish to point out is that an important shift occurs in reception history in terms of which messianic and eschatological views qualify as being "too Jewish" for acceptance by Christians. In the second century, Justin Martyr argued that there was essentially no difference between Christians and Jews in terms of what is expected of the messianic era to come; both, he reasoned, read the same Scriptures that clearly anticipate the Lord's anointed to preside over a restored, earthly kingdom, centered in Jerusalem. The difference concerns not the expectation of what is to happen but the recognition of what has already happened.[48] In *Dialogue with Trypho*, after citing Isa 2's vision of the exalted mountain of the Lord, Justin writes,

> Now I am aware that your teachers grant that all of the words of this passage refer to Christ; and I am also aware that they maintain he has not yet come. Or, if they say that he has come, they contend that it is not known who he is, but when he shall become manifest and glorious [ὅταν ἐμφανὴς καὶ ἔνδοξος γένηται], then it will be known who he is. And then, they say, the events mentioned in this passage shall happen, as though as yet there was no fruit from the words of the prophecy. You unwise people do not understand what has been proved

46. Reed, "Messianism between Judaism and Christianity," 23: "Christianity's origins in Jewish messianism has served as a potent site for reflection on religious identity—not just in the first century, but in Late Antiquity and modernity as well."

47. So Paula Fredriksen on the creation of the "rhetorical Jew," and Jeremy Cohen's earlier idea of the "hermeneutical Jew." Cf. Jeremy Cohen, *Living Letters of the Law: Ideas of the Jew in Medieval Christianity* (Berkeley: University of California Press, 1999), 2 ("a hermeneutically and doctrinally crafted Jew"); Paula Fredriksen and Oded Irshai, "Christian Anti-Judaism: Polemics and Policies," in *Late Roman-Rabbinic Period*, vol. 4 of *The Cambridge History of Judaism*, ed. Steven T. Katz (Cambridge: Cambridge University Press, 2006), 977–1034 (at 984: "Jew" functioned as "a negative code-word within purely Christian internal debate"). See also Leonard Victor Rutgers, *Making Myths: Jews in Early Christian Identity Formation* (Leuven: Peeters, 2009).

48. See discussion in William Horbury, *Messianism among Jews and Christians: Biblical and Historical Studies*, 2nd ed. (London: Bloomsbury T&T Clark, 2016), 311–24.

> by all these passages, that two advents [δύο παρουσίαι] of Christ have been announced: the one, in which he is presented as suffering, without glory, dishonoured, and crucified; but the other, in which he shall come from heaven with glory.[49]

Justin's claim is that he and fellow Christians rightly see that the Scriptures expect the messiah to do *more than* inaugurate the glorious kingdom at the end time; he is *also* to come quietly, humbly, and ingloriously, to suffer and die.[50] Similar claims can be found in other important works from this period. In the Pseudo-Clementine *Recognitions*, Peter states that

> the Jews are mistaken [*erraverunt*] concerning the first coming of our Lord. But between them and us, there is disagreement about this matter only [*hoc est solo discidium*]. They themselves know and expect that the Messiah is coming. They do not know that he has come already in humility, namely, as the one called Jesus.[51]

Tertullian held basically the same view:

> The Jews, too, were well aware that the Christ was coming, as those to whom the prophets spoke. Even now his advent is expected by them, and there is no other contention between them and us [*nec alia magis inter nos et illos conpulsatio*] than that they believe the advent has not yet occurred. For two comings of Christ have been revealed to us: a first, which has been fulfilled in the lowliness of humanity; a second, which looms over the world, now near its close, in all the majesty of deity unveiled. And by misunderstanding the first they have concluded that the second, which, as matter of more manifest prediction, they set their hopes on, is the only one.[52]

Tertullian makes a particularly striking admission here that the prediction of the second coming of Christ—wherein, by his framing, Christians expect Jesus to

49. Justin Martyr, *Dial.* 110 (*ANF* 1:253, with my modifications). For Greek text, see Miroslav Marcovich, ed., *Iustini Martyris Dialogus cum Tryphone*, PTS 47 (Berlin: de Gruyter, 1997), 258.

50. On this contrast, linked to the two respective advents of Christ, see Hippolytus, *Antichr.* 44; Cyril of Jerusalem, *Cat.* 15.1.

51. Ps.-Clem. Rec. 1.50.5–6 (*ANF* 8:90, with my modifications). For Latin text, see Bernhard Rehm and Georg Strecker, eds., *Die Pseudoklementinen*, GCS (Berlin: Akademie-Verlag, 1965), 2:37. See also 1.43.2.

52. Tertullian, *Apol.* 21.14–16 (*ANF* 3:35, with my modifications from the Latin in LCL).

do exactly what Jews hope their messiah will do—is actually "of more manifest prediction" in the Scriptures than the first advent.[53] He makes a similar claim in *Contra Marcion*.[54]

We might call this a Christian messianism of addition—whereby Christians claim merely to add certain overlooked features of the messianic career to what Jews already expect (usually pertaining to his suffering and death and hence biblical texts like Isa 53 and Ps 22). Justin and others still leveraged stereotypes about Jewish carnality and literality to criticize certain biblical interpretations and shape Christian identity, to be sure.[55] So "the rhetorical Jew" is very much operative in Justin's work. Yet such stereotypes do not function to create an alternative Jewish messianic or eschatological foil for Christianity because Justin believed there was much shared in common here.[56] "Jewish carnality" and "literality" are connected in this period more often to biblical interpretation more broadly, and especially to questions of law observance.

But all of this will change. An early messianism of addition becomes, especially after Constantine, and only increasing into the Middle Ages, a more sharp-edged messianism of subtraction. Christians claim to have a view fundamentally different from that of Jews about the nature of the messiah's reign; they believe less—or subtract—those "carnal," "political," "temporal," and "nationalistic" elements (to use common descriptors) presumed to be typical of Jewish hope. The works of Origen and Augustine were paramount for these developments, emerging ini-

53. In this context, we should recall Irenaeus, *Haer.* 4.26.1: after suggesting that Christ is the "treasure hidden in the field" (and "the field" is the Scriptures), he observes that Christ's "human nature could not be understood, prior to the consummation of those things which had been predicted, that is, the advent of Christ" (*ANF* 1:496)! The coming of Jesus, in other words, opens up the proper understanding of the "types and parables" in Scripture that anticipated him.

54. *Marc.* 3.7 (*ANF* 3:326): "to this day they deny that their Christ has come, because He has not appeared in majesty, while they ignore the fact that He was to come also in lowliness." He also here calls predictions of Christ's first advent "the more obscure" in the Scriptures.

55. So Justin, *Dial.* 14, contends that Jews fail to understand the law in a spiritual sense: "you have understood all things in a carnal sense" (*ANF* 1:201). Note also Tertullian, *Marc.* 3.7, who connects the errors of Marcion with Jews: "Our heretic will now have the fullest opportunity of learning the clue of his errors along with the Jew himself, from whom he has borrowed his guidance in this discussion" (*ANF* 3:326). See also 3.6; 3.8. Cf. Marcel Simon, *Verus Israel: A Study of the Relations between Christians and Jews in the Roman Empire (113–425)*, trans. H. McKeating (Oxford: Oxford University Press, 1986), 156–78; Martin C. Albl, "Ancient Christian Authors on Jews and Judaism," in *The 'New Testament' as a Polemical Tool: Studies in Ancient Christian Anti-Jewish Rhetoric and Beliefs*, ed. Riemer Roukema and Hagit Amrav, NTOA 118 (Göttingen: Vandenhoeck & Ruprecht, 2018), 15–56. Cf. Matthijs den Dulk, *Between Jews and Heretics: Reconfiguring Justin Martyr's Dialogue with Trypho*, RSECW (New York: Routledge, 2018).

56. See Reed, "Messianism between Judaism and Christianity," 24.

tially in their critique of other Christian eschatologies, especially the chiliasm of Justin and others.[57] In *First Principles*, for instance, Origen criticizes other Christians who seek "the indulgence of their own desires and lusts" in physical luxury and pleasure in the end time; such persons, he writes, "while believing in Christ, understand the divine Scriptures in a sort of Jewish sense, drawing from them nothing worthy of the divine promises."[58] Augustine advances the same conflation in numerous places. In his discussion of the final things in book 20 of *The City of God*, Augustine stresses the importance of spiritual interpretation, and contends that the millenarians, like Jews, advance "carnal" readings of Scripture.[59] The same assertion appears and reappears, not least in the writings of Athanasius,[60] Eusebius,[61] Basil,[62] Ambrose,[63] Jerome,[64] and Theodoret.[65]

It must be emphasized that often such critiques are housed in attempts to spiritualize and deliteralize various eschatological scenarios held by Christians in their own times.[66] But the cost of that spiritualization, and its accompanying

57. This is not to say they were the first. Hippolytus, *Haer.* 9.25, asserts that Jews hope for the messiah to be "King over them—a warlike and powerful individual."

58. *Princ.* 2.11.2 (SC 252:396–99). Cf. *Comm. Matt.* 17.35. For discussion, see Riemer Roukema, "Origen, the Jews, and the New Testament," in Roukema and Amrav, *'New Testament' as a Polemical Tool*, 241–54. Robert L. Wilken, "Early Christian Chiliasm, Jewish Messianism, and the Idea of the Holy Land," *HTR* 79 (1986): 298–307 (at 302: Origen "presents Christian chiliasm and Jewish Messianism as a single phenomenon"); Paul M. Blowers, "Origen, the Rabbis, and the Bible: Toward a Picture of Judaism and Christianity in Third-Century Caesarea," in *Christianity in Relation to Jews, Greeks, and Romans*, ed. Everett Ferguson (New York: Garland, 1999), 109–11.

59. Cf., e.g., *Civ.* 20.7, 28–29. See also *Adv. Jud.* 7. Cf. Albl, "Ancient Christian Authors," 40.

60. Cf. David Brakke, "Jewish Flesh and Christian Spirit in Athanasius of Alexandria," *JECS* 9 (2001): 453–82.

61. Eusebius, *Hist. eccl.* 7.24.1 (claims that Nepos "taught that the promises to the holy men in the divine scriptures should be understood in a more Jewish manner" [*NPNF* 2/1:308]).

62. Basil accused Apollinarius of introducing a "second Judaism." Cf. *Ep.* 263.4. Note also *Ep.* 265.2.

63. Cf. Maria Doerfler, "Ambrose's Jews: The Creation of Judaism and Heterodox Christianity in Ambrose of Milan's *Expositio evangelii secundum Lucam*," *CH* 80 (2011): 749–72.

64. Jerome, *Comm. Isa.* 66.20, claims that chiliasts replicate "the Jewish error." Cf. Hillel Newman, "Jerome's Judaizers," *JECS* 9 (2001): 421–52; William L. Krewson, *Jerome and the Jews: Innovative Supersessionism* (Eugene, OR: Wipf & Stock, 2017).

65. Theodoret, *Hist. eccl.* 1.9, claims that Melito of Sardis and his followers were corrupted by the views of "Jews and Samaritans."

66. Harnack famously argued that most of the *adversus* literature reflects inner-Christian conflicts. On the impact of this view and its variations, see Horbury, *Messianism among Jews and Christians*, 21–22. Deena Copeland Klepper, *The Insight of Unbelievers: Nicholas of Lyra and Christian Reading of Jewish Text in the Later Middle Ages* (Philadelphia: University of Pennsylvania Press, 2007), 15, suggests that this rhetorical function of anti-Jewish polemic does not really shift until the thirteenth century.

allegorization, was to associate the perceived inverse—literality, materiality, and terrestrial politics—with Judaism.[67]

These tendencies were reinforced, expanded, and further disseminated by means of Christian polemical and apologetical literature throughout the medieval period.[68] Treatises *adversus Judaeos* ("against the Jews"), and (purported) records of public debates between Jews and Christians, develop a predictable format: the Christian author/dialogue partner trots out a standard list of Old Testament texts believed to have been fulfilled in the birth, life, death, resurrection, and ascension of Jesus; the Christian then attends and responds to certain objections to this exegesis from a Jewish perspective, which typically have to do with the assertion that a straightforward reading of said Old Testament texts makes plain Jesus did not fulfill them as expected, and hence he cannot be the true messiah of Israel.[69] The form and content of these works end up reinforcing a Christian messianism of subtraction and suggest that Christians and Jews have irreconcilable visions for the messiah's character and mission. They also often become opportunities for Christian authors to wed exegetical discussion to stereotypes of Jewish carnality, literality, and ethnic particularism while shaping Christian identity around spirituality, humility, and universality.[70]

While we cannot discuss these tendencies comprehensively, we can attend to a few significant examples that are representative of what I am talking about. In the eleventh century, the Benedictine monk and bishop Odo of Tournai composed his *Disputatio contra Iudueum*, which is framed as a debate with a Jew named Leo. At one point, Odo asks Leo what he expects the messiah will do. Leo replies,

> Whatever we read in the prophets, namely that all kingdoms will be subjected to us through him; that we will have perpetual peace under him; that we shall be gathered from all the kingdoms into Jerusalem; that Jerusalem will have dominion over all the kingdoms; and, all other things which the prophets hap-

67. See John G. Gager, *The Origins of Antisemitism: Attitudes toward Judaism in Pagan and Christian Antiquity* (Oxford: Oxford University Press, 1985), 113–73; Paula Fredriksen, "*Secundum Carnem*: History and Israel in the Theology of St. Augustine," in *The Limits of Ancient Christianity: Essays on Late Antique Thought and Culture in Honor of R. A. Markus*, ed. William E. Klingshirn and Mark Vessey (Ann Arbor: University of Michigan Press, 1999), 26–41.

68. Cf. the discussion of Nicholas of Lyra's *Probatio adventus Messia* in Herman Hailperin, *Rashi and the Christian Scholars* (Pittsburgh: University of Pittsburgh Press, 1963), 156–91.

69. Cf., e.g., Robert Chazan, *Barcelona and Beyond: The Disputation of 1263 and Its Aftermath* (Berkeley: University of California Press, 1992), 41–42, 63, on the likely issues covered in debate.

70. For broader discussion, see Robert Chazan, *Medieval Stereotypes and Modern Antisemitism* (Berkeley: University of California Press, 1997); Yaacov Deutsch, *Judaism in Christian Eyes: Ethnographic Descriptions of Jews and Judaism in Early Modern Europe* (Oxford: Oxford University Press, 2012).

> pily enumerate. Since we do not see all these things fulfilled in your Christ, we wonder what you expect from him?[71]

Were Justin Martyr or Tertullian asked this question, they would have replied, "well, we wait for the fulfillment of these things at his return at the end of days." Even Origen, when faced with the accusation of Celsus's "Jew" that Jesus does not actually fulfill the prophetic expectation for a mighty king, appeals to the hope of the second coming.[72] But that is not Odo's response. Odo writes, "We expect the kingdom of heaven through Christ, and we await that felicity which you hope will be earthly, but which through Christ we hope will be heavenly."[73] In other words, Christians have heavenly and spiritual messianic hopes, whereas the Jews' are earthly and political.[74] Odo goes on to suggest that Leo's focus on "glory" and "happiness" does not attend sufficiently to the spiritual realities of sin and the remission of sin, which is what Christ really offers in his messianic work.

An even more influential work in the *adversus* tradition was the *Tractatus adversus Judaeorum inveteratam duritiem* ("Treatise against the Inveterate Obstinacy of the Jews"), composed by Peter the Venerable (abbot of the Benedictine abbey of Cluny) in the twelfth century. We find the same contrast, and even more focus on defining it. He writes,

> because you hear from the prophets that Christ is called a king, because you read in the Scriptures that he has a kingdom, you think that he will be a temporal king and that he will reign in time in the manner of David or Solomon . . . ruler over all or almost all the nations . . . liberate the Jews from such a long-lasting captivity . . . lead you back . . . to your land of ancient promise for which you alone, you brutish men, always yearn.

He continues,

71. Odo of Tournai, *A Disputation with the Jew, Leo, concerning the Advent of Christ, the Son of God*, trans. Iren M. Resnick (Philadelphia: University of Pennsylvania Press, 1994), 85. On the context and background of this work, see Irven M. Resnick, "Odo of Tournai and the Dehumanization of Medieval Jews: A Reexamination," *JQR* 98 (2008): 471–84.

72. Origen, *Cels.* 2.29. The exchange is brief, but significant: "In the preceding pages we have already spoken of this point, namely, the prediction that there were to be two advents of Christ to humanity, so that it is not necessary for us to reply to the objection, supposed to be urged by a Jew, that 'the prophets declare the coming one to be a mighty potentate, Lord of all nations and armies'" (*ANF* 4:443).

73. Odo of Tournai, *Disputation with the Jew*, 86.

74. See here also Theophylact of Ochrid, *Comm. Luc.* at Luke 19:11: apparently the disciples expect liberation.

> you want Christ to be a carnal, temporal king, sitting on a raised throne in the fashion of great kings, resplendent with purple gems, and gold, abundant with riches, subjugating his enemies with arms and men.

But this hope, Peter contends, reveals more about the character of the Jews than about the Scripture or the true nature of the messiah. It reveals a mere "love of earthly things," and a "carnal" interpretive prism.[75] Peter corrects the record: "Unlike what the Jews think, Christ is not a temporal king but the eternal and celestial King."[76] The true Christ is humble and meek, as expected in Zech 9, and he suffers and dies for others, as expected in Isa 53.

Jewish Messianism and the Second Advent

Now one might wonder, How does the common trope that emerges here of pitting a humble and suffering messiah ("the Christian view") over and against a glorious and victorious messiah ("the Jewish view") leave theological space for the expectation for Jesus's triumphant second advent? That would be the logical question. But because the vast majority of these discourses and dialogues focus on the first advent of Christ—especially his (virgin) birth, life and miracles, death, resurrection, and ascension to God's right hand—they often overlook, if not completely ignore, his second coming in the future. Hence, Christian authors are rarely forced to respond to such a natural query.[77] This tendency of focusing on the first advent vis-à-vis Old Testament prophecy is widespread and found

75. Peter the Venerable, *Against the Inveterate Obduracy of the Jews*, ed. and trans. Irven M. Resnick, FC Medieval Continuation 16 (Washington, DC: Catholic University of America Press, 2013), 102, 103, 108.

76. Peter the Venerable, *Against the Inveterate Obduracy of the Jews*, 102. He writes at 104, "you prefer to adapt the Scriptures to your corporeal understanding." Note also at 120: "stop thinking . . . that Christ is a temporal king, that his kingdom is an earthly kingdom." Similar remarks at 123 and 157.

77. In Raymundi Martini's influential *Pugio Fidei*, completed around 1278, the second coming comes up briefly, but it is not clear how the interpretive approach squares with the approach elsewhere. For an early print edition, see *Pugio Fidei adversus Mauros et Judaeos* (Leipzig: Lanckisi, 1687). The second part of this work, chapters 3–15, contrasts Jewish messianism with Christian belief. Chapter 12 argues against "literal" interpretation of biblical prophecies, suggesting instead that "in scriptura multae sint locutiones parabolicae, quae non sunt ad literam exponendae, sed figurate" (259; cf. 426–38). But then chapter 13 responds to other objections that in Dan 7 "adventus ejus [the messiah's] gloriosus & magnificus describitur." He responds that "sermonem ibi esse de secondo & non de primo adventu" (259; cf. 440–44).

already in Cyprian's *Ad Quirinium*, written around 250 CE,[78] as well as in Aphrahat (d. 345 CE).[79] In the fifth century, Pseudo-Gregory of Nyssa's *Testimonies from the Old Testament against the Jews* only once turns to address the second advent in detail, and in that the focus is really on the coming of Elijah. The rest concerns the *fulfillment* of prophecy in Jesus's birth, life, death, resurrection, and the spread of the church.[80] Isadore of Seville's sixth/seventh-century *Against the Jews* highlights Jesus's incarnation and life, with only a short section devoted to the expectation that "he will come to judge the living and the dead."[81] Peter Alphonsi's eleventh-century *Dialogue* works through the scriptural underpinnings of Jesus's first advent, too, including the ascension (where Jesus sits enthroned in the "eternal kingdom" of Dan 7) and its aftermath in the church. The same focus emerges in anti-Christian works penned by Jewish writers, such as the thirteenth-century *Niẓẓaḥon Vetus*.[82]

This tendency is quite understandable on the Christian side when one considers that the main burden in apological and polemical discussions of the Old Testament is to demonstrate that Jesus did in fact fulfill the Scriptures as the Gospels proclaim. Peter the Venerable sums this up succinctly: "I say, he has come; you say, he will come."[83] To focus on outstanding prophetic hopes to be fulfilled in a future advent of Christ, then, actually grants the critique of a Jewish interlocutor that in life, Jesus failed to fulfill the Scripture's expected role for the messiah. To put this another way, the second coming was perilous territory for the Christian arguing for proof from prophecy, because to locate it in the Scriptures required that one admit a significant portion of the messiah's career has not yet occurred. It is interesting to note, in this respect, that when the second advent does make brief appearances in *adversus* literature, it is typical to find it stripped of messianic significance. In Peter Alfonsi's twelfth-century *Against the Jews*, Moses (his Jewish interlocutor) asks about "still one more item in the exposition of your faith, namely, that he will come to judge the living and the dead on the day of judgment," but quickly qualifies with

78. See also Pseudo-Cyprian, *Adversus Judaeos* (*Gegen die Judenchristen*), ed. and trans. Dirk van Damme (Freiburg: Universitätsverlag, 1969).

79. Aphrahat's *Dem.* 17.9–10 focuses on Pss 2, 110; Isa 7:14; 9:6–7; Gen 49:10; Dan 9:26–27; Ps 22; Isa 52–53; Zech 14:7. Cf. Günter Stemberger, "Die Messiasfrage in den christlich-jüdischen Disputationen des Mittelalters," *Jahrbuch für Biblische Theologie* 9 (1993): 239.

80. *Pseudo-Gregory of Nyssa: Testimonies against the Jews*, ed. and trans. Martin C. Albl (Atlanta: Society of Biblical Literature, 2004).

81. *De fide catholica contra Iudaeos* (PL 83:449–538).

82. For text and discussion, see David Berger, *The Jewish-Christian Debate in the High Middle Ages: A Critical Edition of the Niẓẓaḥon Vetus* (Philadelphia: Jewish Publication Society of America, 1979).

83. Peter the Venerable, *Against the Inveterate Obduracy of the Jews*, 137.

"I require neither argument nor a reason for his matter."[84] Why? Because, for Moses, this point does not have to do with messianism, a matter that they have heretofore had much disagreement about. Moses explains, "For if, as you believe, he is both God and man, I admit that it is enough that he is the judge of the world."[85] In other words, the logic of the return of Christ—according to Peter's construal via Moses—stems from Jesus's divine identity, not from the need to complete a previously incomplete messianic mission.[86] That is quite revealing, and, as part 3 will show, it almost completely abandons New Testament claims about the messianic work of Jesus and the intertextual framing of his future coming in scriptural terms.

Impact

Adversus and other apologetical literature ended up deeply impacting the Protestant Reformers and later exegetes, not least Martin Luther, who had read Nicholas of Lyra and drew on his work.[87] Concerning Jewish messianism in particular, Luther's lines are unsurprising. He wrote, "the Jews ask no more of their Messiah than that he be a Kokhba and worldly king who will slay us Christians and share out the world among the Jews and make them lords, and who will finally die like other kings, and his children after him."[88] A similar depiction appears in the Augsburg Confession (1530), which condemns "those who scatter Jewish opinions, that, before the resurrection of the dead, the godly shall occupy the kingdom of the world, the wicked being everywhere suppressed; the saints alone, the pious, shall have a worldly kingdom, and shall exterminate all the godless."[89]

84. Petrus Alfonsi, *Dialogue against the Jews*, FC Medieval Continuation 8, ed. and trans. Irven Michael Resnick (Washington, DC: Catholic University of America Press, 2006), 247.

85. Alfonsi, *Dialogue against the Jews*, 247.

86. Moses asks for some scriptural proof for this, and Peter responds with a few quotations that pertain to the final judgment, including Dan 7.

87. The prolific work of Nicholas of Lyra, as noted by Horbury, "New Testament and Rabbinic Study," 11, crystallizes "the first great age of Christian Hebraism" from the twelfth to the fourteenth century. Lyra himself also drew from the polemical work of Raymundi Martini's *Pugio Fidei*, completed around 1278, which, as already noted, contrasts Jewish messianism with Christian belief.

88. Luther, *About the Jews and Their Lies*, 595. Luther also writes here that Zech 9 has the messiah coming on an ass, peacefully, "that is, not [to] rule in an worldly manner, as the mad Kokhbaites, these bloodthirsty Jews, rave" (586). On *adversus* literature before and after Lyra, see Samuel Krauss, *History*, vol. 1 of *The Jewish-Christian Controversy from the Earliest Times to 1789*, ed. William Horbury (Tübingen: Mohr Siebeck, 1995).

89. Philip Schaff, *The Creeds of Christendom* (Grand Rapids: Baker Books, 1969), 3:18.

In addition, both before and after the Reformation, the work of Christian Hebraists continued to digest and summarize Jewish learning for Christian audiences and "embod(ied) the results of earlier researches" from the medieval period (even if they were more critical and learned) and became major resources for information about Judaism for biblical exegetes.[90] As Horbury has noted, Nicholas of Lyra's work in particular (with subsequent additions by others) became a "standard super-commentary," even sometimes conjoined with the Glossa Ordinaria, and "[it] was often in these forms . . . that mediaeval comment was disseminated in the printed bibles studied by the exegetes and preachers of the late fifteenth and the sixteenth and seventeenth centuries."[91]

We might take a closer look at the construction of Jewish messianism in the work of two particularly impactful exegetes from the sixteenth and seventeenth centuries, respectively. First, John Calvin's exegesis of the apocalyptic discourse in Mark 13 and parallels is an instructive case study. Calvin articulates the structure of the discourse and its logic by ricocheting the teaching of Jesus off the mistaken eschatological expectations held by the disciples and, he presumes, Jews at large. Following Matthew, Calvin stresses the fact that Jesus first predicts the destruction of the temple (24:2), which prompts the question from his disciples, "tell us, when will these things happen, and what will be the sign of your parousia and the end of the age?" (24:3). Calvin remarks,

> it must be observed that, having believed from their infancy that the temple would stand until the end of time, and having this opinion deeply rooted in their minds, they did not suppose that, while the building of the world stood, the temple could fall to ruins. Thus, as soon as Christ said that the temple would be destroyed, their thoughts immediately turned to the end of the world. As one error leads to another, and being convinced that as soon as the reign of Christ should begin they would be happy in every respect, they leave warfare out of the account and fly immediately to the triumph. They associate the coming of Christ and the end of the world as things inseparable from each other; and by the end of the world they mean the restoration of all things, so that nothing may be desired to complete the happiness of the godly.[92]

90. A striking phenomenon that is highlighted in the now-famous essay by George Foot Moore, "Christian Writers on Judaism," *HTR* 2 (1921): 221.

91. Horbury, "New Testament and Rabbinic Study," 15.

92. Calvin, *Comm. Harm. Ev.* at Matt 24:1, English translation modified from John Calvin, *Commentary on a Harmony of the Evangelists*, trans. William Pringle, Calvin's Commentaries 16–17 (Grand Rapids: Baker Books, 2009), 3:117. For Latin, see *Commentarius in Harmoniam*

In other words, Jesus's disciples made two mistakes because they were Jews who had been fed certain ideas "from their infancy" and had certain expectations "deeply rooted in their minds."[93] The first was to think the entire world must be ending on the basis of the prediction of the temple's demise, and the second was to reason further that, if the world is ending, then the messiah must be coming immediately, because the coming of the messiah will mean the beginning of bliss (being "happy") and the restoration of physical comforts. The discourse of Jesus that follows, then, becomes for Calvin an extensive deconstruction of this mistaken associative logic. While the disciples in their question had rushed forward to the "attainment of happiness and rest," Jesus first dwells on coming tribulation, struggle, and persecution, thereby responding to eschatological imminence by "exhorting them to long patience."[94] In terms of the structure of the discourse as a whole, this means that Calvin takes the coming tribulation Jesus describes *not* as the beginning of a genuine response to the disciples—for example, as signs of the nearness of that which the disciples ask about; Calvin rather reads these predictions adversatively, against their question as it were, as exhortations to patience and perseverance, to a life of suffering rather than "happiness." This deconstructive lesson from Jesus further includes the description of the coming of the son of man several verses later, which Calvin assumes is indeed about the parousia. But he thinks Jesus intends this as comfort and encouragement for the long journey ahead, and not as a prediction of what will immediately come to pass as the disciples expected.[95] Moreover, in describing this future advent, Jesus "warns them that the glory of his kingdom will be heavenly, and not earthly, as the disciples had falsely imagined."[96]

Calvin offers, in other words, a mirror reading of the apocalyptic discourse against the backdrop of a presumed Jewish eschatology and messianism. What

---

Evangelicam, vol. 45 of *Ioannis Calvini opera quae supersunt omnia*, ed. Edouard Cunitz, Johann-Wilhelm Baum, and Eduard W. E. Reuss (Brunsvigae: Schwetschke, 1891), 648.

93. See also here Luther, *Hom. Matt.* 45 on Matt 24:1–3: "This is exactly how He preaches here—everything is contrary to the thoughts of the Jews, who believed that all would be calm and tickled themselves with such sweet dreams and trusted that the coming Messiah would bring them the peace they so longed to have" (LW 68:259).

94. Calvin, *Comm. Harm. Ev.* ad loc. (trans. Pringle 3:118).

95. Calvin, *Comm. Harm. Ev.* at Matt 24:24 and parr.: "we ought to learn that no particular time is here fixed, as if the last day were to follow in immediate succession to those events which were just now foretold" (trans. Pringle 3:130). At 24:39 and parr.: "Christ comes now to speak of the full manifestation of his kingdom, about which he was at first interrogated by the disciples, and promises that, after they have been tried by so many distressing events, the redemption will arrive in due time" (trans. Pringle 3:145).

96. Calvin, *Comm. Harm. Ev.* at Matt 24:39 (trans. Pringle 3:148).

Calvin assumes as the mistaken worldview of the disciples informs his understanding of the progression of the discourse as a whole and ensures Jesus is not responsible for any miscalculation about the future. To one who might ask why it is that Jesus would talk about the destruction of the temple and the coming of the son of man in such proximity, Calvin replies that this was not Jesus's decision. "Those two things" (destruction and end, respectively), Calvin notes, "[had] been blended by the disciples . . . [and so] Christ, in replying to the whole question which had been put to him, reminded them that a long and melancholy succession of calamities was at hand, and that they must not hasten to seize the prize."[97]

The work of the prolific commentator and rabbinic scholar John Lightfoot (1602–1675) deserves special mention as well, given our interests. Lightfoot was also a staunch critic of the millenarianism of his time, and his widely read commentaries tend to downplay futurist eschatology and focus on realization and fulfillment.[98] In terms of Jewish messianism, I simply collect a few comments from his oeuvre about conflict with the teaching of Jesus:

- John the Baptist asked Jesus whether he was indeed the messiah because "perhaps he [John] laboured under that dim-sightedness, which the disciples of Christ and the whole nation did concerning his earthly kingdom, victories, and triumphs" (Lightfoot, *Whole Works*, 11:18).
- On Matt 12:15–21's use of Isa 42: "How far different is the Messias, thus described, from the Messias of the expectation of the Jews!" (Lightfoot, *Whole Works*, 11:194; see also 212).
- On the question "who is the greatest?": "the dream of the earthly kingdom of

97. Calvin, *Comm. Harm. Ev.* at Matt 24:14 (trans. Pringle 3:129).

98. On his reading, the apocalyptic discourse in Mark 13 and parr. is entirely about first-century events, especially the destruction of the temple. Jesus's teaching is a response to, and correction of, the query of his disciples that stems wholly from "the opinion of that people concerning the times of the Messias." See John Lightfoot, *The Whole Works of Rev. John Lightfoot. D.D.*, ed. and trans. John Rogers Pitman (London: Dove, 1825), 11:294. He contends that it is common to find in Scripture as a whole "the destruction of Jerusalem . . . very frequently expressed . . . as if it were the destruction of the whole world" (11:303). So, too, "Christ's taking vengeance of that exceeding wicked nation [in the destruction of the temple], is called 'Christ's coming in glory'" (11:303), the "sun being darkened" means "the Jewish heaven shall perish" (11:304), the angels sent to the four corners of the world are human messengers of the gospel (11:304). He reads the comment about the beloved disciple desiring to remain until Jesus returns (21:20) as a reference not to the parousia but the "return" of Jesus to destroy Jerusalem (12:433). Beyond the Gospels, Lightfoot regards the prediction of the "sending of the Messiah among you" for the "times of refreshing" in Acts 3:20 as a reference to the propagation of the gospel in that time (see 8:64–65), the "ends of the ages" in 1 Cor 10:11 refers to the destruction of the temple.

the Messias did so possess their minds (for they had sucked-in this doctrine with their first milk), that the mention of the most vile death of the Messias, repeated over and over again, did not at all drive it thence. The image of earthly pomp was fixed at the bottom of their hearts, and there it stuck; nor by any words of Christ could it, as yet, be rooted out; no, not when they saw the death of Christ, when together with that they saw his resurrection: for then they also asked, 'Wilt thou, at this time, restore the kingdom to Israel?'" (Lightfoot, *Whole Works*, 11:241).

- On Jesus's sending of his disciples in Luke: "It suited well enough with the mean and low estate of that kingdom of heaven, and of that Messiah . . . so that, from the view of the first publishers, the Jews might learn to frame a right judgment concerning both the Messiah and his kingdom" (Lightfoot, *Whole Works*, 12:87; see also 172).
- On the disciples' anxiety in John 10:24: "they looked for a Messias, that should prove a mighty conqueror, should deliver the people from the heathen yoke, and should crown himself with all earthly glory; and saw Jesus, infinite degrees below such pomp; yet, by his miracles, giving such fair specimens of the Messias . . . they could not but hang in great suspense" (Lightfoot, *Whole Works*, 12:345, see also 354).

Lightfoot was a recognized authority on ancient Judaism for generations of subsequent New Testament exegetes and historians.[99] It is particularly troublesome that, as others have noted, eighteenth- and nineteenth-century biblical scholars typically relied on much earlier summaries of Jewish thought and practice, including Lightfoot.[100] In fact, Lightfoot's *Horae* was fundamental for Schoettgen's *Horae Hebraicae et Talmudicae* volumes in 1733 and 1742, which was a standard resource for nineteenth-century Christian historians until it was supplanted by Paul Billerbeck's famous *Kommentar* in the early twentieth century.[101]

99. See Horbury, "New Testament and Rabbinic Study," 22–27.

100. Cf. Moore, "Christian Writers on Judaism," 221, notes that the great period of Hebrew learning in Christian intellectual circles ended "abruptly" around 1750, but, he claims, the earlier studies continued to be used throughout the nineteenth century "without giving sufficient consideration to the fact that it had been gathered for every conceivable motive except to serve as material for the historian." See also Manuel, "Israel and the Enlightenment," 37: "the Enlightenment thinkers disseminated notions of Judaism that rested on information culled from respectable seventeenth century Christian Hebraists at first or second hand. What they did with the data effected a revolution in Christian Europe's perception of Judaism."

101. Though on Billerbeck, too, note Horbury, "New Testament and Rabbinic Study," 29: "Billerbeck . . . sifted the material of Lightfoot and Schoettgen, vastly amplified it, put it into German, and aligned it with modern rabbinical study."

Summation

To sum up the conclusion, then: the negative and stereotypical depiction of "Jewish messianism" that one finds in the literature of Enlightenment Christianity (Thomas Morgan et al.) derives, ultimately, from earlier Christian *adversus* and other apologetical, polemical, and exegetical literature, and, moreover, that earlier literature actively promoted a certain definition of Jewish messianism that ended up laying the groundwork for the later challenge of the second advent expectation itself by those same Enlightenment critics. The earlier *adversus* and polemical literature tended to downplay any meaningful connection between Jesus's messianic work and the second-coming hope, as their main burden was to prove *the fulfillment* of Scripture in his first advent. Enlightenment critics would then sever any connection between Jesus's messianic work and the second coming at all by applying a by-then-conventional critique of Jewish messianism to the parousia itself. The irony here—unappreciated, as far as I can discern, in the history of New Testament criticism—is that the attempt of medieval and early modern Christians to defend orthodoxy and connect the tradition of the church to the biblical witness ended up creating the very categories that later critics would use for the deconstruction of the same. The tools used to dismantle the traditional or creedal eschatological scenario during the Enlightenment were not borrowed from the outside; they were made within the Christian tradition itself. As far as my research can tell, it was not until the more radical criticism of the Enlightenment that such "Jewish opinions" (so the Augsburg Confession) were leveraged against the hope for Christ's return in judgment as found in the work of Morgan and others above.[102]

102. The famous anti-Trinitarian Faustus Socinus (1539–1604) was skeptical of many theological positions considered orthodox in his time, but his skepticism did not extend to the second coming of Christ. He appears to have had no problem affirming this, partly because he believed in the ascension of Jesus after death and his enthronement at God's right hand, whereby the human Christ, he thought, was made to share in God's power to govern and judge the world. See discussion in George Huntson Williams, *The Radical Reformation* (Philadelphia: Westminster, 1962), 752–53. The Rachovian Catechism will not make much of the second coming of Jesus but does affirm it, focusing in particular on Christ's role in judgment. See *The Rachovian Catechism, with Notes and Illustrations, Translated from the Latin*, trans. Thomas Rees (London: Longman, 1818), 81–82, 366–67. Another famous anti-Trinitarian, Michael Servetus (1509–1553), who was burned at the stake in Geneva, held quite radical millenarian views. H. Hotson, "Arianism and Millenarianism: The Link between Two Heresies from Servetus to Socinus," in Laursen and Popkin, *Continental Millenarians*, 9–35, has written about the idiosyncratic connections between Reformation-era Arianism and Millenarianism, which persisted well into the seventeenth and eighteenth centuries. Note that Isaac Newton (1642–1727) and William Whiston (1667–1752), noted for their Arian views, also held millenarian eschatologies.

But the prevalence of this trope about Jewish messianism shows that the later critical move was not a leap in a new direction—it was a small step on the same path. Indeed, the deists and others *relied on* this pejorative description of Jewish messianism as militaristic and earthly minded to bolster their own critique of the second coming. They did not need to offer further argument because they merely leaned into the well-established habit of reading Jesus and his teaching against certain Jewish "Prejudices and false Opinions" (so Morgan). All they did is exercise that move on a Christian doctrine previously free from its gaze. The suggestion was threatening because its premise was so widely accepted.

Back to Reimarus and the Nineteenth-Century Quest

We return, then, to Reimarus, whose work and impact we can now appreciate with greater contextual sensitivity. Reimarus made such a splash in the quest for Jesus not because his arguments were brilliant historically but because they were problematic theologically. What Reimarus effectively did was subvert a widespread, centuries-old tradition of contrasting Jesus with the construct of Jewish messianism—a move shared by staunch defenders of orthodoxy and progressive critics alike.[103] Rather than regard Jewish messianism as the foil against which Jesus's career was to be read as theologically and ethically superior, Reimarus argued that, in actuality, Jesus could not be understood apart from it. Jewish messianism is the key that unlocks all the doors. It is crucial to recognize that the questions and concerns surrounding Jewish messianism that animated Reimarus's project continued to influence subsequent research and shaped the reception history of the second advent in decisive ways (even if Reimarus's own arguments about Jesus as a quasi-revolutionary were fairly quickly dismissed by a handful of notable

103. Charles Leslie, a great critic (!) of the deists, boldly claimed that "the Messiah's undergoing stripes and afflictions . . . is as adverse to the Jews' notion of the Messiah, as death itself; for they suppose him to go on gloriously in conquests and victory, and not to be scourged, or ignominiously treated." Cf. Leslie, *Short and Easy Method*, 15. He even implicated the disciples of Jesus in this false hope, as did the deists he criticized elsewhere: the disciples were "looking out then, as you ['the Jews'] are now, for a temporal fighting Messiah, who should restore again the kingdom to Israel" (88). See a similar depiction in Augustin Calmet's influential *Dictionnaire historique, critique, chronologique, géographique et littéral de la Bible*, rev. ed. (Paris: Emery, 1730 [orig. 1720]), 2:680–86. Note also that Pascal understood two fundamentally opposed manners of reading the messiah's coming in Scripture: the "carnal" Jewish view and the "spiritual" Christian view. Robert P. Kraynak, "The Idea of the Messiah in the Theology of Thomas Hobbes," *JPSR* 4 (1992): 128, connects Pascal's view to Augustine, Aquinas, Luther, Calvin, and Hooker.

critics).[104] Most subsequent questers would challenge the connection Reimarus had made between the aims of the historical Jesus and Jewish messianism,[105] but they would more or less leave unchallenged the association he had made, and that, of course, the deists and others before him, between the second-coming hope and Jewish messianism.[106] And so, predictably, it becomes increasingly rare in subsequent research for critics to link the second-coming hope to the historical Jesus. To do so would be, in effect, to concede to Reimarus and grant the Jewish messianic construct an important foothold in his life and teaching. After Reimarus, a thoroughgoing preoccupation of Jesus research was to resolve a presumed, underlying conflict between Jesus and the messianic expectation of his day that surfaced in numerous ways, not least the notion of a "spiritual messiah."[107] It was very popular in the nineteenth century to argue that Jesus had spoken of the son of man simply to stress his humility and to distance himself from the nationalistic idea of the messiah in Judaism.[108] Indeed, in many of the nineteenth- and even twentieth-

104. So George Wesley Buchanan righty notes that one significant question that came out of Reimarus's work was the meaning of Jesus's teaching about the kingdom of God. See his introduction to Reimarus's work in *The Goal of Jesus and His Disciples*, trans. George Wesley Buchanan (Leiden: Brill: 1970), 1–34. On Reimarus's reception, see Colin Brown, *Jesus in European Protestant Thought, 1778–1860*, SHT 1 (Durham: Labyrinth, 1985), 8–15; Baird, *From Deism to Tübingen*, 170–83.

105. So the main agenda of Johann S. Semler's response to Reimarus in *Beantwortung der Fragmente eines Ungenannten, inbesonders vom Zweck Jesu und seiner Jünger*, rev. ed. (Halle: Erziehungsinstitut, 1780). For a broader discussion of Semler's claims about Judaism and their influence see Gerdmar, *Roots of Theological Anti-Semitism*, 39–49.

106. The way in which Reimarus, *Fragments*, recapitulates earlier stereotypes about carnal Judaism is evident in the way he psychologizes the disciples of Jesus to discern their motives for inventing the second-coming idea. These men "of the lower class and of small means" (240) sought "paths leading to influence and aggrandizement" (247), and the second-coming hope "exactly suited the purpose of the apostles" (249), for they promised "not merely an invisible kingdom of spiritual wealth in heaven, which probably would have made less impression, but it was to be a visible kingdom lasting a thousand years upon earth, in which people were to eat and drink and live as before" (253).

107. Schleiermacher, for instance, argued that the Jewish notion of the messiah—which he characterized as "outward" and "mechanical"—is "childish" in comparison to true Christian teaching. Cf. Gerdmar, *Roots of Theological Anti-Semitism*, 66–67. On Jesus as "ein geistiger Messias" in the thought of de Wette, see Baird, *From Deism to Tübingen*, 228–29.

108. Here Albert Schweitzer, *The Quest of the Historical Jesus*, trans. William Montgomery, ed. John Bowden (Minneapolis: Fortress, 2001), 219, does not mislead: "It had become a dogma of theology that Jesus used the term son of man to veil his messiahship; that is to say, every theologian found in this term whatever meaning he attached to the messiahship of Jesus: the human, humble, ethical, unpolitical, unapocalyptic, or whatever other character was held to be appropriate to the orthodox 'transformed' messiahship." Cf., e.g., Heinrich Paulus, *Philologisch-*

century lives or biographies of Jesus, Jesus's response to the prevalent messianic expectation of his contemporaries was the central drama of his career and the main cause of conflict with potential followers.[109] As I have shown elsewhere with respect to the theory of the Galilean crisis, many scholars believed that Jesus was rejected by the majority of the Galilean masses precisely because his own view of the messiah and the popular Jewish view were so incompatible.[110] Studies of Second Temple Judaism tended to support these reconstructions of Jesus indirectly because they often suggested that there was a particular and widely popular political messianic expectation at the time of Jesus.[111] In the 1879 Hulsean Lectures, Vincent Henry Stanton would even suggest that Christians and Jews

---

kritischer und historischer Commentar über die drey ersten Evangelien, 2nd ed. (Lübeck: Bohn, 1804), 470–71; Ferdinand C. Baur, "Die Bedeutung des Ausdrucks: ὁ υἱὸς τοῦ ἀνθρώπου," *ZWT* 3 (1860): 274–92, esp. 280; Daniel Schenkel, *Das Charakterbild Jesu*, 3rd ed. (Wiesbaden: Kreidel, 1864), 264–65; Orello Cone, "Jesus' Self-Designation in the Synoptic Gospels," *New World* 2 (1893): 511. For further discussion and context, see Mogens Müller, *The Expression 'Son of Man' and the Development of Christology: A History of Interpretation* (London: Equinox, 2008), 115–66. On the caricature of Judaism as nationalistic and/or ethnocentric, see Isaac W. Oliver, *Luke's Jewish Eschatology: The National Restoration of Israel in Luke-Acts* (Oxford: Oxford University Press, 2021), 3–23.

109. Cf., e.g., Johann Jakob Hess, *Lebensgeschichte Jesu* (Zurich: Drell, Fußli, 1822), 1:lxxxiv; 2:235; W. M. L. de Wette, *Lehrbuch der christliche Dogmatik in ihrer historischen Entwicklung dargestellt* (Berlin: Realschulbuchhandlung, 1813), 205, 209; Friedrich von Ammon, *Die Fortbildung des Christenthums zur Weltreligion: Eine Ansicht der höheren Dogmatik* (Leipzig: Vogel, 1833); Schenkel, *Das Charakterbild Jesu*, 87–122; Willibald Beyschlag, *Das Leben Jesu*, 3rd ed. (Halle: Strien, 1893), 1:279–80 (there was "einem unvermeidlichen Zusammenstoß" between Jesus's view and the popular view), 284 (on John 6:66); 2:259–67; 273. Cf. discussion in Luigi Salvatorelli, "From Locke to Reitzenstein: The Historical Investigation of the Origins of Christianity," *HTR* 22 (1929): 263–369, esp. 314 (on Holtzmann).

110. See Tucker S. Ferda, *Jesus, the Gospels, and the Galilean Crisis*, LNTS 601 (London: Bloomsbury T&T Clark, 2019), 95–96. This conflict model continues to inspire studies of Jesus well after the nineteenth century, not least the important work of C. H. Dodd, *The Founder of Christianity* (London: Collins, 1971). On nineteenth-century depictions of Judaism in general, see Heschel, *Abraham Geiger and the Jewish Jesus*, 66–75, 153–57, 190–93, 212–13; Halvor Moxnes, "Jesus the Jew: Dilemmas of Interpretation," in *Fair Play: Diversity and Conflicts in Early Christianity; Essays in Honour of Heikki Räisänen*, ed. Ismo Dunderberg, Christopher Tuckett, and Kari Syreeni (Leiden: Brill, 2002), 83–103, esp. 83–89; James D. G. Dunn, *A New Perspective on Jesus: What the Quest for the Historical Jesus Missed* (Grand Rapids: Baker Books, 2005), 58–63; Heschel, *Aryan Jesus*, 26–66; Annette Yoshiko Reed and Adam H. Becker, "Traditional Models and New Directions," in *The Ways That Never Parted*, TSAJ 95 (Tübingen: Mohr Siebeck, 2003), 7; Winter, "Dissimilar Jesus," 129–42.

111. For discussion and literature see Horbury, *Messianism among Jews and Christians*, 29–57; Matthew V. Novenson, *The Grammar of Messianism: An Ancient Jewish Political Idiom and Its Users* (Oxford: Oxford University Press, 2017), 1–33, 36–40, 116.

differ so substantially in their understanding of the messiah that perhaps they should use different terms.[112] These tendencies are not directly about the second-coming expectation, but they are indirectly consequential for its reception. The sharper the conflict between Jesus and Jewish messianism, the harder it has been to find room for the second-coming hope in his teaching. Having started with the spirit, how could he end with the flesh? Daniel Schenkel was clear: for him, it was "downright impossible."[113]

Perhaps the most poignant expression of these tendencies in the nineteenth century is Timothee Colani's *Jésus-Christ et les croyances messianiques de son temps* (1864), a study that aimed to reconstruct the nature of Jesus's preaching about the kingdom of God and messiahship within the context of Second Temple Judaism.[114] It influenced untold late nineteenth-century and twentieth-century critics and is still sometimes cited by historians and exegetes today.[115] Colani famously concluded that the Olivet Discourse in Mark 13 and parallels was actually an interpolation of a Jewish-Christian apocalypse and is theologically foreign to the teaching of the historical Jesus.[116] So, too, the explicitly eschatological predictions of Matt 10:23 (the return of the son of man), Matt 19:28 and parallels (the disciples on thrones), Matt 23:39 and parallel (you will not see me again until), Mark 14:25 and parallels (will not eat or drink until the kingdom comes), and Mark 14:62 and parallels (you will see the son of man) are either unhistorical or taken by the evangelists in ways that distort Jesus's true message. Material in the Lukan apocalypse (17:22–37) was originally about the destruction of the

112. Published as *The Jewish and the Christian Messiah* (Edinburgh: T&T Clark, 1886).

113. Schenkel, *Das Charakterbild Jesu*, 158 ("Das ist geradezu unmöglich").

114. Timothee Colani, *Jésus-Christ et les croyances messianiques de son temps*, 2nd ed. (Strasbourg: Treuttel & Wurtz, 1864). All translations from this work below are my own. Important for further popularizing Colani was Wilhelm Weiffenbach, *Die Wiederkunftsgedanke Jesu* (Leipzig: Druck, 1873), though in an indirect way. Weiffenbach argues that Jesus did indeed predict his near return—contra Colani—but, like Colani, argues that the entire eschatological and apocalyptic housing of that expectation was foreign to the authentic teaching of Jesus and had been imported from Jewish messianic expectations.

115. See T. Francis Glasson himself in *The Second Advent: The Origin of the New Testament Doctrine*, 3rd ed. (Eugene, OR: Wipf & Stock, 2009), 71–72. Note also the influential study of Albert Réville, *Jésus de Nazareth*, 2 vols. (Paris: Fischbacher, 1897), which denied the content of Mark 13 to Jesus. See also Carl Weizsäcker, *Untersuchungen über die evangelische Geschichte* (Gotha: Besser, 1864), whose threefold outline of Mark 13 became hugely influential, and also Wilhelm Baldensperger, *Das Selbstbewusstein Jesu im Lichte der messianischen Hoffnungen seiner Zeit* (Strassburg: Heitz, 1888).

116. Colani, *Jésus-Christ et les croyances messianiques de son temps*, 203, 207 ("We have under our eyes a short apocalypse from an unknown author that the Synoptics have made a discourse of Jesus and inserted into their reports").

temple and has been misunderstood by the evangelist. To be clear, Colani makes some keen historical and exegetical insights throughout the study to which my arguments in later chapters must attend. But much of this book rehearses the caricatures of Judaism, messianism, and eschatological expectation that part 2 has sought to trace and expose. The qualifier "Jewish" in "Jewish-Christian apocalypse" is crucial for Colani's case because, he argues, "the center of the hopes of all the faithful Israelites" in the time of Jesus was for a messianic leader from the line of David (awaited "with a fervish impatience") who would reinstitute a theocracy.[117] He would be "at the same time priest and king, at once prophet and man of state, at once religious reformer and conquering warrior."[118] Jesus himself had devoted much of his public career to dismantling such "vulgar messianism." Jesus took the messianic and apocalyptic language of his day and invested it with deeper spiritual significance. Rather than fixate on a coming political and temporal kingdom, Jesus claimed the kingdom of God was a "moral power" that was already present and making peace and joy and new life available now. Jesus imagined that the kingdom would "triumph little by little in the world" as "an organic development." Jesus spoke of himself as "the son of man" merely as a way of being humble and stressing his common humanity.[119] "In a word," Colani wrote, Jesus "has broken with the messianism which consists precisely in the confusion of the temporal and the spiritual, in the haughty affirmation of the right of the Jews to their exclusiveness on providence."[120]

But to no avail. The Jewish disciples of Jesus, being unsatisfied with his death as the true achievement of his aims, returned to their old messianic ways and dreamed up the hope for his glorious return from heaven. Colani wrote, "They continued, as all Jews, to expect a triumphant Messiah."[121] The early Christians thereby distorted Jesus's teaching by means of this hope, expecting a future reality

117. Colani, *Jésus-Christ et les croyances messianiques de son temps*, 35, 43, 198, 200–201.

118. Colani, *Jésus-Christ et les croyances messianiques de son temps*, 65, 66 (this expectation "has contributed more than any other religious idea to fixate the Jewish people in the theocratic spirit, and to make them confuse the spiritual and the temporal").

119. Colani, *Jésus-Christ et les croyances messianiques de son temps*, 50, 94, 99, 100, 102, 103, 122, 115, 170 (on "carnal views").

120. Colani, *Jésus-Christ et les croyances messianiques de son temps*, 103. In the conclusion he writes, "the historical study that I terminate here drove me to deny that the messianic ideas of the ancient Jews exercised an influential mark on the work of Jesus. He had borrowed from his people the notion of a royal kingdom of God, but by spiritualizing it, and the term of Messiah, but giving to it a totally other sense. I deny particularly that he drew on the beliefs of his time about the hope of a glorious future on the clouds of heaven" (235).

121. Colani, *Jésus-Christ et les croyances messianiques de son temps*, 144, also 151 (on "the Jewish system").

that is "in manifest contradiction" to what he was all about.[122] Colani at one point criticizes the possibility that Jesus expected a return with these words: "Would he have considered himself as his own precursor, a humble and gentile precursor of a violent and terrible Messiah? Would his life have been the Christian introduction of a Jewish poem?"[123]

In Colani's work, we see a move that was centuries in the making: the second-coming hope is to Jesus what Judaism is to Christianity.

122. Colani, *Jésus-Christ et les croyances messianiques de son temps*, 146, 148, 152 ("incompatible" with "the spirit of Jesus"), 157 ("flagrant contradiction"), 215.

123. Colani, *Jésus-Christ et les croyances messianiques de son temps*, 146.

CONCLUDING THOUGHTS ON PART 2

Paul Ricoeur wrote,

> historians must first stand as heirs of the past. . . . Before even forming the idea of re-presenting the past, we are in debt to the men and women of the past who contributed to making us what we are. Before we can represent the past we must live as beings affected by the past.[1]

The purpose of part 2 was to attend to this wisdom—something that too few have done before when it comes to the topic of the second coming in Christian origins. I have identified particular reception-historical tendencies, theological and contextual realities, and sociological factors that explain why it seemed so eminently reasonable to so many early historians in search of Jesus that the second advent hope originated after and apart from his influence. I highlighted significant theological shifts in the history of Christianity concerning eschatological thought in general and the second advent in particular, as well as inherited assumptions about the nature of Jewish messianism at the time of Jesus that can be traced back to Christian *adversus* and other polemical and exegetical literature. Early historical critics engaged the second-coming hope not in a vacuum but as the expectation was transmitted and shaped by earlier discourse. Part 2 has charted the construction of a plausibility structure in early New Testament scholarship.

To be clear, and this must be emphasized, I do not intend these chapters to function as an argument *for* any particular reconstruction of Christian origins. That onus remains on me in the following chapters. I have throughout part 2 engaged N. T. Wright's reception history of eschatological thought and its impact on New Testament studies. Predictably, perhaps, his description of that history turns out to be quite congenial to his own reconstruction of Jesus, as mine will be to my own. Nevertheless, our different emphases are neither completely self-serving nor completely contradictory, and they certainly do not settle the question of what

1. Paul Ricoeur, "History and Rhetoric," *Diogenes* 168 (1994): 22.

Jesus's eschatological teaching actually entailed. That work remains to be done. My point here is that we cannot hope to offer a reconstruction of the past without acknowledging the ways in which in the early formative stages of modern biblical criticism the second advent hope has been found deficient by scholars on at least two grounds—it has reminded people of "enthusiasts" and "fanatics" in their own time, and it has been thought "too Jewish"—and neither of those has anything to do with the first century. Glasson's and Robinson's books, while far more sophisticated, nuanced, and enduring than many of the old nineteenth-century lives of Jesus, embody some of these same historical and exegetical habits.[2]

Of course, anti-Judaism persists in biblical scholarship,[3] and the intellectual and cultural pressure to "make of Jesus a modern man" (so Schweitzer) have remained, if not intensified, up to the present time.[4] But I would suggest that other aspects of our reception history connect more readily to recent work on the historical Jesus as described in part 1. It is especially peculiar that the eschatological revolution in New Testament Studies, birthed by Weiss and Schweitzer and nurtured by numerous esteemed scholars today, has since Glasson and Robinson only dabbled with the question of how the second-coming hope relates to the teaching of the historical Jesus. I end part 2 with some confidence that this oversight—that consensus of silence, as I have called it throughout—has a great deal to do with the fraught reception history of the second advent as described here, and the fact that historical and theological culture wars are not easily forgotten.[5] As we have seen, the severing of the second-coming hope from the teaching of Jesus led to

2. Glasson and Robinson are close to Colani in several respects, only one of which is their particular view of the apocalyptic discourse. See T. Francis Glasson himself in *The Second Advent: The Origin of the New Testament Doctrine*, 3rd ed. (Eugene, OR: Wipf & Stock, 2009), 71–72; John A. T. Robinson, *Jesus and His Coming: The Emergence of a Doctrine* (New York: Abingdon, 1957), 119–20. The connection between Colani and Glasson is also noted by George R. Beasley-Murray, *Jesus and the Last Days: An Interpretation of the Olivet Discourse* (Vancouver: Regent College, 1993), 30.

3. Cf. Ruben A. Bühner, "The Contested Character of Divine Messianism: From an Inner-Jewish Debate to an Identity Marker," *EC* 13 (2022): 453: "even in modern times scholars have used—and still use—the supposed categorical difference (between 'messianism' and 'christology') as support for their own political or religious beliefs."

4. For a related assessment, see Robert J. Myles, "The Fetish for a Subversive Jesus," *JSHJ* 14 (2016): 52–70.

5. A fact only intensified in recent years by a fascination with biblical eschatology in modern American popular culture, as discussed in two interesting cultural exegeses by David G. Garber Jr., "Biblical Prophecy and Popular Fantasy and Science Fiction," and Shayna Sheinfeld, "Scenes from the End of the World in American Popular Culture," in *The Oxford Handbook of the Bible and American Popular Culture*, ed. Dan W. Clanton Jr. and Terry R. Clark (Oxford: Oxford University Press, 2021), 183–200, 201–18.

heated apologetical counterreactions, making it possible for critical historians, whether by conscious decision or unconscious neglect, to simply leave the thing alone. That, too, is a learned "habit of reading" that must be interrogated.

New Testament Studies continues to grapple with the history and legacy of Christian anti-Judaism. Such efforts have increased in the wake of the atrocities of the Holocaust, the discovery of the Dead Sea Scrolls, and increased Jewish and Christian scholarly collaboration. In historical Jesus studies particularly, the work of E. P. Sanders, Paula Fredriksen, Amy-Jill Levine, and many others has opened new avenues for investigation. I hope that my efforts here to demonstrate that there is a connection between Christian caricatures of Jewish messianism and the reception history of the second advent hope contribute to and advance these larger scholarly efforts. Moreover, our discussion going forward will benefit from the trend in current scholarship to complexify and diversify any monolithic understanding of Jewish messianism.[6] Peter Schäfer has argued that "different Messianic figures cannot be reduced to a uniform underlying pattern; they are to be described adequately only as the dynamic interaction of various and changing configurations within different historical constellations";[7] Matthew Novenson, in his larger critique of the very notion of a "messianic idea," contends that the notion of a "Jewish messiah" and a "Christian messiah" is an exegetical phantom;[8] and Loren Stuckenbruck suggests, "[if] we allow for such diversity in both Christian and Jewish communities, there is no reason to suppose that, beyond the reconciliation of 'Messiah' by Christians to the experiences of Jesus, Jewish and Christian ideas were necessarily very distinct from one another."[9] I find these ob-

6. An important and influential study is Jacob Neusner, William S. Green, and Ernest Frerichs, eds., *Judaisms and Their Messiahs at the Turn of the Christian Era* (Cambridge: Cambridge University Press, 1987). For some reflections on categories and definitions when it comes to "Judaism" and "messianism," see from this volume the essay by James H. Charlesworth, "From Messianology to Christian Christology: Some Caveats and Perspectives," 227–28.

7. See Peter Schäfer, "Diversity and Interaction: Messiahs in Early Judaism," in *Towards the Millennium: Messianic Expectations from the Bible to Waco*, ed. Peter Schäfer and Mark R. Cohen, SHR 77 (Leiden: Brill, 1998), 35.

8. Matthew V. Novenson, *The Grammar of Messianism: An Ancient Jewish Political Idiom and Its Users* (Oxford: Oxford University Press, 2017), 187–216. He writes that sharp definitions here inscribe "a convenient notional boundary where there is otherwise uncomfortable contested territory" (216).

9. Loren Stuckenbruck, "Messianic Ideas in the Apocalypse and Related Literature of Early Judaism," in *The Messiah in the Old and New Testaments*, ed. Stanley E. Porter (Grand Rapids: Eerdmans, 2007), 113 n. 44. See also William Scott Green, "Messiah in Judaism: Rethinking the Question," in Neusner, Green, and Frerichs, *Judaisms and Their Messiahs at the Turn of the Christian Era*, 1–13.

servations on point, even if we must be wary of an overcorrection that essentially empties messianism of content entirely.[10] When it comes to the use of "messiah" or "messianism" in subsequent chapters, I will follow Novenson's suggestion that messianic expressions share not an "essence" but a discursive field—the interpretation of "a common set of scriptural source texts."[11]

When we consider how unreflective assertions about the nature of Jewish messianism have sometimes replaced argument when it comes to reconstructing the origin of the second-coming hope, especially in the nineteenth and early twentieth century, the greater contextual sensitivity of more recent scholarship on messianism clears the way for a fresh reconstruction of Jesus. It is toward that reconstruction we now turn in the next two parts. But as Paul said in 1 Cor 15, "in proper order." For reasons articulated in the opening chapter, I start with careful description of what the earliest Christians claimed about Jesus—thus, historical-critical exegesis (part 3)—and then will seek to infer what historical realities most probably gave rise to those claims—thus, historical reconstruction (part 4).

10. For thoughtful reflections here, see Ruben A. Bühner, *Hohe Messianologie: Übermenschliche Aspekte eschatologischer Heilsgestalten im Frühjudentum*, WUNT 2/523 (Tübingen: Mohr Siebeck, 2020), 12–16.

11. Novenson, *Grammar of Messianism*, 14, also 1 ("common scriptural discourse"). See also Richard Bauckham, *The Testimony of the Beloved Disciple* (Grand Rapids: Baker Books, 2007), 234: "Jewish messianism was not so much a tradition of ideas as a tradition of exegesis." At the same time, since research into such exegesis surfaces repeated patterns and images, we should be able to offer summarizing statements about the contours of messianism without falling prey to the notion of a common messianic idea. For a reliable guide, cf. John J. Collins, *The Scepter and the Star: Messianism in Light of the Dead Sea Scrolls*, 2nd ed. (Grand Rapids: Eerdmans, 2010), 16–20. See also the excellent discussions in James C. VanderKam, "Messianism and Apocalypticism," in *The Origins of Apocalypticism in Judaism and Christianity*, ed. Bernard McGinn, John J. Collins, and Stephen J. Stein, vol. 1 of *The Encyclopedia of Apocalypticism* (New York: Continuum, 1998), 193–228; and Joshua W. Jipp's *The Messianic Theology of the New Testament* (Grand Rapids: Eerdmans, 2020), 15–17.

PART THREE

Awake and at Work

EARLY CHRISTIAN ESCHATOLOGY AND THE COMING OF JESUS

> [The church] has its roots in the future and its branches in the present.
>
> —John Zizioulas[1]

In part 3, we set aside for a moment the question that so many have started with when it comes to the second-coming hope in Christian origins, namely, what did the Jesus of history himself teach about the future? Our focus, instead, is a crucial prior question we must answer before anything else: what were the claims of his early followers about this? For reasons already described (part 1), it is vital to my historical approach that part 3 (exegesis) comes before part 4 (reconstruction). On one level, then, part 3 has little to do with the historical Jesus, since our objective is to describe the eschatological claims of various early Christian sources as carefully and accurately as we can in their own historical contexts. On another level, however, part 3 is essential for any further study of the historical Jesus that might follow, for there is no other way by which we might access him and make inferences about the past. I will ultimately argue that Jesus cannot be so easily sep-

1. John D. Zizioulas, *Being as Communion: Studies in Personhood in the Church* (Crestwood, NY: St. Vladimir's Seminary Press, 1985), 59.

arated from the "wild ideas" (so Annie Dillard) of his followers that we will detail in the following pages.[2] But making that case is not the task of these chapters.

It is also necessary to begin with exegesis because, aside from the question of origination, there are serious disputes about the proper interpretation of numerous so-called eschatological and apocalyptic texts in the New Testament.[3] As noted in part 1, I take issue with the ways in which Glasson, Robinson, and many others have in general deliteralized much of this language and read it as a symbolic or metaphorical way of describing the existential challenge of Jesus's present ministry, the imminent destruction of Jerusalem, or some other historical or social process. But having made that critique, it is now my obligation to offer a more compelling reading of these sources. It is also worth recalling here that I will not attempt to reconstruct "the Jewish background" for Jesus's kingdom proclamation and any putative messianic claim as a self-contained study of its own that is *prior to* our investigation of early Christian sources themselves. The reasons for this were also given in part 1. I think we are on better footing to start with what the early Christians actually claimed about Jesus and the future and to contextualize those claims the best that we can in the complex thought world of Second Temple Judaism and its wider Greco-Roman setting. This procedure respects the "historical constraints" of our sources in their own cultural contexts while also avoiding a situation in which our partial and limited understanding of messianic and eschatological expectations from this period determines the

2. See pp. 55–56 above.

3. There is, of course, no common definition of "eschatology" and "apocalyptic," though sometimes rather minor differences of opinion among scholars are unnecessarily dramatized in this discussion. Paul Foster, "The Eschatology of the Gospel of Matthew," in *"To Recover What Has Been Lost": Essays on Eschatology, Intertextuality, and Reception History in Honor of Dale C. Allison Jr.*, ed. Tucker S. Ferda, Daniel Frayer-Griggs, and Nathan C. Johnson, NovTSup 183 (Leiden: Brill, 2021), 79, articulates a widespread view (drawing upon Robert H. Charles) when he defines eschatology as "the perspectives contained in the writings of those traditions on 'the last things,' or . . . the final condition of the cosmos, or upon the state of being of humanity and the universe at the end of the current temporal spectrum." He further defines "apocalyptic" as broadly concerning heavenly unveiling and/or revelation (including divine manifestation). It is possible, then, he writes, to have noneschatological apocalyptic but "difficult to envisage" nonapocalyptic eschatology (80). See further Jerry L. Walls, introduction to *The Oxford Handbook of Eschatology*, ed. Jerry L. Walls (Oxford: Oxford University Press, 2007), 3–22; Benjamin E. Reynolds and Loren T. Stuckenbruck, introduction to *The Jewish Apocalyptic Tradition and the Shaping of New Testament Thought*, ed. Benjamin E. Reynolds and Loren T. Stuckenbruck (Minneapolis: Fortress, 2017), 1–14 (who rightly challenge the conflation of "apocalyptic" and "eschatology" at 1–2 and rightly emphasize the temporal *and* spatial dimensions of "apocalyptic" at 7).

historical reconstruction offered.[4] I will do much more with Jewish messianic and eschatological expectations in part 4 when I attempt to make a probable historical hypothesis about Jesus as a "believable figure in first-century Palestine."[5]

The thesis of part 3 is relatively straightforward. I aim to show that amid the remarkable theological disagreement, geographical spread, and general diversity of the Jesus movement in its earliest decades, nearly everywhere we look, we find people who were expecting Jesus's future appearance or trying to make sense of that hope in some other way (hence presupposing its existence). The parousia hope was thus not isolated to one small branch of Jesus followers, but it rather appears to emerge throughout the wide and diverse early Christian movement. Moreover, it is apparent that the authors of these texts did not feel the need to prove or defend the general expectation itself, which is quite unlike early Christian views of the Jewish law and gentile inclusion. The historical question arising from this descriptive work will become the focus of part 4: what historical scenarios need we hypothesize to explain how this situation could arise only a short while after the activity of Jesus? The details that emerge from this exegetical discussion will also inform that historical-critical work.

I will proceed in roughly chronological order, starting with Paul's letters, then moving to each of the canonical gospels (in their likely historical order), and finally (and more briefly) taking up some other New Testament and noncanonical texts.[6] I am interested in what these texts claim about Jesus and the future, what they presuppose in doing so, and how they connect to Israel's Scripture and exegetical traditions that grew out of them. I will also attend to these sources diachronically by analyzing their use of source material when that kind of approach is possible. These discussions, then, while not comprehensive, will be fairly in depth. This work, I hope, should preempt any criticism of my argument that is at

4. For this language, and an attempt to walk this line, see the brilliant study of Anthony E. Harvey, *Jesus and the Constraints of History* (Philadelphia: Westminster, 1982).

5. E. P. Sanders, *Jesus and Judaism* (Philadelphia: Fortress, 1985), 166–67.

6. As noted above at p. 27n10, canonical bias in New Testament studies needs to be challenged, but it is nevertheless the case, as most critics agree, that when it comes to reconstructing Jesus, the most important literary sources we have happen to be the Synoptics (John is more debated, and I will say more about this later). For discussion, see Jens Schröter and Christine Jacobi, eds., *The Jesus Handbook*, trans. Robert L. Brawley (Grand Rapids: Eerdmans, 2022), 125–55. In what follows, I assume that the Gospel of Thomas is a second-century text and dependent on the Synoptics. Cf. Simon Gathercole, *The Composition of the Gospel of Thomas: Original Language and Influences*, SNTSMS 151 (Cambridge: Cambridge University Press, 2012), and Mark Goodacre, *Thomas and the Gospels: The Case for Thomas's Familiarity with the Synoptics* (Grand Rapids: Eerdmans, 2012).

times leveled at historical Jesus scholars by New Testament exegetes (with some justification): that they fail to attend adequately to the theological or ideological nature of our sources and their literary complexity.[7] I want to learn the origin of early Christian stories about the end, to be sure. But if I get the origin question wrong, I hope at least to get the stories right.

---

7. See, e.g., Luke Timothy Johnson, *The Real Jesus: The Misguided Quest for the Historical Jesus and the Truth of the Traditional Gospels* (San Francisco: HarperSanFrancisco, 1996), 105–26, 146–58.

8

The Parousia in Paul's Letters and Ministry

From where we sit, with the sources we have, what is the opening scene in Christian origins? In our oldest text to make it into the New Testament, written less than two decades after the crucifixion of Jesus,[1] we find the apostle Paul responding to a challenging situation in Thessalonica. He had already been to Thessalonica and founded a church there before moving south. But while away, apparently some people had died, and Jesus-loyalists there were unsure about what this meant.[2] In particular, it seems that there was some confusion about how this experience of death related to what Paul had told them about something they should expect to happen in the very near future. As Paul often began his letters by reflecting on his past experiences with the particular community addressed (Gal 1:8, 11; Phil 1:5–6; 1 Cor 1:4–9), he gives some hints at the beginning of 1 Thessalonians about this former proclamation there (1:9–10):

1. Cf. Abraham Smith, "First Letter to the Thessalonians," *NIB* 11:682.

2. Rainer Riesner, *Die Frühzeit des Apostels Paulus: Studien zur Chronologie, Missionsstrategie und Theologie* (Tübingen: Mohr Siebeck, 1994), 339–49; Osvaldo D. Vena, *The Parousia and Its Rereadings: The Development of the Eschatological Consciousness in the Writings of the New Testament*, SBT 27 (New York: Lang, 2001), 118. While this is not to say that 4:13–18 is the central focus or purpose of the letter. Here rightly Arthur L. Moore, *The Parousia in the New Testament*, NovTSup 13 (Leiden: Brill, 1966), 108–9. For the term "Jesus-loyalists," see Richard Horsley, *You Shall Not Bow Down and Serve Them: The Political Economic Projects of Jesus and Paul* (Eugene, OR: Cascade, 2021), 114, 130.

> For they [the people of Macedonia and Achaia] report about us what kind of welcome we had among you, and how you turned to God from idols, to serve a living and true God, and to wait for his Son from heaven [ἀναμένειν τὸν υἱὸν αὐτοῦ ἐκ τῶν οὐρανῶν], whom he raised from the dead: Jesus, who rescues us from the wrath that is coming [τὸν ῥυόμενον ἡμᾶς ἐκ τῆς ὀργῆς τῆς ἐρχομένης].[3]

Paul writes this by way of reminder, not instruction. And it takes little literary sophistication or intertextual savvy to get the point, which is why commentators are in agreement at least on this: an essential part of Paul's earlier kerygma in Thessalonica involved the prediction that Jesus, the "son" of God, would return from heaven and deliver his own from fearsome wrath about to be unleashed on the world.[4] Evidently, the Thessalonians had also been informed about the resurrection of Jesus ("whom he raised from the dead"), and probably some account of his passion, as 1:6 seems to imply.[5]

The cause of crisis here is still not evident. What was the problem? While we do not know the full scope and detail of what Paul had shared, it is likely that he had given the Thessalonians the impression that this return of Jesus was so imminent that they would see it happen.[6] It is not necessarily the case that Paul predicted or even assumed that nobody would die in the interim, but his message must have been of such a nature that it was unnecessary to explain in great detail what happened to dead people in that moment of his coming or how their experience corresponded to that of "the living."[7] We learn this from 1 Thess 4:13–18, where

3. All New Testament translations are my own unless otherwise indicated.

4. See F. F. Bruce, *1 and 2 Thessalonians*, WBC 45 (Waco, TX: Word, 1982), 18–19; David Luckensmeyer, *The Eschatology of First Thessalonians*, NTOA 71 (Göttingen: Vandenhoeck & Ruprecht, 2009), 75–114; Michael Zugmann, *Missionspredigt in nuce: Studien zu 1 Thess 1,9b–10* (Linz: Wagner, 2012); Michael Wolter, "Das Evangelium," in *Paulus Handbuch*, ed. Friedrich W. Horn (Tübingen: Mohr Siebeck, 2013), 340.

5. In 1:6, the δεξάμενοι is probably causal: "because you received."

6. Cf. C. H. Dodd, *The Apostolic Preaching and Its Developments* (New York: Harper, 1960), 32 ("His first preaching had left the Thessalonians completely surprised and bewildered when certain of their followers died and yet the Lord had not come"); E. P. Sanders, *Paul: The Apostle's Life, Letters, and Thought* (Minneapolis: Fortress, 2015), 208 ("the substance of his message during this part of his career was not that his converts would be raised after they died, but that Jesus had already been raised, and that he would return while Paul's hearers still lived"), 211; Christof Landmesser, "Parusieverzögerung und die Gegenwart der Glaubenden: Zur Hermeneutik von Ambiguität und Ambivalenz der christlichen Existenz in der Theologie des Paulus," *EC* 9 (2018): 108: "Sie [the Thessalonians] sind in ihrer Gegenwart wesentlich ausgerichtet auf ein noch ausstendendes und für die Zukunft erwartetes Ereignis."

7. Moore, *Parousia in the New Testament*, 108–9, argues that the issue was not that the Thessalonians were surprised by people dying, but they worried the dead would not experience "the

Paul offers what will become one of his most detailed descriptions of the future coming of Jesus to survive:

> We do not want you to be ignorant, brothers, concerning those who have fallen asleep, in order that you might not grieve as the rest who have no hope. For if we believe that Jesus died and was raised, so also God will lead [ἄξει] those who have died through Christ with him. For this we say to you by the word of the Lord: that we who are living, who are left until the appearance of the Lord [εἰς τὴν παρουσίαν τοῦ κυρίου], will by no means precede those who have fallen asleep. For the Lord himself, at the cry of command, at the archangel's call, and at the trumpet of God, will come down from heaven and the dead in Christ will be raised first. Then we who are living, who are left, will be snatched up together with them [ἅμα σὺν αὐτοῖς ἁρπαγησόμεθα] in the clouds to meet the Lord in the air. And so we will be with the Lord always. Thus, encourage one another with these words.

What exactly in 4:13–18 the Thessalonians were formerly ignorant of (4:13: οὐ θέλομεν δὲ ὑμᾶς ἀγνοεῖν) is not clear.[8] We know from 1:9–10 that Paul is not for the first time sharing the idea that Christ would soon return, as confirmed by content elsewhere in the epistle (e.g., 3:13; 5:23), and it also is unlikely that they had never heard of the general resurrection of the dead before (though some have argued this).[9] The focus on order and sequence ("will *by no means precede*" in v. 15, "rise *first*" in v. 16, "*then* we who are alive" in v. 17) suggests that the confusion has to do with *how* Christ's return and the general resurrection of the dead conjoin, or some of the details of that conjunction (in other words, not the parousia hope itself or the resurrection hope itself).[10] In any case, the fact that Paul has to offer

---

first festive phase of the parousia." Even if Moore is right, the fact that we have a church that can exist unawares of how dead persons might experience the return of Jesus is possible only if eschatological imminence (meaning people then alive would see it) is presupposed. Moore's argument is part of a systematic attempt in his book to deny that Paul ever asserted that any then living would experience the parousia.

8. Cf. Willi Marxsen, "Auslegung von 1 Thess 4:13–18," *ZTK* 66 (1969): 22–37; Helmut Merklein, "Der Theologe als Prophet: Zur Funktion prophetischen Redens im theologischen Diskurs des Paulus," *NTS* 38 (1992): 407–8.

9. It is clear that 4:14 begins with what is known: Christ died and has been raised. Paul then adds, and "he will lead those with him." To paraphrase, Jesus died and was raised (as you know), and so I'm telling you he will also lead. Alliteration reinforces the point: ἀπέθανεν . . . ἀνέστη . . . ἄξει. This is not so much about the fact of the coming of Jesus but what will happen to the dead.

10. 2 Bar. 30 is an interesting parallel. It mentions that "those who hope" in the messiah will rise from the dead and connects his appearance with the treasuries of souls in heaven

4:13–18 as supplementary instruction to his original kerygma is quite remarkable, and the need for it tells us a great deal about the eschatological nature of his proclamation about Jesus's coming and the imminence of it. It is further clear that Paul's response in the final two chapters of 1 Thessalonians does not function to soften or take back that sense of imminence very much.[11] Paul appears to assume in 4:13–18 that he will be among the "we" "who are living" (cf. the important pronoun shift from "we the living, who are left [ἡμεῖς οἱ ζῶντες οἱ περιλειπόμενοι]," and the otherwise unnecessary ἡμεῖς, to the substantive participle "those who have fallen asleep [τοὺς κοιμηθέντας]"), even while he continues to reject any attempt to pinpoint the precise time (5:1–23).[12] Paul urges the Thessalonians to keep awake and be sober because "that day" will come "like a thief" at any moment (5:4).

The content Paul relates about the coming of Jesus and the resurrection of the dead needs to be considered in more detail. Despite the fact that recipients of this letter were mostly if not exclusively gentile,[13] it is evident that the description in 4:13–18 presupposes and recycles Jewish eschatological tradition.[14] It may be that παρουσία in 4:15 adopts typical language in the Greco-Roman world for a leader

---

being opened (no mention is made of "the living"). Moreover, there is some concern about equity among the dead, and the similarity of their experience is stressed: "they will be in one assemblage, of one mind," and "the first ones will enjoy themselves and the last ones will not be sad" (30.2).

11. So Sanders, *Paul: Life, Letters, and Thought*, 212.

12. Contra Moore, *Parousia in the New Testament*, 109–18 (that in 1 Thessalonians as well as in 1 Cor 7 and 15 Paul is speaking of "Christians generally"); Mark Keown, "An Imminent Parousia and Christian Mission: Did the New Testament Writers Really Expect Jesus' Return?," in *Christian Origins and the Establishment of the Early Jesus Movement*, ed. Stanley E. Porter and Andrew W. Pitts, TENTS 12 (Leiden: Brill, 2018), 242–63; J. Andrew Doole, "Did Paul Really Think He Wasn't Going to Die? Paul, the Parousia, and the First Person Plural in 1 Thess 4:13–18," *NovT* 62 (2020): 44–59; and Allan Chapple, "The Fantasy of the Frantic Apostle: Paul and the Parousia," *Them* 47 (2022): 288–302. Doole argues that the first-person plural is a soundbite for the Thessalonians to use and encourage each other with—so the "we," then, does not include Paul, Silvanus, and Timothy. Doole's ancient and modern examples of such soundbites, however, do not function to distinguish the speaker from the addressees but rather the opposite: they often express solidarity. It seems to me that Doole's suggestion about a soundbite actually reinforces the traditional interpretation. More convincing is Giesen, "Naherwartung des Paulus in 1 Thess 4, 13–18?," *SNTU* 10 (1985): 123–50; Bruce, *1 and 2 Thessalonians*, 103–5; Earl J. Richard, *First and Second Thessalonians*, SP 11 (Collegeville, MN: Liturgical Press, 1991), 241–42; Vena, *Parousia and Its Rereadings*, 119; Sanders, *Paul: Life, Letters, and Thought*, 211–12.

13. Cf. Jeffrey A. D. Weima, *1–2 Thessalonians*, BECNT (Grand Rapids: Baker Books, 2014), 28–30.

14. Cf. Joseph Plevnik, *What Are They Saying about Paul and the End Time?* (New York: Paulist, 2009), 78–79, 87–88; Candida R. Moss and Joel S. Baden, "1 Thess. 4:13–18 in Rabbinic Perspective," *NTS* 58 (2012): 1–16.

or dignitary's approach to a city (though this has been disputed).[15] But the bulk of the imagery stems from Jewish eschatological thought. Paul writes that Christ will descend from heaven "at the cry of command [ἐν κελεύσματι], at the archangel's call [ἐν φωνῇ ἀρχαγγέλου], and at the trumpet of God [ἐν σάλπιγγι θεοῦ]" (v. 16). The militaristic imagery of "the cry of command" and "the archangel's call" both assume a company of angels; the angels themselves are not mentioned explicitly in vv. 13–18, but they are earlier in the epistle (3:13): Paul prays that God might "strengthen your hearts to be blameless in holiness . . . at the parousia of our Lord Jesus Christ with all his holy ones" (3:13). The parallel here to Zechariah's description of the advent of God on the day of the Lord is patent:

Zech 14:5:	ἥξει κύριος ὁ θεός μου καὶ	<u>πάντες οἱ ἅγιοι μετ᾽ αὐτοῦ</u>
	the Lord my God will come and	all the holy ones with him
1 Thess 3:13:	ἐν τῇ παρουσίᾳ τοῦ κυρίου ἡμῶν Ἰησοῦ	<u>μετὰ πάντων τῶν ἁγίων αὐτοῦ</u>
	at the appearance of our Lord Jesus	with all his holy ones

Zechariah's language itself was inspired by the description of the Sinai theophany, where according to Deut 33:1–2, God "came from Sinai . . . with myriads of holy ones; at his right, a host of his own" (LXX: ἥκει . . . ἐκ δεξιῶν αὐτοῦ ἄγγελοι μετ᾽ αὐτοῦ). The angelic imagery inspired a number of other texts in their descriptions of the last day (cf. 1 En. 1.4–9; Ascen. Isa. 4.14; Apoc. El. 3.4), and appears again in the opening of 2 Thess 1:7–8: "when the Lord Jesus is revealed [ἐν τῇ ἀποκαλύψει] from heaven with his mighty angels in flaming fire [μετ᾽ ἀγγέλων δυνάμεως αὐτοῦ ἐν πυρὶ φλογός], inflicting vengeance on those who do not know God and on those who do not obey the gospel."[16] The appearance of "the trumpet of God" in 4:16 is an eschatological trope, emerging also in the final chapters of Zechariah (9:14). Blowing trumpets can be found in other Jewish end-time speculation (cf., e.g., 1QM II, 16–III, 12; Gen. Rab. 56.9), not least in the New Testament itself (Matt 24:31; 1 Cor 15:52; Rev 10:7; 11:15).[17]

15. The point famously argued by Adolf Deissmann, *Licht vom Osten: Das Neue Testament und die neuentdeckten Texte der hellenistisch-römischen Welt* (Tübingen: Mohr, 1923), 314–20. For a more recent reassessment, see Peter Oakes, "Remapping the Universe: Paul and the Emperor in 1 Thessalonians and Philippians," *JSNT* 27 (2005): 316–17. Given the "day of the Lord" imagery throughout, see below, it is significant to note that Josephus speaks of God's coming at Mount Sinai as the "παρουσία of God." See *Ant.* 3.80. See also παρουσία in T. Jud. 22.2; T. Levi 8.14; 2 En. 32.1.

16. Cf. Weima, *1–2 Thessalonians*, 470–73. See also Jude 14.

17. Tg. 1 Sam. 2.10 rewrites "the Lord shall judge and give strength to his king" with this: "He shall blast them [the adversaries] with a loud noise issuing from Heaven. The Lord shall exact

It is clear, then, that Paul's description of the parousia of Christ in 1 Thessalonians is informed by Jewish tradition about "the day of the Lord" as anticipated in Israel's Scripture.[18] The association is even made explicit in the verses that follow 4:13–18, as Paul addresses questions about "the times and the seasons [περὶ . . . τῶν χρόνων καὶ τῶν καιρῶν] [5:1])" by saying "you yourselves know very well that the day of the Lord [ἡ ἡμέρα κυρίου] will come like a thief in the night" (5:2). The common view that the day of the Lord would bring about both salvation and judgment makes sense of other details in 1 Thessalonians, such as the cryptic claim in 1:10 that the returning Jesus "rescues us from the wrath that is coming" (ἀπὸ τῆς ὀργῆς τῆς ἐρχομένης) (and again in 5:9: "God has destined us not for wrath but for obtaining salvation"), as well as warnings and admonitions throughout (3:13; 5:23).[19]

It is not apparent to me that 1 Thess 4–5 evidences any direct contact with the apocalyptic dream vision of Dan 7, though this is debated.[20] In this famous passage, Daniel describes seeing four beasts rise up from the sea that cause various kinds of destruction on the earth. In both its original context and in reception, these beasts were identified with various political regimes, and in the first century, Rome was a good candidate for the final and "most terrifying" one.[21] But

---

punishment from Gog and from the marauding armies of the nations who come with him from the ends of the earth. He shall give strength to his king, and shall make great the kingdom of his messiah."

18. Influential arguments about the origin of this tradition can be found in Gerhard von Rad, "The Origin of the Day of Yahweh," *JSS* 4 (1959): 97–108, and Sigmund Mowinckel, *Psalmenstudien* (Amsterdam: Schippers, 1961), 2:229–314 (with insights also on its reception). See also A. Joseph Everson, "The Days of Yahweh," *JBL* 93 (1974): 329–37; Vena, *Parousia and Its Rereadings*, 59–106; Nicola Wendebourg, *Der Tag des Herrn: Zur Gerichtserwartung im Neuen Testament auf ihrem alttestamentlichen und frühjüdischen Hintergrund*, WMANT 96 (Neukirchen-Vluyn: Neukirchener, 2003), 28–60. On the influence of the day of the Lord on Paul, see especially Franzjosef Froitzheim, *Christologie und Eschatologie bei Paulus* (Würzburg: Echter, 1979), 9–16; Wendebourg, *Der Tag des Herrn*, 155–214; Larry J. Kreitzer, *Jesus and God in Paul's Eschatology*, JSNTSup 19 (London: Bloomsbury Academic, 2015), 112–28.

19. See Stephen H. Travis, "Wrath of God," *ABD* 6:996–98.

20. For arguments about connections to Dan 7 here, see Béda Rigaux, *Saint Paul: Les Épitres aux Thessaloniciens*, EB (Paris: Gabalda, 1956), 546–47; also Jürgen Becker, *Auferstehung der Toten im Urchristentum* (Stuttgart: KBW, 1976), 53; Becker, "Das Gottesbild Jesu und die älteste Auslegung von Ostern," in *Annäherungen: Zur urchristlichen Theologiegeschichte und zum Umgang mit ihren Quellen*, ed. Ulrich Mell, BZNW 76 (Berlin: de Gruyter, 1995), 42–44; George W. E. Nickelsburg, "Son of Man," *ABD* 6:147; Luckensmeyer, *Eschatology of First Thessalonians*, 259. For doubts, see Maurice Casey, *Son of Man: The Interpretation and Influence of Daniel 7* (London: SPCK, 1979), 153–54.

21. Cf., e.g., Rev 12:3; 13:1–18; 4 Ezra 11.1–12.39; 2 Bar. 39.5–7; probably also Josephus, *Ant.* 10.276. Cf. S. de Boer, "Rome, the 'Translatio Imperii' and the Early-Christian Interpretation of Daniel II and VII," *Rivista di Storia e Letteratura Religiosa* 21 (1985): 181–218; G. K. Beale, *The Use of Daniel*

Daniel also sees the setting up of "thrones," the coming of the God of Israel ("the Ancient One"), and the "opening of the books" for the judgment and destruction of the beasts. He further describes "one like a son of man" coming on or with the clouds of heaven, where he is presented before God at that judgment scene. We will discuss this dream vision more in due course. But insofar as 1 Thessalonians is concerned, the most suggestive detail in 4:13–18 itself has been the mention of "clouds" (v. 18), since the one like a son of man in Dan 7:13 comes on or with "the clouds." It may be, but it is hard to say.[22] It seems more likely to me that such details would, if anything, be remnants of a connection to Dan 7 that is not fully spelled out in this condensed description, rather than be attempts to turn the reader's attention to Dan 7 allusively.

By Word of the Lord

In any case, it is not just the way in which Paul describes Jesus's coming that is important for our purposes but also his express claim, and seeming genuine belief, that Jesus himself had talked about this. Exegetical conversation on the ἐν λόγῳ κυρίου ("by word of the Lord") in v. 15 is sometimes muddled by the quest for authentic words of Jesus in vv. 15–17—a very important consideration, to be sure, but not what we are after here. My interest at this point is not whether Jesus actually said this but whether Paul thinks and claims that Jesus did. And I think that we can be quite confident that Paul did, in fact, believe that.[23] This would mean that Paul framed his description of Jesus's parousia not as his own theological reaction to questions and concerns in Thessalonica, or that of some other leader or prophet speaking in the name of Jesus,[24] but rather ἐν λόγῳ κυρίου ("by the word of the Lord"), which means by the word of Jesus himself. The use of

in Jewish Apocalyptic Literature and in the Revelation of St. John (Eugene, OR: Wipf & Stock, 2010), 67–305.

22. In any case, it is worth noting that the mention of "times and seasons" in 5:1 may further suggest that Daniel is in the background, as this phrasing appears in Daniel and in texts influenced by it (see especially Dan 2:2 LXX). See Gordon D. Fee, *The First and Second Letters to the Thessalonians*, NICNT (Grand Rapids: Eerdmans, 2009), 186. It is also possible that 1 Thess 2:12 ("encouraging you to walk worthily of the God who calls you into his own kingdom and glory") is informed by Dan 7, since it is none other than the one like a son of man who has the "kingdom" and "glory" and the "holy ones of the Most High" ultimately share in that (see 7:22, 27).

23. Sanders, *Jesus and Judaism*, 144: "it is difficult to avoid the conclusion that . . . [the saying in 1 Thess 4] before Paul, was already attributed to Jesus." See also Sanders, *Paul: Life, Letters, and Thought*, 209–11.

24. Contra Christopher Tuckett, "Synoptic Tradition in 1 Thessalonians," in *From the Sayings*

the preposition ἐν suggests that what follows is a summary or paraphrase of this "word" rather than a direct quotation, while there is surely an attempt to frame its beginning and end:[25]

> v. 15: "For this we say to you by the word of the Lord" (ἐν λόγῳ κυρίου)
>
> vv. 16–17: summary/paraphrase
>
> v. 18: "Thus, encourage one another with these words" (ἐν τοῖς λόγοις τούτοις)

Paul also speaks collectively rather than on his own apostolic authority: "for this *we say* [λέγομεν] to you by the word of the Lord" (v. 15, my italics).

Why think that Paul claims to rehearse a teaching of Jesus about his future coming? It cannot be denied that later devotees put words on the lips of Jesus, and that some even had visions of him in which he (or "the Spirit") communicated new things.[26] But we also know that his followers thought it important to differ-

---

to the Gospels, WUNT 328 (Tübingen: Mohr Siebeck, 2014), 339 (Paul cites "a prophetic saying claimed to have been received by [another] prophet").

25. Contrast Michael W. Pahl's monograph devoted to the subject, *Discerning the 'Word of the Lord': The 'Word of the Lord' in 1 Thessalonians 4:15*, LNTS 389 (London: Bloomsbury T&T Clark, 2009), in which he argues that the phrase refers back to the previous message about the death and resurrection of Jesus, not to the lines that follow. On the "word" in what follows, see E. P. Sanders, *The Historical Figure of Jesus* (London: Penguin Books, 1993), 180–82, see also 158 n. 9 (he points to Mark 13:26–27 "but in a version more similar to Mt. 16.27–28 and 24.30–31").

26. Rudolf Bultmann's influence is significant here. See *History of the Synoptic Tradition*, trans. John Marsh, 5th ed. (Peabody, MA: Hendrickson, 1963), 126–30. See also Hans Conzelmann, *An Outline of the Theology of the New Testament* (New York: Harper & Row, 1969), 337–40 (on pneumatic inspiration). For arguments that ἐν λόγῳ κυρίου refers to a Christian prophet (if not Paul himself) speaking with the authority of the risen Jesus, see David E. Aune, *Prophecy in Early Christianity and the Mediterranean World* (Grand Rapids: Eerdmans, 1983), 253–56; Frans Neirynck, "Paul and the Sayings of Jesus," in *L'Apôtre Paul: Personnalité, style et conception du ministère*, ed. A. Vanhoye, SETL 73 (Leuven: Leuven University Press, 1986), 267–321; J. G. Davies, "The Genesis of Belief in an Imminent Parousia," *JTS* 14 (1963): 104–7 (makes the argument that the phrase recalls the prophetic formula from the Old Testament, which suggests that Paul is referring to a prophetic revelation. But there is a crucial difference in form here that Davies overlooks: the prophet, as mouthpiece for said word, speaks in the first person, whereas in this case, Paul is clear to distinguish his own speaking from the word—a point reinforced by the demonstrative at the end "these words"); Ulrich Luz, *Das Geschichtsverständnis des Paulus* (München: Kaiser, 1968), 326–31; Bartholomäus Henneken, *Verkündigung und Prophetie im Ersten Thessalonicherbrief*, SBS 29 (Stuttgart: Katholisches Bibelwerk, 1969), 85–91; Merklein, "Der Theologe als Prophet," 402–29; M. Eugene Boring, *The Continuing Voice of Jesus* (Louisville: Westminster John Knox, 1991), 29, 61–62, 161, 164; Gerd Lüdemann, *Paulus, der Heidenapostel* (Göttingen: Vandenhoeck & Ruprecht, 1983), 254–56; Abraham J. Malherbe, *The Letters to the Thessalonians: A New Translation with Introduction and Commentary*, AB 32B (New York: Dou-

entiate between their own thoughts and the teaching of Jesus himself (at least what they thought it was), as such a basic distinction is more or less necessary to treat some tradition as authoritative. We have no evidence that the words of prophets speaking "in the spirit" or who had communicated with the risen Jesus were easily lumped together with received memories of his earthly teaching as though they were indistinguishable.[27] We might find that scenario in later dialogue gospels (setting aside the genre question), but we are currently twenty years removed from the crucifixion of Jesus and not in the middle of the second or third century CE. In many texts that date from the late-first century, while still decades after 1 Thessalonians, the risen Jesus or the Spirit communicates new instruction for the present moment (cf., e.g., Rev 1:11, 17–20; 2:1–3:22), which means that these insights lack a historiographical dimension and do not claim to be remembered words from his ministry.[28] Even in John's Farewell Discourses, we find verbs that communicate the same: the coming Paraclete will "remind" (ὑπομνήσει) what Jesus had said (14:26), "testify" (μαρτυρήσει) on behalf of Jesus (15:26), and "interpret" (ἀναγγελεῖ) the things that are to come (16:13).[29]

The fact is that the closest parallels to 1 Thess 4:15 are found within the Pauline corpus itself where Paul appears to be exercising care to distinguish his own theological insight from the received instruction of Jesus (or what was thought to be so). In 1 Cor 7, Paul three times draws attention to received teaching of Jesus, each time separating it from his own instruction. In 7:10–11, Paul rehearses with slightly

---

bleday, 2000), 267–69; G. S. Shogren, *1 and 2 Thessalonians* (Grand Rapids: Zondervan, 2012), 184. For another view, see Traugott Holtz, "Paul and the Oral Gospel Tradition," in *Jesus in the Oral Gospel Tradition*, ed. Henry Wansbrough, JSNTSup 64 (Sheffield: Sheffield Academic, 1991), 385.

27. A point rightly stressed by James D. G. Dunn, "The Prophetic 'I'-Sayings and the Jesus-Tradition: The Importance of Testing Prophetic Utterances within Early Christianity," in *The Oral Gospel Tradition* (Grand Rapids: Eerdmans, 2013), 13–40. He asks at 19: "Was there ever a stage when a mass of 'sayings of Jesus' were circulated without any concern as to who first gave them utterance?"

28. In Acts, we most often find people brought to faith through visions (9:1–9; 10:3–6), and leaders receive guidance about next steps (10:10–16; 16:9–10; 18:9–11; 22:17–21; 27:23–24). For discussion, see Earle E. Ellis, "The Role of the Christian Prophet in Acts," in *Apostolic History and the Gospel*, ed. W. Ward Gasque and Ralph P. Martin (Grand Rapids: Eerdmans, 1970), 55–67.

29. On 16:13, Raymond E. Brown, *The Gospel according to John*, AB 29 (Garden City, NY: Doubleday, 1966–70), 2:708, rightly notes that ἀναγγελεῖ here does not refer to the declaration of new content but the disclosure of proper understanding, as frequently in Daniel (cf. Θ 2:2, 4, 7, 9, etc.) and elsewhere, where "*anangellein* . . . is used to describe the interpretation of mysteries *already communicated* in dreams or visions. The declarative interpretation deals with the future by seeking a deeper meaning in what has already happened." See also Andreas J. Köstenberger, *John*, BECNT (Grand Rapids: Baker Books, 2004), 473–74; Jörg Frey, *Theology and History in the Fourth Gospel: Tradition and Narration* (Waco, TX: Baylor University Press, 2018), 144–54.

different wording Jesus's prohibition of divorce as found in synoptic tradition (cf. Mark 10:6–12 and parr.; Luke 16:18), prefaced with this: "to the married I give this command—not I but the Lord [οὐκ ἐγὼ ἀλλὰ ὁ κύριος]." Paul continues in v. 12 with further instruction but notes that it is his own and not Jesus's: "to the rest I say—I and not the Lord [ἐγὼ οὐχ ὁ κύριος]." And a few verses later, Paul writes, "concerning virgins, I have no command of the Lord [ἐπιταγὴν κυρίου οὐκ ἔχω], but I give my opinion [γνώμην] as one who by the Lord's mercy is trustworthy" (7:25). In another context of 1 Corinthians, Paul claims that Jesus commanded that the ones who proclaim the gospel should earn their living by it (9:14), and he also contends that the tradition of the Lord's supper was "received from the Lord" (παρέλαβον ἀπὸ τοῦ κυρίου).[30] While this practice is disproportionately attested in 1 Corinthians, it does appear in other texts (cf. Rom 14:14; cf. Mark 7:19). It should be stressed that to say "I have no command of the Lord" in 1 Cor 7:25 is worth saying only if Paul does, in fact, think he knows more than a handful of things about Jesus. Paul must think he knows enough about Jesus's teaching to regard his lack of knowledge for a particular issue to be a meaningful consideration.

Now it may well be that in all these cases, we are actually hearing the words of a prophet or teacher speaking in the Spirit or in the name of the risen Jesus. I find that conclusion nearly impossible concerning the teaching on divorce, but for now we leave the possibility open.[31] What I mean to stress here, given our interest in the claims of our sources, is only this: when Paul writes "not I but the Lord" in 1 Cor 7, he is surely *not* saying "not I but some other person speaking with the authority of the Lord." It would be news to Paul, I think, were he to hear the conclusion of modern New Testament scholars that the words he cites in 1 Cor 7 do not actually derive from the ministry of Jesus, even should that conclusion be true historically.

These texts are important for the proper understanding of ἐν λόγῳ κυρίου in 1 Thess 4:15, then, because they demonstrate that Paul was otherwise in touch with Jesus tradition (which is not to say it is dominical) and that he was capable of marking it as such and distinguishing it from his own instruction when circumstances required. Paul evidently had no formulaic way of doing this, and

30. Joachim Jeremias, *New Testament Theology: The Proclamation of Jesus*, trans. John Bowden (New York: Scribner's Sons, 1971), 289 (Paul thought the words went "back in a direct chain of tradition to Jesus himself").

31. See John Nolland, "The Gospel Prohibition of Divorce: Tradition History and Meaning," *JSNT* 17 (1995): 19–35; Thomas Kazen, *Scripture, Interpretation, or Authority? Motives and Arguments in Jesus' Halakic Conflicts*, WUNT 320 (Tübingen: Mohr Siebeck, 2014), 195–282.

almost every example above differs from the next in terms of the way in which it introduces the received tradition.[32] But the upshot is the same.

It further suggests that ἐν λόγῳ κυρίου makes this claim when we note that what Paul then summarizes contains numerous parallels to synoptic Jesus tradition.[33] In the Gospels, these are all presented as words of Jesus, meaning Jesus is the speaker.[34]

1 Thess 4:13–18	**synoptic tradition**
v. 14: God will "bring with him" (ἄξει σὺν αὐτῷ) those who sleep	Mark 13:27 // Matt 24:31: the angels "will gather" (ἐπισυνάξει) the elect
v. 15: the Lord will appear v. 16: come down from heaven	Mark 13:26 // Matt 24:30 // Luke 21:27: the son of man comes in the cloud(s)
v. 16: at the trumpet of God	Matt 24:31: "he will send out his angels with a great trumpet"
v. 17: those left will be "caught up" (ἁρπαγησόμεθα)	Matt 24:40–41 // Luke 17:34–35: one will be "taken" (from παραλαμβάνω), the other left

Such parallels persist into 1 Thess 5:[35]

32. Though it is important to note, with Aune, *Prophecy in Early Christianity and the Mediterranean World*, 427 n. 54, that when Paul clearly speaks of revelations received elsewhere, he does not use λόγος. We find rather ἀποκάλυψις (Gal 1:12; 2:2; 1 Cor 14:6; 2 Cor 12:1, 7), ὀπτασία (2 Cor 12:1), ἄρρητα ῥήματα (2 Cor 12:4). Also μυστήριον, though this is in Eph 3:3.

33. Cf. Allan J. McNicol, *Jesus' Directions for the Future: A Source and Redaction-History Study of the Use of the Eschatological Traditions in Paul and in the Synoptic Accounts of Jesus' Last Eschatological Discourse* (Macon, GA: Mercer University Press, 1996), 29–36; Sanders, *Paul: Life, Letters, and Thought*, 210–11; Stephen Motyer, *Come, Lord Jesus! A Biblical Theology of the Second Coming of Christ* (London: Apollos, 2016), 100–103. Tuckett, "Synoptic Tradition in 1 Thessalonians," misses the forest for the trees here. Contrast also P. Nepper-Christensen, "Das verborgene Herrenwort: Eine Untersuchung über 1. Thess. 4,13–18," *ST* 19 (1965): 136–54 (who argues that Paul's "word of the Lord" is actually from John 11:25–26), and Ulrich B. Müller, "Zur Rezeption Gesetzes-Kritischer Jesusüberlieferung im Frühen Christentum," *NTS* 27 (1981): 158.

34. For further discussion here, see George R. Beasley-Murray, "Resurrection and Parousia of the Son of Man," *TynBul* 42 (1991): 298; David Wenham, *Paul: Follower of Jesus or Founder of Christianity?* (Grand Rapids: Eerdmans, 1995), 305–15; Craig S. Keener, *The Historical Jesus of the Gospels* (Grand Rapids: Eerdmans, 2009), 361–71.

35. Cf. McNicol, *Jesus' Directions for the Future*, 15–28; E. Earle Ellis, *Christ and the Future in New Testament History*, NovTSup 97 (Leiden: Brill, 2000), 33–34.

1 Thess 5:1–11	**synoptic tradition**
v. 2: "the day of the Lord will come like a thief in the night" (ὡς κλέπτης ἐν νυκτί)	ὁ κλέπτης, and also at night, in Matt 24:43; Luke 12:39
v. 3: destruction will come "as labor pains [ἡ ὠδίν] come upon a pregnant woman"	eschatological labor pains (from ὠδίν) in Mark 13:8 // Matt 24:8
v. 6: "let us not fall asleep . . . but keep awake" (and again in v. 10)	cf. Mark 13:33–37; Matt 25:5, 13–15; 24:42; Luke 12:37
vv. 6–7: "let us be sober . . . [not] get drunk"	cf. Matt 24:49 // Luke 12:45

As Paul was not dependent on the Gospels, these connections are evidence of Paul's contact with prewritten gospel tradition that eventually made its way into the apocalyptic discourse of Mark 13 and parallels.[36] The connections, in both form and content, support the inference that Paul is drawing from a received pool of eschatological teaching connected to the authority of Jesus.[37] C. P. März also made the keen observation that Paul's specificity about the thief "*in the night*," combined with the "drunk" and "watch" terminology in 5:1–7, mirrors the sequence of three parables in Q 12:35–46 (the watching servants, the thief, the faithful/unfaithful servants).[38] Paul may even, then, have been aware of such a collection of parables about the coming of Jesus.

I would make one further point on this matter. Referring to received teaching of Jesus himself (again, what is assumed to be) makes the most sense on rhetorical grounds in 1 Thess 4–5. The examples above notwithstanding, it is true that sometimes Paul wished to invest his own pronouncements with the authority of Jesus. In 1 Cor 14:37, Paul writes, "If anyone thinks that he is a prophet, or spiritual person, he should acknowledge that what I am writing to you is a command of the Lord [ἃ γράφω ὑμῖν ὅτι κυρίου ἐστὶν ἐντολή]."[39] This text is sometimes cited in

36. It is not exactly clear or important to decide whether Paul is citing saying(s) of Jesus otherwise encountered in the Synoptic Gospels or something similar enough to synoptic tradition to be recognizable to us. Cf. Rigaux, *Saint Paul*, 538–39. Joachim Jeremias, *Unknown Sayings of Jesus*, trans. R. H. Fuller, 2nd ed. (London: SPCK, 1964), 81–83, argued we have an *agraphon* here.

37. Cf. the important essay by Seyoon Kim, "The Jesus Tradition in 1 Thess 4.13–5.11," *NTS* 48 (2002): 225–42. See also McNicol, *Jesus' Directions for the Future*, 43.

38. See C. P. März, "Das Gleichnis vom Dieb," in *The Four Gospels, 1992: Festschrift Frans Neirynck*, ed. F. van Segbroeck et al. (Leuven: Leuven University Press, 1992), 1:633–48.

39. See Aune, *Prophecy in Early Christianity and the Mediterranean World*, 255, who considers 1 Cor 14:37 and 2 Cor 12.

support of the view that 1 Thess 4:15's ἐν λόγῳ κυρίου is simply Paul speaking in a loud voice. But the context of 1 Cor 14 is very different from 1 Thess 4–5 and probably proves the opposite point. In Corinth, Paul is challenging those who, in his estimation, think too highly of themselves and have not properly submitted to his authority. In Thessalonica, Paul is trying to comfort a church that is in crisis about people who have died. He is not writing to admonish the Thessalonians to accept as authoritative something they have heretofore refused to acknowledge; he is correcting their ignorance on a matter of pressing emotional concern. What is the most likely response in such a context? On rhetorical-critical grounds, appealing to Jesus himself is much more fitting in context than asserting the authority of someone else's eschatological prediction (whether from Paul or someone else). I would thus paraphrase 1 Thess 4:13–15 in this way: "Be encouraged, for this situation is not unforeseen. We have it on the authority of Jesus himself that this is what will happen to those who have died."

I wish to clarify once more that nothing in this discussion concerns the actual teaching of the historical Jesus. That is not our aim here. All I am trying to do is reconstruct Paul's claims on this matter. My conclusion is this: roughly twenty years after the crucifixion of Jesus, Paul instructed a church in Thessalonica that Christ would return from heaven so soon that many of them would still be alive to see it, and he believed and told them that Jesus himself had predicted this. Moreover, Paul's description of this event is intelligible within the symbolic universe of Israel's Scriptures, and it is particularly connected to the prophetic expectation of the coming day of the Lord.

1 Corinthians 15 and the Man from Heaven

First Thessalonians 4:13–18 contains Paul's most detailed reflections on the imminent return of Jesus. But as already noted, it is clear that 1 Thessalonians does not contain his first-time teaching on the matter. First Thessalonians 4 clarifies and expands on some base knowledge about the coming of Jesus that was evidently fundamental to his initial proclamation of the gospel.[40] The same is true in the Corinthian correspondence where we find the second most detailed description

40. See Martinus C. de Boer, "Paul and Apocalyptic Eschatology," in *The Origins of Apocalypticism in Judaism and Christianity*, vol. 1 of *The Encyclopedia of Apocalypticism*, ed. Bernard McGinn, John J. Collins, and Stephen J. Stein (New York: Continuum, 1998), 345–83; Seyoon Kim, "Paul as an Eschatological Herald," in *Paul as Missionary: Identity, Activity, Theology, and Practice*, ed. Trevor J. Burke and Brian S. Rosner, LNTS 420 (London: Bloomsbury T&T Clark, 2011), 9–24.

of the parousia in Paul's letters. It is, again, somewhat by accident. In 1 Cor 15, Paul is forced to share some further details about the return of Jesus even though his real focus in context is the resurrection of the dead. In the course of making his argument for the nonnegotiability of the general resurrection of the dead (15:12–34), Paul offers the following (vv. 20–28):

> But now Christ has been raised from the dead as the firstfruits of those who have fallen asleep. For since death came through a man, also through a man comes the resurrection of the dead. For just as all die in Adam, so also in Christ all will be made alive. But each in proper order: Christ the firstfruits, then those who belong to Christ at his appearance, then the end, when he hands over the kingdom to God and to the Father, after he has abolished every ruler and every authority and power. For it is necessary for him to rule until "he puts all enemies under his feet." The last enemy that is destroyed is death. For "he subjects all things under his feet." And when it says that "all things are subjected," it is plain that this excludes the one who subjected all things to him. And when he subjects all things to him, then even the son himself[41] will be subjected to the one who subjected all things to him, in order that God may be all in all.

Paul's dense and focused description of the parousia here appears only because it serves as a subpoint in his main argument that the resurrection of Jesus (which the Corinthians apparently affirm) is inseparable from the general resurrection of the dead (which at least some in Corinth apparently dispute or misunderstand).[42] What is more, the mention of the parousia functions in context to qualify and explain how linking the resurrection of Jesus to the general resurrection of the dead leaves room for some interval between them. For Paul begins with the bold claim

41. The most significant textual variants in the passage occur here, likely because of ambiguity about the subject of ὑποτάσσω in the preceding lines. Cf. Uta Heil, "Theologische Interpretation von 1 Kor 15, 23–28," *ZNW* 84 (1993): 27–35. I have maintained the καί in v. 28, per Sinaiticus, Alexandrinus, numerous church fathers, and the majority text, translated as an ascensive conjunction ("even"). The presence of "the son" in v. 28 is near certain, which makes the αὐτός intensive. Identifying the subject of "put" in v. 25 and "subject" in v. 27 is not necessary for my argument here. Cf. Gordon D. Fee, *The First Epistle to the Corinthians*, rev. ed., NICNT (Grand Rapids: Eerdmans, 2014), 838–42.

42. The reconstruction of Corinthian views of resurrection that Paul aims to correct is complex and not essential for our purposes to examine in detail. See Gerhard Sellin, *Der Streit um die Auferstehung der Toten: Eine religionsgeschichtliche und exegetische Untersuchung von 1 Korinther 15*, FRLANT 138 (Göttingen: Vandenhoeck & Ruprecht, 1986), 21–37; Alexandra R. Brown, "Paul and the Parousia," in *The Return of Jesus in Early Christianity* (Peabody, MA: Hendrickson, 2000), 71–72; K. R. Harriman, "A Synthetic Proposal about the Corinthian Resurrection Deniers," *NovT* 62 (2020): 190–200.

that all die in Adam and all "will be made alive" in Christ (vv. 21–22), which only raises a further question: if Christ has been raised from the dead, and his resurrection is only intelligible within the hope for the general resurrection of the dead, why are Paul and his contemporaries still waiting around? Paul's response is that there is a process underway, and each thing happens "in proper order" (ἐν τῷ ἰδίῳ τάγματι [v. 23]). The eschatological process he articulates is threefold (vv. 23–24):

(1) Christ is raised ("the firstfruits" [ἀπαρχή] of the general resurrection of the dead);
(2) "at his parousia" those in Christ will be raised (οἱ τοῦ Χριστοῦ ἐν τῇ παρουσίᾳ αὐτοῦ);
(3) then "the end" (τὸ τέλος) when Christ "hands over" "the kingdom" to God.

The sequencing is very clear in Greek (ἔπειτα . . . εἶτα), and the process functions to place the Corinthians in between (1) and (2) in eschatological time. Moreover, it is apparent that Paul imagines no significant interval between "the parousia" of Christ (2) and "the end" (3), since the parousia coincides with the general resurrection of the dead and the defeat of death (v. 26).[43] The connection between the two is presupposed throughout 1 Cor 15 and was of course the entire point of 1 Thess 4:13–18.[44] The attempt to articulate an eschatological sequence in these verses, and even the content of the sequence itself, has some interesting parallels in other Jewish texts, notably 2 Bar. 30.1–5, where we find messianic rule, the resurrection, the final judgment, and the establishment of God's final reign, in that order.[45]

43. Contra Henry St. John Thackeray, *The Relation of Saint Paul to Contemporary Jewish Thought* (London: Macmillan, 1900), 121, Albert Schweitzer, *The Mysticism of Paul the Apostle*, trans. William Montgomery (New York: Holt, 1931), 90–100, and Luz, *Das Geschichtsverständnis des Paulus*, 318–58, who argue that Paul expected a messianic reign *between* the parousia and resurrection as in, perhaps, Rev 20:4–6. For convincing responses, see W. D. Davies, *Paul and Rabbinic Judaism: Some Rabbinic Elements in Pauline Theology* (London: SPCK, 1948), 290–98 (he notes at 296, "it is not after but before the Parousia that the Messianic Kingdom lies in the mind of Paul"); Charles E. Hill, "Paul's Understanding of Christ's Kingdom in 1 Corinthians 15:20–28," *NovT* 30 (1988): 297–320; Raymond F. Collins, *First Corinthians*, SP 7 (Collegeville, MN: Liturgical Press, 1999), 552–53; Vena, *Parousia and Its Rereadings*, 131.

44. Telling is the way in which the general resurrection in 1 Cor 15:52 is marked by a trumpet, and a trumpet also sounds at the moment of the parousia in 1 Thess 4:16.

45. On other similarities between 1 Cor 15 and 2 Baruch, see Samuel Vollenweider, "Auferstehung als Verwandlung: Die paulinische Eschatologie von 1 Kor 15 im Vergleich mit der syrischen Baruchapokalypse (2 Bar)," in *Anthropologie und Ethik im Frühjudentum und im Neuen Testament*, ed. Matthias Konradt and Esther Schläpfer, WUNT 322 (Tübingen: Mohr Siebeck, 2014), 463–90.

"According to the Scriptures"

The notion of eschatological process still does not explain why the parousia, the general resurrection, and "the end" have not yet occurred.[46] But Paul has an answer for this, too: the risen Christ has work to do before steps 2 and 3 can occur. With the help of two psalms (Pss 109 and 8 LXX, respectively), Paul explains that Jesus is presently "ruling" and engaged in cosmic battle against superhuman forces opposed to God—the "enemies" from Pss 109 and 8—that must be put "underfoot" and "destroyed."[47] Paul begins with a citation from Ps 109 LXX, an enthronement psalm attributed to David:

1 Cor 15:25	**Ps 109:1 LXX**
βασιλεύειν	cf. v. 2's κατακυρίευε
to reign	to rule
ἄχρι οὗ θῇ	ἕως ἂν θῶ
until he has put	until I put
πάντας τοὺς ἐχθροὺς	τοὺς ἐχθρούς σου
all enemies	your enemies
ὑπὸ	ὑποπόδιον
under	under
τοὺς πόδας αὐτοῦ	τῶν ποδῶν σου
his feet	your feet

The presupposition of Paul's exegesis is that the enthronement scenario envisaged at the opening of Ps 109 LXX ("the Lord said to my lord, sit at my right hand") is

46. Davies, *Paul and Rabbinic Judaism*, 295, suggested that "the end" is "a technical phrase denoting the final consummation."

47. Important studies of Ps 110 in Christian origins include David M. Hay, *Glory at the Right Hand: Psalm 110 in Early Christianity* (Nashville: Abingdon, 1973); Jacques Dupont, "'Assis à la droite de Dieu': L'interprétation du Ps 110, 1 dans le Nouveau Testament," in *Resurrexit: Actes du Symposium international sur la résurrection de Jésus*, ed. Édouard Dhanis, Barnabas M. Ahern, and Giuseppe Ghiberti (Vatican City: Libreria Editrice Vaticana, 1974), 340–422; William R. G. Loader, "Christ at the Right Hand: Ps. XC.1 in the New Testament," *NTS* 24 (1978): 199–217; Donald H. Juel, *Messianic Exegesis: Christological Interpretation of the Old Testament in Early Christianity* (Philadelphia: Fortress, 1988), 135–50; Martin Hengel, "'Sit at My Right Hand!': The Enthronement of Christ at the Right Hand of God and Psalm 110:1," in *Studies in Early Christology* (Edinburgh: T&T Clark, 1995), 119–225.

what happened to the risen Christ. Thus, for Paul, the scenario of Ps 109 LXX is about the continued messianic career of the risen and enthroned Jesus at God's right hand before his return.[48] It is also evident that Paul has apocalypticized the psalm by identifying its "enemies" (which in context appear to be earthly opponents of Israel) with cosmic and superhuman forces (v. 24's πᾶσαν ἀρχὴν καὶ πᾶσαν ἐξουσίαν καὶ δύναμιν).[49] Paul connects the psalm directly to his interest in the resurrection of the dead by claiming that the final "enemy" (ἐχθρός)—drawing on the language of Ps 109 LXX—"is death" itself.

Paul then brings Ps 8 into the mix (v. 27), assuming that it speaks to the same reality, likely because of the linguistic and thematic parallels of putting or subjecting things "under the feet" of God's viceroy:

1 Cor 15:27	**Ps 8:7 LXX**
πάντα γὰρ	πάντα
for all things	all things
ὑπέταξεν	ὑπέταξας
he subjected	you subjected
ὑπὸ τοὺς πόδας αὐτοῦ	ὑποκάτω τῶν ποδῶν αὐτοῦ
under his feet	under his feet

The upshot of the conjunction is that the two psalms now mutually inform each other.[50] The use of Ps 8 in particular could befit Paul's aim in context to contrast the

48. Cf. Jan Lambrecht, "Paul's Christological Use of Scripture in 1 Cor 15:20–28," in *Pauline Studies*, BETL 115 (Leuven: Leuven University Press, 1994), 125–49; Wolfgang Schrage, "Das messianische Zwischenreich bei Paulus," in *Eschatologie und Schöpfung: Festschrift für Erich Grässer*, ed. Martin Evang, Helmut Merklein, and Michael Wolter, BZNW 89 (Berlin: de Gruyter, 1997), 343–54; Lidija Novakovic, *Raised from the Dead according to Scripture: The Role of Israel's Scripture in the Early Christian Interpretations of Jesus' Resurrection*, Jewish and Christian Texts in Contexts and Related Studies Series (London: Bloomsbury, 2012), 150–61.

49. Martinus C. de Boer, *The Defeat of Death: Apocalyptic Eschatology in 1 Corinthians 15 and Romans 5:12–21* (Sheffield: Sheffield Academic, 1988), has shown how punishment of the hosts of heaven and the kings of the earth are common features of traditions about the day of the Lord. In 1 En. 1.3, for instance, when the Holy One comes, the "watchers tremble." Emma Wasserman, "Gentile Gods at the Eschaton: A Reconsideration of Paul's 'Principalities and Powers' in 1 Cor. 15," *JBL* 136 (2017): 727–46, importantly reminds us that Jewish cosmology in this period could envisage lower-ranking powers who actually do God's bidding (and hence are not necessarily evil or demonic), but I am not sure that that insight clarifies what Paul is doing in 1 Cor 15:23–28.

50. Note, in particular, (1) how the "all" from Ps 8:6 LXX has found its way into Ps 109:1 LXX; (2) the "until" of Ps 109:1 has eschatologized Ps 8, such that it no longer describes what humanity/

Jesus who "makes alive" with the Adam "in whom all die" (15:21–22), since Ps 8's paean to "a son of man" and celebration of humanity's dominion over creation clearly evoke Genesis. Jesus's postresurrection activity of exercising messianic authority (Ps 109) would thus also be reclaiming humanity's adamic dominion (Ps 8).[51]

It is highly likely that there is one further witness from Israel's Scripture informing this eschatological scenario—the book of Daniel—though discerning exactly how is complex.[52] The most suggestive lines occur right before Paul alludes to the Psalms, as he is explaining what happens *after* the parousia of Jesus and the resurrection of the dead: "then the end, when he [Jesus] hands over the kingdom to God and to the Father, after he has abolished every ruler and every authority and power." In this short space, Paul refers to "the end" (τὸ τέλος), "the kingdom" (τὴν βασιλείαν), "handing over" (from παραδίδωμι), and the "destruction" (from καταργέω) of anti-God powers. Neither Ps 109 nor Ps 8 contains any of these concepts, but all four appear in Daniel.[53] The absolute use of "kingdom" without any qualifier (e.g., αὐτοῦ ["his"], χριστοῦ ["of Christ"], or θεοῦ ["of God"]) is unusual

---

Christ has, but what he will have in victory; (3) the more confrontational and combative Ps 109 has bled into the more idyllic Ps 8; (4) the creational scope of Ps 8 has broadened the reach of the "enemies" of Ps 109. The conjoining of Ps 8 and 109 appears in many other early Christian texts and may be a tradition Paul has inherited. Cf. Mark 12:35–37 and parr.; Eph 1:20–22; Phil 3:21; 1 Pet 3:22; Heb 1:13; 2:5–9. See discussion in Aquila H. I. Lee, *From Messiah to Preexistent Son: Jesus' Self-Consciousness and Early Christian Exegesis of Messianic Psalms*, WUNT 2/192 (Tübingen: Mohr Siebeck, 2005), 216–23.

51. For traditions about Adam that would support this inference, see Joel Marcus, "Son of Man as Son of Adam," *RB* 110 (2003): 38–61.

52. On the role of Dan 7 here, see Otto Betz, *Die Menschensohnworte Jesu und die Zukunftserwartung des Paulus (Daniel 7, 13–14)*, ANTJ 6 (Frankfurt am Main: Lang, 1985), 121–43; N. T. Wright, "Hope Deferred? Against the Dogma of Delay," *EC* 9 (2018): 37–82 at 62–63. Matthew V. Novenson, *Christ among the Messiahs: Christ Language in Paul and Messiah Language in Ancient Judaism* (Oxford: Oxford University Press, 2012), 143, suggests that several terms in vv. 20–28 derive "from the late-biblical apocalyptic tradition of Daniel" but does not attempt to explain how they relate to the enthronement and/or parousia of Jesus here. For a more detailed discussion, see J. Thomas Hewitt, *Messiah and Scripture*, WUNT 2/522 (Tübingen: Mohr Siebeck, 2020), 119–56. Hewitt's discussion of parallels between 1 Cor 15:20–28 and Dan 7 is quite valuable, but I am not convinced by his thesis that Paul's use of "in Christ" here assumes the notion of solidarity between the one like a son of man and the holy ones of the Most High in Dan 7. It seems to me that Hewitt's investigation gives short shrift to the more immediate parallel for "in Christ" that Paul actually identifies in these lines: "in Adam" (v. 22). Moreover, the Dan 7 connections that Hewitt himself recognizes appear more focused on Christ's activity of subduing hostile powers and the submission of all things to God than forging a connection between Jesus and believers. The notion of solidarity emerges more clearly at the end of Paul's discussion in 15:49–57 rather than here.

53. Of course, the form of Daniel known to New Testament authors is not clear. Cf. important discussions in Pierre Grelot, "Les Versions grecques de Daniel," *Bib* 47 (1966): 383–91, and more

for Paul but finds an exact parallel in both of Daniel's famous visions of the statue and stone (2:44) and the one like a son of man (7:18, 27), respectively.[54] Moreover, the idea of the bestowal of the kingdom—or its "transferability,"[55] so Joel White's term—is distinctive of Daniel,[56] and has influenced other Jewish and Christian texts in the same manner.[57] Nowhere in Daniel is there mention of the handing over of the kingdom *to God*—more on this momentarily—but the general notion of transferability is unquestionably Danielic. Daniel 2 and 7 also detail the destruction of those hostile to God (2:44; 7:11, 26), linked to the inauguration of "the kingdom" that lasts forever and ever, just as in 1 Cor 15:23–28. Finally, given Paul's interest in the resurrection of the dead in context and reference to "the end" (see also Dan 7:26: ἕως τέλους), can it be a coincidence that the book of Daniel concludes with a description of the resurrection of the dead and the coming of "the time of the end" (LXX and Theodotion have ἕως καιροῦ συντελείας)?[58]

> Many of those who sleep in the dust of the earth shall awake. . . . Those who are wise shall shine like the brightness of the sky, and those who lead many to righteousness, like the stars forever and ever. But you, Daniel, keep the words covered (סתם, LXX: κάλυψον) and the book sealed until the time of the end. (Dan 12:2–4)

When Daniel asks two angels when this will happen, he is told to go on his way, "for the words are to remain hidden [סתמים, LXX: κατακεκαλυμμένα] and sealed

recently R. Timothy McLay, "Daniel (Old Greek and Theodotion)," in *The T&T Clark Companion to the Septuagint*, ed. James K. Aitken (London: Bloomsbury T&T Clark, 2015), 544–54.

54. On the kingdom of God in Paul, see the important studies by George Johnston, "'Kingdom of God' Sayings in Paul's Letters," in *From Jesus to Paul: Studies in Honour of Francis Wright Beare*, ed. Peter Richardson and John C. Hurd (Waterloo, ON: Wilfrid Laurier University Press, 1984), 143–56; Günter Haufe, "Reich Gottes bei Paulus und in der Jesustradition," *NTS* 31 (1985): 467–72; Karl Paul Donfried, "The Kingdom of God in Paul," in *The Kingdom of God in 20th-Century Interpretation*, ed. Wendell Willis (Peabody, MA: Hendrickson, 1987), 175–90.

55. Joel White, "Anti-Imperial Subtexts in Paul: An Attempt at Building a Firmer Foundation," *Bib* 90 (2009): 327.

56. As noted by Dominic Rudman, "Authority and Right of Disposal in Luke 4.6," *NTS* 50 (2004): 77–87. See also François Bovon, *Lk 1,1–9,50*, vol. 1 of *Das Evangelium nach Lukas*, EKKNT (Zurich: Benzinger, 1989), 199.

57. Cf. my earlier study: Tucker S. Ferda, "God of the Nations: Daniel, Satan, and the Temptation of Jesus in Luke," *ZNW* 110 (2019): 1–20.

58. As noted by many, it is probable that the end of 1 Cor 15:42–51 draws on Dan 12:1–4, which was one of the most important biblical resources for the belief in the resurrection of the dead. Note especially the comparison of the resurrected to heavenly bodies; "dust of the earth"; "sleep"; and the use of ἀνάστασις throughout (cf. ἀνίστημι in Dan 12:2).

until the time of the end" (12:9). For Paul, however, we might say that, because "the appointed time has grown short" (ὁ καιρὸς συνεσταλμένος [1 Cor 7:29]) and "the end of the ages [τὰ τέλη τῶν αἰώνων] has come" (1 Cor 10:11), "the mystery that was kept secret for long ages is now disclosed and through the writings of the prophets is made known" (Rom 16:25–26).[59]

As further support for the likelihood that Daniel has informed 1 Cor 15:23–28, it is apparent in Paul's response to disputes about lawsuits in the Corinthian churches that he has spent some time with the vision of Dan 7 or traditions that emerged from it.[60] Paul rebukes the Corinthians with this passing remark: "do you not know that the holy ones [οἱ ἅγιοι] will judge [κρινοῦσιν] the world?" (1 Cor 6:2). It is widely acknowledged in the commentaries that the basis of this statement is a line from the middle of Daniel's dream vision (7:22): "the Ancient One came, then judgment (דינא) was given to the holy ones (לקדישי) of the Most High" (LXX: "gave judgment to the holy ones [τὴν κρίσιν ἔδωκε τοῖς ἁγίοις]").[61] The connections are clear and lexically distinctive. Paul's point is that, if such is the future, it is foolish for "the holy ones" now to ask "the world" for advice on solving their in-house problems. We should also note that Paul's allusion to Dan 7:22 here presupposes some knowledge of the larger dream vision in Dan 7. Paul sees a parallel between the future judgment of the holy ones and the present lawsuits in Roman civil courts, which means that he understands the future judgment with the imagery of a lawcourt (and this is explicit with the use of a compar-

59. While I think it likely that Rom 16:25–26 interacts with Dan 12, my point here does not require that these verses were original to the epistle; it is clear in many other passages that Paul believed he was living in the times that the Scriptures predicted, and that previously hidden truths have been "disclosed" (cf. Rom 3:21). Cf. here Christopher Rowland, "Paul as Apocalyptist," in *The Jewish Apocalyptic Tradition and the Shaping of New Testament Thought*, ed. Benjamin E. Reynolds and Loren T. Stuckenbruck (Minneapolis: Fortress, 2017), 131–54.

60. On Daniel in Paul, see Bernard Orchard, "St. Paul and the Book of Daniel," *Bib* 20 (1939): 172–79; Yongbom Lee, "Dominical Shame Tradition in Paul: An Allusion to Jesus' Use of Shame Language from the Book of Daniel," in *Searching the Scriptures: Studies in Context and Intertextuality*, ed. Craig A. Evans and Jeremiah J. Johnson, LNTS 543 (London: Bloomsbury T&T Clark, 2015), 234–45; Hewitt, *Messiah and Scripture*, 140–52. On Paul's knowledge of apocalyptic tradition in general, see J. P. Davies, *Paul among the Apocalypses? An Evaluation of the 'Apocalyptic Paul' in the Context of Jewish and Christian Apocalyptic Literature*, LNTS 562 (London: Bloomsbury T&T Clark, 2016); Brant Pitre, Michael P. Barber, and John A. Kincaid, *Paul, a New Covenant Jew: Rethinking Pauline Theology* (Grand Rapids: Eerdmans, 2019), 64–94.

61. Cf., e.g., C. H. Dodd, *According to the Scriptures* (London: Nisbet, 1952), 68; Hans Conzelmann, *1 Corinthians: A Commentary on the First Epistle to the Corinthians*, trans. James W. Leitch, Hermeneia (Philadelphia: Fortress, 1975), 104–5; Anthony C. Thiselton, *The First Epistle to the Corinthians: A Commentary on the Greek Text*, NIGTC (Grand Rapids: Eerdmans, 2000), 425–26; Fee, *First Epistle to the Corinthians*, 256–57.

ative in v. 2: "if the world is to be judged by you, are you incompetent for the lesser lawcourts [κριτηρίων ἐλαχίστων]?"). That lawcourt imagery for the future judgment is provided in the larger context of Dan 7:22, since the coming of the "Ancient One" (v. 22) was previously described as the moment when "the court sat [דינא יתב, LXX and Θ: κριτήριον ἐκάθισεν], and the books were opened" (v. 10).[62] Moreover, the eschatological way in which Paul frames the judgment by the holy ones presupposes the larger vision of Daniel, since at three different times in the vision and interpretation (7:1–28) the climax of the drama is the *future* bestowal of power, authority, and, in this case, judgment to the "holy ones," who are closely identified with the son of man (7:18, 22, 27). It is the account of the future giving of divine authority as described elsewhere in Dan 7—not actually rehearsed by Paul here—that makes possible the astounding claim that "the holy ones will judge the world," and the future tense of the verb.

Of course, it would be even easier to establish that Paul was well acquainted with the vision of Dan 7 if indeed 2 Thessalonians goes back to him. It is a truism that the lengthy description of what must occur before the return of Jesus (2:3–10) interacts with Daniel (and other traditions) in an intricate and nuanced way, not least Daniel's description of the arrogant "little horn" on Daniel's fourth and final beast that is ultimately destroyed.[63] However, given current dispute about the authenticity of 2 Thessalonians, I do not wish to put too much weight on it in this particular chapter on Paul.[64] Nevertheless, the case for Paul's familiarity with Dan 7 is nearly certain in 1 Cor 6, which makes it probable that Daniel is helping Paul envision the future in 1 Cor 15:23–28 as well. It is repeatedly stressed in Daniel that the destruction of forces hostile to God—whether that be the statue in chapter 2, or the beasts from the sea in chapter 7—is immediately prior to the establishment of God's kingdom and the granting of divine gifts from the Ancient One. In Dan 7 itself, the point is made three times (7:11–14, 17–18, 26–27).

62. On the significance of Daniel for final judgment imagery, note W. D. Davies and Dale C. Allison Jr., *A Critical and Exegetical Commentary on the Gospel according to Saint Matthew*, ICC (Edinburgh: T&T Clark, 1988–1997), 2:214: "Dan 7 is the Tanach's most detailed, most colorful, and most powerful picture of the great assize, and presumably any allusion to the heavenly court and the last judgment might have sent Jewish hearers, steeped as they were in the Bible, back to the *locus classicus*." See also Dale C. Allison Jr., *Jesus of Nazareth: Millenarian Prophet* (Philadelphia: Fortress, 1998), 136.

63. On Daniel in 2 Thessalonians, see Orchard, "St. Paul and the Book of Daniel," 173–79; White, "Anti-Imperial Subtexts in Paul," 332; G. K. Beale and D. A. Carson, eds., *Commentary on the New Testament Use of the Old Testament* (Grand Rapids: Baker Books, 2007), 887–88.

64. Though it is worth noting that some serious studies have begun to rethink the older consensus on this. See especially the influential essay by Paul Foster, "Who Wrote 2 Thessalonians? A Fresh Look at an Old Problem," *JSNT* 35 (2012): 150–75. I am not sure what to conclude.

The same transition is apparent in 1 Cor 15: after "his appearance," Paul describes "the end, when he hands over the kingdom to God and to the Father, when he has abolished every ruler and every authority and power." For Paul, this has not yet occurred, even if the battle for dominion described in Pss 109 and 8 is currently underway.[65] This means that, as in 1 Cor 6, Paul would be reading Daniel in a future-oriented way: it describes realities that, for him and his contemporaries, are still to come.

A question remains about Paul's interaction with Daniel. What do we make of the detail that at "the end" Christ "hands over" the kingdom *to God* (v. 25)? Daniel 7 evidently claims numerous times that authority, power, and much else "are given" to the one like a son of man (7:13–14) and the holy ones of the Most High (7:18, 22, 27), but never is the Ancient One given anything in return.[66] Where does this idea come from? The detail has been insufficiently engaged in the commentaries and related literature.[67] I see a few different possibilities here and ultimately, after much pondering, do not know what to conclude. It may be that Paul's understanding of the exaltation of Jesus according to Ps 109 has influenced his reading of Dan 7, such that he regards the arrival of the one like a son of man before the Ancient One and the "giving" of authority and power and kingship to him in 7:13–14 as having been fulfilled already by the exaltation of Jesus to "the right hand" of God (Ps 109:2 LXX).[68] On this reading, the bestowal scene in Dan 7:13–14 would be presupposed by Paul as having already occurred in heaven, which would make possible the giving *back* of the kingdom to God at "the end." The problem with this reading, though, is that the parousia in 1 Cor 15 is connected to the defeat of Israel's enemies, and in Dan 7, as noted above, the transfer scenes all *follow* the description of the destruction of Israel's enemies (note: "when he hands over the kingdom to God and to the Father, after he has abolished every ruler and every authority

65. This would be natural if Paul identified Rome in some way with the fourth and most terrible beast from the sea, which we know was a widespread interpretive move; see p. 140n21 above.

66. The point is stressed, interestingly enough, by Trypho in Justin, *Dial.* 32: "These and similar Scriptures compel us to wait for him who, as son of man, receives from the Ancient of Days the everlasting kingdom" (*ANF* 1:210). White, "Anti-Imperial Subtexts in Paul," 327, inaccurately summarizes Dan 7 here: "The 'everlasting kingdom' intriguingly changes hands a couple of times within the narrative (from God to the Son of Man to the saints and back), and it is not always easy to follow 'whose' the kingdom is at any given moment." There is no "and back" detailed in Dan 7.

67. Hewitt, *Messiah and Scripture*, does not address this either. Joseph A. Fitzmyer, *First Corinthians: A New Translation with Introduction and Commentary*, AB 32 (New Haven: Yale University Press, 2008), 572, wonders whether this notion "has been inherited from Dan 2:44."

68. See N. T. Wright, *The Climax of the Covenant: Christ and the Law in Pauline Theology* (Minneapolis: Fortress, 1993), 26–28.

and power"). Moreover, as we know from 1 Cor 6 if not elsewhere, Dan 7 for Paul is about the final judgment, something that had not yet occurred, and in Dan 7, the arrival of the one like a son of man roughly coincides with the judgment.[69]

Another possibility that I have not seen seriously entertained before is that the odd giving back of the kingdom to God is itself Paul's summary of Dan 7:13–14 and the presentation of the one like a son of man to God after the defeat of Israel's enemies (thus, still in the future). On this reading, Dan 7:13–14 would indeed describe the parousia and its sequel in the final judgment.[70] But it would idiosyncratically, and surely contrary to the original aim of Dan 7, regard *God* as the recipient of the litany of prerogatives in v. 14.[71] That would, however, be a grammatically possible reading.[72] Daniel 7:14 mentions that authority and glory and much else (our versions disagree on the details) "were given to him" (לה יהיב, LXX: ἐδόθη αὐτῷ, and Θ: αὐτῷ ἐδόθη), while the subject of the verb and the indirect object are unspecified. Both the Ancient One and the one like a son of man appear in v. 13 as potential antecedents.

69. One further text that might support this particular constellation of events is 2 Cor 4:14. According to the NRSV, Paul encourages confidence "because we know that the one who raised the Lord Jesus will raise us also with Jesus, and will bring us with you into his presence." This is not the best translation as it disguises what is likely an underlying connection with Dan 7 here. What Paul wrote is this: ὁ ἐγείρας τὸν κύριον Ἰησοῦν καὶ ἡμᾶς σὺν Ἰησοῦ ἐγερεῖ καὶ παραστήσει σὺν ὑμῖν, which I would translate woodenly, "the one who raised the Lord Jesus will also raise us with Jesus and [*God*] *will present* [*us*] *with you*." Not only does the verb παρίστημι—to make present or publicly display—presuppose a larger setting and series of actions (note this is not a noun as in the NRSV's "presence") that is not actually provided here by Paul, it is the same verb used in Dan 7:13 LXX where the one like a son of man *and others* "were presented" before God at the time of judgment (παρῆσαν αὐτῷ, Θ has ἐνώπιον αὐτοῦ προσηνέχθη). We should further notice that, in 2 Cor 4, Paul is talking about what happens after the resurrection of the dead—so a sure parallel to 1 Cor 15—and he is clearly thinking about the final judgment as well, mentioning only a few lines later "all of us must appear before τοῦ βήματος [the judgment seat] of Christ" (5:10). In this context, note 1 En. 62.8 ("the elect ones shall stand before him [the son of man]) and Luke 21:36 ("in order that you may stand before the son of man").

70. Betz, *Die Menschensohnworte Jesu und die Zukunftserwartung des Paulus*, 130–31, has argued that the use of παρουσία in 1 Cor 15 looks back to Dan 7:13, as the nominal form of the verb πάρειμι appears in the LXX. He also argues use of ἡ παρουσία τοῦ υἱοῦ τοῦ ἀνθρώπου in Matt 24:27 as a summary statement functions in the same way. Matthew Goff, "The Mystery of God's Wisdom, the Parousia of a Messiah, and Visions of Heavenly Paradise," in Reynolds and Stuckenbruck, *Jewish Apocalyptic Tradition and the Shaping of New Testament Thought*, 183, also wonders whether Paul's use of παρουσία here is "a reflex of Danielic tradition."

71. Also noted by Betz, *Die Menschensohnworte Jesu und die Zukunftserwartung des Paulus*, 135.

72. Betz, *Die Menschensohnworte Jesu und die Zukunftserwartung des Paulus*, 135, arrives at a similar place but on different grounds: he has Paul working with the Aramaic and has turned the passive יהיב into an active participle (which he calls "grammatikalisch ohne weiteres möglich").

One further possibility still is that 1 Cor 15:25 is a case of Paul imagining a future with the help of Scripture but in ways that go beyond what any of the texts he references actually state. Daniel 7, Ps 109, and Ps 8 would all end in a place that Paul evidently does not want to: the sharing of divine prerogatives with the one like a son of man and holy ones of the Most High (Dan 7), the ruling of David's "lord" (Ps 109), and the dominion of "a son of man" (Ps 8). For Paul, one might surmise, these are but the penultimate acts. At the end, after the parousia of Jesus and the destruction of those forces opposed to God (15:25), God's authority must be returned, not least from "the son himself" (v. 28). In the same way that the juxtaposition of these different passages from Scripture has meant that they now mutually inform each other, it could be that Paul's view of God has encouraged him to look beyond the vision from Dan 7, and the Psalms, to imagine what comes next.[73] It is also possible, of course, that he is simply dependent on tradition we do not know about.

I do not know what to conclude about this matter, even if I think it highly probable that Dan 7 is in the background somewhere. The more frustrating conclusion is probably the more honest one in this case: as evident by the condensed and abbreviated manner with which Paul presents these details, not least the exegesis of the Psalms, we are surely only seeing in 1 Cor 15 Paul's CliffsNotes on an eschatological scenario that he has evidently thought about before in much more detail, and we have insufficient knowledge of the eschatological background and traditions that might have informed him. There will inevitably be blanks and gaps in our understanding of his exegetical logic, and 1 Cor 15:25 may well be one such case.

1 Thessalonians 4 and 1 Corinthians 15 Compared

We can be more confident in our other conclusions. Were we to compare 1 Cor 15 to 1 Thess 4–5, we might say that 1 Cor 15 views the end-time appearance of Jesus through a wider lens though in a lower magnification. In 1 Corinthians, the parou-

73. The cryptic end of the account of Daniel's vision could easily lead one to think that there is more to come that is not narrated here: "Here the account ends. As for me, Daniel, my thoughts terrified me" (7:28). Ending with divine sovereignty could also be an eschatological topos: the end is like the beginning. Note 1QM VI, 6: "then shall the kingdom belong to the God of Israel, and he will show his power among the holy hosts." See also the much-later Tg. Esth. 1.1, which concludes its rehearsal of the "ten kingdoms" to come in history with this: "The ninth [is] that of the son of David, the Messiah, the tenth [is] that of the Lord of Hosts again, may it be speedily revealed to all the inhabitants of the earth" (trans. *ArBib* 18:96–97).

sia itself is described in the barest of terms—"then those who belong to Christ in his parousia [ἐν τῇ παρουσίᾳ αὐτοῦ]" (15:23)—but we learn more about the bigger story that Paul believes that future coming brings to completion. For Paul, the parousia is essential to a larger divine drama that encompasses Jesus's messianic "reign" at God's right hand and the defeat of God's "enemies." In 1 Cor 15, the "day of the Lord" imagery is not as pronounced as it was in 1 Thess 4–5, but the function of Jesus's return in 1 Cor 15 is much the same in terms of what it accomplishes in salvation history.[74] The parousia for Paul is not a symbolic way to describe the destruction of Jerusalem, the rise of the church, or the bestowal of the Spirit.[75] The parousia is not synonymous with Jesus's resurrection and exaltation to God's right hand; these are clearly differentiated events for Paul that periodize different stages of eschatological time. Rather, for Paul the end-time appearance of Christ is intimately bound up with the resurrection of the dead, the establishment of God's "kingdom," and the reordering of a rebellious creation under God's care (15:26–28). Paul expects a miraculous and transformative event that will decisively shape world history as otherwise experienced, and he appears to believe that some people then living would be alive to experience it.[76]

Eschatology and Mystery in Romans 11

We should make note of one further text from Rom 11 that likely corroborates the general picture that emerges from 1 Thess 4–5 and 1 Cor 15, although, interestingly enough, its description of the parousia draws on different scriptural subtexts still. Also, unlike 1 Thess 4–5 and 1 Cor 15, there is some debate among exegetes about whether Paul even has the parousia in view here (while the majority think that he does).[77] In any case, the key passage appears near the end of Paul's discussion of

74. However, per the combative imagery of 1 Cor 15, the "day of the Lord" tradition often identifies God as the leader of heavenly armies. See Joseph Plevnik, *Paul and the Parousia: An Exegetical and Theological Investigation* (Eugene, OR: Wipf & Stock, 2014), 247.

75. Cf. Allison, *Jesus of Nazareth*, 160: "Paul did not interpret the tradition behind Mk 13:24–27 as does N. T. Wright, that is, as a symbolic prophecy of Jerusalem's destruction."

76. Contra Andrew C. Perriman, "Paul and the Parousia: 1 Corinthians 15:50–57 and 2 Corinthians 5:1–5," *NTS* 35 (1989): 512–21. On the transformative nature of the new age, see Karina Hogan, "The Apocalyptic Eschatology of Romans: Creation, Judgment, Resurrection, and Glory," in Reynolds and Stuckenbruck, *Jewish Apocalyptic Tradition and the Shaping of New Testament Thought*, 157–63.

77. For the common view that Paul has the parousia of Jesus in mind here, see C. E. B. Cranfield, *A Critical and Exegetical Commentary on the Epistle to the Romans* (Edinburgh: T&T Clark, 1979), 2:578; Richard H. Bell, *The Irrevocable Call of God: An Inquiry into Paul's Theology*

the rejection of the gospel and the fate of Israel in Rom 9–11, wherein he unveils a great mystery (11:25–27):

> I do not want you to be ignorant, brothers and sisters, about this mystery . . . that a hardening has happened to part of Israel until the fullness of the gentiles has come in, and in this way all Israel will be saved, just as it is written:
>
> > The redeemer will come from Zion [ἥξει ἐκ Σιὼν ὁ ῥυόμενος],
> > he will turn back ungodliness [ἀποστρέψει ἀσεβείας] from Jacob.
> > And this is my covenant with them,
> > when I take away their sins [ἀφέλωμαι τὰς ἁμαρτίας αὐτῶν].

We learn something remarkable from this passage that might not be evident from 1 Thess 4–5 or 1 Cor 15 alone: Paul believes that the "the fullness of the gentiles coming in" and the subsequent salvation of "all Israel" fulfills scriptural prophecies (v. 26's καθὼς γέγραπται) that pertain (he believes) to the future return of Jesus.[78]

---

of Israel, WUNT 184 (Tübingen: Mohr Siebeck, 2005), 267; James D. G. Dunn, *Romans*, WBC 38 (Nashville: Nelson, 1988), 2:682–83; Robert Jewett, *Romans: A Commentary*, Hermeneia (Minneapolis: Fortress, 2007), 703–5; Christopher D. Stanley, "'The Redeemer Will Come ἐκ Σιών': Romans 11.26–27 Revisited," in *Paul and the Scriptures of Israel*, ed. Craig A. Evans and James A. Sanders (London: Bloomsbury: 2015), 118–42.

78. One perplexing feature of Paul's citation of Isaiah (more on this below) is the description of the redeemer coming ἐκ Σιών rather than ἕνεκεν Σιών ("in behalf of Zion"), which is central to the debate about whether Paul is referring to the parousia in these lines. As Paul's ἐκ Σιών agrees with no extant Greek version of Isaiah, what is the reason for the difference? Most probable to my mind is one of three options: (1) the change is unintentional and does not signal a significant deviation in meaning from Isa 59:20 LXX, (2) Paul has in mind Jesus coming from the *heavenly* Jerusalem/Zion (cf. Gal 4:26–27, where there is also a citation of a Zion text from Isaiah [54:1]), or (3) the change is, whether intentionally or unintentionally, influenced by the far more popular use of ἐκ Σιών when referring to the eschatological restoration of Jerusalem. In any case, either 1, 2, or 3, the parousia remains in view, suggested by the future tense verbs that stand in parallel: "all Israel will be saved [σωθήσεται (something that obviously has not yet happened in Paul's time)], just as it is written, 'the redeemer will come [ἥξει (something that also, then, most likely, has not yet happened in Paul's time)].'" J. R. Daniel Kirk, "Why Does the Deliverer Come ἐκ Σιών (Romans 11.26)?," *JSNT* 33 (2010): 87, is forced to an awkward position when he must argue that the first future verb in the citation (ἥξει) refers to Jesus's ministry in the past, while the future "turning back" (ἀποστρέψει) of ungodliness from Jacob refers to the future. Nevertheless, Kirk's thesis remains preferable to Peter Walker, *Jesus and the Holy City: New Testament Perspectives on Jerusalem* (Grand Rapids: Eerdmans, 1996), 139–42, and N. T. Wright, *Paul and the Faithfulness of God* (Minneapolis: Fortress, 2013), 1234, 1246–52, who find realized eschatology in the whole and believe that Paul is merely talking about Jesus's past ministry and its effects.

That is to say, although Paul had not yet mentioned the return of Jesus in his discussion in Rom 9–11, it is probable that he regards the parousia as the climactic event that will resolve any of the seeming tensions he has been working through since the beginning of chapter 9 concerning the rejection of the gospel and the faithfulness of God to the covenant with Israel.[79] We can make this point without having to resolve or even weigh in on the debated questions about what Paul means by "the fullness of the gentiles" and "all Israel will be saved."[80] However one defines those crucial phrases, it is sufficient for our purposes to note that Paul is thinking of significant events that carry major salvation-historical consequence, and he sees the return of Jesus as a key mechanism by which such outstanding hopes will come to pass. If in 1 Cor 15 Paul shares that Jesus's return culminates his victory over cosmic and superhuman forces, in Rom 11 Paul shares that his return also solves the plight of Israel's rejection of the gospel and accomplishes God's plans for redemption history.

Isaiah and the Future

When we look more closely at the citations from Scripture that Paul provides here, we can understand why he thinks the return of Christ is related to "the fulness of the gentiles coming in" and "all Israel will be saved." We also observe that his scriptural exegesis is not haphazard or piecemeal; he appears to be aware of the larger contexts of these cited lines.[81] Paul strings together two passages from Isaiah, the first from Isa 59:20, almost identical in wording to the LXX (with the exception of ἐκ Σιών, as noted above in note 78):

79. It is not important for my purposes to reconstruct the way in which Paul composed Rom 9–11 (e.g., does Paul end in chapter 11 where he expected at the outset of chapter 9?). There may well have been some discovery in the process of dictating, though I find it implausible that Paul had never thought through the questions animating Rom 9–11 before. In any case, the adventurous thesis of Bent Noack, "Current and Backwater in the Epistle to the Romans," *ST* 19 (1965): 155–66, that Paul thought he received 11:25–26 as a revelation at the moment of composition, has convinced few.

80. For discussion and literature, see Christopher Zoccali, "'And So All Israel Will Be Saved': Competing Interpretations of Romans 11.26 in Pauline Scholarship," *JSNT* 30 (2008): 289–318; John K. Goodrich, "Until the Fullness of the Gentiles Comes In: A Critical Review of Recent Scholarship on the Salvation of 'All Israel' (Romans 11:26)," *JSPL* 6 (2016): 5–32.

81. Cf. J. Ross Wagner, *Heralds of the Good News: Isaiah and Paul 'in Concert' in the Letter to the Romans*, NovTSup 101 (Leiden: Brill, 2002), 23–33, 286–87.

Paul: ἥξει ἐκ Σιὼν ὁ ῥυόμενος,
The redeemer will come from Zion

ἀποστρέψει ἀσεβείας ἀπὸ Ἰακώβ
he will turn back ungodliness from Jacob

καὶ αὕτη αὐτοῖς ἡ παρ᾽ ἐμοῦ διαθήκη
and this is my covenant with them

Isa 59:20–21 LXX: ἥξει ἕνεκεν Σιὼν ὁ ῥυόμενος καὶ
the redeemer will come in behalf of Zion and

ἀποστρέψει ἀσεβείας ἀπὸ Ιακωβ
he will turn back ungodliness from Jacob

καὶ αὕτη αὐτοῖς ἡ παρ᾽ ἐμοῦ διαθήκη
and this is my covenant with them

He then adds one more line that, as noted by many, likely comes from an earlier oracle in Isaiah (27:19):[82]

Rom 11:27:	ὅταν	ἀφέλωμαι	τὰς ἁμαρτίας αὐτῶν
	When	I take away	their sins
Isa 27:9 LXX:	ὅταν	ἀφέλωμαι	αὐτοῦ τὴν ἁμαρτίαν
	When	I take away	his [Jacob's] sin

82. See Otto Michel, *Paulus und seine Bibel* (Darmstadt: Wissenschaftliche Buchgesellschaft, 1972), 281; Plevnik, *Paul and the Parousia*, 684. Some have thought that there is also an allusion to Jeremiah's new covenant:

Paul:	αὕτη αὐτοῖς	ἡ παρ᾽ ἐμοῦ	διαθήκη
Jer 38:33 LXX (31:33 MT):	αὕτη	ἡ	διαθήκη ἣν διαθήσομαι τῷ οἴκῳ Ισραηλ

It is an intriguing possibility, especially given Paul's interaction with this oracle elsewhere. See Richard B. Hays, *Echoes of Scripture in the Letters of Paul* (New Haven: Yale University Press, 1989), 122–53; Pitre, Barber, and Kincaid, *Paul, a New Covenant Jew*, 39–48. But the final line καὶ αὕτη αὐτοῖς ἡ παρ᾽ ἐμοῦ διαθήκη is identical to Isa 59:20 LXX, and so there is no need to think Jer 31 is in play to make sense of the citation in Paul.

The citation from Isa 27:9 functions to repeat and intensify the notion from Isa 59:20 that the coming of Jesus results in the removal of sin (ἀσέβεια in Isa 59 and ἁμαρτία in Isa 27) from Israel. But there are many other connections between these oracles in their original contexts. Both Isaianic oracles in chapters 27 and 59 anticipate the redemption of Israel (and the elimination of Israel's sinfulness and disobedience), the ingathering of the tribes of Jacob, and the conversion of the nations. What is more, both oracles sketch in detail a similar salvation-historical plight: Israel is mired in sin and fails to keep the covenant. In Isa 59, the prophet laments that Israel's iniquities "have been barriers" and "hidden God's face" (59:2). What is to be done? It is worth citing the key transition from Isa 59:15–20 in full (trans. NETS):

> The Lord saw it, and it did not please him
> that there was no judgment.
> And he saw, and there was no man,
> and he took notice, and there was none who helped;
> so he defended them with his own arm,
> and with his compassion he upheld them.
> And he put on righteousness like a breastplate
> and placed a helmet of salvation on his head,
> and he clothed himself with a garment of vengeance
> and with his cloak,
> as one about to render retribution,
> reproach to his adversaries.
> And those from the west shall fear the name of the Lord,
> and those from the rising of the sun, his glorious name,
> for anger will come from the Lord like a rushing river—
> it will come like wrath.
> And the one who delivers will come for Zion's sake,
> and he will turn impiety away from Jacob.

In other words, when there was "no man" and "none who helped," God acted anyway. In Isa 27, we find a similar scenario: the Lord is the subject of all the main verbs. It is easy to see how Paul could believe the Scriptures anticipate his own situation: most of Israel has rejected the gospel, and there is little hope of that changing in the near future. What will be the fix? "The deliverer will come from Zion [ἥξει ἐκ Σιὼν ὁ ῥυόμενος], he will turn back ungodliness [ἀποστρέψει ἀσεβείας] from Jacob . . . [and] take away their sins."[83] If one thinks of the larger argumenta-

83. Paul is clearly dependent on the Septuagint here, which differs from the Hebrew in some

tive sweep of Romans, there is an interesting parallel here between the revelation of the gospel in 3:21 and the future coming of Christ in 11:25–27. In both cases, these two revelations follow and serve to resolve cases of seeming hopelessness: the fact that all are captive to "the power of sin" (3:9), on the one hand, and that Israel has by and large rejected the gospel (9:1–5), on the other. In fact, Paul defines the pregospel state in Rom 3:15–17 with lines drawn directly from the more somber and depressing portion of Isa 59's oracle about the coming of the Lord—*before* the description of that coming (see 59:7).[84] Nevertheless, in the revelation of the gospel (3:21–26), God acts anyway to repair what was broken. Paul seems to expect that, at Christ's future coming, the end will be like the beginning.

It is also important to stress the structural significance of these Isaiah oracles in their original contexts, especially the main passage that Paul cites from Isa 59. The line Paul cites from Isa 59:20–21 about the coming of God appears at the end of a rather extensive discourse on Israel's disobedience and faithlessness that stems all the way back to chapter 56. Indeed, near three chapters of text before 59:15–21 are a consistent lament of Israel's waywardness that is at times despairing. But that tone and focus changes markedly after the description of the intervention of God's own "arm" (59:16–21). The coming of God to banish ungodliness from Jacob issues in a series of subsequent oracles about the restoration of Zion, the ingathering of the tribes of Jacob, and the conversation of the nations—these are the same chess pieces that emerge in Rom 11:25–27. The coming of the Lord in Isa 27 also results in the restoration of Israel and the ingathering of the exiles (and it is worth noting that the larger oracle of which this is a part also mentions the resurrection of the dead [26:19; cf. also 25:7–8, which Paul cites in 1 Cor 15:54–55]).[85]

Perhaps the most distinctive feature of Paul's exegesis is the way in which he has identified in both oracles the coming of the God of Israel with the coming of Jesus, "the deliverer" (ὁ ῥυόμενος). He may not be completely without a traditional basis for this move in Jewish messianic speculation, since Isa 59 also emerges in a later rabbinic discussion about the coming of the messiah after a time of distress.[86] We also find the restoration of Jerusalem and the coming of the messiah linked to-

---

interesting respects. See discussion in Wagner, *Heralds of the Good News*, 280–83. The MT places the accent on Israel's agency, whereas the LXX emphasizes God's action, as elsewhere in this and previous oracles in Isaiah.

84. Also noted by Wagner, *Heralds of the Good News*, 287–88.

85. Similar messianic speculation can be found elsewhere. Cf. the LXX's rewriting of Moses's blessing at Deut 33:4–5 ("there will be a ruler in the beloved, when the rulers of the nations are gathered together at one time with the tribes of Israel"), and also in Tg. Neof. and Frg. Tg. ad loc.

86. Cf. b. Sanh. 98a: "Rabbi Yohanan says: If you saw a generation whose troubles inundate it like a river, await the coming of the messiah, as it is stated: 'When distress will come like a

gether in the Eighteen Benedictions, as the fourteenth reads, "Have mercy, O Lord our God, on Jerusalem your city and on Zion the dwelling place of your glory and on the kingdom of the house of David your righteous Messiah. Blessed are you, O Lord God of David, who builds Jerusalem."[87] The mention of "mercy" in the Palestinian recension is intriguing in light of the conspicuous emphasis on the mercy and compassion of God in Rom 9–11 (cf. 9:23; 11:31; and 12:1 as summary of the previous: "I appeal to you therefore . . . on account of the mercies of God [διὰ τῶν οἰκτιρμῶν]").[88] In any case, this christological exegesis is attested elsewhere in Paul and in some ways takes us back to the beginning of our discussion on 1 Thessalonians. In Paul's first-known epistle, it was evident that Paul identified the coming of the Lord from Zechariah (14:5) with the future coming of Jesus (1 Thess 3:13), which makes sense because in 1 Thess 5:2 he explicitly links "the day of the Lord" with the coming of Jesus.[89] The association between the two allows for a sharing of roles and the reuse of biblical imagery. Paul also identified Jesus as "the deliverer" in 1:10 (a participial form of ῥύομαι)—the same term used in Rom 11:26—who delivers "from the coming wrath" that is expected on the day of the Lord. It is surely no coincidence, then, that the larger oracle of Isa 27 that Paul draws from to predict the return of Jesus is expressly said to describe "that day" (cf. 27:1, 2, 6, 12; see also 26:1). There is a broad and consistent interpretive pattern in Paul of identifying the coming of Jesus with the coming of God on the day of the Lord that will be important for our discussion going forward.

In sum, Rom 11:25–27 is brief and cryptic but points to the climactic and salvation-historical significance of the return of Jesus in Paul's eschatology. Here we learn that the future coming of Jesus would not just initiate the resurrection of the dead (1 Thess 4) and eliminate any remaining cosmic rebellion to the rule of God (1 Cor 15); it would restore the proper covenant relationship between God, Israel, and the nations. It also suggests, though this is less clear, that Jerusalem

river that the breath of the Lord drives' (Isa 59:10), and juxtaposed to it is 'And a redeemer will come to Zion' (Isa 59:20)."

87. For the Hebrew text, see Craig A. Evans, *Jesus and His Contemporaries: Comparative Studies*, AGJU 25 (Leiden: Brill, 1995), 277–80. On the question of dating the Benedictions, see Rainer Riesner, "Vom Messias Jesus zum christlichen Bekenntnis: Jüdische Voraussetzungen und judenchristliche Überlieferungen," *TBei* 32 (2001): 373–92; David Instone-Brewer, "The Eighteen Benedictions and the Minim before 70 CE," *JTS* 54 (2003): 25–44; Joel Marcus, "Birkat Ha-Minim Revisited," *NTS* 55 (2009): 523–51.

88. The potential parallel may further support the thesis of Susan Eastman, "Israel and the Mercy of God: A Re-reading of Galatians 6.16 and Romans 9–11," *NTS* 56 (2010): 367–95, at least for her reading of Romans.

89. Wendebourg, *Der Tag des Herrn*, 158–67.

maintains an important position in Paul's end-time scenario.[90] Paul's larger discussion in Rom 9–11 does not proceed much beyond vv. 25–27, because the return of Jesus is the answer to his question.[91]

Elsewhere in Paul

The rest of Paul's corpus fails to provide further explicit details about the parousia as we find in 1 Thess 4–5, 1 Cor 15, and Rom 11. But it is evident that the other letters are written with very similar eschatological assumptions about the importance of this event.[92] Indeed, we find in every epistle but Galatians and Philemon not only clear statements about Jesus's future appearance but also the rhetorical and formal fact that the expectation is never something that Paul needs to instruct his churches about for the first time in his letters. It comes up by way of reminder. Paul everywhere assumes that his hearers already know and expect the same, as in the following examples:

- 1 Cor 1:6–7: "the testimony of Christ has been strengthened among you, so that you are not lacking in any spiritual gift as you wait for the revealing of our Lord Jesus Christ [ἀπεκδεχομένους τὴν ἀποκάλυψιν τοῦ κυρίου ἡμῶν Ἰησοῦ Χριστοῦ]."[93]
- 2 Cor 1:13–14: "For we write you nothing other than what you can read and also understand; I hope you will understand until the end, as you have already

90. As also in Jub. 31.11–20; Pss. Sol. 17.30–31; 1 En. 26.1–27.5; 2 Bar. 71–73. Cf. discussion and secondary literature in Peter Stuhlmacher, "Die Stellung Jesu und des Paulus zu Jerusalem: Versuch einer Erinnerung," *ZNW* 86 (1989): 140–56, and Samuel Auler, "More Than a Gift: Revisiting Paul's Collection for Jerusalem and the Pilgrimage of Gentiles," *JSPL* 6 (2016): 142–60. The uncertainty in this case stems from the fact that the "from Zion" mentioned by Paul could refer to the heavenly Jerusalem; see p. 160n78 above.

91. Though this is not to say that Paul had worked out exactly "how the Parousia of Christ was related to Israel's final conversion," so rightly Dunn, *Romans*, 2:680.

92. For wider discussion of the parousia in Paul's letters, see Kreitzer, *Jesus and God in Paul's Eschatology*, 93–130; James D. G. Dunn, *The Theology of Paul the Apostle* (Grand Rapids: Eerdmans, 1998), 294–315; Vena, *Parousia and Its Rereadings*, 115–74; Sanders, *Paul: Life, Letters, and Thought*, 379–82; Eve-Marie Becker, "Eschatology: Pauline and Catholic Epistles," in *Eschatology in Antiquity: Forms and Functions*, ed. Hilary Marlow, Karla Pollmann, and Helen Van Noorden (London: Routledge, 2021), 409–21; Michael Wolter, *Paulus: Ein Grundriss seiner Theologie* (Göttingen: Vandenhoeck & Ruprecht, 2021), 182–226.

93. See also 1 Cor 1:8; 3:13; 4:5; 7:29 (on the shortness of the time); 10:11 (on living in the ends of the ages); 11:26.

understood us in part, that on the day of the Lord Jesus [ἐν τῇ ἡμέρᾳ τοῦ κυρίου Ἰησοῦ] we are your boast even as you are our boast."[94]

- Phil 3:20–21: "But our citizenship is in heaven, and it is from there we are also expecting a Savior, the Lord Jesus Christ [ἐξ οὗ καὶ σωτῆρα ἀπεκδεχόμεθα κύριον Ἰησοῦν Χριστόν]. He will transform the body of our humiliation that it may be conformed to the body of his glory, by the power that also enables him to make all things subject to himself."[95]
- Col 3:1–4: "if you have been raised with Christ, seek the things that are above, where Christ is, seated at the right hand of God. Set your minds on things that are above, not on things on earth, for you have died, and your life is hidden with Christ in God. When Christ who is your life is revealed, then you also will be revealed with him in glory [ὅταν ὁ Χριστὸς φανερωθῇ, ἡ ζωὴ ὑμῶν, τότε καὶ ὑμεῖς σὺν αὐτῷ φανερωθήσεσθε ἐν δόξῃ]."

Some of the details about the parousia we hear about in the letters to Thessalonica, Corinth, and Rome may be idiosyncratic and uniquely shared in those settings. It may also be that Paul's thought developed some on the matter over the course of his ministry.[96] But it is evident throughout the entire Pauline corpus that the general hope for Christ's return was a fundamental element of Paul's kerygma. While I disagree with certain exegetical and historical moves in Josef Plevnik's magisterial study, *Paul and the Parousia*, his main conclusion is indisputable: "the Lord's coming is a constituent and permanent part of the Christian faith in the development of Paul's thought."[97] Paul even assumes this hope in churches he did not found, such as in Rome, where he asserts that God will judge people on "the day" through Christ (2:15–16), that salvation "is nearer to us now than when we first believed" (13:11), and that, before one can "be glorified with him," it is necessary to suffer with him (8:17).[98] Paul finds no need to defend himself or even

94. Cf. 2 Cor 5:10.

95. Parallels in this terse description to 1 Cor 15:23–28 are patent. Cf. Phil 4:5.

96. See the famous studies by C. H. Dodd, "The Mind of Paul: I," and "The Mind of Paul: II," in *New Testament Studies* (Manchester: Manchester University Press, 1953), 67–82, 83–128. For further discussion and literature, see Christof Landmesser, "Die Entwicklung der paulinischen Theologie und die Frage nach der Eschatologie," in *Eschatologie—Eschatology: The Sixth Durham-Tübingen Research Symposium; Eschatology in Old Testament, Ancient Judaism and Early Christianity*, ed. Hans-Joachim Eckstein, Christof Landmesser, and Hermann Lichtenberger, WUNT 272 (Tübingen: Mohr Siebeck, 2011), 173–94.

97. Plevnik, *Paul and the Parousia*, xl. See also Brown, "Paul and the Parousia," 51: the return of Jesus is "fundamental to his theological vision, inextricable from his gospel, and pastorally operative even where it is not explicitly narrated."

98. On the reference to Christ being glorified in the future as an allusion to his future coming

present arguments on these matters. The lack of defense and argument here and elsewhere probably explains why the topic never arises in Galatians: Paul's opponents had no major disagreement with him—nor he with them—over Christ's future coming.[99] At issue was the interim: now, before that return, how ought the gentiles be included?

Paul's other letters also are clear to connect the return of Christ to the final judgment (e.g., 2 Cor 5:10: "all of us must appear before the judgment seat of Christ [ἔμπροσθεν τοῦ βήματος τοῦ Χριστοῦ] so that each may receive recompense for what has been done in the body, whether good or evil"; cf. Rom 2:15–16 [judgment on that day "through Jesus Christ"]; 8:34 [Christ is the only ὁ κατακρινῶν]; Phil 1:6, 10 [be pure and blameless "on the day of Christ"]).[100] This point is not made explicitly in 1 Thess 4 and 1 Cor 15, but we are surely not very far away conceptually, as both letters link the parousia to the resurrection of the dead. This matter again appears to have been fundamental instruction in the churches, already by the time of 1 Thessalonians.[101] That point is not particularly controversial in Pauline studies and has been extensively researched.[102]

As historians, we can be thankful that some in Paul's churches were confused about the state of the dead (1 Thessalonians), the nature of the resurrection (1 Corinthians), and the fate of Israel (Rom 11), because it created the need for Paul to explain what he knew about the parousia of Jesus that he otherwise would have had no reason to share. In that respect, these occasional documents are crucial sources for reconstructing Christian origins. They do not present only Paul's views on these eschatological matters; they provide a glimpse into the nature of eschatological

in 8:17, cf. Phil 3:20–21: "our citizenship is in heaven, and it is from there that we are expecting a Savior [ἐξ οὗ καὶ σωτῆρα ἀπεκδεχόμεθα], the Lord Jesus Christ. He will transform the body of our humiliation that it may be conformed to the body of his glory." See also 1 Cor 15:23–41. On the importance of Romans for understanding early Christian diversity of belief, see Jeffrey Peterson, "The Extent of Christian Theological Diversity," *ResQ* 47 (2005): 1–12 at 9–10.

99. Cf. 5:21, which mentions "inheriting" the "kingdom of God" as a future event. See Richard Longenecker, *Galatians*, WBC 41 (Dallas: Word, 1990), 258. It is common to explain the lack of parousia discussion in Galatians to be due to the contingent circumstances of the epistle. See Yon-Gyong Kwon, *Eschatology in Galatians*, WUNT 183 (Tübingen: Mohr Siebeck, 2004), 18–19, 216–17.

100. See John M. G. Barclay, "Believers and the 'Last Judgment' in Paul: Rethinking Grace and Recompense," in Eckstein, Landmesser, and Lichtenberger, *Eschatologie—Eschatology*, 195–208.

101. Why pray that "your spirit and soul and body be kept sound and blameless at the coming of our Lord Jesus Christ [ἐν τῇ παρουσίᾳ τοῦ κυρίου ἡμῶν]" (1 Thess 5:23)? Because the coming of the Lord marks the time of judgment.

102. Cf. Froitzheim, *Christologie und Eschatologie bei Paulus*, 170–71, and the larger study by Brendan Byrne, *Paul and the Economy of Salvation: Reading from the Perspective of the Last Judgment* (Grand Rapids: Baker Books, 2021).

conversation in those earliest decades of the church. Any historical reconstruction of Christian origins needs to account not only for Paul but for the larger situation in which Paul engaged in his ministry of founding and leading new churches. In that environment of intense contestation and debate about a host of topics, there appears to have at least been some widespread agreement about one thing in particular: Jesus will soon appear again, and so the world must get ready. The fact of that larger situation would make good sense if what Paul asserts in 1 Thess 4 about "the word of the Lord" is not as misleading as so many historians in the past two centuries have assumed. But here I would be getting ahead of myself.

9

Jesus and the Future in Mark

The Gospels of Mark, Matthew, and Luke, written decades after the ministry of Paul, aim to and surely do tell us a great deal more about the teaching of Jesus than what we can glean from Paul's occasional letters. But our initial approach to these texts will be the same as our approach to Paul: our question at this point is not what the historical Jesus actually taught about the future but what these texts—creative and intertextually dense narratives with particular theological aims—*claim* about Jesus and the future. I will not seek to answer that question by going immediately for specific texts thought historical (so an atomistic approach) or treating the gospel tradition as a synchronic whole by gathering shared eschatological topoi irrespective of their original placement and context and function (so a thematic approach). I will, instead, treat each of the Gospels individually, on their own terms, and holistically as ideological stories about Jesus. Thus, when we do come to specific texts—and we will look at several—we will not find ourselves in Glasson's and Robinson's precarious situation of overlooking how the very source that contains these verses understood them. I begin with Mark.[1]

1. In what follows, I refer to the writers of the Gospels by their canonical names, but I do not assume anything about the historical reliability of those traditional claims. Moreover, I assume here Markan priority, which has few serious detractors. Andreas Lindemann, "Kommentare zum Markusevangelium 2000–2017," *TRu* 83 (2018): 217–73, shows that among the many points of debate in commentaries of Mark published the last two decades, Markan priority is not one of them.

Story and Time

The first thing to say about Mark's Gospel, written sometime in the throes of the Jewish War with Rome,[2] is that its story is self-consciously aware of its placement in an in-between time after the ministry of Christ and before (I will argue) his imminent return in glory. The narrative thus assumes a particular perspective on time and salvation history, and it tells the story of Jesus from within it.[3] Studies of an already/not-yet eschatological tension in the Gospel of Mark typically focus on the content Mark wishes to relate about Jesus and his ministry in the past, but the already/not-yet includes the very time of Mark's first readers as well.[4] Mark's account both lays stress on what Jesus accomplished in his earthly ministry—in the readers' past—and frequently provides explicit predictions—and subtle foreshadowing—of what is still to take place in the readers' future. Making these assumptions explicit will enable us to better situate this witness to Jesus alongside other sources, including the writings of Paul, as we think of Mark not just for Mark's sake but as part of our larger effort to understand the second advent hope in Christian origins.[5]

For Mark, the accomplishments of Jesus in the readers' past are straightforward. The gospel begins with a catena of scriptural citations, claiming that the "beginning of the gospel" is "just as" the Scriptures foretold. More specifically, the

2. Whether slightly before or after the destruction of the temple does not impact my reading in a notable way. For discussion, see Joel Marcus, *Mark 1–8: A New Translation with Introduction and Commentary*, AB 27 (New Haven: Yale University Press, 2000), 37–39; Stephen S. Kimondo, *The Gospel of Mark and the Roman-Jewish War of 66–70 CE: Jesus' Story as a Contrast to the Events of the War* (Eugene, OR: Pickwick, 2018).

3. For an important study of the construction of time in Mark, though focusing more on Greco-Roman memorial culture, see Eve-Marie Becker, *The Birth of Christian History: Memory and Time from Mark to Luke-Acts*, ABRL (New Haven: Yale University Press, 2017).

4. A point emphasized in the fine study by Cilliers Breytenbach, "Mark's Future Tense," *EC* 12 (2021): 297–321. I will use "readers" here and throughout, though I do not presume the initial audience of any of the Gospels would have necessarily received the story through direct engagement with the text. For a discussion of the issues here, see Chris Keith, *The Gospel as Manuscript: An Early History of the Jesus Tradition as Material Artifact* (Oxford: Oxford University Press, 2020), 163–200.

5. For overviews of eschatology in Mark in general, see Heinrich Baarlink, *Die Eschatologie der synoptischen Evangelien*, BWANT (Mainz: Kohlhmmer, 1986), 30–66; William R. Telford, *The Theology of the Gospel of Mark* (Cambridge: Cambridge University Press, 1999), 54–115; Grant Macaskill, "Apocalypse and the Gospel of Mark," in *The Jewish Apocalyptic Tradition and the Shaping of New Testament Thought*, ed. Benjamin E. Reynolds and Loren T. Stuckenbruck (Minneapolis: Fortress, 2017), 53–78; Reinhard von Bendemann, "Das Markusevangelium als Herausforderung für die Theologie," *ZNT* 24 (2021): 30–31, 38–39.

idea seems to be that the "way" of Jesus of Nazareth embodies in some manner the final and long-awaited arrival of the "Lord" from Isa 40.[6] This is a decidedly eschatological claim in the first century, as Isa 40 was widely read as a prophetic description of God's advent to redeem Zion, gather the lost tribes, and vindicate Israel.[7] Mark's Jesus further contends, only verses later, that his entry to Galilee for public ministry marks the moment at which "the time has been fulfilled." Jesus's first words are these: "The time has been fulfilled and the kingdom of God has drawn near; repent, and believe in the good news" (1:15). As the filling up of time stands in parallel to the coming near of the kingdom, Jesus's message is an assuredly eschatological proclamation about a transition underway in salvation history from one time or age to another.[8] Jesus's activities corroborate that this initial claim is happening in some way already in his work: he engages in victorious battle with the demons (e.g., 1:21–28; 1:34; 1:39; etc., presumably having bound the strong man, so 3:27); he heals and restores people with illnesses characteristic of the old age (1:29–31; 1:40–44; 2:1–13; etc.); he claims to possess in the now (Mark's past) the authority of God to forgive sins (2:5); he calls twelve disciples and constitutes a new family of God bound by obedience to the will of God (3:7–21; 3:31–35).[9] Jesus soon announces that he must suffer and die in order to ransom many (10:45)—something we presume that, Mark's readers would have believed, his death actually did in some way. He has a last meal with his disciples that evokes the covenant Moses made with the Israelites at the base of Mount Sinai (14:17–25; cf. Exod 24:4–8). Readers are encouraged to conclude that his death and resurrection, in the past, mark the end of the era of the temple and its sacrifices (15:38; cf. 12:33).

Mark's Gospel exhibits a rather sophisticated historical and temporal consciousness in that the narrative also anticipates realities that, while *after* the ministry of Jesus and what Mark actually describes, would also have been *past* realities for Mark's first readers. Straightaway in Mark, John the Baptist predicts one coming after him who will "baptize with the Holy Spirit" (1:8)—something that never happens in Mark, though presumably connects to early Christian

6. Cf. Rikki E. Watts, *Isaiah's New Exodus and Mark* (Grand Rapids: Baker Books, 2000), 53–90, 91–122.

7. See Tucker S. Ferda, "John the Baptist, Isaiah 40, and the Ingathering of the Exiles," *JSHJ* 10 (2012): 154–88.

8. Cf. Joel Marcus, "'The Time Has Been Fulfilled!' (Mark 1.15)," in *Apocalyptic and the New Testament: Essays in Honor of J. Louis Martyn*, ed. Joel Marcus and Marion L. Soards (London: Bloomsbury Academic, 2015), 49–68.

9. Cf. Richard B. Hays, *Echoes of Scripture in the Gospels* (Waco, TX: Baylor University Press, 2016), 29–36 (on what he calls "prefigurations of Israel's eschatological restoration").

charismatic or baptismal experience, or both.[10] Jesus predicts a time of fasting when the bridegroom is taken away (2:18–20). Jesus says that the story about the woman who anointed him would be spread throughout the world (14:9), which serves as a kind of self-referential metacommentary on Mark's Gospel itself. And in his final discourse on the Mount of Olives, Jesus predicts that the gospel will be proclaimed to all nations, that his followers will hear of wars and rumors of wars, experience persecution, and be tempted to follow false leaders (13:5–23). These are links, one might say, to experiences at least known to Mark's readership, if not directly experienced.

By the Mouths of Demons

The narrative of Mark also signals, though, in significant ways, how much is yet to happen not just after the ministry of Jesus but after readers of Mark read Mark.[11] Here the discussion becomes more controversial, as it involves the interpretation of some highly debated passages. But I would like initially to frame my exegesis with two observations that take a broader perspective. The first has to do with the utterances of demons. While Jesus is teaching in Capernaum for the first time, a demon-possessed man addresses him with a question and a claim: "What have we to do with you, Jesus the Nazarene! Have you come to destroy us [ἦλθες ἀπολέσαι ἡμᾶς]? I know who you are: the holy one of God!" (1:24). Similarly, the Gerasene demoniac says to Jesus, "What have I to do with you, Jesus the son of God Most High? I adjure you by God, do not torment me [μή με βασανίσῃς]!" (5:7). We have in both instances great examples of dramatic irony in Mark where Jesus, the demons, and the readers know more than the other characters in the story, and the narrative actually requires the readers to supply that assumed knowledge to make sense of the interchange.[12] In these particular instances, the readers must know, too, the

10. For good treatments of these lines that regard both present and future dimensions important, see Rudolf Schnackenburg, *God's Rule and Kingdom* (Montreal: Palm, 1963), 141–42; Robert A. Guelich, *Mark 1–8:26*, WBC 34A (Dallas: Word, 1982), 43–44; Daniel Kosch, "Die Gottesherrschaft erreicht das Jetzt: Eine Annäherung an Mk 1,15 und Lk 11,2 par Mt 6,10," *BK* 62 (2007): 85–88.

11. Right here is Gundrun Guttenberger, "Zur Hermeneutik des Markusevangeliums," *ZNT* 47 (2021): 115–16. See also David S. du Toit, "Prolepsis als Prophetie: Zur christologischen Funktion narrativer Anachronie im Markusevangelium," *WD* 26 (2001): 165–89.

12. This literary feature of Mark is well known and has been extensively researched. An influential study is Jerry Camery-Hoggatt, *Irony in Mark's Gospel: Text and Subtext* (Cambridge: Cambridge University Press, 1992).

true identity of Jesus—that he is "the holy one of God" and "the son of God"—and the readers must know that, as said agent, Jesus's coming brings to mind the destruction or torment of demons. To be sure, this identity and this task are intimately related in both instances. The first demon's "have you come to destroy us?" is immediately followed by "I know who you are: the holy one of God!"

The point I wish to draw out is this: the assumption behind these exchanges is that the arrival of God's kingdom, not least the arrival of its key agent or viceroy, means the defeat of Satan and his minions.[13] The famous opening of T. Mos. 10 captures the idea: "Then [God's] kingdom will appear throughout the whole creation. Then the devil will have his end" (10.1).[14] Such an eschatological expectation is so prominent in the literature of the Second Temple period that it is superfluous to enter a full discussion of it at this point.[15] This knowledge Mark assumes the readers will supply is crucial for our understanding Mark's construal of time, salvation history, and the future, for the destruction or torment of such anti-God powers is an eschatological and apocalyptic event that cannot be reduced to the "founding of the Church" or the "destruction of the temple" or some other historical happening in the first century CE.[16] In other literature of this period, this end-time destruction stands alongside other transcendent events that signal the end (or "transformation," if you will) of normal human history. But here is the thing: that which the demons speak of had not yet occurred when Mark's readers read Mark; the demons speak of a still-outstanding event in Mark's time.[17] It may well be that Mark wishes to suggest that the destruction or torment began to occur in the ministry of Jesus, an example of what Jeremias famously called "sich realisierende Eschatologie."[18] Yet even if the implied answer to the first demon's

13. See Marcus, *Mark 1–8*, 192–93.

14. Cf. T. Sim. 6.5–6: "The Great One in Israel will be manifest upon the earth. . . . Then all the spirits of error shall be given over to being trampled underfoot, and people will have mastery over the evil spirits." Also 4Q174 1–3 II, 7–9 ("rest" from Belial); 1QS IV, 18–23; T. Levi 18:12 (Belial will be "bound" and God will grant authority "to trample on wicked spirits").

15. Cf. 1QS III, 13–IV, 26; 1QM I, 1–15; XIII, 11; T. Levi 18.11–12; T. Dan 5.10–11; T. Jud. 25.3; Jub. 23.29–30; 50.5; 1 En. 10.5–6. Cf. Craig A. Evans, "Inaugurating the Kingdom of God and Defeating the Kingdom of Satan," *BBR* 15 (2005): 49–75.

16. See Tat-siong Benny Liew, *Politics of Parousia: Reading Mark Inter(con)textually*, BibInt 42 (Leiden: Brill, 1999), 46–47 ("for Mark, the development of the entire Gospel is informed by an apocalyptic framework").

17. Cf. Adela Yarbro Collins, *Mark: A Commentary*, Hermeneia (Minneapolis: Fortress, 2007), 272: "Jesus' exorcisms are not the definitive manifestation of the kingdom of God. Rather, they constitute a struggle with Satan that prefigures and anticipates the final, full manifestation of the kingdom of God that will take place with the coming of the Son of Man."

18. Joachim Jeremias, *The Parables of Jesus*, trans. S. H. Hooke, 2nd ed. (New York: Scribner's Sons, 1972), 230. Jeremias notes that this phrase was actually suggested to him by Ernst Haenchen.

question is yes—yes, Jesus has come right now to destroy—that destruction was obviously incomplete. Mark's Gospel signals that its own readership was actively engaged in exorcistic activity (9:29 ["this kind can only come out through prayer"]; cf. 6:13), which means that the plundering of the strong man's house, begun in the ministry of Jesus, had not yet been completed. Satan, to use another of Mark's phrases, has not *fully* "had his end" (3:26). Mark and Mark's readers look forward to that.[19] It is striking to note here that, as much as the opening of Mark signals the fulfillment of long-awaited promises from Isaiah, as noted above, it is also in the very first chapter that the narrative points to something unfulfilled in Jesus's work in the time Mark's readers lived: the destruction of satanic opposition to the rule of God. The story generates anticipation about what is still to come at the same time as it depicts the climactic significance of Jesus's public ministry.

A Transformed World

A second observation leads us in a similar direction. There is a good deal of material in Mark that seems to expect a future in which there is a radically transformed state of life. In Mark 9:43–48, Jesus warns that it is better to cut off your hand or gouge out your eye and thus "enter into life" (εἰσελθεῖν εἰς τὴν ζωήν) or "enter the kingdom" than to "go" or "be thrown" "into gehenna" (εἰς τὴν γέενναν). Moreover, Jesus's later teaching to Peter unveils a clear recognition of "the present age" (ἐν τῷ καιρῷ τούτῳ) and "the age to come" (ἐν τῷ αἰῶνι τῷ ἐρχομένῳ): "there is no one who has left house or brothers or sisters or mother or father or children or fields, for my sake and for the sake of the good news, who will not receive a hundredfold now *in this age*—houses, brothers and sisters, mothers and children, and fields, with persecutions—and *in the age to come* eternal life" (10:29–30, my italics).[20] Here the descriptions of abundant sharing, which surely bring to mind for readers the experience of the church and its persecutions, thus including the time of Mark's readers, are patently described as *prior to* the "age to come."[21] One further gets the

19. Concerning the drowning of the demons in Mark 5, Robert H. Stein, *Mark*, BECNT (Grand Rapids: Baker Books, 2008), 256, writes, "Mark probably intends his readers to see in the destruction of the swine the destruction of the demons as well. . . . What will happen in the final day (Rev. 20:10) has proleptically happened to the demons called Legion, whose destruction is visualized by the fate of the swine."

20. See Joel Marcus, *Mark 8–16: A New Translation with Introduction and Commentary*, AB 27A (New Haven: Yale University Press, 2009), 733 (who refers to 1 En. 48.7; 71.15; 4 Ezra 7.50; 2 Bar. 83.8; and other New Testament texts: Matt 12:32; Rom 12:2; 1 Cor 2:6; etc.). See also Jacques Schlosser, *Le règne de Dieu dans les dits de Jésus* (Paris: Gabalda, 1980), 2:477–507.

21. For a thoughtful treatment of this passage in relation to Mark's eschatology more broadly,

impression that, as "the age to come" is described solely with ζωὴν αἰώνιον (10:30), it is not characterized by normal family life—note, for example, the mothers and children and others listed in "the present age"—which would agree with Jesus's claim later in debate with the Sadducees that "when they rise from the dead, they neither marry nor are given in marriage, but are like the angels in heaven" (12:25). It is also probable, though admittedly less certain, that Mark assumes certain sayings of Jesus would have been read as descriptions of the final judgment, which would of course naturally appear somewhere in or at the divide between these ages. Mark's Jesus explains what will and will not "be forgiven" (3:28–30), he claims "the measure you give will be the measure you get" (4:24), and he declares that "the first will be last and the last first" (10:31) in the very context of describing "the age to come" (10:30). He also warns that scribes who "devour widows' houses" "will receive the greater condemnation" (λήμψονται περισσότερον κρίμα [12:40]). What could this refer to *but* the final judgment?[22]

Now I wish to be clear: Mark's story of Jesus cannot be condensed into some tension-free apocalyptic system. Certain parts of Mark seem much better organized than others, and the literary integrity of the narrative is not everywhere the same.[23] Moreover, the best we can reconstruct may be an already-modified or expanded Mark (should the old Ur-Markus theory have been onto something), and perhaps even Mark was written with the assumption that it would be reused, recycled, and even expanded.[24] At the same time, it was surely an overstatement

see Benjamin A. Edsall, "This Is Not the End: The Present Age and the Eschaton in Mark's Narrative," *CBQ* 80 (2018): 443–45.

22. See, e.g., Werner Zager, *Gottesherrschaft und Endgericht in der Verkündigung Jesu: Eine Untersuchung zur markinischen Jesusüberlieferung einschließlich der Q-Parallelen*, BZNW 82 (Berlin: de Gruyter, 1996), 282–87; Craig A. Evans, *Mark 8:27–16:20*, WBC 34B (Nashville: Nelson, 2001), 279; Stein, *Mark*, 575; Marcus, *Mark 8–16*, 855–56.

23. Cf. F. G. Lang, "Kompositionsanalyse des Markusevangeliums," *ZTK* 74 (1977): 1–24; Dietrich-Alex Koch, "Inhaltliche Gliederung und geographischer Aufriss im Markusevangelium," *NTS* 29 (1983): 145–66; Marcus, *Mark 1–8*, 57–63; Kevin W. Larsen, "The Structure of Mark's Gospel: Current Proposals," *CurBR* 3 (2004): 140–60; M. Eugene Boring, *Mark: A Commentary* (Louisville: Westminster John Knox, 2006), 4–5; Cilliers Breytenbach, "The Gospel of Mark as Episodic Narrative," in *The Gospel according to Mark as Episodic Narrative*, NovTSup 182 (Leiden: Brill, 2020), 11–40. Helen K. Bond, *The First Biography of Jesus: Genre and Meaning in Mark's Gospel* (Grand Rapids: Eerdmans, 2020), argues that Mark is "largely a patchwork of short episodes" (99), as typical of Greco-Roman biographies, while also "more carefully composed than many biographies" (102).

24. The important recent study by Matthew D. C. Larsen, *Gospels before the Book* (Oxford: Oxford University Press, 2018), has shown the ways in which anachronistic exegetical assumptions have led to Mark being read as a "finished book." Mark, he argues instead, was composed as a kind of "collection of notes" and "regularly described and received by its earliest readers and

from the early form critics to suggest that Mark was "ein naiver Volkserzähler" who did not have a sufficient grasp of his own material to know that his story of Jesus was inherently self-contradictory,[25] and that its major eschatological components did not fit together.[26] My conclusion at this point is a simple one, and it seems to me that it follows quite naturally from the above observations: Mark's Gospel, from start to finish, weaves in various threads that it fails to tie off in the ministry of Jesus or in the later historical experiences of the early church. This means that the story line of the gospel not only anticipates but assumes its readers are aware of some climactic denouement that has yet to come.[27] The narrative, in other words, is written from that unrealized eschatological perspective. The abrupt ending of Mark at 16:8—should that be original—would only highlight the still-future character of the kingdom and the outstanding promises of Jesus.[28] Moreover, Mark leaves clear indications throughout that the denouement is characterized by

---

users as less finished, more rough, open, revisable, unpublished, and not very 'bookish'" (122). Larsen's argument is helpful insofar as it complicates certain modes of narrative criticism that read Mark like a modern short story, as in, perhaps, David Rhoads, Joanna Dewey, and Donald Michie, *Mark as Story: An Introduction to the Narrative of a Gospel*, 3rd ed. (Minneapolis: Fortress, 2012). But none of the exegetical claims made in this chapter require us to think of Mark as a "finished book" in the sense that Larsen challenges. Moreover, as Larsen's evidence itself attests, there were varying degrees of "unfinishedness," and there were varying degrees of intentionality and organization in *hypomnemata*. As Larsen leans heavily into Mark's reception by early readers, he glosses too quickly over the fact that Luke clearly called Mark an *attempted* διήγησις—a "narrative" (1:1). We should be able to hold together Mark as an attempted διήγησις—having some literary and ideological intentionality that we can discern—while also admitting (with Larsen) that Luke and many others thought Mark needed reworking.

25. So Karl Ludwig Schmidt, "Die Stellung der Evangelien in der allgemeinen Literaturegeschichte," in *ΕΥΧΑΡΙΣΤΗΡΙΟΝ: Studien zur Religion und Literatur des Alten und Neuen Testaments*, ed. Emil Balla and Hans Schmidt (Göttingen: Vandenhoeck & Ruprecht, 1923), 75.

26. I find compelling the thesis of Elizabeth E. Shively, "The Eclipse of the Markan Narrative: On the (Re)cognition of a Coherent Story and Implications for Genre," *EC* 12 (2021): 369–87, that on the basis of internal textual clues, we should regard Mark a "unified narrative," even while it is apparent that Mark fell short "*according to the standards of Hellenistic historiography that Luke assumes*" (277).

27. Rightly here Franz Mussner, *Was lehrt Jesus über das Ende der Welt?*, rev. ed. (Freiburg: Herder, 1987), 47; Liew, *Politics of Parousia*, 109–32. Contrast Ernest van Eck, "Eschatology and Kingdom in Mark," in *Eschatology of the New Testament and Some Related Documents*, ed. Jan G. van der Watt, WUNT 2/315 (Tübingen: Mohr Siebeck, 2011), 64–91, who argues that most predictions in the gospel as a whole (including Mark 13) are to be regarded as "intratextually fulfilled in Mark's narrative" (84) (which he takes to be about Jesus's replacement of the temple with a new inclusive household).

28. Cf. Richard B. Hays, *The Moral Vision of the New Testament: Community, Cross, New Creation* (San Francisco: HarperSanFrancisco, 1996), 87.

realities unlike normal human history: the destruction of demons, entry into "the age to come" and "eternal life," the angelic existence of those raised from the dead, and the final judgment. It is not a coincidence that the Gospel of Mark starts by identifying John the Baptist with Elijah "who is to come" (1:6; 9:11–13) "*before* the great and terrible day of the Lord" (Mal 3:22, my italics [ET 4:5]). The passion of Jesus appears to initiate "that day" in certain respects (note, e.g., the "darkness at noon" in Mark 15:33 and Amos 8:9 on "that day"), but its culmination looks beyond the horizon of Mark's own narrative and the *Sitz im Leben* of its first readers.

After Peter's Confession

It is within this larger eschatological perspective that we encounter three particular passages that have been at the center of exegetical and historical discussion of the second coming in the New Testament: Mark 8:38–9:1, 13:24–26, and 14:62. If we are to describe the claims of this source accurately before we infer anything about the past, we must at least attempt to read these passages in light of the main contours of the larger source itself, rather than immediately reading them apart from and even against that source, as has so often been the case in historical Jesus research on this question. The first passage appears in the context of Peter's confession and Jesus's initial passion prediction, and thus at a crucial transition point in the overall drama of Mark's Gospel. Jesus has just begun a new stage of his ministry whereby he defines messiahship around the example of his own suffering and death and in the process defines the nature of true discipleship. After encouraging anyone who wishes to follow him to "take up the cross" and "deny self," he ends by issuing this warning, and with it a promise (8:38–9:1):

> "For whoever is ashamed of me and my words in this adulterous and sinful generation, the son of man will also be ashamed of him when he comes in [or with] the glory of his Father with the holy angels [ὅταν ἔλθῃ ἐν τῇ δόξῃ τοῦ πατρὸς αὐτοῦ μετὰ τῶν ἀγγέλων τῶν ἁγίων]." And he said to them, "Amen I say to you that there are some of those standing here who will by no means taste death until they see the kingdom of God has come in power [ἕως ἂν ἴδωσιν τὴν βασιλείαν τοῦ θεοῦ ἐληλυθυῖαν ἐν δυνάμει]."

In these verses, there are two sayings of Jesus conjoined by the characteristically Markan καὶ ἔλεγεν αὐτοῖς in 9:1a.[29] The first (8:38) speaks of some future event

29. Cf. Marcus, *Mark 8–16*, 629.

whereby one's fate (of having Jesus be "ashamed" or not) is conditioned by one's response to Jesus's call to take up the shameful cross (8:34–37; cf. Heb 12:2). The seeming role of Jesus as either judge or advocate strongly implies a judgment scene, as is even more apparent in the close parallel to Mark 8:38 in Q 12:8–9. The second saying (9:1), which the evangelist apparently believes is relevant here, speaks of the future and decisive coming of the kingdom of God. It is evident, then, whatever exactly Mark's Jesus means by "the son of man . . . com[ing] in [or with] the glory of his Father with the holy angels," it coincides with "the kingdom of God hav[ing] come in power." Moreover, it is clear that this future happening is imminent but not immediate, since some may die ("taste death") before it occurs.[30] Since Mark narrates no such deaths in his story of Jesus, the prediction evidently looks beyond Mark's story itself, at the very least, to the post-Easter period.

But what might Mark's Jesus be talking about? Most Markan exegetes argue, at least in terms of Mark 8:38, that Jesus is talking about his own future coming, and a coming down from heaven at that.[31] That is surely right.[32] Not only do the

30. 4 Ezra 6.25–26 is probably close to the sense of Mark as well: "And it shall come to pass that whoever remains after all that I have foretold to you shall himself be saved and shall see my salvation and the end of my world. And they will see the men who were taken up, who from their birth have not tasted death."

31. See discussion in Yarbro Collins, *Mark*, 409–12; Stein, *Mark*, 409–11; Marcus, *Mark 8–16*, 619–21, 628–30. Contra R. T. France, *Mark: A Commentary on the Greek Text*, NIGTC (Grand Rapids: Eerdmans, 2002), 342–43. There is a persistent and theologically convenient move in the interpretation history of Mark to separate 8:38 from 9:1—often suggesting Mark 8:38 refers to the parousia, but Mark 9:1, with its potentially troublesome temporal fixation about "those standing here," to either the transfiguration, the resurrection, or the founding of the church. Cf., e.g., Bede, *Hom. Ev.* 32; in the Glossa Ordinaria, at 9:1, Jesus is speaking of the establishment of the church or the blessedness of heaven, glimpsed in his transfiguration. Cf. *Bibliorum Sacrorum cum Glossa Ordinaria* (Venice: Magnam Societatem, 1603), 5:570: "Idest, ecclesiam contra mundi huius gloria erectam. Vel futuram in celis beatitudinem, quam in monte viderunt." See also Cornelius à Lapide, vol. 2 of *The Great Commentary*, trans. Thomas W. Mossman, 4th ed. (London: Hodges, 1890 [orig. 1681]), 242 (who refers to Hilary, Chrysostom, Jerome, Ambrose, Theophylact, and others). The physical form of manuscripts has supported and perpetuated this idea, which is the reason why the late-medieval chapter and verse system have 9:1 in a new chapter. Already Codex Sinaiticus starts a new line at 9:1 with space remaining on the line above after 8:38. I plan to investigate this phenomenon more fully in a future study.

32. The exegesis of John Calvin deserves special mention here. Calvin argued in his *Commentary on Daniel* at 7:13–14 that the "coming" of the one like a son of man was a prophecy of the ascension of Christ. His explicitly disagrees with "other commentators" who think the setting up of "thrones" and the "opening of the books" at 7:9–11 refers to the final judgment and 7:13–14 to the parousia; this was, indeed, an almost unquestioned exegetical conclusion among the church fathers (so Justin Martyr, Irenaeus, Hippolytus, Tertullian, Eusebius, Aphrahat, Ephraem, Jerome, Theodoret, and others). Cf. Maurice Casey, *The Son of Man: The Interpretation and Influence of*

references to "seeing" and the mention of "in power" strongly suggest that the "coming" is a coming down (rather than a going up to heaven),[33] the directionality is confirmed by the way in which 8:38b ("when he comes in the glory of his Father with the holy angels") recalls Zech 14:5, which reads in the LXX, "and the Lord my God will come and all the holy ones with him."[34] This is an oracle about the day of the Lord and the coming (down) of God to redeem Jerusalem and execute judgment. We have already seen the importance of Zech 14:5 for the return of Jesus in the writings of Paul, as Zech 14:5 also stands behind 1 Thess 3:13. It is further noteworthy that, just as the coming of the kingdom in Mark 9:1 follows the coming of the son of man in 8:38, the passage from Zech 14 continues to predict the establishment of the Lord's kingship over all the earth "on that day" (14:9): "on that day the Lord will be one and his name one" (which the targum takes as, "and the kingdom of the Lord shall be revealed [ותתגלי מלכותא דיוי] upon all the inhabitants of the earth").[35] The connection between Mark 8:38 and 9:1 is readily understandable, then. It is also probable that Dan 7—an important passage for Mark's Gospel as a whole—is at play in Mark 8:38–9:1, and to similar effect.[36]

Daniel 7 (London: SPCK, 1979), 57–77, 92–93. Calvin thinks instead that Daniel imagines the display of God's glory in the incarnation of Christ at 7:9–11 and then describes his exaltation after death at 7:13–14. However, when Calvin then reads the Synoptic Gospels in his *Commentary on the Harmony of the Evangelists*, while he recognizes the Danielic background of the passages at hand, he nevertheless argues that Mark 8:38, 13:24–26, and 14:62 and parr. are about the return of Christ and the final judgment. I am unsure how these two readings relate in his mind, but the point is this: even while Calvin thought Dan 7 referred to the exaltation of this son of man in heaven (akin to some contemporary critics), he was unable to foist the same reading upon these three synoptic passages, nor does he even entertain the possibility of doing so (though he does think that the uniquely Markan reference to the coming of "the kingdom" [9:1] "began" with the resurrection). See also Schlosser, *Le règne de Dieu dans les dits de Jesus*, 1:324–27; Edward Adams, "The Coming of the Son of Man in Mark's Gospel," *TynBul* 56 (2005): 39–61 (who argues that all three of Mark's sayings about the coming of the son of man [8:38; 13:24–27; 14:62] refer to the parousia); Timo Laato, "Der ambivalente Stil und die Eschatologie des Neuen Testaments," *EC* 9 (2018): 91. For reception history, see Martin Künzi, *Das Naherwartungslogion Markus 9,1 par: Geschichte seiner Auslegung* (Tübingen: Mohr Siebeck, 1977).

33. Werner Georg Kümmel, *Promise and Fulfillment: The Eschatological Message of Jesus*, trans. Dorothea M. Barton, 2nd ed. (London: SCM, 1961), 27, rightly argued, contra C. H. Dodd (who thought "you will see" means "you will recognize" [e.g., a change of perspective]), that "in power" is superfluous if it does not refer to the "open appearance" of the kingdom.

34. This connection is missed by R. T. France, *Jesus and the Old Testament: His Application of Old Testament Passages to Himself and His Mission* (Downers Grove, IL: InterVarsity Press, 1971), 139–40, who also disputes that Jesus is talking about the parousia in Mark.

35. Trans. *ArBib* 14:224.

36. So Osvaldo D. Vena, *The Parousia and Its Rereadings: The Development of the Eschatological Consciousness in the Writings of the New Testament*, SBT 27 (New York: Lang, 2001), 178–81;

Mark's Jesus speaks of himself as "the son of man" who "comes," and identifies this event with the arrival of "the kingdom of God"; Dan 7 envisions the "coming" (from ἔρχομαι) of the "one like a son of man" (ὡς υἱὸς ἀνθρώπου) on/with the clouds (7:13), which leads directly to the establishment of "the kingdom" that will never pass away (7:14). The night vision of Dan 7 would also explain the forensic imagery that is presupposed by 8:38.[37] In part 4, I will discuss how this general picture and the use of Dan 7 are corroborated by several other Jewish sources from this period.

Thus, the most straightforward reading of Mark 8:38–9:1 that is attentive to its intertextuality and to pre-Markan eschatological reflection (as we see in Paul) also goes with the grain of exegetical tradition in the history of the church: Mark's Jesus refers to his own future return and identifies that event with the final establishment of the kingdom of God.[38] At the same time, it must be quickly added that far too many exegetes have been able to avoid what is further implied by that very reading: Jesus predicts that the interval before his return will not be indefinite but rather last only the lifetime of some there present. The great exegete Cecil Cadoux was right in this:

> On any reasonable interpretation, and without doing violence to the Greek perfect participle, we must insist that we have here a prediction of a special and spectacular coming of the Kingdom "with power," sufficiently soon and sufficiently late for "some" of the bystanders to live to see that this had happened.[39]

Peter Müller, "Zwischen dem Gekommenden und dem Kommenden: Intertextuelle Aspekte der Menschensohnaussagen im Markusevangelium," in *Gottessohn und Menschensohn: Exegetische Studien zu zwei Paradigmen biblischer Intertextualität*, ed. Dieter Sänger (Neukirchener: Neukirchen-Vluyn, 2004), 130–57. Cf., in addition to the passages discussed below, Mark 2:1–12 (where we find "the son of man," "given," "authority"); 10:35–45 (request of James and John). For discussion see Juel, *Messianic Exegesis*, 151–70; Joel Marcus, *The Way of the Lord* (Louisville: Westminster John Knox, 1992), 164–71; Simon Gathercole, "The Son of Man in Mark's Gospel," *ExpTim* 115 (2004): 366–72; Dunn, *Jesus Remembered*, 753; J. R. Daniel Kirk, *A Man Attested by God: The Human Jesus of the Synoptic Gospels* (Grand Rapids: Eerdmans, 2016), 307–13; Marius Nel, "'Son of Man' in the Gospel of Mark," *IDS* 51 (2017): 1–9.

37. Cf. as an intriguing parallel 1 En. 46.6, wherein the wicked will be covered with "shame" (46.6), and they had "den(ied) the Lord of Spirits."

38. Contrast Kent Brower, "Mark 9:1: Seeing the Kingdom in Power," *JSNT* 6 (1980): 17–41, and Michael Bird, "The Crucifixion of Jesus as the Fulfillment of Mark 9:1," *TJ* 24 (2003): 1–11, who argue that Mark 9:1 refers to the crucifixion of Jesus as the kingdom come "in power." Heinz Giesen, "Mk 9,1—ein Wort Jesu über die nahe Parusie," *TTZ* 92 (1983): 134–48, pointing to the resurrection, is also unconvincing.

39. Cecil J. Cadoux, *The Historic Mission of Jesus* (London: Lutterworth, 1941), 199–200. See also Rudolf Pesch, *Das Markusevangelium*, part 2, *Commentar zu Kap. 8,27–16,20* (Freiburg: Herder, 1977), 66–67.

The truth may be theologically inconvenient, but it sits squarely within the larger eschatological outlook of Mark's Gospel as we have thus far described it. Mark 8:38–9:1 refers to realities that have not yet occurred for the readership of Mark yet were expected to happen soon—before the eyewitness generation (the τινες of 9:1) had passed away. Mark's readers thus live and encounter the story of Jesus from a time *after* the announcement of the kingdom's "drawing near" (ἤγγικεν) in the ministry of Jesus (1:14–15) yet *before* its powerful "arrival" (ἐληλυθυῖαν) at his future return (8:38–9:1). The implied reader lives in between the eschatological frame of 1:14–15 and 8:38–9:1, respectively.

This reading of 8:38–9:1 is confirmed by what follows in the narrative. In the transfiguration of Jesus—a story Mark or Mark's tradition has chosen to place directly after 8:27–9:1—disciples and readers alike receive a foretaste of that which Jesus predicted in 8:38–9:1.[40] After having prophesied he would come again "in the glory of his Father,"[41] using language from Zechariah about a future, Sinai-like theophany (Deut 33:2), Jesus here gives Peter, James, and John a momentary glimpse of that very glory in this Sinai-saturated scene.[42] To say that the transfiguration fulfills the prior prediction would be to make the same mistake as Peter and the disciples, who wish to stay on the mountain (9:5) and are confused about the eschatological timetable (9:11–13).[43] The disciples conclude, in light of what they have seen, that the day predicted by Malachi has been fulfilled, though without the appearance of Elijah as the scribes expected. Jesus must teach them that Malachi's prediction about Elijah is being fulfilled, but suffering is necessary first. Elijah himself, identified with the person of John the Baptist, has indeed come to restore all things, but suffered, as would "the son of man" before his glorious return.[44]

40. Cf. Barry Blackburn, Theios Anēr *and the Markan Miracle Traditions: A Critique of the* Theios Anēr *Concept as an Interpretive Background of the Miracle Traditions Used by Mark*, WUNT 2/40 (Tübingen: Mohr Siebeck, 1991), 120: "the Transfiguration is to be interpreted as a proleptic view of Christ's heavenly glory received upon his resurrection and session at God's right hand and to be revealed publicly in his parousia."

41. Note the description of Jesus in Mark and the Ancient One in Dan 7. Cf. Joshua E. Leim, "In the Glory of His Father: Intertextuality and the Apocalyptic Son of Man in the Gospel of Mark," *JTS* 7 (2013): 213–22.

42. This is also how 2 Pet 1:19 has received the transfiguration story: it is assurance of his coming in glory. Cf. Laato, "Der ambivalente Stil und die Eschatologie des Neuen Testaments," 94.

43. Contrast Enrique Nardoni, "A Redactional Interpretation of Mark 9:1," *CBQ* 43 (1981): 365–84, who argues that, for the evangelist, 9:1 finds fulfillment in the experience of the three disciples in the transfiguration. Contra also Arthur L. Moore, *The Parousia in the New Testament*, NovTSup 13 (Leiden: Brill, 1966), 128, 175–77, who argues this was true even for the historical Jesus! See instead Yarbro Collins, *Mark*, 412–13.

44. How literally Mark understood this connection between John and Elijah is not clear. Cf.

In all, then, the story of Peter's confession up through and including the transfiguration scene communicates a consistent message from Mark about the messiah, his mission, and how his activity fits with the eschatological consummation as predicted in the Scriptures of Israel (according to Mark's view).[45] From start to finish, Mark's Jesus shares that he is the messiah and he will come in power and glory on the last day to establish the kingdom and restore all things. But before that, he must suffer, be rejected, and die. It is telling in this respect that Jesus continues to refer to himself as "the son of man" throughout this unit when predicting both his coming passion and his future glory. From the perspective of Mark's narrative, the messianic mission of the son of man is underway, and some of what Jesus predicted has come to pass, but his work had not yet been completed. The readers of Mark, having heard the prediction of 8:38–9:1, live in an intermediate time, somewhat analogous to the interval of "six days" after 8:38–9:1 and before the transfiguration. They, too, await his appearance in glory.

Messiah and Temple

Exegetes have long noted that Mark 8:38–9:1 closely resembles another utterance of Jesus in the so-called apocalyptic discourse: 13:24–27.[46] In both sayings, Jesus mentions "seeing," "the son of man," "coming," "glory," and "angels." But 13:24–27 is also a longer saying that includes some new information not found in Jesus's earlier prediction, not least citations from apocalyptic oracles in Isa 13 and 34 about "the day of the Lord" that describe strange astral phenomena concerning the sun, moon, stars, and "the powers in heaven":

---

discussion in Christine E. Joynes, "The Returned Elijah? John the Baptist's Angelic Identity in the Gospel of Mark," *SJT* 58 (2005): 455–67.

45. So also Edwin K. Broadhead, *Naming Jesus: Titular Christology in the Gospel of Mark*, JSNTSup 175 (Sheffield: Sheffield Academic, 1999), 133.

46. Some questions of tradition history and the composition of Mark 13 as relevant for my argument will be considered in following chapters. For some important studies and overviews, see Jan Lambrecht, *Die Redaktion der Markus-Apokalypse: Literarische Analyse und Strukturuntersuchung* (Rome: Päpstliches Bibelinstitut, 1967); Pesch, *Markusevangelium 8,27–16,20*, 264–68; Baarlink, *Die Eschatologie der synoptischen Evangelien*, 55–66; George R. Beasley-Murray, *Jesus and the Last Days: An Interpretation of the Olivet Discourse* (Vancouver: Regent College, 1993), 350–76; Yarbro Collins, *Mark*, 594–600; Marcus, *Mark 8–16*, 864–68; Robert H. Stein, *Jesus, the Temple, and the Coming Son of Man: A Commentary on Mark 13* (Downers Grove, IL: InterVarsity Press, 2014), 17–41.

But in those days, after that suffering,
the sun will be darkened,
and the moon will not give its light,
and the stars will fall from heaven,
and the powers that are in the heavens will be shaken.

And then they will see the son of man coming in the clouds with much power and glory. And then he will send the angels, and he will gather together the elect from the four winds, from the edge of the earth until the edge of heaven.

In addition to clear lexical and thematic links to 8:38–9:1, both passages are structurally similar in that they adopt "day of the Lord" imagery from Israel's Scripture—Isaiah here, Zechariah in 8:38—and ascribe to Jesus's future coming images that pertained to the advent of the Lord in their original context.[47] We have seen this move numerous times already in Paul. Moreover, while Mark 8:38 likely alluded to Dan 7:13–14, in Mark 13:26, this connection is even clearer:

Mark 13:26	**Dan 7:13–14 LXX**	**Dan 7:13–14 Θ**
τὸν υἱὸν τοῦ ἀνθρώπου ἐρχόμενον ἐν νεφέλαις μετὰ δυνάμεως πολλῆς καὶ δόξης	ἐπὶ τῶν νεφελῶν τοῦ οὐρανοῦ ὡς υἱὸς ἀνθρώπου ἤρχετο . . . καὶ ἐδόθη αὐτῷ . . . πᾶσα δόξα	μετὰ τῶν νεφελῶν τοῦ οὐρανοῦ ὡς υἱὸς ἀνθρώπου ἐρχόμενος
the son of man coming in the clouds with much power and glory	(one) like a son of man coming upon the clouds of heaven . . . and was given to him . . . all glory	(one) like a son of man coming with the clouds of heaven ["glory" not mentioned in Theodotion]

In Mark 8:38–9:1, the coming of Daniel's son of man is connected to the advent of God in Zech 14:5 and signals the decisive arrival of God's kingly rule "in power"; in Mark 13:24–26, the coming of Daniel's son of man signals the arrival of the Lord's "day" that impacts all of creation, "from the edge of the earth until the edge of heaven."[48]

47. For similar images, beyond Isaiah, of cosmic disturbance in this vein, see Jer 4:23; Ezek 32:7–8; Joel 2:10, 30–31; Amos 5:20; Zeph 1:15; Hag 2:6; LAB 19.13; 23.10; 1 En. 80.2–7; Sib. Or. 2.200–209 and elsewhere; T. Levi 4.1; T. Mos. 10.5; 4 Ezra 5.4–5; Apoc. El. 5.7; etc. For discussion, see Edward Adams, *The Stars Will Fall from Heaven: Cosmic Catastrophe in the New Testament and Its World*, LNTS 347 (London: Bloomsbury T&T Clark, 2007).

48. See Rudolf Pesch, *Naherwartungen: Tradition und Redaktion in Mk 13*, KBANT (Düsseldorf:

Jesus's prophecy in 13:24–27 follows and appears near the end of a lengthy discourse in response to a question from his disciples about the destruction of the temple, at the very least (13:1–4). We will not deal with the complex question of the tradition history of this discourse here but rather treat initially its final form in Mark. Because of that focus on the temple at the outset, that the reference to Daniel's "abomination of desolation" in 13:14 must have something to do with the temple (see Dan 9:25–27; 11:31),[49] and that the use of apocalyptic imagery from Isaiah probably in its original context functioned to "invest history with theological meaning,"[50] some have thought that Mark 13:24–27 refers not to the literal return of Jesus in the future but rather symbolically describes the temple's destruction, or the ascension/vindication of Jesus, or the rise of the church.[51] Such was the view of Glasson and Robinson and numerous others, as we have seen, who believed this was also near the message of the historical Jesus. But this interpretation of Mark is highly unlikely.[52] The connection between 13:24–27 and 8:38–9:1 would

---

Patmos Verlag, 1968), 162, 172–74, on both the judgment and the restoration depicted here. See also Egon Brandenburger, *Markus 13 und die Apokalyptik*, FRLANT 134 (Göttingen: Vandenhoeck & Ruprecht, 1984), 61 (though with some disagreement with Pesch on what symbolizes judgment; he thinks only the ὄψονται of v. 26).

49. On the challenge of identifying the signified for this signifier, see C. Clifton Black, "An Oration at Olivet: Some Rhetorical Dimensions of Mark 13," in *Persuasive Artistry: Studies in New Testament Rhetoric in Honor of George A. Kennedy*, ed. Duane F. Watson, JSNTSup 50 (Sheffield: Sheffield Academic, 1991), 89 ("commentators have despaired of precisely identifying to what or to whom Mark intends this epithet to refer"). See also W. A. Such, *The Abomination of Desolation in the Gospel of Mark: Its Historical Reference in Mark 13:14 and Its Impact in the Gospel* (Lanham: University Press of America, 1999); John S. Kloppenborg, "'Evocatio Deorum' and the Date of Mark," *JBL* 124 (2005): 419–50.

50. N. T. Wright, *The New Testament and the People of God* (Minneapolis: Fortress, 1992), 284 (this phrase appears frequently in his work).

51. Cf. especially France, *Jesus and the Old Testament*, 227–39; George Caird, *The Language and Imagery of the Bible* (Worcester: Duckworth, 1980), 243–71; Wright, *New Testament and the People of God*, 280–99; Wright, *Jesus and the Victory of God* (Minneapolis: Fortress, 1996), 361–68; Wright, "Hope Deferred? Against the Dogma of Delay," *EC* 9 (2018): 73–80; Thomas R. Hatina, "The Focus of Mark 13:24–27: The Parousia, or the Destruction of the Temple?," *BBR* 6 (1996): 43–66; Peter Bolt, *The Cross from a Distance: Atonement in Mark's Gospel*, NSBT 18 (Downers Grove, IL: InterVarsity Press, 2004), 90–99; van Eck, "Eschatology and Kingdom in Mark," 79–84; Ma'afu Palu, *Jesus and Time: An Interpretation of Mark 1.15*, LNTS 468 (London: Bloomsbury T&T Clark, 2012), 175; Sarah Underwood Dixon, "The End of the Temple or the End of the World? First Century Eschatology in the Gospels of Mark and Matthew," in *Eschatology in Antiquity: Forms and Functions*, ed. Hilary Marlow, Karla Pollmann, and Helen Van Noorden (London: Routledge, 2021), 371–82; Colin Brown with Craig A. Evans, *A History of the Quests for the Historical Jesus* (Grand Rapids: Zondervan Academic, 2022), 2:630–36.

52. Already Schleiermacher had argued that Luke 21 referred only to the destruction of the

itself be enough to doubt a purely symbolic reading of these verses (since 8:38–9:1 can clearly not be reduced to the temple's destruction, and/or the ascension/vindication of Jesus, and/or the rise of the church, and it would be odd for Mark to use the same language in completely different ways). But a strong case can be made on three additional grounds. First, while it is probably true that 13:5–23 refers to political and social realities that, for Mark's audience, were either past or contemporary experience (such as the coming of false prophets and messiahs, persecution, and "the abomination of desolation" in the temple),[53] there is an attempt to distinguish vv. 24–27 from that earlier part of the discourse with clear structuring words. Verse 24 begins with an adversative—ἀλλ'—and states that the cosmic signs are "after" the suffering previously described (μετὰ τὴν θλῖψιν ἐκείνην).[54] And the sequencing continues. There appear to be four moves:

- intense suffering, linked in some way with abomination in the temple (prior to v. 24)
    - "after that suffering" (μετὰ τὴν θλῖψιν ἐκείνην) the cosmic imagery from Isaiah (vv. 24b–25)
        - "and then" (καὶ τότε) the coming of the son of man (v. 26)
            - "and then" (καὶ τότε) the sending of the angels and gathering of the elect (v. 27)

Symbolic readings of vv. 24–27 focus on the nouns (and the use of such imagery in Isaiah especially) but tend to overlook the conjunctions.[55] Unless these structur-

---

temple, and the son of man imagery was symbolic. In response, David Friedrich Strauss, *The Life of Jesus Critically Examined*, trans. George Eliot, 4th ed. (London: Sonnenschein, 1902), 589, called this "a violence of interpretation." Strauss's larger reflections on this chapter (cf. 585–91) are still informative. Cf. Joseph Verheyden, "Describing the Parousia: The Cosmic Phenomena in Mark 13, 24–25," in *The Scriptures in the Gospels*, ed. Christopher M. Tuckett (Leuven: Leuven University Press, 1997), 547–50; Simon Gathercole, *The Gospel and the Gospels* (Grand Rapids: Eerdmans, 2022), 83, writes, "Mark's usage of Dan 7 to refer to the parousia of Jesus is undeniable."

53. Micah D. Kiel, "The Open Horizon of Mark 13," *JBL* 136 (2017): 145–62, offers a theoretical analysis that ends up disputing the very idea that the language of Mark 13 refers to specific historical circumstances at all. This is probably a fair point taken too far: interpretive disagreement and confusion in the exegetical literature has been imposed on the evangelist.

54. Note also the summary/concluding statement in v. 23 ("watch out, I have told you everything beforehand"), which anticipates some development in v. 24.

55. So, e.g., Wright, *Jesus and the Victory of God*, 339–67, whose discussion is very general and lacks engagement with these details. Similar in this respect is Scot McKnight, *A New Vision for Israel: The Teachings of Jesus in National Context* (Grand Rapids: Eerdmans, 1999), 135–37, 141–45. See instead Stein, *Jesus, the Temple, and the Coming Son of Man*, 103–20.

ing words are superfluous, however, it must be that vv. 24–27 refer to something different from and subsequent to what was previously described, and that, within vv. 24–27 themselves, the descriptions of the cosmic phenomena, son of man, and sent angels are not metaphorical synonyms for what was previously described.

To be sure, temporal sequence does not necessarily require a literal reading of vv. 24–27; these verses could describe sequentially in apocalyptic metaphor the fall of Jerusalem (vv. 24–25), the vindication/ascension of the son of man (v. 26), and the creation of the church (v. 27). But this leads to my second point: Mark's apocalyptic character in general suggests that the cosmic signs, the "coming of the son of man," and the sending of angels describe actual events that are to come. The temptation in making this point, or arguing the opposite, is to rush to contemporaneous Jewish literature to make a sweeping claim about the literal or metaphorical nature of apocalyptic language in this period.[56] I hesitate to do this. The question before us is, What is the most probable understanding of *this* language in *this* particular source? Putative Jewish parallels in Scripture or postbiblical literature make possible a number of interpretive conclusions, but which is the most probable *here*?[57] In my view, the rest of Mark's Gospel, as described above, gives little reason to doubt that vv. 24–27 describe transcendent realities that cannot be reduced to mere historical or political processes.[58] Jesus's ministry in Mark is framed from the outset as a battle against supernatural forces; he has come to "destroy" demons.

56. Cf. Wright, "Hope Deferred?," 49: "Most contemporary students of Jewish 'apocalyptic' literature understand the idiom to constitute a vivid way of expressing social and political disquiet with the way the world is being run, and the hope and expectation that Israel's God will act dramatically to bring about a rescue for his people and a new kind of world in which justice will dwell at last." See again at 78: (after admitting that people in the first century believed in actual signs and wonders in the heavens) "But the language and imagery in question was in such regular use, and had been in such regular use for a long time, to refer to (what we call) socio-political events and to invest them with (what we might call) their 'cosmic' significance, that we must question whether that is the natural first meaning of such phraseology." Critical of Wright on this point is Adams, *Stars Will Fall from Heaven*, 5–15 (and throughout), and more recently Paula Fredriksen, "*Al Tirah* ('Fear Not!'): Jewish Apocalyptic Eschatology, from Schweitzer to Allison, and After," in *"To Recover What Has Been Lost": Essays on Eschatology, Intertextuality, and Reception History in Honor of Dale C. Allison Jr.*, ed. Tucker S. Ferda, Daniel Frayer-Griggs, and Nathan C. Johnson, NovTSup 183 (Leiden: Brill, 2021), 15–38.

57. This essential move is also lacking in the study by Richard Horsley, *The Prophet Jesus and the Renewal of Israel: Moving beyond a Divisionary Debate* (Grand Rapids: Eerdmans, 2012), who settles for misleading generalizations (e.g., at 39: "the last generation of scholarly specialists have developed more critical perspective and greater precision and literary sensitivity in their reading of particular texts. This includes a much less 'literal' reading of the texts.").

58. Cf. Ferdinand Hahn, "Die Rede von der Parusie des Menschensohnes Markus 13," in *Jesus der Menschensohn*, ed. Rudolf Pesch and Rudolf Schnackenburg (Freiburg: Herder, 1975),

And he signals that the future brings a new state of life whereby not even marriage and procreation are realities. In light of the exorcistic ministry of Jesus in Mark, with all of its eschatological undertones, it would be fitting if not expected to find that the culmination of his ministry in the future continues that battle and brings it to completion.[59] Surely that is the most natural reading of "the powers in heaven will be shaken" in this gospel, as is the inference that "angels" in v. 27 refers to actual angels (not least because of 8:38's μετὰ τῶν ἀγγέλων τῶν ἁγίων) and is not code for Christian missionaries.[60] Moreover, and as others have argued, the remainder of Mark's Gospel shows the reader how to interpret the cosmic language in 13:24–27, because Mark or Mark's tradition has crafted the passion narrative in such a way that Jesus proleptically experiences that which he had formerly predicted on the Mount of Olives.[61] Just as Jesus predicts that his followers will be "handed over" and tried (13:9–11), so he is "handed over" and tried (14:21, 41–42; 15:1); just as Jesus predicts that brother will betray brother (13:12–13), so he is betrayed by one of his closest followers (14:10–11, 18); just as Jesus tells his disciples to "keep awake" (13:23, 33, 35, 37), so he reminds the same in Gethsemane (14:34, 38). When we hear about literal darkness at the crucifixion of Jesus (15:33)—darkness connected to "the day of the Lord" from Amos 8:9, no less—we are to see it as a foreshadowing of what Jesus had predicted in 13:24–26 with its "day of the Lord" imagery from Isaiah. I will have more to say about this in a moment.

Third, what follows in the apocalyptic discourse suggests that 13:24–27 is a prophecy about the climactic return of the son of man. Jesus next offers a parable about learning the signs of the times from the fig tree (vv. 28–31), expresses his own ignorance of the precise day or hour (v. 32), and concludes with a parable about a man who goes away on a journey and puts his slaves in charge of his house (vv. 33–37). The point of the latter is that "the Lord of the house" will indeed return, but his slaves do not know when, so they must "keep awake." The parable is a fairly thin allegory for the situation of his disciples themselves and the readers of Mark, who are also told to "keep awake" in the absence of Jesus.[62] This concluding

---

264–66. See also Hays, *Echoes of Scripture in the Gospels*, 35 ("Jesus prophesies dramatic events that have *not yet* occurred within Mark's narrative world").

59. Rightly here Günther Harder, "Das eschatologische Geschichtsbild der sogenannten kleinen Apokalypse Markus 13," *ThViat* 4 (1952): 71–107; Breytenbach, "Mark's Future Tense," 311–13.

60. Cf. Adams, *Stars Will Fall from Heaven*, 153–64.

61. See especially Dale C. Allison Jr., *The End of the Ages Has Come: An Early Interpretation of the Passion and Resurrection of Jesus* (Philadelphia: Fortress, 1985), 27–39; Peter G. Bolt, "Mark 13: An Apocalyptic Precursor to the Passion Narrative," *RTR* 54 (1995): 10–30.

62. It is not a coincidence that γρηγορεῖτε ("keep awake") ends the discourse at 13:37; it is the final word.

parable, then, which is clearly about Jesus and his followers, tells a story about the presence, absence, and sudden return of the "Lord of the house," using the same language as 13:26 (the son of man "coming" [ἐρχόμενον]; the Lord of the house "comes" [ἔρχεται]).[63] As the parable not only concludes the discourse but serves to summarize and encapsulate it, its focus on the return of Jesus is significant. Since the narrative transitions immediately to the passion narrative (14:1), the parable also serves as a fitting conclusion to the Jerusalem material from 11:1–13:37 in its entirety and actually completes an *inclusio*. Jesus's first entrance to Jerusalem involved a fig tree (11:12–14, 20–21) and a parable about wicked tenants who were given certain responsibilities while the owner of the vineyard was absent (12:1–12). So now, in anticipation of another entrance, Jesus teaches his disciples about reading a fig tree (13:28–31) and warns them to attend to their responsibilities while the Lord of the house is absent (13:34–37). It is not an accident that there is a rich exegetical tradition of reading the triumphal entry and its aftermath as a kind of foreshadowing of the parousia of Jesus.[64]

In sum, Jesus's discourse in Mark 13 as it now stands predicts two different things: (1) historical and political realities that lead up to the destruction of the temple (if not that destruction itself), some of which were recent history or current events for the original readership of Mark, and (2) another and even more climactic event to follow (the "after" of v. 24): the coming of the son of man from heaven.[65] Mark 13 brings these two moves very close together,[66] such that one expects the return of the son of man to follow shortly from what is described in vv. 5–23, and 13:30, looking back over the whole, declares that "all these things" (ταῦτα πάντα [note the ταῦτα in the disciples' question at 13:4]) will occur before "this generation passes away."[67] But there are also the reticence to specify fur-

63. See Evans, *Mark 8:27–16:20*, 339–42; Arland J. Hultgren, *The Parables of Jesus: A Commentary* (Grand Rapids: Eerdmans, 2000), 267; Marcus, *Mark 8–16*, 920–23.

64. For discussion and sources, see Tucker S. Ferda, "Reason to Weep: Isaiah 52 and the Subtext of Luke's Triumphal Entry," *JTS* 66 (2015): 58–59.

65. Here I agree with Marcus, *Mark 8–16*, 874: "although Jesus, then, has prophesied only the destruction of the Temple, not the end of everything, the disciples' question reveals their belief that these two sets of events are conjoined—an impression that the subsequent discourse will do nothing to refute." See also 906. Cf. Pesch, *Markusevangelium 8,27–16,20*, 305.

66. A point emphasized by Brant Pitre, *Jesus, the Tribulation, and the End of the Exile: Restoration Eschatology and the Origin of the Atonement*, WUNT 204 (Tübingen: Mohr Siebeck; Grand Rapids: Baker Books, 2005), 362. Contrast Timothy J. Geddert, *Watchwords: Mark 13 in Markan Eschatology*, JSNTSup 26 (Sheffield: Sheffield Academic, 1989), 113–49, 223–54, 257.

67. Cf. Strauss, *Life of Jesus*, 588 ("it is impossible to evade the acknowledgement, that in this discourse, if we do not mutilate it to suit our own views, Jesus at first speaks of the destruction of Jerusalem, and farther on and until the close, of his return at the end of all things, and that

ther (13:29), the frank acknowledgment of ignorance (13:32), and the expectation for surprise (13:35).[68] In all these ways, Mark 13 is again close to 8:38–9:1, which places a terminus on the return of Jesus within the lifetime of some then living, but offers little concreteness beyond that.[69]

Jesus on Trial

Mark's Jesus is not yet finished prophesying. In the passion narrative that follows the Olivet Discourse, readers of Mark encounter the imagery of 8:38–9:1 and 13:24–27 one final time, but in this case not in the company of would-be followers but amid a hostile audience seeking to kill Jesus (cf. 3:6 and 14:1–2). After some "falsely testify" (ἐψευδομαρτύρουν) that Jesus predicted he would destroy the temple and build another in three days (14:55–59), Caiaphas asks Jesus directly whether he is "the Christ, the son of the Blessed One" (14:61). Jesus replies, "I am, and you will see [ὄψεσθε] the son of man seated at the right hand of the Power [τὸν υἱὸν τοῦ ἀνθρώπου ἐκ δεξιῶν καθήμενον τῆς δυνάμεως], and coming with the clouds of heaven [καὶ ἐρχόμενον μετὰ τῶν νεφελῶν τοῦ οὐρανοῦ]." The mention of "the son of man . . . coming with the clouds of heaven" again draws on Dan 7:13, and there is

---

he places the two events in immediate connexion"); C. K. Barrett, *Jesus and the Gospel Tradition* (London: SPCK, 1967), 83; Yarbro Collins, *Mark*, 616–17; Boring, *Mark*, 375–76; Marcus, *Mark 8–16*, 911–12; Laato, "Der ambivalente Stil und die Eschatologie des Neuen Testaments," 97 ("Wie in Mk 9,1 bezieht sich die Zeitangabe [ἡ γενεὰ αὕτη] hier ganz eindeutig auf das damalige Geschlecht. Jegliche andere Interpretation . . . erweisen sich als artifiziell"). Contra C. E. B. Cranfield, *The Gospel according to St. Mark: An Introduction and Commentary* (Cambridge: Cambridge University Press, 1959), 409, Moore, *Parousia in the New Testament*, 132–33, and many others (including John Calvin), who argue v. 30 does not refer to vv. 24–27 but only the events up to v. 23. Moore's conclusion—"the signs will occur within the immediate future . . . [yet] the End itself is not so delimited" (135)—is forced. See further at 175–90 for his argument that Jesus did not delimit the end. The other alternative interpretation that "this generation" simply refers to the generation living at an unspecified time in the (distant) future is not defended by many exegetes today, though it was a popular interpretation in patristic and medieval exegesis. Cf., e.g., Jerome, *Comm. Matt.* ad loc.; John Chrysostom, *Hom. Matt.* 77.1; and others discussed in Ulrich Luz, *Matthew: A Commentary*, trans. James E. Crouch, Hermeneia (Minneapolis: Fortress, 2005–2007), 3:209.

68. Cf. Cilliers Breytenbach, "Das Wissen und Nicht-Wissen um die Zeit als Verhaltensregel: Eine textpragmatische Analyse der Endzeitrede in Markus 13," in *The Gospel according to Mark as Episodic Narrative*, NovTSup 182 (Leiden: Brill, 2021), 274–91.

69. The sudden shift to the third person in v. 26 has been much discussed. But it in no way pushes the events of vv. 24–26 into the *distant* future. It is fitting within the same timeline assumed in 8:38–9:1: that some, though not necessarily all, will be around for the consummation and the coming of the kingdom in power. Cf. Yarbro Collins, *Mark*, 614–15.

also parity with those earlier sayings in that the prediction before the Sanhedrin looks beyond Jesus's upcoming death and follows the same suffering → glorification pattern that appears in 8:38–9:1 (which follows his first passion prediction) and 13:24–27 (which follows "after that suffering"). What is new is the inclusion of a portion from the opening of Ps 109:1 LXX—"seated at the right hand"—which Mark's Jesus had cited explicitly in an earlier riddle about the messiah being the son of David (12:35–37). The point appears to be that, though Jesus will be killed, he will nevertheless be "seen" as he truly is: the "son of man" from Dan 7 who receives the invitation to "sit at God's right hand." Caiaphas regards such a claim to be blasphemy (14:63–64), just as the scribes had earlier believed the forgiveness of sins by the authority of Dan 7's "son of man" to be blasphemy (2:7).[70] In light of the secrecy motif throughout Mark, the openness of Jesus in responding affirmatively to Caiaphas's question—ἐγώ εἰμι—is jarring, which suggests that the messianic identity revealed by Jesus is of central importance for Mark's Gospel as a whole.

The function of the utterance is to declare that, despite death, Jesus will be vindicated by God before his oppressors. Here all exegetes agree. But vindication in this sense surely includes, rather than excludes, the expectation for his future return.[71] It has been argued that Jesus's reply anticipates something more along the lines of his resurrection or ascension or heavenly exaltation than the scenario Paul hoped for in 1 Thess 4–5.[72] But it is unlikely that Mark's Jesus is simply

70. Much discussed in this context is b. Sanh. 38b and Rabbi Akiva's interpretation of Dan 7's "thrones"—one for God, and one for the messiah—which merited the retort, "Akiva, how long will you profane the Shekinah?" For discussion of the blasphemy charge, see Darrell L. Bock, "Blasphemy and the Jewish Examination of Jesus," *BBR* 17 (2007): 53–114; Michael Theobald, "'Ihr habt die Blasphemie gehört!' (Mk 14:64): Warum der Hohe Rat in Jerusalem auf den Tod Jesu hinwirkte," *NovT* 58 (2016): 233–58.

71. For important treatments, see Karlheinz Müller, "Der Menschensohn im Danielzyklus," in *Jesus und der Menschensohn: Festschrift A. Vögtle*, ed. Rudolf Pesch and Rudolf Schnackenburg (Freiburg: Herder, 1975), 45; George R. Beasley-Murray, *Jesus and the Kingdom of God* (Grand Rapids: Eerdmans, 1986), 300–303; Robert H. Gundry, *Mark: A Commentary on His Apology for the Cross* (Grand Rapids: Eerdmans, 1993), 886–87; Raymond E. Brown, *The Death of the Messiah*, ABRL (New York: Doubleday, 1994), 1:497–98; Cilliers Breytenbach, "Das Markusevangelium, Psalm 110,1 und 118,22f: Folgetext und Prätext," in Tuckett, *Scriptures in the Gospels*, 197–222; Yarbro Collins, *Mark*, 705; Marcus, *Mark 8–16*, 1007–8, 1017; Darrell L. Bock, *Blasphemy and Exaltation in Judaism: The Charge against Jesus in Mark 14:53–65* (Eugene, OR: Wipf & Stock, 2016), 224–29; Murray Smith and Ian J. Vaillancourt, "Enthroned and Coming to Reign: Jesus' Eschatological Use of Psalm 110:1 in Mark 14:62," *JBL* 141 (2022): 513–31.

72. So Timothee Colani, *Jésus-Christ et les croyances messianiques de son temps*, 2nd ed. (Strasbourg: Treuttel & Wurtz, 1864), 20. See also T. W. Manson, *The Teaching of Jesus: Studies of Its Form and Content*, 2nd ed. (Cambridge: Cambridge University Press, 1935), 268; Manson, "The

talking about exaltation after death. Jesus probably speaks of *both* his exaltation, via Ps 109, *and* his future return, via Dan 7.[73] This would accord with the use of Dan 7 elsewhere in Mark, as we have seen,[74] and the use of Ps 109 to describe Jesus's present reign in heaven before his return as we saw already in Paul. Moreover, as C. K. Barrett noted, the sequence is "seated and coming," not "coming and seated," which would be more natural if Mark took both Dan 7 and Ps 109 to refer to Jesus's presentation before God in heaven.[75] When Jesus says "you will see" in 14:62, as in 8:38–9:1 and 13:24–27, he does not merely mean "you will realize" or "you will come to understand" as would be necessary if he were talking about postmortem vindication before God away from human sight.[76] Rather, as in the "day of the Lord" tradition where the coming of God to save and judge is frequently described as *visible* to all (cf. Jub. 1.28; 1 En. 62.3; T. Mos. 10.7)—meaning indisputable—that is the more sensible meaning here as well. Moreover, the use of Dan 7, in the immediate setting of a Sanhedrin trial, implies that Jesus has the final judgment in view in this utterance. The irony would be patent and utterly Markan: while Jesus is seemingly on trial, it is actually the Sanhedrin that is on

Son of Man in Daniel, Enoch, and the Gospels," *BJRL* 32 (1950): 174; Norman Perrin, "Mark 14.62: The End Product of a Christian Pesher Tradition?," *NTS* 12 (1965): 150–55; Morna Hooker, *The Son of Man in Mark* (London: SPCK, 1967), 166–67; John A. T. Robinson, *Jesus and His Coming: The Emergence of a Doctrine* (New York: Abingdon, 1957), 45; Wright, *Jesus and the Victory of God*, 524–25, 642–45; France, *Mark*, 611–13; Thomas Kazen, "The Coming Son of Man Revisited," *JSHJ* 5 (2007): 168 ("says nothing about a return from heaven" but is about "the final victory of God's kingdom"); Hays, *Echoes of Scripture in the Gospels*, 61; Joshua W. Jipp, *The Messianic Theology of the New Testament* (Grand Rapids: Eerdmans, 2020), 77 ("Jesus's response . . . points forward to his vindication by way of resurrection and enthronement").

73. It is somewhat unclear and not really necessary to decide whether Mark regarded "the clouds" as a means of transportation. Mark uses μετά ("with") in 14:62, and ἐν ("in," or "on") in 13:26, both of which draw on Dan 7. In any case, clouds as a mode of transportation are attested elsewhere. Cf. Rev 11:12; Hist. Rech. 17. On the tradition of Baal as "rider on the clouds," see Mark S. Smith, *The Early History of God: Yahweh and the Other Deities in Ancient Israel*, 2nd ed. (Grand Rapids: Eerdmans, 2002), 80–82.

74. So Mussner, *Was lehrt Jesus über das Ende der Welt?*, 52.

75. Barrett, *Jesus and the Gospel Tradition*, 79. See also Bock, "Blasphemy and the Jewish Examination of Jesus," 77, and Smith and Vaillancourt, "Enthroned and Coming to Reign," 524 (who suggest that, while Jesus only alludes to the "sit at my right hand" from Ps 110:1b, the larger context of the psalm implies a process of enthronement, culminating in final victory, which Mark has in view as well).

76. Contra Wright, *Jesus and the Victory of God*, 643, who thinks that Jesus has in mind a "Merkabah-style vision of the divine throne-chariot." Contra also Jane Schaberg, "Mark 14:62: Early Christian Merkabah Imagery?," in Marcus and Soards, *Apocalyptic and the New Testament*, 69–94.

trial, or most certainly will be, at the coming of the son of man.[77] In confirmation of this reading, I would note that "seeing" Dan 7's son of man in the Similitudes of Enoch at the time of the final judgment is stressed, and in many ways close to Mark 14:62: "And there will stand up on that day all the kings and the mighty and the exalted and those who possess the earth. And they will see and recognize that he [the Elect One] sits on the throne of his glory; and righteousness is judged in his presence" (1 En. 62.3).[78]

I further point to an important detail in the crucifixion scene that is often overlooked in this discussion.[79] Just as the darkness at noon (15:33) looks back to Mark 13:24–25 and helps one better understand that earlier prediction, so the mockery of the passersby evokes the Jewish trial in ways that help one understand Jesus's reply to Caiaphas. There is a clear parallel between the mockery and the so-called Jewish trial in that both have two scenes that mirror each other in order and content. In the first round, we hear Jesus critiqued for predicting to destroy and rebuild the temple (15:29–30), just as that "false testimony" began the Jewish trial (14:57–59). In the second, the mockery turns to the messianic identity of Jesus (15:31–32), just as Caiaphas followed the false testimony with a question about Jesus's messiahship (14:61):

	Jewish Trial	**Mockery of the Passersby**
scene 1	"We heard him saying that I will destroy this temple made with hands and after three days build another made without hands"	"Ah! The one who destroys the temple and builds it in three days! Save yourself and come down from the cross"
scene 2	"Are you the Christ, the Son of the Blessed?" And Jesus said, "I am, and you will see the son of man seated at the right hand of the Power and coming with the clouds of heaven"	"He saved others but he cannot save himself. If he is the Christ, the king of Israel, let him come down [καταβάτω] now from the cross, in order that we might see and believe"

Since both cases of mockery are similar in that they throw back at Jesus things he was presumed to have said or implied (e.g., about "saving" oneself [8:34–38]),

77. See Joachim Gnilka, *Das Evangelium nach Markus* (Benziger: Neukirchener Verlag, 1978–1979), 2:282.

78. Translations from 1 Enoch taken from George W. E. Nickelsburg and James C. VanderKam, *1 Enoch: A New Translation* (Minneapolis: Fortress, 2004).

79. For a fuller treatment, see my forthcoming article, "Crucifixion as Parodic Parousia: The Death of Daniel's Son of Man in Mark."

it is striking that the mockery reinscribes Jesus's reply to Caiaphas by asking him to "come down" from the cross.[80] The point would be that, as Jesus had predicted before Caiaphas and the rest that they "will see" him, the messiah, "coming," so here the same chief priests and scribes (14:55) tell him to "come down now from the cross" so that, as he himself had said, they might "see and believe." This parodic parallelism requires us to see that Jesus was talking about his return—a coming *down*—in 14:62.[81] It also makes sense of the emphatic "now" (νῦν) in 15:32; to paraphrase, "you predicted that as the messiah you would come down in the future and be seen, but how about as the messiah you come down *now* from the cross and be seen?" This would be but one of many artful ironies in Mark's crucifixion scene and may in fact function for the evangelist to signal the reversal that is to occur when "the son of man comes with the glory of his Father with the holy angels" (8:38).

Mark in Perspective

If we step back and view the eschatology in Mark as a whole, we see a good deal in common with what we found in Paul.[82] We find imminent eschatological expectation wherein people then alive could expect to see Jesus again. We find the use of "day of the Lord" imagery to inform Jesus's coming. We find the coming of Jesus coincides with the final arrival of the kingdom. We hear about the work of angels, the gathering of followers, and the need to live faithfully in the interim. In addition, there is a striking formal parallel: neither Paul nor Mark sought to contend or prove that Jesus had an important role in the future establishment of the kingdom of God and other end-time realities; rather, their entire theological projects assume this is the case and operate from that basis.[83]

80. Note that Mark specifies the identities of the speakers of this second taunt: "In the same way, the chief priests, along with the scribes, were mocking him, saying. . . ." Cf. 14:53.

81. On parody in Mark's crucifixion scene, see Joel Marcus, "Crucifixion as Parodic Exaltation," *JBL* 125 (2006): 73–87; Jipp, *Messianic Theology of the New Testament*, 78–80.

82. Though I do not see evidence to suppose direct Pauline influence on Mark's understanding of the return of Jesus, as there may be for other matters. The general topic is contested. Cf. Joel Marcus, "Mark—Interpreter of Paul," *NTS* 46 (2000): 473–87 (focuses on Christology and theology of the cross); Eve-Marie Becker, Troels Engberg-Pedersen, and Mogens Müller, eds., *Mark and Paul: Comparative Essays Part II; For and against Pauline Influence on Mark*, BZNW 199 (Berlin: de Gruyter, 2014); Mar Pérez i Díaz, *Mark, a Pauline Theologian: A Re-reading of the Traditions of Jesus in the Light of Paul's Theology*, WUNT 2/251 (Tübingen: Mohr Siebeck, 2020); Heidrun E. Mader, "Narratives Gestalten paulinischer Theologoumena? Paulus und Markus im Vergleich," *ZNT* 24 (2021): 41–58 (focuses on the use of "gospel," gentile inclusion, faith, and the cross).

83. To be sure, the emphasis of Mark, and perhaps the creative contribution of his narrative,

I wish to end this chapter by stressing this final point. Both Mark and Paul believe that the messianic mission of Jesus brought to completion important tasks of great salvation-historical significance, but the present state of things for his would-be followers is incomplete in his absence. The hope of the present is not merely the accomplishments of the past but the soon appearance of Jesus himself in glory.[84] The first written gospel is, of course, very interested in what happened *after* the ministry of Jesus, to be sure. The destruction of the temple, either anticipated or presupposed, receives a good deal of attention. Mark provides an etiology of sorts for the church, expects the spread of the gospel "to all the nations" (13:10), and calls its readers to a cruciform life of discipleship. But it would be a serious mistake to think that the forward momentum and future anticipation of Mark's Gospel centers on any one of these things. For the focus of Mark's narrative, from first line to last, is Jesus, and if the narrative functions to intensify any kind of eschatological longing on the part of the readers, it is for reunion with Jesus. Mark is written from the perspective of christological absence, we might say, that is indistinguishable from Mark's still-future and unrealized eschatology.[85] Readers of the First Gospel live in a time when "the bridegroom is taken away" and hence they fast (2:18–20). Just as those in the ministry of Jesus were often helpless to break free from the old age apart from his intervention and presence, so too, Mark's readers wait in the time of "intense suffering, such as has not been

---

concerns another point: the suffering of the messiah and its role in God's plan. See here Norman Perrin, "The Creative Use of the Son of Man Tradition by Mark," in *A Modern Pilgrimage in New Testament Christology* (Philadelphia: Fortress, 1974), 84–93; Marcus, *Mark 1–8*, 75–79. On what Mark assumes his readers know, see Ulrich Luz, "Looking at Q through the Eyes of Matthew," in *New Studies in the Synoptic Problem: Essays in Honour of Christopher M. Tuckett*, ed. Paul Foster, BETL 239 (Leuven: Peeters, 2011), 587 (he reasons that Mark's interest in Jesus's "teaching," without actually narrating much of it, shows that he was aware of more than he records).

84. Breytenbach, "Mark's Future Tense," 321, offers the following conclusion, which he believes has bearing on the question of the genre of Mark: "Unlike as in tragedy or comedy, the resolution of the plot is not narrated, it is predicted. This distinguishes the Gospel according to Mark fundamentally from almost all biographies scholars draw upon to explain the historical genre of Mark. This also separates Mark's narrative from historiography. The narrator himself does not stand in for the end of the story, he does not look back and tells [*sic*]; he stands back and introduces Jesus as the one who has the authority to announce the end of the story and to bring it to an end."

85. See David S. du Toit, *Der abwesende Herr: Strategien im Markusevangelium zur Bewaltigung der Abwesenheit des Auferstandenen*, WMANT 111 (Neukirchen-Vluyn: Neukirchener Verlag, 2006), 113–49. Mark Goodacre, "The Orthodox Redaction of Mark: How Matthew Rescued Mark's Reputation," in Ferda, Frayer-Griggs, and Johnson, *"To Recover What Has Been Lost"*, 330–31, suggests that one Markan feature that Matthew sought to revise is the impression that, after the ministry of Jesus, he is simply gone.

from the beginning of creation until now" (13:19) and find their hope in his future coming (13:24–26). We might even say that, just as in Mark 6 the disciples in the boat were apart from Jesus, struggling against the wind and the waves that had overtaken them, so later followers lived in a state of turbulence and longed to see Jesus come to them, causing the waves to cease (6:47–52). There is a way in which Mark's descriptions of the past idealize a kind of future: a time when Jesus will again "be with" his followers (3:14) and break the eschatological fast to partake in the messianic banquet (14:25: "I will no longer drink from the fruit of the vine until that day when I drink it new in the kingdom of God"). In the meantime, Mark's readers sit with Peter, James, and John in Gethsemane, striving to "keep awake." To say that eschatology in Mark is about the imminence of "the kingdom," or the judgment, or other final things, without also making mention of the coming of Jesus himself and his followers' reunion with him, is to overlook one of the main claims of the earliest gospel.

10

The Return of the King in Matthew and Luke

Eschatology without Christology is contrary not only to the Gospel of Mark but also to the entire synoptic tradition. The portraits of Jesus in Matthew and Luke, while very different from Mark's, are nevertheless painted with similar eschatological colors, and each narrative's vision for the future extends beyond itself to inform the tomorrow of the readers in a later first-century context. Among exegetes who hold to Markan priority and offer a reading of Mark's eschatology that resembles mine above, I cannot think of one who would suggest that either Matthew or Luke has completely taken back and reframed what one of their main sources asserted about the future coming of Jesus.[1] Moreover, even many critics who think that the eschatology of the earliest gospel tradition was about Jesus merely expressing his hope for vindication by God and the establishment of his movement in symbolic terms will often admit that Matthew and Luke expected more than that, not least that he would come again. In what follows, then, I will not be starting again from ground zero as with Mark, but I will attend to how Matthew and Luke situate the future coming of Jesus within their larger ideological aims to create new but not altogether different images. I will argue that, when their accounts diverge from Mark and from one another, it is not because they presuppose fundamentally different eschatological scenarios but because they narrativize eschatological time in somewhat unique ways and plot Jesus and his

1. See the brief discussion by Osvaldo D. Vena, *The Parousia and Its Rereadings: The Development of the Eschatological Consciousness in the Writings of the New Testament*, SBT 27 (New York: Lang, 2001), 208–11.

followers (including the readers) in varied positions with respect to fulfillment (past) and anticipation (future). These differences can be further explained by the creative ways in which each evangelist has engaged Scripture and situated the story of Jesus and his future coming in relation to the larger story of Israel. I will begin with some broader observations on Matthew's and Luke's Gospels on the whole, as we did for Mark, before turning to discuss the treatment of specific texts they received from Mark and Q.[2]

Eschatology in Matthew

If Isaiah's "way of the Lord" forms one of the crucial scriptural subtexts for Mark's eschatology at the outset, Matthew has broadened that so as to capture the entire covenantal history of Israel. The genealogy that begins the gospel signals that the appearance of Jesus, like that of his ancestors Abraham and David, inaugurates a new stage of salvation history.[3] It also leads one to expect that Jesus's story, "fourteen generations after the Babylonian deportation," will bring about the undoing, in some way, of that exilic low point in the history of Israel.[4] The arrival of the Davidic messiah does not complete anything immediately, however, while it is climactic. Matthew offers a "sich realisierende Eschatologie" within the genealogy itself: there is a claim about fulfillment in the very appearance of the messiah as his coming functions to periodize the history of Israel, but his messianic mission is only beginning to undo what was broken, or "to fulfill all righteousness" (3:15). The early chapters of Matthew confirm this impression.[5] His birth signals the arrival of the expected star of Balaam (2:2–10; cf. Num 24:17)—one of the most famous messianic prophecies in the Second Temple period (cf. Num 24:17 LXX; targumim; T. Jud. 24; etc.)[6]—and in his Galilean ministry, the "light" expected by Isaiah has

2. More on Q and debates about its existence will follow below.

3. See the influential essay by Krister Stendahl, "Quis et Unde? An Analysis of Mt 1–2," in *Judentum Urchristentum Kirche: Festschrift für Joachim Jeremias*, ed. Walther Eltester (Berlin: Töpelmann, 1960), 94–105. See also the compelling reading by Joshua W. Jipp, *The Messianic Theology of the New Testament* (Grand Rapids: Eerdmans, 2020), 25–35.

4. Cf. Nicholas G. Piotrowski, *Matthew's David at the End of Exile: A Socio-rhetorical Study of Scriptural Quotations*, NovTSup 170 (Leiden: Brill, 2016). Here I follow and interpret Matthew's *claim* that there are "fourteen generations" from the exile to "the Christ" (1:17), while noting that the actual number in the genealogy as given is thirteen. For discussion of this much-debated issue, see H. Daniel Zacharias, *Matthew's Presentation of the Son of David: Davidic Tradition and Typology in the Gospel of Matthew* (London: Bloomsbury T&T Clark, 2017), 40–47.

5. For a rich discussion, see Richard B. Hays, *Echoes of Scripture in the Gospels* (Waco, TX: Baylor University Press, 2016), 109–13.

6. It may be Josephus's "ambiguous oracle" in *J.W.* 6.312–313, also referred to by Tacitus,

"dawned" (4:14–16; cf. Isa 9:1–2), which means begun to shine. Thereafter, his healings, exorcisms, and teachings will demonstrate the drawing near of the kingdom of God (4:23–25; 11:2–6; 12:28; 15:29–31), and his death will give expression to the meaning of the name "Jesus," "for he will save his people from their sins" (1:21).[7] But at the same time, for Matthew, the scope of this mission extends beyond the cross and resurrection to anticipate the still-future messianic work of Jesus. This, too, is signaled at the very beginning of Matthew by means of the preaching of John the Baptist, who predicts that "the coming one" "will baptize with the Holy Spirit and fire" and "burn the chaff" of his threshing floor "with unquenchable fire" (3:11–12).[8] While the future referent of "baptize with the Holy Spirit and fire" is ambiguous, "he will burn the chaff with fire" is not. Jesus will do something that, for Matthew's readers, has not happened yet: he will administer, or at least be significantly involved in, the coming judgment of God.[9]

Throughout the gospel, Jesus continues to harken the future-oriented warnings of John the Baptist, which suggests that how people respond to Jesus will determine their fate on "that day" (8:11–12; 11:20–24; 12:36–37; 12:38–42).[10] In full keeping with this larger eschatological vision, all five of Jesus's Moses-like discourses in Matthew end with anticipations of the coming judgment, first in the conclusion of the Sermon on the Mount (7:21–27).[11] In two more of these, Matthew has supple-

Hist. 5.13, and Suetonius, *Vesp.* 4.5. See Ulrich Fischer, *Eschatologie und Jenseitserwartung im hellenistischen Diasporajudentum* (Berlin: de Gruyter, 1978), 161–67. Another intriguing possibility is Isa 11:1–16, especially vv. 10–12, which mention ruling over the nations (cf. Paul's citation of this with reference to Jesus in Rom 15:12).

7. See Tucker S. Ferda, "The Soldiers' Inscription and the Angel's Word: The Significance of 'Jesus' in Matthew's *Titulus*," *NovT* 55 (2013): 221–31.

8. See Donald Hagner, *Matthew*, WBC 33 (Dallas: Word, 1993–1995), 1:50.

9. Cf. Alexander Sand, "Die Gemeinde zwischen 'jenen Tagen Jesu' und 'dem Tag des Gerichts': Zum Geschichtsverständnis des Matthäusevangeliums," *TTZ* 99 (1990): 49–71. On the fire language and its relation to judgment, see Daniel Frayer-Griggs, *Saved through Fire: The Fiery Ordeal in New Testament Eschatology* (Eugene, OR: Pickwick, 2016), 131–44.

10. On the final judgment in Matthew, see Ulrich Luz, *Matthew: A Commentary*, trans. James E. Crouch, Hermeneia (Minneapolis: Fortress, 2005–2007), 3:285–96; Anders Runesson, *Divine Wrath and Salvation in Matthew: The Narrative World of the First Gospel* (Minneapolis: Fortress, 2016).

11. On the end of the Sermon on the Mount and the final judgment, see Hans Dieter Betz, "Eine Episode im Jüngsten Gericht (Mt 7, 21–23)," *ZTK* 78 (1981): 1–30; W. D. Davies and Dale C. Allison Jr., *A Critical and Exegetical Commentary on the Gospel according to Saint Matthew*, ICC (Edinburgh: T&T Clark, 1988–1997), 1:719–24, 728–30; Daniel J. Harrington, *The Gospel of Matthew*, SP 1 (Collegeville, MN: Liturgical Press, 1991), 109–11; R. T. France, *The Gospel of Matthew*, NICNT (Grand Rapids: Eerdmans, 2007), 292–97; David L. Turner, *Matthew*, BECNT (Grand Rapids: Baker Books, 2008), 213–23; Paul Foster, "The Eschatology of the Gospel of Matthew," in *"To Recover What Has Been Lost": Essays on Eschatology, Intertextuality, and Reception History*

mented Mark in a very revealing manner: he adds eschatological parables about the return of Jesus and the final judgment to Mark's parable chapter (4:1–34) and to his Olivet Discourse (13:1–37). Mark's parable chapter, which also likely looked forward to the final eschatological harvest (4:26–29) and the ingathering of all the nations in God's kingdom (4:30–32), now ends in Matthew with explicit predictions of the son of man's future coming with his angels to judge "all evildoers" (13:36–43), and the sorting of the righteous and the unrighteous "at the end of the age" (13:47–50). Moreover, Mark's Olivet Discourse, which concluded with a parable about the sudden return of "a man" going away on a journey (13:33–37), now ends with four further parables about the faithful and wise slave (24:45–51), the ten virgins (25:1–13), the talents (25:14–30), and the sheep and the goats (25:31–46).[12] These additions, strategically placed at the precise point where Mark had a similar parable about the return of "the Lord of the house," nearly double the size of the Olivet Discourse itself and place even more focus on the future appearance of Jesus (which Matthew refers to four times with παρουσία, a term not found in Mark).[13] There are few exegetes of Matthew who would dispute this summary.[14]

The importance of the future for Matthew extends beyond the warnings to encompass ethical material as well. In the Beatitudes of the Sermon on the Mount, the Lord's Prayer, and elsewhere, the future indicative ("your kingdom come, your will be done") informs the present imperative ("on earth as in heaven"). In the first spoken word of Jesus's public ministry—"repent, for the kingdom of heaven has drawn near" (4:17)—the γάρ is the hinge word. Repentance is necessary because of the nearness of the kingdom.

In Matthew's eschatological scheme, then, Jesus inaugurates the kingdom and its requisite communal ethic while never losing sight of the future denouement where his activity will again be center stage.[15] Matthew's readers live in between

---

in Honor of Dale C. Allison Jr., ed. Tucker S. Ferda, Daniel Frayer-Griggs, and Nathan C. Johnson, NovTSup 183 (Leiden: Brill, 2021), 85–87.

12. Cf. John Paul Heil, "Final Parables in the Eschatological Discourse in Matthew 24–25," in *Matthew's Parables: Audience-Oriented Perspectives*, ed. Warren Carter and John Paul Heil (Washington, DC: Catholic Biblical Association of America, 1998), 177–209.

13. See Foster, "Eschatology of the Gospel of Matthew," 77–79.

14. Though one persistent point of disagreement concerns the nature and/or extent of eschatological violence in Matthew's depiction. David J. Neville, *A Peaceable Hope: Contesting Violent Eschatology in New Testament Narratives* (Grand Rapids: Baker Books, 2013), argues that Mark's eschatological scenario is "relatively peaceful" in comparison to Matthew's, wherein he finds a "deep-seated discrepancy between moral vision and eschatology" (249; see further 17–90).

15. Contrast Mark Harris, "The Comings and Goings of the Son of Man: Is Matthew's Risen Jesus 'Present' or 'Absent'?," *BibInt* 22 (2014): 51–70, who goes so far as to argue that the parousia hope in Matthew can be read as a statement of the continuous presence of Jesus after the resur-

this past and future messianic work of Jesus, which means their own discipleship in the present—their "producing fruit" (3:10; 7:16–20; 13:23, 30; 21:41) and "obedience to all that I have commanded you" (28:20)—is swept into and made intelligible by the larger covenantal myth of God rescuing dispersed Israel and redeeming the nations through Abraham's seed.[16] For Matthew, the resurrection of the dead, the final judgment, and the reunion with Jesus still to come are as integral to Jesus's epoch-shaping work as anything accomplished in his earthly ministry.[17] To be sure, Matthew signals the onset of these last things in Jesus's very life, death, and resurrection, a point made most clearly by the earthquake and resurrection of the holy ones of old that follow the moment of his death (27:51–53).[18] Moreover, Matthew's risen Jesus contends that he has received all the authority promised to Dan 7's son of man ("all authority in heaven and earth have been given to me [ἐδόθη μοι πᾶσα ἐξουσία]" [28:18]), and thereby sends out his followers to disciple the nations (28:19). But as his followers go about fulfilling such tasks, and living out this new state of things, the promise of the earlier commission still rings in their ears: "Truly I say to you, you will by no means finish the cities of Israel until the son of man comes" (10:23).[19] That is, Matthew's Gospel contends, the followers of Jesus will not complete the tasks he has set before them before he comes again. The ultimate end of "the deportation to Babylon" (1:17) and the regathering of those lost in exile, we might say, will not be finished until the angels of the son of man "gather [ἐπισυνάξουσιν] the elect from the four winds" (24:31).[20]

---

rection. See instead Andries van Aarde, "'On Earth as It Is in Heaven'—Matthew's Eschatology as the Kingdom of the Heavens That Has Come," in *Eschatology of the New Testament and Some Related Documents*, ed. Jan G. van der Watt, WUNT 2/315 (Tübingen: Mohr Siebeck, 2011), 35–63, whose emphasis on the notion of inauguration is not at the expense of consummation.

16. See here especially Matthias Konradt, *Israel, Church, and the Gentiles in the Gospel of Matthew* (Waco, TX: Baylor University Press, 2014).

17. David C. Sim, *Apocalyptic Eschatology in the Gospel of Matthew*, SNTSMS 88 (Cambridge: Cambridge University Press, 1996), 93–128.

18. See Dale C. Allison Jr., "The Scriptural Background of a Matthean Legend: Ezekiel 37, Zechariah 14, and Matthew 27," in *Life beyond Death in Matthew's Gospel: Religious Metaphor or Bodily Reality?*, ed. Wim Weren, Huub van de Sandt, and Joseph Verheyden, BTS 13 (Leuven: Peeters, 2011), 153–88.

19. Cf. Otto Betz, *Die Menschensohnworte Jesu und die Zukunftserwartung des Paulus (Daniel 7, 13–14)*, ANTJ 6 (Frankfurt am Main: Lang, 1985), 75–80. Betz further attempts to connect this prediction to the famous messianic oracle of Gen 49:10 ("bis der Schiloh kommt"), which I find intriguing in light of Matthew's use of Gen 49 in the triumphal entry. See Tucker S. Ferda, "Doubling Down: Zechariah's Oracle, Judah's Blessing, and the Triumphal Entry in Matthew," *JTS* 71 (2020): 1–27.

20. As noted at p. 3n6, the reading of Matthew offered by Jipp, *Messianic Theology of the New Testament*, tends to downplay the significance of future eschatology simply by virtue of what he

Eschatology in Luke

In the work of the Third Evangelist, we find a similar eschatological scheme, albeit with far more emphasis on what Jesus's coming, and going (in the ascension), has *realized* for the history of Israel and the nations.[21] Already in the prologue, Luke announces that his narrative will be about "the things that have been fulfilled among us" (1:1), and at the end of the gospel, Jesus reprimands the weary travelers on the road to Emmaus for failing to see that what had happened to Jesus in Jerusalem actually fulfilled "all that the prophets have declared" about the messiah (24:44–49).[22] Here the death of Jesus is neither a past failure nor a mere pretext for what is to come in the future; it is, rather, "necessary that the messiah should suffer and then enter his glory" (24:26). Between this beginning and ending, the narrative is persistent in its stress on the same. In Luke's infancy narrative, Jesus's coming is heralded as the arrival of God's "salvation" (2:30) and the long-awaited "light" from Isa 49 (2:32), and Mary's Magnificat and Zechariah's Benedictus celebrate the fulfillment of a dizzying number of prophetic expectations (1:46–55; 1:67–79). Luke has decided to open the public ministry of Jesus with a dramatic reading of Isa 61, in which Jesus declares that the coming of one "anointed" by the Spirit to initiate the long-awaited time of jubilee "has been fulfilled today in your hearing" (4:16–21).[23] And Jesus's subsequent activity is true to that opening declaration. His miracles and teachings manifest the presence of the kingdom of God (6:17–19; 7:18–23; 10:9). His exorcisms demonstrate that "the kingdom of God has arrived [ἔφθασεν]." One particular saying unique to Luke sums this up better than any other: Jesus dismisses attempts to calculate the future coming of the kingdom by redirecting attention to the present, because "the kingdom of God is among you" (17:21).

We would seriously misread the much-discussed realized eschatology of Luke, however, if we failed to see that the "already" in this narrative is intelligible only within a process of realization that looks beyond the ministry of Jesus in Luke,

---

includes for discussion. In his discussion of the messianic work of Jesus and the restoration of Israel in Matthew (21–56), for instance, there is not a single discussion of Matt 24.

21. As is well known. Cf., e.g., Joel B. Green, *The Theology of the Gospel of Luke* (Cambridge: Cambridge University Press, 1991), 76–101; Earle. E. Ellis, *Christ and the Future in New Testament History*, NovTSup 97 (Leiden: Brill, 2000), 105–19; Michael Wolter, "Eschatology in the Gospel according to Luke," in van der Watt, *Eschatology of the New Testament*, 97–100.

22. See Hays, *Echoes of Scripture in the Gospels*, 191–95, 275–77.

23. 11Q Melchizedek (11Q13)—which will be discussed in more detail in part 4—conflates Isa 61 and Lev 25 in ways that closely parallel Luke 4. This fragment deepens our understanding of the eschatological significance of Luke 4, which is also expressed in other ways (e.g., "today this Scripture is fulfilled in your hearing").

the history of the church in Acts, and even the experiences of the readers of Luke and Acts in the final decades of the first-century CE.[24] In this respect, Luke's work is similar to Mark and Matthew in that its narrative not only directs its readers to the past; it also shapes their expectations for the future.[25] The notion of eschatological process—underway but not yet completed—is likely true for Luke's use of Isa 61 in the annunciation scene itself, since Jesus's reading breaks off at the precise moment the prophet turns to mention the coming "day of vengeance" (Isa 61:2).[26] In Luke's eschatological scenario, this coming "day of vengeance" is not rejected but deferred to the future, as Jesus will later describe the events surrounding the destruction of Jerusalem as "the days of vengeance, to fulfill all that is written" (21:22). Moreover, it is clear that Luke's John the Baptist predicts not just the Spirit and fire of Pentecost (Luke 3:16; Acts 2:1–4) but, as in Matthew, the final judgment beyond that (Luke 3:17). Jesus himself will routinely speak of "the judgment" that is to come (10:14; 11:31, 32; see also 13:22–29), as Paul in Acts will warn his Athenian hearers that God "has fixed a day on which he will have the world judged in righteousness by a man whom he has appointed" (17:31). Luke and Acts clearly anticipate the resurrection of the dead (e.g., Luke 14:14; 20:35; Acts 17:32; etc.) and reunion with the patriarchs of old (Luke 16:19–31). The account signals throughout that the defeat of Satan and his minions is underway but not yet completed.[27] Luke is certainly interested in the political history of Judea and

24. Simon Gathercole, *The Gospel and the Gospels* (Grand Rapids: Eerdmans, 2022), 181, is helpful in noting that while Luke and Acts are not treated as a single work in their early reception (cf. Andrew F. Gregory and C. Kavin Rowe, eds., *Rethinking the Unity and Reception of Luke and Acts* [Columbia: University of South Carolina Press, 2010]), "there is a certain artificiality in keeping Acts out of the picture altogether, since it can of course shed light on Luke's thought."

25. For some important studies that challenge Conzelmann's understanding of the "delay of the parousia" in a way that minimizes future expectation, see S. G. Wilson, "Lukan Eschatology," *NTS* 16 (1970): 330–47; Beverly Roberts Gaventa, "The Eschatology of Luke-Acts Revisited," *Enc* 43 (1982): 27–42; Craig S. Keener, *Acts*, NCBC (Cambridge: Cambridge University Press, 2020), 69–70.

26. See discussion in Hays, *Echoes of Scripture in the Gospels*, 225–30.

27. Luke has emphasized exorcism in Jesus's ministry, and he has also emphasized Jesus's clear, no-contest victory in these struggles (cf. Luke 4:40–41). Only Luke explicitly notes that, while Beelzebul is the "strong man," Jesus is "the stronger one" (ὁ ἰσχυρότερος [11:22]). Moreover, Jesus gives the Twelve "power and authority" (δύναμιν καὶ ἐξουσίαν) over "all" the demons (9:1), he gives the seventy-two authority "over every power of the enemy" (10:19), and he declares, in a context discussing exorcism no less, that "all things have been handed over to me by my Father" (10:22). It seems to me that these details challenge Susan R. Garrett's brilliant study, *The Demise of the Devil* (Minneapolis: Fortress, 1989), in its understanding that Luke narrativizes the progressive recovery of Jesus's authority over the world from Satan (who, she thinks, in 4:6, actually possesses it). She contends that "as the Kingdom of Satan diminishes, the Kingdom of God grows proportionately" (45), and that this narrative culminates in Jesus's victory over Satan

the destruction of Jerusalem, but the eschatological imagination of this source is not limited to the past. The open ending of Acts 28 itself bears witness to this.

The messianic mission of Jesus as conceived by Luke is, also, only intelligible within a process of realization. This is signaled at the outset of Luke, where we find a typological parallel between the story of Jesus and the story of David's rise.[28] The angel Gabriel tells Mary that God will "give to him [Jesus] the throne of his ancestor David" (1:32)—in fulfillment of Nathan's promise to David in 2 Sam 7—and that "his kingdom will last forever" (1:33), as envisioned in Daniel's dream vision about the son of man in Dan 7.[29] But this does not happen overnight. Luke has understood the resurrection and ascension of Jesus to God's right hand, at the end of the gospel narrative, to be a significant moment in the "forever" enthronement of David's heir.[30] Luke emphasizes and reemphasizes this in the somewhat theologically repetitive speeches of Acts, which often focus on the same two claims: the messiah's rejection by mortals, and his resurrection and exaltation by God in fulfillment of the Scriptures.[31] But that, too, is not the end of the story of the messiah's rise for Luke—from that heavenly place of exaltation, there is more

---

in the resurrection and ascension. But how does one explain Jesus's clear authority over Satan already during his ministry and his claim to have already received authority over him and his hoard? Moreover, it is not apparent that the narrative of Luke-Acts supports identifying such a key transition point in the resurrection and ascension when it comes to Satan's dethronement. In Acts, things continue as before: (1) Satan still has "authority" (Acts 26:18); (2) Satan infiltrates the church (5:3); (3) Satan and his demons still oppress and overpower people (8:6–7; 19:11–20). Garrett's master reading of Luke-Acts may overreach in terms of both the extent of Satan's power in the world and the idea that Satan's defeat is signaled (implicitly, that would be) in some narrative event. Garrett, *Demise*, 60, admits some weakness with her thesis here: "if this story is so important for Luke, why has the evangelist nowhere made it more plain? This is a difficult question."

28. Note the clear parallels between Hannah's song in 1 Sam 2 and the Magnificat. Cf. Cristina Buffa, "The Magnificat and the Song of Hannah," *RevScRel* 92 (2018): 377–92. As Hannah's song served to anticipate David's rise, so does Mary's. Also suggestive is the side note that Jesus was "about thirty" when he began his ministry (Luke 3:23), as David was "about thirty years old when he began to reign" (2 Sam 5:4). For a broader discussion, see Yuzuru Miura, *David in Luke-Acts: His Portrayal in the Light of Early Judaism*, WUNT 2/232 (Tübingen: Mohr Siebeck, 2007).

29. On the conflation of 2 Sam 7:12–13 and Dan 7:14 in Gabriel's word to Mary, see Karl A. Kuhn, "The 'One like a Son of Man' Becomes the 'Son of God,'" *CBQ* 69 (2008): 36–37.

30. See the rich discussion by Jipp, *Messianic Theology of the New Testament*, 86–89 (on Luke), 101–8 (on Acts).

31. As highlighted by Charles H. Talbert, *Literary Patterns, Theological Themes, and the Genre of Luke-Acts* (Missoula, MT: Scholars Press, 1975). See also Marion L. Soards, *The Speeches in Acts: Their Content, Context, and Concerns* (Louisville: Westminster John Knox, 1994); Janusz Kucicki, *The Function of the Speeches in the Acts of the Apostles: A Key to Interpretation of Luke's Use of Speeches in Acts* (Leiden: Brill, 2018).

to come for Daniel's son of man.[32] Jesus responds on two notable occasions to expectations about the future establishment of his kingdom: once when nearing Jerusalem and the people "supposed that the kingdom of God was to appear immediately" (Luke 19:11), and again after his resurrection when the disciples ask, "is this the time when you will restore the kingdom to Israel?" (Acts 1:6). In both cases, his response is the same. He does not deny the premise—for example, that the kingdom is coming and hence "not yet" here—but simply redirects the focus to the tasks of the present.[33] You have been given minas to invest before the king returns, he says (Luke 19:12–27), and you will soon receive power to be my witnesses to the end of the earth, he says again (Acts 1:8). In neither case does Jesus say that his hearers are wrong to expect the coming kingdom but rather that it is not happening right now (Luke 19:11), and "it is not for you to know the times and seasons" (Acts 1:7). This opening scene of Acts concludes with angels providing the only further commentary needed: "Men of Galilee, why do you stand gazing into heaven? This Jesus, who has been taken up from you into heaven, will come in the same way as you saw him go into heaven" (1:11). In other words, Luke suggests, you can rest assured that Jesus will be coming back, so bring your eyes back down to earth and get to work. This going, and predicted coming, provides the eschatological timeline for the rest of Acts and for its readers.[34]

We should conclude that, in comparison with Mark and Matthew, eschatological time in Luke has been stretched to a further degree but not bent into an

32. Cf. Isaac W. Oliver, *Luke's Jewish Eschatology: The National Restoration of Israel in Luke-Acts* (Oxford: Oxford University Press, 2021), 45. Luke emphasizes more frequently than the other gospels the identity of Jesus as the son of man from Dan 7 (5:24; 9:22; 12:8, 40; 17:24, 30; 18:8; 21:27; 22:22). See here Crispin H. T. Fletcher-Louis, *Luke-Acts: Angels, Christology and Soteriology*, WUNT 2/94 (Tübingen: Mohr Siebeck, 1997), 225–50; Craig A. Evans, "Inaugurating the Kingdom of God and Defeating the Kingdom of Satan," *BBR* 15 (2005): 49–75; Christopher Tuckett, "The Lucan Son of Man," in *From the Sayings to the Gospels*, WUNT 328 (Tübingen: Mohr Siebeck, 2014), 557–73. Luke often draws on several other details from that famous vision: "authority" (4:32, 36; 5:24; 9:1; 10:19; 20:2), "handing over" (10:22), "giving" (1:32; 12:32), and "glory" (9:26; 21:27; 24:26).

33. Oliver, *Luke's Jewish Eschatology*, 3–6, shows how frequently in the history of interpretation Jesus essentially rejects the disciples' question along the lines of a "spiritual" redefinition of the kingdom or realized eschatology. As Oliver shows, this does not make sense of the text.

34. There may even be a similar dynamic at play in the uniquely Lukan account of Jesus's exchange with the brigand on the cross, though it is not necessary for my overall case to demonstrate this fully. In my view, the crucified man's question to Jesus probably alludes to his future coming "in," meaning *with*, his kingdom: "Jesus, remember me when you come in your kingdom" (ἐν τῇ βασιλείᾳ [23:42]). So Darrell L. Bock, *Luke 9:51–24:53*, BECNT (Grand Rapids: Baker Books, 1996), 1856–57. Jesus's reply, then, is another case of realizing eschatology, which we might paraphrase in this way (v. 43): "I will remember you much earlier than that; I tell you truly, you will be with me this very day in paradise."

altogether different shape.[35] There is more emphasis in Luke on life in *die Mitte der Zeit*, that is, in the space created between Jesus's rise and return.[36] Here his followers are to continue "all that Jesus began to do and to teach" (Acts 1:1),[37] embodying in themselves the mission of Isaiah's servant (from Isa 42, cf. Luke 3:22; 9:35; 23:35; Acts 26:18; from Isa 53, cf. Luke 18:31–33; 22:37; 24:26; Acts 3:13–14), empowered by the resurrection of Jesus and Joel 2's poured-out Spirit (Acts 2:16–21).[38] But the subsequent activity of Jesus in the future is not thereby deferred or even downplayed; it is, rather, important enough that it can be assumed and utilized to do other rhetorical work.[39] In Acts 3, Peter urges his opponents to "repent" and "turn to God" "so that your sins might be wiped out, so that the times of refreshing might come from the presence of the Lord, and that he may send the messiah appointed for you, that is, Jesus, who must remain in heaven until the time of universal restoration that God announced long ago through his holy prophets" (3:19–21).[40] And in Luke 12, Jesus recalls before his disciples Dan 7's investiture scene—"Do not be afraid, little flock, for it is your Father's good pleasure to give you the kingdom" (12:32)—followed immediately with this: "Sell your possessions, and give alms. Make purses for yourselves that do not wear out, an unfailing treasure in heaven, where no thief comes near and no moth destroys. For where your treasure is, there your heart will be also" (12:33–34). Before outsiders in the first case (Acts 3),

35. Cf. Young Ho Kim, *Die Parusie bei Lukas: Eine literarisch-exegetische Untersuchung zu den Parusieaussagen im lukanischen Doppelwerk*, BZNW 217 (Berlin: de Gruyter: 2016) (who reads Luke-Acts synchronously and identifies the parousia hope throughout). See also Ellis, *Christ and the Future in New Testament History*, 112–19; Wolter, "Eschatology in the Gospel according to Luke," 93–97 (at 93: "Luke shares more or less the expectations that can be found in other New Testament writings").

36. Though, *pace* Hans Conzelmann in *Die Mitte der Zeit: Studien zur Theologie des Lukas*, 6th ed. (Tübingen: Mohr, 1977), Luke does not appear to divide history into "parts." Cf. Wolter, "Eschatology in the Gospel according to Luke," 97–98 ("the Lucan narrative is part of one single overall history"). Moreover, as commonly noted, the impact of the delay of the parousia was overstated by Conzelmann.

37. On this translation, see Richard B. Hays, *The Moral Vision of the New Testament: Community, Cross, New Creation* (San Francisco: HarperSanFrancisco, 1996), 120.

38. Cf. Holly Beers, *The Followers of Jesus as the 'Servant': Luke's Model from Isaiah for the Disciples in Luke-Acts*, LNTS 535 (London: Bloomsbury T&T Clark, 2015).

39. Nor is it necessarily the case that the Third Evangelist eliminates eschatological imminence altogether. C. E. B. Cranfield, "Thoughts on New Testament Eschatology," *SJT* 35 (1982): 499, wrote memorably about Luke 18:1–8, "If Luke was really intent on getting rid of the idea of the nearness of the Parousia, he has surely done his work with extraordinary maladroitness here." See also K. B. Haacker, "Der Geist und das Reich im Lukanischen Werk: Konkurrenz oder Konvergenz zwischen Pneumatologie und Eschatologie?," *NTS* 59 (2013): 325–45.

40. On the depiction of the return of Jesus in these lines, see Carl R. Holladay, *Acts: A Commentary*, NTL (Louisville: Westminster John Knox, 2016), 120.

and insiders in the second (Luke 12), the future coming of Jesus and the kingdom invests the present with urgency, and discipleship with radicalism.[41]

Use of Mark: After Peter's Confession

To gain a deeper understanding of the eschatological claims of Matthew and Luke as they pertain to the coming of Jesus specifically, I turn now to consider how they have made use of their two main sources. The first of these, of course, is Mark. How have Matthew and Luke received those three crucial Markan passages discussed above that have dominated discussion about the parousia in historical Jesus research?[42] These texts appear in Matthew and Luke in the same general location in the ministry of Jesus—that is, after Peter's confession, at the end of the Olivet Discourse (though, for Luke, this occurs "in the temple," 21:1–38), and before Caiaphas—and, I will argue, we find much continuity with Mark in general, while also creative elaboration and change that is understandable given the tendencies of these two gospels as already described.[43] Matthew and Luke rework the first prediction of Jesus as follows:

41. For these reasons, I disagree with Christopher Tuckett, "The Christology of Luke-Acts," *From the Sayings to the Gospels*, 603, that Luke's "claims about Jesus involve changing almost every element in the nature of this [messianic] hope . . . Jesus is a 'royal' figure, but not in any political sense at all and his reigning has absolutely no consequences for the political status quo. . . . his throne is in heaven, not on earth." It is true that Luke completely absorbs the suffering and death of the messiah within his scripturally inspired mission (cf. 24:46–47). But that is not the end of the story. Note the logic of Luke 17:24–25: "For as lightning flashing shines from one side of the sky to another, thus also will be the son of man. *But first* [πρῶτον δέ] it is necessary for him to suffer many things." The suffering and death here are a prelude and not a total spiritualization of the messianic task. There is no reason to spiritualize the clear allusions to Dan 7:13–14, 22, 27 in the Last Supper in Luke 22:28–30. Cf. Craig A. Evans, "The Twelve Thrones of Israel: Scripture and Politics in Luke 22:24–30," in *Luke and Scripture*, ed. Craig A. Evans and James A. Sanders (Minneapolis: Augsburg, 1993), 155–60. See also Franz Mussner, "Die Idee der Apokatastasis in der Apostelgeschichte," in *Lex Tua Veritas: Festschrift für Hubert Junker zur Vollendung des siebigsten Lebensjahres am 8. August 1961*, ed. Heinrich Gross and Franz Mussner (Trier: Paulinus, 1961), 293–306; J. Bradley Chance, *Jerusalem, the Temple, and the New Age in Luke-Acts* (Macon, GA: Mercer University Press, 1988), 127–38; David Ravens, *Luke and the Restoration of Israel*, JSNTSup 119 (Sheffield: Sheffield Academic, 1995); Oliver, *Luke's Jewish Eschatology*, 69–70, 83–93, 97–102, 142.

42. And in receiving, we are not looking merely at change. The view that only redaction can be used to identify the theology of the Gospels is problematic, as now commonly acknowledged. Cf. Graham N. Stanton, *The Gospels and Jesus*, 2nd ed. (Oxford: Oxford University Press, 2002), 29–30.

43. On the similarities, see Wilhelm Weiffenbach, *Die Wiederkunftsgedanke Jesu* (Leipzig: Druck, 1873), 180–82.

Mark 8:38–9:1	Matt 16:27–28	Luke 9:26–27
ὃς γὰρ ἐὰν ἐπαισχυνθῇ με καὶ τοὺς ἐμοὺς λόγους ἐν τῇ γενεᾷ ταύτῃ τῇ μοιχαλίδι καὶ ἁμαρτωλῷ		ὃς γὰρ ἂν ἐπαισχυνθῇ με καὶ τοὺς ἐμοὺς λόγους
καὶ ὁ υἱὸς τοῦ ἀνθρώπου ἐπαισχυνθήσεται αὐτόν,		τοῦτον ὁ υἱὸς τοῦ ἀνθρώπου ἐπαισχυνθήσεται
ὅταν ἔλθῃ ἐν τῇ δόξῃ τοῦ πατρὸς αὐτοῦ μετὰ τῶν ἀγγέλων τῶν ἁγίων	μέλλει γὰρ ὁ υἱὸς τοῦ ἀνθρώπου ἔρχεσθαι ἐν τῇ δόξῃ τοῦ πατρὸς αὐτοῦ μετὰ τῶν ἀγγέλων αὐτοῦ	ὅταν ἔλθῃ ἐν τῇ δόξῃ αὐτοῦ καὶ τοῦ πατρὸς καὶ τῶν ἁγίων ἀγγέλων
	καὶ τότε ἀποδώσει ἑκάστῳ κατὰ τὴν πρᾶξιν αὐτοῦ	
Καὶ ἔλεγεν αὐτοῖς· ἀμὴν λέγω ὑμῖν ὅτι εἰσίν τινες ὧδε τῶν ἑστηκότων οἵτινες οὐ μὴ γεύσωνται θανάτου ἕως ἂν ἴδωσιν τὴν βασιλείαν τοῦ θεοῦ ἐληλυθυῖαν ἐν δυνάμει	Ἀμὴν λέγω ὑμῖν ὅτι εἰσίν τινες τῶν ὧδε ἑστώτων οἵτινες οὐ μὴ γεύσωνται θανάτου ἕως ἂν ἴδωσιν τὸν υἱὸν τοῦ ἀνθρώπου ἐρχόμενον ἐν τῇ βασιλείᾳ αὐτοῦ	λέγω δὲ ὑμῖν ἀληθῶς, εἰσίν τινες τῶν αὐτοῦ ἑστηκότων οἳ οὐμὴ γεύσωνται θανάτου ἕως ἂν ἴδωσιν τὴν βασιλείαν τοῦ θεοῦ
"For whoever is ashamed of me and my words in this adulterous and sinful generation		"For whoever is ashamed of me and my words
also the son of man will be ashamed of that person		the son of man will be ashamed of this person
when he comes in the glory of his Father with the holy angels"	"For the son of man is about to come in the glory of his Father with his angels	when he comes in his glory and [the glory of] the Father and of the holy angels
	And then he will repay each according to his deeds	

Mark 8:38–9:1	Matt 16:27–28	Luke 9:26–27
And he was saying to them, "Amen I say to you that there are some standing here who will by no means taste death until they see the kingdom of God has come in power"	Amen I say to you that there are some standing here who will by no means taste death until they see the son of man coming in his kingdom"	And I truly say to you, there are some standing here who will by no means taste death until they see the kingdom of God"

Matthew emphasizes the future coming of the son of man by better integrating Mark 8:38 and 9:1.[44] Matthew omits Mark's editorial καὶ ἔλεγεν αὐτοῖς and substitutes ἀμὴν λέγω ὑμῖν, with the result that 16:28 functions to build on and clarify the preceding line. For Matthew, "the kingdom of God come in power" *is* "the son of man coming in his kingdom," which was Mark's point, too, but now more clearly communicated. Matthew has also connected this prediction to the preceding discourse about suffering and discipleship in a slightly different way. In Mark, the line about "being ashamed" functions as a warning to those who fail to heed Jesus's call to take up the shameful cross and likely imagines the final judgment. Matthew omits Mark's line about the son of man "being ashamed" (having a very similar saying elsewhere in his gospel, which was likely from Q [more on this below]) but retains if not emphasizes the anticipation of the final judgment by adding the line "he [the son of man] will repay [ἀποδώσει] each person according to his deeds." This addition connects to the prior question of Jesus in 16:26, "what can a person give [δώσει] in return for his life?" The upshot is that Mark's warning against disobedience becomes in Matthew a word of encouragement for obedience: do not worry what you might lose, for when the son of man comes, he will give back anything you have given (so δώσει . . . ἀποδώσει). That is an intriguing rhetorical and functional shift in Matthew, though the basic content from Mark is maintained if not emphasized: Jesus is talking about his own future coming, which is imminent and connected to the final judgment.[45] To be sure, Matthew can also

44. I see no reason to think Matt 16:27 contains independent tradition, though some others have thought this. Cf. E. P. Sanders, *Jesus and Judaism* (Philadelphia: Fortress, 1985), 144–45. On Matthew's use of Daniel, see Daniel M. Gurtner, "Danielic Influence at the Intersection of Matthew and the Dead Sea Scrolls," in *Matthew within Judaism: Israel and the Nations in the First Gospel*, ed. Anders Runesson and Daniel M. Gurtner, ECL 27 (Atlanta: SBL Press, 2020), 309–28.

45. So also Foster, "Eschatology of the Gospel of Matthew," 92.

leverage the future coming of Jesus as a threat or challenge (e.g., 24:36–51), but that is not what the text emphasizes here.[46]

Luke maintains Mark 8:38 more or less unchanged, where it still refers to the future coming of Jesus.[47] Luke's editorial hand is more evident in the reception of Mark 9:1, which betrays the penchant for realized eschatology. The future prediction of the parousia (v. 26) is followed by an opportunity for a nearer fulfillment (v. 27): Jesus speaks not merely of a future fact that is to happen (the kingdom come in power) but invites his hearers to deeper perception now (seeing the kingdom), much like the exchange in 17:20–21 wherein Jesus proclaims the kingdom is presently "among you."[48] Luke's new conjunction holds the logic: Mark's clunky καὶ ἔλεγεν αὐτοῖς becomes in Luke λέγω δὲ ὑμῖν ("but I say to you"), where the contrastive δέ is crucial. To be clear, this is not a case where Luke has rejected or completely reinterpreted the expectation for Jesus's coming in the future; it is, rather, in characteristically Lukan fashion, using the future (v. 26) to inform the present (v. 27). Given the transfiguration scene that follows, it may be that Luke has the resurrection of Jesus particularly in mind here, as Mark's "after six days" becomes "about eight days after"—the first day of the new week (cf. 24:1)—and Jesus's "glory" is emphasized (9:31, 32). In any case, the expectation for the parousia is maintained in Luke's version of the transfiguration, made clear by means of a unique addition to Mark's account: "Peter and those with him were heavy with sleep, but because they kept awake [διαγρηγορήσαντες] they saw his glory" (9:32; cf. 22:45–46).[49] Luke's parables about the future coming of Jesus are near to hand (cf. especially 21:34–36).

Use of Mark: Messiah and Temple

In their reception of Mark 13, Matthew and Luke have both maintained the climactic prediction of the "coming of the son of man," though not without taking some creative license with the wording.[50]

46. This is not to say threat is totally eliminated, as the final judgment is depicted. This is a matter of emphasis. See Hagner, *Matthew*, 2:485–88; Luz, *Matthew*, 2:385–88; Turner, *Matthew*, 413.

47. See Arthur L. Moore, *The Parousia in the New Testament*, NovTSup 13 (Leiden: Brill, 1966), 128; Bock, *Luke 9:51–24:53*, 856.

48. Cf. Darrell L. Bock, *A Theology of Luke and Acts* (Grand Rapids: Zondervan, 2012), 391–94.

49. The NRSV rightly takes the participle causally, "because"; contrast the KJV and NASB.

50. See Benjamin W. Bacon, *Studies in Matthew* (London: Constable, 1930), 236–49; Moore, *Parousia in the New Testament*, 84–89; Joseph A. Fitzmyer, *The Gospel according to Luke X–XXIV*, AB 28A (Garden City, NY: Doubleday, 1985), 1348–51; John T. Carroll, *Response to the End of His-*

Mark 13:24–27	**Matt 24:29–31**	**Luke 21:25–28**
Ἀλλ᾽ ἐν ἐκείναις ταῖς ἡμέραις μετὰ τὴν θλῖψιν ἐκείνην	Εὐθέως δὲ μετὰ τὴν θλῖψιν τῶν ἡμερῶν ἐκείνων	Καὶ ἔσονται
But in those days after that tribulation	And immediately after the tribulation of those days	And there will be
ὁ ἥλιος σκοτισθήσεται	ὁ ἥλιος σκοτισθήσεται	σημεῖα ἐν ἡλίῳ
the sun will be darkened	the sun will be darkened	signs in the sun
καὶ ἡ σελήνη οὐ δώσει τὸ φέγγος αὐτῆς	καὶ ἡ σελήνη οὐ δώσει τὸ φέγγος αὐτῆς	καὶ σελήνῃ
and the moon will not give its light	and the moon will not give its light	and the moon
καὶ οἱ ἀστέρες ἔσονται ἐκ τοῦ οὐρανοῦ πίπτοντες	καὶ οἱ ἀστέρες πεσοῦνται ἀπὸ τοῦ οὐρανοῦ	καὶ ἄστροις
And the stars will fall from heaven	and the stars will fall from heaven	and the stars
		καὶ ἐπὶ τῆς γῆς συνοχὴ ἐθνῶν ἐν ἀπορίᾳ ἤχους θαλάσσης καὶ σάλου, ἀποψυχόντων ἀνθρώπων ἀπὸ φόβου καὶ προσδοκίας τῶν ἐπερχομένων τῇ οἰκουμένῃ
		and upon the earth distress of nations in confusion at the roaring of the sea and the waves, people fainting with fear and with foreboding of what is coming on the world

tory: Eschatology and Situation in Luke-Acts, SBLDS 92 (Atlanta: Scholars Press, 1988), 104–17; John Nolland, *The Gospel of Matthew: A Commentary on the Greek Text*, NIGTC (Grand Rapids: Eerdmans, 2005), 956–57, 981–86; Luz, *Matthew*, 3:183, 200–204; Edward Adams, *The Stars Will Fall from Heaven: Cosmic Catastrophe in the New Testament and Its World*, LNTS 347 (London: Bloomsbury T&T Clark, 2007), 166–69, 172–75; Jan Lambrecht, "The Line of Thought in Matthew 24:1–35," *ETL* 84 (2008): 519–28.

Mark 13:24–27	**Matt 24:29–31**	**Luke 21:25–28**
καὶ αἱ δυνάμεις αἱ ἐν τοῖς οὐρανοῖς σαλευθήσονται	καὶ αἱ δυνάμεις τῶν οὐρανῶν σαλευθήσονται	αἱ γὰρ δυνάμεις τῶν οὐρανῶν σαλευθήσονται
And the powers in the heavens will be shaken	And the powers of the heavens will be shaken	for the powers of the heavens will be shaken
	καὶ τότε φανήσεται τὸ σημεῖον τοῦ υἱοῦ τοῦ ἀνθρώπου ἐν οὐρανῷ, καὶ τότε κόψονται πᾶσαι αἱ φυλαὶ τῆς γῆς	
	Then will appear the sign of the son of man in heaven, and then all the tribes of the earth will wail	
καὶ τότε ὄψονται τὸν υἱὸν τοῦ ἀνθρώπου ἐρχόμενον ἐν νεφέλαις μετὰ δυνάμεως πολλῆς καὶ δόξης	καὶ ὄψονται τὸν υἱὸν τοῦ ἀνθρώπου ἐρχόμενον ἐπὶ τῶν νεφελῶν τοῦ οὐρανοῦ μετὰ δυνάμεως καὶ δόξης πολλῆς	καὶ τότε ὄψονται τὸν υἱὸν τοῦ ἀνθρώπου ἐρχόμενον ἐν νεφέλῃ μετὰ δυνάμεως καὶ δόξης πολλῆς
And then they will see the son of man coming in the clouds with much power and glory	and they will see the son of man coming on the clouds of heaven with power and much glory	And then they will see the son of man coming in a cloud with power and much glory
		ἀρχομένων δὲ τούτων γίνεσθαι ἀνακύψατε καὶ ἐπάρατε τὰς κεφαλὰς ὑμῶν, διότι ἐγγίζει ἡ ἀπολύτρωσις ὑμῶν
		And when these things begin to happen, look up and raise your heads, because your redemption draws near

Mark 13:24–27	Matt 24:29–31	Luke 21:25–28
καὶ τότε ἀποστελεῖ τοὺς ἀγγέλους καὶ ἐπισυνάξει τοὺς ἐκλεκτοὺς [αὐτοῦ] ἐκ τῶν τεσσάρων ἀνέμων ἀπ᾽ ἄκρου γῆς ἕως ἄκρου οὐρανοῦ	καὶ ἀποστελεῖ τοὺς ἀγγέλους αὐτοῦ μετὰ σάλπιγγος μεγάλης, καὶ ἐπισυνάξουσιν τοὺς ἐκλεκτοὺς αὐτοῦ ἐκ τῶν τεσσάρων ἀνέμων ἀπ᾽ ἄκρων οὐρανῶν ἕως [τῶν] ἄκρων αὐτῶν	
And then he will send out the angels and gather his elect from the four winds, from the ends of the earth to the ends of heaven	And he will send out his angels with a loud trumpet call, and they will gather his elect from the four winds, from one end of heaven to the other	

The core of the prediction is maintained in the threefold progression of astral signs, the coming of the son of man, and the rescue of people. The connection to Dan 7:13–14 in the description of the son of man is also retained.[51] Matthew even clarifies this further, adjusting Mark's wording to more closely align with Daniel (Mark's ἐν νεφέλαις becomes in Matthew ἐπὶ τῶν νεφελῶν τοῦ οὐρανοῦ, which is identical to Dan 7:13 LXX).[52] Matthew and Luke will also follow Mark by including after this saying a few parables about the signs of the times, and the need for watchfulness and diligence. As already noted, Matthew has decided to greatly expand this conclusion to the Olivet Discourse by adding additional parables on the same eschatological themes.

Deviations from Mark come in the form of both additions and subtractions.[53] Matthew's astral signs evoke Isa 13 and 34 as in Mark, whereas Luke's abbreviated lines lose much of that Isaianic intertextuality. Nevertheless, Luke keeps the "powers in heaven will be shaken" from Isa 34:4, and there may be other connec-

51. See Hays, *Echoes of Scripture in the Gospels*, 136–37.

52. While the connection to Dan 7 is clear in Mark, Mark's preposition (ἐν) is found in no extant Greek version, and he lacks "of heaven." However, Mark 14:62 has μετὰ τῶν νεφελῶν τοῦ οὐρανοῦ, which agrees with Theodotion. Luke's motive for making Mark's plural "clouds" a singular "cloud" is not clear, but it parallels Acts 1:9. It may be relevant that, in the theophany of Exod 19:9, 16, there is a singular "thick" or "dense" cloud that descends on Sinai.

53. See Heinrich Baarlink, *Die Eschatologie der synoptischen Evangelien*, BWANT (Mainz: Kohlhammer, 1986), 118–21, 158–63.

tions to the "day of the Lord" tradition in the unique mention of perplexity and distress on the earth (see especially Isa 24:19 LXX; cf. Ps 65:7).[54] Luke's version is also distinctive in its omission of the reference to the gathering work of angels, replaced with an imperative to "lift up your heads" in light of the coming "redemption."[55] The reference to "redemption" recalls the expectations of Simeon (Luke 2:28–32) and Anna (Luke 2:36–38), and looks forward to Acts 1:6 ("is this the time you will restore the kingdom to Israel?"), thus showing the ultimate connection of those expectations to the future coming of Jesus for Luke.[56] The imperative to "lift up your heads" is a striking and revealing inverse of the suggestion of the angels in Acts 1 that the apostles cease "staring into heaven." The angels imply, and Luke 21 confirms, that "staring into heaven" is the proper posture at the future coming of Jesus but not for the present life of "witness" (Acts 1:8).

Matthew does not lose one jot or tittle from Mark but rather, as with the Torah, "fulfills" this predecessor by adding to and intensifying it.[57] Matthew's additions, and three in particular, create an even more scripturally evocative passage. (1) Matthew mentions not just the son of man but "the sign [τὸ σημεῖον] of the son of man" "shining" (φανήσεται) in the heavens (24:30a).[58] This odd detail, which has

54. In any case, Luke's laconic rewriting clearly evidences that miraculous activity in the heavens is in mind here. It is also worth noting that Luke's citation of Joel 2 in Peter's Pentecost speech (Acts 2:17–21) shows an understanding that those cosmic signs about the day of the Lord are fulfilled, in part, by the supernatural gift of the Spirit, which further impresses the realized eschatology of Luke and Acts.

55. The reason for omitting the mission of the angels is not self-evident, though intriguing in light of the mission of the church as Acts narrates it. Others have noted that angels disappear from some other material (such as parables) that are shared with Matthew.

56. Cf. Tucker S. Ferda, "Reason to Weep: Isaiah 52 and the Subtext of Luke's Triumphal Entry," *JTS* 66 (2015): 34–40; Oliver, *Luke's Jewish Eschatology*, 95–102; Wolter, "Eschatology in the Gospel according to Luke," 103 (Jesus "will redeem Jerusalem" and "restore the kingdom to Israel" "when he as the son of man 'comes in his glory and in the glory of the Father and the holy angels'"). Contra Steve Walton, "The End: What and When? Eschatology in Luke-Acts," in *Eschatology in Antiquity: Forms and Functions*, ed. Hilary Marlow, Karla Pollmann, and Helen Van Noorden (London: Routledge, 2021), 387, 392 (who reads the language symbolically, citing Caird). On Luke 21 and the narrative of Acts, see Carroll, *Response to the End of History*, 118.

57. Though I do not find compelling the thesis of Vicky Balabanski, *Eschatology in the Making: Mark, Matthew, and the Didache* (Cambridge: Cambridge University Press, 1997), that Matthew's eschatological expectation was more imminent than Mark's.

58. In the Qur'an, Jesus is the "sign" of the hour of judgment at Sura 43:61, though the import is not immediately clear. The expectation for his second coming is frequent in the Hadith. Cf. Johannes Triebel, "Das koranische Evangelium: Kritische Anmerkungen zur koranischen Darstellung der Person und Botschaft Jesu," *TBei* 38 (2007): 269–82.

confounded commentators, is likely the result of messianic exegesis (whether from the evangelist or the evangelist's tradition).[59] In Isa 11, one of the richest reservoirs for messianic speculation in the Second Temple period,[60] we find at v. 10, "on that day the root of Jesse shall stand as a sign [HB: נס] to the peoples, the nations shall inquire of him, and his dwelling shall be glorious," and further at v. 12, God "will raise up a sign [HB: נס, LXX: σημεῖον] for the nations, and assemble the dispersed of Israel."[61] Suggestive here is not just the identification of the "root of Jesse" with the "sign" but the way in which Isaiah's "sign" issues forth an eschatological ingathering—11:11–12—just as, in Matthew, the coming of Jesus brings about the same (v. 31: the angels "gather his elect from the four winds, from one end of heaven to the other"). Moreover, since Matthew mentions Isa 11's messianic sign "shining" (from φαίνω), it is also possible that Matthew has identified Isaiah's "sign" with Num 24:17's messianic "star," the "shining" of which the infancy narrative has shown clear interest in (cf. Herod asks about τὸν χρόνον τοῦ φαινομένου ἀστέρος [2:7]). The connection between these messianic oracles is already present in the LXX, which appears to have linked the "raising up" of the sign to the "rising up" of Balaam's star.[62] The same can be found in the Testament of Judah and the targumim.[63] Such an intertextual move would also make sense in context in Matthew, where Jesus will come from heaven and there will be other cosmic disturbances in the skies above, not least the stars. Should this reading be on target, Matthew has understood Jesus's beginning to be like his end and thus found both his birth and his

59. In the history of interpretation, "the sign" has commonly been thought to be the sign of the cross, so Cyril of Jerusalem, *Cat.* 15.22; Chrysostom, *Hom. Matt.* 76.3; Jerome, *Comm. Matt.* ad loc.; Theophylact, *Comm. Matt.* ad loc. ("the cross will then be seen in heaven shining more brightly than the sun"). Some commentators support this still, so Davies and Allison, *Matthew*, 3:359–60. See discussion in Marius Nel, "What Is 'the Sign of the Son of Man in Heaven' (Mt 24:30)?," *IDS* 49 (2015): 1–9. On the whole as a prediction of the parousia, see Augustine, *Ep.* 199.41; Hilary of Poitiers, *Comm. Matt.* 25.8; Gloss. Ord. ad loc.

60. Cf., e.g., Isa 11:1–11 LXX; Gen 49:9–10 LXX; T. Jud. 22–24; 1QS^b V, 20–29; 4Q161 8–10 III, 11–25; 4Q285; Pss. Sol. 17.35–42; Rev 5:5; b. Sanh. 93 (Kokhba cannot "smell and judge" per Isa 11); etc. Cf. Dunn, *Romans*, WBC 38 (Nashville: Nelson, 1988), 2:850.

61. Paul himself cites from this passage and reads it messianically in Rom 15:12, though he does not include the mention of the sign. For discussion, see J. Ross Wagner, *Heralds of the Good News: Isaiah and Paul 'in Concert' in the Letter to the Romans*, NovTSup 101 (Leiden: Brill, 2002), 317–27. It appears that Paul believes this oracle is being fulfilled in the mission to the gentiles of which he is a part.

62. Isa 11:10 LXX reads, "On that day the root of Jesus also will rise up to rule the gentiles [ὁ ἀνιστάμενος ἄρχειν ἐθνῶν], and upon him the gentiles will hope, and his rest will be glorious."

63. Cf. T. Jud. 24:1 and Tg. Isa. 11 ad loc. Unclear, but still noteworthy, is Philo, *Praem.* 95, "a man will come forth," which some have read messianically.

future parousia predicted in Num 24:17.[64] A similar messianic and eschatological interpretation of Isa 11's "sign" appears to stand behind the linkage between Jesus and the bronze snake in Num 21 as it appears in the Fourth Gospel (3:14–15).[65]

(2) Matthew also uniquely has it that, at the appearance of the shining sign, "then all of the tribes of the earth will mourn" (τότε κόψονται πᾶσαι αἱ φυλαὶ τῆς γῆς). As noted by commentators far and wide, this line is drawn directly from an eschatological "oracle" at the end of Zechariah (12:1–14:21), where we find that on the day of the Lord (12:3, 4, 6, 8, 9), "I [God] will pour out a spirit of compassion and supplication on the house of David and the inhabitants of Jerusalem, so that, when they look on the one whom they have pierced, they will mourn for him, as one mourns for an only child" (12:10).[66] The relevance of this passage for Matthew's purposes is evident in the line that the evangelist does not actually cite here—"when they look on the one whom they have pierced"—which we know others had understood to refer to the crucified Jesus. As Rev 1:7 also conjoins Dan 7:13–14 with Zech 12:10 ("Behold, he comes with the clouds, every eye will see him, even those who pierced him, and on his account all the tribes of the earth will wail"), though is not dependent on the Gospel of Matthew, this linkage is evidently traditional.[67] Though Luke does not have this line in 21:25–28, the evangelist may, too, have been aware of this eschatological tradition and realized it at least partially at the time of the crucifixion or "piercing" of Jesus, where those who "saw" it, afterward "went home, beating their breasts" (23:48). The Fourth Gospel achieves a similar realized result at the crucifixion scene via different means still: the mention of Jesus's unbroken bones and the stream of blood that flowed from his pierced side (19:36, 34), both of which draw from Zech 12:10–13:1.[68]

64. Matthew has also understood Jesus's earthly ministry as a fulfillment of Isa 9's prediction about a "great light" that will shine on those who sit in darkness. On the "sign" in Matt 24:30 as light, see Herman C. Waetjen, *The Origin and Destiny of Humanness: An Interpretation of the Gospel according to Matthew* (Corte Madera: Omega, 1976), 229.

65. Isa 11's "sign" is נס, which also appears in Num 21:8 ("set the fiery serpent על נס"). John's exegesis of Num 21 may be less idiosyncratic than at first glance, then, should his messianic reading of Num 21's נס be guided by the נס of Isa 11. In other words, Num 21 stands out on the assumption that נס is a messianic designation, which Isa 11 would provide, and as we have seen, there was precedent for reading Isa 11's "sign" in that way. On the realized eschatology evident here, see discussion below. Cf. Robert H. Gundry, *Matthew: A Commentary on His Handbook for a Mixed Church under Persecution* (Grand Rapids: Eerdmans, 1994), 488.

66. Cf., e.g., Davies and Allison, *Matthew*, 3:360–61; Luz, *Matthew*, 3:201.

67. For Zech 12 imagery applied to the parousia elsewhere, see Barn. 7.9; Justin, *1 Apol.* 52.12; *Dial.* 14.8; 32.2; 64.7; 118.1; Pseudo-Hippolytus, *On the End of the World* 40.

68. See Andreas J. Köstenberger, *John*, BECNT (Grand Rapids: Baker Books, 2004), 553–54; Sebastian A. Carnazzo, *Seeing Blood and Water: A Narrative-Critical Study of John 19:34* (Eugene, OR: Pickwick, 2012).

(3) Finally, Matthew adds to Mark not only new sights but new sounds: the son of man will send forth his angels "with a great trumpet" (μετὰ σάλπιγγος μεγάλης). As already noted, a trumpet sound coincides with the return of Jesus and the resurrection of the dead in 1 Thess 4:16 and 1 Cor 15:52 (cf. Did. 16.6; Apoc. Ab. 31.1) and appears to be a "day of the Lord" motif elsewhere in Scripture (e.g., Isa 27:13). So Matthew is again drawing on tradition here.[69] The most immediate connection may be liturgical, however, as the linkage of the trumpet to the "gathering" of the elect in Matthew finds a remarkably close parallel in the tenth benediction of the Shemoneh Esreh, which also, interestingly enough, alludes to the raising of the "sign" from Isa 11:10–12: "Sound the great shofar for our freedom; lift up the sign [נס] to gather our exiles, and gather us from the four corners of the earth."[70] It is doubtful that this is a coincidence.

The upshot of these three additions to Mark is not a wholly new depiction of the return of Jesus but one that, like Matthew's account of Jesus in general, is more deeply rooted in the Scriptures and traditions of Israel. For Matthew, the coming of Dan 7's son of man (as in Mark) is at the same time the messianic "rising" of the "sign" and "star" from Isa 11 and Num 24, which results in fulfillment of Zech 12's mourning on the day of the Lord and the long-awaited ingathering of the people of God. Luke's changes to Mark are also intelligible within the same scriptural subtexts present in Mark, and logical given Lukan tendencies we otherwise know about. What Matthew and Luke have done to Mark 13:24–27 resembles their treatment of the larger discourse, where they have seized on different aspects of the Markan *Vorlage* present there—so, future-oriented eschatology (Matthew), and life in the interim before Christ's return (Luke)—and developed those aspects in different ways. Matthew's interest emerges at the outset by a rewording of the disciples' question to refer more clearly to the destruction of Jerusalem *and* "your parousia and the completion of the age" (τῆς σῆς παρουσίας, καὶ τῆς συντελείας τοῦ αἰῶνος [24:3]).[71] Matthew offers various clarifications and scriptural elaborations throughout in keeping with that.[72] Luke, on the other hand, retains the prediction

69. Cf. Herbert W. Basser with Marsha B. Cohen, *The Gospel of Matthew and Jewish Traditions: A Relevance-Based Commentary*, BRLJ 46 (Leiden: Brill, 2015), 623–38.

70. For text, see Craig A. Evans, *Jesus and His Contemporaries: Comparative Studies*, AGJU 25 (Leiden: Brill, 1995), 277–80.

71. Much like Matthew's rewording of Mark 8:38–9:1, as noted above. See Allan J. McNicol, *Jesus' Directions for the Future: A Source and Redaction-History Study of the Use of the Eschatological Traditions in Paul and in the Synoptic Accounts of Jesus' Last Eschatological Discourse* (Macon, GA: Mercer University Press, 1996), 77–114.

72. Others: (1) Matthew adds to Mark imagery from the eschatological tribulation at 24:10–12, specifically the "increase of lawlessness" at the end time (cf. 1QpHab III, 14–15; CD VI, 10–14; 4 Ezra 5.10; 2 Bar. 30.5–6; 48.38; m. Soṭa 9.15; b. Sanh. 97a); (2) Matthew adds to Mark a saying about the coming of the son of man being like lightning (24:27)—which Luke has elsewhere—

of the future return of Jesus but lessens the sense of eschatological imminence in Mark's discourse.[73] Luke's Jesus warns of people who predict "the time is near" (21:8); Luke changes Mark's "the end is not yet" to "the end is not coming immediately" (21:9), which heightens the sense of eschatological process; Luke omits "the beginning" from Mark's "the beginning of birth pangs," thereby making it more difficult to draw up an eschatological timetable around the coming wars, earthquakes, and famines;[74] Mark's "the one who endures to the end will be saved" (13:13) becomes in Luke "by your endurance you will gain your lives" (21:19), which avoids suggesting that some who experience this eschatological travail will live to see "the end"; and Luke depicts the destruction of Jerusalem as part of a stage of salvation history—"the times of the gentiles" and the "trampling" of the sanctuary (21:24)—that, presumably, will last some time, and have its end (e.g., "be fulfilled") at the return of Jesus.[75] For this final detail, Luke has dropped Mark's "abomination of desolation" from Daniel but nonetheless got Mark's point and found this notion of a period of "trampling" (from πατέω) Jerusalem by the gentiles from Daniel itself.[76] Matthew's heightened interest in the future notwithstanding, both Matthew and Luke have carefully reworded Mark's transition to the description of the coming of the son of man so as to avoid any immediate connection between

---

signifying perhaps both aspect (sudden) and content (light). This increases the sense of the suddenness of Jesus's arrival, which is also important for Mark 13. Cf. F. W. Beare, "The Synoptic Apocalypse: Matthean Version," in *Understanding the Sacred Text: Essays in Honor of Morton S. Enslin*, ed. John Henry Reumann (Valley Forge: Judson, 1972), 115–33; Victor Kossi Agbanou, *Le discours eschatologique de Matthieu 24–25: Tradition et rédaction* (Paris: Gabalda, 1983); Ingo Broer, "Redaktionsgeschichtliche Aspekte von Mt. 24:1–28," *NovT* 35 (1993): 209–33; Luz, *Matthew*, 3:182–83.

73. Cf. Michael Wolter, "Israels Zukunft und die Parusieverzögerung bei Lukas," in *Theologie und Ethos im frühen Christentum: Studien zu Jesus, Paulus und Lukas* (Tübingen: Mohr Siebeck, 2009), 311–33.

74. This evokes Luke 17:20: "The kingdom of God is not coming μετὰ παρατηρήσεως."

75. See Jan Lambrecht, "Naherwartung in Luke?," *ETL* 87 (2011): 428. On the likely background of the times of the gentiles and the notion of the trampling of the sanctuary, see John Nolland, "'The Times of the Nations' and a Prophetic Pattern in Luke 21," in *The Gospel of Luke*, vol. 3 of *Biblical Interpretation in Early Christian Gospels*, ed. Thomas R. Hatina, LNTS 376 (London: T&T Clark International, 2006), 133–47.

76. Luke elsewhere makes similar additions to sources by drawing on Daniel. Note (1) language from the vision of the messianic stone that will "break to pieces" and "will crush" (λικμήσει) the statue (Dan 2:34–35, 44–45; cf. Josephus, *Ant.* 10.210; Sib. Or. 3.767–768; 4 Ezra 13.36) appears in the conclusion to the parable of the wicked tenants (20:18). (2) Satan's claim that he has received the right to "give" to "whomever he wishes" the kingdoms of the world draws from a refrain found throughout Dan 4. See Tucker S. Ferda, "God of the Nations: Daniel, Satan, and the Temptation of Jesus in Luke," *ZNW* 110 (2019): 4–8.

the events of 70 CE and the parousia, as could be implied by Mark's ἀλλ᾽ ἐν ἐκείναις ταῖς ἡμέραις μετὰ τὴν θλῖψιν ἐκείνην (13:24).[77]

Use of Mark: Jesus on Trial

Matthew's and Luke's reception of Mark 13 is characterized by both creativity and constraint. They work with, and within, their Markan *Stoff.* The same is true of the final Markan text to consider here: the reply of Jesus at the so-called Jewish trial.

Mark 14:62	**Matt 26:64**	**Luke 22:67–69**
ἐγώ εἰμι	σὺ εἶπας. πλὴν λέγω ὑμῖν	ἐὰν ὑμῖν εἴπω, οὐ μὴ πιστεύσητε· ἐὰν δὲ ἐρωτήσω, οὐ μὴ ἀποκριθῆτε
I am	You say so. But I say to you	If I tell you, you will by no means believe, and if I ask, you will by no means answer
	ἀπ᾽ ἄρτι	ἀπὸ τοῦ νῦν δὲ
	but from now on	but from now
καὶ ὄψεσθε	ὄψεσθε	
and you will see	you will see	
τὸν υἱὸν τοῦ ἀνθρώπου ἐκ δεξιῶν καθήμενον τῆς δυνάμεως	τὸν υἱὸν τοῦ ἀνθρώπου καθήμενον ἐκ δεξιῶν τῆς δυνάμεως	ἔσται ὁ υἱὸς τοῦ ἀνθρώπου καθήμενος ἐκ δεξιῶν τῆς δυνάμεως τοῦ θεοῦ
the son of man seated at the right hand of the power	the son of man seated at the right hand of the power	the son of man will be seated at the right hand of the power of God

77. Luke avoids any timetable here with the simple "and there will be" (καὶ ἔσονται). Matthew keeps Mark's wording, even adding "immediately" (εὐθέως), but to a very different effect. Matthew's "immediately after the suffering of those days" (εὐθέως δὲ μετὰ τὴν θλῖψιν τῶν ἡμερῶν ἐκείνων) is not the same as "after that suffering" (μετὰ τὴν θλῖψιν ἐκείνην) as in Mark, where the "that" looks back to the tumult of 70 CE in general if not the destruction of the temple in particular. Matthew's demonstrative pronoun does not point to a particular event but a period of time, "those days," meaning, after the suffering of those days, some of which was described in the previous lines, the son of man will come.

Mark 14:62	Matt 26:64	Luke 22:67–69
καὶ ἐρχόμενον μετὰ τῶν νεφελῶν τοῦ οὐρανοῦ	καὶ ἐρχόμενον ἐπὶ τῶν νεφελῶν τοῦ οὐρανοῦ	
and coming with the clouds of heaven	and coming upon the clouds of heaven	

As noted above, Mark's Jesus conjoins two passages, Ps 109:1 LXX, and Dan 7:13, likely referring to Jesus's enthronement in heaven and his future coming, either sequentially, or viewed together. Matthew retains the intertextuality and the same meaning: the "coming on the clouds" surely refers to the parousia as it has elsewhere in his gospel.[78] Matthew does, however, make more of the enthronement scenario of Ps 110 by adding to Mark "from now on" (ἀπ' ἄρτι), implying that the exaltation of David's "Lord" to God's right hand *begins* to occur, paradoxically, in the passion narrative itself.[79] This striking claim makes sense of the way in which Matthew frames the crucifixion of Jesus as a messianic enthronement (here following Mark), perhaps aiming to evoke the installation of Ps 2:6–7's "king" and "son" on Zion (as I have argued elsewhere).[80] Luke also emphasizes Mark's citation of Ps 110 and similarly suggests it is proleptically fulfilled in what follows (22:69: ἀπὸ τοῦ νῦν δέ) but goes further than Matthew in eclipsing any connection to Dan 7:13 and any reference to the return of Jesus.[81] Luke's Jesus speaks here only of his vindication, despite rejection, in fulfillment of Scripture, just as Luke's Jesus will say in response to the travelers on the road to Emmaus (24:26), the apostles will say repeatedly in the speeches of Acts (2:22–36; 13:32–41), and Stephen will confirm in his near-death vision (7:56).[82]

78. Contra Hagner, *Matthew*, 2:800; France, *Gospel of Matthew*, 1027–28. On the preposition "on" or "with" in various versions of Daniel and their significance, see discussion in James A. Montgomery, *A Critical and Exegetical Commentary on the Book of Daniel*, ICC (Edinburgh: T&T Clark, 1964), 304–5.

79. While it is also possible that the Greek should be taken as ἀπαρτί, meaning "certainly," rather than ἀπ' ἄρτι, meaning "from now on." To read "certainly" here would simply emphasize the future prediction.

80. Tucker S. Ferda, "Matthew's Titulus and Psalm 2's King on Mount Zion," *JBL* 133 (2014): 561–81.

81. See discussion in Tuckett, "Lucan Son of Man," 565–66 (on son of man sayings being pulled "into the service of Luke's views on the present exaltation of Jesus as well as the parousia of Jesus"). See also Joseph Plevnik, "Son of Man Seated at the Right Hand of God: Luke 22,69 in Lucan Christology," *Bib* 72 (1991): 331–47; John Nolland, *Luke 18:35–24:53*, WBC 35C (Dallas: Word, 1993), 1111–12.

82. See Hengel, "'Sit at My Right Hand!,'" 187.

Glasson, Robinson, and many others have seized on the response of Luke's Jesus, in particular, claiming that this is also what Matthew and Mark's Jesus intends to say, and even suggested that we have in this prediction of vindication an alternative eschatological scenario that runs against the grain of the hope for Jesus's parousia.[83] But this, we can now confidently say at the end of our exegetical discussion, is specious. To put it bluntly, Matthew and Mark's Jesus does not actually say the same thing as Luke's Jesus. Luke avoids speaking about the parousia precisely by having Jesus avoid Dan 7:13 in his reply (and, with it, the claim that "you will see").[84] Moreover, Luke's emphasis on vindication/enthronement is only an alternative eschatological scenario that stands in tension with the parousia if you isolate 22:67–69 from its larger context and read it against the grain of the very source that contains it, which clearly expects Jesus's future coming. Luke's Jesus simply does not speak of that future coming in this instance, and that is in keeping with a larger and pervasive penchant for realized eschatology in this gospel.[85] Here we see the importance of reading these passages in context, and these sources holistically.

Eschatology in the Double Tradition

In addition to reworking the Gospel of Mark, the eschatologies of Matthew and Luke draw on some additional material—so-called double tradition—whose provenance, background, and form are complicated and remain highly debated. I continue to affirm the Q hypothesis, even if I am skeptical of elaborate theories in the subfield of Q studies concerning this document's tradition history, its redactional strata, and even the history of the community ("the Q people") responsible

83. Cf. discussion above at pp. 17–18. Contra also Joachim Jeremias, *New Testament Theology: The Proclamation of Jesus*, trans. John Bowden (New York: Scribner's Sons, 1971), 273 (who argues that Luke's version is from L and actually more primitive and nearer to what Jesus had actually said); N. T. Wright, *Jesus and the Victory of God* (Minneapolis: Fortress, 1996), 360–65, 642–43.

84. On reducing connections to Dan 7 in Luke, see Mogens Müller, *Der Ausdruck "Menschensohn" in den Evangelien: Voraussetzungen und Bedeutung* (Leiden: Brill, 1984), 142. See also Gathercole, *Gospel and the Gospels*, 225.

85. See Jerome H. Neyrey, *The Passion according to Luke: A Redaction Study of Luke's Soteriology* (New York: Paulist, 1985), 74. The upshot of Luke's reworking of Mark is that his Jesus is not predicting that his accusers would see his return. A similar outcome is achieved by Luke's reworking of Mark 9:1. Relevant here is the uniquely Lukan 17:22 ("The days are coming when you will desire to see one of the days of the son of man, and you will not see it"), though the meaning is unclear and disputed. Cf. discussion in Ryan P. Juza, "One of the Days of the Son of Man: A Reconsideration of Luke 17:22," *JBL* 135 (2016): 575–95.

for it.[86] I have written about this elsewhere and will not repeat my reasons for skepticism here.[87] In any case, I assume in what follows the least possible or a lowest common denominator approach to Q, and, following Christopher Tuckett, assume that any inferences we make about Q must begin with its putative final form.[88] I also believe, though, that many of my conclusions below could still be accepted by those persuaded of the case against Q, although the import may be less significant.[89] That is because my aim here, after all, is not to double down on a particular reconstruction of Q, or even to reconstruct an earlier tradition history with the help of Q. I am talking at this point about *reception* (as with Matthew and Luke's reception of Mark) and trying to understand better the eschatological claims of some early Jesus followers by attending to the ways in which this non-Markan material has shaped Matthew and Luke. I begin with two observations before turning to discuss some specific texts.

First, if there is anything that Q theorists agree on, it is that eschatology pervades the source known to Matthew and Luke.[90] What Q critics debate is how that eschatology got there: was there an initial document or documents characterized

86. For cogent arguments on the need for modesty on these matters, see Paul Hoffmann, *Studien zur Theologie der Logienquelle*, 3rd ed. (Münster: Aschendorff: 1982); Daniel Marguerat, "Pourquoi s'intéresser à la Source? Histoire de la recherche et questions ouvertes," in *La source des paroles de Jésus (Q): Aux origins du christianisme*, ed. Andreas Dettwiler and Daniel Marguerat (Paris: Labor et Fides, 2008), 43–46; Dale C. Allison Jr., *Constructing Jesus: Memory, Imagination, and History* (Grand Rapids: Baker Books, 2010), 118–21; Christopher Tuckett, "On the Stratification of Q," *From the Sayings to the Gospels,* 143–52.

87. Tucker S. Ferda, *Jesus, the Gospels, and the Galilean Crisis*, LNTS 601 (London: Bloomsbury T&T Clark, 2019), 142–44.

88. Cf. Christopher Tuckett, *Q and the History of Early Christianity: Studies on Q* (London: T&T Clark, 2004), 75–82; Tuckett, "The Son of Man and Daniel 7: Q and Jesus," *From the Sayings to the Gospels,* 267.

89. Especially influential here have been Mark Goodacre, *The Case against Q: Studies in Markan Priority and the Synoptic Problem* (Harrisburg, PA: Trinity, 2002), and Francis Watson, *Gospel Writing: A Canonical Perspective* (Grand Rapids: Eerdmans, 2013), 117–216. In my view, John S. Kloppenborg's response to Goodacre, in "On Dispensing with Q? Goodacre on the Relation of Luke to Matthew," *NTS* 49 (2003): 210–36, is weighty (particularly his emphasis that ultimately the case against Q depends on the plausibility of Luke's direct use of Matthew, and the case for Q on the basic implausibility of that). Moreover, in the debate between Christopher Tuckett and Francis Watson—see Tuckett's "Francis Watson, Q and 'L/M'" and Watson's "Seven Theses on the Synoptic Problem, in Disagreement with Christopher Tuckett," in *Gospel Interpretation and the Q-Hypothesis*, ed. Mogens Müller and Heike Omerzu, LNTS 573 (London: Bloomsbury T&T Clark, 2018), 115–38, 139–47—I believe that Tuckett has the stronger arguments.

90. For a fine study, see Albert Hogeterp, *Expectations of the End*, STDJ 83 (Leiden: Brill, 2009), 154–62, and literature there. See also Olegs Andrejevs, *Apocalypticism in the Synoptic Sayings Source: A Reassessment of Q's Stratigraphy*, WUNT 2/499 (Tübingen: Mohr Siebeck, 2019), who argues that an apocalyptic perspective is present in all putative layers of Q.

by sapiential instruction, to which later eschatological material was added (perhaps even in stages)?[91] Or was that order reversed?[92] Or was there no redaction at all? Or is it impossible to discern the recension history for this "grab bag" of traditions?[93] It is hard to dispute, however, that what Matthew and Luke knew (assuming the validity of the Q hypothesis) contained these elements: the apocalyptic preaching of John the Baptist and his prediction of the coming judgment (Q 3:2–22),[94] eschatological reversal in the Beatitudes (Q 6:20–54), the threat of judgment on those who reject the gospel (Q 6:43–45, 46–49; 10:10–15; 11:29–30; 11:49–51; 13:24–27), predictions of the sudden coming of the son of man (Q 17:23–25), the expectation of the messianic banquet with the patriarchs (Q 13:28–29), the promise that the disciples will sit on thrones (22:28–30). This tradition also contains some of the most studied indicators of realized eschatology in the Synoptics:

91. Cf. Helmut Koester, "One Jesus and Four Primitive Gospels," *Trajectories through Early Christianity* (Philadelphia: Fortress, 1971), 186; Koester, *Ancient Christian Gospels* (Philadelphia: Trinity International, 1990), 133–71; Heinz Schürmann, "Beobachtungen zum Menschensohn-Titel in der Redequelle," in *Jesus und der Menschensohn: Festschrift A. Vögtle*, ed. Rudolf Pesch and Rudolf Schnackenburg (Freiburg: Herder, 1975), 124–47; Llewellyn Howes, *Judging Q and Saving Jesus: Q's Contribution to the Wisdom-Apocalypticism Debate in Historical Jesus Studies* (Durbanville: AOSIS, 2015), 326 ("the formative stratum is essential sapiential and completely lacks not only any apocalyptic and/or futurist eschatology, but also any prophetic material"). In addition to Koester and Schürmann, the work of John Kloppenborg on the topic has been particularly influential, *The Formation of Q: Trajectories in Ancient Wisdom Collections*, 2nd ed. (Minneapolis: Fortress, 2007), though Kloppenborg does not categorically deny the presence of futurist eschatology in Q—he rather disputes the appropriateness of calling that eschatology "apocalyptic" in nature. Cf. Kloppenborg, "Symbolic Eschatology and the Apocalypticism of Q," in *Synoptic Problems*, ed. John S. Kloppenborg, WUNT 329 (Tübingen: Mohr Siebeck, 2014), 164–73.

92. Siegfried Schulz, *Q: Die Spruchquelle der Evangelisten* (Zurich: Theologischer Verlag, 1972), 481–89, argues that the first stage of Q framed Jesus as the son of man, and the second, from a Hellenistic rather than Jewish context, added sapiential ideas. See also Migaku Satō, *Q und Prophetie: Studien zur Gattungs- und Traditionsgeschichte der Quelle Q*, WUNT 29 (Tübingen: Mohr Siebeck, 1988), 406–11 (Q resembles the prophetic books of the Old Testament, to which sapiential material was later added); Satō, "Wisdom Statements in the Sphere of Prophecy," in *The Gospel behind the Gospels: Current Studies in Q*, ed. Ronald A. Piper, NovTSup 75 (Leiden: Brill, 1995), 139–58; Arland D. Jacobson, "The Literary Unity of Q," *JBL* 101 (1982): 365–89 (a deuteronomistic perspective supplemented an earlier apocalyptic focus on the imminent arrival of the son of man).

93. So John P. Meier, *Mentor, Message, and Miracles*, vol. 2 of *A Marginal Jew: Rethinking the Historical Jesus* (New York: Doubleday, 1994), 181 and 271 n. 1. Cf. Maurice Casey's "chaotic model" of Q in *An Aramaic Approach to Q: Sources for the Gospels of Matthew and Luke*, SNTSMS 122 (Cambridge: Cambridge University Press, 2002).

94. Critics will, of course, dispute which particular lines in these blocks are actually from Q, but I will not be that granular here with my citations, as I am simply making some broader observations. For further discussion about the range of debate, one should consult the *Critical Edition of Q*.

Jesus's reply to John with its allusions to Isaiah (Q 7:18–19), the pronouncement of blessing on "what your eyes see" (Q 10:23–24), the claim that exorcisms by the finger or spirit of God evidence the kingdom's arrival (Q 11:20). Those who see an irresolvable eschatological tension here between the "not-yet" and the "already" approach these passages with reified categories. In Q, future and realized eschatology sit side by side in the final form and thus were not considered to be in tension for whoever put this together.[95] As with Mark, and with Paul, what we find in Q makes good sense on the assumption that some kind of eschatological process is underway, wherein Jesus's coming brings certain expectations to pass while others remain outstanding. Though the particulars of the content differ, we can say that the eschatologies of Paul, Mark, and Q share the same symbolic universe: they see on the horizon the coming of Jesus after a (brief) time of absence.[96] I cannot improve on Cadoux's summary conclusion: "it seems impossible to draw any other conclusion than that, with or without the use of the word 'Parousia', Q represented Jesus as foretelling his future reappearance."[97]

My second point is this: it is apparent that both Matthew and Luke use the eschatological material in Q in similar ways. That is to say, even though double tradition appears in diverse narrative locations in these gospels, and with numerous differences in wording and emphasis, the eschatological nature and purpose of those units appears to be retained. What we do not find is shared tradition that is future oriented in one, and related solely to the present in the other, or about the future coming of Jesus in one, and related to something else entirely in the other. In my assessment, there is only one possible exception to this—the lament over Jerusalem (Q 13:34–35)—which we will consider further below.

The insight has bearing on the question of the reception of eschatological tradition over time. Without denying in any way the realities of development, expansion, and even blatant invention, we must observe the retention of core elements in the midst of change, much like what we found in Matthew's and Luke's

95. Cf. Dennis Ingolfsland, "Kloppenborg's Stratification of Q and Its Significance for Historical Jesus Studies," *JETS* 46 (2003): 217–32.

96. Some critics have tried to distance Q theologically from other early Christian texts, often with respect to ethics, Christology, and atonement; so Burton Mack, *The Lost Gospel: The Book of Q and Christian Origins* (San Francisco: HarperSanFrancisco, 1993). More careful here is John S. Kloppenborg, *Excavating Q: The History and Setting of the Sayings Gospel* (Minneapolis: Fortress, 2000), 345–79. More on this below. On the future coming of the son of man specifically, see Harry T. Fleddermann, *Q: A Reconstruction and Commentary*, BTS 1 (Leuven: Peeters, 2005), 129–32, 140–43; Andrejevs, *Apocalypticism in the Synoptic Sayings Source*, 210–12.

97. Cecil J. Cadoux, *The Historic Mission of Jesus* (London: Lutterworth, 1941), 290.

use of Mark. There would be different implications of this for both deniers and affirmers of the existence of Q, respectively. For deniers of Q, one might conclude that Luke has not drastically de-eschatologized the material received from Matthew—a meaningful but perhaps not astonishing insight. For Q theorists, it would imply that Matthew and Luke have independently accessed and maintained the eschatological nature of their shared tradition, even while reworking that material to suit their own purposes. Within Q studies, there is room for further disagreement still depending upon how one understands the form and structure of Q as known to Matthew and Luke, of course.[98] If Q had no stable form or structure to speak of, or even was not a single document, Matthew and Luke would then have made similar editorial decisions in grouping together various eschatological units according to common theme and purpose (notably the parables of Q 12 and the apocalyptic teachings in Q 17). Should Luke preserve something of the original order of a more stable Q, then the groupings of Q 12 and 17 (whatever exactly they were) would have already been present in Q itself, while Matthew would more freely reorganize Q material according to its putative formal and thematic connections to the rest of Matthew's tradition and aims (much like in Matthew's use of Mark).[99] I find the latter scenario more probable, but either would be an important conclusion, and for our purposes it is not important to decide.

Use of Q: Some Specifics

A few examples are worth discussing at this point. We find in Q 12:8–9 a saying of Jesus that sounds a lot like Mark 8:38 and may be a variant of the same (see also Rev 3:5; 2 Clem. 3.2):

Luke 12:8–9	**Matt 10:32–33**
πᾶς ὃς ἂν ὁμολογήσῃ ἐν ἐμοὶ ἔμπροσθεν τῶν ἀνθρώπων	Πᾶς οὖν ὅστις ὁμολογήσει ἐν ἐμοὶ ἔμπροσθεν τῶν ἀνθρώπων
whoever acknowledges me before people	Therefore everyone who acknowledges me before people

98. See Delbert Burkett, *The Unity and Plurality of Q*, vol. 2 of *Rethinking the Gospel Sources* (Atlanta: Society of Biblical Literature, 2009), 51–60, 87–92.

99. The more popular understanding. Cf. Fleddermann, *Q*, 69–71; Kloppenborg, *Formation of Q*, 64–88.

Luke 12:8–9	**Matt 10:32–33**
καὶ ὁ υἱὸς τοῦ ἀνθρώπου ὁμολογήσει ἐν αὐτῷ	ὁμολογήσω κἀγὼ ἐν αὐτῷ
also the son of man will acknowledge that person	and I also will acknowledge that person
ἔμπροσθεν τῶν ἀγγέλων τοῦ θεοῦ	ἔμπροσθεν τοῦ πατρός μου τοῦ ἐν [τοῖς] οὐρανοῖς
before the angels of God	before my Father who is in heaven

Matthew and Luke have utilized this saying to different ends in their narratives.[100] Matthew places it in the middle of the mission charge where the audience is only the Twelve, and it serves to motivate their work of proclaiming the kingdom (10:32–33). Luke has the logion not in the mission charge but simply amid broader instructions to "his disciples" (12:1), though there it also has an encouraging function.[101] There are also interesting differences in the wording of the saying—"son of man" or "I," "before my Father" or "the angels of God"—and so speculation about the original wording of Q is understandable.[102] But a narrow focus on these details can distract from the broader agreement between Matthew and Luke in content and claim here: (1) Jesus is speaking about himself (2) and his future activity (3) that is contingent on one's behavior in the present, (4) and, as with Mark 8:38, the use of courtroom imagery suggests that the day of judgment is in view. All of these points stand regardless of whether one sees Dan 7 in the background of this saying.[103]

100. The connection between Q 12:8 and its present literary contexts is somewhat artificial. Luke uses the formulaic λέγω δὲ ὑμῖν, while Matthew πᾶς οὖν. We are likely dealing here with an originally detached saying of Jesus. For discussion, see Henk Jan de Jonge, "The Sayings on Confessing and Denying Jesus in Q 12:8–9 and Mark 8:38," in *Sayings of Jesus: Canonical and Noncanonical*, ed. William L. Petersen, NovTSup 89 (Leiden: Brill, 1997), 105–21; Brian Han Gregg, *The Historical Jesus and the Final Judgment Sayings in Q*, WUNT 2/207 (Tübingen: Mohr Siebeck, 2006), 161–90; Kloppenborg, *Formation of Q*, 208–16; François Bovon, *Luke 2: A Commentary on the Gospel of Luke 9:51–19:27*, trans. Donald S. Deer, Hermeneia (Minneapolis: Fortess, 2002), 182–84.

101. In both Matthew and Luke, and thus likely Q, the immediately preceding saying is "Do not be afraid, you are of more value than many sparrows" (Q 12:7).

102. Cf. Paul Hoffmann, "Der Menschensohn in Lukas 12:8," *NTS* 44 (1998): 357–79; Christopher Tuckett, "Q 12.8 Once Again—'Son of Man' or 'I'?," *From the Sayings to the Gospels*, 232–49.

103. For an affirmative answer, see Dale C. Allison Jr., *The Intertextual Jesus: Scripture in Q* (Harrisburg, PA: Trinity International, 2004), 130–31; Tuckett, *Q and the History of Early Christianity*, 246; Gregg, *Historical Jesus and the Final Judgment Sayings in Q*, 166.

We find similar commonality amid difference in Q 22:30:

Luke 22:30	**Matt 19:28**
	ὑμεῖς οἱ ἀκολουθήσαντές μοι ἐν τῇ παλιγγενεσίᾳ, ὅταν καθίσῃ ὁ υἱὸς τοῦ ἀνθρώπου ἐπὶ θρόνου δόξης αὐτοῦ
	you who followed me, in the renewal of all things, when the son of man is seated upon the throne of his glory
καθήσεσθε ἐπὶ θρόνων τὰς δώδεκα φυλὰς κρίνοντες τοῦ Ἰσραήλ	καθήσεσθε καὶ ὑμεῖς ἐπὶ δώδεκα θρόνους κρίνοντες τὰς δώδεκα φυλὰς τοῦ Ἰσραήλ
you will sit on thrones judging (or governing) the twelve tribes of Israel	you will be seated also upon twelve thrones, judging (or governing) the twelve tribes of Israel

Placement and wording betray Matthew's and Luke's eschatological tendencies as already described. Luke has this at the Last Supper, where it now sits beside Jesus's teaching about greatness and service from Mark 10:41–45, and hence functions to motivate servant-like discipleship in the present.[104] Matthew, however, adds the logion to Peter's complaint of having left everything to follow Jesus (from Mark 10:23–31), where it promises eschatological reward. Given Matthew's interest in Scripture, and the evangelist's willingness to expand the scriptural resonance of sources at every turn, critics are understandably skeptical of assigning the opening of this saying and its clear allusion to Dan 7 to Q.[105] But what remains? A significant agreement: Jesus promises his intimate circle a privileged place on the last day, where they will share a notable role in either the judging or governing of ingathered Israel. To be sure, even without Matthew's more obvious introduction, the notion of human agents sitting on thrones and receiving the prerogative

104. Jesus even gives "a kingdom" to his disciples at this point. The passage reads in full: "I assign to you, as my Father assigned to me, a kingdom, that you may eat and drink at my table in my kingdom, and sit on thrones judging the twelve tribes of Israel." For discussion see Nolland, *Luke 18:35–24:53*, 1066–68; François Bovon, *Luke 3: A Commentary on the Gospel of Luke 19:28–24:53*, trans. James E. Crouch, Hermeneia (Minneapolis: Fortess, 2012), 175–76.

105. This remains one of the major pieces of evidence for critics who think Matthew knew 1 Enoch. For broader discussion, see Amy E. Richter, *Enoch and the Gospel of Matthew* (Eugene, OR: Pickwick, 2012), and Loren T. Stuckenbruck and Gabriele Boccaccini, eds., *Enoch and the Synoptic Gospels: Reminiscences, Allusions, Intertextuality*, EJL 44 (Atlanta: SBL Press, 2016).

κρίνειν remains evocative of Daniel's dream vision, which mentions "thrones" and explicitly the "giving" of "the judgment" to "the holy ones of the Most High."[106] Paul knew this, too, as we have seen (cf. 1 Cor 6:2). Matthew's Danielic opening most likely magnifies what was latent.

We should also take note of numerous parables of Jesus in the double tradition that both Matthew and Luke take to be about his absence and future return.[107] Mark has only one of these, quite similar to Q 12:27–28, which appears at the end of the apocalyptic discourse (13:33–37). In Q, there are five worthy of note:[108]

- the parable of the lamps lit and the wedding feast (Q 12:35–36)
- the parable of slaves alert when the master comes (Q 12:37–38)
- the parable of the coming thief at an unexpected hour (Q 12:39–40)
- the parable of the faithful and wise person (Q 12:42–48)
- the parable of the pounds (Q 19:12–27)

Matthew and Luke have added these parables to the Markan narrative at different points and in ways that demonstrate their own editorial creativity. Since the first four in the list appear in immediate succession in Luke 12, and three of them appear again in the same relative order in Matt 24, I find it likely they were already combined in Q. Assuming the Q hypothesis, then, Matthew preserves most of the cluster in Q 12:35–48 but moves it to the end of the Olivet Discourse for obvious thematic reasons. Matthew then adds two more, one from Q (the parable of the talents [pounds]) and one from Matthew's own special tradition (the parable of the sheep and the goats), to round off Jesus's fifth and final discourse in this gospel in this way:

- the parable of the coming thief at an unexpected hour (24:42–44)
- the parable of the faithful and wise person (24:45–51)
- the parable of the lamps lit and the wedding feast (25:1–13)
- the parable of the talents (25:14–30)
- the parable of the sheep and the goats (25:31–46)

This is a lot of shared material with a very similar punch line. At the same time, there is creative expansion and probably blatant invention here. Two cases stand out in

106. So George R. Beasley-Murray, *Jesus and the Kingdom of God* (Grand Rapids: Eerdmans, 1986), 275–76; Craig A. Evans, "Sitting on the Twelve Thrones of Israel: Scripture and Politics in Luke 22:24–30," in *Jesus in Context: Temple, Purity, and Restoration*, ed. Bruce Chilton and Craig A. Evans, AGJU 39 (Leiden: Brill, 1997), 455–80; Allison, *Intertextual Jesus*, 138–40.

107. See Dieter Roth, *The Parables in Q*, LNTS 582 (London: Bloomsbury T&T Clark, 2018), 87–144, 164–75, 394.

108. See Schulz, *Q: Die Spruchquelle der Evangelisten*, 268–322.

particular: Matthew has greatly extended and developed the parable of the lamps lit and the wedding feast (or, as it is more commonly known, the parable of the ten virgins, 25:1–13),[109] and Luke reworks the parable of the pounds/talents such that it plays off the well-known saga of Herod Archelaus (Q 19:12–27).[110] These two become, for all intents and purposes, new parables. But the evangelists did not make them parables about something else. They remain parables about the departure and return of Jesus that teach the need for faithfulness, diligence, and readiness in the interim.

There is one more batch of texts to consider. We find in the double tradition a number of sayings of Jesus that use vivid imagery to refer to the suddenness of his future coming.[111] The use of these sayings in Matthew and Luke presents a situation similar to the above: the sayings appear together—which could imply they were already grouped in Q—but have been placed into different narrative contexts.

Luke	**Matthew**
son of man and "lightning" (17:24)	son of man and "lightning" (24:27)
son of man and "the days of Noah" (17:26–27)	son of man and "the days of Noah" (24:37–39)
son of man and "the days of Lot" (17:28–30)	(not in Matthew)
one "taken," the other "left" (17:34–37)	one "taken," the other "left" (24:40–41)

The relative order of these is identical in both Matthew and Luke, and Matthew, as with the Q parables, places them in Mark's Olivet Discourse, though dispersed. Some differences in wording again raise the question of what was originally in Q, but this should not distract from the broader agreement here. The collective claim is that the coming of the son of man will be surprising and unexpected, like lightning,[112] that it will interrupt life as usual, as the great flood for the contemporaries of Noah,[113] and it will result in the rescuing of some and the abandonment

109. For discussion of tradition and redaction, see Davies and Allison, *Matthew*, 3:391–94; Luz, *Matthew*, 3:227–32.

110. Cf. Brian Schultz, "Jesus as Archelaus in the Parable of the Pounds (Lk. 19:11–27)," *NovT* 49 (2007): 105–127; Bovon, *Luke* 2, 606–10.

111. Sudden appearance was a messianic trope, so with some humor in b. Sanh. 97a: [R. Zeira would say to sages debating the coming of the messiah] "please do not delay his coming by calculating the end of days. As we learn in a *baraita*: there are three matters that come only by means of diversion of attention: the messiah, a found piece of clothing, a scorpion."

112. Whether his coming is like lightning (so Matthew) or his appearance will be like lightning (so Luke), the suddenness of his arrival is indicated. See Bovon, *Luke* 2, 518–19.

113. While the focus here appears to be on suddenness and not the character of that "generation," it is worth noting that the generation of Noah was remembered as stereotypically

of others (likely to judgment).[114] In this final perplexing saying, it is probable that the "taking" (from παραλαμβάνω) assumes a gathering to meet the son of man (similar in this respect to 1 Thess 4:17), perhaps by means of the angels mentioned elsewhere but not in this saying (see especially Mark 13:31 parr.; Matt 24:27; cf. Matt 13:41: "the son of man will send his angels, and they will collect. . . .").[115] It is impossible to say for sure, because we are seeing the CliffsNotes here, as with Paul in 1 Thess 4 and 1 Cor 15. These sayings of Jesus all assume some knowledge on the part of the readers, which they point to and signify, rather than state outright. Nevertheless, the fact that a Q saying may require a Markan or M saying to create a complete thought would tell us something important about the breadth and depth of eschatological tradition in the Gospels.

As noted above, there is one saying in Q that could be an important exception to this recurring pattern of Matthew and Luke using Q material in similar ways. This is the lament of Jesus over Jerusalem (Q 13:34–35):

Luke 13:34–35	**Matt 23:37–39**
Ἰερουσαλὴμ Ἰερουσαλήμ, ἡ ἀποκτείνουσα τοὺς προφήτας καὶ λιθοβολοῦσα τοὺς ἀπεσταλμένους πρὸς αὐτήν, ποσάκις ἠθέλησα ἐπισυνάξαι τὰ τέκνα σου ὃν τρόπον ὄρνις τὴν ἑαυτῆς νοσσιὰν ὑπὸ τὰς πτέρυγας, καὶ οὐκ ἠθελήσατε	Ἰερουσαλὴμ Ἰερουσαλήμ, ἡ ἀποκτείνουσα τοὺς προφήτας καὶ λιθοβολοῦσα τοὺς ἀπεσταλμένους πρὸς αὐτήν, ποσάκις ἠθέλησα ἐπισυναγαγεῖν τὰ τέκνα σου, ὃν τρόπον ὄρνις ἐπισυνάγει τὰ νοσσία αὐτῆς ὑπὸ τὰς πτέρυγας, καὶ οὐκ ἠθελήσατε
Jerusalem, Jerusalem, the one who kills the prophets and stones those who are sent to it. How often did I desire to gather your children together as a hen gathers her brood under her wings, and you were not willing	Jerusalem, Jerusalem, the one who kills the prophets and stones those who are sent to it. How often did I desire to gather your children together as a hen gathers her brood under her wings, and you were not willing

sinful (cf. Jub. 20.5–6; 1 En. 67.10; LAB 3.1–3; Josephus, *Ant.* 1.72–76), and the generation of the flood was sometimes thought a type of the judgment to come (cf., e.g., 2 Pet 3:6–7; LAE 49.3 [V]; LAB 3.9–10).

114. Cf. Hilary of Poitiers, *Comm. Matt.* ad loc. For discussion see Luz, *Matthew*, 3:214, who thinks the "taken" ones are those "taken" *to* the Lord, and hence rescued.

115. The exegetical tradition has commonly placed Matt 24:40–42 and parr. in conversation with 1 Thess 4:13–18. Cf., e.g., Ambrose, *Exp. Luc.* 8.47; Theophylact, *Comm. Matt.* (on 24:31); Johann Albrecht Bengel, *Gnomon of the New Testament*, 3rd ed., trans. James Bandinel and Andrew R. Fausset (Edinburgh: T&T Clark, 1858), 1:433–34.

Luke 13:34–35	**Matt 23:37–39**
ἰδοὺ ἀφίεται ὑμῖν ὁ οἶκος ὑμῶν	ἰδοὺ ἀφίεται ὑμῖν ὁ οἶκος ὑμῶν ἔρημος
See, your house is left to you	See, your house is left to you, desolate
λέγω ὑμῖν, οὐ μὴ ἴδητέ με ἕως εἴπητε· εὐλογημένος ὁ ἐρχόμενος ἐν ὀνόματι κυρίου	λέγω γὰρ ὑμῖν, οὐ μή με ἴδητε ἀπ᾽ ἄρτι ἕως ἂν εἴπητε· εὐλογημένος ὁ ἐρχόμενος ἐν ὀνόματι κυρίου
I tell you, you will not see me until you say, "Blessed is the one who comes in the name of the Lord"	For I tell you, you will not see me from now on until you say, "Blessed is the one who comes in the name of the Lord"

Though the wording is nearly identical in Matthew and Luke,[116] its placement may suggest very different interpretations by the evangelists. Matthew has it at the end of Jesus's tirade against the Pharisees and the scribes in Jerusalem (23:1–39)—hence after the triumphal entry when the crowds shout precisely the line from Ps 118:26 (cf. 21:9)—and it becomes the last thing Jesus ever says "in the temple" (24:1). As such, Matthew clearly intends Jesus to be talking about his future coming. Jerusalem's unwillingness to be "gathered" (from ἐπισυνάγω)—evoking the end-time hope for the ingathering of Israel (cf. Deut 30:4; Isa 11:10–12; Jer 3:7–8; etc.) parallels the future coming of Jesus when the elect will be "gathered" (from ἐπισυνάγω) by the angels (24:31). While some have thought that Matt 23:37–39 implies Jesus's return is conditional, which would require Israel's confession of his messiahship, I remain unconvinced that *Matthew* assumes such a scenario.[117]

116. Though the use of γάρ to connect Ps 118:26 to the assertion of the "abandoned house" (as Jesus himself is departing from the temple; see 24:1) may imply that Matthew identifies Jesus in some way with the divine presence. Cf. Boris Repschinski, "Re-imagining the Presence of God: The Temple and the Messiah in the Gospel of Matthew," *ABR* 54 (2006): 37–49, esp. 44–49.

117. Cf. H. van der Kwaak, "Die Klage über Jerusalem (Matth. xxiii. 37–39)," *NovT* 8 (1966): 156–70 (argues only Matthew's version is conditional); Chance, *Jerusalem, the Temple, and the New Age*, 130–32; Davies and Allison, *Matthew*, 3:323–24. I would make two points in disagreement with Davies and Allison's conditional reading of the passage. (1) Concluding this discourse with a conditional prophecy about Jesus's return would sit awkwardly beside the Olivet Discourse that comes immediately next, which says not a word about repentance hastening the day but, if anything, the opposite: before Jesus returns, things will get worse! Matthew even draws on eschatological tradition about lawlessness increasing at the end time that he adds to Mark 13 (24:10–12). (2) Moreover, when Matthew describes the return of Jesus only lines later, he adds to Mark the line, "then all the tribes will wail," from Zech 12:10, as discussed above. So how does a collective turning to "the one who comes in the name of the Lord" to initiate Jesus's own return relate to the "wailing" expected when he comes? It is likely that what is depicted in Matt 24 is

Because Luke has the utterance in the middle of the travelogue (13:34–35) and before the triumphal entry in Jerusalem, it could be that Luke's Jesus refers only to his arrival in 19:29–44 but not to anything beyond that.[118] I would wager, however, that we probably have here another instance of realized eschatology in Luke that does not collapse future expectation altogether. Luke's placement functions to create a new layer of meaning in the triumphal entry: it becomes a proleptic parousia and a foretaste of the final visitation (see 19:44). In Luke 13, we learn what Jerusalem ought to do, and in Luke 19, we see that demand both satisfied and subverted: the "multitude of the disciples"(19:37) is on key with Ps 118:26, while the city and its leaders are not.[119]

I could be wrong in this reading of Luke, but even if so, Q 13:34–35 would be the only case where material in the double tradition has been taken in noticeably different eschatological directions: one wholly future (Matthew), one wholly present (Luke). Everywhere else we look, we find large-scale patterns of agreement and creative development, wherein expansion and invention accentuate what the sources already contain.[120] The synoptic tradition, varied and diverse though it is, is bound together by a similar eschatological vision of the future coming of Jesus, the son of man. Many studies of eschatology in Christian origins have looked at some of the material discussed thus far to argue that the hope for "the coming kingdom" was widespread. That is true but also misleading. In synoptic tradition, the future is all about Jesus.

---

the sight of Jesus, which causes varied reactions, as typical in descriptions of the coming day of the Lord, and the same is true in 23:37–39. For two different nonconditional readings of Matt 23:37–39 in context, see Nolland, *Gospel of Matthew*, 952–93, and Luz, *Matthew*, 3:163–64.

118. Cf. Frederick W. Danker, *Jesus and the New Age: A Commentary on Luke's Gospel* (Philadelphia: Fortress, 1988), 266–67.

119. See Ferda, "Reason to Weep," 38–40. See also Manfred Korn, *Die Geschichte Jesu in veränderter Zeit: Studien zur bleibenden Bedeutung Jesu im lukanischen Doppelwerk*, WUNT 51 (Tübingen: Mohr Siebeck, 1993), 98; Brent Kinman, "Parousia, Jesus' 'A-Triumphal' Entry, and the Fate of Jerusalem (Luke 19:28–44)," *JBL* 118 (1999): 279–94; Bovon, *Luke 2*, 331–32.

120. Speaking of the First Evangelist, note Luz, *Matthew*, 2:17: "for Matthew's Christian readers . . . this expression [the son of man] was filled with everything that they already knew from Christian tradition . . . especially about his coming as judge."

11

Jesus and Eschatology in the Fourth Gospel

If we extend our gaze beyond the Synoptic Gospels, do we find a different picture? Does the Gospel of John, in particular, contain a divergent perspective on Jesus and his message that would evidence more disagreement in early Christian eschatological hope than has thus far been apparent? In this chapter, I will argue that it does not. John's eschatology, while certainly distinctive, is not wholly discontinuous with what we have found in Paul and the Synoptics. To be sure, we find in John a creative realized eschatology that goes beyond anything we have seen thus far. Yet John maintains several future hopes that were shared in other Christian circles, not least the expectation for Jesus's future coming and his involvement in the final judgment and the resurrection of the dead. Moreover, a close reading of John shows that one best appreciates the rhetorical force of its realized eschatology when one reads Jesus's claims against the backdrop of—and in response to—various future-oriented hopes that were extant in Jewish circles and among Jesus followers (Jewish and non-Jewish). In other words, the playing field of John's Gospel itself is chalked with future-oriented hopes that were widely known. One marvels at Jesus's pronouncements only if one assumes certain future expectations, and many of these expectations are contained in the sources we have studied already. I can make this case without taking a firm position on the highly debated question of John's relation to the Synoptics, which seems to be undergoing a seismic shift at present.[1] In what follows, I assume only this widely

1. A few important heralds of such change include Wendy E. S. North, *What John Knew and What John Wrote: A Study in John and the Synoptics* (Lexington: Fortress, 2020); Eve-Marie

held scenario: John was written near or at the end of the first century CE and with extant Jesus tradition in mind, some of which also appears in the Synoptic Gospels. Whether John was dependent or independent of one or more of the Synoptics is not, at this point, important to establish for my argument.

Realized Eschatology

We would seriously misconstrue the Fourth Gospel if we thought that one of its objectives was to encourage its readers to long for a yet-to-be-accomplished future. The emphasis of the narrative is clearly on what, for the readers, had already happened in the coming of Jesus in the past and on the continual work of the Paraclete in the present.[2] Line after line of this gospel labors to show that the most important event in history has already transpired: the *logos* present at creation had come down and "become flesh" (1:14), "lived among" humanity, revealed heavenly truth (1:9; 1:51; 3:12–13; etc.), took away the sins of the world (1:29), "completed" or "perfected" the Father's work (see 4:34; 19:30), and "returned" to the Father (13:1; 17:11; 20:17). The salvation-granting descent and ascent of the preexistent Word was an event of the past. Moreover, John's Gospel begins and ends with creation (1:1–5) and new creation (19:41; 20:1, 15), respectively, such that the story of Jesus in itself concretizes the eschatological trope that the end time will be like the beginning time. The first hearers of the story are rhetorically positioned in the aftermath of that work, and they are invited to live accordingly. The main verbs of discipleship in John are "believe" (in Jesus and what he had revealed about himself), "abide" (in Jesus and in the Father), and "love" (as Jesus had modeled himself and given as his sole "commandment" [13:34–35; 15:12]); it is not accidental that "hope" is absent from this list.

Becker, Helen K. Bond, and Catrin H. Williams, eds., *John's Transformation of Mark* (London: Bloomsbury T&T Clark, 2021).

2. As is well known. Cf. John T. Carroll, "The Parousia of Jesus in the Johannine Literature," in *The Return of Jesus in Early Christianity* (Peabody, MA: Hendrickson, 2000), 78–84; John Ashton, *Understanding the Fourth Gospel* (Oxford: Oxford University Press, 2007), 386–87 (calls John an "upside down apocalypse"); R. Alan Culpepper, "Realized Eschatology in the Experience of the Johannine Community," in *The Resurrection of Jesus in the Gospel of John*, ed. Craig R. Koester and R. Bieringer, WUNT 222 (Tübingen: Mohr Siebeck, 2008), 253–76; John Ashton, "Intimations of Apocalyptic: Looking Back and Looking Forward," in *John's Gospel and Intimations of Apocalyptic*, ed. Catrin H. Williams and Christopher Rowland (London: Bloomsbury T&T Clark, 2013), 3–35; Ruben Zimmermann, "Eschatology and Time in the Gospel of John," in *The Oxford Handbook of Johannine Studies*, ed. Judith M. Lieu and Martinus C. de Boer (Oxford: Oxford University Press, 2018), 292–310.

In the course of making this claim, John's Gospel weaves various eschatological threads into its descriptions of Jesus's teachings and activities.[3] The logic is in some ways the mirror image of Matthew's fulfillment formulas but from the perspective of the future. In John, Jesus realizes in his earthly activity not just the hopes from the past but the expectations for the future. The end-time buzz words of "the hour" (ἡ ὥρα) and "the time" (ὁ καιρός) are clearly identified with Jesus's passion and crucifixion (7:8; 12:23), even phrased on two occasions in ways that explicitly acknowledge and rework a future orientation: "the hour is coming and now is" (ἔρχεται ὥρα καὶ νῦν ἐστιν [4:23; cf. 5:25]). The hope for "eternal life" can be experienced now (one can "have" it, so 3:15; 5:24; 6:40; etc., and even "enter," so 3:4) as people respond in faith to Jesus and his message (cf. especially "now this is eternal life, that they might know you the only true God, and Jesus Christ whom you sent" [17:3]).[4] No longer does one merely wait for the resurrection of the dead on the last day, but one can experience resurrection now through Jesus who says, "I am the resurrection and the life" (11:25; cf. 5:21–25). And Jesus says his crucifixion marks "the judgment of the world" and casts out Satan, "the ruler of the world" (12:31).[5] John's *Erzählungstechnik* encourages the readers to experience these claims as striking rather than commonsensical, which means that John presupposes future eschatological hopes in order to refashion them. The passage just noted reads in full, "now [νῦν] is the judgment of this world, now [νῦν] the ruler of this world will be cast out" (12:31)—with two emphatic nuns, each placed at the beginning of each clause. A similarly emphatic "already" (ἤδη) appears in the aftermath of Jesus's conversation with the Samaritan woman at the well, where Jesus announces the arrival of the end-time harvest: "Do you not say, 'Four months more, then comes the harvest?' But I tell you, look around you, and see how the fields are ripe for harvesting already [ἤδη]" (4:35).[6] The Fourth Evangelist also glo-

3. See Jan van der Watt, "Eschatology in John—a Continuous Process of Realizing Events," in *Eschatology of the New Testament and Some Related Documents*, ed. Jan G. van der Watt, WUNT 2/315 (Tübingen: Mohr Siebeck, 2011), 116–18.

4. Cf. Catrin H. Williams, "Faith, Eternal Life, and the Spirit in the Gospel of John," in Lieu and de Boer, *Oxford Handbook of Johannine Studies*, 347–62.

5. Carroll, "Parousia of Jesus in the Johannine Literature," 83; Joshua W. Jipp, *The Messianic Theology of the New Testament* (Grand Rapids: Eerdmans, 2020), 140–43. Note that the baptizing activity of John in the Fourth Gospel is not predictive of a future baptism by fire.

6. The point seems to be that, while it is normal to wait for an interval between sowing and reaping—usually four months (see C. K. Barrett, *The Gospel according to St. John*, 2nd ed. [London: SPCK, 1978], 202)—no such interval is needed now. Interestingly, Matthew identifies the harvest with the return of Jesus and the work of his angels at 13:39 ("the harvest is the end of the age, and the reapers are angels"), though see also the use of this imagery for the sending of the Twelve in the double tradition (Matt 9:37–38 // Luke 10:1–2).

ries in having characters voice future expectations so that Jesus might announce their more immediate fulfillment. John's Samaritan woman lobs this slow pitch at Jesus: "I know that messiah is coming," which means yet to come. Jesus swings away: "I am he, the one speaking to you" (4:25–26).[7]

It is particularly important for our purposes to note that John's tendency to realize future eschatological hopes has also meant that the evangelist associates with Jesus's earthly activities various actions and motifs that other streams of tradition linked to his future coming.[8] The revelation of Jesus's "glory" (δόξα), for instance, is commonly connected to the parousia in both synoptic tradition and in Paul, as we have seen, but in John, Jesus "reveals his glory" in his "signs" (1:14; 2:11) and most spectacularly on the cross. In one climactic pronouncement, Jesus triangulates his crucifixion, his glorification, and his identity as "the son of man": "the hour has come that the son of man might be glorified" (ἐλήλυθεν ἡ ὥρα ἵνα δοξασθῇ ὁ υἱὸς τοῦ ἀνθρώπου [12:23]).[9] John also suggests that "judgment" is meted out now as people respond positively or negatively to Jesus (see especially 12:31). And last, whereas in Paul and in the Synoptics the future work of Jesus signals eschatological "gathering" (Mark 13:27 and parr.), John's Jesus "gathers" at the moment of his crucifixion. The narrator explains at one point that Jesus was about to die to "gather into one [συναγάγῃ εἰς ἕν] the dispersed children of God" (11:51–52), and Jesus himself explains in another that "when I am lifted up from the earth, I will draw all people to myself" (πάντας ἑλκύσω πρὸς ἐμαυτόν [12:32]). In making these claims, it is evident that John is working with some of the same scriptural

7. Cf. a similar dynamic in the exchange with Martha about "the resurrection of the dead" at 11:23–25, where Jesus pronounces, "I am the resurrection and the life." See Raymond E. Brown, *The Gospel according to John*, AB 29 (Garden City, NY: Doubleday, 1966–1970), 1:433–35; Andreas J. Köstenberger, *John*, BECNT (Grand Rapids: Baker Books, 2004), 335.

8. See C. H. Dodd, *The Apostolic Preaching and Its Developments* (New York: Harper, 1960), 121; Jörg Frey, "Eschatology in the Johannine Circle," in *Theology and Christology in the Fourth Gospel: Essays by the Members of the SNTS Johannine Writings Seminar*, ed. Gilbert van Belle, Jan G. van der Watt, and Petrus J. Maritz, BETL 184 (Leuven: Leuven University Press, 2005), 47–82. Though I will not consider it further here, there is, in addition to the examples below, the interesting case of John 10:1–5 where we find the images of shepherd, thief, and doorkeeper. See C. H. Dodd, *Historical Tradition in the Fourth Gospel* (Cambridge: Cambridge University Press, 1963), 382–85.

9. See Martinus C. de Boer, "Johannine History and Johannine Theology: The Death of Jesus as the Exaltation and the Glorification of the Son of Man," in *The Death of Jesus in the Fourth Gospel*, ed. G. Van Belle, BETL 200 (Leuven: Leuven University Press, 2007), 293–326; Jörg Frey, "Die 'theologia crucifixi' des Johannesevangeliums," in *Die Herrlichkeit des Gekreuzigten: Studien zu den Johanneischen Schriften*, ed. Juliane Schlegel, WUNT 307 (Tübingen: Mohr Siebeck, 2013), 485–554.

subtexts (and the traditions that grew out of them) that appeared in other sources above and informed their end-time scenarios, especially Isaiah, Zechariah, and Daniel.[10] For the latter, one especially revealing remark appears in 5:26–27 when Jesus says, "for just as the Father has life in himself, so also he gave [ἔδωκεν] the son to have life in himself. And he gave authority to him to execute judgment [ἐξουσίαν ἔδωκεν αὐτῷ κρίσιν ποιεῖν], because he is the son of man." This final explanatory clause—"because he is the son of man" (ὅτι υἱὸς ἀνθρώπου ἐστίν)—is meaningful only if one knows Daniel's dream vision about that figure and the "giving" of "judgment" in turn.[11] The passage assumes rather than explains; it signifies without offering the signified. Were that not enough, the grammar of the utterance itself is drawn directly from Dan 7 and its distinctive images of bestowal (especially ἐξουσίαν ἔδωκεν αὐτῷ), and this will recur at other points in John's account.[12] It is also evident, as Benjamin Reynolds has shown in his important study, that John's use of "son of man" several times assumes the apocalyptic connotations of that figure in Dan 7 and its later reception.[13] This seems especially clear when John uses "the son of man" at those precise moments Jesus speaks of himself as a heavenly traveler, such as to Nicodemus in 3:13 ("no one has gone up into heaven except the one who came down from heaven [ὁ ἐκ τοῦ οὐρανοῦ καταβάς], the son of man").[14] Here, of course, the flight of Dan 7's son of man is identified with the enfleshment of the Word as described in the prologue (1:14). But it appears that

10. As suggested on p. 216 above, it may be that the exegesis of Num 21's bronze serpent in John 3:14–15 presupposes a realized reading of the end-time sign mentioned in Isa 11:10, 12 (where we find "he will raise up a sign [ונשא נס]"). This exegesis may also be connected to John's idiosyncratic reading of the raising up (נשא, LXX: ὑψωθήσεται) of the servant in Isa 52:10 in reference to the crucifixion of Jesus (12:32). On John's use of Isaiah, see Catrin H. Williams, "Isaiah in John's Gospel," in *Isaiah in the New Testament*, ed. Steve Moyise and Maarten J. J. Menken (London: T&T Clark, 2005), 101–16; on Zechariah, see Adam Kubis, *The Book of Zechariah in the Gospel of John*, EBib 64 (Paris: Gabalda, 2012); and on Daniel, see Stefanos Mihalios, *The Danielic Eschatological Hour in the Johannine Literature*, LNTS 436 (New York: T&T Clark, 2011).

11. Note also 9:35, where the question "do you believe in the son of man?" leads to this pronouncement moments later: "I came into this world for judgment" (v. 39).

12. Note 3:35; 13:3; 17:2.

13. See Benjamin E. Reynolds, *The Apocalyptic Son of Man in the Gospel of John*, WUNT 249 (Tübingen: Mohr Siebeck, 2008). Though I am not convinced that the eightfold typology Reynolds identifies at the outset is ultimately helpful for understanding every son of man saying in the Gospel of John. For another take, see Francis J. Moloney, *The Johannine Son of Man*, 2nd ed. (Eugene, OR: Wipf & Stock, 2007), who argues that son of man for John is an incarnational descriptor and has little meaning for the Fourth Evangelist beyond "the glorification of the Son of Man on the cross" (213). See also Richard B. Hays, *Echoes of Scripture in the Gospels* (Waco, TX: Baylor University Press, 2016), 332 ("John presupposes this apocalyptic Son of Man tradition").

14. See also 6:61. Cf. Reynolds, *Apocalyptic Son of Man in the Gospel of John*, 160.

Dan 7 and the heavenly associations of its "one like a son of man" has informed the scenario just the same.

The Johannine pull toward realization is not completely without precedent in the synoptic tradition, to be sure. On three occasions in the narrative (John 3:14; 8:28; 12:32), John's Jesus speaks of himself as "the son of man" and declares the necessity (cf. δεῖ in 3:14 and 12:34) that he be "lifted up" (from ὑψόω). As this refers to his coming death by crucifixion and probably also his subsequent resurrection, Jesus makes the paradoxical assertion that his crucifixion is actually the beginning of his exaltation. As many have noted, these utterances conjoin the "son of man" language from Dan 7 with the "lifting up" of God's "servant" from Isa 52–53. In Isa 52:13 LXX we find "behold . . . my servant will be lifted up [ὑψωθήσεται] and glorified [δοξασθήσεται] greatly," before further descriptions of this figure's suffering and rejection. The intertextuality is striking because the Synoptic Gospels, while lacking the exact language of "lifting up" with reference to the cross, nevertheless have Jesus, and on three occasions as well (cf. Mark 8:31; 9:30–32; 10:32–34 and parr.), predict his coming death with statements that conjoin language from Dan 7 and Isa 53.[15] In each of these, Jesus speaks of himself as "the son of man" and predicts his suffering with images drawn (most likely) from Isa 53. Whether John's three ὑψόω statements are refashioned synoptic passion predictions, or drawn most likely from another tradition, we see here an intertextual conjoining that predates John and works to similar ends. The more realized use of "son of man" language, not least to describe Jesus's rejection and suffering, is not a Johannine invention.

Unrealized Eschatology?

What remains to happen, then? Is there any room left for the future? Some have thought not and that John might be theologically nearer some later apocryphal gospels, so-called gnostic or not,[16] that downplay the eschatological nature of

15. On this conjoining, see Otto Betz, *Die Menschensohnworte Jesu und die Zukunftserwartung des Paulus (Daniel 7, 13–14)*, ANTJ 6 (Frankfurt am Main: Lang, 1985), 103–20. On John, see Adam W. Day, *Jesus, the Isaianic Servant: Quotations and Allusions in the Gospel of John* (Piscataway, NJ: Gorgias, 2018).

16. On the value of this descriptor, see especially M. A. Williams, *Rethinking "Gnosticism": An Argument for Dismantling a Dubious Category* (Princeton: Princeton University Press, 1996) (who proposes "biblical demiurgical"). For a better suggestion, see Roelof van den Broeck,

Jesus's utterances to the point of elimination, or near it.[17] Bultmann famously regarded any hint of future eschatology in John as evidence of a later "ecclesiastical redactor" who tried to conform the gospel's rogue eschatology to the church's more widespread teaching about the end. It seems fair to say, though, that most subsequent Johannine critics have acknowledged that John does contain future expectations without resorting to elaborate stratification theories.[18] There is dis-

---

"Gnosticism I: Gnostic Religion," in *Dictionary of Gnosis and Western Esotericism I*, ed. Wouter J. Hanegraaf (Leiden; Boston: Brill, 2005), 403–16, esp. 404.

17. See, e.g., numerous sayings in the Gospel of Thomas, whose dependence on the Synoptics is probable. See Jens Schröter, "B.IV.1. Das Evangelium nach Thomas," in *Antike christliche Apokryphen in deutscher Übersetzung, 1.1–2, Evangelien und Verwandtes*, ed. Christoph Markschies and Jens Schröter (Tübingen: Mohr Siebeck, 2012), 483–526. Cf. Gos. Thom. 18 ("The disciples said to Jesus, 'Tell us how our end will come about.' Jesus said, 'Have you uncovered the beginning, then, that you are now seeking the end? For where the beginning is the end will come to be. Blessed is the one who stands at the beginning: that one will know the end and he will not taste death'"), 37 ("His disciples said, 'When will you appear to us and when shall we see you?' Jesus said, 'When you strip naked without being ashamed and take your clothes and place them under your feet like little children and stamp on them, then you will see the Son of the Living One, and you will not be afraid'"); see also sayings 61, 111, 113. Similar is Gos. Mary 8, where Jesus says, "Peace be to you, may my peace be born to you. Be on guard lest one leads you astray by saying, 'Look here' or 'Look over there.' For the Son of Man is within you." In Treat. Res. 45–46 there is mention of "arising" and "ascending" with Jesus; no parousia is necessary. See also Gos. Phil. 71.15. Contrast Orig. World 123.16–24; 127.5–10, which expects the appearance of "the glory of the unbegotten one." For further studies on the later reinterpretation of eschatology, see F. C. Burkitt, *Church and Gnosis* (Cambridge: Cambridge University Press, 1932); Robert M. Grant, *Gnosticism and Early Christianity* (New York: Columbia University Press, 1959), 29–38; Malcolm L. Peel, "Gnostic Eschatology and the New Testament," *NovT* 12 (1970): 141–65; Tobias Nicklas, "Gnostic 'Eschatologies,'" in van der Watt, *Eschatology of the New Testament*, 601–28. April DeConick, "Reading the Gospel of Thomas as a Repository of Early Christian Communal Memory," in *Memory, Tradition, and Text: Uses of the Past in Early Christianity*, ed. Alan Kirk and Tom Thatcher, SemeiaSt 52 (Atlanta: Society of Biblical Literature, 2005), 207–20, argues that Thomas reinterprets apocalyptic tradition.

18. For a history of research, see the important work of Jörg Frey, *Die johanneische Eschatologie: Ihre Probleme im Spiegel der Forschung seit Reimarus*, WUNT 96 (Tübingen: Mohr Siebeck, 1997). See also Urban C. von Wahlde, "C. H. Dodd, the Historical Jesus, and Realized Eschatology," in *Engaging with C. H. Dodd on the Gospel of John: Sixty Years of Tradition and Interpretation*, ed. Tom Thatcher and Catrin Williams (Cambridge: Cambridge University Press, 2013), 149–62. For readings of John in this vein, see Arthur L. Moore, *The Parousia in the New Testament*, NovTSup 13 (Leiden: Brill, 1966), 62–63; Jörg Frey, "Eschatology in the Gospel of John and in the Johannine Epistles," in *Eschatology in Antiquity: Forms and Functions*, ed. Hilary Marlow, Karla Pollmann, and Helen Van Noorden (London: Routledge, 2021), 396–408; van der Watt, "Eschatology in John," 124 ("John's eschatology is neither exclusively futurist nor realized").

agreement about which texts in John refer to the future and which metaphorically try to describe the impact of his ministry or the work of the Paraclete after Easter. But the *dass* of some future eschatology in John is commonly admitted. One important case appears near the end of the Sabbath healing in John 5:24–29:

> Truly truly I say to you that the one who hears my word and believes in the one who sent me has eternal life and does not come into judgment, but has passed from death to life. Truly truly I say to you that the hour is coming and now is when the dead will hear the voice of the son of God and those who hear will live. For just as the Father has life in himself, so also he gave to the son to have life in himself, and he gave him authority to execute judgment, because he is the son of man. Do not marvel at this, because the hour is coming in which all those who are in the tombs will hear his voice, and the ones who did good will go out to the resurrection of life and those who did evil to the resurrection of judgment.

Some have argued that this is all realized eschatology—that is, from start to finish, Jesus is speaking metaphorically about offering spiritual "resurrection" to the spiritually "dead" through his teaching.[19] That is unlikely.[20] The opening of the saying (vv. 24–26) is definitely metaphorical and there is no disputing that; those who hear Jesus's voice in his ministry have already passed (μεταβέβηκεν) from a state of "death" to "eternal life" (see 5:24). But as the end of the saying (vv. 28–29) has "the hour is coming [ἔρχεται ὥρα]" but *not* the line "and now is," and mentions "those in the tombs [οἱ ἐν τοῖς μνημείοις]" who hear, Jesus is surely talking about the future. This reading is supported by the fact that throughout the bread of life

19. H.-C. Kammler, *Christologie und Eschatologie: Joh 5, 17–30 als Schlüsseltext johanneischer Theologie*, WUNT 126 (Tübingen: Mohr Siebeck, 2000); Hugo Méndez, "Mixed Metaphors: Resolving the Eschatological Headache of John 5," *JBL* 137 (2018): 711–32. It seems to me that Méndez's reading, rather than finding "mixed metaphors," creates a tautology. It is also troublesome that he intentionally sets aside the rest of the gospel and does not allow other last day sayings to inform the exegesis of this passage.

20. Cf. M. É. Boismard, "L'évolution du thème eschatologique dans les traditions Johanniques," *RB* 68 (1961): 514–18, who argues vv. 26–30 are more primitive and resemble the Synoptics. See also Josef Blank, *Krisis: Untersuchungen zur johanneischen Christologie und Eschatologie* (Freiburg: Lambertus, 1964), 172–80; Brown, *Gospel according to John*, 1:220; Carroll, "Parousia of Jesus in the Johannine Literature," 88; Jörg Frey, *Die johanneische Eschatologie: Die eschatologische Verkündigung in den johanneischen Texten*, WUNT 117 (Tübingen: Mohr Siebeck, 2000), 389; Craig S. Keener, *The Gospel of John: A Commentary* (Peabody, MA: Hendricksen, 2003), 1:321–23, 652–55; Tim O'Donnell, "Complementary Eschatologies in John 5:19–30," *CBQ* 70 (2008): 750–65.

discourse, Jesus repeats almost as a refrain that he will "raise up on the last day" those who accept him and his word (see 6:39, 40, 44, 55).[21] Moreover, in John 12, moments after offering the bold claim that "now is the judgment of the world" (12:31), Jesus continues to warn about the future: "The one who rejects me and does not receive my word has a judge; on the last day the word that I have spoken will serve as judge" (12:48).[22] On the whole, there is no indication in John that realized "resurrection" and "judgment" replace hope for the future resurrection and the final judgment,[23] or that the "casting out" of Satan by the cross meant that evil had been uprooted from the world completely.[24] The present and the future can be maintained, and sit side by side as in 5:24–29, on the assumption that positive response to Jesus in the present enables one to participate in "eternal life" and guarantees "resurrection to life" on the last day, whereas rejection entails the inverse. The narrator very nearly expresses this outright at 3:36: "the one who believes in the son has eternal life, but the one who disobeys the son will not see life, but the wrath of God remains upon that person." Mention of "the wrath," and the way in which Jesus saves "the one who believes" from it, is near the thought world of 1 Thess 1:10 and where we started part 3, which speaks of the Jesus "who rescues us from the wrath that is coming" (ἐκ τῆς ὀργῆς τῆς ἐρχομένης).

Farewell and Reunion

John's realized eschatology, then, is best understood as a stretching or pulling of the future to include the present, rather than the transfer of the future into the present.[25] But what of the expectation of the future coming of Jesus himself? Is the same logic at work? The claims in John 5, 6, and 12 about the future judgment

21. Jaime Clark-Soles, "'I Will Raise [Whom?] Up on the Last Day': Anthropology as a Feature of Johannine Eschatology," in *New Currents through John: A Global Perspective*, ed. Francisco Lozada Jr. and Tom Thatcher, RBS 54 (Atlanta: Society of Biblical Literature, 2006), 29–53, strains to read all of these passages as further cases of realized eschatology.

22. Also relevant here is 5:45: "do not think that I have come to accuse you before the Father, your accuser is Moses, in whom you hoped."

23. See Reynolds, *Apocalyptic Son of Man in the Gospel of John*, 197. I am grateful for the insight of Daniel Frayer-Griggs in a personal correspondence that the raising of Lazarus may be relevant here as a foretaste of what is to come.

24. See here Brown, *Gospel according to John*, 1:477: "To suggest that the Fourth Gospel is so much in the atmosphere of realized eschatology that the writer expects no further victory over evil than that won in the victorious hour of Jesus' life is to reduce him to a hopeless romantic who cannot recognize existing evil in the world."

25. Jörg Frey, *Die johanneische Eschatologie: Das johanneische Zeitverstandnis*, WUNT 110

and resurrection in John presuppose Jesus's involvement if not his administration of those events, and in this respect, John is not far from what we found in both Paul and synoptic tradition (while neither Paul nor the Synoptics claim that Jesus himself will raise the dead on the last day).[26] But the coming of Jesus itself is not described in those Johannine passages. There are other places in John, however, where a future coming of Jesus himself appears to be expected, and, interestingly, these cluster in John's Farewell Discourse(s) (critics often distinguish 13:31–14:31 and 15:1–16:33), which bears certain parallels in form and content to the Olivet Discourse in Mark 13 and parallels.[27] Formally, both John and the Synoptics resemble many Jewish texts in having the main character offer a final monologue near the end of life wherein that person calls for certain (noble) behaviors in that figure's absence as well as predicts things that are to come (cf. especially Testaments of the Twelve Patriarchs; also 1 Macc 2:49–70; Tob 14:3–11; Philo, *Mos.* 2.288–292).[28] It is standard in such "farewell discourses" that at least some of the predictions from the character would be experienced by the readers as either past or present realities. This of course raises the challenging interpretive task to discern which of the predictions described past and present realities for the reading audience and which would have looked beyond them. Such is precisely the dilemma facing interpreters of Mark 13 and parallels, as we have seen, who debate how much, if any, of that discourse looks beyond the events of 70 CE. In John, the question is even more pressing and challenging, however, because of the figural nature of Jesus's language, as well as John's known penchant for realizing future hopes.

(Tübingen: Mohr Siebeck, 1998), 295, has sought to connect present and future by speaking of a "modell zweier temporaler Brennpunkte."

26. Daniel Frayer-Griggs, "The Johannine Reception of a Matthean Legend" (paper presented at the Annual Meeting of the Society of Biblical Literature, San Antonio, TX, November 20, 2023), makes the interesting argument that John 5:28–29 and 11:43 creatively refract Matthew's account of the resurrection of the dead at the moment of Jesus's "loud shout" and death on the cross (27:50–53).

27. For various views on the question about the literary integrity of this discourse and/or multiple discourses in these chapters of John, see George Parsenios, *Departure and Consolation: The Johannine Farewell Discourses in Light of Greco-Roman Literature*, NovTSup 117 (Leiden: Brill, 2005), 36–48; Udo Schnelle, "Johannes 16 im Rahmen der Abschiedsreden," in *Studies in the Gospel of John and Its Christology: Festschrift Gilbert van Belle*, ed. Joseph Verheyden (Walpole: Peeters, 2014), 425–46; Wayne A. Brouwer, "The Chiastic Structure of the Farewell Discourse in the Fourth Gospel, Part I," *BSac* 175 (2018): 195–214.

28. See Kari Syreeni, *Becoming John: The Making of a Passion Gospel*, LNTS 590 (London: Bloomsbury T&T Clark, 2018), 166–94. See also Andreas Dettwiler, *Die Gegenwart des Erhöhten: Eine exegetische Studie zu den johanneischen Abschiedsreden (Joh 13,31–16,33) unter besonderer Berücksichtigung ihres Relecture-Charakters*, FRLANT (Göttingen: Vandenhoeck & Ruprecht, 1995); Ernst Bammel, "The Farewell Discourse of the Evangelist John and Its Jewish Heritage," *TynBul* 44 (1993): 103–16.

John's Farewell Discourses also resemble Mark 13 and parallels in terms of the content in the instruction itself. There are a number of interesting parallels to note, which I list according to their order of appearance in synoptic tradition:

Stated prediction	**synoptic tradition**	**John**
Jesus warns of falling away	Mark 13:5 and parallels	16:1: "I have spoken these things to you in order that you may not stumble"
Jesus uses the imagery of labor pains	Mark 13:8; Matt 24:8	16:21: "when a woman is in labor, she has pain, because her hour has come"
Jesus predicts persecution in synagogues	Mark 13:9 and parallels	16:2: "They will put you out of the synagogue"
persecution will occur "on account of" Jesus	Mark 13:9 and parallels	15:20–21: "they will persecute you . . . on account of my name [διὰ τὸ ὄνομά μου]"
Jesus's followers will offer witness to the world	Mark 13:9–10 (εἰς μαρτύριον αὐτοῖς) and parallels	15:27: "And you also are to bear witness [μαρτυρεῖτε]"
the Holy Spirit will guide and instruct	Mark 13:11	15:26–27; 16:7; etc. (Jesus will send the Paraclete)
following Jesus will lead to death	Mark 13:12 and parallels	16:2: "the one who kills you will think he is offering a sacrifice to God"
Jesus's followers will be hated	Mark 13:13 and parallels	15:19: "the world hates you"
Jesus speaks about "that day" or "in those days"	Mark 13:17, 20, 24 and parallels	14:20: "on that day you will know"; cf. 16:23
Jesus speaks of his followers as specially chosen	Mark 13:20; Matt 24:22	15:16: "I chose you [ἐξελεξάμην ὑμᾶς]"; cf. v. 19

Stated prediction	synoptic tradition	John
Jesus says that he shares the future before it happens	Mark 13:23; Matt 24:25	14:29: "now I have told you this before it occurs, so that when it does, you may believe"
Jesus speaks of a future coming and his followers being gathered	Mark 13:26 and parallels	14:3: "I will come again [πάλιν ἔρχομαι] and take you to myself"; cf. 14:18, 28
Jesus says he will be seen again	Mark 13:26 and parallels	16:16: "in a little while, you will see me"; cf. 16:17–24; 14:19
Jesus speaks about going away	Mark 13:34 ("the master left [ἀφείς] his house"); cf. Matt 25:15 ("he went away [ἀπεδήμησεν]"); Luke 19:12 (ἀπεδήμησεν)	(cf. 13:33–36; 14:2–4, 18, 28, etc.)
Jesus speaks about his followers as "servants" or "slaves"	Mark 13:34–37 (uses δοῦλος); Matt 25:14 (δοῦλος); cf. Luke 19:13–27 (δοῦλος), as well as Luke 12:41–46 // Matt 24:45–51 (δοῦλος)	15:15: "No longer do I call you servants [δούλους], because the servant does not know what his master does; but I have called you friends [φίλους]"; though cf. 15:20 ("a δοῦλος is not greater than his master")
Jesus uses wedding imagery to describe their reunion	Matt 25:1–13	14:3: "I go to prepare a place for you"

Amid these numerous and striking parallels, there would be one glaring lacuna in the Johannine column: John's Jesus says nothing about the destruction of the temple and the political discord leading up to its fall.[29] But it is otherwise apparent

29. Though too much is made of this silence by Mark Jennings, "The Fourth Gospel's Reversal of Mark in John 13:31–14:3," *Bib* 94 (2013): 210–36, who overstates the evidence. The absence of

that in this most Johannine of Johannine portions of the gospel, the Fourth Evangelist is in touch with earlier tradition about Jesus, whether that be one or more of the Synoptic Gospels directly, or simply another tradition or several traditions that share much in common with Mark 13 and parallels.[30] I remain unsure what to think about this specific question. C. H. Dodd considered some of the putative connections in the chart above in *Historical Tradition in the Fourth Gospel*, arguing as expected that none of them betray evidence of direct contact between John and the Synoptics but rather John's reliance on an independent "strain of tradition." My hesitancy on the matter stems from the fact that often these debates about John's relationship to the Synoptics disagree less about the textual minutiae themselves and far more about what kind of writer they think that "John" was and what kind of liberties they think the evangelist or the evangelist's group was willing to take with known tradition. The hermeneutical circle of Johannine criticism will necessarily require both aspects—the texts inform our understanding of the tradent, and the tradent the texts. But since the background and character of the Johannine tradent is simply something we do not know, there is a real risk that assumptions about this will end up influencing if not determining how one sees the relationship between John and the Synoptics as a whole.[31]

In any case, synoptic tradition or not, there is a more pressing question to consider here: does John, like the Synoptics (as argued above), have Jesus predict a future coming in the Farewell Discourses? I think we can be confident that

temple destruction material in the Farewell Discourses is probably due in part to the fact that John has relocated and repurposed the troublesome temple saying (cf. Mark 14:58 and parr.) at the beginning of the narrative (2:19).

30. Dodd, *Historical Tradition in the Fourth Gospel*, 8, 406–20. More recently, see Johannes Beutler, "Synoptic Jesus Tradition in the Johannine Farewell Discourse," *Jesus in Johannine Tradition*, ed. Robert T. Fortuna and Tom Thatcher (Louisville: Westminster John Knox, 2001), 165–74, though it is not as detailed as Dodd's study and in my opinion takes the discussion no further. See also Paul N. Anderson, "Incidents Dispersed in the Synoptics and Cohering in John: Dodd, Brown, and Johannine Historicity," in Thatcher and Williams, *Engaging with C. H. Dodd on the Gospel of John*, 176–202.

31. When writing about the dialogues in John proper, Dodd, *Historical Tradition in the Fourth Gospel*, 329, noted, "it is theoretically possible either that John was acquainted with dialogues of the Synoptic type, and deliberately remoulded them, or that he had at his disposal a tradition still partly fluid, not yet fully crystallized into fixed forms, which he could deal with as he chose. There are some indications in favour of the latter alternative." Those options are relevant to the present circumstance because John's parallels to the synoptic tradition are, while clear, in no discernible order. As the synoptic discourse is, clearly, a literary product, and stitches together items that must have at one point been independent, it is possible that we see in John a different reception of that tradition. In any case, that is not clear.

John's Jesus does.[32] It is not the climax or even the main focus of anything Jesus says in these chapters, to be sure, and the literary structure of the discourse(s) would not highlight it as in Mark 13 where vv. 24–27 appear near the end of the discourse. Jesus in John is much more focused on his disciples' character of life in his absence, especially their love for one another (13:34; 15:12), their abiding in him and the Father (15:1–17), and their relation to "the world" (17:6–26). But the hope for his future coming is maintained. We see this voiced at the outset of chapter 14, as Jesus explains for the first time that he must "go away":[33]

> Do not let your heart be troubled. Believe in God and believe in me. In my Father's house are many dwelling places, and if not, would I have told you that I go to prepare a place for you? And if I go and prepare a place for you, I will come again [πάλιν ἔρχομαι] and take you to myself [παραλήμψομαι ὑμᾶς πρὸς ἐμαυτόν], in order that where I am also you may be.

Raymond Brown made the obvious yet poignant observation: "it is not apparent that Jesus ever did return to take his disciples along with him."[34] Some have suggested that John's Jesus speaks of bringing individual people to heaven at the hour of their death, but this overlooks the corporate nature of this prediction and its emphasis on corporate reunion.[35] Jesus speaks not of returning to gather disciples one by one but coming to "take you all [ὑμᾶς] . . . in order that where I am you all also may be [ὑμεῖς ἦτε]." The image is, uncoincidentally, reminiscent of what we found in 1 Thess 4, where Jesus's parousia issues in a corporate regathering

32. See Moore, *Parousia in the New Testament*, 62–63; Frey, *Die johanneische Eschatologie: Die eschatologische Verkündigung*, 137–45; Osvaldo D. Vena, *The Parousia and Its Rereadings: The Development of the Eschatological Consciousness in the Writings of the New Testament*, SBT 27 (New York: Lang, 2001), 221–22.

33. This verb itself (John 14:28) could be evidence of John's reliance on tradition, as in Mark 14:21 Jesus says that the son of man ὑπάγει. Cf. Joel Marcus, *Mark 8–16: A New Translation with Introduction and Commentary*, AB 27A (New Haven: Yale University Press, 2009), 951.

34. Brown, *Gospel according to John*, 2:625. See also Leon Morris, *The Gospel according to John*, rev. ed., NICNT (Grand Rapids: Eerdmans, 1995), 568; Carroll, "Parousia of Jesus in the Johannine Literature," 90–92; George R. Beasley-Murray, *John*, 2nd ed., WBC 36 (Nashville: Nelson, 1999), 250; Köstenberger, *John*, 427; J. Ramsey Michaels, *The Gospel of John*, NICNT (Grand Rapids: Eerdmans, 2010), 771–72.

35. For discussion and literature, see Johannes Neugebauer, *Die eschatologischen Aussagen in den johanneischen Abschiedsreden: Eine Untersuchung zu Johannes 13–17*, BWANT 140 (Stuttgart: Kohlhammer, 1995). On the importance of reunion, see Heinrich Greeven, "Kirche und Parusie Christi," *KD* 10 (1964): 116–22; William R. G. Loader, *Jesus in John's Gospel: Structure and Issues in Johannine Christology* (Grand Rapids: Eerdmans, 2017), 55.

where being "with him" (σὺν αὐτῷ in v. 14) is stressed. In fact, being "with" Jesus is the οὕτως, the so what, of 1 Thess 4:13–18: "And thus [οὕτως] we will be with the Lord always [πάντοτε σὺν κυρίῳ ἐσόμεθα]," Paul concludes, so "encourage one another with these words." Hope for future reunion is also at the forefront of the Last Supper traditions in the Synoptics and the eschatological prospect saying (Mark 14:25 and parr.),[36] as well as in Paul, where the meal "proclaims the Lord's death until he comes [ἄχρι οὗ ἔλθῃ]" (1 Cor 11:26).

John's Jesus does not just mention "coming again" in 14:1–3, he speaks of "coming" two more times before the end of the first Farewell Discourse. It is likely that these next two instances, however, refer to the postresurrection appearances of Jesus (14:18–24) and the indwelling of the Paraclete (14:25–31), respectively.[37] In 14:18–24, it is only Jesus's followers who will "see" him in this moment and not the world (14:22)—a reality that makes good sense of the resurrection appearances but not the return of Jesus. And in 14:25–31, Jesus's "coming" appears to be synonymous with the "sending" of the Paraclete who comes "in the name" of Jesus (and, fittingly, shares his grammar: is sent [from πέμπω], teaches [from διδάσκω], comes [from ἔρχομαι]). The comings mentioned in 14:18–24 and 14:25–31 cohere with the style of John's realized eschatology thus far encountered, where the future (in this case, the future "coming" of Jesus) is pulled back toward the present to find more immediate fulfillment (e.g., the "coming" of the risen Christ and the "coming" of the Paraclete).

In the second Farewell Discourse (15:1–16:33), we find another series of sayings that mention "seeing" Jesus in "a little while" (πάλιν μικρόν), which have caused confusion among the disciples (16:16–24) and later commentators alike.[38] "A little while, and you will no longer see me [οὐκέτι θεωρεῖτέ με], and again in a little while, you will see me [ὄψεσθέ με]," Jesus begins (16:16). What exactly is he talking about, and why the change in verbs (θεωρέω and ὁράω)? To follow Ruben Zimmermann and others, it seems to me that a double meaning is actually precisely the point here.[39] The Farewell Discourse has two audiences: on the narrative level,

36. Matthew is especially clear here: "I will not drink again of this fruit of the vine until that day when I drink it new with you (μεθ᾽ ὑμῶν) in my Father's kingdom" (26:29).

37. There is interesting divergence here in the history of interpretation. As Brown, *Gospel according to John*, 2:645–46, notes, many of the Latin fathers thought these passages were about the parousia, while many in the east looked to the postresurrection appearances of Jesus. Compare, e.g., John Chrysostom, *Hom. Jo.* 75; Cyril of Alexandria, *Comm. Jo.* ad loc.; Augustine, *Tract. Ev. Jo.* 67, 75.

38. For discussion, see Johanna Rahner, "Vergegenwärtigende Erinnerung: Die Abschiedsreden, der Geist Paraklet und die Retrospektive des Johannesevangeliums," *ZNW* 91 (2000): 72–90.

39. Zimmermann, "Eschatology and Time in the Gospel of John," 299–300. See also Udo

the disciples themselves, and on the historical level, the recipients of the Gospel of John. The text is written in such a manner that Jesus's words can be heard in two ways. Within the narrative, Jesus appears to be speaking to his disciples about his upcoming death (where they flee and no longer "see" him) and their reunion after the resurrection. But for the historical readers of John, the same words mean something else: to "see" Jesus again after "a little while," using the same poignant verb (ὄψεσθέ) that appears in several of the synoptic parousia predictions (cf. Mark 9:1; 13:26; 14:62 and parr.), is to talk about his future return.[40] To say that, upon seeing Jesus again, the disciples would no longer "have grief" and their "joy" would be such that "no one will be able to take it away from you" (16:22) is rather dramatic commentary for the resurrection appearances but makes good sense if their final and more-lasting reunion with Jesus is in view.[41] It is not clear whether "a little while" here would imply for John's readers a sense of imminence about Jesus's coming as we have seen elsewhere, especially in Paul, Mark, and Matthew, all of whom assumed that the return of Jesus was near.[42] That sense of imminence seems unlikely to me in John, because John's Jesus nowhere else explicitly encourages that notion, and in other places, the text might actually try to reject that idea. It is possible that, as Joachim Jeremias suggested and Dale Allison has argued in detail, in John 21, Jesus refutes earlier tradition that expected John the son of Zebedee—assuming he is the beloved disciple—would be alive for Jesus's

---

Schnelle, *Das Evangelium nach Johannes*, THKNT 4 (Leipzig: Evangelische Verlagsanstalt, 1998), 227–28, 250–51.

40. Joachim Jeremias, "Die Drei-Tage-Worte der Evangelien," in *Tradition und Glaube: Das Frühe Christentum in seiner Umwelt; Festschrift für Karl Georg Kuhn*, ed. Gert Jeremias, Heinz Wolfgang Kuhn, and Hartmut Stegemann (Göttingen: Vandenhoeck & Ruprecht, 1971), 224–25 (the sight language is "altes Kennwort für die Parusie"). Some have thought that John 1:51, with its sight language, conjoined with "the son of man" as well, repurposes an earlier parousia saying (something like Mark 14:62). See Brown, *Gospel according to John*, 1:89. For further discussion, see Christopher Rowland, "John 1:51, Jewish Apocalyptic and Targumic Tradition," *NTS* 30 (1984): 498–507; David R. Kirk, "Heaven Opened: Intertextuality and Meaning in John 1:51," *TynBul* 63 (2012): 237–56.

41. It is worth noting that Paul in 1 Thess 4 refers to the future coming of Christ precisely in order to comfort and encourage, even telling the Thessalonians they should not grieve as those who have no hope. Christine Trotter, "Consolatory Rhetoric in 1 Thessalonians 4:9–12" (paper presented at the Annual Meeting of the Eastern Great Lakes Biblical Society, March 18, 2022), convincingly argues that Paul begins to address Thessalonian reactions to grief in vv. 9–12 before turning to the eschatological teaching in 4:13.

42. Luke's position on the matter is less clear to me, though it has been argued by John Carroll that Luke's softening of certain imminent expectations in his sources has the effect of moving that imminence to his own time, rather than omitting it altogether. See Carroll, *Response to the End of History*. See also Anders E. Nielsen, *Until It Is Fulfilled: Lukan Eschatology according to Luke 22 and Acts 20*, WUNT 2/126 (Tübingen: Mohr Siebeck, 2000), 134–39, 280–86.

return. This is exactly what Jesus appears to predict in Mark 9:1 // Matt 16:28 before John the son of Zebedee is singled out for the transfiguration episode (Mark 9:2 and parr.).[43] It may also be that Jesus's saying in John, "whoever keeps my words will never see death" (8:51), reworks to similar ends the potentially problematic prediction that appears in synoptic tradition as "some who are standing here will not taste death until they see" Jesus's return.[44] Should these suggestions be near the truth, John would maintain the hope for Jesus's future coming but work to soften the imminence of the expectation, though in doing so actually attest to the presence of imminence in earlier tradition. More on this to come.

John in Context

As those parallels between John's Farewell Discourses and the Synoptics might have led us to suspect, then, we see that John's Jesus, too, talks about his future coming when predicting other events to come after his upcoming death. As readers of Mark 13 and parallels heard in that discourse the description of things that had already happened and at least one crucial thing that had not, so also the readers of John 13–17 who lived after the resurrection of Jesus and the sending of the Paraclete. There is, John's Gospel agrees, more to come in this story, and the central character will again be Jesus.[45] It is important to note that nowhere does John use the imagery of Dan 7's son of man in order to describe this future coming, nor are there future-oriented traces of Zechariah or Isaiah behind Jesus's words on the matter.[46] Language about the return of Jesus is, in comparison to the Synoptics

43. See Joachim Jeremias, *New Testament Theology: The Proclamation of Jesus*, trans. John Bowden (New York: Scribner's Sons, 1971), 137 ("the expectation expressed in John 21.23a . . . is a reinterpretation of the Marcan saying influenced by the delay of the Parousia"); Dale C. Allison Jr., "'Jesus Did Not Say to Him That He Would Not Die': John 21:20–23 and Mark 9:1," in *The Gospel of John and History* (forthcoming).

44. In Mark's version of this saying (followed by Luke), Jesus had just mentioned being ashamed of "his words" (8:38), which is another potential connection to John 8:51 ("my word"). See Dodd, *Historical Tradition in the Fourth Gospel*, 366–69, 338–43; Brown, *Gospel according to John*, 1:471–73; Herbert Leroy, *Rätsel und Missverständnis: Ein Beitrag zur Formgeschichte des Johannesevangeliums* (Bonn: Hanstein, 1968), 76–80.

45. On point here is van der Watt, "Eschatology in John," 134: "In the person of Jesus, the realized eschatology and futuristic eschatology are entwined in a process that realizes itself through time. These things are completely bound to Jesus' presence and promises. He is the guarantee of the eschatological presence and future."

46. Markus Sasse, *Der Menschensohn im Evangelium nach Johannes* (Tübingen: Francke, 2000), 243–45, lists eleven differences between the son of man in John and in the Synoptics.

and Paul, somewhat stripped down and lacking those brilliant intertextual colors. We might say—to switch metaphors—that the gravitational weight of John's Christology has pulled to itself not just the future eschatology of earlier tradition but its intertextuality as well, such that Daniel, Zechariah, and Isaiah now work together to inform the meaning of Jesus's earthly ministry, and especially his passion and death. But hope for a similar future remains in John, nonetheless.

Johannine Christianity obviously changed and developed as it encountered new circumstances, and we can see that process at work in 1, 2, and 3 John. But the exegesis offered here shows that, with respect to at least one issue, the Epistles of John and the Gospel of John are on the same page (1 John 2:28–3:3):

> And now, children, remain in him, in order that when he is revealed [φανερωθῇ] we might have boldness and not be put to shame before him at his coming [ἐν τῇ παρουσίᾳ αὐτοῦ]. If you know that he is righteous, you know that everyone who does righteousness has been born from him. Behold what kind of love the Father has given to us, in order that we might be called children of God, and we are. On this account the world does not know us, because it did not know him. Beloved, now we are children of God [νῦν τέκνα θεοῦ ἐσμεν], and not yet [οὔπω] has what we will be been revealed. We know that when he is revealed [φανερωθῇ], we will be like him, because we will see [ὀψόμεθα] him as he is. And everyone who has this hope in him purifies himself, just as he is pure.

There it is: the νῦν ("now") of the love of God and the surety of being "children of God," alongside the οὔπω ("not-yet") of the "revealing" of Jesus and his "coming."[47]

Where does this leave us, then, if we consider the claims of the Four Gospels as a whole? Their theological diversity and unique narrative profiles are patent, but so also is this: all four commemorate a Jesus who anticipated a further coming after his death, and this expectation is difficult to distinguish from the eschatological hopes they otherwise contain. It is also apparent that these narratives were written under the assumption that their readers already believed this to be true and frankly knew more about it than was necessary to say. In both of these respects, the claims of the Gospels cohere with what we can reconstruct about the eschatology of Paul and the situation on the ground in his churches decades earlier. Moreover, these claims cohere with what we can infer about almost every

47. Cf. Andrew J. Byers, "Johannine Readings of the Johannine Gospel: Reception Theology and Practice in John's Epistles," in *Gospel Reading and Reception in Early Christian Literature*, ed. Madison N. Pierce, Andrew J. Byers, and Simon Gathercole (Cambridge: Cambridge University Press, 2022), 208–9.

other text that made it into the New Testament and are roughly contemporaneous with or later than the Gospels.[48] It would distract too much from our purposes to give these other sources a detailed read, and they would not ultimately be that useful for reconstructing the historical Jesus. But the core exegetical claim is not particularly controversial concerning Colossians, 2 Thessalonians, all three Pastoral Epistles, Hebrews, James, 1 Peter and 2 Peter, Jude, and Revelation.[49] This includes as well early noncanonical texts like the Didache and 1 and 2 Clement.[50]

48. Cf. Wilfried Joest, "Die Kirche und die Parusie Jesu Christi," in *Gott in Welt: Festgabe für Karl Rahner*, ed. Herbert Vorgrimler (Freiburg: Herder, 1964), 1:536–50. And for those that do not, such as Ephesians, it is not as though the text presents an alternative eschatological scenario. See Andrew T. Lincoln, *Paradise Now and Not Yet: Studies on the Role of the Heavenly Dimension in Paul's Thought with Special Reference to His Eschatology*, SNTSMS 43 (Cambridge: Cambridge University Press, 1991), 167. Contrast Andreas Lindemann, *Die Aufhebung der Zeit: Geschichtsverständnis und Eschatologie im Epheserbrief*, SNT 12 (Gütersloh: Mohn, 1975), 209–10, who argues that Paul's eschatology has been transformed in Ephesians to such a degree that there is no longer any meaningful future dimension.

49. See Col 1:22, 27; 3:1–4; 4:5. Cf. Benjamin Wold, "Apocalyptic Thought in the Epistles of Colossians and Ephesians," in *The Jewish Apocalyptic Tradition and the Shaping of New Testament Thought*, ed. Benjamin E. Reynolds and Loren T. Stuckenbruck (Minneapolis: Fortress, 2017), 219–32 at 220–21. On 2 Thessalonians, see Janusz Kucicki, *Eschatology of the Thessalonian Correspondence: A Comparative Study of 1 Thess 4,13–5,11 and 2 Thess 2,1–12 to the Dead Sea Scrolls and the Old Testament Pseudepigrapha* (Bern: Lang, 2014). The Pastoral Epistles, while lacking any hint of eschatological imminence, as well as common terms used for Jesus's coming (like παρουσία), nevertheless exhort the reader "to keep the commandment without spot or blame until the manifestation [μέχρι τῆς ἐπιφανείας] of our Lord Jesus Christ, which he will bring about at the right time" (1 Tim 6:14–15). See also 2 Tim 4:1, 8; Tit 2:13. Cf. Mark Harding, "Apocalypticism in the Pastoral Epistles," in Reynolds and Stuckenbruck, *Jewish Apocalyptic Tradition and the Shaping of New Testament Thought*, 265, 266–68. In Hebrews, see 9:27–28 (the only time in the New Testament that the adjective "second" is applied to Jesus's future coming); 10:12–13. Cf. Gert J. Steyn, "The Eschatology of Hebrews—as Understood within a Cultic Setting," in van der Watt, *Eschatology of the New Testament*, 433–36. In James, see 5:7–9 and discussion in John T. Carroll, "The Parousia of Jesus in Other New Testament Writings," in *Return of Jesus in Early Christianity*, 121–30. In the Petrines, see 1 Pet 1:7, 13; 2 Pet 1:16; 3:3–9, and discussion in Fika J. van Rensburg, "The Eschatology of 1 Peter—Hope and Vindication for Visiting Resident Strangers," in van Der Watt, *Eschatology of the New Testament*, 472–92; Romeo Popa, "Parusieverzögerung und Generationenkonflikt im Zweiten Petrusbrief," *BZ* 61 (2017): 164–72. In Revelation, see 3:11; 16:15; 19:11–21; 22:13, 20. Cf. Mathias Rissi, "Die Erscheinung Christi nach Off. 19:11–16," *TZ* 21 (1965): 81–95; Carroll, "Parousia of Jesus in the Johannine Literature," 99–112; Jan A. du Rand, "Depicting Eschatology in the Gospel of John," in van der Watt, *Eschatology of the New Testament*, 535–66 at 548–52, 559–61.

50. See Did. 16.6–8 and discussion in Murray Smith, "The Lord Jesus and His Coming in the Didache," in *The Didache: A Missing Piece of the Puzzle in Early Christianity*, ed. Jonathan A. Draper and Clayton N. Jefford, ECL 14 (Atlanta: SBL Press, 2015), 363–407. See also 1 Clem. 23.2–5

In all of these texts, the hope for Jesus's future coming is present and often abbreviated in description (excluding Revelation). That is possible only on the basis of shared expectations between the authors and readers; it is possible, in other words, only if the readers, like Luke's Theophilus, have already "been instructed" to see Jesus on the horizon of the future. These texts were written, and this without exception, not to inform about Jesus's return but to use that hope for some other end, typically parenesis.[51]

---

and 2 Clem. 17.4–6. Cf. Wolfgang Pratscher, "Die Parusieerwartung im 2. Klemensbrief," in *Apokalyptik als Herausforderung neutestamentlicher Theologie*, ed. Michael Becker and Markus Öhler, WUNT 2/214 (Tübingen: Mohr Siebeck, 2006), 197–210.

51. As Kurt Erlemann, *Naherwartung und Parusieverzögerung im Neuen Testament: Ein Beitrag zur Frage religiöser Zeiterfahrung* (Tübingen: Francke, 1995), argued, the language of imminence is not just about temporal concerns but has a practical function, as does the language of delay.

CONCLUDING THOUGHTS ON PART 3

My hope is that the exegesis of these chapters offers an important contribution to the discussion of the place of the second-coming hope in early Christianity. My core contention in terms of method is that we must attend carefully at first to the claims of the sources themselves and how they appear to have understood the very eschatological traditions that they contain before we move to offer hypotheses about the past behind them. As already discussed in part 1, many studies have either begun with history and treated the sources atomistically in an effort to reconstruct a particular Jesus, which gets things backward, or they have combed through the sources synchronically in search of particular eschatological topoi that appear widely shared, which does not adequately attend to how these sources understand, frame, and develop these topoi on their own terms. In these chapters, we have sat with texts much longer than is typical in historical Jesus books. But it has brought us to an important place that recognizes what is common, shared, and assumed by New Testament authors without mitigating what is distinctive, unique, and innovative. While it would be tedious to summarize the results of part 3 in their entirety, I offer the following highlights by way of conclusion and in anticipation of part 4, where we will rely on and frequently revisit the exegeses of these chapters.

(1) Eschatology in Paul, the Gospels, and other noted sources has particular christological content.[1] And in terms of our extant sources, this is the earliest eschatology that we have. First Thessalonians already assumes the future coming of Jesus as tradition. Moreover, we do not find in these early decades other Christian groups emerging who hold to drastically different eschatological scenarios wherein Jesus plays no important role. They could have existed but we have no evidence of it.[2]

1. Cf. Arthur L. Moore, *The Parousia in the New Testament*, NovTSup 13 (Leiden: Brill, 1966), 92.

2. It is worth noting that, in Q studies, where there has been great debate about how Q's theology might diverge from that of the canonical gospels, especially with reference to the significance of Jesus's death, there is less debate about Q's interest (at least in its final form) in the future coming of Jesus. This is not to endorse the view of some that the Q people had a noticeably different understanding of Jesus's death but simply to observe an interesting tendency in scholarship that probably hints at something about the nature of our texts. Some stratification theories of Q have, of course, suggested this eschatological interest in Q is secondary. Cf. Leif E.

The return of Jesus is often connected to the expectation for the day of the Lord and the coming of God in Israel's Scriptures.[3] This also makes sense of why the coming of Jesus is often linked to the resurrection of the dead, the final judgment, and the ingathering of Israel or the nations, while our sources do not agree on the precise nature of Jesus's involvement in these events.

(2) In the Gospels, their claim is not just that the authors or the disciples or later followers believe Jesus will come again but that Jesus himself had talked about this in short utterances, extended teachings, and even parables. Paul himself appears to have believed that the scenario he details in 1 Thess 4:13–17 comes from the teaching of Jesus.

(3) In all the sources discussed in part 3, the coming of Jesus can be alluded to in the barest of terms, sometimes with simply a single word: his "coming" (from ἔρχομαι) or "appearance" (from παρουσία) or "revelation" (from φανερόω and cognates). This is similar to how texts can refer to "the judgment" and "the resurrection" under the assumption that the audience is in the know.[4] At the same time, however, there is no formulaic way of talking about the future coming of Jesus; numerous terms appear and sometimes within the same sources.[5]

(4) In reception, we see expansion and development in kind, and that is true for both additions and subtractions. Matthew and Luke creatively expand Mark in quite different ways when it comes to the future work of Jesus, often with the help of Israel's Scriptures as well as messianic and eschatological traditions that grew out of them. But they do not create something entirely new. And John refracts the

---

Vaage, "The Son of Man Sayings in Q: Stratigraphical Location and Significance," *Semeia* 55 (1991): 103–29; James M. Robinson, "The Critical Edition of Q and the Study of Jesus," in *The Sayings Source Q and the Historical Jesus*, ed. A. Lindemann, BETL 158 (Leuven: Leuven University Press; Sterling: Peeters, 2001), 39, 42–43, 45; Bernard Brandon Scott, "How Did We Get Here?," in *Jesus Reconsidered: Scholarship in the Public Eye*, ed. Bernard Brandon Scott (Santa Rosa, CA: Polebridge, 2007), 47–64; Douglas E. Oakman, *The Political Aims of Jesus* (Minneapolis: Fortress, 2012), 119–23. But this argument has convinced few outside a rather narrow circle of critics. Moreover, even should a stratification of Q that leaves little to no eschatology in its earliest version be correct, why think this small document captures everything this Q group thought about the future? On the perils of such an argument from silence, see Harold W. Attridge, "Reflections on Research into Q," *Semeia* 55 (1992): 228–29. John Kloppenborg himself has noted, in *Excavating Q: The History and Setting of the Sayings Gospel* (Minneapolis: Fortress, 2000), 371, that "Q does not offer a complete catalogue of the Q group's beliefs."

3. Cf. Richard Bauckham, *Jude and the Relatives of Jesus in the Early Church* (London: T&T Clark, 2004), 96 ("seems to have been a widespread practice in primitive Christianity").

4. Cf., e.g., Luke 11:29–32: "at the judgment" and "at the resurrection."

5. On terminology, see Albrecht Oepke, "παρουσία, κτλ," *TDNT* 5:858–71; Greeven, "Kirche und Parusie Christi," 113–15; Osvaldo D. Vena, *The Parousia and Its Rereadings: The Development of the Eschatological Consciousness in the Writings of the New Testament*, SBT 27 (New York: Lang, 2001), 107–14 (see the helpful chart at 112–13).

prior futurist eschatology of the traditions known to him not by setting it aside entirely but by realizing it in the earthly ministry of Jesus.

(5) We also see in all of our sources a mixture of present and future eschatology when it comes to describing the activity of Jesus, while with notable differences in terms of what has been accomplished and where the emphasis lies. The "already" and the "not-yet" make sense on the assumption that an eschatological process of fulfillment is underway that includes the life experience of the text and its readers and looks beyond it. All the sources considered here plot the readers in an interim time wherein Jesus's absence is thought a temporary phenomenon.

(6) There is disagreement among our sources in terms of the question of imminence. Paul expected to still be alive (at least at the beginning of his ministry), and it seems that Mark and Matthew also thought the time was very short indeed. Luke, to my mind, is more enigmatic, though this is highly debated, and John does not appear to share the imminence of earlier tradition (but appears to react to it, especially with the "in a little while" sayings, and thus betrays knowledge of its existence). Other later sources vary. While it is dubious to sketch a clear line of development from more imminence to less, it does seem that our earliest sources expect Jesus to come very soon.[6]

(7) One striking feature of nearly every source, minus the Gospel of John, is the degree to which the future coming of Jesus was informed by Israel's Scripture, and that with great diversity in terms of the particular intertexts engaged (though we hear especially from Isa 11, 27, 59, 66, Zech 12, 14, Dan 7, and Pss 2, 8, 89, 110). There were some common patterns, to be sure, especially the association between Jesus's future coming and the "day of the Lord" tradition and the coming of God therein. We find texts conjoined with others in highly creative ways that betray intentional thought and perhaps even scribal activity and knowledge of the Greek Bible.

(8) There is also consistent interest in well-known messianic texts from Isaiah and especially the dream vision about the son of man in Dan 7 (although Paul remains somewhat enigmatic on this front). In the Gospels, Jesus is clearly that son of man Daniel saw, and his enactment of that vision sometimes includes his present activity and sometimes his future activity. This is true even in the Synoptic Gospels, while their use of Dan 7 is most often futuristic. The Gospels simply presume that Jesus is the son of man, and they are comfortable speaking of his identity as such in both present and future activities. In part 3, I have not followed the common procedure—since Bultmann[7]—of distinguishing three categories

6. So Paula Fredriksen, *Jesus of Nazareth, King of the Jews: A Jewish Life and the Emergence of Christianity* (New York: Knopf, 1999), 89.

7. Rudolf Bultmann, *Theology of the New Testament*, trans. Kendrick Grobel (New York: Scribner's Sons, 1955), 1:28–32. After him, cf., e.g., Hans Conzelmann, *Jesus*, ed. John Reumann,

of son of man sayings (present, suffering, future), because the Gospels make no such differentiation.[8]

(9) It is somewhat misleading to say that the early Christians thought of "two advents" of Jesus in the ways of later patristic theologizing, and the intertextuality tells a different story. I have used "second advent" throughout this study by way of concession to its common usage, but the phrase itself is too schematic.[9] The point we find again and again is about one mission with consummation expected after an interim.

As already discussed in part 1, E. P. Sanders popularized a common argument about eschatology in Christian origins: because John the Baptist and the early church sandwich the historical Jesus, and because both the before and the after expected an imminent consummation, we should think that Jesus did, too.[10] It is a good argument. But, in light of the work of part 3, we see that there is also a problem with it. The early followers of Jesus, if we read their literature carefully, did not expect the imminent consummation in general, or the arrival of "the kingdom" alone. They had a very particular hope that their messiah would figure prominently in whatever was still left to happen. So Sanders's wording of this argument, which is really an argument about historical continuity, disguises an underlying discontinuity in a common reconstruction of Christian origins. Can the core insight be salvaged, albeit nuanced and sharpened around what the earliest Christian literature actually claims? Is there a better historical scenario we might hypothesize that accounts for the "wild ideas" of the early Christians? I think that there is.

---

trans. J. Raymond Lord (Philadelphia: Fortress, 1973), 43; Helmut Merklein, *Jesu Botschaft von der Gottesherrschaft: Eine Skizze*, SBS 111 (Stuttgart: Katholisches Bibelwerk, 1983), 153; Jürgen Becker, *Jesus of Nazareth*, trans. James E. Crouch (Berlin: de Gruyter, 1998), 204; Georg Strecker, *Theology of the New Testament*, trans. M. Eugene Boring (Louisville: Westminster John Knox, 2000), 257.

8. For similar skepticism of the usefulness of this threefold division, see Robert Maddox, "The Functions of the Son of Man according to the Synoptic Gospels," *NTS* 15 (1968): 45–74; Christopher Tuckett, "The Present Son of Man," in *From the Sayings to the Gospels*, WUNT 328 (Tübingen: Mohr Siebeck, 2014), 506–7. It is also specious to pit son of man sayings that have the suffering of Jesus in view against those that are more future oriented, as noted also by Tuckett, "On the Stratification of Q," *From the Sayings to the Gospels*, 151; Tuckett, "The Son of Man and Daniel 7: Q and Jesus," *From the Sayings to the Gospels*, 275. Cf. C. F. D. Moule, *The Origin of Christology* (Cambridge: Cambridge University Press, 1977), 13–14.

9. Cf. Oscar Cullmann, "Die Hoffnung der Kirche auf die Wiederkunft Christi nach dem Neuen Testament" (1944), in *Vorträge und Aufsätze 1925–1962*, ed. K. Fröhlich (Tübingen: Mohr Siebeck, 1966), 385: "In Neuen Testament ist allerdings nirgends von der *Wieder*kunft Christi die Rede, sonder immer nur von seiner *An*kunft."

10. E. P. Sanders, *Jesus and Judaism* (Philadelphia: Fortress, 1985), 91–94.

PART FOUR

The Future Kingdom and Its Messiah

DEATH, MISSION, AND THE END OF THE AGE

In the face of these testimonies, to doubt would be an act of violence.

—Theodor Keim[1]

I would like to pause to reflect for a moment on the situation in which we find ourselves. We have identified in the New Testament an expectation for the future coming of Jesus that is present in the ministry of Paul (and not unique to Paul), found in each layer of the gospel tradition, and appears in almost every other text that made it into the New Testament. The hope emerges even when it is not theologically advantageous for the source in question and the author would rather talk about something else (such as, in the Gospel of John, what Jesus *already* accomplished). When there is otherwise and lamentably so little explicit contact between the letters of Paul and the Gospels, we have, in our earliest Pauline epistle, a saying attributed to Jesus himself that presents numerous parallels with synoptic tradition. Moreover, already by the time of 1 Thessalonians, the imminence of this expectation was raising questions that needed answers, and by the time of 2 Peter, outright mockery.[2]

1. Theodor Keim, *The History of Jesus of Nazara, Freely Investigated in Its Connection with the National Life of Israel, and Related in Detail*, trans. Arthur Ransom, 2nd ed. (London: Williams & Norgate, 1876–1883), 4:287.

2. See Fernando Bermejo Rubio, "Calling the Parousia into Question: Doubters and Skeptics

With what other issue in Jesus studies do we find this level of attestation, coherence, and potentially embarrassing material? I do not think there is a single one, minus the crucifixion of Jesus. At the very least, we should be able to see afresh that the consensus of silence on this topic is a truly remarkable thing, and it is in part explicable, as I have argued, by the reception history of the expectation over the course of several centuries.

The task before us now is to offer a probable historical scenario that explains how these claims came to exist (in general) and came to exist as they do (respecting their various particularities and tendencies). And it needs to be stressed that this task is incumbent on any and all engaged in Christian origins research, not just on those who might tie the genesis of these claims to the Jesus of history in some way. All historians can do is craft competing historical scenarios about the past to explain the emergence of the Jesus movement as it appears in our sources and determine which one among them is the most probable.[3] We might not always be able to tell and move the needle beyond a number of possibilities, to be sure. But we need to have grounds for suspicion, as well as for claims about historicity; otherwise we are just assuming a portrait of Jesus at the outset and using that to guide our conclusions. Electing to tell no story at all is not an option at the luxury of anyone. As noted in part 1, it turns out that, on a close read, John A. T. Robinson was actually not quite sure how to explain the origin of this hope in the post-Easter period, but he tries to avoid the significance of that by shifting the burden of proof onto those who would make a positive argument about the historical Jesus. That is dubious, and it throws into question his entire argument. The burden of proof is on anyone making any argument about anything.[4]

---

in Some Early Christian Texts," *Archiv für Religionsgeschichte* 23 (2022): 173–87. Note in this clear Christian addition to the Mart. Ascen. Isa. 3.21: "And afterwards . . . his disciples will abandon the teaching of the twelve apostles, and their faith, and their love, and their purity. And there will be much contention at his coming and at his approach." Cf. 1 Clem. 23.1–5; 2 Clem. 11.2–7. Contra Edward Adams, "'Where Is the Promise of His Coming?' The Complaint of the Scoffers in 2 Peter 3:4," *NTS* 51 (2005): 106–22, who argues that the complaint is not about the failure of the parousia to materialize but rather the advent of God as expected in the biblical prophets.

3. Robert L. Webb, "The Historical Enterprise and Historical Jesus Research," in *Key Events in the Life of the Historical Jesus: A Collaborative Exploration of Context and Coherence*, ed. Darrell L. Bock and Robert L. Webb, WUNT 247 (Tübingen: Mohr Siebeck, 2009), 81, is right to stress that hypotheses about the past should be preferred by the degree to which they provide a "better explanation of the evidence" on not just the micro but also the macro in the context of Christian origins.

4. So famously Morna Hooker, "On Using the Wrong Tool," *Theology* 75 (1972): 580. See also John P. Meier, *The Roots of the Problem and the Person*, vol. 1 of *A Marginal Jew: Rethinking the Historical Jesus* (New York: Doubleday, 1991), 183; Gerd Theissen and Dagmar Winter, *The Quest for the Plausible Jesus: The Question of Criteria* (Louisville: Westminster John Knox, 2002), 204.

As I analyze the evidence in what follows, I will make a case that the most probable explanation for the early and widespread belief in Jesus's future coming before the generation then living had expired is the teaching of Jesus himself. My approach is simple. First, I believe, with James Crossley, that the best way through the current method wars in Jesus studies is to follow "an old-fashioned view of interpretation, argument, and the combining of arguments for collective weight to make a general case,"[5] and second, that historical arguments, like pyramids, should be constructed with a wide base, and not balance precariously on a single tip. Before critiques of the criteria of authenticity were standard fare, E. P. Sanders wisely wrote,

> The method which is being followed more and more, and the one which seems necessary to follow in writing about Jesus, is to construct hypotheses which, on the one hand, do rest on material generally considered reliable without, on the other hand, being totally dependent on the authenticity of any given pericope.[6]

As will become apparent in what follows, I am often skeptical of our ability to answer the question, "did Jesus say or do that," but I do think we can make probabilistic arguments, based upon the kinds of things that recur in our sources, make sense within first-century Palestinian Judaism, and explain the later rise of the church, that Jesus said and did things "like" that.[7] Making such arguments will necessarily involve at times drawing on the logics that undergird the criteria of authenticity, even while a dogmatic and atomistic use of the criteria (as, e.g., a "method" used "to prove") has been justly criticized.[8] On the whole, and as the

5. James Crossley, *Jesus and the Chaos of History: Redirecting the Life of the Historical Jesus* (Oxford: Oxford University Press, 2015), 44–45.

6. E. P. Sanders, *Jesus and Judaism* (Philadelphia: Fortress, 1985), 3.

7. Eric Eve, *Behind the Gospels: Understanding the Oral Tradition* (Minneapolis: Fortress, 2014), 182, has wisely suggested that "the very concepts of authentic and inauthentic material need rethinking" because "a great deal of the material that now appears in the Gospels" is "a blend of recollection, reinterpretation, reflection, conflation, confusion and distortion that simply cannot be reverse-engineered." Rather than use "authentic" to mean "a literal transcription of historical fact as it might have been recorded by a video camera," we should use authenticity with reference to "the sort of things Jesus typically said and did." Cf. Morna Hooker, "Foreword: Forty Years On," in *Jesus, Criteria, and the Demise of Authenticity*, ed. Chris Keith and Anthony Le Donne (London: T&T Clark, 2012), xv: "If we concentrate on the whole rather than the details . . . we shall find that we know quite a lot about Jesus, even though we may not be able to reconstruct with certainty any of his sayings or actions." See further discussion and literature on pp. 30–32 above.

8. I have written about this elsewhere. See Tucker S. Ferda, *Jesus, the Gospels, and the Galilean Crisis*, LNTS 601 (London: Bloomsbury T&T Clark, 2019), 10–14; Ferda, "The Galilean Crisis

historiographer Johann Droysen once wrote, I offer in the following pages not "the exact historical fact"—as that is unattainable—but "a relatively safe and correct view" that stems from, and circles back to explain, the tendencies of early Christian memories about Jesus.[9]

Because there are a number of different interlocking historical and exegetical issues involved in pursuing our question, I will proceed in several steps and take up different issues in turn for clarity's sake. It should be stressed at the outset that I have equally strong disagreements with critics on the other side of Glasson, Robinson, and others, who think that everything early Christians claimed about Jesus in terms of eschatology goes back to him in some fashion. This is most certainly false. As I will argue in detail, it cannot be said that the same mind that was in the early Christians was in Jesus Christ. Moreover, in the final chapter of part 4, I will suggest that there are at least two competing scenarios for how and when this hope emerged in the activity of Jesus—one that finds some kind of "crisis" of rejection in the ministry that changed his mind (like the old Galilean crisis theory—the subject of my first book), and one that assumes more continuity throughout. I will reiterate and build on my earlier skepticism of the Galilean crisis theory, but I personally cannot decide with much confidence which is preferable between these scenarios. In any case, while both scenarios cannot be true, either one is still *more probable* than another that would have the disciples of Jesus coming up with the expectation themselves in the post-Easter period. And that is where I will leave this fascinating and complex topic, having done the best with it that I can and having gone as far as I believe is historically responsible.

---

and Jesus Research Past and Present: A Response to Paula Fredriksen, Sarah Rollens, and Jens Schröter," *JSHJ* 20 (2022): 134–36.

9. Johann Gustav Droysen, *Outline of the Principles of History*, trans. E. Benjamin Andrews (New York: Fertig, 1893), 25–26.

12

Tendencies, Trajectories, and Tradition Histories

We begin where part 3 left off: with the eschatological claims of early Jesus followers in literary sources spanning various decades of the first and early second centuries CE. Having sympathetically described the most important of these sources individually and on their own terms,[1] what might we learn about the relationships among these traditions, and the contours of their transmission, in hopes to run the tape backward and infer their most probable origination?[2]

I think the core results of part 3 are clear, and any hypothesis about the past that gave rise to the claims needs to account for a twofold reality. On the one hand, we found a widespread and shared hope for Jesus's messianic role in outstanding future events, and, on the other hand, we found change, development, and even

1. Here my views on which sources are potentially more promising for helping to reconstruct Jesus are conventional in the field—even though debate persists about the Gospel of Thomas—and I have little to add to that conversation. For discussion, and literature, see pp. 27n10, 133n6 above.

2. The procedure here is similar to that which Jürgen Becker, "The Search for Jesus' Special Profile," in *Handbook for the Study of the Historical Jesus*, ed. Tom Holmén and Stanley Porter (Leiden: Brill, 2010), 1:71, has outlined: "we can uncover the processes of reinterpretation and contextualization in the various ways in which the same material is treated, and even transfer these insights to material to which we have no parallels. By means of comparisons, we can shed light in many cases on the options which govern the reception of the tradition in the texts, thereby distinguishing between the interpretation and the antecedent material which is interpreted."

some outright disagreement among the sources in terms of what those roles and realities might entail. I will take some time to explore both of these features and their putative historical implications in this chapter.

Change

I begin with something T. F. Glasson wrote: "One consideration to be borne in mind in discussing the eschatological sayings reported in the Gospels is that the original words of Jesus may have been coloured by the beliefs of the early Church."[3] We can be bolder than this. It is not that the words "may" have been so shaded; they most certainly *were*. And we know this for no other reason than that the words of Jesus, according to our earliest witnesses, do not all agree with each other. To be more precise, in the gospel tradition itself we found, assuming nothing more than Markan priority, that the evangelists were somewhat flexible in rephrasing sayings of Jesus that pertained to his future coming. In Matthew's treatment of Mark, for instance, we found for each of Mark's three climactic sayings (8:38–9:1; 13:24–27; 14:62) sharper and more pointed language and the clear addition of new motifs. Luke was a bit more conservative with Mark (in terms of additions), but the Third Evangelist made changes, too. The same reality was present with double tradition material, assuming the Q hypothesis. Now some of these differences were relatively minor, but others were of greater significance. For instance, what about the contents and details of these parables about someone leaving for a time and then returning after an interval? Did Jesus offer the analogy of keeping your "lamps lit" in the space of two modern verses (Luke 12:35–36) or thirteen (Matt 25:1–13)? These are not trivial questions if we are interested in the teaching of the historical Jesus.

The upshot of part 3's exegesis is an indisputable truth: the words of Jesus about the future have been changed before our very eyes.[4] Moreover, it is evident that a major resource for such changes and additions was Jewish eschatological tradition, whether from Israel's Scriptures or elsewhere (e.g., Matthew's "trumpet" could be inspired by the Shemoneh Esreh, as noted above; see also Targum Pseudo-Jonathan on Num 23:21 [on "the trumpet call of king messiah"]).

3. T. Francis Glasson, *The Second Advent: The Origin of the New Testament Doctrine*, 3rd ed. (Eugene, OR: Wipf & Stock, 2009), 62.

4. It is likely, of course, that some of these changes were attempts to revert to other known, non-Markan retellings and hence are not redactional in the pure sense. This important point is stressed throughout the work of James D. G. Dunn, *Jesus Remembered* (Grand Rapids: Eerdmans, 2003), but it is not a panacea, nor does it do away with the value of redaction criticism entirely.

This means that eschatological tradition otherwise known was added to and supplemented the words of Jesus in the process of transmission. Did this creativity, flexibility, and propensity for expansion suddenly appear only when Matthew and Luke got ahold of Mark? It would be unwise to think so. There is no reason to doubt that this same creativity characterized Mark's use of sources, and even typified the transmission of Jesus material before that, when the process is hidden from our view.

Kinds of Change

There is, however, a crucial follow-up question that many have failed to ask. We must go beyond merely identifying change to ask *what kinds of* change we find, and what might we infer from that in terms of tradition history? Some have assumed that we might deduce a process of eschatological development that, if run in reverse, leaves nothing left at the beginning. But the nature of the differences themselves speaks strongly against this notion, for the additions and subtractions work within something larger shared in common, whose form, while changed, is not wholly remade. Three results from the exegesis of part 3 stand out and, it seems to me, must be accounted for in any historical reconstruction.

(1) We found growth and expansion *in kind*. Matthew's additions to Mark and Q, for instance—such as "the son of man is seated on the throne of his glory" (19:28; 25:31), numerous changes to the apocalyptic discourse ("end of the age," the increase of lawlessness, etc.), and the expansion and redeployment of parables (especially in Matt 24–25)—accentuate the eschatology and underlying hope for Jesus's coming that was already in Matthew's sources. We saw this in detail in part 3 as we considered how Matthew and Luke rewrote Markan texts by working with the language and logic of those texts.[5] This is not to deny newness or difference but simply to point out that newness and difference are not wholly discontinuous with the old. A good example concerns the role of Jesus at the final judgment. According to the Gospels, is he the judge, meaning, he administers the judgment, or is he some kind of heavenly advocate or celestial lawyer before God, who remains the true judge?[6] Mark 8:38 seems to assume that Jesus is some kind of advocate, while the gospel never anywhere denies that Jesus takes a more active role (and I

5. Cf. pp. 207–21 above.

6. See discussion and literature in Sigurd Grindheim, *God's Equal: What Can We Know about Jesus' Self-Understanding in the Synoptic Gospels?*, LNTS 446 (London: T&T Clark International, 2011), 77–80.

hesitate to read anything more into the silence of the text). The same may be true of Q 12:8, which likely Luke maintains. But in Matthew, it is clear that Jesus serves as the judge (e.g., 16:27; 25:31–32), even while he gives to the Twelve the ability κρίνειν (19:28). This is also true for Paul (see 2 Cor 5:10), while he also speaks of God judging (e.g., Rom 2:16 [though here διὰ Χριστοῦ Ἰησοῦ]).[7] It may well be that we cannot neatly distinguish between these two roles in the judgment, and this is a futile exercise based on a false distinction. But should the distinction be true, and Matthew's presentation goes beyond what Mark, the more primitive witness, in this case, ever claimed, *what kind of* development is that? We would go from, in Mark's presentation, Jesus involved in a crucial and unique way in the final judgment (as some manner of heavenly lawyer), to another presentation in which Jesus himself pronounces the judgment. This is a step, not a leap. We would have here a case of both change and continuity. What would be foolish is to play these off against each other in order to reconstruct some entirely other tradition—such as Jesus not being involved in a special way in the judgment at all.

There is a related point to make here that involves comparing Paul with the Gospels. Thanks to 1 Thess 4:13–18, and the likelihood that Paul's "word of the Lord" draws from extant Jesus tradition that resembles what we find in the Synoptics (which says nothing about historicity), we are in the unique situation of being able to peer into received Jesus material twenty to thirty years before the composition of the Gospels themselves.[8] And what do we find happened in this span of time when it comes to this particular expectation? Not much. In fact, if anything, we might say that this exercise should make us wary of assuming a predictable and linear process of gradual expansion and development alone,[9] since some of Paul's details are closer to Matthew's (24:29–31), while Mark's depiction (13:24–27) is less adorned.[10]

7. See discussion and literature on p. 168 above.

8. On Paul's use of gospel tradition here, see discussion in Dale C. Allison Jr., "The Pauline Epistles and the Synoptic Gospels: The Pattern of the Parallels," *NTS* 28 (1982): 10–11, 19–25; Nikolaus Walter, "Paulus und die urchristliche Jesustradition," *NTS* 31 (1985): 507–8, 513–18; Richard Bauckham, "The Study of Gospel Traditions Outside the Canonical Gospels: Problems and Prospects," in *The Jesus Tradition outside the Gospels*, vol. 5 of *Gospel Perspectives* (Sheffield: JSOT Press, 1985), 378–80, 383; David Wenham, *Paul: Follower of Jesus or Founder of Christianity?* (Grand Rapids: Eerdmans, 1995), 289–337.

9. As a general criticism of such a model, see Larry Hurtado, "Interactive Diversity: A Proposed Model of Christian Origins," *JTS* 64 (2013): 445–62.

10. On the larger question of the relationship between Paul and Matthew's Gospel, see Paul Foster, "Paul and Matthew: Two Strands of the Early Jesus Movement with Little Sign of Connection," in *Paul and the Gospels: Christologies, Conflicts and Convergences*, ed. Michael F. Bird and Joel Willitts, LNTS 411 (London: Bloomsbury T&T Clark, 2011), 86–114. I find Foster more

(2) We also found a creative and dynamic interplay between received tradition and new experience, wherein tradition shapes reflection while new experience also reshapes tradition. In Rom 9–11, the sudden and abrupt mention of the coming of "the redeemer" in the midst of Paul's complex scenario for the inclusion of the gentiles and the salvation of "all Israel" is surely due, in part, to the fact that Paul is bringing disparate things together and connecting the experience of the rejection of the gospel in his ministry to received material about the Lord's future coming. The result is the situating of that coming in a new and larger story. In 1 Thess 4 and 1 Cor 15, Paul leverages the future coming of Jesus to address new crises, resulting in a further elaboration of the parousia's connection to the resurrection of the dead (1 Thess 4) and the present reality of Jesus's cosmic reign in heaven as depicted in Ps 110 (1 Cor 15). In the Gospels, we find sayings of Jesus that, while intelligible in the overall eschatological outlook of the source in question, nevertheless push back somewhat against their immediate literary contexts, which shows that they had some life independent of those contexts and maintained some of their earlier integrity. We see this, for instance, with Q 12:8–9 in its context, and possibly also for Mark 8:38 and 9:1 (with 9:1 being, perhaps, connected redactionally to 8:38), and both positioned by the evangelist right before the transfiguration.[11] The same is true with the editorial processes at work in the apocalyptic discourse. Matthew and Luke update Mark 13, we might say, in light of later experience, yet maintain, in their retellings, the same threefold structure of the discourse (birth pangs, abomination, parousia).[12] The details confirm the same. The Third Evangelist, for example, inserts predictions of the coming imprisonment of Jesus's followers and their presentation before "kings and governors" (21:12, both, of course, significant features of Acts), and decodes "the abomination of desolation" by describing Jerusalem "surrounded by armies" (21:20). These clear

---

compelling on this question than David C. Sim, *The Gospel of Matthew and Christian Judaism: The History and Social Setting of the Matthean Community*, SNTW (Edinburgh: T&T Clark, 1998), 188–211, and other publications.

11. See discussion above, pp. 178–79, 226n110.

12. Cf. Joachim Jeremias, *New Testament Theology: The Proclamation of Jesus*, trans. John Bowden (New York: Scribner's Sons, 1971), 123, and further discussion in Vittorio Fusco, "Problems of Structure in Luke's Eschatological Discourse," in *Luke and Acts*, ed. Gerald O'Collins and Gilberto Marconi (New York: Paulist, 1991), 72–92. Evidence is slim (and for some critics theologically convenient) that Luke 21 is in fact dependent on another source besides Mark, which spoke only of the destruction of Jerusalem and not the parousia; so John A. T. Robinson, *Jesus and His Coming: The Emergence of a Doctrine* (New York: Abingdon, 1957), 122–27. The question of Luke's incorporation of other sources in the composition of chapter 21, however, remains open. Cf. Paul T. Penley, *The Common Tradition behind Synoptic Sayings of Judgment and John's Apocalypse*, LNTS 424 (London: T&T Clark International, 2010), 89–124.

attempts to refashion tradition *ex eventu* and in light of later experience work with and within the received Jesus material; Luke is making sense of "the abomination of desolation" in light of what actually occurred. In this case, Luke takes "the abomination" to refer to the destruction of Jerusalem itself, whereas Mark likely had something else—more temple centered—in mind.

Discerning Mark's use of tradition in chapter 13 is a more fraught endeavor, yet there is here, too, obviously a great deal of *ex eventu* reworking that served to make Jesus speak directly to Mark's context, not least the literary presentation of this "speech" in a testament-like genre (though whether that is Mark's unique contribution is not clear).[13] Nevertheless, prediction and first-century reality do not exactly align—to the great consternation of Christian exegetes over the centuries—and Mark and Mark's readership would have shown little interest in this material if they did not believe that they were receiving, and responding to, a message that informed their own present (willful invention ex nihilo, that is, destroys the entire premise of Mark 13 in the first place). I am skeptical that we can do much more with the tradition history of Mark 13 than this, but the general point is sufficient for my present purposes.

The key takeaway, then, is that later experience consistently reframes received traditions, but what is received also informs the experience. To be clear, I am claiming nothing here about historicity.[14] We are talking only about tendencies in the reception of Jesus material.

13. See discussion at pp. 183–90.

14. I can be more explicit. I agree with T. W. Manson, *The Teaching of Jesus: Studies of Its Form and Content*, 2nd ed. (Cambridge: Cambridge University Press, 1935), 260: "it is highly improbable that it [Mark 13] was ever delivered by Jesus in the form in which we have it." Manson's reasoning for his judgment is flawed, however, because he takes as evidence of inauthenticity the presence of the idea of "the imminent return of the Lord," which begs the entire question. See also Jeremias, *New Testament Theology*, 124 (though he evaluates Luke 17:20–37 differently, calling it "a nucleus of the proclamation of Jesus," even if he thinks the evangelist misunderstood what Jesus was talking about). I think the general assessment of David E. Aune, *Prophecy in Early Christianity and the Ancient Mediterranean World* (Grand Rapids: Eerdmans, 1983), 184, is probably the best we can do: "The Olivet Discourse . . . was not delivered by Jesus in the form in which it has come down to us. The present unity of Mark 13 is the result of the editorial work of the evangelist, who welded together previously discrete sayings of Jesus into a relatively unified composition." This conclusion is close to Werner Georg Kümmel, *Promise and Fulfillment: The Eschatological Message of Jesus*, trans. Dorothea M. Barton, 2nd ed. (London: SCM, 1961), 98 (constructed "out of detached sayings or small groups of sayings of different origin"). For more conservative treatments, see Rudolf Pesch, *Das Markusevangelium*, part 2, *Commentar zu Kap. 8,27–16,20* (Freiburg: Herder, 1977), 267 (calls Mark a "conservative redactor"); George R. Beasley-Murray, *Jesus and the Last Days: An Interpretation of the Olivet Discourse* (Vancouver: Regent College, 1993), 350–76.

(3) Last, when we found more divergent eschatologies in the New Testament, they were often of a reactionary nature, realizing in the ministry of Jesus or in the experience of the church what had been reserved for the future coming of Jesus. In the Gospels, we find this most clearly in Luke and John, while it reaches new extremes in the Gospel of Thomas and later second-century texts.[15] Luke is clearly aware of and endorses the fact that, in the evangelist's sources, Dan 7 is associated with the future coming of Jesus. That is why Luke maintains Dan 7's imagery at the conclusion of the apocalyptic discourse at 21:27 (because here Luke's Jesus *is* talking about his future coming) and omits it from Jesus's reply to Caiaphas at 22:69 (because here Luke's Jesus *is not* talking about his future coming but rather his enthronement and exaltation).[16] Given Luke's interest in realized eschatology throughout and clear redactional tendencies in this direction as noted in part 3, it is specious to take the focus of the speeches in Acts on the enthronement/ascension of Jesus in heaven after death to be some pristine witness to the historical preaching of the earliest church before the hope for Jesus's future coming crept in.[17] In John, Jesus speaks as the eschatological son of man in order to inform his

15. See Petr Pokorny, "Die Eschatologie des Thomasevangeliums," *ZAC* 13 (2009): 48–54, who argues that the Gospel of Thomas is a platonic reinterpretation of earlier tradition in a timeless frame.

16. This hypothesis is far preferable to one that (1) claims Luke's version stems from independent, non-Markan tradition, and (2) is more primitive if not historical. Cf. Jeremias, *New Testament Theology*, 273–74. This is not to say Mark's version is historical, to be clear; I doubt that anyone would have known what happened should such a trial have occurred, while the mockery of Jesus as a would-be "king" and failed "prophet" may have been intentionally public events, and so the Gospels' claims about these matters could indeed stem from memory. On Lukan redaction in this scene, see John J. Kilgallen, "Jesus' First Trial: Messiah and Son of God (Luke 22,66–71)," *Bib* 80 (1999): 401–14; Martin Bauspiess, "Die Gegenwart des Heils und das Ende der Zeit: Überlegungen zur lukanischen Eschatologie im Anschluss an Lk 22,66–71 und Apg 7,54–60," in *Eschatologie—Eschatology: The Sixth Durham-Tübingen Research Symposium; Eschatology in Old Testament, Ancient Judaism and Early Christianity*, ed. Hans-Joachim Eckstein, Christof Landmesser, and Hermann Lichtenberger, WUNT 272 (Tübingen: Mohr Siebeck, 2011), 125–48.

17. Cf., e.g., Glasson, *Second Advent*, 154–59; Robinson, *Jesus and His Coming*, 28–29 ("we are left with the surprising conclusion that no evidence is to be found that the Parousia expectation formed part of the earliest strata of Apostolic Christianity"), 136–37, 144–59; Hans Grass, "Zur Frage der Wiederkunft Christi," in *Altes Testament und christliche Verkündigung*, ed. Antonius H. J. Gunneweg, Manfred Oeming, and Axel Graupner (Stuttgart: Kohlhammer, 1987), 136–47. C. H. Dodd, *The Apostolic Preaching and Its Developments* (New York: Harper, 1960), 33, 42, 69, while still somewhat credulous in his use of the speeches in Acts, was at least more careful here: he does not claim the parousia hope was absent but that it was not "emphasized." Most convincing exegetically is C. K. Barrett, *Jesus and the Gospel Tradition* (London: SPCK, 1967), 69 ("there is not a word in this outline account of what [according to Acts] happened in early

present coming, even while the influence of Dan 7's apocalyptic vision on this mission and task is evident.[18]

We should not oversimplify a diverse and complex early Jesus movement by constructing a linear model for eschatological development that moves from more to less, and from future-focused to present-focused, to be sure.[19] But that there is some movement in this direction cannot be denied. I find the conclusion of James Carleton Paget entirely appropriate: "de-eschatologization," he writes, is not "the key to understanding the development of early Christianity," and yet we should "accept that Christian expectations of a return of Christ diminished in their intensity over time . . . [and] there are indications of adjustments being made to the idea of when this end will occur."[20] This point has been recognized by students of early Christian eschatology for some time, though often stated in generalities (about "the kingdom" or "the end") and stripped of its particular content concerning the future coming of Jesus.

The collective upshot of the three results from part 3 is this: for the texts that we have and can compare, we find innovation, exaggeration, and even shrinkage in tradition—that is, undeniable change—but change that works with and within the logics of what came before. That is true even for the more emphatic realized eschatology we find in John and Luke, which are responding to and hence presupposing the existence of earlier, more future-oriented expectations. It needs to be

---

Christianity that does not have its counterpart in the gospels, in either the form of prediction or of command").

18. It is indicative of how far both Glasson and Robinson have gone astray when they regard the realized eschatological outlook of John 14–16, with its emphasis on the resurrection and the coming of the Spirit, as capturing the true nature of the teaching of Jesus about the future. See T. Francis Glasson, "The Second Advent—25 Years Later," *ExpTim* 82 (1971): 309.

19. So, for instance, the reconstruction that emerged from Schweitzer's thoroughgoing eschatology—he wrote in *The Quest of the Historical Jesus*, trans. William Montgomery (New York: Macmillan, 1955), 360: "The whole history of 'Christianity' down to the present day . . . is based on the delay of the Parousia, the non-occurrence of the Parousia, the abandonment of eschatology, the progress and completion of the 'de-eschatologising' of religion which has been connected therewith." Martin Werner ended up writing a history of early Christianity around the premise in *Die Entstehung des christlichen Dogmas* (Bern: Haupt, 1954). Similar to Werner in this respect was Erich Grässer, *Das Problem der Parusieverzögerung in den synoptischen Evangelien und in der Apostelgeschichte*, 3rd ed. (Berlin: de Gruyter, 1977). See also Osvaldo D. Vena, *The Parousia and Its Rereadings: The Development of the Eschatological Consciousness in the Writings of the New Testament*, SBT 27 (New York: Lang, 2001), 257–61.

20. James Carleton Paget, "Some Observations on the Delay of the Parousia in the Historiography of Its Discussion," *EC* 9 (2018): 34. See also David Aune, "The Significance of the Delay of the Parousia for Early Christianity," in *Current Issues in Biblical and Patristic Interpretation*, ed. G. F. Hawthorne (Grand Rapids: Eerdmans, 1975), 87–109.

stressed that nowhere do we have evidence of nonparousia sayings suddenly becoming parousia sayings in reception (with one potential exception, Luke 13:34–35, as discussed in part 3, though the case is unclear);[21] the noticeable movement is, instead, a changing of parousia sayings into nonparousia sayings (as in, for instance, Luke 22:69 and, perhaps, John 1:51). The situation is a great case study of what Anthony Le Donne has described with the phrase "memory refraction": the idea that "initial perceptions" of Jesus can still be identified in "multiple (and sometimes contradictory) interpretations of Jesus."[22] He points out that subsequent interpretations of Jesus were shaped by "previous and cognate refractions,"[23] even if that shaping took the form of negatively reacting against other interpretations of Jesus. It indeed appears that, for some tradents, the future coming of Jesus was not so much a concept of convenience but a feature of Jesus material that had to be dealt with and explained whether the tradent liked it or not. Even the Gospel of John, as we saw, could not completely repurpose it. The hope abides.

Perspective and Limits

There follow, I think, two significant implications for the work of historical reconstruction when we seek to move beyond the texts to hypothesize the past behind them. And these cut in somewhat contrary directions. On the one hand, the large-scale tendencies provide some perspective on what we might call "microchanges" in the tradition. A great deal of attention has been paid to certain redactional changes, such as the rewriting of "I" as "son of man" and vice versa. Attention to those details is important, to be sure. But given broader trends in the transmission of Jesus material and how widespread the hope for Jesus's future coming appears to be in the early Jesus movement, we should be skeptical of arguments that construct elaborate tradition histories on the basis of such "microchanges" and posit not only the presence but actually the primacy and priority of an entirely contrary tradition about Jesus and the future.[24] This is a matter of both probability and epistemology.

21. Matt 23:37–39 // Luke 13:34–35.

22. Anthony Le Donne, *The Historiographical Jesus: Memory, Typology, and the Son of David* (Waco, TX: Baylor University Press, 2009), 13.

23. Le Donne, *Historiographical Jesus*, 73.

24. As a good example of this kind of approach, see the now famous essay by Heinz Schürmann, "Beobachtungen zum Menschensohn-Titel in der Redequelle," in *Jesus und der Menschensohn: Festschrift A. Vögtle*, ed. Rudolf Pesch and Rudolf Schnackenburg (Freiburg: Herder, 1975), 124–47. More recently, see Matthias Kreplin, "The Self-Understanding of Jesus," in Holmén and Porter, *Handbook for the Study of the Historical Jesus*, 3:2473–2516. Kümmel, *Promise and*

I do not think that the historical evidence supports such a conjecture, but I am even more certain that, should it be true, we are in no position to now Sherlock-Holmes our way to the truth in the way that this hypothesis would require.

On the other hand, the facts and frequency of change should make us leery of any attempt to recover the actual words of Jesus.[25] If we can see logia change from Mark to Luke, and from Q to Matthew (I would argue), they surely did before that as well. There is something of an irony in my position, perhaps, in that I am the one making the case in part 4 that the parousia expectation in some form goes back to Jesus, but I am much more skeptical than Glasson, Robinson, and many others about both the staticity of the tradition and our abilities as historians two thousand years removed. But here is precisely where we see the benefit of our approach of working backward from claims and interpretation to inferring probable causes. For if one starts with Paul and the Gospels and works backward, the pressing historical question becomes *not* "is this or that saying historical as written" but rather "what historical Jesus need we hypothesize to make sense of the beliefs of Christ groups that appear early and ubiquitously in our sources?" I do not imply that we cannot ever speak of specifics. The point is the nature of the specifics.[26] We are after not the *ipsissima verba Jesu* but, as Brant Pitre has helpfully phrased it, the *substantia verba Jesu*: the substance of the words of Jesus.[27]

Primitivity

These insights about tendencies in the transmission of Jesus material need to be paired with a few others that demonstrate, at the very least, the extreme antiq-

---

Fulfillment, 17, responded to this line of argument: "the oldest tradition can only be drawn out conjecturally from the deposit of the traditions in the gospels. The correctness of the decision in particular cases must therefore hold good within the framework of the picture as a whole."

25. In this respect, I am sympathetic with Aune, *Prophecy in Early Christianity and the Ancient Mediterranean World*, 187: "Many of the prophecies of Jesus have been so altered in transmission that their original form and often the full scope of their content can no longer be determined."

26. Cf. Anthony E. Harvey, *Jesus and the Constraints of History* (Philadelphia: Westminster, 1982), 5: when "there is so much information which all points in the same direction" one's attention moves "away from establishing the truth or falsity of any particular report about Jesus, and is now directed more towards the impression made by the narrative as a whole."

27. For this formulation and its logic, see Brant Pitre, *Jesus and the Last Supper* (Grand Rapids: Eerdmans, 2015), 47. The point is theoretically helpful, though in Pitre's application in *Jesus and the Last Supper*, it would be more convincing if he ever once pointed to something in the Gospels that *fails* to capture the *substantia verba Jesu*, such that one might grasp both its constructive and deconstructive utility for him. The category must have both functions if it is to be more than a way of guaranteeing historicity.

uity of the hope for Jesus's coming in Christian origins. Jesus-loyalists disagreed about many things of great importance in the earliest years, but our sources give no indication that there was ever any serious disagreement about the future reappearance of Jesus. Despite variation in detail, and shifts in emphasis, there was a widespread general hope. Moreover, our earliest and best witnesses not only contain the expectation; they also testify to the fact that readers are already in the know and expect the same, and the authors are not compelled to try to convince or persuade their readers to adopt it.

It is improbable that one could explain this kind of agreement on the basis of a collective misunderstanding of Jesus's teaching in a later time, as though communities of Jesus followers, upon receiving traditions about his words and reflecting on them, took them to mean something about the future that he really did not, and they were mirrored in this misunderstanding by other communities elsewhere, resulting in a shared mistake that was so widespread and uniform that it became a new standard narrative. Moreover, it is improbable that one could explain this kind of agreement on the basis of a shared theological inference or exegetical conclusion made years later as believers reflected on the life of Jesus and his significance, again assuming that different Christ groups stumbled upon the same idiosyncratic patterns of reading Scripture and revised the teaching of Jesus accordingly. This is where Glasson (whose argument is exegetical) and Robinson (whose argument is theological-inferential) ended up, as noted in part 1, and they did not believe that the hope for Jesus's speedy return characterized the preaching of the earliest community.

My suggestion is this: the most probable explanation for the widespread hope for Jesus's future coming and the nature of its transmission in our literary sources as described above is a shared tradition that goes back, at the very least, to the original post-Easter community of Jesus's followers in Jerusalem and, moreover, to a tradition that presumed to contain, in various forms, the teaching of Jesus about the future (rather than the implications or consequences of Jesus's teaching). Paul's letters are important evidence here.[28] In 1 Thessalonians, we observed that the future coming of Jesus was fundamental to Paul's initial kerygma there, and this appears true for communities he writes to elsewhere. Given the importance of the hope for Paul, and the way that he assumes rather than argues for it, it is doubtful that the apostles in Jerusalem whom he had met on at least two occa-

28. It is again fascinating to note how infrequently, and often how late, Paul's letters are brought into the conversation. A few exceptions that attempt to combine the discussion of Jesus and Paul include Arthur L. Moore, *The Parousia in the New Testament*, NovTSup 13 (Leiden: Brill, 1966), 160–74; Stephen S. Smalley, "The Delay of the Parousia," *JBL* 83 (1963): 41–54; Ben Witherington III, *Jesus, Paul, and the End of the World* (Downers Grove, IL: InterVarsity Press, 1992).

sions (Gal 1:18–20; 2:1–10) would have been surprised to find that Paul believed this. Concerning Paul's initial fifteen-day jaunt to Jerusalem to "visit Peter," we may still presume, as Dodd so memorably put it, that "they did not spend all the time talking about the weather."[29] Moreover, when Paul says that on his next visit he "laid before them . . . the gospel that I proclaim about the gentiles" (2:2), would the future coming of Jesus have failed to come up?[30] "James and Cephas and John" must have "extended the right hand of fellowship" (2:9) in full awareness of what Paul was saying about Jesus and the future.[31] In *The Birth of the Messiah*, Raymond Brown states the following concerning Paul's claim in Rom 1:3 about Jesus's messianic credentials:

> it [the Davidic formula of faith] is cited by Paul who knew the Palestinian situation and was always sensitive to correction from Jerusalem. Would he have used it if he knew that Jesus was not really descended from David? Would not this have left him vulnerable to the Jerusalem followers of James (Gal 2:12) or to those who were questioning his apostolate precisely on the grounds that he knew little of the earthly Jesus?[32]

It seems to me that the same insight applies to our topic.

But that is not all. Paul nowhere states or implies that he or some other Jesus follower came up with the notion of the future coming of Jesus and that he had the duty of informing others about it. Rather, Paul assumes that the coming of Jesus is a traditional belief he himself had received and that he shares in common with the wider movement, much like Paul contends in 1 Cor 15 about the resurrection (v. 3: "for I handed on to you as of first importance what I in turn had received,

29. Dodd, *Apostolic Preaching*, 16. Dodd himself believed that the kerygma Paul received included the expectation for the parousia (23), but he thought a significant change from the original teaching of Jesus had already occurred.

30. Though we do not know enough to follow Peter Tomson, "Paul as a Recipient and Teacher of Tradition," in *Studies on Jews and Christians in the First and Second Centuries*, WUNT 418 (Tübingen: Mohr Siebeck, 2019), 409–410, who argues that Peter was Paul's main source for Jesus tradition.

31. Cf. Dale C. Allison Jr., *Constructing Jesus: Memory, Imagination, and History* (Grand Rapids: Baker Books, 2010), 49, wrote that the "agreement" on the gospel in Gal 2 must tell us that "apocalyptic-kerygmatic Christianity" included such figures who knew Jesus himself. Note also the likelihood that Peter himself had visited Corinth. See C. K. Barrett, "Cephas and Corinth," in *Essays on Paul* (Philadelphia: Westminster, 1982), 28–39, which makes Paul's undramatic and nonpolemical reflections on the parousia in 1 Corinthians all the more intriguing.

32. Raymond Brown, *The Birth of the Messiah: A Commentary on the Infancy Narratives in Matthew and Luke* (Garden City, NY: Doubleday, 1977), 508.

that Christ died").[33] The use of (παρα)λαμβάνω and παραδίδωμι (+ dative) parallel rather closely מסר ל ... קבל מן used for the passing on of tradition in rabbinic literature.[34] Dependence on tradition is the implication of 1 Thess 4:15, where Paul writes that his scenario about Jesus's coming from heaven is "by word of the Lord," as I argued in part 3. It is also stated, and even more explicitly, in Paul's discussion of the Lord's Supper in 1 Cor 11, a passage we did not consider in part 3 but is relevant here. Paul writes (11:23–26),

> For I received from the Lord [παρέλαβον ἀπὸ τοῦ κυρίου] what also I handed on to you [ὃ καὶ παρέδωκα ὑμῖν], that the Lord Jesus on the night in which he was betrayed took bread, and after giving thanks broke it and said, "This is my body in behalf of you all, do this in my memory." Similarly also the cup after eating, saying, "this cup is the new covenant in my blood, do this, as often as you drink, in my memory." For as often as you eat this bread and drink the cup, you proclaim the death of the Lord until he comes [ἄχρι οὗ ἔλθῃ].

For Paul, fundamental to the meaning of this meal, whose words and practices he "received" and "passed on" in common with the wider movement, is the way in which it anticipates the future coming of Jesus: "until he comes."[35] In "until he comes" we find again an abbreviated, understated description only possible on the assumption that readers know what Paul is talking about.[36] This is not Paul's spin—he does nothing with that expectation here—it is part of the tradition he

33. See here Simon Gathercole, *The Gospel and the Gospels* (Grand Rapids: Eerdmans, 2022), 51–54.

34. Especially notable is m. ʾAbot 1.1: "Moses received the Torah at Sinai and transmitted it to Joshua, Joshua to the elders, and the elders to the prophets, and the prophets to the men of the great assembly." The parallel is interesting in light of Paul's background as a Pharisee (Phil 3:5). For discussion, see Traugott Holtz, "Paul and the Oral Gospel Tradition," in *Jesus and the Oral Gospel Tradition*, ed. Henry Wansbrough, JSNTSup 64 (London: T&T Clark International, 1991), 382–92; David Aune, "Jesus Tradition and the Pauline Letters," in *Jesus, the Gospel Tradition and Paul in the Context of Jewish and Greco-Roman Antiquity*, WUNT 303 (Tübingen: Mohr Siebeck, 2013), 303–30.

35. Contrast Francis Watson, "'I Received from the Lord . . .': Paul, Jesus, and the Last Supper," in *Jesus and Paul Reconnected: Fresh Pathways into an Old Debate*, ed. Todd D. Still (Grand Rapids: Eerdmans, 2007), 103–24, who argues that Paul received 11:23–25 by a revelation of the risen Jesus.

36. Paul also calls Christ a Passover sacrifice here. On the role of Passover in messianic and eschatological speculation, see Christopher Rowland, *Christian Origins: An Account of the Setting and Character of the Most Important Messianic Sect of Judaism* (London: SPCK, 1985), 41–42; Pitre, *Jesus and the Last Supper*, 382–89.

is rehearsing. He only turns to address the crisis at Corinth directly in light of this supper tradition (vv. 23–26) in vv. 27–34.

What Paul claims and implies about the future coming of Jesus, then, leads us to the same place that the nature of transmission as described above would lead us to suspect: this is an expectation that goes back to the original Palestinian church and hence the apostles who had known Jesus "according to the flesh."[37] This may be indirectly confirmed by the likelihood that the "Maranatha" (our Lord, come!) exclamation refers to Jesus's future appearance and stems from early Aramaic-speaking Christians (1 Cor 16:22; cf. Rev 22:20; Did. 10.6; Apos. Con. 7.26.5).[38] This is not a particularly controversial view, and I have little to add to that conversation.

Origin Stories

While we have said nothing so far about the historical Jesus, we are confidently in the orbit of the earliest followers in the post-Easter period in Jerusalem. But why might *they* have thought this? Can we say anything more at this juncture? I would like to end this chapter and transition to the next by weighing some possibilities.

Scholars have essentially told five stories about the origin of the second-coming hope (and these can be mixed and matched). Early Christians came to the expectation

1. by rereading the Old Testament;
2. by thinking theologically about their new post-Easter situation;
3. by reflecting on the resurrection appearances;

37. This point is admitted by many who do not trace the parousia expectation to Jesus himself. Cf., e.g., T. W. Manson, *Studies in the Gospels and Epistles* (Philadelphia: Westminster, 1962), 27; C. H. Dodd, "'The Primitive Catechism' and the Sayings of Jesus," in *More New Testament Studies* (Manchester: Manchester University Press, 1969), 11–29; Barnabas Lindars, "Re-enter the Apocalyptic Son of Man," *NTS* 22 (1975): 52–72; Ulrich B. Müller, "Parusie und Menschensohn," *ZNW* 92 (2001): 2–3. See also W. D. Davies, *Paul and Rabbinic Judaism: Some Rabbinic Elements in Pauline Theology* (London: SPCK, 1948), 286 ("the belief in the Second Advent was integral to that eschatological faith which Paul shared with the early church").

38. For discussion and literature, see C. F. D. Moule, "Reconsideration of the Context of Maranatha," *NTS* 6 (1960): 307–10; Joseph A. Fitzmyer, *To Advance the Gospel: New Testament Studies*, 2nd ed. (Grand Rapids: Eerdmans, 1998), 218–35; Martin Hengel, "Abba, Maranatha, Hosanna und die Anfänge der Christologie," in *Studien zur Christologie*, vol. 4 of *Kleine Schriften*, ed. Claus-Jürgen Thornton, WUNT 201 (Tübingen: Mohr Siebeck, 2006), 496–534.

4. by incorporating new prophetic/charismatic inspiration;
5. by remembering and developing what Jesus had taught.

So long as any one of these captures the activity of that early Jerusalem community of Jesus followers, which is not always the case—so Robinson (2) and Glasson (1), for instance—it could theoretically explain the widespread nature of the hope and the fact that the expectation quickly becomes assumable already by the earliest extant Pauline epistle.[39] But it is not just the widespread nature of the tradition that requires historical explanation; it is its form. Jesus-loyalists purported to have teachings of Jesus on the matter. The Gospels assume this at every turn, containing parables, apothegms, and more extended teachings devoted to the topic. Paul also thought the same, comforting the Thessalonians with a future scenario about Jesus's coming that he believed was "by word of the Lord."[40] Both of these points I have argued for in part 3. What historical scenario best explains these twin facts of breadth and appearance?

I think that the first three stories (pointing to the Old Testament, general theological reflection, and the resurrection appearances, respectively) struggle at this point. Should any one of these be true, one would have to argue in one of two implausible directions. In the one, Jesus followers basically left the words of Jesus intact but gave them a completely different spin.[41] My response to this approach is part 3. I simply disagree, on interpretive grounds, that despite the evangelists' misguided expectation for Jesus's return (so the theory goes), they conveniently left enough crumbs on the trail for us to find authentic words of Jesus that were *actually* about the "crisis" of his coming then (so Dodd), or the destruction of Jerusalem (so Wright), or his exaltation to heaven, for example, "going up" rather than "coming down" (so Jeremias and Dunn and many others).[42] More on this later. The

39. For an assessment that resembles Robinson's arguments about theodicy in some interesting ways, see Enrico Morelli, "Why Did Early Believers in Jesus Write Apocalypses?," *ZAC* 20 (2016): 63–83.

40. E. P. Sanders, *Jesus and Judaism* (Philadelphia: Fortress, 1985), 229, agrees, and goes further: he thinks the saying "is quite possibly a genuine saying of Jesus which Paul already knew."

41. Cf. C. H. Dodd, *The Founder of Christianity* (London: Collins, 1971), 123 (Jesus followers were "understandably anxious to find his words relevant to their own urgent preoccupations, have given them a twist away from their original intention"); Donald Hagner, *Matthew*, WBC 33 (Dallas: Word, 1993–1995), 2:711 (on the disciples misattributing the imminence of the temple's demise to Jesus's return).

42. Cf., e.g., Jeremias, *Proclamation*. In the earliest sayings, he wrote, we have "an underlying idea of a movement from below upwards" (273) and that Jesus "speaks only of a single event: the glorification of the Son of man takes place through his exaltation to God" (274). Dunn, *Jesus Remembered*, 428–31, 747–54, 757–58, believes that the parousia hope resulted from "a post-Easter

other is more incredible: upon 1, 2, or 3, early Christians then wrote up entirely fictional sayings of Jesus about the topic, and so many of them in such diverse form that they ended up making their way into every strand of the written gospel tradition and ultimately defined the way in which the Gospels themselves—especially the Synoptics—conceive of time and construct their symbolic universes. To make this argument, one would have to assume that the gospel tradition was at that very early stage almost completely pervious to fictionalization, and that the early community (composed of people who had known Jesus, no less) had little interest in preserving his teaching. Moreover, this seems to be ultimately a self-defeating position for someone who hopes, in the end, to say something about the historical Jesus.[43] For sources in which history has been so thoroughly swallowed up by imagination, what hope is there for Jesus research?[44] In that case, we should just call it what it is: the sources are too bad.[45]

There were other options available to Jesus followers in telling stories about him should they have arrived at the second-coming hope by means of 1, 2, or 3 alone. We know that the gospel authors could introduce new, post-Easter understandings in the form of clarification or elaboration, as happened in, for instance,

---

merging of the Son of Man coming motif with the return motif of the crisis parables." That is, it is a kind of hybrid doctrine—a combination of two things that are both historical but meant something different in the ministry of Jesus. He wrote, "talk of a 'second coming' belongs more to the perspective of the subsequent retelling of the parables of 'return' and other 'coming' sayings, rather than to the perspective of the first utterance" (794). Dunn relies heavily on Jeremias here. See Joachim Jeremias, *The Parables of Jesus*, trans. S. H. Hooke, 2nd ed. (New York: Scribner's Sons, 1972). More on this below. See also Ben F. Meyer, *The Aims of Jesus* (London: SCM, 1979), 206, who describes "the triumph (enthronement) of the Son of man," defining enthronement as "transcendent exaltation conceived as messianic investiture." And also Thomas Kazen, "The Coming Son of Man Revisited," *JSHJ* 5 (2007): 160, 172 ("experiences of his resurrection and continued spiritual presence modified their vision of the kingdom and triggered a re-interpretation in which exalted and coming Son of Man sayings were understood as promises of a future fulfillment of Jesus' kingdom vision through his personal return").

43. So, e.g., Robert Funk, *Honest to Jesus: Jesus for a New Millennium* (San Francisco: HarperSanFrancisco, 1996), 168: "they [Jesus's followers] had not understood the subtleties of Jesus' position, they had not captured the intensity of his vision, and so reverted to the standard, orthodox scenario once Jesus had departed from the scene." By "orthodox scenario," Funk means Jewish apocalypticism.

44. As a methodological point, note Alexander J. M. Wedderburn, *Jesus and the Historians*, WUNT 269 (Tübingen: Mohr Siebeck, 2010), 171: "It would . . . be hard to believe that so many different witnesses should be similarly mistaken. And, if we dispute these motifs or themes that are best attested, can we know anything at all about Jesus or say anything about him?"

45. There is more on 1–3 to consider, of course, and will be in what follows; here I am making some initial points related to tradition history.

Mark 7, where the evangelist or the evangelist's tradition explains the putative meaning of the words of Jesus (7:19) in a way that surely goes beyond what the historical Jesus ever claimed about the law of Moses.[46] We find intrusions throughout the Gospels that serve a similar function, not least in the narrative asides in the Gospel of John, which are forthright in sharing that some insights about Jesus did not emerge until after the resurrection (2:22; 20:9). Luke does the same but in a different way (9:45; 18:34; 24:45). Would there not be *some* trace in the Gospels of this phenomenon connected to the future coming of Jesus, should this indeed have been what had happened?[47]

Speaking for Jesus

Option 4 (prophetic or charismatic inspiration) potentially explains both the breadth and form of the tradition in a more convincing manner and hence is a more intriguing and promising hypothesis. Story 4 assumes a post-Easter origin for the hope for Jesus's return, but it could have been very early, and the prophetic figure(s) in question, speaking for and as the risen Jesus or by the inspiration of the Spirit, could have been thought to communicate Jesus's own thoughts on the matter (just the *risen* Jesus, in this case). Thus, the entry of unhistorical, post-Easter sayings of Jesus into the gospel tradition would not have been as dramatic of a transformation as, say, writing up sayings of Jesus on the basis of scenarios 1, 2,

46. The point being that Mark *interprets* the saying of Jesus, "whatever goes into a person from outside cannot defile," as "he thus declared all foods clean," which Matthew of course understands quite differently (Matt 15:10–11). Mark does not have his Jesus say, "I thus declare all foods clean."

47. Sanders, *Jesus and Judaism*, implies an *inferential* cause rooted in the resurrection experiences, though he gives the matter little attention, as already noted. He wrote, "It seems intrinsically likely that beliefs about Jesus' relation to God and his imminent return depend very heavily on the resurrection appearances" (21), and, "We can explain Paul's conviction that the Lord would return from heaven and that the resurrection would not be of a physical body by the resurrection appearance. It is more difficult to attribute to the same cause the general eschatological framework in which he lived and worked" (21), and further, "We can understand better how the disciples could so readily shift their hopes to awaiting the return of the Lord from heaven. If they had always expected an eschatological miracle, it is easy to understand the role of the resurrection appearances in the creation of Christian belief in a heavenly kingdom" (233). But it is not clear why seeing Jesus risen again "intrinsically" (21) requires one to posit something else about his future coming, for the same reasons that the resurrection of Jesus would likely not suddenly create a new eschatological vision for the Christian movement (a good point that Sanders himself makes). I will have more to say about this in the next chapter.

or 3. I argued in part 3 that Paul's "word of the Lord" in 1 Thess 4:15 likely purported to summarize an actual teaching from Jesus, but Paul could have been mistaken in this, as I noted, and the origin could actually have been some prophetic figure speaking with the authority of the risen Jesus.[48]

Yet there are several problems with scenario 4. We know, without a doubt, that Christians put words on the lips of Jesus, and we have good reason to think that prophetic or pneumatic inspiration occurred in the earliest communities (cf. 1 Thess 5:19–22; 1 Cor 12–14; cf. Did. 10–13).[49] But we have no evidence that the two went together on the scale that would be necessary to explain the state of Jesus material on this question. That is, there is no evidence that Jesus tradition was so easily populated with sayings of the risen Christ by means of prophetic inspiration (which, again, is *not* to say the phenomenon did not occur at all).[50] Some have asserted that to have early Jesus followers distinguish between the pre- and post-Easter periods when thinking about the ministry of Jesus is a completely modern projection, but this is simply not true (even while the distinction has, indeed, been reified by later theological developments). Paul betrays some anxiety in various places in his writings that he, unlike other apostles, did not actually know Jesus before the resurrection experiences. He wrote in Gal 2:6, "but from those who are seeming to be something—as much as *they formerly were* [ποτε ἦσαν] matters nothing to me, for an image of a person God does not receive—for to me these persons added nothing." This admission, and in the midst of a conversation about the content of Paul's gospel at that, shows that Paul had to address the fact that James, Cephas, and John knew Jesus in the flesh and hence could potentially claim access in a more immediate way than Paul to the true nature of the gospel. This anxiety would be hard to place if the pre- and post-Easter "lives" of Jesus had been so thoroughly collapsed. Moreover, the view that early Christians did not really care to distinguish between the pre- and post-Easter periods in terms

48. See Aune, *Prophecy in Early Christianity and the Ancient Mediterranean World*, 253–56 (argues the saying stems not from Jesus but from an unknown prophet).

49. In 1 Cor 12–14, it seems like prophetic activity happened during and as a part of Christian gatherings and worship (see also 11:4–5).

50. Contra Norman Perrin, *Rediscovering the Teaching of Jesus* (New York: Harper & Row, 1967), 15–53, who wrote at 15, "The early Church made no attempt to distinguish between the words the earthly Jesus had spoken and those spoken by the risen Lord through a prophet in the community, nor between the original teaching of Jesus and the new understanding and reformulation of that teaching reached in the catechesis or parenesis of the Church under the guidance of the Lord of the Church." For a more convincing analysis, see Aune, *Prophecy in Early Christianity and the Ancient Mediterranean World*, 245 (his conclusion: "it appears unlikely that many oracles of the risen Lord became assimilated to sayings of the historical Jesus" and "the historical evidence in support of the theory lies largely in the creative imagination of scholars").

of Jesus's teaching struggles to explain where the impulse to write history-like narratives about his ministry ultimately came from.[51] If Jesus followers had no issue with the risen Jesus freely communicating and providing new instruction through prophetic inspiration, and it is only a modern bias that privileges the pre-Easter Jesus, then why did the early Christians not simply tell it as it was and have the risen Jesus communicate such things and present them as such? In other words, why disguise what actually happened by expunging the inspired prophet or series of prophets from the historical record and make it look as if Jesus had given these teachings while in Galilee and Jerusalem, speaking to followers and debating opponents?[52]

Many early Christians appear to have thought that the risen Jesus was alive and could communicate, to be sure, but they also remembered him as a Galilean "teacher"—the most common descriptor that appears in the Gospels[53]—who had called disciples and committed some body of instruction to them.[54] We need not follow Birger Gerhardsson, and more recently Craig Keener, in thinking they slavishly memorized what he had said, or even wrote it down.[55] But to call someone a teacher is meaningful only if one thinks he taught something worth preserving, however imperfect the process of preservation.[56] Moreover, we have to attend

51. Contra Eugene Boring, who argues that it was actually the writing of the Gospel of Mark that created a new distinction between the pre- and post-Easter periods that was not in existence before. See "The Paucity of Sayings in Mark," in *SBL 1977 Seminar Papers*, ed. Paul J. Achtemeier (Missoula, MT: Scholars Press, 1977), 371–77.

52. The question of form is crucial. Odes Sol. 42.6, which has Christ speaking as "I," is just as clear that this is the risen Christ speaking as "I," and does not pretend to be anything else.

53. See Dunn, *Jesus Remembered*, 697, who also recalls here Josephus's description of Jesus as "a wise man" and "a teacher of the people" (διδάσκαλος ἀνθρώπων [*Ant.* 18.63]).

54. Cf. Manson, *Teaching of Jesus*, 3–21; W. R. Herzog, *Prophet and Teacher: An Introduction to the Historical Jesus* (Louisville: Westminster John Knox, 2005), 71–98; Rainer Riesner, "From the Messianic Teacher to the Gospels of Jesus Christ," in Holmén and Porter, *Handbook for the Study of the Historical Jesus*, 1:405–46; Aune, "Oral Tradition and the Aphorisms of Jesus," in *Jesus, the Gospel Tradition and Paul in the Context of Jewish and Greco-Roman Antiquity*, 282–83. There is evidence that some expected the messiah to be a teacher. Cf. Rainer Riesner, *Jesus als Lehrer: Eine Untersuchung zum Ursprung der Evangelien—Überlieferung*, WUNT 2/7 (Tübingen: Mohr Siebeck, 1984), 304–30. Note Pss. Sol. 17.47 expects that the son of David will be raised up "over the house of Israel to instruct [παιδεῦσαι] them." See also 11Q13, II, 20 ("instructing them").

55. Cf. Birger Gerhardsson, *Memory and Manuscript: Oral Tradition and Written Transmission in Rabbinic Judaism and Early Christianity*, trans. Eric J. Sharpe (Uppsala: Gleerup, 1961), 329–35; Craig S. Keener, *Christobiography: Memory, History, and the Reliability of the Gospels* (Grand Rapids: Eerdmans, 2019), 401–501.

56. Keener, *Christobiography*, 416–17, 436 ("ancient pupils valued the preservation of their master's teachings"). Cf. Riesner, *Jesus als Lehrer*, 408–99. Note the potential parallel here be-

to the ways in which Jesus's followers regarded him as a uniquely authoritative teacher, as this makes it less likely they would continue to speak for and as him without any differentiation. In fact, we do find positive evidence in Paul's letters that there were efforts to maintain a distinction between the teaching of Jesus and the "opinion" of his followers (1 Cor 7:25, here, of Paul), as discussed in part 3. The very fact that this emerges in 1 Corinthians only because circumstances required it make it all the more important as a window into the early transmission of Jesus material, for this is a candid moment. We should pair that with the insight of C. K. Barrett that "the quantity of explicit prediction of the life of the Church in the time after his death and resurrection that is put in the mouth of Jesus is relatively small." That is, we have little about the work of the Spirit, only "hints" at the gentile mission, nothing about circumcision, "complete silence" about church structure.[57] Was the future coming of Jesus treated in a wholly different manner?[58]

It seems to me that, even for critics who have argued for the significance of prophetic and charismatic inspiration in early Christian communities, their arguments would not support the tying of *the origin* of the second-coming idea to this activity. Eugene Boring, whose work on this topic has been influential for many years, argues that Christian prophets did not necessarily come up with "new" material but rather continued and sometimes represented in different and varied form known words of Jesus for new situations.[59] There is a crucial difference between Christian prophets elaborating on and developing an underlying notion that Jesus would appear again for the final consummation, and Christian prophets coming up with that core idea itself as a novel contribution.[60] Indeed, one could

tween memories of Jesus and memories of the *Moreh Ṣedeq* at Qumran, who was commemorated as an unrivaled teacher and interpreter of Scripture (cf. 1QpHab VII, 1–5). See 1QH VIII, 4–10, 16–26 on his being a fountain on which the planting/community depends for its life. See John Yueh-Han Yieh, *One Teacher: Jesus' Teaching Role in Matthew's Gospel Report*, BZNW 124 (Berlin: de Gruyter, 2004), 95–184; Per Bilde, *The Originality of Jesus: A Critical Discussion and a Comparative Attempt*, SANt 1 (Göttingen: Vandenhoeck & Ruprecht, 2013), 183–88.

57. Barrett, *Jesus and the Gospel Tradition*, 71.

58. Dale C. Allison Jr., *The End of the Ages Has Come: An Early Interpretation of the Passion and Resurrection of Jesus* (Philadelphia: Fortress, 1985), 135, and Darrell L. Bock, "The Use of Daniel 7 in Jesus' Trial, with Implications for His Self-Understanding," in *'Who Is This Son of Man?' The Latest Scholarship on a Puzzling Expression of the Historical Jesus*, ed. Larry W. Hurtado and Paul L. Owen, LNTS 390 (London: Bloomsbury T&T Clark, 2011), 92, infer from the (relative) dearth of later christological titles in the Gospels that early Christians did not easily retroject later terminology onto Jesus.

59. M. Eugene Boring, *The Continuing Voice of Jesus* (Louisville: Westminster John Knox, 1991), 270.

60. Moreover, it appears that prophetic activity was frequently received in communal contexts

follow those who suppose Paul's "word of the Lord" in 1 Thess 4:15 actually stems from an unknown Christian prophet, and perhaps that is right. I find it astonishing that historical Jesus critics so readily ignore or quickly brush aside such a claim from our earliest extant source. But who knows? That argument, in any case, would not explain the origin of the entire expectation, and it would certainly not suffice to explain why the gospel tradition is populated with sayings of Jesus about his future coming at every layer, in pedagogical and polemical contexts, and in an array of forms (parables, isolated sayings, extended teachings, etc.).[61]

It also strikes me that scenario 4 claims that, at essentially the origins of the Christian movement, some person, or maybe several people, thought they were inspired enough to predict the future, and their predictions ended up shaping the rest of early Christian thinking on the matter in a very formative way. Is this not, in terms of the structure and form of a historical argument, the swapping of the quest for the historical Jesus for the quest for an unnamed prophet or series of prophets? If all we can do is weigh relative probabilities, we must attend to the fact that we know very little about the nature of this prophetic activity, while we do have, at the very least, sources that claim to relate, however theologically and imaginatively, stories about a historical person named Jesus of Nazareth. As a matter of historiography, I do not see how the charismatic-pneumatic prophet thesis could be regarded *more probable* than tracing the hope ultimately to Jesus.[62]

---

and thereby subject to those communal dynamics. Cf. especially 1 Thess 5:19–22 ("test everything"); 1 Cor 14:29 ("Let two or three prophets speak, and let the others weigh what is said"); Rom 12:6 (if one has the gift of prophecy, let that person use it "in agreement to the faith" [κατὰ τὴν ἀναλογίαν τῆς πίστεως]); 1 John 4:1–3 ("do not believe every spirit, but test the spirits"). See James D. G. Dunn, "The Prophetic 'I' Sayings and the Jesus-Tradition: The Importance of Testing Prophetic Utterances within Early Christianity," in *The Oral Gospel Tradition* (Grand Rapids: Eerdmans, 2013), 13–40. Cf. also Aune, *Prophecy in Early Christianity and the Ancient Mediterranean World*, 222: "the most important informal criterion set forth by Paul for the judgment of prophetic speech . . . was the content of the message. Such messages must be in agreement with what Paul himself had previously taught . . . or with the generally accepted beliefs and customs of the Christian community."

61. Relevant here are several important articles by Richard Bauckham early in his career, in which he claimed to observe in the book of Revelation—and hence by its spirit-inspired seer—the "deparabolization" of synoptic parables about the parousia. Bauckham took this as evidence of the continued use and reuse of Jesus tradition by Christian prophets but not the wholesale invention of said tradition. He argues, in fact, that the evidence suggests the formation of new words of Jesus by such activity was quite limited. Cf. Richard Bauckham, "Synoptic Parousia Parables and the Apocalypse," *NTS* 23 (1977): 162–76; Bauckham, "Parousia Parables Again," *NTS* 29 (1983): 129–34.

62. Aune, *Prophecy in Early Christianity and the Ancient Mediterranean World*, 252–56, suggests that the "unknown prophet" responsible for delivering this "word of the Lord" may have been none other than Silvanus, coauthor of 1 Thessalonians!

To be sure, the plausibility of the prophetic/charismatic scenario hinges, and perhaps in large part, on the implausibility of tying the hope to the Jesus of history as discerned *on other grounds*. That is fair enough. All of these arguments are, as my own will be, holistic, and that means based on what positively supports them but also what is lacking or weak in competing views. It is up to me to deal with such objections in subsequent chapters. But at this point, it is fair to register this: there are major problems with stories 1, 2, 3, and 4 as hypotheses that seek to explain the tendencies and trajectories of Jesus material as we have it.

13

Messianic Exegesis, Imagination, and History

Despite the fictitious nature of the Lukan scene where the risen Jesus appears to the eleven apostles and their companions and, miraculously and in a moment's time, "opened their minds to understand the Scriptures" (24:45), the episode captures a certain development in the post-Easter period that we know is true. After and in light of the resurrection appearances of Jesus, early Christians read Scripture with fresh eyes and therein "uncovered a second narrative."[1] It is a truism of New Testament scholarship that all of the sources that we have from insiders, from Paul's letters to the Gospels, are written from that postresurrection perspective and so refract the story of Jesus through the lens of certain scriptural convictions that emerged only later. This simple fact, however, creates an obvious challenge for historians who deem early Christian exegesis worthy of study on its own terms but also want to know which scriptural claims come from Jesus and which come from the post-Easter church.[2] This is a particularly pressing issue for our topic because, as highlighted in part 3, at almost every turn, early Christians were drawing on the language of Israel's Scripture to describe the future coming of Jesus. The use of Dan 7 and prophetic "day of the Lord" imagery were particularly prominent. Moreover, these exegeses appear in Greek, not the Aramaic of Jesus, and several are highly creative, literary, and, in a word, scribal. What is to prevent us from fol-

1. To use a phrase of David Steinmetz, "Uncovering a Second Narrative: Detective Fiction and the Construction of Historical Method," in *The Art of Reading Scripture*, ed. Ellen F. Davis and Richard B. Hays (Grand Rapids: Eerdmans, 2003), 54–65.

2. On this dilemma, see Gerbert S. Oegema, "Jesus' Use and Interpretation of Scripture: What Was 'Scripture' to Jesus and How Did Such Texts Influence Him?," in *Jesus Research: New Methodologies and Perceptions*, ed. James H. Charlesworth (Grand Rapids: Eerdmans, 2007), 802–26.

lowing some kind of scenario (1) as described above, in which case Jesus followers, after his death, went to the Bible and there found the answer to their questions and new insights about the future: this Jesus, who was crucified, will surely "come again" "with the glory of his holy angels" "on the clouds of heaven"?

Paula Fredriksen once posed a question to me in a review issue of my first book hosted by *Journal for the Study of the Historical Jesus*: "How can we know how *Jesus* used Israel's scriptures, if what we are working with are the later representations of biblically literate authors. . . . *How* does one discern 'Jesus's [biblical] script' from the ones that the evangelists gave him?"[3] It is worth repeating my response to that good question by way of framing my objectives in this chapter. My response is that I do not think that we often can successfully distinguish the two if we regard our core task as an atomistic endeavor to demonstrate that *this one* (saying or cluster of sayings) comes from Jesus and *that one* comes from the early church. But, as noted already in part 4, I am skeptical about the prospects of the atomistic quest for the historical Jesus in general. I have found most persuasive, in terms of approach, the work of E. P. Sanders and Paula Fredriksen herself, critics similarly skeptical of hitching their carts to individual sayings of Jesus and who rather sought to reconstruct a plausible Jesus within an overall portrait of Christian origins—one that fits within Second Temple Judaism yet also explains the rise of the church and its idiosyncrasies.[4] Can we talk about Jesus and Scripture in a similar manner, not in effort to answer the question "did Jesus actually say that," but rather what is the most reasonable explanation for why Paul and the Gospels remember Jesus in the scriptural ways that they do? What is the most probable historical scenario that explains the interest in these specific scriptural patterns?[5] This question may lead to "fuzzier" results,[6] but I think we can be more confident in them.

3. Paula Fredriksen, "*Jesus, the Gospels, and the Galilean Crisis*, by Tucker Ferda," *JSHJ* 20 (2022): 123.

4. See, e.g., E. P. Sanders, *Jesus and Judaism* (Philadelphia: Fortress, 1985), 18–22; Paula Fredriksen, *Jesus of Nazareth, King of the Jews: A Jewish Life and the Emergence of Christianity* (New York: Knopf, 1999), 40–41. For a similar approach, see already T. W. Manson, "Is It Possible to Write a Life of Christ?," *ExpTim* 53 (1942): 250.

5. And the scriptural subtexts of the actions of several of the so-called sign prophets in Josephus demonstrate the general plausibility of the suggestion that Jesus, too, also in a nonscribal context, would act out Scripture with an eye toward eschatological fulfillment (cf. *J.W.* 2.258–260, 261–263; 6.285; *Ant.* 18.85–89; 20.97–98; 20.169–171; 20.188). The popularity of the so-called ambiguous oracle mentioned by Josephus (*J.W.* 6.312–313), reflected also in Tacitus (*Hist.* 5.13) and Suetonius (*Vesp.* 4.5), further shows that there was a popular-level interest in scriptural prophecy in first-century Palestine. Note also Anthony Le Donne, *The Historiographical Jesus: Memory, Typology, and the Son of David* (Waco, TX: Baylor University Press, 2009), 77: "it can be argued that typological narrativization is often a means of remembering itself and not necessarily a literary device employed in a far-removed context."

6. For this language, see Jens Schröter, *Jesus of Nazareth: Jew from Galilee, Savior of the World*, trans. Wayne Coppins and S. Brian Pounds (Waco, TX: Baylor University Press, 2014), 17.

In the case of the future coming of Jesus, is it not inherently likely that the Greek exegesis of Scripture as we find it in Paul and the Gospels has gone well beyond anything Jesus had said, and that the expansion of such scriptural connections, in turn, created history? I think that is nearly certain, even if I hesitate to try at this stage to point to definitive cases and harvest prematurely the wheat from the weeds. But just because we cannot neatly divide memory and invention does not mean we cannot probabilistically infer where early Christian interest in Dan 7 and the "day of the Lord" tradition comes from ultimately.

Jesus and Daniel's Dream

I begin with Dan 7. There are a number of sayings in the Gospels that use the peculiar Greek phrase ὁ υἱὸς τοῦ ἀνθρώπου and look back to that "one like a son of man" mentioned in Daniel's dream vision. In addition to frequency, there is breadth: Dan 7's son of man emerges in triple, double, and special Matthean and Lukan material, as well as in John.[7] In addition to breadth, there is a consistency of usage: in these Dan 7–inspired "son of man" passages (and all the others, for that matter), we are dealing with sayings of Jesus, that is, Jesus is the speaker (he is never addressed, by character, or narrator, as "the son of man").[8] In addition to

7. For a helpful organization of the data, albeit with an idiosyncratic and unconvincing interpretation, see John Dominic Crossan, *The Historical Jesus: The Life of a Mediterranean Jewish Peasant* (New York: HarperCollins, 1991), 238–55, 454–56. Half of Crossan's apocalyptic son of man sayings are in what he calls the "first stratum." See also C. F. D. Moule, "'The Son of Man': Some of the Facts," *NTS* 31 (1995): 277–79; Darrell L. Bock, "The Use of Daniel 7 in Jesus' Trial, with Implications for His Self-Understanding," in *'Who Is This Son of Man?' The Latest Scholarship on a Puzzling Expression of the Historical Jesus*, ed. Larry W. Hurtado and Paul L. Owen, LNTS 390 (London: Bloomsbury T&T Clark, 2011), 91 ("well-attested" "in every level"); Christopher Tuckett, "The Son of Man and Daniel 7: Q and Jesus," in *From the Sayings to the Gospels*, WUNT 328 (Tübingen: Mohr Siebeck, 2014), 266–89 (at 285: a "ubiquitous feature of all strands of the gospel tradition"). Contra Leif E. Vaage, "The Son of Man Sayings in Q: Stratigraphical Location and Significance," *Semeia* 55 (1991): 103–29; John S. Kloppenborg, "The Sayings Gospel Q and the Quest of the Historical Jesus," *HTR* 89 (1996): 318 (who thinks that the son of man sayings in Q are untouched by Dan 7); Matthias Kreplin, *Das Selbstverständnis Jesu: Hermeneutische und christologische Reflexion—historisch-kritische Analyse*, WUNT 2/141 (Tübingen: Mohr Siebeck, 2001), 102–32, 140–72 (who argues that all connections to Dan 7 stem from the scribal activity of the post-Easter community).

8. Joachim Jeremias, *New Testament Theology: The Proclamation of Jesus*, trans. John Bowden (New York: Scribner's Sons, 1971), 266 ("exclusively on the lips of Jesus" and "anchored in the sayings of Jesus"). See also Gerd Theissen and Annette Merz, *The Historical Jesus: A Comprehensive Guide*, trans. John Bowden (Minneapolis: Fortress, 1998), 549: "already in primitive Christianity it was regarded as a characteristic feature of Jesus' language."

that consistency of usage, there is the striking absence of the titular use of "son of man" in Paul's letters and elsewhere in early Christian literature.[9]

All of this makes it very hard to argue that the early church, after Easter, came up with a Dan 7 "son of man" Christology and retrojected it back into Jesus's sayings early, frequently, and consistently enough to impact the gospel tradition in such a thorough way, only before easing up on their use of the phrase themselves.[10] And this is aside from the further problem of reasonable motive: it is not at all evident why Easter would suddenly make Jesus the son of man from Dan 7.[11] Our

9. Tuckett, "Son of Man and Daniel 7," 285. Note that Rev 1:13 and 14:14 draw on Dan 7:13 to describe Jesus "like a son of man" (ὅμοιον υἱὸν ἀνθρώπου)—using language that differs from the idiomatic and consistent ὁ υἱὸς τοῦ ἀνθρώπου in the Gospels.

10. Some other notable critics who think that Jesus used son of man with reference to Dan 7 (though they understand the sense differently) include Eduard Schweizer, "Der Menschensohn," *ZNW* 50 (1959): 185–209; Morna Hooker, *The Son of Man in Mark* (London: SPCK, 1967), 182–98; C. F. D. Moule, *The Origin of Christology* (Cambridge: Cambridge University Press, 1977), 11–22; Marinus de Jonge, *Jesus, the Servant Messiah* (New Haven: Yale University Press, 1991), 51–54; Peter Stuhlmacher, *Grundlegung von Jesus zu Paulus*, vol. 1 of *Biblische Theologie des Neuen Testaments* (Göttingen: Vandenhoeck & Ruprecht, 1992), 122–23; Martin Hengel, "Jesus as Messianic Teacher of Wisdom and the Beginnings of Christology," in *Studies in Early Christology* (Edinburgh: T&T Clark, 1995), 105–8; David Wenham, *Paul: Follower of Jesus or Founder of Christianity?* (Grand Rapids: Eerdmans, 1995), 110–12; Theissen and Merz, *Historical Jesus*, 548–53; Brian Han Gregg, *The Historical Jesus and the Final Judgment Sayings in Q*, WUNT 2/207 (Tübingen: Mohr Siebeck, 2006), 181–86; Dale C. Allison Jr., *Constructing Jesus: Memory, Imagination, and History* (Grand Rapids: Baker Books, 2010), 293–94; Chrys C. Caragounis, *The Son of Man: Vision and Interpretation* (Eugene, OR: Wipf & Stock, 2011), 168–243; Tuckett, "Son of Man and Daniel 7," 283–87; Tobias Hägerland, "Jesus and the Scriptures—Problems of Authentication and Interpretation," in *Jesus and the Scriptures: Problems, Passages and Patterns*, ed. Tobias Hägerland, LNTS 552 (London: Bloomsbury T&T Clark, 2016), 3–32.

11. Contra Norman Perrin, *The Kingdom of God in the Teaching of Jesus* (Philadelphia: Westminster, 1963), who famously denied the authenticity of all the apocalyptic son of man sayings (suggesting they originated from "Christian exegetical tradition connected with the resurrection" at 173). See also Perrin, "Mark 14.62: The End Product of a Christian Pesher Tradition?," *NTS* 12 (1965): 150–55. For a similar conclusion about the influence of Easter, see Delbert R. Burkett, *The Son of Man Debate: A History and Evaluation* (Cambridge: Cambridge University Press, 1999). For some others who think Jesus used *bar naša* but doubt any connection with Dan 7 and/or apocalypticism, see Ragnar Leivestad, "Exit the Apocalyptic Son of Man," *NTS* 18 (1972): 243–67; Chris Mearns, "The Son of Man: Trajectory and Eschatological Development," *ExpTim* 97 (1985): 8–12; Donald. H. Juel, *Messianic Exegesis: Christological Interpretation of the Old Testament in Early Christianity* (Philadelphia: Fortress, 1988), 151–71; Hans Bietenhard, "Der Menschensohn," *ANRW* 25.1:265–350; Marcus Borg, *Conflict, Holiness and Politics in the Teachings of Jesus*, 2nd ed. (Harrisburg, PA: Trinity International, 1998), 221–27; Crossan, *Historical Jesus*, 238–59. Even less convincing is the view that Jesus did not use "son of man" at all; so, e.g., Philipp Vielhauer, "Gottesreich und Menschensohn in der Verkündigung Jesu," and "Jesus und der Menschensohn,"

sources do not imply this logic as they now stand either. Norman Perrin, who famously invested Easter with this generating power, wrote that "the resurrection of Jesus is now interpreted as his ascension to God as Son of man,"[12] but this is patently *not* what we find in the New Testament.[13] It is conspicuous, in fact, how rarely the resurrection is connected to Dan 7 in our sources (I will have more to say about this in a later chapter).

While some have contended that the articular use of "son of man"—*the* son of man—is impossible in Aramaic at the time of Jesus,[14] this is a dubious judgment (not least because our evidence is so fragmentary and late),[15] and few agree.[16] The

---

in *Aufsätze zum Neuen Testament*, TB 31 (Munich: Kaiser, 1965), 55–91, 92–140. Cf. Burkett, *Son of Man Debate*, 50–56, for additional literature. It is fair to say that the debate has focused, instead, on what he meant by the phrase, granting its general historicity.

12. Perrin, *Kingdom of God in the Teaching of Jesus*, 179.

13. Contra Helmut Merklein, "Die Auferweckung Jesu und die Anfänge der Christologie," in *Studien zu Jesus und Paulus*, WUNT 43 (Tübingen: Mohr Siebeck, 1987), 241, who suggests that it is commonplace, even a topos, to see Jesus as exalted as the son of man, even while he admits that there are no texts that explicitly refer to the appointment of Jesus as the son of man. Contra also John A. T. Robinson, *Jesus and His Coming: The Emergence of a Doctrine* (New York: Abingdon, 1957), 57.

14. Cf. many works by Maurice Casey over the years, e.g., *The Solution to the "Son of Man" Problem*, LNTS 343 (London: Bloomsbury T&T Clark, 2007).

15. Susceptible to this critique is Geza Vermes, *Jesus the Jew* (London: Collins, 1973), 163–68, 188–91, who relied heavily on later rabbinic evidence for his argument that Jesus used *bar naša* only as a circumlocution for "I." See an assessment of his work in Hilde Brekke Moller, *The Vermes Quest: The Significance of Geza Vermes for Jesus Research*, LNTS 576 (London: Bloomsbury T&T Clark, 2017), 109–22. Vermes was preceded by two influential essays in *Expository Times* that both suggested, on the basis of later Aramaic texts, that "the regular sense which barnash had come to have in Palestinian Aramaic" was "'one'" or "'a man'"; so Matthew Black, "The 'Son of Man' in the Teaching of Jesus," *ExpTim* 60 (1948): 35, and also John W. Bowman, "The Background of the Term 'Son of Man,'" *ExpTim* 60 (1948): 286. Similar insights appeared in the work of Erik Sjöberg, "בן אדמ und בר אנש im Hebräischen und Aramäischen," *AcOr* 21 (1950): 57–65, 91–107, and were further disseminated by Carsten Colpe in his *TDNT* essay, "ὁ υἱὸς τοῦ ἀνθρώπου," *TDNT* 8:400–477, esp. 401–5. For a recent defense of a circumlocutional use of υἱὸς τοῦ ἀνθρώπου by Jesus, see Llewellyn Howes, *Judging Q and Saving Jesus: Q's Contribution to the Wisdom-Apocalypticism Debate in Historical Jesus Studies* (Durbanville: AOSIS, 2015), 53–61.

16. So even before Maurice Casey, note Cecil J. Cadoux, *The Historic Mission of Jesus* (London: Lutterworth, 1941), 91: "we must . . . be on guard against hastily adopting false clues, especially those that give results irreconcilable with what we know on less ambiguous evidence." See also Jeremias, *New Testament Theology*, 262 ("traditio-historical analysis is much more penetrating than philological analysis"); Joseph A. Fitzmyer, "The New Testament Title 'Son of Man' Philologically Considered," in *A Wandering Aramean: Collected Aramaic Essays*, vol. 1 of *The Semitic Background of the New Testament* (Missoula, MT: Scholars Press, 1979), 143–60; Bruce Chilton, "(The) Son of (the) Man, and Jesus," in *Authenticating the Words of Jesus*, ed. Bruce Chilton and

Greek article likely functions deictically, meaning, it points to a particular "son of man," namely, *that* son of man from Daniel.[17] Moreover, while "the son of man" does not appear to be a fixed title in pre-Christian Judaism,[18] there was widespread eschatological interest in Dan 7's vision,[19] and a messianic interpretation of its star character is indeed extant.[20] On the whole, we can say with confidence that

Craig A. Evans (Leiden: Brill, 1999), 259–66; Tuckett, "Son of Man and Daniel 7," 287–89 (argues that we do not know enough on the philological front to overturn the gospel evidence). Paul Owen, "Problems with Casey's 'Solution,'" in Hurtado and Owen, *'Who Is This Son of Man?'*, 29, contends that the emphatic state was in force at the time of Jesus and that he could have used the phrase with "definite and specified meaning." Note also P. J. Williams, "Expressing Definiteness in Aramaic: A Response to Casey's Theory concerning the Son of Man Sayings," in Hurtado and Owen, *'Who Is This Son of Man?'*, 61–77, who writes at 72, "even if I were to concede the unlikely position that the definite state had no force that still would not lead me to the view that definiteness was not expressed."

17. This is similar to several passages in 1 Enoch that mention "this/that son of man." See especially 46.2, 3, 4; 48.2, and note also 62.5; 69.26, 27, 29; 71.14 (though there is some variation in the manuscript tradition, cf. Matthew Black, *The Book of Enoch or 1 Enoch*, SVTP 7 [Leiden: Brill, 1985], 206–7). See also Lester L. Grabbe, "'Son of Man': Its Origin and Meaning in Second Temple Judaism," in *Enoch and the Synoptic Gospels: Reminiscences, Allusions, Intertextuality*, ed. Loren T. Stuckenbruck and Gabriele Boccaccini, EJL 44 (Atlanta: SBL Press, 2016), 182–88. Convincing is Adela Yarbro Collins, "Daniel 7 and the Historical Jesus," in *Of Scribes and Scrolls*, ed. Harold W. Attridge, John J. Collins, and Thomas H. Tobin (Lanham, MD: University Press of America, 1990), 190, who suggests the idiosyncratic Greek translation attempts to point to Dan 7, and in that respect captures what Jesus was after, too.

18. See summary of arguments in Kreplin, *Das Selbstverständnis Jesu*, 88–108.

19. Cf. Jürgen Becker, *Jesus of Nazareth*, trans. James E. Crouch (Berlin: de Gruyter, 1998), 203 ("the Book of Daniel . . . as a whole was influential in Early Judaism and Christianity to a degree that can hardly be exaggerated").

20. Cf. e.g., 4Q246; 1 En. 37–71; 4 Ezra 11–13; Sib. Or. 5.414–33; b. Ḥag. 14a; b. Sanh. 38b; Justin Martyr, *Dial.* 32. See also Tg. Chr. 3.24 (which appears to draw on the "clouds" of Dan 7). I will discuss some of these texts more fully below. Ruben A. Bühner, *Messianic High Christology: New Testament Variants of Second Temple Judaism* (Waco, TX: Baylor University Press, 2021), 84, has put this more boldly, and he appears to be right: "it is hard to find a non-messianic understanding of Dan 7 in Second Temple Judaism." He notes at 71, "regardless of the initial meaning of Dan 7, every available early Jewish source that interprets the figure from Dan 7:13 understands him as a messianic figure possessing several superhuman attributes." Cf. Bühner, *Hohe Messianologie: Übermenschliche Aspekte eschatologischer Heilsgestalten im Frühjudentum*, WUNT 2/523 (Tübingen: Mohr Siebeck, 2020), 123 ("die messianische Interpretation . . . mindestens gängig war, wenn nicht sogar das verherrschende Verständnis"). For some important studies, in addition to Bühner, see William Horbury, "The Messianic Associations of 'The Son of Man,'" *JTS* 36 (1985): 34–55; Peter W. Flint, "The Daniel Tradition at Qumran," in *Eschatology, Messianism, and the Dead Sea Scrolls*, ed. Craig A. Evans and Peter W. Flint (Grand Rapids: Eerdmans, 1997), 41–60; Christopher Rowland, *The Open Heaven: A Study of Apocalyptic in Judaism*

the historical Jesus, should he have shown interest in Daniel's vision for imagining the future, would not have been unique in doing so.[21] Putative Jewish parallels to the Gospels support, rather than challenge, tracing an interest in Dan 7 back to Jesus. I should stress that this argument in no way attempts to solve the larger son of man debate in the Gospels. I am not offering a master theory of everything but making a case about a particular.

In support of this line of argument, I would stress something else often missed in discussions of Jesus and Dan 7: the "one like a son of man" of Dan 7 is only one of several images from that passage, and related portions of Daniel, to emerge in the Jesus tradition. One should highlight the following: (1) Luke 12:32 ("do not be afraid, little flock, because your Father is well pleased to give [δοῦναι] you the kingdom [τὴν βασιλείαν]") draws on the transfer scenes of Dan 7, using the same verb and absolute form of "the kingdom" (as in Dan 7:18, 27);[22] (2) Q 22:28–30 (par. Matt 19:28) has Jesus speak of his disciples on "thrones" "judging" or "ruling" (κρίνοντες) the twelve tribes, which draws on Dan 7's description of the placement of "thrones" (plural) and, likely, the giving of judgment (MT: דינא, LXX has τὴν κρίσιν, and Θ has τὸ κρίμα) to the "holy ones of the Most High";[23] (3) the request of James and John to sit at

---

and Early Christianity (Eugene, OR: Wipf & Stock, 2002), 104–07, 183–86; James D. G. Dunn, *Jesus Remembered* (Grand Rapids: Eerdmans, 2003), 730 (Dan 7 "became very influential in Jewish apocalyptic thinking"); G. K. Beale, *The Use of Daniel in Jewish Apocalyptic Literature and in the Revelation of St. John* (Eugene, OR: Wipf & Stock, 2010), 12–153; John J. Collins, *The Scepter and the Star: Messianism in Light of the Dead Sea Scrolls*, 2nd ed. (Grand Rapids: Eerdmans, 2010), 196–214; Collins, "The Son of Man in Ancient Judaism," in *Handbook for the Study of the Historical Jesus*, ed. Tom Holmén and Stanley Porter (Leiden: Brill, 2010), 2:1545–68 (at 1547: "The text of Daniel's vision was well known, and it inspired further reflections and imaginative elaborations," and also at 1568 on "ongoing speculation" about Dan 7 at the turn of the era). See also Peter Schäfer, *Two Gods in Heaven: Jewish Concepts of God in Antiquity* (Princeton: Princeton University Press, 2020), 54–58.

21. Cf. Josephus, *Ant.* 10.267 (LCL): "the books that [Daniel] wrote and left behind are still read by us even now, and we are convinced by them that Daniel spoke with God, for he was not only wont to prophesy future things, as did the other prophets, but he also fixed the time at which these would come to pass. . . . Daniel was a prophet of good tidings to them, so that through the auspiciousness of his predictions he attracted the goodwill of all."

22. On Daniel and kingdom in Jesus's proclamation, see David Wenham, "The Kingdom of God and Daniel," *ExpTim* 98 (1987): 132–34; Craig A. Evans, "Daniel in the New Testament: Visions of God's Kingdom," in *The Book of Daniel: Composition and Reception*, ed. John J. Collins and Peter W. Flint (Leiden: Brill, 2002), 2:510; Evans, "Inaugurating the Kingdom of God and Defeating the Kingdom of Satan," *BBR* 15 (2005): 49–75.

23. While reconstructing the wording of Q here is challenging, it is most likely that we have Matthew and Luke accentuating an existing connection to Dan 7 in different ways. Cf. Dale C.

Jesus's "right and left in glory" (see Mark 10:35–45; Matt 20:20–28) presupposes the enthronement scenario in Dan 7, confirmed by the fact that Jesus's reply draws on the same: he says he does not have the authority "to give" (δοῦναι [cf. Dan 7:14]), and Jesus actually subverts the image of the son of man being "served" by others (7:13–14) by saying "even" (καί) "the son of man" came to "serve";[24] (4) the comparison of the kingdom of God to a "great tree" where birds nest in its branches (Mark 4:30–32 [though here, ironically, "shrub"]; cf. Matt 13:31–32 and Luke 13:18–19) probably draws on an earlier eschatological vision of Daniel about the coming kingdom (4:10–12, 19–27);[25] (5) Q 10:22 (cf. Matt 11:25–27) has Jesus exclaim that "all things have been handed over [παρεδόθη] to me by my Father" (cf. Dan 7:14); (6) the apocalyptic discourse in Mark 13 and parallels is riddled with phrases drawn from Dan 7–12 that have to do with suffering, persecution, and the temple.[26]

To these examples must be added two further facts: (1) Paul himself drew on Daniel when he reminded the Corinthians that the "holy ones" "will judge the world" (1 Cor 6:2) and when making sense of the eschatological timetable of Jesus's resurrection, reign, parousia, and "the end" (1 Cor 15:20–28) (all discussed in part 3);[27] (2) the Gospels themselves not only draw on Daniel, but they presuppose

---

Allison Jr., *The Intertextual Jesus: Scripture in Q* (Harrisburg, PA: Trinity International, 2004), 138. Matthew explicitly mentions "the son of man," and has him "seated on the throne of his glory" (cf. 1 En. 45.3), which has suggested to some that Matthew knew 1 Enoch. Cf. Amy E. Richter, *Enoch and the Gospel of Matthew* (Eugene, OR: Pickwick, 2012).

24. As noted by many in the commentaries. See, e.g., Craig A. Evans, *Mark 8:27–16:20*, WBC 34B (Nashville: Nelson, 2001), 115–25. Cf. also Joshua W. Jipp, *The Messianic Theology of the New Testament* (Grand Rapids: Eerdmans, 2020), 67.

25. A similar image appears in Ezek 17:22–24, interpreted messianically in the targum ad loc. (where the "twig" on the cedar is actually the messiah himself, and the birds are "the humble who dwell in the shade of his kingdom").

26. As is well known. Cf., e.g., Joel Marcus, *Mark 8–16: A New Translation with Introduction and Commentary*, AB 27A (New Haven: Yale University Press, 2009), 867 ("the chapter abounds in echoes of the book of Daniel, especially the apocalyptic sections").

27. Some have wanted to say more about Paul in particular; so Jeremias, *New Testament Theology*, 265, on Paul's knowledge of "the son of man" title. He makes the interesting argument that Jesus's identity as "son of man" undergirds his exegesis of Ps 8 (about בן אדם), as well as (ὁ) ἄνθρωπος in 1 Cor 15:21–28 and Rom 5:12–21. I am not sure what to think about this. Though it is worth noting the observation of Frederick Houk Borsch, *The Christian and Gnostic Son of Man*, SBT 14 (London: SCM, 1970), 38–42, that the final hand to work on the Didache was in touch with sayings about the son of man even though the title itself does not appear. For the argument that Paul was influenced by son of man traditions that appear in the Similitudes of Enoch (which the author dates earlier than Paul), see James A. Waddell, *The Messiah: A Comparative Study of the Enochic Son of Man and the Pauline Kyrios* (London: T&T Clark International, 2011).

readers (at least some of them) who were making sense of the Jesus story with the prophecies of Daniel near to hand.[28] Daniel, in other words, is central to the Gospels' "encyclopedia of reception."[29]

Where did this collective interest in Daniel—and most often a future-oriented and eschatological interest, we should add—come from? It may not be that all of the six gospel units above go back to Jesus, and I am personally quite skeptical about the Johannine thunderbolt saying (Q 10:21–22) and much of the Mark 13 discourse as it stands.[30] But whoever wrote up Mark 13 was surely interested in Daniel and thought it spoke to the present situation and what was yet to come.[31] This interest and conviction requires a historical explanation.[32] Given the abundance of evidence, it is probable that Jesus had already placed their feet on that path. Naturally, in light of later experience and new insight, as Jesus followers

28. So, e.g., the entire conversation in Mark 2:1–12 about Jesus's "authority" as "the son of man" to forgive sins, including the charge of blasphemy, plays on Dan 7. Cf. Adela Yarbro Collins, *Mark: A Commentary*, Hermeneia (Minneapolis: Fortress, 2007), 186–87. Daniel Boyarin, "How Enoch Can Teach Us about Jesus," *EC* 2 (2011): 52, argues that "the son of man" in the Gospels is "inexplicable" and "unintelligible" apart from its subtext in Dan 7.

29. For this language, see Stefan Alkier, "Intertextuality and the Semiotics of Biblical Texts," in *Reading the Bible Intertextually*, ed. Richard B. Hays, Stefan Alkier, and Leroy A. Huizenga (Waco, TX: Baylor University Press, 2009), 3–21.

30. On Q 10:21–22, I remain ambivalent concerning the thesis of the important study by Brant Pitre, "From Reimarus to Allison: The Quest for Jesus and the Christological 'Thunderbolt' (Matt 11:25–27 // Luke 10:21–22)," in *"To Recover What Has Been Lost": Essays on Eschatology, Intertextuality, and Reception History in Honor of Dale C. Allison Jr.*, ed. Tucker S. Ferda, Daniel Frayer-Griggs, and Nathan C. Johnson, NovTSup 183 (Leiden: Brill, 2021), 373–404, that these lines preserve an utterance of the historical Jesus.

31. Cf. the thesis of Lars Hartman, *Prophecy Interpreted: The Formation of Some Jewish Apocalyptic Texts and of the Eschatological Discourse Mark 13 Par.* (Lund: Gleerup, 1966), on Mark 13 and midrashic interpretation of Daniel. See also David S. du Toit, "Die Danielrezeption in Markus 13," in *Die Geschichte der Daniel-Auslegung in Judentum, Christentum und Islam: Studien zur Kommentierung des Danielbuches in Literatur und Kunst*, ed. Katharina Bracht and David S. du Toit, BZAW 371 (Berlin: de Gruyter, 2007), 55–78. The hypothesis of David Friedrich Strauss, *The Life of Jesus Critically Examined*, trans. George Eliot, 4th ed. (London: Sonnenschein, 1902), 582–98, is still intriguing. Despite being skeptical of the chapter as a whole, he thought a core pattern in Mark 13 goes back to Jesus, inspired by Daniel. He suggested that Daniel would lead one to expect something bad to happen to the temple (albeit desecration, not necessarily destruction) and other "calamities caused by the kingdom of iron and clay" right before the heavenly kingdom's advent (595)—that is, he noted, the basic movement of Mark 13.

32. Hartman himself in *Prophecy Interpreted* thinks that Mark 13's use of Daniel goes back ultimately to Jesus.

continued to read, they found new trails that opened up to new vistas. But the trailhead was on the other side of Easter.

Now to say it is probable that the historical Jesus drew on Dan 7 does not demonstrate that Jesus predicted his own future coming after death. This is for the simple reason that there are many critics who would likely agree with nearly everything that I just wrote but think that, instead, Jesus was actually (1) talking about some other "son of man" soon to come on the clouds of heaven, (2) speaking of his own "coming" in the sense of a "going (up)"—for example, vindication or heavenly enthronement after death—rather than a "coming (down)," or (3) hoping to be revealed as the son of man during his own lifetime and not after some delay or interim in the way that Paul and the Gospels consistently maintain. I will deal with (3) and the question of Jesus's death and an interim period in the next chapter, but in what follows, I want to address 1 and 2 in turn.

The argument that Jesus talked about some other son of man, and early Christians, in light of the resurrection, identified Jesus with this figure, was famously made by Rudolf Bultmann and entertained even earlier by David Friedrich Strauss and Julius Wellhausen.[33] Several of Bultmann's students or those heavily influenced by Bultmann continued to advance the argument, and it has, since then, not gone extinct.[34] E. P. Sanders, Bart Ehrman, Jürgen Becker, Adela Yarbro Collins, Bruce Chilton, and others maintain some variant of the notion.[35] While argu-

33. Rudolf Bultmann, *Theology of the New Testament*, trans. Kendrick Grobel (New York: Scribner's Sons, 1955), 1:29–32. See also Bultmann, *History of the Synoptic Tradition*, trans. John Marsh, 5th ed. (Peabody, MA: Hendrickson, 1963), 122; Strauss, *Life of Jesus*, 283 (wonders whether Jesus began to speak of himself as the son of man only after he believed himself to be the messiah); Julius Wellhausen, *Evangelienkommentare* (Berlin: de Gruyter, 1987), 123–30.

34. Cf. H. E. Tödt, *The Son of Man in Synoptic Tradition*, trans. D. M. Barton (Philadelphia: Westminster, 1965), 222–83; Ferdinand Hahn, *The Titles of Jesus in Christology*, trans. Harold Knight and George Ogg (London: Lutterworth, 1969), 23–34.

35. J. M. McDermott, "Luke xii, 8–9: Stone of Scandal," *RB* 84 (1977): 523–37; Helmut Merklein, *Jesu Botschaft von der Gottesherrschaft: Eine Skizze*, SBS 111 (Stuttgart: Katholisches Bibelwerk, 1983), 155–65; David E. Aune, *Prophecy in Early Christianity and the Ancient Mediterranean World* (Grand Rapids: Eerdmans, 1983), 181–84; Sanders, *Jesus and Judaism*, 145, 229, 233; Becker, *Jesus of Nazareth*, 200–11; Joachim Gnilka, *Jesus of Nazareth: Message and History*, trans. Siegfried S. Schatzmann (Peabody, MA: Hendrickson, 1997), 249–50, 258–62; Bart D. Ehrman, *Jesus: Apocalyptic Prophet of the New Millennium* (Oxford: Oxford University Press, 1999), 135, 144–48; Henk Jan de Jonge, "Les Origines Historique de l'Attente du Retour de Jesus," *ETR* 74 (1999): 491–504; Yarbro Collins, "Daniel 7 and the Historical Jesus," 191; John J. Collins, "The Second Coming," *Chicago Studies* 34 (1995): 262–74; Chilton, "(The) Son of (the) Man, and Jesus," 281; Adela Yarbro Collins and John J. Collins, *King and Messiah as Son of God: Divine, Human, and Angelic Messianic Figures in Biblical and Related Literature* (Grand Rapids: Eerdmans, 2008), 172 ("After the death of Jesus, the exalted Jesus and the heavenly manlike figure whose coming Jesus had

ments vary, the core contention is rooted on a particular saying—Q 12:8–9 and Mark 8:38—that is commonly thought to be multiply attested and may very well go back to Jesus. It is worth citing again here:

Q 12:8–9

And I say to you, all who confess me before others, also the son of man will confess that person before the angels of God, but the one who denies me before people will be denied before the angels of God.

Λέγω δὲ ὑμῖν, πᾶς ὃς ἂν ὁμολογήσῃ ἐν ἐμοὶ ἔμπροσθεν τῶν ἀνθρώπων, καὶ ὁ υἱὸς τοῦ ἀνθρώπου ὁμολογήσει ἐν αὐτῷ ἔμπροσθεν τῶν ἀγγέλων τοῦ θεοῦ· ὁ δὲ ἀρνησάμενός με ἐνώπιον τῶν ἀνθρώπων ἀπαρνηθήσεται ἐνώπιον τῶν ἀγγέλων τοῦ θεοῦ.

Mark 8:38

For whoever is ashamed of me and my words in this adulterous and sinful generation, also the son of man will be ashamed of that person, when he comes in the glory of his Father with the holy angels.

ὃς γὰρ ἐὰν ἐπαισχυνθῇ με καὶ τοὺς ἐμοὺς λόγους ἐν τῇ γενεᾷ ταύτῃ τῇ μοιχαλίδι καὶ ἁμαρτωλῷ, καὶ ὁ υἱὸς τοῦ ἀνθρώπου ἐπαισχυνθήσεται αὐτόν, ὅταν ἔλθῃ ἐν τῇ δόξῃ τοῦ πατρὸς αὐτοῦ μετὰ τῶν ἀγγέλων τῶν ἁγίων.

The common suggestion is that this saying differentiates Jesus from "the son of man." Since early Christians would be unlikely to make up a saying in which Jesus is talking about some other figure having this role, the utterance probably goes back to Jesus.

That is a strong argument if its premises are sure. But they are not. The suggestion labors under four significant difficulties. (1) The argument is only as strong as its interpretation of Q 12:8–9 // Mark 8:38, which is far from evident. It is simply not the case that Q 12:8–9 // Mark 8:38 requires one to think that Jesus was talking about someone else.[36] That is clearly not how the very sources that preserved this saying understood it, of course, and presented it in the manner in which we now read it. We have here a species of all the son of man sayings, where the Gospels

---

announced were easily collapsed into one"); Olegs Andrejevs, *Apocalypticism in the Synoptic Sayings Source: A Reassessment of Q's Stratigraphy*, WUNT 2/499 (Tübingen: Mohr Siebeck, 2019), 219 ("in Q² Jesus becomes identified as ὁ υἱὸς τοῦ ἀνθρώπου").

36. I agree with Stuhlmacher, *Grundlegung von Jesus zu Paulus*, 122, that the point of Luke 12:8–9 is not to distinguish Jesus and the son of man but actually the opposite—to stress their "Zusammengehörigkeit." See also Mogens Müller, *Der Ausdruck "Menschensohn" in den Evangelien: Voraussetzungen und Bedeutung* (Leiden: Brill, 1984), 107; Gregg, *Historical Jesus and the Final Judgment Sayings in Q*, 174.

have Jesus speaking in the third person.[37] In this case, the expression is sensible if one thinks Jesus is simply talking about present versus future realities—that is, Jesus distinguishes between not two different figures but between present and future activities[38]—or earthly versus heavenly realities, as did Paul when speaking of himself in 2 Cor 12.[39] Moreover, the notion that the response to Jesus now impacts one's fate on the last day is widely attested, if not inseparable from the way in which the final judgment appears in the Gospels as a whole.[40] (2) We also need to consider what this hypothesis requires of us as historians, and what it implies about our sources. It requires us to believe that, in the midst of a gospel tradition thoroughly clouded by a later and misleading connection between Jesus and the son of man, a few authentic sayings that go against the grain have been preserved essentially as they were uttered. I find the chances slim that the early Christians were so thoroughly revisionary and simultaneously careless.[41] In addition, it would require us to believe that, despite the fact that these sayings were unproblematic to the gospel writers who included them, we remain in position to extract them from their narrative contexts and infer their true and contrarian meaning.[42] Jeremias was right: Luke 12:8 "cannot bear this burden."[43] I think that a more honest

37. But one example to press the question: how is Luke 12:8–9 significantly different from Luke 18:8: "When the son of man comes, will he find faith on earth?" While I disagree with the larger thesis of R. E. C. Formesyn, "Was There a Pronominal Connection for the Bar Nasha Self-Designation?," *NovT* 8 (1967): 1–35, he is right about the following observation as a matter of interpretation: "there is no single exception: *all* Son of Man titles are replaceable by a personal pronoun of the first person" (27–28).

38. Rightly Jeremias, *New Testament Theology*, 276. This was also the position of Albert Schweitzer, *The Quest of the Historical Jesus*, trans. William Montgomery (New York: Macmillan, 1950), 343–44, 365–71.

39. Cf. especially 2 Cor 12:5, where Paul, speaking of himself, of course, writes "of such a one [ὑπὲρ τοῦ τοιούτου] I will boast, but on my own behalf [ὑπὲρ δὲ ἐμαυτοῦ] I will not boast, except of my weakness." This presents a much stronger contrast than anything in Q 12:8–9.

40. Cf., e.g., Q 10:13–15; Mark 8:35; Matt 7:21–23; 18:18 [cf. John 20:23]; 25:31–46. Note Marius Reiser, *Jesus and Judgment: The Eschatological Proclamation in Its Jewish Context*, trans. Linda M. Maloney (Minneapolis: Fortress, 1997), 317–18: "Even if we should conclude that the confessional situation here addressed (Luke 12:8–9 and par.) belongs to the post-Easter period, or that the Son of man sayings are absolutely not to be credited to Jesus, we must consider it established that this saying, in its imagery and expression, agrees completely with the preaching of Jesus that is certainly attested." See also Christian Stettler, *Das letzte Gericht: Studien zur Endgerichtserwartung von den Schriftpropheten bis Jesus*, WUNT 2/299 (Tübingen: Mohr Siebeck, 2011), 200–218.

41. Indeed, had Jesus spoken about this other individual as frequently as the Gospels presume, why is there no trace of the idea in Paul's letters or in other texts?

42. Ulrich B. Müller, "Parusie und Menschensohn," *ZNW* 92 (2001): 17, is forced to this awkward position.

43. Jeremias, *New Testament Theology*, 275.

conclusion would be that, if the sources have been so reworked in ways that are at odds with the actual teaching of Jesus, recovering his eschatological message is beyond our grasp. (3) Moreover, if it were the case that the resurrection appearances and subsequent theological reflection led Christians to believe that Jesus himself actually was the son of man, and so they revised the material accordingly, we should expect to find closer association between the resurrection of Jesus and Dan 7. But this is not the case. More on this later. (4) Because Jesus was most likely crucified as "king of the Jews" (Mark 15:26 and par.), his followers soon referred to him as "Christ" as a kind of shorthand, stressed his Davidic lineage (Rom 1:3; 15:12; Matt 1:1–17; Luke 3:23–38), and applied to him known messianic prophecies, many recent historians have concluded that a basic messianic claim, however understood or defined, probably goes back to Jesus.[44] I agree.[45] But if this is true, how could there be "room . . . for a further eschatological figure besides Jesus himself

44. Paula Fredriksen, *When Christians Were Jews* (New Haven: Yale University Press, 2018), 68, skeptical of connecting the messianism of the later movement to Jesus, writes, "Had Jesus of Nazareth actually and forthrightly claimed the role for himself—a teaching that the later gospel writers would have happily used, had it existed—the evangelical depictions would be more uniform." This is an overstatement. I query why Fredricksen connects "actually" (*whether* he did) and "forthrightly" (*how* he spoke of it) with a simple conjunction. How is lack of evidence for forthrightness—and one might want to dispute some of the particulars here—connected to whether he "actually" had any messianic pretensions? In the end, there are two facts we have to explain, and Fredricksen focuses on only one of the two: we have to explain *both* the nonuniform presentations of the evangelists vis-à-vis Jesus's messianic claims (so Fredriksen) *and* their uniform assumption that he is in some sense the messiah, and that they tell the story of Jesus from that conviction. Some have argued that Mark's Gospel challenges and seeks to subvert the messianic status of Jesus, but this is possible only on a highly selective reading of Mark. Max Botner's important study, *Jesus Christ as the Son of David in the Gospel of Mark*, SNTSMS 174 (Cambridge: Cambridge University Press, 2019), should put this view to rest.

45. One of the best treatments on this question remains Martin Hengel and Anna Maria Schwemer, *Der Messianische Anspruch Jesu und die Anfänge der Christologie*, WUNT 138 (Tübingen: Mohr Siebeck, 2001), esp. 1–80 ("Jesus der Messias Israels"). Cf. Jostein Ådna, "The Messianic Claim of Jesus: An Appreciation and Appraisal of Martin Hengel's Portrayal of the Historical Jesus," in *The Mission of Jesus*, ed. Samuel Byrskog and Tobias Hägerland, WUNT 2/391 (Tübingen: Mohr Siebeck, 2015), 59–76. Jörg Frey, "Continuity and Discontinuity between 'Jesus' and 'Christ': The Possibilities of an Implicit Christology," *RCT* 36 (2011): 81–83, makes the important insight—which my work on reception history in part 2 confirms—that scholars who denied a messianic element in the career of the historical Jesus were often strongly influenced by the assumption that there was a normative messianic idea, or *Messiasdogmatik*, usually regarded as militaristic and zealot-like. If Jesus was not so disposed, the logic went, then he surely could not have claimed or even entertained the prospect of being the messiah. But with the understanding of far greater diversity of messianic opinion in Second Temple Judaism, thanks not least to the discovery of the Dead Sea Scrolls, that manner of argument is now impossible. See also Craig A.

to complete the picture"?[46] Strauss, interestingly enough, did not think there was such room, but he was able to entertain the possibility that Jesus was speaking of someone else in Luke 12:8 because he thought there may have been a time during Jesus's career when he did not believe he was the messiah.[47] This speculative dive into the development of Jesus's messianic consciousness shows what may be required of this reading. And Bultmann, we should recall, could hold to this interpretation of Luke 12:8 because he did not think that Jesus believed he was the messiah at all; he thought the resurrection created the messianism of the early Christian movement. This reconstruction creates a whole new series of problems.[48] I would follow Jeremias again: "it is quite impossible that in the 'Son of man' Jesus should have seen a future saving figure who was to be distinguished from himself."[49]

Again, to be fair, the plausibility of this reading of Q 12:8 // Mark 8:38 and the larger reconstruction that has Jesus pointing to some other eschatological agent depends a great deal on the implausibility (so it is thought) of Jesus predicting his own future coming. This was certainly true for Bultmann, who wrote, "[Jesus] would have had to count upon being removed from the earth and raised to heaven before the final End, the irruption of God's Reign, in order to come from there on the clouds of heaven to perform his real office. But how would he have conceived his removal from the earth?"[50] I have a response to Bultmann about that, which we will get to in a later chapter of part 4. But if Bultmann's core criticism is on target, then it does, indeed, increase the likelihood of his reconstruction of Jesus's eschatological message, even while there remains the problem of what such a view

---

Evans, "Prophet, Sage, Healer, Messiah, and Martyr: Types and Identities of Jesus," in Holmén and Porter, *Handbook for the Study of the Historical Jesus*, 2:1236–39, 1243.

46. So Hans Conzelmann, *Jesus*, ed. John Reumann, trans. J. Raymond Lord (Philadelphia: Fortress, 1973), 77, was at least right in this.

47. Strauss, *Life of Jesus*, 283. See also Rudolf Otto, *The Kingdom of God and the Son of Man: A Study in the History of Religion*, trans. Floyd V. Filson and Bertram Lee Woolf (Grand Rapids: Zondervan, 1938), who argued that Jesus changed his mind about this: he first regarded the son of man as a figure distinct from himself (so Luke 12:8) but later believed that he must suffer to bring about the kingdom.

48. Ehrman, *Apocalyptic Prophet*, 218, ends up in a rather contorted posture: the son of man will come, who is someone different from Jesus, but then Jesus himself will be the king in the kingdom that is inaugurated. The son of man, for Ehrman, functions as a kind of eschatological middleman who is involved in the inauguration of the end and the judgment before handing the baton back to Jesus.

49. Jeremias, *New Testament Theology*, 276, also notes that if the son of man were some other figure, and should the pericope containing the reply to John the Baptist go back to Jesus, the question from John (Q 11:5) would be "senseless," and Jesus's answer should have been, "'No, I am not he. I am only his forerunner and his prophet.'"

50. Bultmann, *Theology of the New Testament*, 1:29.

requires us to think about our sources and our capabilities as historians. And here I must make a very important point related to our discussion in part 1 concerning overlooked disagreements amid the inheritors of Schweitzerian eschatology (where I compared and contrasted the views of E. P. Sanders, Paula Fredriksen, and Dale Allison).[51] It should not be missed that the eschatological reconstruction of Bultmann and Sanders and others is in many respects closer to the actual claims of the Gospels than are the views of some others in this eschatological school. In particular, rather than collapsing the coming of the son of man into a general prediction about the imminent coming of "the kingdom," Bultmann, Sanders, and others in this camp generally affirm as historical what the Gospels hold out, and they follow the details more carefully: Jesus is talking about an eschatological figure, coming in the future (and soon), and his arrival will coincide with the establishment of the kingdom. Bultmann and company just think that, contra the Gospels, the historical Jesus must have been talking about someone else. Otherwise, however, the sources do not seriously mislead us.[52] To be sure, I think it is fair to say that, despite my strong disagreement with Bultmann's reading of Q 12:8 and the displacement of Jesus from his eschatological expectation,[53] Bultmann's view will be ultimately nearer my own conclusion than some other eschatological reconstructions of Jesus because of its closer attention to the claims of the sources themselves.

Up or Down?

Others, as we have seen, argue Jesus drew on Dan 7 and further believe he saw himself in the role of its star character. But they contend he spoke of his coming in the sense of "going (up)," rather than "coming (down)." I want to rephrase this debate. The "coming (down)" or "going (up)" distinction, while helpful in some ways, also distracts from the real question at hand and the interpretive disagreement before us. The crucial question is not the directionality of movement but whether the coming of the son of man is coordinated with the establishment of the kingdom of God, on the one hand, or with something prior to that, such as the son of man's vindication or enthronement (before the consummation of the

51. See pp. 42–53 above.

52. And it is worth observing here that, among Bultmann's three categories of son of man sayings ("earthly," "suffering," and "coming"), the eschatological sayings are those most consistently regarded as authentic by scholars. So Aune, *Prophecy in Early Christianity and the Ancient Mediterranean World*, 181, whose summary/assessment is still accurate.

53. Here I agree with the general conclusion of Allison's chapter, "The Christology of Jesus," in *Constructing Jesus*, 303: "[Jesus] was the center of his own eschatological scenario."

kingdom and the final judgment), on the other. Bultmann and like-minded critics have closely connected the coming of the son of man with the final arrival of the kingdom and the judgment, while others (such as Glasson, Robinson, Dodd, Wright, Dunn, and many more) have not, even if the latter have not necessarily explicitly named this as the implication of their reading.[54]

I will say more in a later chapter about why the question of the direction of movement is distractionary and ultimately ambiguous. But for our purposes here, let us consider the complexity of the question of the kind of cosmological space being imagined, and see how this impacts the discussion. If Candida Moss and Joel Baden are right that Paul in 1 Thess 4 and other Jews expected a transformed state of existence "in the air"[55]—hence a reality not fully terrestrial but also not wholly heavenly in the sense of nonearthly—then there are multiple ways to get *there*, including a going up (notice ἁρπάζω in 1 Thess 4:17) and a coming down ("from heaven"). But is not the establishment of *the there* the more important question than how to get there? The key issue is this: when the son of man comes (from wherever), is this the end of the age (not in the sense of "end of the space time universe," contra Wright, but "undeniable transformation")? Or is this only one event in a sequence of still more transformative events that are yet to come?

There are four reasons why we should coordinate the coming of the son of man with the establishment of the kingdom and the final judgment in the eschatology of Jesus. (1) Regardless of whether Dan 7 originally referred to the son of man's going up or coming down in 7:13–14, the point of the vision is that the presentation scene is the great climax to and end of the sequence of beasts arising from the sea and the trampling and oppression that they inflict. The sequence of the vision is clear:

(a) the emergence of the beasts and their dominion (vv. 1–8);
(b) the vision of the Ancient One and the opening of the books (vv. 9–10);
(c) the stripping of power from the beasts (vv. 11–12)
(d) the bestowal to the one like a son of man and the holy ones of the Most High (vv. 12–14, cf. v. 17).[56]

54. Cf., e.g., T. Francis Glasson, *The Second Advent: The Origin of the New Testament Doctrine*, 3rd ed. (Eugene, OR: Wipf & Stock, 2009), 63–75, 151–56, 162–66; Robinson, *Jesus and His Coming*, 59–103; N. T. Wright, *Jesus and the Victory of God* (Minneapolis: Fortress, 1996), 513–19; Dunn, *Jesus Remembered*, 758 ("there has been a tendency to reverse the direction of travel in the course of transmission of the Jesus tradition"), 761.

55. Candida R. Moss and Joel S. Baden, "1 Thessalonians 4.13–18 in Rabbinic Perspective," *NTS* 58 (2012): 199–212. Cf. Heikki Räisänen, "Did Paul Expect an Earthly Kingdom?," in *Paul, Luke and the Graeco-Roman World*, ed. Alf Christophersen, JSNTSup 217 (Sheffield: Sheffield Academic, 2002), 2–20.

56. It seems to me most probable that the original aim of Dan 7 was to describe the "one

The climactic nature of 7:13–14 is reinforced by the fact that the seer intrudes immediately in v. 15: "As for me, Daniel, my spirit was troubled within me, and the visions of my head terrified me." In other words, the vision is now completed.[57] The rest of the chapter functions as an interpretation of the vision, with further clarifications (e.g., not the continuation of the vision). The sequence here is almost identical to that earlier vision in Dan 2, which shows that 7:13–14 stands in climactic parallel to the arrival of the great "stone that struck the statue [and] became a great mountain that filled the whole earth" (2:35). Both visions, in other words, are about the establishment of God's "eternal kingdom."[58] The interpretation offered in Dan 2:44 is decisive: "and in the days of those kings the God of heaven will set up a kingdom that shall never be destroyed, nor shall this kingdom be left to another people. It shall crush all these kingdoms and bring them to an end, and it shall stand forever." That Josephus himself hesitated to state the implications of this "stone" for the future of the Roman Empire suggests he was thinking about climactic and irreversible "future" realities (as he says, τὰ μέλλοντα).[59]

(2) The coordination of the coming of the son of man with the arrival of the kingdom and the judgment of God is not only clear in Dan 7; it is what the Synoptics themselves actually claim, as argued in detail in part 3. It is only on very shaky exegetical grounds that one can take the Dan 7–inspired son of man sayings as references to Jesus's enthronement or exaltation only, and hence on even shakier grounds still to argue that the historical Jesus believed something our sources do not even assert. For the evangelists, as for Paul, Ps 110 most often does that work of pointing to heavenly enthronement—a passage that is *not* treated synonymously (or tautologically) with Dan 7. It is telling, as also noted in part 3, that when Luke

like a son of man" as a representative figure for "the holy ones of the Most High," just as the four beasts represent the peoples in those empires. It is also quite possible, however, that the one like a son of man is a leading figure, who represents but is also distinct from the people, just as the beasts might stand in for leaders while also representing their empires. For discussion, see Nathaniel Schmidt, "The 'Son of Man' in the Book of Daniel," *JBL* 19 (1900): 22–28 (for summary of earlier literature); Klaus Koch, *Das Buch Daniel*, EdF 144 (Darmstadt: Wissenschaftliche Buchgesellschaft, 1980), 214–55; John J. Collins, *Daniel: A Commentary on the Book of Daniel*, Hermeneia (Minneapolis: Fortress, 1993), 304–10; G. K. Beale and D. A. Carson, eds., *Commentary on the New Testament Use of the Old Testament* (Grand Rapids: Baker Books, 2007), 133–39. It is clear, in any case, that one like a son of man was individualized and messianized in reception, irrespective of original aim. Cf. Horbury, "Messianic Associations of 'The Son of Man,'" 34–55.

57. See Collins, *Daniel*, 311.

58. Cf. James A. Montgomery, *A Critical and Exegetical Commentary on the Book of Daniel*, ICC (Edinburgh: T&T Clark, 1964), 317–24; Collins, *Daniel*, 311.

59. Josephus, *Ant.* 10.210. For discussion of this "hidden transcript" in Josephus, see Alexandria Frisch, *The Danielic Discourse on Empire in Second Temple Literature*, JSJSup 176 (Leiden: Brill, 2016), 186–92.

seeks to realize the eschatology of Mark by having Jesus speak in the so-called Jewish trial of a more immediate fulfillment in the ascension, he does so by *omitting* the allusion to Dan 7's "coming" (cf. 22:69).[60] It is also crucial to observe that the Fourth Gospel never realizes the eschatology of apocalyptic son of man material by having Jesus speak of his (immediate) heavenly enthronement as Dan 7's son of man. Would that not have been natural, had other Gospels made this move, and the historical Jesus, to boot?

(3) Related to this, should Jesus have used Dan 7's vision of the coming of the son of man to describe merely his own vindication, it would really be about something that happens to him apart from and even invisible to the rest of the world. But this, again, is counter to the consistent testimony of our sources, which frequently stress that his coming will be "seen," link it to reunion with his followers, and use Dan 7 language to talk about their own future activities (such as being enthroned and judging/ruling). Reunion is also emphasized in John and Paul's letters (see 1 Thess 4:17: "thus we will be with the Lord always"), as we have seen in part 3, even though Dan 7 does not appear in these cases (I think, at least; others would dispute this). Both sets of texts are, in any case, describing future, final, transformative things (so Paul thought the "judging" by Dan 7's "holy ones" in 1 Cor 6:2 had not yet happened). Moreover, if cross-cultural studies of apocalyptic and millenarian movements are of any value for understanding the Jesus group, and if a common feature of these movements is the expectation for the radical transformation of social conditions, does it not cast some doubt on the idea that the initial hope of the leader of this movement was for heavenly vindication?[61] While I do not wish to press the point too strongly, it is intriguing that, in some other situations, claims about hidden and heavenly fulfillment are a secondary reaction to the initial failure of an earlier expectation, and an attempt to salvage it.[62]

60. And in Luke 9:26–27, the evangelist separates the description of the future coming of Jesus (v. 26, with its clear pointers to Dan 7) from the present possibility of "seeing the kingdom" (v. 27) by introducing an adversative ("*but* [δέ] truly I tell you"). See p. 210 above.

61. For some important studies, see Norman Cohn, *The Pursuit of the Millennium: Revolutionary Millenarians and Mystical Anarchists of the Middle Ages*, rev. ed. (Oxford: Oxford University Press, 1970); Ronald L. Numbers and Jonathan M. Butler, eds., *The Disappointed: Millerism and Millenarianism in the Nineteenth Century* (Bloomington: Indiana University Press, 1987); Dale C. Allison Jr., *Jesus of Nazareth: Millenarian Prophet* (Philadelphia: Fortress, 1998), 78–94; Albert I. Baumgarten, "Four Stages in the Life of a Millennial Movement," in *War in Heaven/Heaven on Earth: Theories of the Apocalyptic*, ed. Glen S. McGhee and Stephen D. O'Leary (London: Equinox, 2005), 61–76.

62. Of many studies that could be mentioned here, see the important work on cognitive dissonance by Leon Festinger, Henry W. Riecken, and Stanley Schachter, *When Prophecy Fails* (New York: Harper & Row, 1964), 3–32.

(4) The coordination of Dan 7's son of man with consummating end-time realities is also the repeated pattern of its exposition in other Jewish texts from this period, their important differences notwithstanding. Near the end of the Animal Apocalypse, a king arises who rules the world on God's behalf, and after the judgment the nations who survived "fell down and worshipped those sheep, making petition to them and obeying them in every respect" (90.30)—an image likely inspired by the activity of "the holy ones" in Dan 7:27.[63] In 4Q246, which I believe interacts with Dan 7, the mention of a messianic "son of God" is conjoined with the overcoming of the "trampling" by the nations (4Q246 II, 3; cf. the identical דוש in Dan 7:23), leading to "his/its kingdom is an eternal kingdom" (4Q246 II, 5; cf. the identical מלכותה מלכות עלם in Dan 3:33 [ET 4:3] and 7:27), and "his/its dominion is an eternal dominion" (4Q246 II, 9; cf. the identical שלטנה שלטן עלם in Dan 4:31 [ET 4:34]; 7:14).[64] The vision of the vine in 2 Bar. 35–40 is clearly modeled on Dan 2 and 7 (where "four kingdoms" will arise before being destroyed). The destruction of the most terrible fourth kingdom (39:5) happens "at that time [when] the dominion of my Anointed One . . . will be revealed"—a sure allusion to the "dominion" of the son of man in Dan 7:13–14—and we find a few lines later that "his dominion will last forever" (40.3, cf. Dan 7:27).[65] In the Similitudes of Enoch, the messianic son of man, while present in heaven (and thought preex-

63. Gregg, *Historical Jesus and the Final Judgment Sayings in Q*, 42–43, and J. R. Daniel Kirk, *A Man Attested by God: The Human Jesus of the Synoptic Gospels* (Grand Rapids: Eerdmans, 2016), 172, rightly observe the same. Confirming this allusion to Dan 7 is the description a few lines earlier at 90.20: "a throne was erected" upon which a kingly figure sits "for the Lord of the sheep," and then "he took all the sealed books and opened those very books in the presence of the Lord of the sheep" (90.20). This is undoubtedly the further symbolization of Dan 7:9–10. So Beale, *Use of Daniel in Jewish Apocalyptic Literature*, 81–88. These connections to Daniel are important because this portion of 1 Enoch is indisputably earlier than the Similitudes (the date of which remains highly disputed, as already noted). For a messianic reading of "a white bull" who appears at 90.37, see James C. VanderKam, "Messianism and Apocalypticism," in *The Origins of Apocalypticism in Judaism and Christianity*, ed. Bernard McGinn, John J. Collins, and Stephen J. Stein, vol. 1 of *The Encyclopedia of Apocalypticism* (New York: Continuum, 1998), 200 (also argues this is inspired by Dan 7).

64. Cf. Seyoon Kim, *"The Son of Man" as the Son of God*, WUNT 30 (Tübingen: Mohr Siebeck, 1983), 21; Johannes Zimmermann, *Messianische Texte aus Qumran: Königliche, priesterliche und prophetische Messiasvorstellungen in den Schriftfunden von Qumran*, WUNT 104 (Tübingen: Mohr Siebeck, 1998), 165–68; Collins, *Scepter and the Star*, 176–79; Karl A. Kuhn, "The 'One like a Son of Man' Becomes the 'Son of God,'" *CBQ* 69 (2007): 22–42; Tucker S. Ferda, "Naming the Messiah: A Contribution to the 4Q246 'Son of God' Debate," *DSD* 21 (2014): 158–63.

65. Cf. Beale, *Use of Daniel in Jewish Apocalyptic Literature*, 144–53; Matthias Henze, *Jewish Apocalypticism in Late First Century Israel: Reading Second Baruch in Context*, TSAJ 142 (Tübingen: Mohr Siebeck, 2011), 264.

istent), is expected to enact God's judgment per Dan 7 in the future and receive the homage of the nations (1 En. 46.1–4; 48.2–10; etc.).[66] In 4 Ezra, the messianic figure, inspired by Dan 7,[67] defeats the nations who oppose Israel and establishes an idyllic four-hundred-year messianic "reign" that culminates with the resurrection of the dead and even further blessedness (12.31–39; 13.1–56). In 4 Ezra 11, the destruction of the fourth beast/Rome (drawing from Dan 7:11) is differentiated from the final judgment, to be sure, but still an undeniably transformative event in human history that is closely tied to the messianic era and its sequel.

The implication of reading the coming of the son of man and the coming of the kingdom of God together in the proclamation of Jesus is that we are talking about things that did not happen as expected in the first century. Many have managed to pull the future coming of the kingdom into the present by misreading the son of man sayings as references to Jesus's immediate vindication or exaltation. I think a more natural reading of our sources, and one in line with Dan 7 itself and its *Wirkungsgeschichte* in Judaism at or near the time of Jesus, is to see that the coming of Dan 7's son of man was regarded as coterminous with a transformed future state. To take the "coming of the son of man" language in the Gospels as references merely to Jesus's exaltation ("going up") prior to the consummation of history is a distinctly modern reading and one that has emerged at about the same time that Christian eschatology was being problematized on scientific, philosophical, and theological grounds.

I pause at this point to summarize. It is probable that Jesus, like many of his contemporaries, was influenced by Dan 7's dream vision, and, moreover, it is probable that, before the resurrection appearances and the attainment of new scriptural insight by his early followers, Jesus had already identified with the "one like a son of man" there described. The implications of this for reconstructing Jesus's overall eschatological message are still potentially multiplex, to be sure. While, as argued, it is unlikely that Jesus believed Dan 7's son of man was someone other than himself, and even more improbable that the coming described was a "going (up)" distinct from the final establishment of the kingdom and the final judgment, I have not yet shown how this constellation of future events—kingdom, judgment, the "giving" of privileges to the "holy ones," and so on—might relate to the death of Jesus and the potential of some interim period after that. Nothing I have argued so far would necessarily challenge the theses of, say, Albert Schweitzer or Paula Fredriksen, who have argued that Jesus expected all of those things within his own lifetime. There is more to come, then, in the next chapters of part 4.

66. On the use of Daniel here, see Beale, *Use of Daniel in Jewish Apocalyptic Literature*, 96–112.

67. Cf. Beale, *Use of Daniel in Jewish Apocalyptic Literature*, 112–44; Michael E. Stone, *Fourth Ezra: A Commentary on the Book of Fourth Ezra*, Hermeneia (Minneapolis: Fortress, 1990), 383–85.

Jesus and the Day of the Lord

But before that I need to consider another significant exegetical pattern we observed in our exegesis of early Christian literature in part 3: the association between Jesus's coming and the coming of God in traditions about the day of the Lord. Numerous passages from Israel's Scripture putatively *about God* in the future were mined for details *about Jesus* in the future, not least oracles from Isa 26–27, 59, 66, Zech 14, and others.[68] Jesus followers had borrowed these passages, in some cases verbatim from a Greek version, and thereby twisted them away from their original meaning, as I have shown. Does this not demonstrate that early Christians had created the expectation of Jesus's future coming by relying on, and misreading, Old Testament texts that were really about the God of Israel?[69]

This was Glasson's view, we recall. "The Christians took over the OT doctrine of the Advent of the Lord," he wrote, "[and made] the single adjustment that the

68. There is also the striking case of ascribing the universal acclamation of God in Isa 45:23 to Jesus in the Christ hymn of Phil 2:6–11, which we did not discuss in detail in part 3. See Stephen Fowl, "The Use of Scripture in Philippians," in *Paul and Scripture: Extending the Conversation*, ed. Christopher D. Stanley, ECL 9 (Atlanta: Society of Biblical Literature, 2012), 165–71. While the parousia of Jesus is not described, this tradition must depict the homage paid to Jesus as some reality to come after—and hence not synonymous with—the heavenly exaltation of Jesus in 2:9 ("therefore God highly exalted him"). On the potential assumption of the parousia here, see Morna Hooker, "Philippians 2:6–11," in *Jesus und Paulus: Festschrift für W. G. Kümmel*, ed. E. E. Ellis and Erich Grässer (Göttingen: Vandenhoeck & Ruprecht, 1975), 156; Frank J. Matera, *New Testament Christology* (Louisville: Westminster John Knox, 1999), 125–31. Note a similar use of Isa 45 in Tg. 1 Sam. 22.32: "because of the miracle and the deliverance you will perform for your messiah and for the remnant of your people who remain, all peoples, nations, and tongues will confess and say, 'There is no God but the Lord' . . . and your people will say, 'There is none mighty except our God.'"

69. While it has never been seriously considered as a historical hypothesis (to my knowledge), one could argue that the hope for Jesus's future return was modeled on—in the sense of created by—Greco-Roman mythology, where it is common to find tales of the gods "coming down" and "appearing" to mortals. Cf., e.g., Homer, *Od.* 1.96–105; 2.267; 17.484–487; 22.205; Ovid, *Metam.* 1.212–213; 3.251–313; 8.620–724. For some other potential parallels, cf. the brief reflections by Osvaldo D. Vena, *The Parousia and Its Rereadings: The Development of the Eschatological Consciousness in the Writings of the New Testament*, SBT 27 (New York: Lang, 2001), 49–52. Note that in Acts 14:11, the people of Lystra exclaim after witnessing a miracle, "the gods have come down to us [κατέβησαν πρὸς ἡμᾶς] in the likeness of men!" However, there would be two immediate and fatal flaws with such an argument: (1) the mythology is not eschatological in nature—e.g., there is no stress on a climactic return of the gods in the future, and (2) it overlooks the formative influence of Jewish Scripture and traditions on New Testament claims about Jesus. We also find a lexical distinction here: the typical term used for the appearance of the gods is "epiphany" (ἡ ἐπιφάνεια), which appears in the New Testament only in the Pastoral Epistles and in 2 Thessalonians with reference to Jesus.

Lord was the Lord Jesus."[70] More recently, N. T. Wright, his higher Christology notwithstanding, has argued in a very similar direction: the early Christians, and Paul specifically, drew on the "coming of God" tradition to generate an eschatological expectation that Jesus himself had never spoken about.[71] This is one way that Wright moves from the symbolic, realized eschatology of his historical Jesus to the literal, futurist eschatology of the early church with its parousia expectation.

To my mind, Glasson's attention to Scripture is one of the strongest aspects of his argument.[72] Glasson preferred to speak about the "theophany" tradition, while I would prefer "day of the Lord" tradition (we will come back to this in a moment). But his exegesis is often insightful, and my own work in part 3 would affirm much of his own on the intertextuality of the New Testament as it pertains to this topic. But here is the question: What are the conditions and presuppositions that made this exegesis possible? Glasson was perfectly clear here: the fundamental premise of such exegesis was the conviction that Jesus was the κύριος—a reality that, he suspected, goes well beyond anything the historical Jesus ever claimed for himself.[73] He memorably wrote, "Jesus comes not because He is Christ, but because He is Lord."[74] Linking Old Testament passages to Jesus the κύριος was, he argues, possible only in a later and more advanced stage of christological development, and it has nothing to do with Second Temple Jewish messianism or even Jewish apocalyptic tradition.[75] We have here a kind of early Christian *gezerah shavah*, he thought, where κύριος functions as the crucial linking term.

Here I must protest—not his exegesis but his assumptions about their motives, how they fail to fit in Jewish messianic tradition, and their conceptual distance from the teaching of the historical Jesus otherwise. I lay out an alternative case in four steps.

70. Glasson, *Second Advent*, 183.

71. N. T. Wright, *Paul and the Faithfulness of God* (Minneapolis: Fortress, 2013), 1078–95, and esp. 1084–85 ("since Paul identified Jesus as the one in and through whom YHWH had become personally present, it was not difficult *to transfer* to him the still-future expectation of YHWH's 'day' or 'coming' or 'appearing'" [my italics]).

72. For similar exegetical conclusions, see Edward Adams, "The 'Coming of God' Tradition and Its Influence on New Testament Parousia Texts," in *Biblical Traditions in Transmission: Essays in Honour of Michael A. Knibb*, ed. Charlotte Hempel and Judith M. Lieu, JSJSup 111 (Leiden: Brill, 2006), 1–20.

73. See also T. Francis Glasson, "Theophany and Parousia," *NTS* 34 (1988): 260 ("Is it not possible, or indeed obvious, that this is the origin of the whole idea of Christ's Parousia?").

74. Glasson, *Second Advent*, 176. See also 195. Cf. Müller, "Parusie und Menschensohn," 8 ("Die theophan vorgestellte Parusie des Erhöhten liegt in der besonderen Kontur des Osterglaubens begründet").

75. Glasson, *Second Advent*, 261.

Eschatology and the Day of the Lord

First, what we find in early Christian texts—the claims—is not the recycling of a theophany tradition only but the liberal use of texts about the day of the Lord. This tradition included, to be sure, the notion of divine "appearance," but it was also about more than that. The use of "day of the Lord" and cognate phrases in the classical prophets and also in Lamentations typically looked forward, to the future, to a climactic moment wherein the God of Israel would act decisively (often using verbs "come" [בוא], "go out" [יצא], "come down" [ירד]) to redeem Israel and defeat Israel's oppressors.[76] In describing that future, such passages often paint with a remarkably similar palette of images: there are fire, gathering, cosmic disturbances (whether understood literally or metaphorically), sometimes a heavenly court or angels, acts of judgment and destruction, and acts of salvation and restoration.[77] This latent eschatological sense is only further intensified in reception, and that already in later biblical texts (cf. especially Zech 14 and its great battle for Zion, Isa 26–27 where the Lord "comes forth" to punish the inhabitants of the earth, and Isa 66 where the Lord comes in fire to save and judge).[78] As noted by many critics, the phrase "day of the Lord" sometimes still appears in later, noncanonical texts (cf., e.g., 2 En. 18.6 [J]; Apoc. Zeph. 12.7), but others speak simply of "the day of judgment," or "the great day of judgment," or "the day of God," or "your/his day," or even "the day."[79]

Speaking of a "day of the Lord" tradition rather than a "theophany" tradition is important because it highlights the eschatological aspect that was so important for New Testament authors. It is not just that Jesus followers were finding texts that speak of the appearance of the Lord; they were finding texts that speak of the future work of the Lord in a particularly climactic and decisive way.

76. On "day of the Lord," see Frank Schnutenhaus, "Das Kommen und Erscheinen Gottes im Alten Testament," *ZAW* 76 (1964): 1–22; Richard H. Hiers, "The Day of the Lord," *ABD* 2:82–83; J. D. Barker, "Day of the Lord," in *Dictionary of the Old Testament: Prophets*, ed. Mark J. Boda and J. Gordon McConville (Downers Grove, IL: InterVarsity Press, 2012), 132–43.

77. Cf. Amos 5:18–20; 8:9–14; Isa 2:12–17; 13:1–22; 34:1–17; 61:1–3; 63:1–6; Ezek 7:1–27; 30:1–9; Obad 1–21; Joel 1–4; Mal 3:13–24; Zeph 1:1–9; Zech 14:1–21; etc.

78. See 1 En. 1.2–9 (cited by Jude 14); 90.14–15 ("the Lord of the sheep came upon them in wrath"); 91.7; 100.4; 2 En. 32.1 (J); 2 Bar. 48.39 (on the "coming" of "the judge," who "will not hesitate"); Jub. 1.28 ("the Lord will appear in the sight of all"); LAB 19.12 ("until I visit the world"); T. Jud. 22.1–3 ("until the coming of the God of righteousness"). A. Joseph Everson, "The Days of Yahweh," *JBL* 93 (1974): 336, also notes that in the postexilic period the tradition became more future oriented.

79. Cf. Gerhard Delling, "ἡμέρα," *TDNT* 2:947–53; David E. Aune, *Revelation*, WBC 52 (Nashville: Nelson, 1997–1998), 2:412–23.

Early Christian texts described the future coming of Jesus within that imagined eschatological space.

There is, then, a great deal of continuity between this eschatological "day of the Lord" tradition and the eschatological teaching of Jesus, apart from the question of his own future coming. As the "day of the Lord" was further eschatologized in reception, it was linked specifically with the future "day" of the resurrection of the dead or the "day" of final judgment.[80] It is not particularly controversial to say that these were common hopes in Palestinian Judaism that were surely held by the historical Jesus as—if our sources can be trusted at all—they frequently emerged in his teaching.[81] Moreover, it is probable that John the Baptist before Jesus expected the imminent arrival of the day of the Lord, which is one reason why he was out in the Jordan with such an urgent message of repentance. John's proclamation is riddled with "day of the Lord" images: "gathering," "fire/burning," "coming," "wrath." I see no reason to challenge the conclusion of James Dunn that John was inspired in particular by the book of Malachi (cf. chapters 3–4), with its warnings about the sudden "coming" of the Lord "on the day of his coming" when God will "refine" with "fire" and draw near for "judgment."[82] This would make even more sense if, as the Synoptics presume, John either identified himself with or was identified by others as "Elijah who is to come" (cf. Mark 9:11–13 and par.), since according to the end of Malachi, Elijah is to come "before the great and terrible day of the Lord" (cf. Mal 3:19–24 [ET 4:1–6]) and hopefully limit its damage.[83]

80. For one or both of these together, cf. Jdt 16:17; Jub. 5.10; 23.11; 1 En. 10.6; T. Levi 3.3, 23.11; Pss. Sol. 15.12; 4 Ezra 7.38; 7.102; 12.34; 2 Bar. 48.47; 49.2; 55.6; Apoc. Adam 13.3; 37.5. Cf. Nicola Wendebourg, *Der Tag des Herrn: Zur Gerichtserwartung im Neuen Testament auf ihrem alttestamentlichen und frühjüdischen Hintergrund*, WMANT 96 (Neukirchen-Vluyn: Neukirchener, 2003), 86–154.

81. See Richard H. Hiers, *Jesus and the Future: Unresolved Questions for Understanding and Faith* (Atlanta: John Knox, 1981), 19–49; Gregg, *Historical Jesus and the Final Judgment Sayings in Q*, 269–78; Stettler, *Das letzte Gericht*, 198–268.

82. Cf. James D. G. Dunn, "John the Baptist's Use of Scripture," in *The Gospels and the Scriptures of Israel*, ed. Craig A. Evans and W. Richard Stegner (Sheffield: JSOT Press, 1994), 42–54, and also Jeffrey A. Trumbower, "The Role of Malachi in the Career of John the Baptist," 28–41, in the same volume.

83. On the expectation for Elijah's return, see Mal 3:22–24 (ET 4:5–6); Sir 48:10; 4 Ezra 6.26–28; 4Q558 1 II, 4; 1 En. 90.31, 37; Sib. Or. 2.187–189; LAB 21; Tg. Num. 25.12; Justin Martyr, *Dial.* 8.4; 49.1; b. Sanh. 96b–99a. I argued in "The Historicity of Confusion: Jesus, John the Baptist, and the Construction of Public Identity," *JBL* 139 (2020): 747–67, that the association between John and Elijah goes back to the historical Jesus himself, even if John had not declared as much for himself. See also discussion in Joseph Klausner, *Jesus of Nazareth: His Life, Times, and Teaching*, trans. Herbert Danby (New York: Macmillan, 1925), 244, 247; Markus Öhler, "The Expectation

For further evidence of contact with the teaching of Jesus, we should also point out that the notion of the future establishment of the kingdom or reign of God had been associated with the day of the Lord in this period. Testament of Moses 10.1–7 begins, "then his kingdom will appear throughout his whole creation," and continues with this:

> For the Heavenly One will arise from his kingly throne.
> Yea, he will go forth from his holy habitation
> with indignation and wrath on behalf of his sons.
> And the earth will tremble, even to its ends shall it be shaken.
> And the high mountains will be made low.
> Yea, they will be shaken, as enclosed valleys they will fall.
> The sun will not give light,
> and in darkness the horns of the moon will flee. . . .
> For God Most High will surge forth,
> the Eternal One alone.
> In full view will he come to work vengeance on the nations.
> Yea, all their idols he will destroy.[84]

While the exact phrase "day of the Lord" does not appear here, all of these images about the Lord's coming are drawn from texts in the Bible that describe the day of the Lord from Micah, Joel, and Isaiah. We can multiply examples with ease. In T. Jud. 22, Judah declares that the "coming of the God of righteousness" (ἕως παρουσίας τοῦ θεοῦ τῆς δικαιοσύνης) will "preserve the power of my kingdom forever" (κράτος βασιλείας μου ἕως τοῦ αἰῶνος) in fulfillment of Gen 49:10. In the targum, Zech 13–14's elaborate description of "that day," which includes the bold claim that "the Lord will become king over all the earth" (14:9), is rewritten as, "and the kingdom of the Lord will be revealed upon all the inhabitants of the earth."[85] We find more of the same in Tg. Isa. 24.23 ("the kingdom of the Lord of hosts will be revealed on the Mount of Zion in Jerusalem"), Tg. Isa. 31.4 ("so the kingdom of the Lord of hosts will be revealed to settle upon the Mount of Zion . . . as the bird soars"), Tg. Obad. 21 (at Mount Zion, "the kingdom of the Lord shall be revealed

of Elijah and the Presence of the Kingdom of God," *JBL* 118 (1999): 461–76; Joel Marcus, *John the Baptist in History and Theology* (Columbia: University of South Carolina Press, 2018), 46–61.

84. *OTP* 1:932.

85. *ArBib* 14:224. This was evidently a wider tradition. Note Mekilta de-Rabbi Ishmael on Exodus 17:14: "R. Eleazar says, when will the name of these people [Israel's enemies] be blotted out? At the time when idolatry will be eradicated together with its worshippers, and God will be recognized throughout the world as One, and his kingdom will be established for all eternity."

over all the inhabitants of the earth"),[86] Tg. Ezek. 7.7 (where the "doom" of the day of the Lord is written as, "the kingdom of God is revealed upon you"), and related texts about the Lord's "coming" or "going forth," as in battle (cf. Tg. Onq. and Neof. on Exod 15:18; Tg. Isa. 40.9; 52.7; Tg. Mic. 4.7–8).[87] Fourth Ezra 2.34 anticipates the "shepherd" who will "come at the end of the age," and follows in the next line with, "Be ready for the rewards of the kingdom" (2.35). All of this increases the likelihood that, between the proclamation of John the Baptist and the expectations of Paul that drew from the "day of the Lord" tradition, the teaching of Jesus of Nazareth about the "kingdom of God" was a middle term and not an outlier.

Coagency

Now to a second point. There is another crucial matter on which Glasson and followers have been mistaken: the contention that identifying Jesus with the actions of the Lord in these scriptural texts derives from a unique christological development that departs from Jewish messianism or apocalyptic tradition.[88] The reality is that, throughout the Second Temple period and after, it is common to find human and angelic figures described as sharing, cooperating with, or performing acts and duties that, in Scripture, are reserved for the Lord.[89] We even find this in the biblical text itself, as certain characters perform God's work or

86. *ArBib* 11:49, 62; 14:102.

87. See also Jub. 1.28 (though "kingdom" does not appear here); Pss. Sol. 17.3 ("the kingdom of our God is forever over the nations in judgment"); T. Dan 5:13 (the Holy One "will rule"); Sib. Or. 3.47–48 (the "great kingdom of the immortal King will become manifest"). See also 1QM VI, 6; XII, 7.

88. Glasson meant this point in critique, but it has also been made in service of Christian theology, such as Mark D. Vander Hart, "The Transition of the Old Testament Day of the LORD into the New Testament Day of the Lord Jesus Christ," *Mid-America Journal of Theology* 9 (1993): 3–25, who stresses that in Old Testament texts (the limit of his study), "it should be clearly noted that the Day of YHWH is one in which YHWH is seen as the sole actor" (8). He presses this to ascribe a high Christology to the historical Jesus.

89. While I am not convinced by all aspects of Kirk's master reading of the Christology of the Synoptics in *Man Attested by God*, he is certainly right in this: "Jewish literature in the biblical and Second Temple periods repeatedly assigns to human figures the roles and attributes that are typically seen as being reserved uniquely for God alone" (45). He is also right that "being identified *with* God is not the same as being identified *as* God" (174). Cf. Maurice Casey, "Chronology and the Development of Pauline Christology," in *Paul and Paulinism: Essays in Honour of C. K. Barrett*, ed. Morna D. Hooker and S. G. Wilson (London: SPCK, 1982), 128 (on what he calls the "elaboration" of various figures: Davidic king, eschatological high priest, eschatological prophet, Abel, Elijah, Enoch, Melchizedek, Michael, Moses, Wisdom). See also Mary E. Mills, *Human*

seemingly stand in for God,[90] and some such passages are related to messianism.[91] This becomes even more pronounced in later, nonbiblical texts, including the Dead Sea Scrolls, where we find the following. (1) In 11Q13, which concerns the mysterious Melchizedek figure mentioned in Gen 14:18–24 (cf. Ps 110:4),[92] the "year of the Lord's favor" from Isa 61:2 becomes "the year of Melchizedek's favor," and this figure also assumes God's role of judge in Ps 82:1 (and maybe also Ps 7:8–9). Moreover, Isa 52:7's description of the coming of "your God" is now Melchizedek himself.[93] (2) In 1QpHab (Pesher Habakkuk), on Hab 2:4b ("the righteous will live by their faith/faithfulness to him"), the Teacher of Righteousness is now the object of that faith/faithfulness (probably "loyalty"), rather than God (VII, 1–VIII, 3). (3) In 4Q167 (Pesher Hosea), Hos 5:14 ("for I will be like a lion to Ephraim [and like a lion cub to the house of Judah]") receives this gloss: "[Its interpretation con]cerns the last priest who will stretch out his hand to strike Ephraim" (frag. 2 line 3). Here this eschatological "last priest," whoever he might be, appears to work out the judgment that Hos 5 attributes to God (indeed, in context, Hos 5:1–15 contains

---

Agents of Cosmic Power in Hellenistic Judaism and the Synoptic Tradition, JSNTSup 41 (Sheffield: JSOT Press, 1990).

90. Cf. especially Moses in Exod 4:15–16 ("You [Moses] will be God for him [Pharoah]"); 8:19. Cf. Philo, *Mos.* 1.155–158; Ezek. Trag. 70–82.

91. Note, for instance, in Ezek 34, at first we read that God will be the shepherd (vv. 10–16), and then near the end of the passage that God will appoint "David" to shepherd the people (vv. 23–24). See also Jer 23:3 ("I myself shall gather the remnant"), 5 ("I will raise up for David a righteous branch, and he shall reign"). This figure's very name is "the LORD is our righteousness" (v. 6), which the targum exploits (see also Lam. Rab. 1.51). Other important texts include Isa 9:6–7; Jer 30:8–11; Ps 45:1–6; 72:1–19; 89:1–37; 110:1–7; 1 Chr 29:20. Cf. Yarbro Collins and Collins, *King and Messiah as Son of God*, 1–24; Derek Kidner, *Psalms 73–150* (Downers Grove, IL: InterVarsity Press, 2014), 431.

92. Note also that, in 4Q401 frag. 11 line 3, Melchizedek is said to be "in the assem[bly of God]." Critics debate whether Melchizedek in 11Q13 is a human or angelic figure. Given the text assumes the reader's familiarity with the biblical Melchizedek, David Flusser, "Resurrection and Angels in Rabbinic Judaism, Early Christianity, and Qumran," in *The Dead Sea Scrolls Fifty Years after Their Discovery*, ed. Lawrence H. Schiffmann et al. (Jerusalem: Israel Exploration Society, 2000), 568, may be right to argue that that the eschatological judge Melchizedek is "at the same time the biblical Melchizedek."

93. It has been argued that the "one anointed with the spirit" that emerges in lines 5–12, and hence this connection to Isa 52, refers to someone distinct from Melchizedek. This is argued by Zimmermann, *Messianische Texte aus Qumran*, 389–412. See also Andrew Chester, *Messiah and Exaltation: Jewish Messianic and Visionary Traditions and New Testament Christology*, WUNT 207 (Tübingen: Mohr Siebeck, 2007), 261, who claims this "anointed one" is a royal messiah. But it seems more likely to me that we are dealing with one figure here, given that both are connected intertextually with stock phrases from Isa 61. See the excellent discussion and literature in Bühner, *Hohe Messianologie*, 223–27; Bühner, *Messianic High Christology*, 52–53.

multiple declarations about coming judgment spoken by God in the first person). (4) 1QM (War Scroll) routinely has the human armies of the Lord performing God's work, so Num 24's declaration, "Yours is the battle!" (XI, 1 etc.), is interpreted as, "by the hand of" various figures (XI, 2, 3), including "your anointed ones" (XI, 7), and the "banners" that accompany the armies to and fro contain inscriptions such as, "the truth of God," "the justice of God," "the glory of God," "the judgment of God," "the right hand of God," "the greatness of God," "the praise of God," and more (cf. especially IV, 6–17). (5) The Self-Glorification Hymn (4Q491; see also 4Q471b, 4Q427, and 1QH XXV–XXVI) appears to describe a human being sitting on a throne in heaven among the angels, "reckoned with the *elim*," who asks, "who is like me in my glory?" (4Q491c frag. 1 line 8). These descriptions are striking in light of Exod 15:11 ("Who is like you, Yahweh, among the *elim*?") and related texts (cf. Isa 44:7; Ps 89:7).[94]

None of these texts are necessarily messianic, though I do think it likely that the Melchizedek fragment and the Self-Glorification Hymn refer to messianic figures.[95] Unfortunately the "messianic or not" debate quickly becomes a semantic game. The important point is that there is a much wider phenomenon of describing the activity of figures who are not God with biblical language, and even specific prophetic expectation, that was originally about God.[96]

94. For a careful discussion, see Collins, *Scepter and the Star*, 155–64.

95. See also Bühner, *Messianic High Christology*, 40–41, 52–52. On defining messianism, see pp. 129–30 above. In addition to "common scriptural discourse" (Matthew V. Novenson, *The Grammar of Messianism: An Ancient Jewish Political Idiom and Its Users* [Oxford: Oxford University Press, 2017], 1), I agree with Simon Gathercole, *The Gospel and the Gospels* (Grand Rapids: Eerdmans, 2022), 40, that certain "themes . . . are prominent." Helpful here is Gerbern S. Oegema, *The Anointed and His People: Messianic Expectations from Maccabees to Bar Kochba* (Sheffield: Sheffield Academic, 1998), 26: "A messiah is a priestly or royal figure, or one that can be characterized otherwise, who will play a liberating role at the end of time." Cf. also Jacob Neusner, preface to *Judaisms and Their Messiahs at the Turn of the Christian Era*, ed. Jacob Neusner, William S. Green, and Ernest Frerichs (Cambridge: Cambridge University Press, 1987), ix; Zimmermann, *Messianische Texte aus Qumran*, 16–18.

96. In the Palestinian recension of the Shemoneh Esreh (the Eighteen Benedictions), the eleventh includes in the same breath: "Restore . . . our judges as at first and our counselors as at the beginning, and rule over us, you alone." Here the restoration of proper leadership and divine "reign" go together. A similar idea appears in the explicitly messianic fourteenth benediction, which petitions for God's "mercy" to be shown to Israel, to Jerusalem, and "on the kingdom of the house of David your righteous anointed." While the messianic heir of David is sometimes understood as the future temple builder (cf. 2 Sam 7:13; Zech 6:12–13; cf. 4Q522 9 II, 3–9; Sib. Or. 5.414–33; Tg. Isa. 53.5; Lev. Rab. 9.6), this petition appears to petition God specifically as "rebuilder of Jerusalem." On the use of the benedictions for reconstructing messianic expectations, see Philip S. Alexander, "The King Messiah in Rabbinic Judaism," in *King and Messiah*

Some of these claims drew from the "day of the Lord" tradition in making this move. I highlight the following (and, again, not all of these are necessarily about a "messianic" figure, nor is that essential to my argument here. The point is about agency):

- Isaiah 19's oracle against Egypt and prediction of God's coming "on a swift cloud" to judge expects that, when Israel calls out for deliverance from their oppressors, God will send them a "savior" (v. 20), who is clearly the Lord: "The LORD will make himself known to the Egyptians" (v. 21). But in the LXX we find "the Lord will send them a man [ἀποστελεῖ αὐτοῖς κύριος ἄνθρωπον]," and it is this figure "who will save them" (ὃς σώσει αὐτούς), and who "judges" (from κρίνω).
- In a similar way, Isa 62's vision for the redemption of Jerusalem anticipates the Lord's "salvation" coming and "his reward is with him, and his recompense before him" (62:11). In the LXX, this "salvation" is personified: "behold, the savior appears [ὁ σωτὴρ παραγίνεται], having his reward and his deed before him."[97]
- In Pss. Sol. 17's paean to the "son of David" (17.21), we find in vv. 29–32 expectations about judgment, glorification, and the purification of Jerusalem that draw from the final chapter of Isaiah, particularly 66:18–21. This is striking because these lines are about actions of God when "the LORD will come in fire" (cf. 66:15).[98] Isaiah 66:18 claims that God knows the thoughts of the people, but in Pss. Sol. 17.25 the king has this ability, just as Isa 66:18 claims the nations will "see my [God's] glory," but in Pss. Sol. 17.31, the nations "see his [the king's] glory." Moreover, in the final chapter of the Psalms of Solomon, the author puts the "day" of God's mercy and the "day" of the arrival of David's heir in parallel: "May God cleanse Israel for the day of mercy in blessing, for the appointed day when his messiah will reign" (18.5).
- In 4Q521 (Messianic Apocalypse), an "anointed one" is introduced (2 II, 1) before descriptions of restoration drawn from Isaiah and other texts appear (enthroning, freeing prisoners, giving sight to blind, raising the dead; cf., e.g., Isa 26:19; 29:18; 35:5–6; 42:7).[99] In the Scriptures evoked, God is the agent. While

in Israel and the Ancient Near East, ed. John Day (Sheffield: Sheffield Academic, 1998), 456–73. Reuven Kimelman, "The Messiah of the Amidah: A Study in Comparative Messianism," *JBL* 116 (1997): 313–24, rightly emphasizes the interest in divine agency in the Amidah, but he is overly schematic in his descriptions.

97. Cf. William Horbury, *Jewish Messianism and the Cult of Christ* (London: SCM, 1998), 246–48.

98. Also noted by Horbury, *Jewish Messianism and the Cult of Christ*, 103.

99. For discussion on identifying this figure, cf. F. García Martínez, "Messianische Erwartungen in den Qumranschriften," in *Jahrbuch für Biblische Theologie* 9 (1993): 171–208 at 182–86;

that might also be true in 4Q521 (it is not always clear), it is likely that the anointed figure is depicted as performing some of these actions.[100]

- In 4Q246 (Apocryphon of Daniel), the positively identified "son of God" and "son of the Most High" (II, 1) eventually works in tandem with God's self: he will "judge the earth" (II, 5–6), "make peace" (II, 6), receive homage (II, 7), and establish "an eternal dominion" by the power of God who "will wage war for him" (II, 8–9).[101]
- In CD (Damascus Document), the "time of visitation"—a scripturally evocative reference about God's advent (cf., e.g., Isa 29:6; LAB 19.12)—is identified with the "coming" of "the messiah of Aaron and Israel" (XIX, 10–11).[102]
- In the Animal Apocalypse, a sheep with a large horn (90.9), some kind of kingly figure arising from Israel, fights for Israel, gathers Israel, and then is enthroned: "a throne was erected in a pleasant land, and he sat upon it for the Lord of the sheep." That language is striking: this figure sits upon a throne in behalf of the Lord of the sheep. Moreover, this figure is involved in the opening of the books for judgment (90.20), a scene that perhaps draws on Dan 7.
- In the Similitudes of Enoch, the "day of the Lord" has become "the day of the Chosen One" (1 En. 61.5; see also "that day" at 62.9 [when kings and the mighty fall down and pay homage to the son of man] and 62.13 [when the righteous are saved]). This figure has glory (49.2) and receives the homage or worship of all who inhabit the earth (48.5; 62.9). At the time the Lord of the Spirits sits down "on the throne of his glory" (62.2), the son of man sits down "on the throne of his glory" (62.5; cf. 51.3–4). To deny the son of man is to deny the Lord of Spirits (48.10), while to praise and glorify the son of man is to praise and glorify the

---

Zimmermann, *Messianische Texte aus Qumran*, 343–88; Collins, *Scepter and the Star*, 131–41 (who suggests Elijah *redivivus*).

100. The allusions to Isa 61:1 strongly suggest that "the anointed" is the subject of at least some of the verbs. On this debate, see Martínez, "Messianische Erwartungen in den Qumranschriften," 184–85; Collins, *Scepter and Star*, 133–35.

101. I have argued elsewhere for a messianic reading of this fragment. Cf. Ferda, "Naming the Messiah," 150–75, and see also John J. Collins, "The Son of God Text from Qumran," in *From Jesus to John: Essays on Jesus and New Testament Christology in Honour of Marinus de Jonge*, ed. Martinus C. De Boer, JSNTSS 84 (Sheffield: JSOT Press, 1993), 76–82; Johannes Zimmermann, "Observations on 4Q246—the 'Son of God,'" in *Qumran-Messianism: Studies on the Messianic Expectations in the Dead Sea Scrolls*, ed. James H. Charlesworth, Hermann Lichtenberger, and Gerbern S. Oegema (Tübingen: Mohr Siebeck, 1998), 175–90; Schäfer, *Two Gods in Heaven*, 38–44.

102. The question whether the Damascus Document refers to one or two messiahs here is not important for our purposes. For discussion, see Shemaryahu Talmon, "Waiting for the Messiah: The Spiritual Universe of the Qumran Covenanters," in Neusner, Green, and Frerichs, *Judaisms and Their Messiahs at the Turn of the Christian Era*, 122.

Lord of Spirits (46.5–6). He plays a significant role on the day of judgment, weighing deeds in the balance (61.8–9; cf. 49.4).[103] It is even said that at the appearance of the righteous and elect one, the "mountains shall become wax" (53.7), as is written in Mic 1:3 about the coming of the Lord ("Behold, the Lord is coming out of his place, he will come down and tread upon the high places of the earth. Then the mountains will melt under him and the valleys will burst open, like wax near the fire"). See also 1 En. 52.6.

- In 4 Ezra, a messianic figure (cf. "my son" in 13.32–33, 51–52) "will come and speak against" the unrighteousness of Rome (12.31–32)—an interesting repurposing of the ריב tradition from prophetic literature.[104] In the same vein, he then "will set them living before his [that is, the messiah's] judgment seat, and when he has reproved them, then he will destroy them," before also "deliver[ing] in mercy the remnant of my people" (12.33–34). (This "judgment" is not, however, the final judgment, which this text regards as still yet to come.) In the next vision, the messiah is "something like the figure of a man" who rises up from the sea and, per Dan 7:13, "flew with the clouds from heaven" (13.1–3). The text immediately continues, "and wherever he turned his face to look, everything under his gaze trembled, and whenever his voice issued from his mouth, all who heard his voice melted as wax melts when it feels the fire" (13.4). The use of "day of the Lord" imagery for God's own coming is unmistakable here (in addition to Mic 1:3 cited above, cf. Ps 97:5: "melt like wax before the Lord, before the Lord of all the earth"). In the battle that ensues, this figure "neither lifted his hand nor held any spear or any weapon of war, but I saw only how he sent forth from his mouth as it were a stream of fire, and from his lips a flaming breath, and from his tongue a storm of sparks" (4 Ezra 13.9–10). This description is clearly modeled on the famous messianic image of Isa 11:4 (where we read that "with the breath of his lips he shall kill the wicked"), but the fire imagery, not found in Isaiah, draws from descriptions of the Lord's coming (e.g., Ps 18:8), and perhaps even the vision of the Ancient One in Dan 7, where the fire that issues from the throne of God is now linked to the messiah. Perhaps most remarkably, in 13.35, we hear in the interpretation of this vision that "an innumerable multitude will be gathered together . . . desiring to come and conquer him. But he will stand on the top of Mount Zion." This battle, and the distinctive "standing," is clearly

103. Cf. Larry W. Hurtado, *One God, One Lord: Early Christian Devotion and Ancient Jewish Monotheism*, 3rd ed. (London: Bloomsbury T&T Clark, 2015), 53–58: this figure "is seen as performing the eschatological functions associated with God and is therefore God's chief agent, linked with God's work to a specially intense degree" (56).

104. On the rebuke of God when God "comes down," see 2 Sam 22:16 and Ps 18:16, eschatologized in Isa 66:15.

inspired by Zech 13–14, but there it is the "feet" "*of the Lord*" that "will stand upon the Mount of Olives" opposite the temple.[105] It is fitting, in all, that 4 Ezra 13.52 speaks of "his day" with reference to the messiah.[106]

- 2 Baruch uses theophanic language to describe the messiah's advent. He will be "revealed" (29.3; cf. also 39.7), and "at the time of [his] appearance . . . he returns with glory" (30.1).[107] This coincides with the resurrection of the dead (vv. 2–5). As expected of the Lord's coming, "when the time of my Anointed One comes, he will call all nations, and some of them he will spare, and others he will kill" (72.2). As with Pss. Sol. 17, there is probably a specific allusion to Isa 66:15–21 here.[108]
- The description of the coming of the LORD from Edom with garments stained crimson from Isa 63:1–6 was given a messianic interpretation, and linked to the blessing of Judah in Gen 49:8–12 (one of the most influential messianic passages in the Hebrew Bible). This interpretation was known to the writer of Revelation (19:11–16) and appears in all the Palestinian targumim except Onqelos.[109]
- Fragmentary Targum and Targum Pseudo-Jonathan on Numbers provide more detail about the content of the lost prophecy of Eldad and Modad (Num 11:26).[110] According to both, they had talked about the final battle of Gog and Magog (cf. Ezek 39:9–10) and, in the Fragmentary Targum, that the enemies of Israel shall "fall by the hand of king messiah." Targum Pseudo-Jonathan depicts the battle in this way: "But the Lord shall be ready for them by burning the breath of life out of them with the flame of fire that issues from beneath the throne of glory." The manner of battle reminds of God's manner of slaying Nadab and Abihu according to Lev 10:1–3.[111]

105. This might be encouraged by the reading of Zech 13–14 alongside the "battle" of Ps 2 (which the author knew; cf. 4 Ezra 13.32, 35–37), where it is plain that God and the anointed one operate together and are opposed together (e.g., the nations rage "against the Lord and his anointed").

106. For further discussion, see Michael E. Stone, "The Question of the Messiah in 4 Ezra," in Neusner, Green, and Frerichs, *Judaisms and Their Messiahs at the Turn of the Christian Era*, 209–24; Bühner, *Messianic High Christology*, 79–82.

107. Chester, *Messiah and Exaltation*, 348, calls the language theophanic.

108. In support of this, note "I will set a sign among them" in Isa 66:19 and 2 Bar. 70.7, right before the above cited, "the Most High will then give a sign to those nations he has prepared before. . . ."

109. See Roger Syrén, *The Blessings in the Targums: A Study on the Targumic Interpretations of Genesis 49 and Deuteronomy 33* (Åbo: Åbo Akademi, 1986), 111–12.

110. For a tentative reconstruction, see Dale C. Allison Jr., "Eldad and Modad," *JSP* 21 (2011): 99–131.

111. Samson Levey, *The Messiah: An Aramaic Interpretation* (Cincinnati: Hebrew Union Col-

- Deuteronomy 30:4 predicts that "even if you [Israel] are exiled to the ends of the world, from there the LORD your God will gather you, and from there he will bring you back. The LORD your God will bring you into the land," emphasizing the agency of God. In Targum Pseudo-Jonathan, however, this happens "by the hand of Elijah" and "by the hand of king messiah."
- Micah 2:12–13 has God predict ingathering with the repeated use of the first person ("I"), concluding with a classic case of poetic parallelism: "Their king will pass on before them, the LORD at their head." The LORD, here, is the king. But in Targum Micah, this is "a king," the messiah.[112] See also Tg. Mic. 4.8.
- Habakkuk ends with a rousing prediction of the "coming" of God to "tread the earth," to punish, and to save (3:1–16), concluding with a note about the prophet rejoicing and exulting in the LORD (vv. 18–19) even should troubles persist in the present (v. 17). Targum Habakkuk rewrites v. 18 to make clear that this earlier coming also involved God's messiah, while the original text never stated that clearly: "Therefore they shall give praise for the sign and deliverance which you will perform for your Anointed One and for the remnant of your people who are left."[113]
- Lamentations 4:22 predicts coming punishment on Edom, apparently from the hand of God, but in the targum, this will come from the messiah.

Andrew Chester for good reason wrote the following: "in the case of Qumran, so also with Judaism more generally, hope and deliverance rest fully and ultimately with God; he can act via a specific form of agency, or he can act directly by himself. Hence also to play off texts that speak of direct divine action or deliverance against those that have a 'messianic' figure is misplaced."[114] We should also emphasize just how closely many of these passages parallel the intertextuality of New Testament

lege, 1974), 150 n. 47, has noted that "Lord" here appears not as the typical ייי used for God but rather קירים, which is "perhaps a veiled messianic hint."

112. A similar messianic interpretation of this passage appears in Gen. Rab. 48.10; Lev. Rab. 32.8; Qoh. Rab. 4.1.

113. *ArBib* 14:161. For additional discussion of messianism in the targumim, see Bruce D. Chilton, *The Glory of Israel* (Sheffield: JSOT Press, 1982), 86–96, 112–17; Torleif Elgvin, *Warrior, King, Servant, Savior: Messianism in the Hebrew Bible and Early Jewish Texts* (Grand Rapids: Eerdmans, 2022), 292–98.

114. Chester, *Messiah and Exaltation*, 296. See Bühner, *Messianic High Christology*, 49–64, 123–42. Also Wendebourg, *Der Tag des Herrn*, 160 (on judgment and mediator figures). For an influential example of the "playing off" that Chester here decries, see Vielhauer, "Gottesreich und Menschensohn in der Verkündigung Jesu," 55–91, whose arguments rely heavily on the theological supposition that Jesus's proclamation was so theocentric that there is no space left for an intermediary figure.

texts when they describe the future coming of Jesus. In several cases, we are even dealing with the same "day of the Lord" passages, notably from Zechariah and Isaiah. Perhaps the most remarkable parallels in this respect emerge in the Similitudes of Enoch and 4 Ezra. As noted in part 1, Glasson claimed these two texts were essentially irrelevant for the reconstruction of Christian origins and ultimately out of bounds for consideration by virtue of their post-70 date[115]—a fact more or less sure for 4 Ezra,[116] while still highly disputed for the Similitudes (and the tide on this question has dramatically fluctuated in recent years, with most critics now arguing they are pre-70).[117] Even if, however, a later first-century date for the Similitudes is preferred (I remain unsure about this), we are still dealing here with very ancient texts that are nearly contemporaneous with New Testament texts. It is methodologically precarious and historically specious to allow the hypothetical dating of texts so near the origins of Christianity to determine the date and value (for comparative purposes) of the traditions that they contain. Are we really to think that the events of 70 created such messianic intertextuality ex nihilo (which we know is not true, since Paul and the Dead Sea Scrolls already provide attestation) or, even more incredibly, that it was borrowed from the Jesus movement itself?[118]

A twofold conclusion follows from the above-referenced passages that requires some nuance as it pertains to our topic. On the one hand, it was hardly a novel

115. See Glasson, "Theophany and Parousia," 262–63. For a similarly dismissive attitude, see Leivestad, "Exit the Apocalyptic Son of Man," 246–48; Thomas Kazen, "The Coming Son of Man Revisited," *JSHJ* 5 (2007): 160.

116. See Stone, *Fourth Ezra*, 1–11.

117. Cf. George W. E. Nickelsburg and James C. VanderKam, *1 Enoch 2*, Hermeneia (Minneapolis: Fortress, 2012), 58–64 (with extensive bibliography); Darrell L. Bock and James H. Charlesworth, eds., *Parables of Enoch: A Paradigm Shift* (London: Bloomsbury T&T Clark, 2013); Darrell D. Hannah, "The Elect Son of Man in the Parables of Enoch," in Hurtado and Owen, *'Who Is This Son of Man?'*, 133–34: "Today most would place the Parables at the turn of the eras, while a significant minority would argue for later in the first century AD." Hannah also rightly notes that, while much is sometimes made of the absence of the similitudes from the cache at Qumran, the significance of that must be tempered by the fact that we have recovered only a tiny portion of what was originally there (134). See also Loren T. Stuckenbruck and Gabriele Boccaccini, "Introduction: 1 Enoch and the Synoptic Gospels: The Method and Benefits of a Conversation," in Stuckenbruck and Boccaccini, *Enoch and the Synoptic Gospels*, 6–8; Olegs Andrejevs, "The Background of the Term 'Son of Man' in Light of Recent Research," *ExpTim* 130 (2019): 480: "Currently, the consensus of scholars studying this document is that it was composed at the turn of the era" and "predates the activity of the historical Jesus."

118. One should note that, while there is debate about whether 1 Enoch and 4 Ezra expect readers who understand "son of man" in a titular sense (see discussion in Stone, "Question of the Messiah in 4 Ezra," 213, and Collins, "Son of Man in Ancient Judaism," 1558–63), it seems clear that both texts expect readers who know and bring a working knowledge of Dan 7.

idea to expect that a coming redeemer figure would join or coparticipate in what the prophets had expected about God's future "day." What we find in the New Testament about Jesus and the future, then, is not necessarily the unique product of an exalted κύριος Christology possible only after the resurrection experiences.[119] (Of course, I imagine that some critics would want to pause here and challenge Glasson's christological premise, arguing that the historical Jesus himself had held a divine self-conception. But that is not my argument, nor is it necessary to make my case.) On the other hand, there is nothing here that would suggest the existence of a standard scenario about a coming messiah or redeemer figure. For historians working in this area, this fact is by now well known.[120] This is important for our purposes because it suggests that, while Christian claims about Jesus are readily understandable and plausible within extant patterns of scriptural exegesis, they are by no means necessary simply on the basis of a messianic claim itself. We still need to explain *why* Jesus followers believed what they did about Jesus and the future so early and ubiquitously, when there were other options available.

Daniel 7 Once Again

Third, it is probable that the answer to our question ("what are the conditions and presuppositions that made early Christian exegesis about the day of the Lord possible?") has to do with the teaching of the historical Jesus, if for no other reason than, as already argued, his eschatological proclamation was inspired by Dan 7. The phrase "day of the Lord" does not appear in Dan 7, but the vision describes a climactic manifestation of the Ancient One (so v. 9: "thrones were set in place, and the Ancient One took his throne," followed by a description of his appearance), the opening of the books for judgment, the twin arms of punishment and salvation.[121] Moreover, the participation of the one like a son of man in that eschatological theophany is crucial for the vision as a whole. Daniel makes the startling discovery that the glory, dominion, and kingship—all appropriate, we might say, for the Lord and creator of all that is—are "given" to the one like a son of man and the holy ones he either represents or is identified with (7:13–14, 18, 27). It is not an accident

119. John J. Collins, *The Apocalyptic Imagination*, 2nd ed. (Grand Rapids: Eerdmans, 1998), 263, concerning 1 Enoch and 4 Ezra: "There is no reason in principle why Jesus should not have made similar use of Daniel 7."

120. Cf. Frey, "Continuity and Discontinuity between 'Jesus' and 'Christ,'" 88–89.

121. Contra Dunn, *Jesus Remembered*, 757, who writes that it is "obvious" that the setting of Dan 7:9–14 is in heaven. More on this at pp. 360–61 below.

that, in the reception of Dan 7, the roles and appearances of the son of man figure and the Ancient One are blurred in rather startling ways.[122]

We should further note that, in several of those climactic gospel texts that speak of Jesus's future coming by evoking different Old Testament passages about the day of the Lord, Dan 7 is present as the middle term.

Saying of Jesus	**Old Testament Scripture**
Mark 8:38 // Luke 9:26	Dan 7:13 + Zech 14:5's angels
Mark 13:24–27	Dan 7:13 + Isa 13:10; 34:4; Joel 2:10 (4:15)'s cosmic signs
Matt 13:41–43	Dan 7:13 + Zech 14:5's angels; "gathering" language (cf. Isa 27:1, Ps 50:4–5)
Matt 16:27	Dan 7:13 + Zech 14:5's angels + biblical trope about God's judgment[123]
Q 17:24	Dan 7:13 + lightning image (cf. Ps 97:4; Zech 9:14)[124]
Matt 25:31–32	Dan 7:13 + Zech 14:5's angels + Isa 66:18's "gathering" ("I am coming to gather all the nations")[125]

122. So, e.g., perhaps, the Old Greek of Dan 7:13 (where the son of man comes <u>ὡς</u> παλαιὸς ἡμερῶν, as opposed to <u>ἕως</u> τοῦ παλαιοῦ τῶν ἡμερῶν in Θ). On the question whether the Old Greek's ὡς is intentional or was made in error, see discussion and literature in Bogdan Gabriel Bucur, *Scripture Re-envisioned: Christophanic Exegesis and the Making of a Christian Bible* (Leiden: Brill, 2019), 208–46. Note also Mark 8:38–9:8 and parr. (on Jesus coming "in the glory of the Father"); cf. Joshua E. Leim, "In the Glory of His Father: Intertextuality and the Apocalyptic Son of Man in the Gospel of Mark," *JTS* 7 (2013): 213–22. See, too, Rev 1:12–16 (on the appearance of Jesus).

123. The phrase τότε [the son of man] ἀποδώσει ἑκάστῳ κατὰ τὴν πρᾶξιν αὐτοῦ, unique to Matthew's version, is a biblical trope concerning the judgment of God (cf. Ps 62:13; Eccl 3:22; Prov 24:12) and need not point to one specific passage (though see Rev 22:6, which gets it from Isa 40:10). But on its import, note LAB 3.10, where God says after the flood, "when the years appointed for the world have been fulfilled, then the light will cease and the darkness will fade away. And I will bring the dead to life and raise up those who are sleeping from the earth. . . . I will render to each according to his work."

124. See also the association between lightning and God's coming down in Exod 19:16 (cf. Philo, *Mos.* 2.56; LAB 11.4); Ps 18:14; 144:6. Lightning also appears to be associated with the messiah's coming (down) in 2 Bar. 53.8–11; cf. 72.1–73.1.

125. This is a popular image for the day of the Lord. Cf. also Joel 3:2, 11–12; Zech 3:8; 14:2; 4 Ezra 7.33–37 (where it is "the Most High" on "the seat of judgment"). In 2 Bar. 72.1–3, it is associated with the messiah's advent. In T. Benj. 9.2–3, the phrase is associated with the "sending forth of [God's] salvation through the ministration of the unique prophet."

It is not necessary to argue that these sayings go back to Jesus as written, though we should not be too hasty in rejecting that possibility. E. P. Sanders, despite his skepticism about the sayings tradition, linked 1 Thess 4:15–17, Matt 16:27, and Mark 8:38 and argued that we have multiple attestation.[126] He suggested that the core idea behind these sayings goes back to Jesus: "ordinarily . . . this kind of attestation counts in favour of authenticity."[127] He further acknowledged a double standard in historical Jesus scholarship here: "the general tendency in recent scholarship has been to give it [referring in this case to Matt 16:27; Luke 9:26; and Mark 8:38] little weight in depictions of Jesus . . . but I fear that it has receded in importance not so much because it has been proved to have played a small role in Jesus' message as because of scholarly preference for less dramatic material."[128]

Nevertheless, I only need to stress this point: if Jesus believed that he was, or would become, that son of man, then associating his coming with the coming of the Lord merely elaborates what is already there.[129] It may well be, in other words, that Jesus himself did not draw on such "day of the Lord" texts in this manner, and such allusions stem from early Christian exegesis of the Old Testament. But that would actually change the resultant image little. Concerning this possibility, I would highlight an important and overlooked fact: the associative logic that binds these mixed scriptural allusions together presupposes that the connective spokes come out from Dan 7.[130] In addition to the thematic cohesion between Dan 7 and these different "day of the Lord" texts, there is for some a word connection—a form of *gezerah shava*—that likely further encouraged such exegetical linkages. That word is not "Lord"—contra Glasson—but "coming" (from ἔρχομαι). And in every instance, the "coming" appears in conjunction with Dan 7, not the other "day of the Lord" texts:

126. Sanders, *Jesus and Judaism*, 144–45. Sanders argues that Matt 16:27 in its difference from Mark is not due to redaction.

127. Sanders, *Jesus and Judaism*, 145.

128. Sanders, *Jesus and Judaism*, 143. Fredriksen, *Jesus of Nazareth*, 78–80, and Yarbro Collins and Collins, *King and Messiah as Son of God*, 172, have likewise suggested that the saying could go back to Jesus.

129. Note John Goldingay, *Daniel*, WBC 30 (Dallas: Word, 1989), 167: "The court is seated on earth (vv. 9–10), and 'among the clouds of the heavens' denotes the position of the figure about to be described as it moves toward that court. The description then compares with the coming of God to earth in, e.g., Isa 19:1; Ps 18:10–13."

130. Some have suggested that, in the dual citation from Ps 110 and Dan 7 in Mark 14:62 and parr., there are clues that the Dan 7 reference is primary and Ps 110:1 has been supplemented to it. See discussion and literature in Dunn, *Jesus Remembered*, 750.

Mark 8:38 // Luke 9:26:	ὁ υἱὸς τοῦ ἀνθρώπου	. . . ὅταν ἔλθῃ
Matt 16:27:	μέλλει γὰρ ὁ υἱὸς τοῦ ἀνθρώπου	ἔρχεσθαι
Mark 13:26:	ὄψονται τὸν υἱὸν τοῦ ἀνθρώπου	ἐρχόμενον
Luke 12:40:	ὁ υἱὸς τοῦ ἀνθρώπου	ἔρχεται
Matt 25:31:	[ὁ υἱὸς τοῦ ἀνθρώπου]	[Ὅταν δὲ ἔλθῃ][131]

This pattern includes, also, Mark 14:62 and parallels, though here with no corresponding intertextuality with the "day of the Lord" tradition (it is conjoined with Ps 110:1 instead):

Mark 14:62:	ὄψεσθε τὸν υἱὸν τοῦ ἀνθρώπου	. . . ἐρχόμενον

All of this is modeled on the arrangement of Dan 7:13, which appears as follows in our notable versions:

MT:	עם ענני שמיא	כבר אנש	אתה
LXX:	ἐπὶ τῶν νεφελῶν τοῦ οὐρανοῦ	ὡς υἱὸς ἀνθρώπου	ἤρχετο
Θ:	μετὰ τῶν νεφελῶν τοῦ οὐρανοῦ	ὡς υἱὸς ἀνθρώπου	ἐρχόμενος ἦν[132]

The preservation of this Danielic detail is, moreover, not unique to the Gospels in the reception of Dan 7:13–14.[133]

My contention, then, is that the "coming" from Dan 7 is primary in these intertextual connections, and roads to various other texts emerge from and out of Dan 7, rather than end back at Dan 7 from somewhere else.[134]

131. Order of the phrases is inverted.

132. Justin Martyr in *Dial.* 31 has ἐρχόμενος καὶ ἦλθεν.

133. Cf. Sib. Or. 5.414–415: "there came from the expanses of heaven [ἦλθε γὰρ οὐρανίων νώτων] a blessed man [ἀνὴρ μακαρίτης] having a scepter in his hands, which God had given to him, and he seized all things well." Other texts, while they substitute Dan 7's אתה or ἔρχομαι for another verb, nevertheless were interested in the movement envisaged here. Cf. John 3:13 ("the one who has come down from heaven [ὁ ἐκ τοῦ οὐρανοῦ καταβάς], the son of man"); 4 Ezra 13.3 ("something like the figure of a man . . . that man flew with the clouds of heaven").

134. It also must be remembered that as messianic speculation was largely biblical exegesis (so Novenson, *Grammar of Messianism*, 1, 13–14, and others), texts were routinely, if not ordinarily, read together with others in hopes to clarify and expound them. Note, e.g., that in 1 Enoch and 4 Ezra, the son of man is given messianic attributes from Ps 2 and eschatological tasks from

John the Baptist

Last, we can be assured that the conceptual linkage between Jesus and the coming day of the Lord has traction in the pre-Easter period because of the activity of John the Baptist. According to the Synoptics, John not only anticipated the coming wrath and salvation of God as expected on the Lord's day, he predicted that a fiery baptism to come would be mediated by "the coming one" (ὁ ἐρχόμενος), "the stronger one" ([ὁ] ἰσχυρότερός), the one whose sandals John is not worthy to loosen (cf. Luke 3:16 and Matt 3:11; cf. Luke 7:19 and Matt 11:3). Some have argued that the historical John merely predicted the advent of God, and it was Jesus's followers who made him predict a human figure so that it might be fulfilled in their own messiah, Jesus.[135] But this is a weak argument. The titles John uses are not distinctive of the later Jesus movement,[136] the language is more befitting a human figure than God (especially the memorable sandals saying, which is nonsensical if not irreverent if used for God), and it is hard otherwise to explain why Christians would take such efforts to claim John as the forerunner of Jesus and think it carried any weight if the entire prediction were their own creation. The claim that Jesus is "the coming one" that John expected is likely a case of forced fulfillment, rather than the outright invention of both prediction and fulfillment.[137]

Deutero-Isaiah (for 1 Enoch, note, e.g., Isa 42:6 and 49:6 in 1 En. 48.4; Isa 42:1 in 1 En. 39.6 and 40.5; Isa 49:2 in 1 En. 48.3 and 62.6–7). For broader discussion, see the valuable essays in Sean A. Adams and Seth M. Ehorn, eds., *Jewish, Greco-Roman, and Early Christian Uses*, vol. 1 of *Composite Citations in Antiquity*, LNTS 525 (London: Bloomsbury T&T Clark, 2016), and Adams and Ehorn, eds., *New Testament Uses*, vol. 2 of *Composite Citations in Antiquity*, LNTS 593 (London: Bloomsbury T&T Clark, 2018).

135. Cf. C. H. Kraeling, *John the Baptist* (New York: Scribner's Sons, 1951), 57; M. Eugene Boring, *Mark: A Commentary* (Louisville: Westminster John Knox, 2006), 41.

136. Quite unlike what we find in the Fourth Gospel, that is: "Behold the lamb of God who takes away the sins of the world!" (John 1:29). Though see also 1:15 (ὁ ὀπίσω μου ἐρχόμενος).

137. Some have wondered whether the language of "the coming one" (ὁ ἐρχόμενος) itself has messianic overtones. In addition to its use in the Synoptics, note John 1:15, 27; 6:14; 11:27 (where a titular meaning may be assumed: σὺ εἶ ὁ χριστὸς ὁ υἱὸς τοῦ θεοῦ ὁ εἰς τὸν κόσμον ἐρχόμενος); 12:13. Other key texts include Ps 118:25–26; Hab 2:3 LXX (Aquila); 1QS IX, 9–11; CD VII, 18–21; XIX, 10–11. Note also Gen 49:10 and its reception in texts such as 4Q252 V, 1–4 ("until the coming of the messiah of righteousness, the branch of David"). For discussion, see Michael F. Bird, *Are You the One Who Is to Come? The Historical Jesus and the Messianic Question* (Grand Rapids: Baker Academic, 2009), 112–14. See also Gerbern S. Oegema, *Apocalyptic Interpretation of the Bible: Apocalypticism and Biblical Interpretation in Early Judaism, the Apostle Paul, the Historical Jesus, and Their Reception History* (London: T&T Clark International, 2012), 64–72 (who explores the language of ἡ ἔλευσις τοῦ δικαίου from Acts 7:52).

As I have argued elsewhere, John almost certainly did *not* point publicly to Jesus as the continuation and fulfillment of his work in the way that Matthew (3:14–15) and the Gospel of John (1:29–34, 36; 3:27–36) maintain, and yet Jesus sought to connect their activities in various ways, often to his own benefit and to bolster his own public reputation.[138]

Should this be on target, it would mean that we have already present in the movement that kickstarted Jesus's own activity an eschatological vision for the future coming of God that involved the unique participation of a special, likely messianic, figure.[139] Some have even argued that John himself was inspired by Dan 7, and "the coming one" was his way of talking about the "coming" son of man. That would make good sense of much of John's language, including the threefold linkage of fire and judgment and baptism (note the "fiery stream" in Dan 7:10). But I ultimately do not believe there is enough extant material about John to say either way with confidence.

The Conversion of the Imagination

Once the association was made between the activity of Jesus and the long-awaited day of the Lord, early Christian texts bear witness to what we might call a conversion of the imagination.[140] The rich and vast "day of the Lord" and "coming of God" tradition in the Old Testament enabled the forging of all sorts of new intertextual connections that were theologically generative. Naturally, such exegesis added new details to early Christian eschatological scenarios and surely shaped their claims about the identity of Jesus in important ways.[141] We might visualize the process in this way:

138. See Ferda, "Historicity of Confusion," 747–67.

139. On John's expectation for a human figure who would act as God's special agent, see Robert L. Webb, *John the Baptizer and Prophet*, JSOT 62 (Sheffield: JSOT Press, 1991), 286; Marcus, *John the Baptist in History and Theology*, 81–82.

140. To borrow the phrase from Richard B. Hays, *The Conversion of the Imagination: Paul as Interpreter of Israel's Scripture* (Grand Rapids: Eerdmans, 2005).

141. Here I agree with Fredriksen, *When Christians Were Jews*, 101: "the more that biblical verses were pressed into this service [of filling out Jesus's messianic identity], the more articulate the shape of Jesus' awaited future appearance grew," while I disagree with the larger argument she is making here about origin.

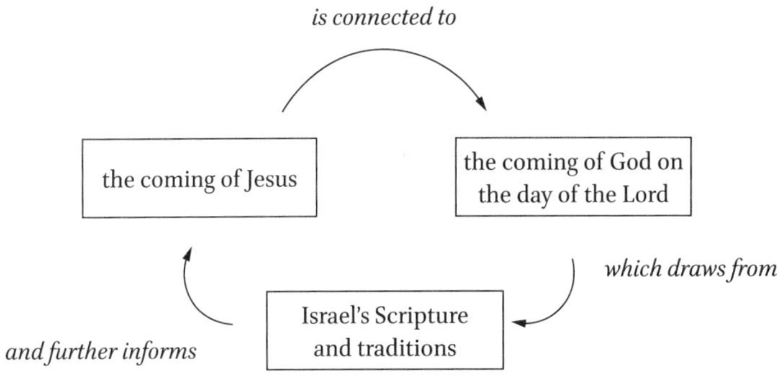

From where we sit as historians, this spiral has already been underway for some time, which any honest assessment must admit makes it challenging to discern which images stem from Jesus and which emerged in the creative, post-Easter activity or rereading Scripture with "opened minds" (so Luke 24:45). But there is nothing inevitable about the fact that we find this kind of messianic exegesis in our sources, and it is not apparent how the resurrection experiences would suddenly create both the interest in and conviction behind such scriptural engagements. In such an argument, Easter would function as "a magic wand that, being waved, somehow explains things."[142] Glasson stated that theophany motifs in Christian claims about the parousia "cannot be explained by anything in the teaching of Jesus but they are clearly from the OT."[143] This statement is not only false in terms of Jesus's proclamation of the kingdom of God, it is an overstatement based on a false distinction (that is, it is not the teaching of Jesus *or* the Old Testament but the teaching of Jesus *and* the Old Testament). And Glasson, too, in the end, is unable to explain where the motive for early Christian exegesis of Scripture comes from.[144]

I think there is before us a more probable historical scenario that is far simpler and makes sense of more data. Jesus, following in the footsteps of John the Baptist's eschatologically laden ministry, believed that he was some kind of special

142. Allison, *Constructing Jesus*, 242 (in critique of Bultmann's argument that Easter made Jesus the messiah).

143. Glasson, "Theophany and Parousia," 261.

144. Arthur L. Moore, *The Parousia in the New Testament*, NovTSup 13 (Leiden: Brill, 1966), 59, makes an important point that is relevant here: "there is a qualitative distinction between recognizing that the early church increasingly applied Old Testament passages to the risen Lord and supposing that, by the application of certain passages to him, the church created for itself a hope foreign to Jesus' teaching."

figure who would have a unique role in the unfolding and arrival of God's expected day. He also was inspired by Dan 7's vision of the coming of God's kingdom and the "one like a son of man," whom he believed himself to be. After his ministry, his followers approached the Scriptures with the conviction that this was true—emboldened by the resurrection experiences—and they discovered in their reading far more than Jesus had said about the future and about himself. Consequently, they remembered his ministry and retold stories about it with the clarity of that later light. They even read *back* into the ministry of Jesus (and found in their own experiences) "day of the Lord" motifs that invested the past with new meaning.[145] This happened particularly with the crucifixion and resurrection of Jesus—so the darkness at noon, earthquakes, and so on—as has been noted by others.[146] But it was the prior association between Jesus's activity and the eschatological coming of God that enabled the kinds of scriptural connections that they made. The Scriptures, themselves, did not create them. Put otherwise, the early Christians did not approach Scripture with the future of Jesus as the question and go to Scripture to find the answer. They approached Scripture with Jesus as the answer, and Scripture filled out, and further informed, what they already believed to be true. That is why and how they found Jesus in passages that had nothing to do with him and probably would not have suggested anything more unless one were looking for it. One recalls here what Joseph Klausner once wrote: "*a passage of Scripture* (unless it indicates a certain fact with complete clarity) *does not create a new idea; but the new idea, which is already emerging, finds proof and support in the Scriptural passage.*"[147] Klausner misstated this as a general truth, but it does appear to apply in our case.

I imagine that Schweitzer and several other more recent critics would find much to applaud in this chapter, and perhaps part 4 as a whole so far, but reply

145. Examples, we might say, of "reinterpretation" that grapple with "cognitive dissonance" in eschatological expectation, to borrow language from the famous study by John G. Gager, *Kingdom and Community: The Social World of Early Christianity* (Englewood Cliffs, NJ: Prentice Hall, 1975), 20–49.

146. Cf., e.g., Douglas J. Moo, *The Old Testament in the Gospel Passion Narrative* (Sheffield: Almond, 1983), 173–224; Dale C. Allison Jr., *The End of the Ages Has Come: An Early Interpretation of the Passion and Resurrection of Jesus* (Philadelphia: Fortress, 1985), 115–41; Mark Black, "The Messianic Use of Zechariah 9–14 in Matthew, Mark, and the Pre-Markan Tradition," in *Scripture and Traditions: Essays on Early Judaism and Christianity in Honor of Carl R. Holladay*, ed. Patrick Gray and Gail R. O'Day, NovTSup 129 (Leiden: Brill, 2008), 97–114. For a helpful chart of Zechariah connections in Mark, see Gathercole, *Gospel and the Gospels*, 124.

147. Joseph Klausner, *The Messianic Idea in Israel: From Its Beginning to the Completion of the Mishnah*, 3rd ed., trans. W. F. Stinespring (New York: Macmillan, 1955), 485.

that I have not yet demonstrated that Jesus expected a future coming after death in the way that the Gospels presume. That is true. Based on what I have argued so far, one could conclude that Jesus expected to be revealed as Dan 7's son of man during his lifetime, and he had taught that the day of the Lord would arrive before he himself had tasted death. What are we to say about these things?

14

Death, Interim, Resurrection, and the Sitz im Leben Jesu

Despite my critiques of other origin stories about the second-coming hope,[1] these alternative scenarios become, if not suddenly more plausible, at least necessary, should it be true that there are even more insurmountable difficulties with tracing the idea to Jesus himself. Julius Wellhausen named a potential big one: "If it is true that Jesus did not in advance teach his disciples of his death and resurrection, it is even more certain that he did not teach about his parousia."[2] The argument is that because the predictions of Jesus's death and resurrection are clearly *ex eventu*, and the parousia requires Jesus being dead, raised, and gone, it follows that the parousia hope must originate after the time of Jesus.

Does not Wellhausen have a point? He most certainly does. The apostle Paul and many in the movement before him believed that, when Christ returns, and the general resurrection of the dead commences, Jesus himself comes in his risen glory.[3] "We will also bear the image of the man of heaven," Paul wrote to the Corinthians, expecting "all will be changed" to assume the form Christ has already (1 Cor 15:49–51). But I imagine there are very few critical scholars who would want to argue that the Jesus of history expected his individual resurrection before the

1. See pp. 274–82 above.

2. Cited by Werner Georg Kümmel, *The New Testament: The History of the Investigation of Its Problems*, 2nd ed., trans. S. McLean Gilmour and Howard C. Kee (Nashville: Abingdon, 1972), 283.

3. Though this was not, evidently, a universal view. More on this below.

general resurrection of the dead.[4] The threefold passion and resurrection predictions are highly suspect as they conveniently predict what exactly took place in Jerusalem (Mark 8:31, 9:30–32, 10:32–34, and parr.);[5] the resurrection of the dead was a corporate event for the end time, it seems, not something that would happen to individuals before that time;[6] and the followers of Jesus, after his death, were certainly not acting as though their teacher had told them multiple times that he would rise again after three days according to the plan of God. These are old arguments, around since the time of Reimarus and Strauss, and they are still compelling.[7]

4. Contra Hans F. Bayer, *Jesus' Predictions of Vindication and Resurrection*, WUNT 2/20 (Tübingen: Mohr Siebeck, 1986), who argues that Jesus expected an interim between his own individual resurrection from the dead and the eschaton. Contra also Oscar Cullmann, "Die Hoffnung der Kirche auf die Wiederkunft Christi nach dem Neuen Testament" (1944), in *Vorträge und Aufsätze 1925–1962*, ed. K. Fröhlich (Tübingen: Mohr Siebeck, 1966), 378–402; Christian Stettler, *Das letzte Gericht: Studien zur Endgerichtserwartung von den Schriftpropheten bis Jesus*, WUNT 2/299 (Tübingen: Mohr Siebeck, 2011), 235–36. On this point I also disagree with Werner Georg Kümmel, whose overall conclusions about the origins of the second-coming hope are informative and are much closer to my own than many other modern critics. In *Promise and Fulfillment: The Eschatological Message of Jesus*, trans. Dorothea M. Barton, 2nd ed. (London: SCM, 1961), Kümmel argues that Jesus expected the near arrival of the kingdom, by which he meant a transformed world, as this would be marked by the resurrection of the dead, the final judgment, and the coming/return of the son of man. But Kümmel contends that Jesus predicted his own individual resurrection from the dead, linked to the predictions of coming suffering and death, which is quite unlikely. It is also problematic for Kümmel's case that his approach is atomistic and follows a predictable pattern: he identifies individual sayings, asserts they are detached sayings and thus stem from earlier tradition, claims they are historical, and then paints a larger portrait of Jesus's eschatological teaching from them.

5. So Rudolf Bultmann, *History of the Synoptic Tradition*, trans. John Marsh, 5th ed. (Peabody, MA: Hendrickson, 1963), 152; Bultmann, *Theology of the New Testament*, trans. Kendrick Grobel (New York: Scribner's Sons, 1955), 1:29; Gerd Theissen and Annette Merz, *The Historical Jesus: A Comprehensive Guide*, trans. John Bowden (Minneapolis: Fortress, 1998), 550–52; Paula Fredriksen, *When Christians Were Jews* (New Haven: Yale University Press, 2018), 75–76.

6. Lidija Novakovic, *Resurrection: A Guide for the Perplexed* (London: Bloomsbury T&T Clark, 2016), 43: "There is not a single text that envisions the resurrection of a single individual ahead of the general resurrection, however holy and righteous that person may be, and there is not a single text that envisions the resurrection of the Messiah." See also N. T. Wright, *The Resurrection of the Son of God* (Minneapolis: Fortress, 2003), 204.

7. Hermann Samuel Reimarus, *Reimarus: Fragments*, ed. Charles H. Talbert, trans. Ralph S. Fraser (Chico, CA: Scholars Press, 1985), 165–66; David Friedrich Strauss, *The Life of Jesus Critically Examined*, trans. George Eliot, 4th ed. (London: Sonnenschein, 1902), 567, 574 (the conduct of the disciples "speaks against such a prediction on the part of Jesus"), 582 ("the foreknowledge, as well as the prediction of the resurrection, was attributed to Jesus only after the issue"). See also Joseph Klausner, *The Messianic Idea in Israel: From Its Beginning to the Completion of the*

In addition to the question of the death and resurrection of Jesus, there is a closely related stumbling block for many: the unlikelihood that Jesus expected an interim period after his death and before the consummation of the kingdom. Is it not true that to admit an interim period destroys the entire apocalyptic character of the early Christian movement? Is it not to sacrifice an eschatological Jesus in favor of the old nineteenth-century lives of Jesus, or even for the view of Timothee Colani, who thought Jesus expected the kingdom to "triumph little by little in the world"?[8]

All historians are faced with the task of discerning the proper historical relationship between the parousia hope and (1) the death of Jesus, (2) the question of an interim period, and (3) the claim of Jesus's individual resurrection from the dead, for the simple reason that all appear in the only sources that we have. This chapter will take up these matters, in that order, and argue that not only is there a fitting *Sitz im Leben Jesu* for the hope for Jesus's future coming to emerge before Easter, but recognizing that ends up unraveling other knots in the study of Christian origins.

The Prospect of Death

First, death. Albert Schweitzer noted that you can divide the old lives of Jesus in two based upon how they answer the question of why Jesus went up to Jerusalem at the end: to work or to die.[9] Schweitzer pressed hard for the latter, even suggesting that Jesus, as determined by his eschatological beliefs, staged the temple incident to put himself deliberately in harm's way. This idiosyncratic reconstruction has convinced few.[10] But the question whether Jesus expected to die, or, at least,

---

Mishnah, 3rd ed., trans. W. F. Stinespring (New York: Macmillan, 1955), 358; Cecil J. Cadoux, *The Historic Mission of Jesus* (London: Lutterworth, 1941), 286 ("the fact that they were completely taken by surprise forces us to ask whether Jesus really did say and mean that he would rise from the dead on the third day, in the literal sense of the words"); David E. Aune, *Prophecy in Early Christianity and the Ancient Mediterranean World* (Grand Rapids: Eerdmans, 1983), 177–79 (who also recalls here the important motif in Greco-Roman folklore about heroes being able to predict their own death). Contra Wright, *Resurrection of the Son of God*, 408–11 (though he does not contend the predictions are verbatim reports); Craig S. Keener, *The Historical Jesus of the Gospels* (Grand Rapids: Eerdmans, 2009), 289.

8. Timothee Colani, *Jésus-Christ et les croyances messianiques de son temps*, 2nd ed. (Strasbourg: Treuttel & Wurtz, 1864), 100.

9. Albert Schweitzer, *The Quest of the Historical Jesus*, trans. William Montgomery (New York: Macmillan, 1950), 388–92.

10. Though see one of the last essays from Ulrich Luz, "Der unbequeme Jesus. Nochmals:

was aware of the possibility that he might die in Jerusalem, is another matter and also distinct from the question of the authenticity of Mark 8:31, 9:30–32, 10:32–34, and parallels (which were clearly formulated after the fact).[11] Christians very early on were convinced that Jesus's death was meaningful, and they devised all kinds of different explanations not only to excuse the cross but to explain how it was actually fundamental to his mission.[12] We should be leery of tracing all of these claims and their supporting scriptural exegeses back to Jesus. But it remains unlikely that Jesus's death in Jerusalem caught him by complete surprise,[13] and he may have made some sense of it beforehand. In making this case, I follow initially C. H. Dodd, who wrote,

> We may observe (1) that the whole prophetic and apocalyptic tradition, which Jesus certainly recognized, anticipated tribulation for the people of God before the final triumph of the good cause; (2) that the history of many centuries had deeply implanted the idea that the prophet is called to suffering as a part of his mission; (3) that the death of John the Baptist had shown that his fate was still part of the prophetic calling; (4) that it needed, not supernatural prescience, but the ordinary insight of an intelligent person, to see whither things were tending, at least during the later stages of the ministry.[14]

We might briefly expand on a few of these arguments that add up to a weighty case.[15] The notion of an eschatological tribulation—that things will get worse for

---

Warum zog Jesus nach Jerusalem?," in *Exegetische Aufsätze*, WUNT 357 (Tübingen: Mohr Siebeck, 2016), 133–48, who explicitly tries to resurrect Schweitzer's thesis. Rather than find this Jesus noble, as did Schweitzer, Luz admits at the end that he finds this frightening. See his probing conclusion at 147–48.

11. As already discussed. Cf. Strauss, *Life of Jesus*, 567, and helpful overview in Raymond E. Brown, *The Death of the Messiah*, ABRL (New York: Doubleday, 1994), 2:1473–82.

12. See Marinus de Jonge, *God's Final Envoy: Early Christology and Jesus' Own View of His Mission* (Grand Rapids: Eerdmans, 1998), 12–33; Barry D. Smith, *The Meaning of Jesus' Death: Reviewing the New Testament's Interpretations* (London: Bloomsbury T&T Clark, 2017).

13. Helpful here is Joachim Gnilka, "Wie urteilte Jesus über seinen Tod?," in *Der Tod Jesu*, ed. Johannes Beutler and Karl Kertelge, QD 74 (Freiburg: Herder, 1976), 13–50, who distinguishes between readiness for death (Todesbereitschaft) and certainty of death (Todesgewissheit). Earlier, see Benjamin Bacon, *The Story of Jesus and the Beginnings of the Church* (New York: Century, 1927), 217. See also Heinz Schürmann, *Jesus, Gestalt und Geheimnis: Gesammelte Beiträge*, ed. Klaus Scholtissek (Paderborn: Bonifatius, 1994), 161–62 ("Jesus angesichts dieses seines Engagements mit der *Möglichkeit* eines gewaltsamen Todes realistisch rechnen mußte").

14. C. H. Dodd, *The Parables of the Kingdom*, rev. ed. (New York: Scribner's Sons, 1961), 40.

15. Other important studies that reach a similar conclusion include Raymond E. Brown, "How Much Did Jesus Know?," *CBQ* 29 (1967): 9–39; Leonhard Goppelt, *Jesu Wirken in seiner*

the people of God before they get better—is widespread in Second Temple Judaism and, as others have argued convincingly, finds several points of contact in the Jesus tradition.[16] Moreover, there may be a connection here to some of the work we have already done on Dan 7. In Daniel's dream vision, he describes not just the destruction and oppression caused by the beasts that arise from the sea but a particularly climactic suffering caused by the fourth beast right before the "giving" of the kingdom (7:23–27 NRSV, modified):

> [the fourth beast] shall devour the whole earth,
> And trample it down, and break it to pieces . . .
> [and the little horn] shall speak words against the Most High,
> [and] shall wear out the holy ones of the Most High. . . .
> And they shall be given [from יהב] into his hand [בידה] for a time,
> two times, and half a time.

---

theologischen Bedeutung (Göttingen: Vandenhoeck & Ruprecht, 1976), 234–47; Jostein Ådna, *Jesu Stellung zum Tempel: die Tempelaktion und das Tempelwort als Ausdruck seiner messianischen Sendung*, WUNT 2/119 (Tübingen: Mohr Siebeck, 2000), 412–19; E. P. Sanders, *The Historical Figure of Jesus* (London: Penguin Books, 1993), 264 ("Jesus knew he was a marked man"); Theissen and Merz, *Historical Jesus*, 359–83; Scot McKnight, *Jesus and His Death: Historiography, the Historical Jesus, and Atonement Theory* (Waco, TX: Baylor University Press, 2005); James D. G. Dunn, *Jesus Remembered* (Grand Rapids: Eerdmans, 2003), 796–805; Michael Patrick Barber, "Did Jesus Anticipate Suffering a Violent Death? The Implications of Memory Research and Dale C. Allison's Methodology," *JSHJ* 18 (2020): 191–219. For other views, see David E. Aune, "Christian Beginnings and Cognitive Dissonance Theory," in *Jesus, the Gospel Tradition and Paul in the Context of Jewish and Greco-Roman Antiquity*, WUNT 303 (Tübingen: Mohr Siebeck, 2013), 165 (on "the unanticipated execution of Jesus"); Dale Martin, "Jesus in Jerusalem: Armed and Not Dangerous," *JSNT* 37 (2014): 19–20; Fernando Bermejo Rubio, "The Day of the LORD Is Coming: Jesus and the Book of Zechariah," in *Jesus and the Scriptures: Problems, Passages and Patterns*, ed. Tobias Hägerland, LNTS 552 (London: Bloomsbury T&T Clark, 2016), 111–31; Arthur J. Dewey, *Inventing the Passion: How the Death of Jesus Was Remembered* (Salem: Polebridge, 2017), 26.

16. For some important texts, see Dan 12:1–2; Jub. 23.1–31; T. Mos. 9.1–7; 4Q171 II, 9–12; 4Q174 1 I, 18–19; 1, II, 1–8; 1QH III, 7–10; CD XIX, 7–10 (which also draws on Zech 13:7); Pss. Sol. 17.11–20; 1 En. 94–99; 4 Ezra 5.1–13; 9.1–4; 2 Bar. 25–29; 70–72; m. Soṭa 9.15. Cf. Joachim Jeremias, *New Testament Theology: The Proclamation of Jesus*, trans. John Bowden (New York: Scribner's Sons, 1971), 127–31, 241–44; Dale C. Allison Jr., "Q 12:51–53 and Mark 9:11–13 and the Messianic Woes," in *Authenticating the Words of Jesus*, ed. Bruce Chilton and Craig A. Evans (Leiden: Brill, 2002), 289–310; Brant Pitre, *Jesus, the Tribulation, and the End of the Exile: Restoration Eschatology and the Origin of the Atonement*, WUNT 204 (Tübingen: Mohr Siebeck; Grand Rapids: Baker Books, 2005), 163–76, 180–86, 212–16.

> Then the court shall sit in judgment,
> And his dominion shall be taken away, to be consumed and totally destroyed.
> The kingship and dominion . . . shall be given [from יהב] to the holy ones of the Most High; their kingdom shall be an everlasting kingdom.

There is more going on in Dan 7 than the giving of God's kingdom and power and glory. Daniel expects not just a limited time of intense suffering but suffering for precisely those who inherit the kingdom at the time of the judgment (the timeline harkens back to Dan 7:9, and the son of man bestowal scene at 7:13–14). This was not lost on later interpreters. In 4Q246, we find (II, 1–5),

> He will be called the son of God, and the son of the Most High they will call him. As the comets of the vision, thus their kingdom will be, years they will rule on the land and everything they will trample. People will trample people and province [will trample] province, until he will raise up the people of God and everyone will rest from the sword. His kingdom is an eternal kingdom and all his paths in truth. He will judge the earth and all will make peace.[17]

What is particularly interesting about this passage is that the recognition of this "son of God"—a positive figure—comes *before* the time of suffering caused by this alternative kingdom, the descriptions of which are drawn directly from Dan 7 (for "trample" in II, 3, cf. the identical דוש in Dan 7:23). That use of Dan 7 includes the denouement: "his kingdom is an eternal kingdom" (II, 5; see also II, 9: שלטנה שלטן עלם in Dan 7:14, also 4:31 [ET 4:34]). Also noteworthy here is 1 En. 47, where Enoch witnesses the following in heaven (vv. 1–4):

> In those days there had arisen the prayer of the righteous, and the blood of the righteous one, from the earth into the presence of the Lord of Spirits . . . [they] were interceding and praying in behalf of the blood of the righteous that had been shed, and the prayer of the righteous, that it might not be in vain in the presence of the Lord of Spirits; that judgment might be executed for them, and endurance might not be their (lot) forever. In those days I saw the Head of Days as he took his seat on the throne of his glory, and the books of the living were

17. My translation from "Naming the Messiah: A Contribution to the 4Q246 'Son of God' Debate," *DSD* 21 (2014): 152.

> opened in his presence, and all his host, which was in the heights of heaven, and his court, were standing in his presence. And the hearts of the holy ones were filled with joy, for the number of the righteous was at hand; and the prayer of the righteous had been heard, and the blood of the righteous one had been required in the presence of the Lord of Spirits.[18]

The sequence of images is striking: the recognition of the suffering righteous right before the setting up of the throne of the Ancient One and the opening of the books of judgment—descriptions clearly inspired by Dan 7.[19]

In this light, we might, along with T. W. Manson, Morna Hooker, and others, take a closer look at those clearly *ex eventu* passion and resurrection traditions in Mark and parallels.[20] For amid these conspicuous predictions, it is noteworthy that all of them are in touch with Dan 7, and not for the details of what happened to Jesus but their framing:[21]

18. Translation from George W. E. Nickelsburg and James C. VanderKam, *1 Enoch: A New Translation* (Minneapolis: Fortress, 2004).

19. Cf. George W. E. Nickelsburg and James C. VanderKam, *1 Enoch 2*, Hermeneia (Minneapolis: Fortress, 2012), 163–65. For another text that seems to draw on Daniel to describe the eschatological tribulation, see 1Q33 I, 11–12, which mentions a "time of suffering" and that "of all their sufferings, none will be like this." G. K. Beale, *The Use of Daniel in Jewish Apocalyptic Literature and in the Revelation of St. John* (Eugene, OR: Wipf & Stock, 2010), 71, argued the reference to animals fighting Israel and causing their distress in the Animal Apocalypse (1 En. 90.11), recalls "Israel's eschatological distress in Daniel 7:21, 25."

20. T. W. Manson, *The Teaching of Jesus: Studies of Its Form and Content*, 2nd ed. (Cambridge: Cambridge University Press, 1935), 229–31; Morna Hooker, *The Son of Man in Mark* (London: SPCK, 1967), 103–9; C. F. D. Moule, *The Origin of Christology* (Cambridge: Cambridge University Press, 1977), 11–22; Jane Schaberg, "Daniel 7.12 and the New Testament Passion-Resurrection Predictions," *NTS* 31 (1985): 208–22; Simon Gathercole, "The Son of Man in Mark's Gospel," *ExpTim* 115 (2004): 366–72; Scot McKnight, *Jesus and His Death: Historiography, the Historical Jesus, and Atonement Theory* (Waco, TX: Baylor University Press, 2005), 234; Christopher Tuckett, "The Present Son of Man," in *From the Sayings to the Gospels*, WUNT 328 (Tübingen: Mohr Siebeck, 2014), 507–9. And long before any of them, see Wilhelm Baldensperger, *Das Selbstbewusstein Jesu im Lichte der messianischen Hoffnungen seiner Zeit* (Strassburg: Heitz, 1888), 259.

21. Another intriguing detail here is the "three days" language, which some have tried to trace to Jesus on the grounds that it would have meant something like "a little while" (cf. John 16:16–19) and was already connected to the resurrection of the dead (so Hos 6:2: "on the third day he will raise us up"). See especially Joachim Jeremias, "Die Drei-Tage-Worte der Evangelien," in *Tradition und Glaube: Das Frühe Christentum in seiner Umwelt; Festschrift für Karl Georg Kuhn*, ed. Gert Jeremias, Heinz Wolfgang Kuhn, and Hartmut Stegemann (Göttingen: Vandenhoeck & Ruprecht, 1971), 221–30; Ben F. Meyer, *Christus Faber: The Master Builder and the House of God* (Allison Park, PA: Pickwick, 1992), 135; Dale C. Allison Jr., *The Resurrection of Jesus: Apologetics, Criticism, History* (New York: Bloomsbury T&T Clark, 2021), 188–90. It is not important for our

8:31: "*the son of man* must suffer many things, and be rejected by the elders and the chief priests and scribes, and be killed."

9:31: "*the son of man* will be *handed over* [παραδίδοται] *into the hands* [εἰς χεῖρας] of men, and they will kill him."

10:33: "*the son of man* will be *handed over* [παραδοθήσεται] to the chief priests and the scribes, and they will condemn him to death; then they will *hand him over* [παραδώσουσιν] to the gentiles."

We have here not just "son of man," but the "handing over" or "giving" up of him, with one passage mentioning giving "into the hands of"; compare the "giving" (from יהב) of the holy ones of the Most High into the hand (יד) of the final beast.[22] And these passages are not unique in these ways (cf. Mark 14:21 and par.; Mark 14:41 ["*the son of man* is *handed over* into *the hands of* sinners"]; also John 3:14 and 12:23 [which both use son of man]). In such texts, we are surely looking at the end result of a process of theological and scriptural reflection, to be clear, and there are other allusions involved here we might be quite skeptical about tracing to Jesus (so Isa 53's "servant," though this is highly disputed, and I have nothing to add to the discussion).[23] But I suspect that we are in a situation akin to the relationship between Dan 7 and the "day of the Lord" tradition as described above: the fact of creative elaboration that goes well beyond what Jesus ever said is not to be denied, yet it remains probable that an initial connection with Dan 7 is precisely what made possible later Christian exegesis (indeed, the "giving" or

purposes to defend a particular position on this question. I think it is possible that Jesus used the "three days" language—in the sense of "in a little while"—with reference to the "raising up" of a new temple, as this appears in the troublesome temple saying that Christians struggled to make sense of (cf. Mark 14:57–58 and parr.; 15:29–30 and parr.; John 2:18–19; cf. also Acts 6:14 and Gos. Thom. 71 [though lacking "three days"]). In light of what happened after the death of Jesus, did Christians reread that prediction and see new meaning in it, precisely as we find in the Fourth Gospel, where Jesus connects the temple to the raising up of his own body? It seems more likely to me that the post-Easter expansion was from temple prediction to resurrection prediction, rather than from resurrection prediction to temple prediction. But this is of course speculative.

22. Also noted by Simon Gathercole, *The Gospel and the Gospels* (Grand Rapids: Eerdmans, 2022), 126.

23. A few important studies include Morna Hooker, *Jesus and the Servant* (London: SPCK, 1959), 134–63; Hans Walter Wolff, *Jesaja 53 im Urchristentum* (Berlin: Evangelische Verlagsanstalt, 1950), 55–70; Marinus de Jonge, *Jesus, the Servant Messiah* (New Haven: Yale University Press, 1991), 48–50; and essays in William Bellinger, Jr., and William R. Farmer, eds., *Jesus and the Suffering Servant: Isaiah 53 and Christian Origins* (Eugene, OR: Wipf & Stock, 2009).

"handing over" in Dan 7 may be what enabled a connection to the "handing over" of Isa 53's servant).[24]

There is one feature of the gospel tradition that I think more or less settles this question, though it does require me to make a particular claim about a particular episode. In Mark 10:35–40, we find an exchange between James and John and Jesus that assumes the glorification and the suffering depicted in Dan 7 as its subtext: they ask to be enthroned with him, and he replies by asking whether they are ready first to suffer with him. The images for suffering, uncoincidentally, draw on other extant images for the eschatological tribulation (cup and baptism).[25] But here is the thing: Jesus predicts that, while it is not his to "give" (δοῦναι) positions of glory, these two will indeed suffer with him. The symbolic language does not indicate what kind of suffering Jesus has in mind—death by crucifixion is hardly a necessary implication—but this is something that did not happen. James and John did not, in fact, drink the same drink as Jesus and receive the same baptism. James died in the 40s (Acts 12:2), but John, as far as we know, lived to an old age.[26] So it is hard to imagine early Christians inventing this exchange from whole cloth after the fact. It does, however, make good sense before the fact, and especially in light of Dan 7, since it is "the holy ones of the Most High" who will be "worn out" by the final beast and be "given" into his hand before the kingdom comes.

On the whole, I would say, Jesus surely expected suffering to precede the coming of God's kingdom, as did others in his time, not least Dan 7 and some of its interpreters, and it is probable that he was open to the likelihood that he (and others) would not be spared.[27]

24. The "handed over" language in the Gospels—from παραδίδωμι—that many exegetes have connected to Isa 53:6 works only in the LXX (also in 53:12). The MT of 53:6 reads, "the LORD laid on him [הפגיע בו] the iniquity of us all" (LXX: "handed him over for our sins" [παρέδωκεν αὐτὸν ταῖς ἁμαρτίαις ἡμῶν]). See discussion in David A. Sapp, "The LXX, 1QIsa, and MT Versions of Isaiah 53 and the Christian Doctrine of Atonement," in Bellinger and Farmer, *Jesus and the Suffering Servant*, 170–92. Thus, if the "handed over" language goes back to Jesus, it is more likely to have stemmed from the יהב of Dan 7, which could be connected to Isaiah in a Greek version.

25. On the cup as a metaphor for judgment, see Pss 11:6; 75:7–8; Isa 51:17; Jer 25:15–29; Zech 12:2; 1QpHab XI, 14–15; Pss. Sol. 8.14; Mart. Ascen. Isa. 5.13. Cf. Bayer, *Jesus' Predictions of Vindication and Resurrection*, 70–77; McKnight, *Jesus and His Death*, 119–10, 124–29.

26. On John's death, see Irenaeus, *Haer.* 2.22.5; 3.3.4. See discussion in W. D. Davies and Dale C. Allison Jr., *A Critical and Exegetical Commentary on the Gospel according to Saint Matthew*, ICC (Edinburgh: T&T Clark, 1988–1997), 3:90–92.

27. Cf. Jeremias, *New Testament Theology*, 243–44; Dunn, *Jesus Remembered*, 805; Barber, "Did Jesus Anticipate Suffering a Violent Death?," 191–219. See also Aune, *Prophecy in Early Christianity and the Ancient Mediterranean World*, 178: "though the Markan passion predictions betray the hand of the Christian community in their present form, we have argued that they may in fact conceal a prophecy of Jesus concerning his own fate."

Dodd's three other arguments—about Jesus's knowledge of John's demise, traditions about the fate of the prophets, and the general animosity Jesus faced—point us in the same direction. Concerning John the Baptist, it is not just the fact of John's execution but that Jesus actively continued to link his ministry and message to John.[28] How could he do this and not be aware that he was potentially putting himself in a similar position?[29] Concerning the vocation of the prophets, Dodd may have overstated how widespread the rejected prophet motif was in the Second Temple period, but it is nonetheless true that such a tradition existed,[30] and we find traction at several points in the Gospels, such as the rejection story at Nazareth (Mark 6:1–5 and parr.; cf. John 4:44), the parable of the wicked tenants (Mark 12:1–9 and parr.) and the parable of the great supper (Q 14:16–24) (two of the four "happy few" that even made it through the gauntlet of John Meier's critique),[31] and some isolated sayings (Luke 13:31–33; Mark 9:11–13; Q 6:22–23, 26; 7:31–35; 11:49–51; 16:16).[32] Moreover, the basic notion that rejection and religious vocation go together is widespread in the righteous martyr tradition in Second

28. See Tucker S. Ferda, *Jesus, the Gospels, and the Galilean Crisis*, LNTS 601 (London: Bloomsbury T&T Clark, 2019), 165–73; Ferda, "The Historicity of Confusion: Jesus, John the Baptist, and the Construction of Public Identity," *JBL* 139 (2020): 758–60.

29. Especially if it is true that, as Luke 13:31 reports, he was aware that Antipas was out for him. Mark's presentation of Antipas as a curious dupe is politically convenient and at odds with what we find elsewhere (so Josephus, *Ant.* 18.109–119; Matt 14:5). Cf. Joseph B. Tyson, "Jesus and Herod Antipas," *JBL* 79 (1960): 239–46.

30. Some key texts outside the New Testament include Neh 9:26; 1 Kgs 18:4; Jer 2:30; 26:5 (as well as the general story of his biography); Jub. 1.12; LAB 1.1; 2.1; 3.2; 6.1; 7.2; 23.1; Josephus *Ant.* 10.38; Sib. Or. 1.130–136; Mart. Ascen. Isa. 2.16; 5.1–14; Tg. Jer. 7.11–15 ("because you have done all these things says the Lord, and when I spoke to you persistently you did not listen, and when I called you, you did not answer" is rewritten as "I have sent to you all my servants the prophets, rising up and speaking, but you did not heed them; and they prophesied to you, but you did not repent"); cf. 1 Clem. 7.5–7. Cf. Odil H. Steck, *Israel und das gewaltsame Geschick der Propheten*, WMANT 23 (Neukirchen-Vluyn: Neukirchener, 1967), 60–264; Johannes M. Nützel, "Zum Schicksal der eschatologischen Propheten," *BZ* 20 (1976): 59–94; Aune, *Prophecy in Early Christianity and the Ancient Mediterranean World*, 157–59, 176 ("a tradition which appears to have played a central role in Jesus' understanding of his own mission and destiny"); Michael Tilly, *Johannes der Täufer und die Biographie der Propheten: die synoptische Täuferüberlieferung und das jüdische Prophetenbild zur Zeit des Täufers*, BZANT 7 (Stuttgart: Kohlhammer, 1994), 236–47; David L. Turner, *Israel's Last Prophet: Jesus and the Jewish Leaders in Matthew 23* (Minneapolis: Fortress, 2015), 13–54.

31. John P. Meier, *Probing the Authenticity of the Parables*, vol. 5 of *A Marginal Jew: Rethinking the Historical Jesus* (New Haven: Yale University Press, 2016), 240–53, 253–73.

32. On the enigmatic "men of violence" saying (Q 16:16), which marks the onset of violence with the coming and/or end of John's ministry, Pitre, *Jesus, the Tribulation, and the End of Exile*, 166, has suggested that the language draws from depictions of the eschatological tribulation.

Temple Judaism, which often depicts obedience to God's will as leading to suffering and even death (2 Macc 7:1–23, 30–38, 40; 4 Macc 1:10–11; 6:16–22; 9:1–9, 15, 23–25; 17:11–22). We must account for the fact that nearly everywhere we look in early Christianity, Jesus was remembered as having gone to death as an act of obedience to God (Phil 2:7–8; Rom 5:18–19),[33] and willingly (Gal 1:3–4, 2:20 ["gave himself"]; Rom 15:3 ["did not please himself"]; cf. Eph 5:2; 1 Tim 2:5–6; Tit 2:14).[34] We also have a few brief and memorable sayings to this effect that could very well go back to Jesus—especially intriguing is the multiply attested saying about losing one's life to save/gain/preserve it (Mark 8:35 and parr., Q 17:33, and John 12:25), and the description of a coming baptism to endure (Luke 12:50; Mark 10:38)[35]—not to mention the Gethsemane narrative that was very soon problematic for Christians.[36] Concerning this overall impression, Dale Allison rightly concluded, "to entertain the suggestion that Jesus did not go to his death willingly requires positing a widespread conscious cover-up or a catastrophic memory failure in the early Christian sources."[37]

Last, concerning the animosity Jesus faced, we must oppose the widespread anti-Jewish tendency in Christian biblical interpretation of regarding Jesus's disputes with the Pharisees and scribes about torah and table fellowship as instrumental in his death (supported, of course, by texts like Mark 3:6 and parr.; John 5:18; etc.). The idea that Jesus was so full of love and grace for the outcast and had such a desire for justice that the bigots who opposed him could respond only by killing him is obviously a ridiculous anti-Jewish cartoon. But Jesus did, indeed, offend some people, and he found himself at the end of two particular

33. See the interesting study by James F. McGrath, "Obedient unto Death: Philippians 2:8, Gethsemane, and the Historical Jesus," *JSHJ* 14 (2016): 223–40.

34. On the importance of martyrological traditions for Paul, see Douglas A. Campbell, *The Deliverance of God: An Apocalyptic Rereading of Justification in Paul* (Grand Rapids: Eerdmans, 2009), 648–51; Jarvis Williams, *Maccabean Martyr Traditions in Paul's Theology of Atonement: Did Martyr Theology Shape Paul's Conception of Jesus' Death?* (Eugene, OR: Wipf & Stock, 2010). I discovered after writing this chapter that James Crossley and Robert J. Myles, *Jesus: A Life in Class Conflict* (Winchester: Zero, 2023), 178–91, argue that Jesus himself held a martyr theology.

35. The latter is particularly important for Luz, "Der unbequeme Jesus," 144–46.

36. Already by the time of the Fourth Gospel (12:27), whose Jesus rejects what Mark's Jesus requests (14:36). There may also be echoes of Gethsemane in Rom 8:1; Gal 4:6; Col 4:2; Heb 5:7–8. Cf. Rafael Rodríguez, "Your Will Be Done: Remembering Jesus' Submission to the Father," in *"To Recover What Has Been Lost": Essays on Eschatology, Intertextuality, and Reception History in Honor of Dale C. Allison Jr.*, ed. Tucker S. Ferda, Daniel Frayer-Griggs, and Nathan C. Johnson, NovTSup 183 (Leiden: Brill, 2021), 294–318.

37. Dale C. Allison Jr., *Constructing Jesus: Memory, Imagination, and History* (Grand Rapids: Baker Books, 2010), 433. See also Barber, "Did Jesus Anticipate Suffering a Violent Death?," 219.

attacks that early Christians would surely not have invented: that he was in league with the devil (Mark 3:22; Q 11:19), and that he was a "glutton and a drunkard" (Q 7:34). These are serious matters. Sorcery, and being a "rebellious son" from Deut 21 (which is where the "glutton and drunkard" line comes from),[38] were punishable by death according to the Torah (cf. Lev 20:27; Deut 18:9–14; 21:21) and m. Sanh. 7.4.

None of this, of course, supports Schweitzer's bold claim that Jesus went up to Jerusalem with a death wish, and we have not yet attempted to fit this expectation into the rest of his public activity (next chapter). But we have ample evidence to conclude with confidence that Jesus must have known it was possible, if not actually expected outright, that the cost of his activity would be his very life, and that this made sense in light of the expectation for the coming eschatological tribulation.

Interim and Imminence

How, then, does the prospect of death relate to Jesus's larger eschatological message about the coming of the kingdom? As noted in part 1, this question has been either overlooked or inadequately explored by critics who would place themselves in the family tree of Albert Schweitzer and his eschatological interpretation of Jesus.[39] Some have argued that Jesus expected to die, *and also* that Jesus expected

38. Deut 21:18–21: "If someone has a stubborn and rebellious son who will not obey his father and mother, who does not heed them when they discipline him, then his father and his mother shall take hold of him and bring him out to the elders of his town at the gate of that place. They shall say to the elders of his town, 'This son of ours is stubborn and rebellious. He will not obey us. He is a glutton and a drunkard [זולל וסבא].' Then all the men of the town shall stone him to death." Cf. Joseph B. Modica, "Jesus as Glutton and Drunkard," in *Who Do My Opponents Say That I Am? An Investigation of the Accusations against the Historical Jesus*, ed. Scot McKnight and Joseph B. Modica, LNTS 327 (London: T&T Clark, 2008), 50–75.

39. This oversight is likely a symptom of the fact that Jesus research since the advent of form criticism was increasingly atomistic in nature. Indeed, the success of the form-critical project is perhaps most clearly seen in the way in which subsequent Jesus research has focused on the authentication of specific sayings, deeds, or even themes in the tradition without feeling the need to explain how these parts fit together. See Ferda, *Jesus, the Gospels, and the Galilean Crisis*, 144. The coherence envisioned in the "criterion of coherence" has typically been about conceptual or ideological harmony, not about thinking realistically and sociologically about how the activity of Jesus hangs together. For discussion see Anthony Le Donne, "The Criterion of Coherence: Its Development, Inevitability, and Historiographical Limitations," in *Jesus, Criteria, and the Demise of Authenticity*, ed. Chris Keith and Anthony Le Donne (London: T&T Clark, 2012), 95–114. For critique of a "kriteriologische Modell" of Jesus studies that marginalizes the role of inference and

the kingdom to come "imminently," but not explained how the two connect to each other.[40] Here is my suggestion: the prospect of death not only permits but actually requires that an interim period featured into Jesus's larger eschatological scenario. For if Jesus reckoned with the possibility of death but did not thereby assume that history would end when he died, we have an interim period de facto: a time when people are living and Jesus is not. That is it. The notion of an interim period has a fitting, even necessary, *Sitz im Leben Jesu*, if Jesus thought that he might die.[41]

The topic of an interim period has been controversial in New Testament scholarship and repeatedly rejected by proponents of an eschatological Jesus because it has often been set by interpreters in opposition to the view that Jesus expected the kingdom "imminently." Hans Conzelmann speaks for many: Jesus left "*no room* for another interim figure between the present time and the in-breaking of the kingdom . . . [and] *neither is there time* for his own preceding removal and 'parousia.'"[42] But to pit imminence against interim is to be caught in the extremes of the nineteenth-century quest and think that our options are Ritschl (a world without end) and Schweitzer (a world ending tomorrow). Indeed, to appreciate the rationale for rejecting an interim period in the teaching of Jesus, one must recognize that what is typically being opposed is the notion that Jesus expected history to continue for eons after his death.[43] So Seeley in his famous *Ecce Homo* (1867) says that what has happened is what Jesus intended: "the divine society has been founded, that has lasted nearly two thousand years, that has extended over a large and the most highly civilized portion of the earth's surface, and that

---

imagination, see Eckhard Rau, *Jesus, Freund von Zöllnern und Sündern: Eine methodenkritische Untersuchung* (Stuttgart: Kohlhammer, 2000), 49, 74–75.

40. See pp. 44, 46 above.

41. Cf. Anton Vögtle, "Exegetische Erwägungen über das Wissen und Selbstbewusstein Jesu," in *Gott in Welt: Festgabe fur Karl Rahner*, ed. Herbert Vorgrimler (Freiburg: Herder, 1964), 1:626–27. See also Oscar Cullmann, *Peter: Disciple-Apostle-Martyr*, trans. Floyd V. Filson (Philadelphia: Westminster, 1953), 200–201 ("a rather brief period of time"); Kümmel, *Promise and Fulfillment*, 64–82; Ben F. Meyer, *The Aims of Jesus* (London: SCM, 1979), 202–6.

42. Hans Conzelmann, *Jesus*, ed. John Reumann, trans. J. Raymond Lord (Philadelphia: Fortress, 1973), 46 (my italics). See also Günther Bornkamm, *Jesus of Nazareth*, trans. Irene and Fraser McLuskey, with James M. Robinson (New York: Harper, 1960), 187. C. K. Barrett, *The Holy Spirit and the Gospel Tradition* (London: SPCK, 1947), 160, wrote that Jesus did not expect any space "between the period of humiliation and that of complete and final glorification." See also C. K. Barrett, *Jesus and the Gospel Tradition* (London: SPCK, 1967), 76.

43. So, e.g., the critique of Charles Guignebert, *Jesus*, trans. S. H. Hooke (New York: Knopf, 1935), 323: "what Jesus obviously expected, and that in the near future, was the advent of the Kingdom, and not the establishment, for countless centuries, of a Church constituted by a group of the elect in an apostate world."

continues full of vigor at the present day."[44] Here we find an interim period that effectively destroys eschatology and explicitly endorses European colonialism.[45] To this polluted view, Schweitzer's apocalyptic Jesus is fresh air.[46] But it is simply not the case that we must choose between imminence and interim, even if Schweitzer was much nearer the truth on this question than the liberal lives of Jesus. The reaction of Schweitzer was an overreaction.

If we take seriously that Jesus thought he might die, but that history would continue, we have the conditions for a brief interim period wherein Jesus expects that his followers continue his work in his absence before the end of that generation and the coming of the kingdom in power. This scenario hardly eliminates eschatological imminence; the assumption is that this is the last generation and there are some living who will not taste death. But there is indeed "room" (contra Conzelmann) for his followers to continue his work for a short time, "awake" and "at work" before the coming of the son of man, the resurrection of the dead, and the final judgment.[47] The expectation would be that, should Jesus perish in the great tribulation, he would, nonetheless, be revealed as the son of man in the near future at a specific time known only to God.

To one who would respond that this proposed scenario sacrifices imminence at the behest of an interim period, I must first reply: where is it, exactly, that we find evidence of an eschatology *more* imminent than what I have proposed? Jeremias was right that "we have no saying of Jesus that postpones the end into the distant future,"[48] but neither do we have a saying of Jesus that says the end is so soon that it excludes even the prospect of his own death. We should consider, in this light, three particular sayings of Jesus that have been at the center of debates about imminent eschatology:

> Mark 9:1: "Truly I say to you that there are some standing here who will by no means taste death until they see the kingdom of God has come in power."

44. John Seeley, *Ecce Homo: A Survey of the Life and Work of Jesus Christ* (Boston: Roberts Brothers, 1867), 50.

45. A common move. See Halvor Moxnes, *Jesus and the Rise of Nationalism: A New Quest for the Nineteenth Century Historical Jesus* (London: Tauris, 2012), 8–13, 31–38, 44–55, 69–95.

46. Which is not to deny the problems with Schweitzer's own reconstruction, or to overlook his own endorsement of colonialism in his own time. Cf. discussion in Andrew M. Mbuvi, *African Biblical Studies: Unmasking Embedded Racism and Colonialism in Biblical Studies* (London: Bloomsbury T&T Clark, 2023), 40–57.

47. Contrast Stettler, *Das letzte Gericht*, 24 (who attributes to Jesus "die Lehre von der unbestimmten Zwischenzeit"), and also Alistair I. Wilson, *When Will These Things Happen? A Study of Jesus as Judge in Matthew 21–25* (Eugene, OR: Wipf & Stock, 2004), 237.

48. Jeremias, *New Testament Theology*, 139.

> Mark 13:30: "Truly I say to you that this generation will by no means pass away until all these things happen."
>
> Matt 10:23: "when they persecute you in this city, flee to the next, for truly I say to you, you will by no means finish the cities of Israel until the son of man comes."

These remarkable sayings have for good reason figured prominently in arguments for an eschatologically minded Jesus.[49] But we must note that while they all depict a coming *soon*, it is not so soon as to be *immediate*. Mark 9:1 actually expects that "some" will die before the kingdom and son of man (8:38) comes.[50] Mark 13:30 looks to the horizon of the "generation" then living. And Matt 10:23 expects that there is work to do before the coming of the son of man; the point is that the disciples will not finish that work before the son of man comes.[51] It is actually on such grounds that some have argued that one, or more, of these sayings is unhistorical: they assume, it is said, the "delay of the parousia," and hence a later *Sitz im Leben*.[52]

49. So, e.g., Dale C. Allison Jr., "A Plea for Thoroughgoing Eschatology," *JBL* 113 (1994): 651–56; Allison, *Jesus of Nazareth: Millenarian Prophet* (Philadelphia: Fortress, 1998), 47–51, where they are discussed in a subsection entitled "imminence." Allison's descriptions are fair but also vague: "sands of time had run out" (147), "the eschatological harvest was ripe" (148), "temporally near" (149). Cf. Allison, *Constructing Jesus*, 33 (with the collective summary that the three "openly declare that the sands of ordinary time have just about run out"). See also Jacques Schlosser, *Le règne de Dieu dans les dits de Jesus* (Paris: Gabalda, 1980), 1:323–50; Aune, *Prophecy in Early Christianity and the Ancient Mediterranean World*, 171–72; Franz Mussner, *Was lehrt Jesus über das Ende der Welt?*, rev. ed. (Freiburg: Herder, 1987), 59; Robert H. Gundry, *Mark: A Commentary on His Apology for the Cross* (Grand Rapids: Eerdmans, 1993), 466–70; Theissen and Merz, *Historical Jesus*, 255–56.

50. And, it is interesting to note that, in Allison's Matthew commentary with Davies, *Matthew*, 2:189, they argue that "some" and "here" are secondary. So the saying has been tampered with, they think, in ways that soften the imminence.

51. So rightly Kümmel, *Promise and Fulfillment*, 29, 75–82. See also Cullmann, "Die Hoffnung der Kirche auf die Wiederkunft Christi nach dem Neuen Testament," 391.

52. Cf., e.g., Bultmann, *History of the Synoptic Tradition*, 121 (on Mark 9:1); Erich Grässer, *Das Problem der Parusieverzögerung in den synoptischen Evangelien und in der Apostelgeschichte*, 3rd ed. (Berlin: de Gruyter, 1977), 174 (though here on Mark 14:62, but for the same reasons); Norman Perrin, *Rediscovering the Teaching of Jesus* (New York: Harper & Row, 1967), 199–202; Heinz Schürmann, *Gottes Reich, Jesu Geschick: Jesu ureigener Tod im Licht seiner Basileia-Verkündigung* (Freiburg: Herder, 1983), 38–41; Helmut Merklein, *Jesu Botschaft von der Gottesherrschaft: Eine Skizze*, SBS 111 (Stuttgart: Katholisches Bibelwerk, 1983), 54–56; Joachim Gnilka, *Jesus of Nazareth: Message and History*, trans. Siegfried S. Schatzmann (Peabody, MA: Hendrickson, 1997), 147–49; Gerd Lüdemann, *Jesus after Two Thousand Years: What He Really Said and Did* (Amherst: Prometheus, 2001), 59–60.

But this begs the very question under consideration. It assumes a Schweitzerian sense of imminence as the baseline and describes any deviation from that as "delay," despite the fact that Schweitzer's own evidence for the imminence of Jesus's proclamation depended in large part on these very sayings.

Perhaps these sayings are not historical.[53] I personally think it is unlikely that a later follower invented Mark 9:1, and Matt 10:23 is clearly an isolated logion that is being asked to do work in Matthew's mission discourse that it was not created for.[54] In any case, if the sayings are not historical, we look elsewhere in vain for clear evidence of a more imminent eschatology.[55] Jesus is purported to have pronounced woes on his contemporaries (e.g., Q 10:13–15), warned of the coming

53. For an in-depth discussion, see John P. Meier, *Mentor, Message, and Miracles*, vol. 2 of *A Marginal Jew: Rethinking the Historical Jesus* (New York: Doubleday, 1994), 336–48 (who ultimately denies the authenticity of all three). See also Martin Künzi, *Das Naherwartungslogion Markus 9,1 par: Geschichte seiner Auslegung* (Tübingen: Mohr Siebeck, 1977), 179, 340; M. Eugene Boring, *The Continuing Voice of Jesus* (Louisville: Westminster John Knox, 1991), 236, 250–51. Barry Crawford, "Near Expectation in the Sayings of Jesus," *JBL* 101 (1982): 225–44, suggests all three sayings stem from prophetic inspiration, but he does not thereby sever their eschatological outlook from the historical Jesus.

54. So also Aune, *Prophecy in Early Christianity and the Ancient Mediterranean World*, 183–84 (he concludes, "a saying of this nature appears authentic precisely because of its difficulty"). Mark labors to give Mark 9:1 a more immediate fulfillment by placing it right before the transfiguration, as commonly noted. See Joel Marcus, *Mark 8–16: A New Translation with Introduction and Commentary*, AB 27A (New Haven: Yale University Press, 2009), 635. And the Fourth Gospel likely responds to it in its own way (cf. 8:51–52, and perhaps also 21:22–23). On John 1:51 as possibly a repurposed parousia saying, see Raymond E. Brown, *An Introduction to New Testament Christology* (New York: Paulist, 1994), 55. On Matt 10:23, see Volker Hampel, "Ihr werdet mit den Städten Israels nicht zu Ende kommen," *TZ* 45 (1989): 1–31; Ulrich Luz, *Matthew: A Commentary*, trans. James E. Crouch, Hermeneia (Minneapolis: Fortress, 2005–2007), 2:91–94 (with brief history of interpretation).

55. Stettler, *Das letzte Gericht*, 243 (rightly against "eine konsequente Eschatologie im Sinne einer extremen Naherwartung"). One might think of Luke 19:11 ("he went on to tell a parable, because he was near Jerusalem, and because they supposed that the kingdom of God was to appear immediately [παραχρῆμα]"); so Allison, *Jesus of Nazareth*, 165, and Allison, *Constructing Jesus*, 65–66, which he groups with John 21:20–23, Mark 9:1, and Mark 13:30, despite the very different eschatological outlooks of these verses vis-à-vis Luke 19:11. While Luke 19:11 does indeed (*unlike* John 21:20–23, Mark 9:1, and Mark 13:30) appear to assume the kingdom imminently in the sense of "tomorrow," one must emphasize three things: (1) this verse is a redactional introduction to Luke's parable that attempts to psychologize "the crowd" with a generalization—a stylistic feature typical of the Third Evangelist, (2) this passage theologically coheres with Acts 1:6—in which a blunder by the disciples permits Luke to assert his more enlightened eschatological vision (with emphasis on delay), and (3) like Acts 1:6, the aim here is to rebuke and correct eschatological perspectives extant in Luke's own time. All of this would make Luke 19:11 shaky ground on which to reconstruct the kind of imminent eschatological hope present among the

judgment and called for repentance (e.g., Mark 1:15 and parr.; Luke 5:32; 13:1–5), said the kingdom has "come near" (Mark 1:15 and parr.) or even "arrived" (Q 11:20), said "let the dead bury the dead" (Q 9:60), observed that the harvest is "plentiful" (Q 10:2; John 4:35–38), and did not permit his disciples to greet others on the road (Q 10:4). One *could* read into these statements a horizon of expectation that is only days or weeks long, but they certainly do not require that. One accounts for all of the tradition, including the imminence of Paul's own eschatological message, on the simple assumption that this is the last generation.[56] Should one say that this undercuts the urgency of Jesus's activity, I do not see how. If persons believe that they are living in the last generation, even should they think the sun might rise tomorrow, is that not sufficient reason to get one's life in order?

But we should be precise here: none of the three sayings cited above or any other traditions predict *that* history will last for the duration of that living generation but rather state a *limit*, or terminus ad quem.[57] Beyond that, there is an eschatological openness that undergirds a call for readiness and watchfulness.[58] Some critics have read temporally marked sayings like Mark 9:1 ("some will not taste death") against temporally open sayings like Mark 13:32 ("concerning that day or hour no one knows, neither the angels in heaven, nor the son, but only the Father"), suggesting that only the marked sayings are historical and the open sayings are secondary responses to the delay of the parousia, or the inverse, that only the open sayings are historical and the marked sayings are secondary reflections from the eschatological enthusiasm of the early church.[59] But there is no

historical followers of Jesus at a specific time during his activity, and even more so the actual eschatological teaching of Jesus himself.

56. Contrast Arthur L. Moore, *The Parousia in the New Testament*, NovTSup 13 (Leiden: Brill, 1966), 108–59. A major weakness of this otherwise learned study is Moore's thoroughgoing attempt to deny that Paul's letters or the Gospels or any New Testament text ever evidence the belief that people then living would witness the end. He settles for what he calls "undelimited nearness" (164), which he further defends in largely theological terms (cf. 168–72). For other highly theological discussions in this book, cf. 67–79 (on Bultmann and demythologization), 93–94 (on the humanity of Jesus), 198 (on Jesus's eschatological teaching as oblique, rooted in his self-consciousness).

57. Contra Meier, *Mentor, Message, and Miracles*, 343. Jeremias, *New Testament Theology*, 137, has suggested that the reference to death here is not about passing away peacefully in old age, but rather to martyrdom, such that Jesus's statement is a prediction that "before the tribulation introduced by the passion of Jesus . . . has reached its climax, the intervention . . . will occur."

58. See Anthony E. Harvey, *Jesus and the Constraints of History* (Philadelphia: Westminster, 1982), 87–88.

59. Contra, e.g., Wilhelm Hadorn, *Zukunft und Hoffnung: Grundzüge einer Lehre von der christlichen Hoffnung* (Gütersloh: Bertelsmann, 1914), 124; Wilhelm Michaelis, *Der Herr verzieht nicht die Verheißung: Die Aussagen Jesu über die Nähe des Jüngsten Tages* (Bern: Buchhandluner

contradiction here and no need to read such sayings against each other. There is a consistent picture that this is the final generation, yet when the curtain will close is known only to God. We have nearness and openness, together. This is just what we find in 1 Thessalonians, where Paul presumably expected the return of Christ before that generation passed on (and expected himself to be alive still) but also warned, in the very same context no less, that there is nothing else for them to know about the "times and seasons" since they should be ready for the coming of Jesus "as a thief in the night" (1 Thess 5:1–2). We find the same dynamic elsewhere in Second Temple Judaism, where eschatological time is often marked generationally,[60] while knowing the exact time of the end is beyond mortals.[61]

But all of this merely scratches the surface in terms of the question of an interim period in the eschatological outlook of Jesus. For in addition to the above, we have an abundance of material in the Gospels—teaching material putatively from Jesus, that is—that assumes some interim time in which he will be absent.[62]

---

der Evangelischen Gesellschaft, 1942), 45; Geza Vermes, "The Jewish Jesus Movement," in *Partings: How Judaism and Christianity Became Two*, ed. Hershel Shanks (Washington, DC: Biblical Archaeological Society, 2013), 10–13.

60. 4Q171, in its interpretation of Ps 37, identifies the community's present with the forty years of wandering in the wilderness. It interprets Ps 37:10 in this way: "Its interpretation concerns all the wickedness at the end of the forty years, for they will be completed and upon the earth no [wic]ked person shall be found" (II, 7–8). This resembles CD XX, 13–15 ("from the day of the gathering in of the unique teacher, until the end of all the men of war who turned back with the man of lies, there shall be about forty years"). Cf. also Tg. Ps.-J. on Exod 17:16. In the biblical text, see Exod 16:35; Num 32:13; Judg 3:11; 1 Kgs 11:42; etc.

61. Note Tg. Ps.-J. on Gen 49:1: "Jacob called his sons and said . . . 'Purify yourselves . . . and I will tell you the hidden secrets, the concealed date of the end, the reward of the righteous and the punishment of the wicked, and what the pleasure of paradise will be' . . . [but after his sons gather] as soon as the date of the end when the king messiah would arrive was revealed to him, it was immediately concealed from him; and therefore, instead he said: 'Come, and I will relate to you what will happen to you at the end of days.'" This also appears in the Frg. Tg. on Gen 49. In some cases, eschatological ignorance includes angels, too. So in b. Sanh. 99a, the angels are said to be ignorant of the date of Israel's deliverance. Cf. also LAB 19.14–15 (where what is disclosed to Moses only at the moment of his death appears to be intentionally obscured for the readers); 4 Ezra 4.52 (Uriel does not know whether Ezra himself will live to see the end of the age); 2 Bar. 24.3 ("a man does not know the number of things which pass away nor those which come"); 69.2 ("for only the Most High knows what will happen in the future"); b. Sanh. 97b (Elijah does not know when the messiah will come); Mek. on Exod 16:32 ("hidden from people" is "when the kingdom of David will be restored"); Tg. Eccl. 7.24 (no one knows when the messiah comes). For positive assertions of God's knowledge of the future, see Pss. Sol. 17.21; 2 Bar. 21.8; 54.1. Cf. Harvey, *Jesus and the Constraints of History*, 96.

62. Cf. Cadoux, *Historic Mission of Jesus*, 307; Moore, *Parousia in the New Testament*, 97–98; David Bosch, *Die Heidenmission in der Zukunftsschau Jesu: Eine Untersuchung zur Eschatologie*

I offer four summary statements. First, Jesus is reported to have predicted future activity for his disciples where he does not seem to be part of the picture. This activity concerns both the simple notion of the disciples as successors of Jesus's mission—which Tobias Hägerland has defended strongly[63]—as well as persecution and hardship. The general expectation for the latter appears in all layers of the gospel tradition and cannot be easily removed without major surgery (cf. Mark 13:9–13; Q 6:22; Q 13:24–25; Matt 10:16–23, 28; John 15:20; etc.). Some of these are more obviously *ex eventu* than others, but the core notion requires only the existence of an expectation about the eschatological tribulation.[64] Early Christians continued to make sense of their present struggles in this light (see 1 Cor 7:26–29; 1 Thess 3:4; 2 Thess 2:7; Col 1:24; Rev 1:9; 6:10–11; 7:14; etc.).[65] Second, there are a number of parables of Jesus that really make sense only if they are about Jesus's departure and then return after a brief absence: the parable of a man on a journey (Mark 13:33–37), the parable of the householder and the thief (Q 12:39–40), the parable of the faithful and wise person (Q 12:41–48), the parable of the pounds/ talents (Q 19:12–27), the parable of the virgins (Matt 25:1–13; cf. Luke 12:35–37). There has been a strong tendency in historical Jesus scholarship since Dodd and Jeremias to interpret *all* these parables like the parable of the wicked tenants (Mark 12:1–12 and parr.) and the parable of the wedding feast (Q 14:16–24) as "crisis parables" that were actually about Jesus's "coming" *at that time* and only later were

der synoptischen Evangelien (Zurich: Zwingli-Verlag, 1959), 139; R. Newton Flew, *Jesus and His Church: A Study of the Idea of the Ecclesia in the New Testament* (London: Epworth, 1960), 30–35.

63. Tobias Hägerland, "The Role of the Disciples in the Prophetic Mission of Jesus," in *The Mission of Jesus*, ed. Samuel Byrskog and Tobias Hägerland, WUNT 2/391 (Tübingen: Mohr Siebeck, 2015), 177–202. Two specific points in his essay are worth recalling here. First, in terms of method: "this, again, appears to be an instance where the concept of 'recurrent attestation' is applicable: if there is any historical value at all to the gospel tradition, the notion of Jesus' disciples as his successors has to be rooted in his own mission by virtue of the sheer frequency with which it occurs in the tradition" (195). Second, in terms of implications for eschatology: "[Jesus did not rule out] a continuing prophetic mission carried out by his disciples. A consequence of this is that the crude Schweitzerian understanding of eschatology must be modified . . . his eschatological proclamation did not entail the imminent cessation of prophetic activity or the superfluousness of a succession of prophet-disciples" (200). I agree with both points.

64. See p. 330n16 above and literature cited.

65. As argued convincingly throughout Dale C. Allison Jr., *The End of the Ages Has Come: An Early Interpretation of the Passion and Resurrection of Jesus* (Philadelphia: Fortress, 1985). See also John M. Court, "Paul and the Apocalyptic Pattern," in *Paul and Paulinism: Essays in Honour of C. K. Barrett*, ed. Morna D. Hooker and S. G. Wilson (London: SPCK, 1982), 57–66; C. M. Pate and D. W. Kennard, *Deliverance Now and Not Yet: The New Testament and the Great Tribulation*, StBibLit 54 (New York: Lang, 2003).

misinterpreted with reference to the parousia.[66] But the parables do not fit inside that straitjacket, as Georg Kümmel noted long ago.[67] And Cecil Cadoux remarked that, if the parables were simply admonitions to pay attention,

> it is surely very extraordinary that he should have felt it necessary to throw on to the screen so often the same scene of servants whose absent master has left them in charge, who do not know when he will return, but do know that, when he returns, he will expect to find not only that they are then ready to receive him, but that they have been loyally doing their duty in his absence.

Moreover, he continued, the details of the parables do not fit "a *present* crisis . . . for which the hearers must be prepared" but rather "suggest on the contrary a crisis near to hand, but not yet actually present."[68] Cadoux's reading is more natural.

Third, we have several "you will" sayings that look beyond the time of Jesus: Q 13:34–35 ("you will not see me . . . you will say, 'Blessed is the one . . .'"); Luke 17:22 ("you will long to see the days of the son of man . . ."); John 16:16 ("a little while, you will no longer see me, and again in a little while, you will see me"; cf. vv. 17–28); Mark 14:7 ("the poor you will always have with you"). The last of these is quite peculiar and occurs in the context of the anointing of Jesus by an unnamed woman—a story that appears in all four gospels, though with striking differences in detail (see Mark 14:3–9; Matt 26:6–13; John 12:1–9; likely, too, Luke 7:36–50). The perplexing saying "the poor you will always have with you, but you will not always have me [ἐμὲ δὲ οὐ πάντοτε ἔχετε]" appears in three of these accounts (Mark 14:7; Matt 26:11; John 12:8) and may well go back to Jesus.[69]

66. See Dodd, *Parables of the Kingdom*, 122–39; Joachim Jeremias, *The Parables of Jesus*, trans. S. H. Hooke, 2nd ed. (New York: Scribner's Sons, 1972), 48–58, 115–24, 169–80; Jeremias, *New Testament Theology*, 138–39; John A. T. Robinson, *Jesus and His Coming: The Emergence of a Doctrine* (New York: Abingdon, 1957), 69; Dunn, *Jesus Remembered*, 428–31 (who endorses "crisis parables"). Others have argued that many of these parables do have the parousia in mind and for that reason are unhistorical. See discussions in Günther Bornkamm, "Die Verzögerung der Parusie," in *In Memoriam Ernst Lohmeyer*, ed. Werner Schmauch (Stuttgart: Evangelisches Verlagswerk, 1951), 121–25; John Dominic Crossan, *In Parables: The Challenge of the Historical Jesus* (New York: Harper & Row, 1973), 24–27; Lüdemann, *Jesus after Two Thousand Years*, 233–34; Meier, *Probing the Authenticity of the Parables*, 189–229.

67. Kümmel, *Promise and Fulfillment*, 54. Contrast also Arland J. Hultgren, *The Parables of Jesus: A Commentary* (Grand Rapids: Eerdmans, 2000), 162–68, 262–68, 272–80, 282–90, who suggests four of these were originally parables about God.

68. Cadoux, *Historic Mission of Jesus*, 314.

69. See C. H. Dodd, *Historical Tradition in the Fourth Gospel* (Cambridge: Cambridge University Press, 1963), 162–65. Cf. also C. E. B. Cranfield, "Thoughts on New Testament Eschatology,"

Fourth and last, we must consider the so-called eschatological prospect saying in the context of the Last Supper.[70] Jesus is made to say the following:

	Mark 14:25	Matt 26:29	Luke 22:16	Luke 22:18
preamble	truly I say to you	I tell you	for I tell you	for I tell you
termination	no longer shall I drink from the fruit of the vine	I shall not drink from now on from this fruit of the vine	I shall not eat it (the Passover)	from now on I shall not drink from the fruit of the vine
duration	until that day when I drink it new	until that day when I drink it new with you	until it is fulfilled	until
context	in the kingdom of God	in the kingdom of my Father	in the kingdom of God	the kingdom of God comes

The differences are exegetically interesting,[71] but the upshot remains the same across the board: in anticipation of death, Jesus predicts a time of separation from his disciples before a reunion in the coming kingdom.[72] The imagery is surely

---

SJT 35 (1982): 497–512 at 508, though he is wrong in his larger attempt to discredit the notion that the early church was animated by the hope for Jesus's imminent return in their days.

70. Meier, *Mentor, Message, and Miracles*, 302, writes, "suffice it to say that the historicity of a final farewell meal held by Jesus with his disciples is generally accepted by scholars across the spectrum." E. P. Sanders, *Jesus and Judaism* (Philadelphia: Fortress, 1985), 307, writes that the historicity of the Last Supper is "almost equally [as] certain" as the temple action. Some have been skeptical of the historicity of the words of institution but nonetheless regarded the prospect saying considered below to go back to Jesus in some form. See Jens Schröter, *Das Abendmahl: Frühchristliche Deutungen und Impulse für die Gegenwart*, SBS 210 (Stuttgart: Katholisches Bibelwerk, 2006), 132–33. Brant Pitre, *Jesus and the Last Supper* (Grand Rapids: Eerdmans, 2015), 499, offers that "the vast majority of scholars" believe that Mark 14:25 is "substantially historical."

71. It is not clear whether Luke 22:16 is a secondary rewriting of Mark 14:25, or something Luke found in tradition. For discussion, see Schlosser, *Le règne de Dieu*, 2:387–89.

72. Davies and Allison, *Matthew*, 3:968, are right to call this another passion prediction. See also Rudolf Pesch, *Das Abendmahl und Jesu Todesverständnis* (Freiburg: Herder, 1978), 101–2; Schürmann, *Jesus, Gestalt und Geheimnis*, 161–62. Contra Joachim Jeremias, *The Eucharistic Words of Jesus*, 3rd ed. (London: SCM, 1966), 207–18 (that Jesus hoped the kingdom would come at any moment and vowed

influenced by the expectation of the messianic banquet, which remains in the future and closely identified with "the kingdom."[73] Paul in 1 Cor 11 reflects a similar understanding in his rehearsal of the tradition, emphasizing reunion with Jesus: "For as often as you eat this bread and drink the cup, you proclaim the death of the Lord until he comes [τὸν θάνατον τοῦ κυρίου καταγγέλλετε ἄχρι οὗ ἔλθῃ]."[74] That Jesus here expects a time of separation from his disciples (duration unspecified) would be reinforced if the imperative to "do this in remembrance of me" (ποιεῖτε εἰς τὴν ἐμὴν ἀνάμνησιν)—as reported by Luke (22:19) and Paul (1 Cor 11:24–25)—captures something that Jesus had said. But this remains unclear.

To my knowledge, Brant Pitre has noted more clearly than any the significance of the Last Supper tradition for our understanding of the eschatology of Jesus. At the outset of *Jesus and the Last Supper*, he makes a number of poignant observations that are directly relevant to our subject. He writes,

> One serious problem with the hypothesis of Jesus as an apocalyptic prophet of the imminent end of history is that scholars who adopt this point of view have substantial difficulty in making sense of the words of institution recorded in our earliest accounts of the Last Supper. In these words, Jesus apparently looks *beyond* his own imminent suffering and death.

Pitre goes on to accuse "scholarly advocates of Schweitzer's hypothesis" of "consistently ignor[ing] the words of institution in their reconstruction of Jesus' es-

to fast until it happened). This is similar to Paula Fredriksen, *Jesus of Nazareth, King of the Jews: A Jewish Life and the Emergence of Christianity* (New York: Knopf, 1999), 118–19, 244–45, 251, 257 (who suspects the supper may be historical but stresses that Jesus expected the kingdom to come that very Passover). For an effective response to Jeremias, see Meier, *Mentor, Message, and Miracles*, 306–9, though there are issues with his analysis, particularly that the notion of reunion with the disciples has to be read into the text (371). Here he follows Grässer, *Das Problem der Parusieverzögerung*, 54.

73. See also Q 13:28–29. Important texts for reconstructing the expectation for some kind of banquet in the world to come include 1QS II, 11–22; 1 En. 25.4–6; 62.13–16; T. Levi 18.10–11; 2 Bar. 29.1–30.4. For discussion, see Lawrence H. Schiffman, *The Eschatological Community of the Dead Sea Scrolls*, SBLMS 38 (Atlanta: Scholars Press, 1989), 53–67; Philip J. Long, *Jesus the Bridegroom: The Origin of the Eschatological Feast as a Wedding Banquet in the Synoptic Gospels* (Eugene, OR: Pickwick, 2013), 148–83; Claudia D. Bergmann, *Festmahl ohne Ende: Apokalyptische Vorstellungen vom Speisen in der Kommenden Welt im antiken Judentum und ihre biblischen Wurzeln*, BWANT 222 (Stuttgart: Kohlhammer, 2019), 53–137. It is also worth noting that, while the particulars of pre-70 Passover practice remain disputed, at the time of Jesus, the Passover was clearly not just a time of remembering but also had an eschatological orientation and significance. This is noted by Josephus himself, who wrote that all three pilgrimage festivals were opportunities for the people to "intercede for future mercies" (*Ant.* 4.203–204).

74. See also Did. 9.4; 10.5–6.

chatology," pointing specifically to E. P. Sanders and Dale Allison. He marvels at the fact that Sanders thought it was "almost . . . certain" (Sanders's language) that Jesus held a last meal with his disciples but "never explains how the words of institution can be reconciled with his overall reconstruction of Jesus' eschatology." As for Allison, Pitre notes that "the reader will search Allison's reconstruction in vain for any detailed discussion of the words of institution . . . in his many writings . . . [he] never explains how the words of institution do or do not fit into his overall reconstruction of Jesus' eschatology."[75]

Pitre's scope is wider than mine in thinking of the words of institution as a whole, but he has his finger on a crucial issue, and I could not put it better. His own solution, however, creates a whole new bag of problems. Ironically, Pitre ends up following T. F. Glasson in suggesting not just that Jesus expected history to continue but to continue for a long period of time.[76] He suggests that a "short interval" does not make sense of Jesus using "covenant" language (and specifically the "new covenant" as found in Luke and Paul) with reference to his death, since the Sinai covenant "had lasted for well over a thousand years."[77] But this argument (1) requires the authenticity of "new covenant" in the words of institution (which is unique to Luke and Paul and hence disputed), (2) needs a peculiar interpretation of that "new covenant" language to indicate an extended duration (which is not apparent), (3) overlooks the eschatological imminence that emerges elsewhere in the Jesus tradition (which commits the same fallacy he accuses Sanders and Allison of—namely, failure to integrate), and (4) ultimately cannot account for the imminent eschatology of Paul and the earliest community (which takes us back to the core insights of Sanders and Allison about Christian origins, where they are surely preferable).

Is there a way that we might better account for the Last Supper, and specifically the eschatological prospect saying, as Pitre does, without putting ourselves in a position where we cannot explain why Paul would ever have to respond to worry

75. Pitre, *Jesus and the Last Supper*, 17, 20. Helen K. Bond, *The Historical Jesus: A Guide for the Perplexed* (London: Bloomsbury T&T Clark, 2012), argues that Jesus did anticipate his death, and that the meal is historical and was a handing over of the reins to the disciples (her image) so that they might "continue his work" (147). But, recalling Pitre's critique of Sanders and Allison, it is not clear how this view relates to Bond's take on the eschatology of Jesus elsewhere. She writes on the immediately preceding page that the Last Supper tradition may have undergone "considerable transformation," since, she asserts, "Jesus preached the coming of God, rather than his own return" (146).

76. Specifically T. F. Glasson's *Jesus and the End of the World* (Edinburgh: St. Andrews, 1980). Also contra Cranfield, "Thoughts on New Testament Eschatology," 508 (Jesus expected "a significant interval between his resurrection and Parousia").

77. Pitre, *Jesus and the Last Supper*, 19.

about why Christ has not returned in 1 Thess 4? I think there is, and it is what we have suggested already: the bell lap of history has begun, but the time is not so short that Jesus cannot anticipate his own death and prepare his disciples for some activity in his potential absence.[78] This hypothesis accounts for the most gospel data while it also explains how Jesus fits between the activity of John the Baptist and the apostle Paul.

The Resurrection of the Dead

Now one particularly interesting feature of the eschatological prospect saying, and something that surely counts in favor of its general authenticity, is the fact that Jesus does not speak here about reunion with his disciples after his individual resurrection of the dead. The negative (separation) and positive (reunion) counterweights of this saying, or, to use different terms, the suffering (anticipated death) and the vindication (its overcoming) depicted here, straddle not the death and the individual resurrection of Jesus but death and reunion in the future kingdom of God. In this respect, Mark 14:25 and parallels are different from the threefold passion and resurrection predictions, which we have already historically problematized, as they localize suffering and vindication around Jesus's death and his resurrection after three days. Moreover, Mark 14:25 and parallels differ from how the Gospels depict the individual resurrection of Jesus and its aftermath where there is, in fact, reunion with the disciples (and for the timeline of the Gospels, of course, this is only a few days away).

In other words, the eschatological picture we see in Mark 14:25 and parallels has nothing to do with the individual resurrection of Jesus but expects only suffering/death and the final coming of the kingdom after some time in which the disciples are on their own. This makes sense in light of everything we have argued so far: Jesus embarked on a mission of announcing the kingdom of God was near (in the sense that people living in that generation would experience the transformation of history) and calling people to repent; at some point, though, he thought he might or would die in the eschatological tribulation and that history would continue until the kingdom would come; and he expected that, when that kingdom came, he would have a role to play. His own story, that is, would not end

78. Contra Bultmann, *History of the Synoptic Tradition*, 266, "in the immediate future," and also Allison, *Constructing Jesus*, 146 n. 518 ("if Mark 14:25 reflects something that Jesus said during Passover week, we might wonder whether he hoped that the end would come in the next few days").

in death. In Mark 14:25, that role is participating in the messianic banquet. Other sayings would fill in that picture to explain how he gets there, and how that reunion is possible: the coming of the kingdom coincides with Jesus's own coming as Dan 7's son of man.[79]

But what about the individual resurrection of Jesus? How do we account for the belief of early Jesus-loyalists about that, as well as what the Gospels do with it? I do not think this is very complicated. As far as we can tell, the resurrection of the dead was a common hope in Second Temple Judaism—by no means universal but certainly entertained by more than a sliver of the population.[80] The resurrection of the dead was to be a corporate event at the end time and often coincided with other significant end-time events (particularly the final judgment and whatever blissful existence followed for the righteous), even while disagreements persisted about the nature of the resurrected body.[81] The historical Jesus, we should have no doubt, expected the general resurrection of the dead, not only because the Gospels have him say so but because of the very fact that early Christians interpreted the appearances of Jesus with the language of "resurrection."[82] Paul's logic in 1 Cor 15 was not his own: Christ's resurrection makes sense only as connected to the notion of the general resurrection of the dead, such that Paul can even say that "if the dead are not raised [in the general resurrection], then not even Christ has been raised" (15:16).[83] In light of Jesus's expectation for the imminent arrival

79. De Jonge, *God's Final Envoy*, 68, unnecessarily reads Mark 14:25 against the parousia expectation, arguing that the former is more primitive than the latter.

80. See discussion in Sanders, *Jesus and Judaism*, 237; C. D. Elledge, "Resurrection of the Dead: Exploring Our Earliest Evidence Today," in *Resurrection: The Origin and Future of a Biblical Doctrine* (New York: T&T Clark, 2006), 36–41. Contra Geza Vermes, *The Resurrection: History and Myth* (New York: Doubleday, 2008), 55.

81. Cf. C. D. Elledge, *Resurrection of the Dead in Early Judaism: 200 BCE–CE 200* (Oxford: Oxford University Press, 2017), 19–43.

82. Pheme Perkins, "The Resurrection of Jesus," in *Handbook for the Study of the Historical Jesus*, ed. Tom Holmén and Stanley Porter (Leiden: Brill, 2010), 3:2430: "religiously interpreted experiences are inextricably entwined with the cultural vocabulary available to participants." See also Novakovic, *Resurrection*, 153; Fredriksen, *When Christians Were Jews*, 85–87. Contra Rudolf Pesch, "Zur Entstehung des Glaubens an die Auferstehung Jesu," *TQ* 153 (1973): 201–28, who argues that early Christian language about the resurrection of Jesus stems from a preexisting tradition about the individual resurrection of holy people, martyrs, and prophets. See also Klaus Berger, *Die Auferstehung des Propheten und die Erhöhung des Menschensohnes* (Göttingen: Vandenhoeck & Ruprecht, 1976). Pesch later modified this view in response to criticism. See "Zur Entstehung des Glaubens an die Auferstehung Jesu: Ein neuer Versuch," *FZPhTh* 30 (1983): 82–98.

83. Contrast Jürgen Becker, *Die Auferstehung Jesu Christi nach dem Neuen Testament: Ostererfahrung und Osterverständnis im Urchristentum* (Tübingen: Mohr Siebeck, 2007), 94–118, who argues that there is a more primitive view that understood Jesus as a vindicated martyr, not the

of the kingdom of God and the great assize, it makes sense that he also expected the general resurrection in the near future as part of the same constellation of events.[84] The early followers of Jesus, then, in saying that Jesus individually had been raised from the dead—for reasons we need not go into here—did indeed go beyond what Jesus had predicted, but they were not inventing a new end-time hope. Their theological work was about naming in the present what Jesus had told them to look out for. The subtext of the earliest formula, "he was raised," is that what Jesus expected is coming to pass, and what happened to Jesus himself after death is the surest proof. There is discontinuity between the preaching of Jesus and the proclamation of the early church as it pertains to the resurrection of Jesus, to be clear, but it is a discontinuity of placement rather than sheer invention. The belief in the resurrection of Jesus functions to pull back, into the present, what Jesus saw still on the horizon (though soon), such that the resurrection of Jesus, like a new center of gravity, does not create new planets but rather changes their orbits and draws more distant things nearer.

None of these arguments are original, to be sure, and the general sketch of the last paragraph is commonly found in discussion of resurrection beliefs in Christian origins. But the bearing of this view on the question of the parousia is significant and largely unexplored. As noted at the outset of this chapter, Julius Wellhausen argued that the parousia hope cannot go back to Jesus because Jesus did not expect to be individually raised from the dead—the former, he thought, is dependent on the latter. He is right that Jesus did not speak of being raised by himself after three days.[85] But he is wrong to think that this says anything about the parousia. In fact, disentangling the parousia from Jesus's individual resurrection of the dead actually illuminates some notorious idiosyncrasies in the gospel tradition and even Paul's letters and strengthens the overall thesis of this study.

Unlike the expectation for Jesus's future coming, the prediction of Jesus's individual resurrection of the dead is rather easy to remove from the gospel tradition without much disturbance, which I think is possible precisely because of its secondary nature. The expectation obviously appears in the three passion and resurrection predictions already discussed, but beyond that only a few other times (cf., e.g., Luke 13:32; 16:31; possibly Mark 12:10 and par.; John 12:23–24), typically

---

firstfruits of the general resurrection. This hypothesis does not account for the eschatological nature of early Christian belief.

84. See Ulrich B. Müller, "Auferweckt und erhöht: Zur Genese des Osterglaubens," *NTS* (2008): 201–20; Maurice Casey, *Jesus of Nazareth: An Independent Historian's Account of His Life and Teaching* (London: T&T Clark International, 2010), 380–81.

85. As noted above (p. 327n4), here I disagree with Kümmel, *Promise and Fulfillment*, who assumes that Jesus predicted his own individual resurrection from the dead.

tacked onto the end of other sayings of Jesus. Moreover, it is significant that, in terms of form, none of these predictions of individual resurrection are connected to the parousia of Jesus. That is, nowhere do we find the prediction that Jesus will suffer, die, be raised after three days, and then come in glory at a future time. It is striking that the Gospel writers never have Jesus say, in the same place, what they themselves actually believed about the sequence of these important things.[86]

Others have observed and written about this phenomenon. Joachim Jeremias remarked that "in no saying of Jesus do resurrection and parousia stand side by side as two events," and further suggested it was "the Easter experience which led to the systematization of the course of events into a sequence of resurrection, exaltation, and parousia."[87] C. H. Dodd ended up in a similar place, which is interesting because of the otherwise significant disagreements between Dodd and Jeremias concerning eschatology. Dodd noted that the future predictions in the Synoptics are of two kinds: predictions of death and resurrection, and predictions of the "coming of the son of man." He summarized the situation in this way: "In none of the passages which forecast resurrection is there any reference to *parousia*, and similarly in the forecasts of the coming of the Son of Man there is no reference to resurrection."[88]

Given this separation, it is initially hard to see, contra Wellhausen, how the parousia could be found guilty by association with the individual resurrection of Jesus, and thereby historically suspect. But how might we make sense of the state of the tradition as it stands? Dodd offered the following:

> The phenomena [of the predictions never having the sequence of suffering, death, resurrection, parousia] would so far be consistent with the view that Jesus spoke in broad, general terms, suggestive rather than precise, with the use of varying imagery, of a renewal of life and activity upon an enhanced level after death, and that these terms were understood, sometimes as referring to a return from the grave to his followers, and restored fellowship with them on earth, and sometimes as referring to a final consummation beyond history; that in fact resurrection and *parousia* are, in these predictions, different aspects of the same reality.[89]

86. It is also striking that the creedal formulas in other New Testament texts that are concerned with Jesus's resurrection from the dead do not connect his resurrection to his coming in the future. This is also noted by de Jonge, *God's Final Envoy*, 74.

87. Jeremias, *New Testament Theology*, 286.

88. Dodd, *Historical Tradition in the Fourth Gospel*, 413–14. Again at 414: "There is thus no place where the Synoptic predictions give the sequence: sufferings, death, resurrection, *parousia*."

89. Dodd, *Historical Tradition in the Fourth Gospel*, 414. See Dodd, *Parables of the Kingdom*, 74–77.

So for Dodd, what remained general and unified for Jesus became, for his followers, specific and diffused.[90] This view, or something quite close to it, has found numerous supporters over the years, including among proponents of the so-called eschatological interpretation of Jesus.[91] But I am not convinced for several reasons.

(1) Dodd accurately describes the formal features of the tradition—that parousia and resurrection are never conjoined—but then offers a historical explanation that actually goes against the very features he identified (for Jesus, he thinks, parousia and resurrection were not only conjoined but actually conflated). If the thing that got us to ask this historical question is the striking fact that parousia and resurrection are always *distinguished* in our sources, how does it work, as a matter of historical argumentation, to say that they actually grew from a singular expectation? (2) Moreover, appealing to a general vagueness of prediction on Jesus's part is similarly problematic. There is actually little in our sources that is vague on these matters; it is their clarity, again, assumed here by Dodd himself, that raises this intriguing historical question. Dodd's claim about vagueness and generality is therefore an appeal to the unknown—an appeal to a vagueness and generality that has presumably been replaced by the only sources we have, which are not vague or general. (3) In addition, I wager, with fear and trembling, that at least for Dodd (not necessarily all who agree with him on this), there is an underlying theological advantage to saying that Jesus's eschatological teaching was characterized by generality, vagueness, and imprecision: it rescues him from error about the future. C. K. Barrett wrote that, for Jesus, "how this vindication would happen mattered little, and Jesus seems to have used the conventional apocalyptic language of resurrection and of parousia to describe it."[92] It strikes me as a dis-

90. See also C. H. Dodd, *The Apostolic Preaching and Its Developments* (New York: Harper, 1960), 31: "In one respect it appears that even within a very few years the perspective of the kerygma must have altered, namely, in respect of the relation conceived to exist between the death, resurrection, and exaltation of Christ on the one hand, and His second advent on the other." See also 33.

91. See, e.g., George Duncan, *Jesus, Son of Man* (New York: Macmillan, 1949), 140; Jeremias, *New Testament Theology*, 274 ("the distinction between resurrection and Parousia derives from the post-Easter Christology . . . both events were alternative ways of describing the final triumph of God." And again, "while ultimate clarity is impossible to achieve, there is much to suggest that the earliest conception was that the revelation of the Son of man would come about in the form of an assumption to God"), 310; Robinson, *Jesus and His Coming*, 136; Eduard Schweizer, *Jesus*, trans. David E. Green (Atlanta: John Knox, 1971), 20; Meyer, *Aims of Jesus*, 202–6; Barrett, *Jesus and the Gospel Tradition*, 82–83 ("the two forms of prediction were not carefully distinguished"); Allison, *End of the Ages*, 160 ("Jesus . . . did not distinguish between the resurrection and the Parousia of the Son of man"); Allison, *Resurrection of Jesus*, 200–201 (with reference to Dodd).

92. Barrett, *Jesus and the Gospel Tradition*, 99.

tinctly modern, Western, and academic understanding of eschatology, battered by its turbulent reception history as we have seen in part 2, to say that interest in how things happen matter little. What other text from the Second Temple period refers vaguely and generally to the "vindication" of Israel and shows no interest in how that might happen and what it may entail? Barrett, like Dodd, confuses shared imagery with distinct events. This is a category mistake. We have lots of shared imagery in Second Temple Jewish eschatology, but seers knew full well when they were talking about the resurrection of the dead vis-à-vis the defeat of Israel's enemies, the reconstitution of the tribes, the rebuilding of the new temple, and the final judgment, among other things. (4) Furthermore, if Dodd is right, we struggle to explain the intertextuality of the New Testament, and especially the consistent linkage of Dan 7 to the future coming of Jesus and *not* to his resurrection from the dead.[93] If the resurrection of Jesus and the parousia of Jesus, as depicted in our sources, are actually two branches that emerged from the same stump, we would expect to find the same nutrients feeding both. But where, then, is the coming of Dan 7's son of man applied to the resurrection of Jesus?[94] Why is his "coming" never identified with his vindication after death and exit from the tomb?[95] (5) Finally, there remains the simple matter of motive. If Jesus did in fact

93. Dan 7 is absent from 1 Cor 15:3–8 as well as the resurrection narratives in the Gospels, minus one line in the Great Commission in Matthew (28:18: ἐδόθη μοι πᾶσα ἐξουσία ἐν οὐρανῷ καὶ ἐπὶ [τῆς] γῆς). It is telling in this respect that the masterful study by Lidija Novakovic, *Raised from the Dead according to Scripture: The Role of Israel's Scripture in the Early Christian Interpretations of Jesus' Resurrection*, Jewish and Christian Texts in Contexts and Related Studies Series (London: Bloomsbury, 2012), 172, discusses Dan 7 in the entire study only in relation to Matt 28:18.

94. Though it is not a significant feature of her historical reconstruction, Fredriksen, *When Christians Were Jews*, 105, suggests at one point that for the earliest community after Jesus's death, animated by imminent eschatological hopes, the "resurrection appearances of Jesus should have 'counted' as his second, messianic revelation in glory. For a brief period of time, I have argued, the community probably did interpret these appearances in this way. Time disabused them of that interpretation, however, especially once the appearances ceased." The qualification "probably did" is necessary because there is no evidence for this linkage anywhere in the New Testament. She writes again at 106, "the expectation of Jesus' second and public manifestation as messiah was dictated by the failed Parousia of his initial resurrection appearances."

95. Lack of evidence has not prevented some critics from asserting just that. Hans-Werner Bartsch, *Das Auferstehung: Sein historisches und sein theologisches Problem*, TF 41 (Hamburg: Reich, 1965), 9–15, speculated that the New Testament fails to recount the appearance of the risen Christ to Peter because in that event, Jesus announced the fulfillment of the parousia, and this did not square with Christian eschatological beliefs later in the first century. Less speculative, but still unconvincing, is Rudolf Pesch's argument, *Simon Petrus: Geschichte und geschichtliche Bedeutung des ersten Jüngers Jesu Christi* (Stuttgart: Hiersemann, 1980), 52–55, that early Christians believed the enthronement of Jesus in heaven after death was the fulfillment

say what Dodd and others have asserted, then it is hard to understand why the resurrection experiences would have modified the beliefs of Jesus followers in the ways suggested. For what reason would followers create the idea of a still-future parousia in the sense of a return from heaven and distinguish that so sharply from his resurrection?

There is a much simpler scenario that better explains the same phenomenon that Dodd and many others have identified. The original Jesus group operated on the assumption that this was the last generation, and when Jesus spoke about the near future, he spoke about the coming of the kingdom of God, the resurrection of the dead, and the final judgment. Since Jesus likely at some point entertained the possibility he would lose his life in the eschatological tribulation, he taught that he, too, would come as the son of man at the same time that those final events in history transpired. The future coming of Jesus, then, along with the final arrival of the kingdom, the resurrection of the dead, and the final judgment, would constitute, together and roughly contemporaneously, the climactic arrival of the Lord's day as predicted by the prophets. What Jesus appears *not* to have expected, but his followers nevertheless believed was true, is that shortly after his death, the general resurrection of the dead would begin with Jesus himself alone. Jesus, I think, would have been just as surprised as the women at the empty tomb (according to the Gospels' retelling).[96] But the impact of the resurrection appearances of Jesus on the theological imaginations of his early followers is predictable: if what Jesus expected in the future was coming to pass, even the resurrection of the dead, then they began to search for further evidence in their present for the realization of outstanding hopes. The spirit of God had been liberally poured out, too, they came to believe. Jesus's messianic "reign," or his enthronement, which he identified with the final consummation and the coming of the kingdom in power, had begun with Jesus's own resurrection from the dead. They further remembered Jesus's own ministry and activity in light of future expectations like the coming day of

---

of his predictions about the coming of the son of man from Dan 7. See also Adolf von Harnack, "Die Verklärungsgeschichte Jesu, der Bericht des Paulus (I. Kor 15,3ff) und die beiden Christusvisionen des Petrus," in *Zur neutestamentlichen Überlieferung von der Auferstehung Jesu*, ed. Paul Hoffmann (Darmstadt: Wissenschaftliche Buchgesellschaft, 1988), 89–117. Ulrich B. Müller, "Parusie und Menschensohn," *ZNW* 92 (2001): 17, is creative but fails to compel: while observing that there is no evidence of regarding the exaltation of Jesus to be the coming of the son of man, he takes this as evidence that viewing Jesus as the coming son of man does not belong at the earliest stages of christological development.

96. Rightly C. E. B. Cranfield, "The Resurrection of Jesus Christ," *ExpTim* 101 (1990): 170: "neither the women nor the disciples had the slightest expectation of their Master's being raised from the dead before the general eschatological resurrection."

the Lord, linking his own crucifixion with its onset. The "gathering" expected at the end time was underway in the mission of his followers, forming assemblies, and speaking about the good news prophesied by Isaiah.

An Analogy

If one imagines eschatological expectation like a chapter book, my argument is that Jesus and his followers had books with essentially the same final chapter. Before Easter, and after Easter, the final chapter did not change much formally: it was still about the coming of the son of man, the arrival of the kingdom of God, the resurrection of the dead, the final judgment. Dodd and followers have Jesus composing a vague final chapter, and his followers rewriting that chapter in light of later experience, thereby creating the notion of his future return. I disagree. The bulk of the creative theological work of the early Christians was spent not in writing a new final chapter but in adding more penultimate chapters. The early Christians thought that there was more to the story, *before* the end, because of the resurrection of Jesus. To draft this content, they went to the Scriptures for help and listened to the voice of the spirit of God in the present. But the chapters they composed make sense only if one knows where the story is going—if one knows the final chapter. Paul makes the most sense in this light. As we have seen in part 3, much of Paul's theological work in his letters presupposes the final coming of Jesus, the resurrection of the dead, and the final judgment. What Paul had to contend, advocate, and make arguments about was what was going on in the in-between—after the death and resurrection of Jesus in the past, and before the coming of Jesus and the arrival of the kingdom in the future. Paul's exegesis of Scripture is particularly revealing in this respect, especially his use of the Psalms. For Paul, the Psalms—namely, Pss 8 and 110—do *not* answer the question, What comes next, now that Jesus is dead and gone and we have to write the next chapter? The Psalms, rather, answer this: Knowing that Jesus has died and risen, and knowing we will meet him again in the coming of the kingdom, *what is he doing now*?[97] Put otherwise, What is the risen Christ up to in the in-between of his earthly activity and what he said would happen in the future? Here we are back at our exegesis of 1 Cor 15, where Paul asserted with the aid of Pss 8 and 110 that, *before* "the end," Jesus was "reigning"—albeit from heaven—and putting "all his enemies under his feet"—albeit cosmic enemies rather than earthly ones.

97. Contra Terrance Callan, "Psalm 110:1 and the Origin of the Expectation That Jesus Will Come Again," *CBQ* 44 (1982): 622–36.

This, I think, is not exactly the kind of "reign" Jesus expected and told his followers about (nor, as far as we can tell, were these psalms read messianically in this fashion before the Christian movement).[98] But the eschatological scenario of 1 Cor 15 and the cosmic reign of Christ has been created on the basis of what Jesus held out in the future about the coming kingdom, and realized before that only because of what the rest of 1 Cor 15 is about: that Χριστὸς ἐγήγερται ("Christ has been raised").[99]

The reason that the predictions of the individual resurrection of Jesus and the parousia expectation are distinct in the Gospels, then, is not that they were originally different ways of describing the same thing, or that the latter somehow grew out of the former. They are distinct in our sources because they have different origins. The more primitive parousia hope functioned to structure the imagined future and was so widespread and presupposable because, I think, it goes back to Jesus himself. The belief in Jesus's resurrection emerged from the early Christian Easter experiences (however we understand and describe those). So Jesus followers ended up telling two different suffering and vindication stories as they pertain to Jesus—one about his death and vindication in the (future) coming kingdom as the son of man, and another about his death and vindication in his individual res-

98. Though note Ruben A. Bühner, *Messianic High Christology: New Testament Variants of Second Temple Judaism* (Waco, TX: Baylor University Press, 2021), 85–93, thinks he can spy a messianic interpretation of Ps 110 in the LXX and from there infers, "Ps 110 was probably an integral part of the messianic discourse of Second Temple Judaism even long before the Jesus movement" (93). Cf. more fully in Bühner, *Hohe Messianologie: Übermenschliche Aspekte eschatologischer Heilsgestalten im Frühjudentum*, WUNT 2/523 (Tübingen: Mohr Siebeck, 2020), 51–75. Martin Hengel, "'Sit at My Right Hand!,'" in *Studies in Early Christology* (Edinburgh: T&T Clark, 1995), 185–89, believes that Dan 7 and Ps 110 were already combined in 1 Enoch. It has also been argued that Jesus's question about David's son in Mark 12:35–37 presupposes a messianic understanding of this passage, even while we lack external evidence to illuminate that. Cf. David M. Hay, *Glory at the Right Hand: Psalm 110 in Early Christianity* (Nashville: Abingdon, 1973), 30 ("the argument of Jesus . . . is most easily understood if a messianic interpretation prevailed").

99. This hypothesis also makes sense of the only passage in the Gospels (Matt 28:18) that connects Dan 7 to the resurrection (where it is not really connected to the resurrection itself but Jesus's glorified state, postresurrection). On the use of Dan 7 in Matt 28:18, see Davies and Allison, *Matthew*, 3:682–83; Richard B. Hays, *Echoes of Scripture in the Gospels* (Waco, TX: Baylor University Press, 2016), 183–85. "Depicting Jesus after his resurrection by speaking of his heavenly status in terms borrowed from Daniel 7," so Chilton, "(The) Son of (the) Man, and Jesus," 277, is possible by reading backward into the past/present what is expected will one day be, or, to put it otherwise, realizing future eschatological hopes. In Matt 28, the exaggerated claim that Jesus currently has "all authority on heaven and on earth" is surely a case of rereading past/present realities in light of future hopes. See also the description of Jesus in Rev 1:12–16, and possibly 1 Pet 1:21 (in which I would wager that the δόξαν αὐτῷ δόντα is inspired by Dan 7).

urrection from the dead after three days. We only confuse matters if we think the parousia presupposes Jesus's individual resurrection of the dead (so Wellhausen), or parousia and resurrection were originally more or less synonyms (so Dodd). We make the most sense of the most data if we conclude that the parousia was an expectation *prior to* the belief in Jesus's individual resurrection and *distinct from* the resurrection in general. It did not derive from later experience, but it helped organize and make sense of later experience.

15

The Ambiguities of the "Coming" of the Son of Man

At this point, I want to explore a potential implication of the argument that we separate the parousia hope from the belief of Jesus's individual resurrection of the dead. If, as I have argued, it is unlikely that Jesus expected to be individually raised from the dead after three days but probable that he did speak of a future "coming" after a brief interim, we might well ask, Whence and whither might he come, then? To put this another way, How would Jesus's future "coming" relate to the resurrection of the dead if these were in fact expected to be distinct events that would happen at the end of the age?

I want to entertain in what follows two different possibilities, and it may not be wise to systematize and separate them categorically: his "coming" was a way of speaking generally of his return after the general resurrection, or his "coming" was indeed initially regarded as a coming from heaven that would coincide with the general resurrection in some way. While I will submit that the latter may be preferable, the more important point is that either option supports the probability of the basic sequence in Jesus's eschatological expectation that I have argued for already: potential death, brief period of absence, "coming" at the consummation of the age. The details on whence and whither he "comes," that is, will remain somewhat ambiguous, and it may well have been so at the beginning. What I hope to show is that, either way we go, the inferences I have made about Jesus on other grounds make good sense in historical context. Moreover, either of these two options appears to be more congruent with extant Jewish views about the end and the afterlife than the scenario we find in many sources produced by the Jesus movement, which have him being individually raised from the dead, present in heaven, and expected to come to earth in his risen body.

"Coming" as Arrival

It is important to make an initial point about the coming of the son of man in Dan 7 that we can be more confident about. Many historical Jesus critics have argued that it makes little sense to read the coming of the one like a son of man in 7:13–14 as originally envisioning a coming down to earth. What we have here is not a "coming down," it is argued, but a "going up."[1] We recall that this argument is often made by those who seek to connect Dan 7 to the expectation for Jesus's vindication in his resurrection or ascension to God's right hand (often reading Dan 7:13–14 and Ps 110:1 as depicting more or less synonymous realities).[2] While we should not permit Dan 7's original import to dictate its reception in subsequent centuries, it may well be that Dan 7 in its original context does not depict the one like a son of man "coming down" to earth. However, Dan 7 does not clearly depict the one like a son of man "going up" either. It is ambiguous, so John Collins: the text "does not indicate whether the [figure] is ascending or descending or moving horizontally."[3] The crucial point is that concentrating on the direction of movement, whether up or down, distracts from the real focus of the vision, which is where the one like a son of man ends up. The coming of this figure is about his *arrival* before the Ancient One at this judgment scene:

> MT: "behold, with the clouds of heaven there came [אתה] one like a son of man, and he came [מטה] to [עד] the Ancient One, and was presented [הקרבוהי] before him"

Now, to be clear, it is far from obvious that we are in heaven here.[4] The vision begins with beasts who are "coming up out of the sea," walking, trampling, and devouring

1. See Norman Perrin, *Rediscovering the Teaching of Jesus* (New York: Harper & Row, 1967), 173–85.

2. See pp. 191–92 above.

3. John J. Collins, *Daniel: A Commentary on the Book of Daniel*, Hermeneia (Minneapolis: Fortress, 1993), 311.

4. See Maurice Casey, *The Son of Man: The Interpretation and Influence of Daniel 7* (London: SPCK, 1979), 22–29; Brian Han Gregg, *The Historical Jesus and the Final Judgment Sayings in Q*, WUNT 2/207 (Tübingen: Mohr Siebeck, 2006), 42: "The final judgment is clearly executed on the earth. Both the destruction of oppressors and the consequent resurrection make this

on the earth. The vision continues seamlessly to v. 9: "as I watched, thrones were set in place, and the Ancient One took his throne."[5] To say that thrones were "set in place" means they were not formerly in that place, which would be a peculiar description of God in the heavenly realm.[6] We should also note that the Ancient One is midmotion, "taking his seat." The widespread motif of God coming in the "day of the Lord" tradition, wherein God is depicted as being on the move, is near to hand. It seems to me that it is not only possible but preferable to imagine the judgment scene of vv. 9–10 taking place upon or near the earth (in some kind of liminal space, perhaps) where the rest of the drama has unfolded, including the consequences of the judgment that follows the opening of the books. That includes, too, then, what happens in vv. 13–14, which appears in its details to be a public event. This figure is "given" "peoples, nations, and tongues" that will "serve him," paralleled in the same book by the stone of Dan 2 that became a mountain that fills *the whole earth*.

The takeaway for Dan 7:13–14 is that, while it remains unclear where the one like a son of man is coming from, the point is that he *arrives at* this climactic scene of judgment. He is "presented before" the Ancient One where the thrones have been set up, where the verdict is given on the injustice and oppression caused by the beastly kingdoms.[7] Concerning the use of Dan 7 in the Jesus tradition as

plain." Note that 4Q530 II, 16–18 envisages Dan 7 on the earth, though there is no messianic interpretation here. It reads, "I saw something amazing in my dream this night: The Ruler of the heavens came down to earth [לארעא נחת], and thrones were erected and the Great Holy One sa[t down. A hundred hun]dreds were serving him, a thousand thousands [were . . .] him, [and ten thousand times ten thousand be]fore him were standing. And behold, [bo]oks were opened and the sentence was proclaimed." Cf. also 1 En. 90.20 ("a throne was constructed in the pleasant land, and the Lord of the sheep sat upon it . . . and the sealed books were opened"), which clearly evokes Dan 7:9–10—so G. K. Beale, *The Use of Daniel in Jewish Apocalyptic Literature and in the Revelation of St. John* (Eugene, OR: Wipf & Stock, 2010), 81—and has the throne not in heaven but "in the pleasant land" (itself drawn from Dan 11:16, which refers to Palestine). Ruben A. Bühner, *Messianic High Christology: New Testament Variants of Second Temple Judaism* (Waco, TX: Baylor University Press, 2021), 9, has concluded that "except for the Parables of Enoch . . . we lack clear evidence that any Jew in the Second Temple period understood it in the way many modern scholars conclude from the Danielic text itself, that is, as a heavenly ascent."

5. So also John Goldingay, *Daniel*, WBC 30 (Dallas: Word, 1989), 164–65: "there is no reason to suppose that the scene on earth that Daniel has been watching has changed. . . . Daniel continues to look in the direction he had been looking. That the scene takes place on earth is presupposed by v. 22."

6. Also note by Gregg, *Historical Jesus and the Final Judgment Sayings in Q*, 42: "it is less clear whether the 'trial' is set in heaven or on earth. The fact that 'thrones were set in place' may indicate that the heavenly tribunal has come to earth in order to render judgment."

7. See James A. Montgomery, *A Critical and Exegetical Commentary on the Book of Daniel*, ICC (Edinburgh: T&T Clark, 1964), 304. C. F. D. Moule, *The Origin of Christology* (Cambridge: Cambridge University Press, 1977), 18, wisely observed, "it is objected, [that] the human figure of Dan. 7 is brought *to* God, whereas, in the apocalyptic passages of the Gospels, the Son of Man

discussed thus far, *"coming" as "arrival"* makes good sense, and we can state that without needing to settle definitively the question of where he is coming from.

Raised Then Arrive?

In any case, I do want to press a bit further on the question of the direction of movement, even if it requires some speculation, in order to show that two different possibilities would still support the arguments advanced so far. The first is the simple idea that when Jesus spoke about the coming of the son of man after an interim, the assumption was that he had been raised from the dead. This is actually not too different from what his later followers would claim—the crucial distinction being that, in light of the resurrection appearances, they thought he had been raised before and apart from the general resurrection of the dead and taken up to heaven, and so they talked about his future coming from that perspective. In support of the notion that "coming" referred to his return after being raised, one could observe the general fact that, amid the diversity of Jewish eschatology, the general resurrection (when it is affirmed) typically precedes the judgment (as is logically fitting, of course).[8] And Dan 7, as already noted, is the *locus classicus* for the final judgment in Second Temple Jewish literature and in the Jesus movement. Moreover, since it is probable that Jesus talked about suffering in the eschatological tribulation—and was perhaps influenced by Dan 7 itself in this notion, as entertained above—it is easy to see why his coming/arrival before the Ancient One would assume that resurrection had occurred. Interestingly, the eschatological description of the resurrection later in Daniel (12:1–3), which was also important for the early Jesus movement, seems to assume something close to that very thing: Dan 12 begins with predictions about "a time of anguish, such as has never occurred since nations first came into existence" (v. 1), just as Dan 7

---

comes *from* heaven. How, then, can the two be associated—let alone identified? It seems to me that the vindication of the Son of man in the court of heaven (when he is brought *to God*) is identical in meaning with his manifestation in judgement *on* earth (or *to* the dwellers on earth), and that it is not difficult to make the link between the two. His coming to God for vindication *is* his being shown on earth in judgment. The glory of the human figure *is* his investiture as Judge of the earth. I would dare call it prosaic and unimaginative to object that the one cannot be identical with the other."

8. Cf. Marius Reiser, *Jesus and Judgment: The Eschatological Proclamation in Its Jewish Context*, trans. Linda M. Maloney (Minneapolis: Fortress, 1997), 43–163; Christian Stettler, *Das letzte Gericht: Studien zur Endgerichtserwartung von den Schriftpropheten bis Jesus*, WUNT 2/299 (Tübingen: Mohr Siebeck, 2011), 112–84.

depicts anguish and suffering for "the holy ones" before the granting of the kingdom (vv. 21, 23, 25), and Dan 12 continues to describe deliverance for those mentioned "in the book" (v. 1), just as Dan 7:10 describes "the books" at the judgment. Daniel 12:2 then concludes, "many of those who sleep in the dust of the earth shall awake, some to everlasting life, and some to shame and everlasting contempt."

If the original Jesus movement expected something along these lines, there would be continuity but also some discontinuity with eschatological expectations in the post-Easter period as far as we can reconstruct them. In terms of continuity, there would be, as already mentioned, the coming of Jesus expected after resurrection, as well as his coming linked to the judgment (while, as we noted in part 3, there may be some disagreement in New Testament literature about whether Jesus is the judge or a kind of celestial lawyer). In terms of discontinuity, Jesus may not have so clearly specified that his coming would be a coming "from heaven" as his followers soon believed, but simply spoke of the "coming of the son of man" to refer to a future *arrival* before God at the end of the age. It is worth recalling here that New Testament sources do not universally claim that Jesus's coming precedes and causes the general resurrection of the dead. In fact, the Synoptic Gospels do not explicitly coordinate the coming of Jesus with the general resurrection in this way, while Paul does, and the Gospel of John seems to assume it as well (5:28–29). This is a striking fact that has received little attention.[9] The structure of early Christian memory could reflect the fact that Jesus himself had not coordinated his coming in such a causal way with the general resurrection, and our sources diverge because early Christians made that connection in light of their belief that Jesus himself had been raised beforehand.

This would be a fairly significant difference between the eschatological expectations of the original Jesus group and those of the post-Easter church, to be sure. But it would not challenge the core eschatological scenario that I have argued goes back to Jesus and is about his potential death, brief absence, and future arrival at the consummation.

"Coming" from Heaven?

That is but one option. Another possibility would imply more continuity with early Christian claims. Here Jesus, like his post-Easter followers, expected a com-

9. Though see Thomas Kazen, "The Coming Son of Man Revisited," *JSHJ* 5 (2007): 59, who notes that nowhere in the synoptic sayings is the coming of the son of man "*expressly* associated" with the general resurrection.

ing *from heaven* that precedes or initiates the general resurrection of the dead. The main difference between Jesus and his early followers would be a simple matter of timing: based on the resurrection appearances, they thought Jesus had been raised well before his coming, whereas, for Jesus, the general resurrection and his coming must have been expected in closer succession.

One might immediately object, however, with this: if Jesus thought that he might die, but he did not predict his individual resurrection from the dead after three days, how could he expect to be in heaven before his future coming? I want to pause and take some time to explore this question.

Excursus: Death and Heaven

In the Gospel of Luke, Jesus famously tells the dying man next to him on the cross that he will not merely remember him when he comes in his kingdom, but "you will be with me today in paradise" (23:43).[10] The idea, problematic as it was to later Christians who wanted to defend the *descensus Christi ad inferos*, is that Luke's Jesus plans to be in heaven "today" (and he expects that others will be there, too).[11] Luke also contains a parable about an unnamed rich man and a poor man named Lazarus that assumes a similar situation: upon death, Lazarus "was carried away by the angels to be with Abraham" (16:22). Concerning these two uniquely Lukan episodes, whose historicity we might justifiably question, what is to prevent us from summoning the gray bead from the Jesus Seminar of old: "Jesus did not say this, but the ideas contained in it are close to his own"?[12]

Amid the diversity of views of life after death in Second Temple Judaism, it was not uncommon, it appears, to expect that the righteous dead would be present in some way in the heavenly realm after

10. On whether the bandit speaks of Jesus coming "into" ($\mathfrak{P}^{75}$, B) or coming "in" (א, A) his kingdom, cf. Norval Geldenhuys, *Commentary on the Gospel of Luke* (London: Marshall, Morgan & Scott, 1950), 611; Darrell L. Bock, *Luke 9:51–24:53*, BECNT (Grand Rapids: Baker Books, 1996), 1856–57.

11. Contrast the strained exegesis of E. Earle Ellis, *Christ and the Future in New Testament History*, NovTSup 97 (Leiden: Brill, 2000), 139–46, who argues that "with me in paradise" does not actually mean the man will be "with Jesus in paradise" but that the man will somehow "participate" in the resurrected life of Jesus by "shar[ing] in Jesus' exaltation corporately" (145).

12. Robert W. Funk, Roy W. Hoover, and the Jesus Seminar, *The Five Gospels: The Search for the Authentic Words of Jesus* (New York: Macmillan, 1993), 36.

death. This view was held by those who affirmed an afterlife but denied (or did not otherwise explicitly affirm) the resurrection of the dead,[13] as we find in Wisdom of Solomon, Jubilees, some of the Dead Sea Scrolls, Testament of Abraham, 4 Maccabees, and Philo.[14] But it was also held by those who affirmed the resurrection of the dead (such as the evangelist Luke in the examples above). In some texts, this heavenly state is rather nondescript, focused more on place than experience.[15] But we also find the following:

13. On the methodological questions involved here, see James H. Charlesworth, "Where Does the Concept of Resurrection Appear and How Do We Know That?," in *Resurrection: The Origin and Future of a Biblical Doctrine* (New York: T&T Clark, 2006), 1–21.

14. See Wis 3:1–7 ("the souls of the righteous are ἐν χειρὶ θεοῦ"); 4:7–15 ("the righteous, though they die early, will be at rest"). In Jub. 23.30–31, it remains unclear whether the "rising up" in these lines refers to resurrection and, if so, how it might relate to the assertion that "their bones will rest in the earth, but their spirits will increase joy." In the Dead Sea Scrolls, see 1QS IV, 7–8 (which mentions "eternal enjoyment with endless life, and a crown of glory with majestic raiment in eternal light"). See also 1QH XII, 26–27; XIV, 14–17. For broader discussion, see David C. Sim, "Life after Death? The Question of Immediate Life after Death in the Dead Sea Scrolls and in the Gospel of Matthew," in *Matthew within Judaism: Israel and the Nations in the First Gospel*, ed. Anders Runesson and Daniel M. Gurtner, ECL 27 (Atlanta: SBL Press, 2020), 329–46. There appears to be a diversity of views about the afterlife operative at Qumran; see discussions in Albert Hogeterp, *Expectations of the End*, STDJ 83 (Leiden: Brill, 2009), 247–334; C. D. Elledge, *Resurrection of the Dead in Early Judaism: 200 BCE–CE 200* (Oxford: Oxford University Press, 2017), 150–74. Resurrection appears, in my opinion, but may not have been the dominant understanding.

See also T. Ab. 10.1–14.15 and discussion in Dale C. Allison Jr., *Testament of Abraham*, CEJL (Berlin: de Gruyter, 2003), 236–93; 4 Macc 7:19; 16:25; 18:23 ("the sons of Abraham with their victorious mother are gathered together [συναγελάζονται] into the chorus of the fathers and have received pure and immortal souls from God"), and discussion in Jan A. Sigvartsen, *Afterlife and Resurrection Beliefs in the Pseudepigrapha* (London: Bloomsbury T&T Clark, 2019), 104–59; and Philo, *Mos.* 2.228; *QG* 1.86; *Conf.* 78; *Her.* 274; *Sacr.* 1.5–3.10. Cf. Alan F. Segal, *Life after Death: A History of the Afterlife in Western Religion* (New York: Doubleday, 2004), 368–75.

15. So, e.g., (1) In the oldest portions of 1 Enoch, perhaps even earlier than the book of Daniel, Enoch learns that the souls of the dead, who await the final judgment, are kept in holes on a celestial mountain above (22.1–13). There are four such holes, and their occupants are divided according to their righteousness (or lack thereof). There is some debate about the presence of resurrection in 1 En. 22 before the judgment. For discussion see Elledge, *Resurrection of the Dead in Early Judaism*, 130–49. (2) Josephus once contends that the souls of the righteous, those "remaining spotless and obedient, are allotted the most holy place in heaven, whence, in the revolution of the ages, they are introduced as new inhabitants [ἀντενοικίζονται] in pure bodies" (*J.W.* 3.374–375 [LCL, my modifications]). This is similar to *Ag. Ap.* 2.218 (LCL): "those who observe the laws and, if they must needs die for them, willingly meet death, God has granted a renewed existence and in the revolution of the ages the gift of a better life." For discussion, cf. Joseph Sievers, "Josephus and the Afterlife," in *Understanding Josephus: Seven Perspectives*, ed.

- In the final scene of the Similitudes of 1 Enoch, Enoch is taken up and sees "the first fathers and the righteous of old, dwelling in that place" (70.4).[16]
- In 4 Ezra, the seer is instructed that at the moment of death, "the spirit leaves the body to return again to him who gave it . . . it adores the glory of the Most High" (7.78; see also 4.35–37; 7.91–101).[17]
- In Hebrews, the author encourages the audience by telling them "you have come to Mount Zion and to the city of the living God, the heavenly Jerusalem, and to innumerable angels in festal gathering, and to the assembly of the firstborn who are enrolled in heaven, and to God the judge of all, and to the spirits of the righteous made perfect" (12:22).
- Several times in Revelation the readers are given glimpses into heaven before the resurrection(s) of the dead where there are descriptions of those who had died in obedience to God (6:9–11; 7:9–17).
- In the Martyrdom and Ascension of Isaiah, Isaiah says that in the seventh heaven, he saw "all the righteous ones from the time of Adam" (9.7).[18]
- In Zech 14's prediction of God's coming to Zion with "all the holy ones with him" (v. 5), it is probable that, in its original context, the "holy ones" are angels.[19] But we know that some read this as a

---

Steve Mason (Sheffield: Sheffield Academic, 1998), 20–34; Elledge, *Resurrection of the Dead in Early Judaism*, 175–98. (3) In LAB, the souls of the righteous are "stored" "in peace" "until the time allotted the world to be complete" (23.13), whereupon the resurrection of the dead will occur (3.10). (4) In 2 Baruch, the coming of the messiah coincides with the resurrection of the dead, and "it will happen at that time that those treasuries will be opened in which the number of the souls of the righteous were kept" (30.1). See Jared Ludlow, "Death and the Afterlife in *2 Baruch*," in *Interpreting 4 Ezra and 2 Baruch: International Studies*, ed. Gabriele Boccaccini and Jason M. Zurawski, LSTS (London: Bloomsbury T&T Clark, 2014), 116–23.

16. See Lidija Novakovic, *Resurrection: A Guide for the Perplexed* (London: Bloomsbury T&T Clark, 2016), 20–21.

17. Cf. Daniel J. Harrington, "Afterlife Expectations in Pseudo-Philo, 4 Ezra, and 2 Baruch, and Their Implications for the New Testament," in *Resurrection in the New Testament: Festschrift for J. Lambrecht*, ed. Reimund Bieringer (Leuven: Leuven University Press, 2002), 21–34. See also 7.32 ("the earth shall give up those who are asleep in it; and the chambers shall give up the souls which have been committed to them").

18. Cf. Mart. Ascen. Isa. 7.22; 8.26; 9.12; 11.40.

19. Collins, *Daniel*, 316, also concludes that the "holy ones" in the sectarian literature of Qumran are normally angels or heavenly beings.

> reference not just to angels but to human figures ("holy persons" or "the righteous"), coming with God on the last day.[20] That understanding of "holy ones" may even be implied in certain New Testament texts.[21] It could also be that our attempt to distinguish neatly between angels, on the one hand, and human "holy ones," on the other, in the reception of this passage is misguided and was not a concern for some ancient readers.[22]

There are also two significant passages in Paul's letters. In Philippians, Paul writes concerning the possibility of his own death that he does not know what to hope for: "my desire is to depart and be with Christ, for that is far better; but to remain in the flesh is more necessary for you" (1:23–24). Paul assumes without feeling it necessary to explain or justify himself that death would mean being ushered into the presence of Christ in heaven (without Paul abandoning his hope for the resurrection of the dead in the future).[23] We find a similar notion in a dense and difficult portion of 2 Cor 5, which contains imagery of tents and buildings and clothing (vv. 1–4):

> We know that if our earthly tent-house is destroyed, we receive a building from God, an eternal house made without hands in the heavens. For in this tent we groan, longing to be clothed with our heavenly dwelling—if indeed, upon taking it off, we will not be found naked. For while we are still living in the tent, we groan

20. Joel Marcus, *The Way of the Lord* (Louisville: Westminster John Knox, 1992), 155, who cites several midrashim. This interpretation is already there in Did. 16.6–8 as well.

21. The idea that 1 Thess 3:13 ("at the coming of our Lord Jesus Christ with all his holy ones [μετὰ πάντων τῶν ἁγίων αὐτοῦ]") refers to human saints has an impressive pedigree. Cf., e.g., 2 Thess 1:7, which also draws on Zech 14, specifies "angels." In a later text, note the depiction of the return of Jesus in Mart. Ascen. Isa. 4.14–22, which has him coming with both angels and saints.

22. In the depiction of Christ's return in Rev 19:14, which draws on Zech 14, he comes with "the armies of heaven"—presumably angelic beings. However, in Rev 14:1–5, the lamb is on "Mount Zion" accompanied by the 144,000. In the Testaments of the Twelve Patriarchs, "holy ones" is used to refer both to humans and to angels (cf. T. Levi 3.3; 18.11; T. Iss. 5.4; T. Dan 5.11). Cf. Collins, *Daniel*, 316.

23. Cf. C. J. de Vogel, "Reflexions on Philippians i.23–24," *NovT* 19 (1977): 262–74; Stefan Schreiber, "Paulus im 'Zwischenzustand': Phil 1.23 und die Ambivalenz des Sterbens als Provokation," *NTS* 49 (2003): 340–41. On this view not replacing Paul's expectation for the resurrection, see Martin Hawthorne and Ralph P. Martin, *Philippians*, rev. ed., WBC 43 (Grand Rapids: Zondervan Academic, 2015), 60–61.

> under our burden, because we wish not to be unclothed but further clothed, in order that the mortal might be swallowed up by the living.

Most exegetes agree that Paul is not simply talking about the resurrection of the body in the future. At least a portion of this passage is referring to something that happens at death.[24] This interpretation is supported by a sentence that follows a few lines later: "we know that while we are at home in the body we are away from the Lord" (2 Cor 5:6). This is close to what Paul writes in Phil 1:21–23: "For to me to live is Christ, and to die is gain. If it is to be life in the flesh, that means fruitful labor for me. Yet which I shall choose I cannot tell. I am hard pressed between the two. My desire is to depart and be with Christ, for that is far better." Pauline scholars have struggled to fit this heavenly interim state into Paul's larger eschatological scenario (as in 1 Cor 15), with some suggesting he developed or changed his views.[25] But to my mind, W. D. Davies remains compelling (and he is not alone in this view): what Paul writes here makes sense within common beliefs of life after death in Judaism, and it appears here because Paul is more earnestly considering his own death be-

24. See the influential study by Jan Nicolass Sevenster, "Some Remarks on the GYMNOS in II Cor. V 3," in *Studia Paulina: In honorem Johannis de Zwaan Septuagenarii*, ed. Jan Nicolass Sevenster and W. C. van Unnik (Haarlem: Bohn, 1953), 202–14 (argues Paul presupposes three states of being: the present life, the disembodied status of the dead, and the resurrected/transformed life). How Sevenster's second state relates to the resurrected body remains highly debated. Cf. D. E. H. Whiteley, *The Theology of St. Paul* (Philadelphia: Fortress, 1966), 260, who argued that the heavenly form is transformed into the resurrected body, while Wilhelm Bousset, *Kyrios Christos: A History of the Belief in Christ* (Nashville: Abingdon, 1970), 184, believed the assumption was that individual believers possess a preexisting body in heaven that is received at death. For discussion, see John Gillman, "A Thematic Comparison: 1 Cor 15:50–57 and 2 Cor 5:1–5," *JBL* 107 (1988): 439–54; Margaret E. Thrall, *A Critical and Exegetical Commentary on the Second Epistle to the Corinthians*, ICC (Edinburgh: T&T Clark, 1994), 1:356–70; Nikolaus Walter, "Hellenistische Eschatologie bei Paulus? Zu 2 Kor 5, 1–10," *TQ* 176 (1996): 53–64.

25. See R. H. Charles, *Eschatology, the Doctrine of a Future Life in Israel, Judaism, and Christianity* (New York: Schocken, 1963), 437–63 (a rationalist take: Paul changed his mind because he discovered a tension in his thought, namely, there is no continuity between the present and the future without an interim period); W. L. Knox, *St. Paul* (New York: Appleton, 1932), 121–45 (argues Paul made a departure to Hellenistic thought); Murray J. Harris, "2 Corinthians 5:1–10: Watershed in Paul's Eschatology?," *TynBul* 22 (1971): 32–57 (suggests Paul expected to receive his "spiritual body" at death, which was a development from his earlier views); E. P. Sanders, *Paul: The Apostle's Life, Letters, and Thought* (Minneapolis: Fortress, 2015), 430–31.

fore the parousia than he was in other letters. While it is of course possible, even likely, that Paul changed his mind on various matters over the course of his activity, it is not necessary to argue that he has substantially changed his views of the afterlife here.[26]

When one digs a bit at the arguments of those who find difficulty in making sense of Phil 1 and 2 Cor 5 in the context of Paul's larger thought, it is often the case that one uncovers a presumed distinction between "Jewish views" of the body (as unity) and "Hellenistic views" of the body (as duality) at the root of it.[27] But we must be wary of such oversimplifications that are the product of their own peculiar reception history and are simply not fair descriptions of the material that we have.[28] While we need to take seriously the Hellenization of Palestine, we also need not import an entire platonic cosmology and corresponding anthropological systems into any Jewish text that we find from this period that happens to believe a person continues to exist in some sense after death and before the resurrection of the dead (even should they use "soul" or "spirit" language—terms loaded for modern scholars with anachronistic baggage). Moreover, this area of research is sometimes sorely lacking in imagination. Many texts from Jewish circles that did affirm the resurrection of the body and also held to some kind of postmortem existence were fine with embodied descriptions of such

26. W. D. Davies, *Paul and Rabbinic Judaism: Some Rabbinic Elements in Pauline Theology* (London: SPCK, 1948), 310–18. Among many other texts, Davies cites b. Ber. 28b, which has Johannan ben Zakkai crying in preparation for his death because he expected to be "led before the supreme King of Kings, the Holy One, blessed be He, Who Lives and endures forever." Davies also makes the interesting argument that the "age to come" was commonly regarded as eternally existent, such that "Paul, like other Rabbis, would have thought of the Age to Come as awaiting him at death and at the same time he could and did conceive of it as a final consummation of all created being" (317).

27. The argument being: (1) Paul was a Jew (and so held to "Jewish views" of the body as a unity), (2) he expected the resurrection of the dead and not the disembodied immortality of the soul, (3) he therefore could never have entertained the prospect of some continued life after death without his flesh and blood body before the resurrection. There are flaws in all three steps. For an influential early study that claimed to identify two distinct and irreconcilable branches in Paul's eschatology—Jewish and Hellenistic—cf. Otto Pfleiderer, *Paulinism: A Contribution to the History of Primitive Christian Theology*, trans. Edward Peters, 2 vols. (London: Williams & Norgate, 1877).

28. Cf. Bart D. Ehrman, *Heaven and Hell: A History of the Afterlife* (New York: Simon & Schuster, 2020), 125: "the neat differentiation between pagan and Jewish views does not always hold." See also Sim, "Life after Death?," 330.

prerisen persons in heaven. So in Revelation, for instance, we have the ψυχαί of martyrs in heaven who wear clothes and can talk, and in numerous other apocalyptic and visionary texts we find descriptions of people who are in heaven without their flesh-and-blood bodies, presumably, but nonetheless have a humanlike form and are still recognizable (cf., e.g., 1 En. 39.3–14 of the righteous in heaven: "their mouth shall be full of blessing and their lips will praise" and some "stand before him").[29] This ambiguity even appears, interestingly enough, in descriptions of the afterlife in Homer and Virgil—two authors who were significant in shaping Greco-Roman views of the afterlife.[30]

It is again crucial to stress that there were no standard and universally held views about life after death in Judaism. But it is fair to say that, for those who *did* affirm some afterlife, it was not uncommon to believe that the righteous dead continued to exist in some kind of heavenly or transcendent sphere above.[31] The precise nature, or anthropology, of the deceased in this state is not clear. But it is also not apparent that many authors were too concerned about that. Depicting the hereafter is better suited to the imagination, which operates by its own rules.

---

29. So David E. Aune, *Revelation*, WBC 52 (Nashville: Nelson, 1997–1998), 2:404: "The problem of how it is possible for John to see a (presumably) disembodied ψυχή immediately suggests itself, though this never appears to be a problem for visionaries in either Jewish or Hellenistic texts." See also LAE 33, 37 (A). Moreover, Paul evidently had a view of heaven that permitted both somatic and nonsomatic experience: "I know a man in Christ who fourteen years ago was caught up to the third heaven, whether in the body [ἐν σώματι] or out of the body [ἐκτὸς τοῦ σώματος] I do not know—God knows" (2 Cor 12:2). Note also that it was common to think that there were bodies in heaven, e.g., those who never had died, like Elijah, Enoch, Moses, etc.

30. Cf. especially books 10–11 in Homer, *Iliad*, and book 6 of Virgil, *Aeneid*. See Mark T. Finney, *Resurrection, Hell and the Afterlife: Body and Soul in Antiquity, Judaism and Early Christianity* (New York: Routledge, 2016), 6–24.

31. N. T. Wright, *Surprised by Hope: Rethinking Heaven, the Resurrection, and the Mission of the Church* (New York: HarperOne, 2008), 171, writes, at death, the "real person—however we want to describe him or her—continues." See also Wright, *The Resurrection of the Son of God* (Minneapolis: Fortress, 2003), 203, 216, 312–74. See also Cecil J. Cadoux, *The Historic Mission of Jesus* (London: Lutterworth, 1941), 223; Sim, "Life after Death?," 331–44.

Back to Jesus

All of this would be circumstantial and potentially irrelevant for the study of the historical Jesus in the absence of any link to the Jesus tradition (beyond the word to the brigand on the cross and the parable of the rich man and Lazarus).[32] But that we probably have. Jesus is reported to have debated with some Sadducees about the resurrection of the dead in the Synoptics (Mark 12:18–27 and parr.). In this account, he appeals to the story of the burning bush from Exod 3, which Mark records as follows (12:26–27):

> And concerning the dead that they are raised, have you not read in the book of Moses concerning the bush, how God said to him, "I am the God of Abraham and the God of Isaac and the God of Jacob"? God is not God of the dead but of the living. You are greatly deceived.

In Moses's day, Abraham, Isaac, and Jacob were long dead, and the general resurrection had not yet occurred. So how does Jesus's scriptural argument work? Joel Marcus wrote, "the Lord is *presently* the God of Abraham, Isaac, and Jacob, who are therefore still alive."[33] Marcus links this to the notion of an "interim state of blessedness before the final resurrection" that we find in other Jewish and early Christian texts.[34] Marcus is right. To say the patriarchs have already been raised from the dead would completely spiritualize the resurrection, and this cannot be. Confirming Marcus's interpretation is the fact that it was a common view that the patriarchs in particular were present with God in heaven.[35] It may be, moreover,

32. In addition to the passage below, Sim, "Life after Death?," 336–44, believes that the evangelist Matthew held to the belief of immediate life after death on the basis of Matt 10:28, 17:1–8.

33. Joel Marcus, *Mark 8–16: A New Translation with Introduction and Commentary*, AB 27A (New Haven: Yale University Press, 2009), 828–29.

34. See also Robert H. Gundry, *Mark: A Commentary on His Apology for the Cross* (Grand Rapids: Eerdmans, 1993), 446; W. D. Davies and Dale C. Allison Jr., *A Critical and Exegetical Commentary on the Gospel according to Saint Matthew*, ICC (Edinburgh: T&T Clark, 1988–1997), 3:231 ("The argument seemingly implies not resurrection but continued existence and therefore an interim state. The two things were, however, not mutually exclusive; indeed, many no doubt thought the one to imply the other."). On the resurrection of the patriarchs on the last day (as well as Enoch and Seth), see T. Zeb. 10.1–4; T. Jud. 25.1–4; T. Benj. 10.5–6.

35. See Heb 11:40, 12:13; LAB 4.11; T. Isaac 2.1–9; 1 En. 60.2 (Enoch sees God on the throne surrounded by angels and the righteous); 70.4 (Enoch sees "the first fathers and the righteous"); 2 En. (A) 42.3; 3 En. 44.7; Exod. Rab. 25.8 ("the patriarchs and all the righteous sit in God's midst"); Philo, *Sacr.* 1.5–6; 4 Macc 7:19 ("To God they do not die, as our patriarchs Abraham, Isaac, and

that Jesus thought the patriarchs presently experienced in heaven some manner of angelic existence.[36] It may not be a coincidence that Jesus in this very context appears to describe the resurrected body as an angelic body. One also wonders whether lingering in the background here is the view we find in some Jewish texts that persons on earth have an angelic double in heaven with whom they may or may not be identified with in the future.[37] Although it is quite speculative, a few scholars have even suggested that Jesus thought the same about Dan 7's son of man—that figure being Jesus's heavenly double and the person whom he would later become.[38] First Enoch 71 makes a similar move: Enoch, once taken from the earth, is identified as the very son of man he has seen operative in heaven.

Be that what it may, the key point is that Mark 12:18–27 and parallels, which probably contain memory of a dispute Jesus had about the resurrection,[39] hold out the belief of postmortem existence after death and before the general resurrection. It is not a leap to think that Jesus would have expected the same for himself should he perish before the general resurrection of the dead had occurred.[40]

Jacob did not die") and 16:25; T. Ab. 20.8–14. Note also the reference to the "bosom of Abraham" in Luke 16:22; cf. b. Qidd. 72a–b (which mentions to be "in Abraham's bosom") and Apoc. Sedr. 14.5 ("the nations that have no law, yet fulfill the law. . . . I shall receive with my righteous ones in the bosom of Abraham"). Is a similar notion implied by the notion of being "gathered to/with the ancestors"? Cf. CD XIX, 33–XX, 1 (which mentions the "gathering in" of the Teacher of Righteousness); Jub. 23.1.

36. Cf. 1 En. 104.2–6; 2 Bar. 51.5, 10 ("they will be like angels, equal to the stars"). See also Mart. Pol. 2.3; Herm. Sim. 9.25.1; 9.27.3. Perhaps implied by 1QS XI, 7–8; 1QH XI, 19–21? See John J. Collins, "The Angelic Life," in *Metamorphoses: Resurrection, Body and Transformative Practices in Early Christianity*, ed. Turid Karlsen Seim and Jorunn Økland (Berlin: de Gruyter, 2009), 291–310.

37. See texts and discussion in Dale C. Allison Jr., *Constructing Jesus: Memory, Imagination, and History* (Grand Rapids: Baker Books, 2010), 296–303.

38. Cf. David Catchpole, "The Angelic Son of Man in Luke 12:8," *NovT* 24 (1982): 255–65, who argues the son of man is the heavenly sponsor or representative of Jesus. Note also Bruce Chilton, "(The) Son of (the) Man, and Jesus," in *Authenticating the Words of Jesus*, ed. Bruce Chilton and Craig A. Evans (Leiden: Brill, 1999), 281; Allison, *Constructing Jesus*, 303 (finds the hypothesis intriguing but "[does] not pretend to know").

39. As it has no clear connections to later Christian beliefs about Jesus, it does not appear to grant the fleshly nature of the resurrection as we see stressed in Luke and John. This view is common in historical Jesus scholarship. Cf. Maurice Casey, *Jesus of Nazareth: An Independent Historian's Account of His Life and Teaching* (London: T&T Clark International, 2010), 468.

40. Given arguments above that Jesus expected to or thought he might die, it is worth noting that in some texts, it is the righteous, and sometimes specifically those who died in obedience to God, who are named residing in heaven. For the righteous, see 1 En. 39.3–8; 71.16–17; Apoc. El. 1.8 ("everyone who will obey me will receive thrones and crowns"); Mart. Ascen. Isa. 7.22; 9.6–12. Ps.-Clem. Rec. 1.27–71; 1.52.5; b. Šabb. 152b; b. Ber. 17a; 'Abot R. Nat. 12. For martyrs, see Rev 7:9–17 (the multitude clothed in white are those "who have come out of the great ordeal; they have washed their robes and made them white in the blood of the Lamb. For this reason

Again, it is not clear how Jesus would have conceived of the anthropology of this state, nor is it clear for other Jewish texts of this period. Moreover, it is not clear how Jews in this period imagined the transition from heavenly existence to resurrected life. But we know from multiple sources that, for those who expected the general resurrection of the dead, it was thought that the event would impact people differently depending upon their circumstances and location. For Paul, the dead will be "raised," but the living will be "changed" (ἀλλαγησόμεθα [cf. 1 Cor 15:50–54]).[41] Paul also speaks about the "putting on" (from ἐνδύω) of immortality (cf. 1 Cor 15 and 2 Cor 5)—an image that befits varied circumstances (note that both transformation language and clothing language also appear in 1 En. 62.15, 90.33–38, and 2 Bar. 49.1–51.6). In the Apocalypse of Elijah, it is said that Enoch and Elijah, who were thought to be in heaven and never died, will "come down" and receive their "spiritual flesh" at the time of the resurrection (5.32). Moreover, while the resurrection was expected to be a corporate event, some apparently thought that certain persons would experience it before others (cf. Paul again in 1 Thess 4:16: "the dead will be raised *first*"). In the Testament of Benjamin, the patriarch predicts some kind of sequence in his final words to his children: "you will see Enoch and Seth and Abraham and Isaac and Jacob raised up at the right hand in great joy. Then we shall also be raised, each of us over our tribe, and we shall prostrate ourselves before the heavenly king. . . . Then all shall be changed, some destined for glory, others for dishonor" (10.6). This text appears to hold out that leaders and important figures would be raised first before all the rest are "changed." Should Jesus, in a similar way, have expected to experience the

---

[διὰ τοῦτό], they are before the throne of God, and worship day and night within his temple"); 1 En 108.12 (God brings into heaven those who suffered in obedience and says, "I will seat each on the throne of his honor"); see also Josephus, *J.W.* 1.65, and Tacitus, *Hist.* 5.5 (on those killed/martyred). Some have argued that the notion of heavenly reward for martyrs is behind Paul's reflections in the opening of Philippians, where he clearly is open to the possibility of death and also expects to be "present with the Lord." See Albert Schweitzer, *The Mysticism of Paul the Apostle*, trans. William Montgomery (New York: Holt, 1931), 135–37. Cf. also Ernst Lohmeyer, "*Syn Christō*," in *Festgabe für Adolf Deissmann zum 60. Geburtstag*, ed. Karl Ludwig Schmidt (Tübingen: Mohr, 1927), 218–57; de Voguel, "Reflexions on Philippians i.23–24," 262–74.

41. See Joachim Jeremias, "Flesh and Blood Cannot Inherit the Kingdom of God," *NTS* 2 (1955–1956): 151–59; Hans Conzelmann, *1 Corinthians: A Commentary on the First Epistle to the Corinthians*, trans. James W. Leitch, Hermeneia (Philadelphia: Fortress, 1975), 289–93; C. K. Barrett, *A Commentary on the First Epistle to the Corinthians* (London: Black, 1971), 381; Ben F. Meyer, "Did Paul's View of the Resurrection of the Dead Undergo Development?," *TS* 47 (1986): 375–78 (he contends the "mystery" of v. 51 is this: "*although those still living at the Parousia would not die, they too—like those raised from the dead—would at that same moment be transformed*"); Novakovic, *Resurrection*, 73. For another view, see David E. Garland, *1 Corinthians*, BECNT (Grand Rapids: Baker Books, 2003), 740–42.

general resurrection first, thereupon coming "from heaven," what his early followers wrote about him coming "in glory" would not be far off the mark at all.

We do not have the evidence to move the needle in this discussion anywhere beyond "it is possible." But I would make one further important point about this. If it be at all near the truth that Jesus expected to be in some sense present in heaven after death, it would go a long way in explaining something that we have not yet stressed much in this study: the common belief among his followers in the post-Easter period that Jesus is presently, before the end, in heaven with God. Historians of Christian origins need to find some way of getting Jesus into heaven. Simply having him raised from the dead is not in itself sufficient to do that, as Timo Eskola has noted: "in Jewish writings resurrection was never actually identified with any heavenly enthronement."[42] So how do we get an individually raised Jesus in heaven with God before his return?[43] It could be rather straightforward: Jesus believed, like many other Jews, that if and when he died prematurely in the eschatological tribulation, he would nonetheless be with God in heaven in the interim before his coming from heaven as the son of man on the last day.[44] After Jesus's death, early Christians continued to hold the same basic framework. Or, to use the analogy last offered above, they kept the same final chapter. What they did is *add* the new belief that Jesus himself had already experienced the resurrection of the dead. But they accommodated this view of Jesus's individual resurrection to the more primitive one about presence of some kind in heaven after death, which

42. Timo Eskola, *Messiah and the Throne: Jewish Merkabah Mysticism and Early Christian Exaltation Discourse*, WUNT 2/142 (Tübingen: Mohr Siebeck, 2001), 248. See also Allison, *Constructing Jesus*, 248 ("resurrection in and of itself did not entail enthronement. Those raised from the dead do not, in Jewish sources, automatically sit on thrones, in heaven or anywhere else"). A purely exegetical origin is also unconvincing, so John H. Hayes, "The Resurrection as Enthronement in the Earliest Church Christology," *Int* 22 (1968): 333–45.

43. Disagreeing here with Ulrich Kellermann, *Auferstehung in den Himmel: 2 Makk 7 und die Auferstehung der Martyrer*, SBS 95 (Stuttgart: Katholisches Bibelwerk, 1978), and Joost Holleman, *Resurrection and Parousia: A Traditio-Historical Study of Paul's Eschatology in 1 Corinthians 15*, NovTSup 84 (Leiden: Brill, 1996), 139–57, who argue that early Christians drew on an extant tradition of the individual resurrection of the righteous (distinct from the eschatological general resurrection at the end) in making sense of what happened to Jesus.

44. This is near where Cadoux, *Historic Mission of Jesus*, 284, ends up (though he comes close to conflating Jesus's coming with his resurrection). This view could have been reinforced by the notion of the postmortem enthronement of pious persons in Greco-Roman religion as argued by D. Clint Burnett, *Christ's Enthronement and Its Greco-Roman Cultural Context*, BZNW 242 (Berlin: de Gruyter, 2021). Cf., e.g., Diodorus Siculus, *Bibl. hist.* 13.1–17.2 (on Uranos, Kronos, and Zeus, those who Euhermeros claims were formerly humans). See also James Buchanan Wallace, "Benefactor and Paradigm: Viewing Jesus' Ascension in Luke-Acts through Greco-Roman Ascension Traditions," in *Ascent into Heaven in Luke-Acts: New Explorations of Luke's Narrative Hinge*, ed. David K. Bryan and David W. Pao (Minneapolis: Fortress, 2016), 83–110.

is how they created the situation of an individually raised person in heaven with God before the last day. They might have been further encouraged in this belief if Jesus had talked about enthronement in the future.[45] This hope, too, then, was thought partly realized in the present, before the parousia.

Of the two possibilities explored in this chapter, it is the second that I would, if pressed, prefer to the first. It is supported by common views of life after death in Judaism, and it keeps intact the consistent spatial imagery of early Christian eschatology, which is about coming down: for example, "your kingdom come, your will be done on earth as it is in heaven" (Matt 6:10 // Luke 11:2), the spirit of God coming down (Mark 1:10 and parr.; John 1:33; Acts 2:1–4), the heavenly Jerusalem coming down (Rev 21:2). So too, we might expect, the son of man, when he comes. Jeremias's suggestion that "an underlying idea of a movement from below upwards" is the most primitive one requires serious exegetical gymnastics.[46]

I could be wrong in preferring the second scenario, and the above discussion has required some speculation. But if I am wrong, and the first hypothesis explored above is preferable (raised then arrive), the overall probability of my thesis in this study about tying the parousia hope to Jesus changes little. The first hypothesis would imply more discontinuity between the eschatological hopes of Jesus and the beliefs of his early followers after his death, but the general sequence of death, brief absence for an interim, and reunion at the consummation, would remain. The key point, then, is that there are two reasonable ways we might connect the coming of the son of man to the judgment and the general resurrection of the dead, and both of these leave us with a Jesus who is a wholly "believable figure in first-century Palestine."[47] That is what I hoped to demonstrate in this chapter.

45. This is the argument of Dale C. Allison Jr., *The Resurrection of Jesus: Apologetics, Criticism, History* (New York: Bloomsbury T&T Clark, 2021), 194–96.

46. Joachim Jeremias, *New Testament Theology: The Proclamation of Jesus*, trans. John Bowden (New York: Scribner's Sons, 1971), 273. This is evident by his reliance on Luke 22:69 here ("but from now on the son of man will be seated at the right hand of the power of God") as this is a redacted version, as already noted, and omits Mark's reference to Dan 7. Jeremias claims that Luke's version is "simpler" than what we find in Mark and has "not been influenced by the early Christian christological pattern of exaltation and parousia." This not only begs the question; it ignores Luke's larger theological *Tendenzen* (Jeremias even relies on Acts 7:56 and the vision of Stephen). He also suggests that Mark 13:26 envisages a movement upward, which is quite unlikely, before suggesting that perhaps other passages "originally" had a similar conception before the evangelists got their hands on them (citing Mark 8:38; Matt 10:23; Matt 19:28; Matt 25:31). That is an astounding admission: the texts as they stand disagree with his view, but he nonetheless infers that, behind them, at a stage we cannot access, the message was different.

47. E. P. Sanders, *Jesus and Judaism* (Philadelphia: Fortress, 1985), 166–67.

16

Two Scenarios and Das Leben Jesu *Revisited*

I have pointed out several times in this study that many proponents of an eschatological Jesus have inadequately accounted for the prospect of Jesus's death—and thereby a period of his absence—for reconstructing his teaching about the future. I have also suggested that this oversight is due in part to the dominant way in which Jesus research has been conducted after the life-of-Jesus heyday in the nineteenth century and the advent of form criticism in the early twentieth century. Critics generally gave up on the attempt to write a biography of Jesus (for good reason) and shifted focus instead to specific passages or even themes in the tradition with less concern for the big picture.[1] I have argued that there is indeed "room" (contra Conzelmann) for Jesus to expect a brief interim period before the establishment of the kingdom on the simple grounds that Jesus thought that he might die. In other words, there is a fitting *Sitz im Leben Jesu* for an interim period and for Jesus's future coming as the son of man if we grant that the prospect of death did not completely catch Jesus by surprise. Making this argument does not assume that much more clarity is possible about the particulars, to be sure. There is no going back to the overconfident historiography of the nineteenth-century lives of Jesus. But, contra the atomization of Jesus research in the wake of form

1. See discussion in Tucker S. Ferda, *Jesus, the Gospels, and the Galilean Crisis*, LNTS 601 (London: Bloomsbury T&T Clark, 2019), 106–13, 144. I also argue here that, while the rejection of the older biographical approach was rightly more skeptical of our sources and our historical abilities, the newer atomistic approach to Jesus assumed something that it had not demonstrated: that Jesus was generally consistent in message and aims throughout the course of his activity.

criticism, it is essential that we seek to integrate to the best we are able, even if in broad strokes, what we have good reason to think is historical about Jesus. The rationale here is that the best reconstructions of the past are those that make the most sense of the most data.[2]

In this final chapter, then, I continue this attempt at integration to ask how this hope for the future coming of Jesus after death could have reasonably emerged during his activity.[3] If this is implausible, or if it would make his life seem suspiciously scripted, then the hypothesis should be abandoned, despite the positive arguments made so far and the weaknesses I have identified with competing theories.[4] But I hope to show that this is far from the case.

While most studies of the historical Jesus have tried to make a compelling case for one particular reconstruction of his profile or message, I will do something different in what follows given the nature of our evidence. I will entertain two different scenarios. I favor the second of these, for reasons I will explain, but want to stress that either one is still *more probable* than the alternative that the expectation for Jesus's future coming emerged only after his death in the post-Easter period. Such is the nature of the "fuzzy sphere" that Jesus research must inhabit as we offer hypotheses about the past to make sense of the sources that we have.[5] I doubt that we can do any better than that when it comes to this issue. The first scenario is that the hope for Jesus's future coming was a response to the rejection that he faced—it was reactionary—and hence not in view all along. The second holds that Jesus's message is best described by what I would call a process

2. Cf. N. T. Wright, *The New Testament and the People of God* (Minneapolis: Fortress, 1992), 98–100: hypotheses about the past should make sense of all available data, be simple, and explain/help resolve other known problems.

3. Another weakness of the study by Arthur L. Moore, *The Parousia in the New Testament*, NovTSup 13 (Leiden: Brill, 1966), due in part to its atomistic approach, is he never once attempts to connect Jesus's expectation for the parousia (which he thinks is authentic) to larger questions concerning death, messianism, and developments during his ministry.

4. Of course, some Christian historians have ascribed to Jesus a kind of preternatural clarity about the course of his ministry, such as Oscar Cullmann, *The Christology of the New Testament*, rev. ed., trans. Shirley C. Guthrie and Charles A. M. Hall (Philadelphia: Westminster, 1963), 67 ("Jesus therefore became conscious at the moment of his baptism that he had to take upon himself the *ebed Yahweh* role").

5. For this language, see Jens Schröter, *Jesus of Nazareth: Jew from Galilee, Savior of the World*, trans. Wayne Coppins and S. Brian Pounds (Waco, TX: Baylor University Press, 2014), 17: "historical-critical Jesus research moves within a certain 'fuzzy sphere,' since it details as a historical endeavor with sources that do not mediate an unambiguous picture of the past. Therefore, its goal cannot be to reach the *one* Jesus *behind* the texts but to reach a conception grounded on the weighing of plausibilities, which as an abstraction from the sources always moves *in front of* the sources."

eschatology, which may have made room for if not figured in the prospect of suffering and even death without requiring an adjustment of his entire eschatological expectation. I will explore each in turn.

Reenter the Galilean Crisis Theory?

While it is strangely overlooked in recent New Testament scholarship, there is a fascinating genealogy for the view that Jesus's expectation for a future coming was actually a plan B after the failure of his initial hopes for success. This genealogy includes perhaps most prominently the old theory of a Galilean crisis, which held that there was an increase in opposition to Jesus over the course of his activity that led to *changes* in his outlook and rhetorical tone. I have written about this extensively elsewhere, and I noted in the preface of this book that researching and writing about the crisis theory was what initially interested me in the parousia tradition in Christian origins.[6] Several notable historians well into the twentieth century continued to hold that Jesus did indeed speak of a future parousia but only *after* and *in response to* a crisis of rejection.[7] There is a close relative of this view that regards Jesus's eschatological message as conditional in nature—meaning, dependent on positive response—and that Jesus was forced to make sense of poor results that he may not have initially expected (while these critics do not speak of a Galilean crisis per se). This argument necessarily presumes, though, somewhat like the crisis theory, that there were different periods in Jesus's activity defined by his public reception, even if we may remain unable in our position to sort them out neatly. In any case, this reconstruction still holds that Jesus initially cherished the hope that his message would find acceptance, and only later grappled with rejection and failure that changed his mind. It is rarely noted that this was, in fact, the conclusion of Johannes Weiss, whose consistent eschatology anticipated Albert Schweitzer's by over a decade.[8] Rudolf Otto, Joseph Klausner,

6. Ferda, *Jesus, the Gospels, and the Galilean Crisis*, 15–146. I explored some initial conclusions in "The Origin of the Second Advent Reconsidered," at the Annual Meeting of the Eastern Great Lakes Biblical Society (New Testament section) in Perrysville, OH, March 12, 2015.

7. Cf. literature in Ferda, *Jesus, the Gospels, and the Galilean Crisis*, 63–146. Particularly notable in the late nineteenth century is the work of Theodor Keim, *The History of Jesus of Nazara, Freely Investigated in Its Connection with the National Life of Israel, and Related in Detail*, trans. Arthur Ransom, 2nd ed. (London: Williams & Norgate, 1876–1883). A quotation from this work concerning the parousia hope began part 4.

8. As noted in Ferda, *Jesus, the Gospels, and the Galilean Crisis*, 93. Johannes Weiss, *Jesus' Proclamation of the Kingdom of God*, trans. Richard H. Hiers and David Larrimore Holland (Phil-

Cecil Cadoux, and many others advanced similar positions in subsequent years.[9] A few other more recent studies also belong in this line of interpretation, namely,

---

adelphia: Fortress, 1971), argued that Jesus believed the "end had been postponed" due to "the pressure of certain circumstances" (86). These circumstances include the following: there was little fruit of repentance, the crowds mistook him for a revolutionary messiah, and the religious leaders rejected him. Jesus then expected to die to remove "the guilt of the people" that had postponed the coming of the kingdom (87), and that his disciples would continue his ministry. When the expected repentance had occurred, Jesus the son of man would come in glory to usher in the kingdom of God and the final age.

9. Cf., e.g., R. H. Charles, *Eschatology, the Doctrine of a Future Life in Israel, Judaism, and Christianity* (New York: Schocken, 1963), 376–78: "At the outset of His ministry He had, we can hardly doubt, hoped to witness the consummation of this kingdom without passing through the gates of death. But the accomplishment of His task was dependent on the conduct of the people. In the earlier days when His preaching was received with enthusiasm and the nation seemed to be pressing into the kingdom of God, His teaching dwells mainly on the present kingdom of God on earth. . . . But when the temper of the people changed and His rejection and death appeared as an inexorable necessity, He began to speak of the future kingdom. . . . The prophecy of His second coming appears in connection with His first mention of His approaching death" (he is thinking of Mark 8:38). See also Rudolf Otto, *Life and Ministry of Jesus: According to the Historical Critical Method, Being a Course of Lectures*, trans. H. J. Whitby, 3rd ed. (Chicago: Open Court, 1908), 45 (argues that, as Jesus's death loomed in Jerusalem, and it became apparent that he was not accepted, he expected that he would come on the clouds of heaven and hold divine judgment and establish an everlasting kingdom); Paul Wernle, *Jesus* (Tübingen: Mohr, 1916), 237; Joseph Klausner, *The Messianic Idea in Israel: From Its Beginning to the Completion of the Mishnah*, 3rd ed., trans. W. F. Stinespring (New York: Macmillan, 1955), 302, 313, 402–3 (he thinks that Jesus preached repentance and hoped that it would bring about the messianic era); Cecil J. Cadoux, *The Historic Mission of Jesus* (London: Lutterworth, 1941), 229, 307 (Jesus initially hoped for the inauguration of the kingdom on earth, but on account of rejection he predicted death and a short interim period before his return). See also Xavier Léon-Dufour, *The Gospels and the Jesus of History*, ed. and trans. John McHugh (New York: Desclee, 1968), 221 (rejection led Jesus to begin to preach of "a time of waiting" rather than the imminence of the kingdom); Athanasius Polag, *Die Christologie der Logienquelle*, WMANT 45 (Neukirchen-Vluyn: Neukirchener Verlag, 1977), 121, 195 (on the impact of the rejection of Jesus on his message); Mark Saucy, *The Kingdom of God in the Teaching of Jesus* (Dallas: Word, 1997), 338 ("the Kingdom that was first preached as 'at hand' now becomes 'at hand' only to certain, distant future events. It is still the Davidic Kingdom of the ancestral Jewish hope, but it would not come immediately through Jesus' ministry"). Vincent Taylor, "The Son of Man Sayings Relating to the Parousia," *ExpTim* 58 (1946–47): 12–15, argued the opposite: the parousia sayings stem from the early part of the career, before Jesus interpreted the son of man concept alongside Isaiah's "servant." For additional views on conditionality, see Olshausen, cited in David Friedrich Strauss, *The Life of Jesus Critically Examined*, trans. George Eliot, 4th ed. (London: Sonnenschein, 1902), 591 (argues the return of Christ "depends on the conduct of men, consequently on their free will"); Joachim Jeremias, *New Testament Theology: The Proclamation of Jesus*, trans. John Bowden (New York: Scribner's Sons, 1971), 139–40.

When the Son of Man Didn't Come: A Constructive Proposal on the Delay of the Parousia, by Christopher Hays, with Brandon Gallaher, Richard J. Ounsworth, Julia S. Konstantinovsky, and C. A. Stine, which seeks to recover the conditional nature of biblical prophecy in general,[10] and Barry Smith's *Jesus' Twofold Teaching about the Kingdom of God*, which attempted an interpretation of Jesus's teachings within what he calls their original "non-rejection" (the earlier) and "rejection" (the later) contexts.[11] Unexplored in Hays's and Smith's interesting studies are the ways in which their exegetical ancestry for this view stretches back well before the nineteenth-century quest for Jesus.[12]

These views may seem idiosyncratic, but as a matter of historiography, it is crucial to note how similar these reconstructions of Jesus are to very common studies of Christian origins that posit the generative role of disappointment in the theological development of the movement. As we have seen in this study, many critics have argued that grappling with the death of Jesus encouraged Jesus followers after Easter to come up with the notion of his second advent as a remedy for the failure of his messianic mission. This hypothesis is actually not very far from the Galilean crisis theory in that it narrates a similar account of theological change but sees that change occurring not during the life of Jesus but after it. Reconstructions of the early church and its theological rationalizations of fail-

10. Christopher M. Hays et al., *When the Son of Man Didn't Come: A Constructive Proposal on the Delay of the Parousia* (Minneapolis: Fortress, 2016).

11. Barry D. Smith, *Jesus' Twofold Teaching about the Kingdom of God* (Sheffield: Sheffield Phoenix, 2009).

12. Well before Reimarus, we find arguments that Jesus had hoped for Israel to be restored by "ethical renewal" rather than "supernatural intervention"—we see this in the work of certain Enlightenment rationalists, for instance, who pitted Jesus's ethical teaching over and against a supernatural or atoning death. For discussion and texts, see Ferda, *Jesus, the Gospels, and the Galilean Crisis*, 44–53. This view also emerges in Old Testament scholarship from Christian circles that praised the prophets as the true religious geniuses of Israel because they focused on ethical behavior in the present rather than trusting their contemporaries to hope for God's supernatural intervention (through the temple cult, or in the future by God). Cf. Henning Graf Reventlow, *From the Enlightenment to the Twentieth Century*, vol. 4 of *History of Biblical Interpretation*, trans. Leo G. Perdue (Atlanta: Society of Biblical Literature, 2010). Note also that, in Hugo Grotius's 1627 *The Truth of the Christian Religion, with Jean Le Clerc's Notes and Additions*, trans. John Clarke, ed. Maria Rosa Antognazza (Indianapolis: Liberty Fund, 2012), he appeals to conditional prophecy as an "answer to what is alleged, that some things were not fulfilled." He wrote, "There are some Promises which appear from the foregoing and following Words, or from their own Sense, to contain in them a tacit Condition. Thus God promised many things to the *Hebrews*, if they would receive and obey the Messiah when he came, which if they do not come to pass, they must impute it to themselves. And if there be any, which are expressly and unconditionally promised, and are not yet fulfilled, they may yet be expected" (218).

ure, then, can be eerily similar to old lives of Jesus that fit similar ups and downs into Jesus's ministry by constructing a figure who had grappled seriously with disappointment already. Matthew Novenson summarizes a very common view in *The Grammar of Messianism* when he writes, "the early Christian belief in the parousia of Jesus had a kind of compensatory function, enabling the preservation of certain utopian aspects of the messiah myth alongside the many concessions to the circumstances of Jesus' life."[13] The nineteenth-century historian Theodor Keim might have replied to Novenson that the historical Jesus was already making "concessions to the circumstances" of his life during what Keim famously called "the Galilean storms."[14]

Eschatology and Agency

An initial reason why we must seriously entertain the notion that Jesus revised his proclamation due to the negative reception of his message is that conditional prophecy and conditional end-time scenarios do indeed appear elsewhere in Jewish sources.[15] (And to clarify, by conditional prophecy and eschatology I am not speaking of the common view that God's judgment [on the day of judgment or in history generally] is regarded a response to human sin, or that by means of righteous behavior one might expect to forgo the judgment of God. That was a widely held view. We are considering here something bolder: the view that righteous behavior can encourage or guide God's eschatological redemption. We might specify, then, that conditional eschatology is not about avoiding punishment but about triggering positive divine action by means of righteousness.)

Such conditional expectations have certainly been overlooked and underappreciated by New Testament scholars, probably because of the field's formative Protestant-Christian heritage and the legacy of a Reformation-era binary between

13. Matthew V. Novenson, *The Grammar of Messianism: An Ancient Jewish Political Idiom and Its Users* (Oxford: Oxford University Press, 2017), 213.

14. Cf. Ferda, *Jesus, the Gospels, and the Galilean Crisis*, 81–83.

15. This view appears presupposed by Acts 3:19–21 (μετανοήσατε οὖν καὶ ἐπιστρέψατε εἰς τὸ ἐξαλειφθῆναι ὑμῶν τὰς ἁμαρτίας ὅπως ἂν ἔλθωσιν καιροὶ ἀναψύξεως ἀπὸ προσώπου τοῦ κυρίου καὶ ἀποστείλῃ τὸν προκεχειρισμένον ὑμῖν χριστὸν Ἰησοῦν). Cf. Zech 12:10–13:2; Bar 2:30–34; Tob 13:5; Jub. 1.13, 15 (cf. 1.22–25); 23.26–30; Pss. Sol. 18.4–7; T. Dan 6.4; T. Sim. 6.2–7; T. Zeb. 9.7–9; T. Jud. 23.5; T. Iss. 6.3–4; T. Benj. 10.7, 11; T. Mos. 1.18; 3.4–6; 2 Bar. 78.6–7; 84.2; 4 Ezra 13.9–13; Apoc. Ab. 29–31; Sib. Or. 4.152–170; Philo, *Praem.* 162–165; CD IV, 2; VI, 4; VIII, 16; XV, 7–17; XX, 17; 1QS III, 2–12; X, 20; 1QH II, 9; XIV, 24; b. Sanh. 97b–98a ("If Israel were to repent, they would straightaway be redeemed" [as one of several views on the question]); b. Yoma 86b ("Great is repentance which hastens the redemption"); y. Ta'an. 63d.

grace (understood as God's labor) and works (understood as human labor). In a 2012 article on John the Baptist, I gathered numerous texts that give witness to the apparently popular view that the ingathering of the exiles at the end time *was dependent on* (that is, awaited) Israel's repentance.[16] Indeed, in many texts, repentance appears to condition all sorts of eschatological realities, and in some, this includes the appearance of the messiah himself.[17] Other texts, learning perhaps from deuteronomistic theology and the meritorious nature of covenantal blessing in biblical texts like Deut 28, assume that increased righteousness in Israel will spur God to action.[18] Of course, we also find the call for repentance, interest in eschatological ingathering, and the expectation for an eschatological higher righteousness in great supply in the Jesus tradition. So Christopher Hays's attempt to situate Jesus in this prophetic context is hardly implausible on its face.

In my book-length study of the Galilean crisis, however, I ultimately found the evidence wanting that Jesus had revised his message in a significant way in response to rejection. I did argue that Jesus experienced rejection in ways that many recent historians have overlooked and that there are features of the tradition that

16. Cf. Tucker S. Ferda, "John the Baptist, Isaiah 40, and the Ingathering of the Exiles," *JSHJ* 10 (2012): 154–88, and also Jacques Schlosser, *Le règne de Dieu dans les dits de Jesus* (Paris: Gabalda, 1980), 1:101–4. See, e.g., Jub. 1.22–25; 23.26 ("return to the way of righteousness"); T. Jud. 23.5; T. Dan 5.9–10; 1QS III, 6–12. See also CD V, 20–VI, 7 and the self-description as the שבי ישראל that García Martínez and Tigchelaar take as "converts of Israel," but it could equally be "the repentant of Israel." Also CD XV, 5–13 mentions "returning to the law of Moses" (again with שוב here), which has eschatological connotations. For additional discussion, see Mark Jason, *Repentance at Qumran: The Penitential Framework of Religious Experience in the Dead Sea Scrolls* (Minneapolis: Fortress, 2015), 201–32.

17. See Tg. Mic. 4.8; b. Sanh. 98a (drawing on Ps 95:7: "today, *if* you would heed his voice"); b. Šabb. 118b; b. B. Bat. 10a; b. Yoma 86b (which draws on Isa 59:20, which intrigues in light of Paul's use of the same in Rom 11:26); b. Ber. 57a (which reads Dan 7:13 against Zech 9:9); Exod. Rab. 25.16. It eventually became a very popular view that repentance can hasten the coming of the messiah, due in part to the influence of Saadia Gaon (882–942 CE) in his *The Book of Beliefs and Opinions*, trans. Samuel Rosenblatt (New Haven: Yale University Press, 1976), which was the clearest attempt to crystallize and define messianic belief within rabbinic tradition to his time. See discussion in Philip S. Alexander, "The King Messiah in Rabbinic Judaism," in *King and Messiah in Israel and the Ancient Near East*, ed. John Day (Sheffield: Sheffield Academic, 1998), 456.

18. On my read, the apocalypse of Jub. 23 (which never mentions a messianic figure) is a wholly conditional eschatology. Things begin to turn around when "children will begin to search the law . . . and return to the way of righteousness" (v. 26) and so their days and longevity will eventually increase (the text understands the steep decline in longevity from the earliest biblical accounts to be due to human sinfulness). There will be "no Satan and no evil one" and "all their days will be days of blessing and healing" (v. 29). See again, at the close of the book, 50.5. Cf. James Kugel, "The Jubilees Apocalypse," *DSD* 3 (1994): 322–37; Jason, *Repentance at Qumran*, 204.

are most understandable on the grounds that they are *reactions* to disappointing developments (the best example being the Galilean woes in Q 10:13–15). But that is not the same as saying that Jesus, on account of rejection that was perhaps greater than he anticipated (a perfectly plausible idea), took up a new course of action and began to talk about the future in a noticeably different way. I veer toward a similar conclusion in this study as we consider specifically the claim that unforeseen rejection generated the parousia expectation, and for similar reasons.

Some Difficulties

In large part, my skepticism is exegetical in nature. As noted above, it is not challenging to find parallels in Jewish texts that contend human repentance or righteousness trigger end-time blessing. But it seems to me that the risk of parallelomania here is real.[19] The reality is that we find a variety of views about the end in existence, with some texts even outright rejecting the notion of conditional outcomes.[20] In some cases, we find these conflicting views in the very same texts,[21] while others remain unclear.[22] I noted this as well in my earlier study of John the

19. Samuel Sandmel, "Parallelomania," *JBL* 81 (1962): 1–13.

20. See the comparison of 4 Ezra and 2 Baruch in Francis Watson, *Paul and the Hermeneutics of Faith*, 2nd ed. (London: Bloomsbury T&T Clark, 2016), 448. In b. Sanh. 97–98, various conditional and nonconditional views are grouped together, including at 97a the explicit claim that the messiah will not come until things are hopeless for Israel (including the proliferation of apostates, diminishment of torah students, and general "despair of the redemption"). See also 4 Ezra 4.38–43; Ps. Rab. at 45.3. In m. Soṭa 15 we read, "in the footsteps of the messiah insolence will increase," and, we should observe, this is an extended reflection on Ps 89, whose arc is about the seeming collapse of the promise to David's seed and the ensuing despair that ends with hope in God to remember the promise to David (15.49–51).

21. On 2 Baruch, Matthias Henze, "Torah and Eschatology in the Syriac Apocalypse of Baruch," in *The Significance of Sinai: Traditions about Sinai and Divine Revelation in Judaism and Christianity*, ed. George Brooke, Hindy Najman, and Loren Stuckenbruck, TBN 12 (Leiden: Brill, 2008), 204, writes, "Deuteronomic theology, particularly the call on Israel to live in accordance with the Mosaic Torah and to choose life over death, has become the central aspect of the book's apocalyptic world view. Our author manages to harmonize two distinct strands of early Jewish thought which, by modern literary standards, are not harmonious but appear to be mutually exclusive, to the extent that they are normally kept separate: the *Deuteronomic promise* to those who follow Torah that they will be rewarded with a long and prosperous life, and the *apocalyptic promise* that this life will soon come to an end."

22. I would include here Philo's hope (*Praem.* 162–165) that the dispersed will one day understand that their afflictions are disciplinary measures sent from God, and, fittingly, "feel shame"

Baptist: some texts indeed expect repentance to initiate the ingathering of the lost tribes, but others hoped for an act of God irrespective of human initiative.[23] It is also likely that in some texts, the notion of mass repentance is simply an eschatological trope and not systematized and factored into larger scenarios about divine causation that interest modern historians.[24] Here is the key point, then: the fact we find various viewpoints in the air only forces us back to the task of discerning the most probable reading of the texts before us on the topic in question—the first step in any historical reconstruction. This is much like the debate about how literally we should take the apocalyptic language in the Gospels; that controversy can only be settled by exegesis, not by gathering putative parallels. And compelling exegesis of New Testament texts is lacking, to my mind, in the interesting studies by Barry Smith and Christopher Hays. Smith offers a plausible idea but never actually explains how and why he decided to reorganize the teaching of Jesus into its respective "non-rejection" and "rejection" contexts. The reader picks up the book to find the gospel tradition already divided into these contexts, while the logic for such reorganization, and the rationale by which Smith came to these determinations, are never disclosed. In fact, Smith will often discuss a particular episode or logion at length without *ever* explaining why it best fits a "non-rejection" or "rejection" context.[25] This assumes what should be the very central argument of the study.

---

and "change their ways" and "confess all the sins," and that this "conversion [μεταβολῆς] in body to virtue" will "strike awe into their masters, who will set them free." The unclarity stems from the fact that, while change of behavior is stressed, it also appears to be miraculous in nature. See discussion in James M. Scott, "Philo and the Restoration of Israel," in *Society of Biblical Literature 1995 Seminar Papers*, SBLSP 34 (Atlanta: Scholars Press, 1995), 553–75. I also find ambiguous Bar 4:27–29; 4Q174 1 I, 13–14 (on those who turn aside from the path of wickedness "in the last days"); 4Q215a 1 II, 4–10 ("the age of wickedness is fulfilled and all injustice will [pass a]way . . . the time of justice has arrived"); 4Q397 (4QMMT[d]) 14–21, 12–15 ("will turn [to him with al]l your heart and with [al]l [your] soul at the end [of time]"); 11Q19 LIX, 9–13 ("they shall come back to me with all their heart and soul"). In all of these texts, repentance is important, to be sure, and eschatological, but the effects are unclear, as is, in some cases, whether the question of causation is even in view.

23. And as argued in Ferda, "John the Baptist, Isaiah 40, and the Ingathering of the Exiles," it is not apparent that John was calling for repentance in order to trigger the onset of God's day, even though his proclamation of repentance surely had an eschatological subtext. The emphasis, rather, appears to be calling for repentance because God's day was near.

24. See, e.g., Tg. Ps.-J. on Deut 30:8, where a prediction of future repentance sits alongside predictions about God's ingathering of the dispersed and replacing the evil impulse with a good impulse (30:4, 6).

25. I offered a similar critique in my review of Smith's work. See Tucker S. Ferda, review of *Jesus' Twofold Teaching about the Kingdom of God*, by Barry D. Smith, *JSHJ* 14 (2016): 274–76.

Hays's book showed more work here, and it is different from Smith's in that Hays is not trying to reconstruct different periods in Jesus's activity. But crucial questions remain, mostly because none of the New Testament examples he points to (minus three, to my mind: Luke 13:6–9 [parable of the fig tree]; Luke 18:1–8 [arable of the persistent widow]; Acts 3:19–21 [Peter's speech in the temple])[26] are cases of conditional prophecy or conditional eschatology as Hays has defined it.[27] That is, Hays sometimes forces conditionality where it does not appear to be a natural reading of the text. He notes, for instance, that Jesus's "prophecies regarding the time of the end are all followed by imperatives to the disciples, demanding they proclaim the good news to all the nations . . . bear witness to Jesus . . . be ethically and existentially awake and alert."[28] But the Gospels never state or even imply that said prophecies *depend upon* the disciples doing these things; it is, rather, the very conviction that the time is short that provides the seriousness of the imperatives themselves. Of course, the Gospels could have distorted the originally conditional teaching of Jesus on this matter, but how could we ever know if the only evidence that we have does not actually claim that? Hays's thesis basically depends upon his ability to redefine prophecy—in terms of genre—as essentially or typically conditional.[29] But even the biblical survey early in the book by C. A. Strine does not justify such a sweeping conclusion.

For those who believe Jesus's message changed in a noticeable way, I also fear there is an underestimation of how fragmentary our evidence is for Jesus while simultaneously an overestimation of our ability as historians to get into Jesus's head and reconstruct the ups and downs of his activity.[30] As in the case of a Gal-

26. While it also raises questions for me that all of these texts come from Lukan literature.

27. Hays et al., *When the Son of Man Didn't Come*, 83, acknowledges the possible exegetical critique before engaging some texts: the "reader may well object that our explanation, though consonant with how prophecy works elsewhere in Scripture, is simply not derived from the Synoptic Gospels themselves." Hays highlights the petition for the kingdom to come in the Lord's Prayer (Q 11:2), the prediction about the gospel being proclaimed throughout the whole world before the end comes (Matt 24:14), Jesus thinking of his ministry in Jeremianic terms, and later New Testament claims about the timing of the eschaton being delayed on account of God's character (e.g., 2 Pet 3:8–10). Prayer for God to act, as well as the general notion of the flexibility of the end, may well conflict with eschatological determinism, but it is a stretch to say they imply a larger understanding of the future in which God's action is contingent on human response.

28. Hays et al., *When the Son of Man Didn't Come*, 83.

29. So Hays et al., *When the Son of Man Didn't Come*, 83: "we are reframing what it means for Jesus to 'prophesy,' on the basis of how prophecy works throughout much of Scripture and the ancient world."

30. See the fascinating final thoughts in the important study by Kim Huat Tan, *The Zion Traditions and the Aims of Jesus*, SNTSMS 91 (Cambridge: Cambridge University Press, 1997),

ilean crisis, the notion that we can actually identify a change of mind on Jesus's part requires us to be able to reconstruct with relative precision a tension in his teaching concerning eschatology, such that we might assign these conflicting elements to different stages of his activity.[31] But this is a very speculative and tenuous procedure, not wholly unlike some reconstructions of Q and its recension history (which are at least dealing with texts). For heuristic purposes, and to strip an argument about periodizing Jesus's activity to its essential moves, it is fair to say that a historian must do the following:

1. claim that Jesus expected x concerning the kingdom of God in the future and we can know pretty clearly what he meant;
2. be equally confident that x does not square with future scenario y, also known pretty clearly, in which the parousia hope is present;
3. then assign the parousia material y to a different historical stage (either in the life of Jesus, or in the post-Easter period), in order to maintain the coherence, and presumed primitivity, of x.[32]

The initial diagnosis of such thematic tensions between x and y is, of course, an interpretive decision. While all history writing is inherently interpretive, the consequences of the subjectivity of this process are heightened because the reconstruction is largely dependent on one's ability to first accurately interpret and then distinguish these "eschatologies" as different conceptual schemes.[33] Can we really

---

224–25. He asks, "would Jesus have expected to die if his ministry was well received by the nation and especially by Jerusalem?" He responds, "Here we come to a great puzzle which demands an abundance of data for its resolution but, unfortunately, such data are unavailable." He does, in any case, offer tentatively that "he would probably not have deemed his death to be necessary if Israel, and especially Jerusalem, responded positively to his ministry."

31. See discussion in Ferda, *Jesus, the Gospels, and the Galilean Crisis*, 97, 140, 142–44.

32. Cf. Philipp Vielhauer, "Gottesreich und Menschensohn in der Verkündigung Jesu," and "Jesus und der Menschensohn," in *Aufsätze zum Neuen Testament*, TB 31 (Munich: Kaiser, 1965), 55–91, 92–140, argued that the proclamation of the kingdom and the expectation of the son of man are mutually exclusive in content, and so the conclusion: Jesus did not speak of the latter. For similar positions, see Ernst Käsemann, "The Beginnings of Christian Theology," in *New Testament Questions of Today* (London: SCM, 1969), 101–2 (because Jesus "proclaimed the immediacy of God who was near at hand," he could not have anticipated the future coming of the son of man); Norman Perrin, *Rediscovering the Teaching of Jesus* (New York: Harper & Row, 1967), 164–73.

33. Such is the main problem with the argument of Joel Marcus, "The Beelzebul Controversy and the Eschatologies of Jesus," in *Authenticating the Activities of Jesus*, ed. Bruce Chilton and Craig A. Evans (Leiden: Brill, 2002), 247–78, that there is embedded in the Beelzebul controversy two contradictory perspectives on the exorcisms. One assumes Satan's house has not been over-

know enough about Jesus's eschatological message to exclude the parousia on the grounds that it is contrary to other kingdom teachings?[34] Where exactly do we find that clarity in the tradition? Moreover, simply identifying conditional elements in the teaching of Jesus is one thing, and I do not deny their presence categorically, as noted above.[35] But it is quite another thing to say that conditional elements in Jesus's teaching are sufficiently different from other aspects of his message that one must conclude he could not have held both views at the same time, or that we must periodize his activity accordingly.[36] This schematic view that first emerged in the nineteenth-century lives of Jesus probably reflects a modern bias that is influenced by hardened philosophical understandings of divine and human agency.[37]

---

thrown ("Satan's house is not divided"), and the second that the strong man has been bound. He argues both sayings are historical and come from different stages of the ministry, indicating some development in the thought of Jesus about eschatological fulfillment.

34. Contra Cadoux, *Historic Mission of Jesus*, 203, who claimed there was "a very considerable difference" between saying the kingdom has "drawn near" (Mark 1:15) and that some will not "taste death" before seeing the kingdom in power (Mark 9:1). He moderates this claim somewhat in later lines on 203.

35. Nor should one deny a priori the likelihood that Jesus was inconsistent about certain things. Contra Lewis A. Muirhead, *The Eschatology of Jesus, or, The Kingdom Come and Coming: A Brief Study of Our Lord's Apocalyptic Language in the Synoptic Gospels* (London: Melrose, 1904), 48: "I assume with moral certainty, that Jesus is not chargeable with intellectual inconsistency." Cf. Jack T. Sanders, "The Criterion of Coherence and the Randomness of Charisma: Poring through Some Aporias in the Jesus Tradition," *NTS* 44 (1998): 1–25; Gerd Theissen and Dagmar Winter, *The Quest for the Plausible Jesus: The Question of Criteria* (Louisville: Westminster John Knox, 2002), 236 n. 7 ("figures who think less systematically, including Jesus, probably have at least as many contradictions in their utterances as does Paul, if not more"). See further Ferda, *Jesus, the Gospels, and the Galilean Crisis*, 100–101, and 150–57.

36. On this point, see the important essay by C. F. D. Moule, "The Influence of Circumstances on the Use of Eschatological Terms," *JTS* 15 (1964): 1–15, which challenges common attempts to systematize eschatological views in New Testament texts without sufficient attention to the circumstances in which they were said/written. He suggests that one might stress different aspects at different times (e.g., present vs. future, free will vs. determinism, pessimism vs. optimism) depending on the situation being addressed. "Different formulations have to be enlisted in the service of different affirmations, all of which may prove to be simultaneous aspects of a single great conviction too large to be expressed coherently or singly" (9).

37. Most discussions of agency in New Testament criticism have focused on the apostle Paul. But there are some instructive studies. Cf. John M. G. Barclay and Simon J. Gathercole, eds., *Divine and Human Agency in Paul and His Cultural Environment*, LNTS 335 (London: Bloomsbury T&T Clark, 2007); Jason Maston, *Divine and Human Agency in Second Temple Judaism and Paul: A Comparative Study*, WUNT 2/297 (Tübingen: Mohr Siebeck, 2010); Kyle B. Wells, *Grace and Agency in Paul and Second Temple Judaism*, NovTSup 157 (Leiden: Brill, 2015); Yoonjong Kim, *The Divine-Human Relationship in Romans 1–8 in the Light of Interdependence Theory*, LNTS 635 (London: Bloomsbury T&T Clark, 2020), 32–52.

Moreover, it is also dubious to claim that there are qualitatively different senses of imminence in the tradition—imminent in the sense of tomorrow, and imminent in the sense of within this generation—such that we might position the imminent-meaning-tomorrow material at an earlier stage of the ministry, and the imminent-meaning-this-generation material at a postrejection stage later in the ministry. I have already argued above that we search in vain in the Gospels for evidence of an eschatology that is more imminent than the view that the generation then living is the last.

In the end, then, to claim that a parousia scenario does not fit with what we otherwise know of Jesus's message, and it must thereby only have emerged after a crisis (or crises) of rejection, is problematic because it actually claims to know *more* than we can know. In many respects, the argument is a mirror image of a once-common reconstruction of Jesus's relationship to John the Baptist, wherein Jesus's announcement of grace and forgiveness was frequently contrasted to the Baptist's message of judgment. The latent anti-Judaism of that move aside, we hardly know enough about John the Baptist to wager such a systematic analysis of what his message entailed, such that we can identify what is foreign to it.[38] So, too, we hardly know enough about Jesus to contrast two different eschatologies in his teaching.[39]

Eschatology and Process

I would favor a second historical scenario. This second scenario is supported by greater evidence in the Gospels and equally vast parallels in Jewish eschatological thought. It concerns the common expectation that the eschatological fulfillment of God's purposes in history would involve some kind of process, with various events expected to transpire with varied transformative effects.[40] My sense is

38. Fernando Bermejo Rubio, "Why Is John the Baptist Used as a Foil for Jesus? Leaps of Faith and Oblique Anti-Judaism in Contemporary Scholarship," *JSHJ* 11 (2013): 170–96.

39. It is possible, of course, that an initial conditional eschatology has been suppressed by post-Easter theology and hence the witness of the Gospels. But, (1) methodologically, it is precarious to read less-frequent contingent elements over and against the grain of other and more prominent strains of eschatological thought in the New Testament and to prioritize them (this would be the inverse of a gist approach), and (2) historically, there is no reason why such a conditional eschatology would have been repressed in that manner. In fact, it might have been quite useful theologically for the fledgling movement as a means of heightening the culpability of those who rejected Jesus. The theological emphasis of the Gospels and Paul's letters is more idiosyncratic, and thus historically curious: to explain how the death of Jesus was actually the plan of God.

40. See Jürgen Becker, *Jesus of Nazareth*, trans. James E. Crouch (Berlin: de Gruyter, 1998), 105–7, 118–19.

that, once again, modern constructs of divine and human agency, and particularly fraught theological debates from the nineteenth century onward between apocalyptic and developmental understandings of the kingdom of God in Protestant Christianity, have created a false and anachronistic impression that historians face a binary choice between instantaneity and process when it comes to the manifestation of the kingdom. But this choice has been constructed by years of Western Christians picking teams between Barth and neoliberalism, on the one hand, and the social gospel and liberation theology, on the other, and it has very little to do with ancient Jewish sources. What we find instead with some frequency is that the expectation for a radical action of God in history to change it for good can sit with, and alongside, an interest in timelines, sequences, and the expectation of more observable changes, including the ethical labor of persons. It was not uncommon in Jewish eschatological expectation, that is, to expect a process of inauguration, working toward a more decisive, climactic, and irreversible end.

Such a notion might be the most natural impression left by the cascade of images that comprise Second and Third Isaiah, beginning with the preparation for return "in the wilderness," through the oracles of the restoration of Zion, and concluding with the "new heavens and new earth."[41] It is significant that coins minted by Jewish leaders during the Jewish-Roman War intentionally evoke Isaiah with inscriptions "Jerusalem the Holy" (ירושלים הקדושה, cf. Isa 52:1: "Awake, awake! Put on your strength, O Zion! Put on your beautiful garments, O Jerusalem the Holy City [ירושלם עיר הקדש]!"), and "for the Redemption of Zion" (לגאלת ציו). Some are dated "Year 1" through "Year 4." This suggests that these revolutionaries understood Isaiah to forecast an eschatological process they thought underway, and hence datable, but, obviously, not yet completed.[42] The books of Baruch (4:21–5:9) and Tobit (13:1–17) also imagine God's longed-for future to involve a sequence of events[43]—heavily influenced by Isaiah as well—as does the apocalypse of Jub. 23 (which, per the discussion above, does indeed appear to regard the transformed future state as contingent on Israel's obedience).[44]

41. Cf. Lloyd Gaston, *No Stone on Another: Studies in the Significance of the Fall of Jerusalem in the Synoptic Gospels*, NovTSup 23 (Leiden: Brill, 1970), 414: "One can even speak of the coming of salvation in Deutero-Isaiah as a process."

42. Cf. Donald T. Ariel, "Identifying the Mints, Minters and Meanings of the First Jewish Revolt Coins," in *The Jewish Revolt against Rome: Interdisciplinary Perspectives*, ed. Mladen Popović, JSJSup 154 (Leiden: Brill, 2011), 373–97.

43. And, in Tobit, already underway, so Jill Hicks-Keeton, "Already/Not Yet: Eschatological Tension in the Book of Tobit," *JBL* 132 (2013): 97–117.

44. Cf. James C. VanderKam, *Jubilees: A Commentary*, Hermeneia (Minneapolis: Fortress, 2018), 2:694–702.

In Daniel, the apocalyptic establishment of the world-filling stone (2:35) and the giving of the kingdom to the one like a son of man (7:13–14, 18, 27) occur within a document that also shows a concerted interest in periods of time, as do other apocalyptic texts inspired by it, such as 4 Ezra and Revelation.[45] A similarly apocalyptic kingdom appears famously in T. Mos. 10.1–10, but this is *after* a description of the suffering and martyrdom of Taxo and his sons (9.1–7), which implies some kind of movement from suffering to vindication. At Qumran, 1QpHab (Pesher Habakkuk) asserts that "all the ages of God [כול קיצי אל] will come at the right time" (VII, 13), and earlier speaks of the "age of wickedness" that precedes the time of salvation (V, 7–8).[46] In CD, the author assumes that the existence of the sect belongs to a certain "period" (קץ) of history that ushers in the eschaton—an "intermediate step," so Lawrence Schiffman.[47] Similar transitional processes are depicted in later texts like the Apocalypse of Weeks in 1 En. 93, 91.12–17, and Apocalypse of the Clouds in 2 Bar. 53–74, which forecast the future via a sequence of ten weeks (so 1 Enoch) or twelve weather systems (so 2 Baruch).[48] These passages invest the present with eschatological significance by situating the readers somewhere within the timeline.[49]

It is also important to note that messianic hopes, varied though they were, frequently envisioned some kind of process of inauguration, whereby the coming of a messianic figure is climactic but does not necessarily change history instantaneously. In 4Q246, the naming of the "son of God" occurs *before* the "trampling" by the nations (inspired by Daniel) and then the establishment of God's peace and

45. Cf., e.g., 4 Ezra 4.36–51; 5.7–10; 9.1–2; etc. See also Sib. Or. 3.656–795.

46. Cf. also 4Q215a II, 3–4 expects that the "age of wickedness" will be "fulfilled" and "all unrighteousness will pass away." For discussion, see Årstein Justnes, *The Time of Salvation: An Analysis of 4QApocryphon of Daniel ar (4Q246), 4QMessianic Apocalypse (4Q521 2), and 4QTime of Righteousness (4Q215a)* (Frankfurt: Lang, 2009), 281–390.

47. See Lawrence H. Schiffman, *Qumran and Jerusalem: Studies in the Dead Sea Scrolls and the History of Judaism* (Grand Rapids: Eerdmans, 2010), 272. He further argues that "the author saw the eschaton as having already partially dawned" (272).

48. See James C. VanderKam, "Studies in the Apocalypse of Weeks (1 Enoch 93:1–10; 91:11–17)," *CBQ* 46 (1984): 511–23; Mark A. Elliott, *The Survivors of Israel: A Reconsideration of the Theology of Pre-Christian Judaism* (Grand Rapids: Eerdmans, 2000), 528–33; George W. E. Nickelsburg, "Response: Context, Text, and Social Setting of the Apocalypse of Weeks," in *Enoch and Qumran Origins: New Light on a Forgotten Connection*, ed. Gabriele Boccaccini (Grand Rapids: Eerdmans, 2005), 234–41; Matthias Henze, *Jewish Apocalypticism in Late First Century Israel: Reading Second Baruch in Context*, TSAJ 142 (Tübingen: Mohr Siebeck, 2011), 266–74.

49. Though it is important to note that, in the "twelve calamities" of 2 Bar. 26–30, it says that some of the times "will be mixed, one with another," such that people on the earth will not be able to understand where exactly they reside. In 29.3, the anointed one "will begin to be revealed."

kingdom (also inspired by Daniel).[50] (Note that, in the War Scroll at Qumran, the final battle takes forty years—that is, a biblical generation.)[51] Mention of struggle is absent from Pss. Sol. 17's idealization of the son of David, but the passage nonetheless imagines that the "raising up" of David's seed will include a series of events (e.g., purging Jerusalem, gathering the tribes, etc.) that would obviously transpire over the course of some time, while the duration is not clear. The concluding summary statement in 17:44 fittingly reads, "blessed are those born *in those days*. . . ." Near identical expressions designating some period of time are frequently found in targumim and rabbinic literature, including "the days of the messiah," and "the footprints of the messiah," and "the tribulation of the messiah."[52] Second Baruch even speaks of a time at which God's "messiah" will "begin to be revealed."[53] It is also telling that, like the leaders in the Jewish-Roman War, the messianic claim-

50. See discussion in Tucker S. Ferda, "Naming the Messiah: A Contribution to the 4Q246 'Son of God' Debate," *DSD* 21 (2014): 150–75. Another important text from Qumran that may be relevant here is 1QH XI, 6–12, though its interpretation is fraught. The passage depicts the birth of someone called the "wonderful counselor" from Isa 9:6 amid crushing pains for a mother—e.g., in a time of tribulation. For a messianic reading of this figure, see Andrew Chester, *Messiah and Exaltation: Jewish Messianic and Visionary Traditions and New Testament Christology*, WUNT 207 (Tübingen: Mohr Siebeck, 2007), 263. Against a messianic reading, see Marinus de Jonge, "The Role of Intermediaries in God's Final Intervention in the Future according to the Qumran Scrolls," in *Jewish Eschatology, Early Christian Christology, and the Testaments of the Twelve Patriarchs*, NovTSup 63 (Leiden: Brill, 1991), 42–43.

51. See also the pesher on Ps 37:10 in 4Q171 II, 6–8, which expects a forty-year period after which wickedness will be destroyed. See also CD XX, 13–15.

52. Tg. Ps.-J. and Frg. Tg. on Gen 3:15; Tg. Neof. on Gen 49:10–12; Frg. Tg. on Exod 12:42 (on the "four nights"); Tg. Ps.-J. on Exod 17:16; Tg. Ps.-J. on Num 24:20; Tg. Ps.-J. on Deut 25:19; Tg. 1 Sam. 2.35; Tg. Isa. 9.6 ("the messiah in whose days peace will increase upon us"); 11.6; 53.8; Tg. Ps. 61.7; Tg. Eccl. 1.11. For footprints, see m. Soṭa 9.15 and days see m. Ber. 1.5 (which are two of only a few messianic references in the Mishnah); Tg. Ps. 89.52. See also b. Sanh. 91b, 98b (R. Gidel declares "Israel will in the future enjoy the years of the messiah"), 99a ("all the prophets prophesied only of the days of the messiah"); b. Ber. 34b.

53. On 2 Bar. 29.3, Henze, *Jewish Apocalypticism in Late First Century Israel*, 296, speaks of "the initial stage of the messianic presence." See also 39.7. In 40.3–4, the dominion of the Anointed One is predicted to last "until the world of corruption has ended" and "until the times mentioned before have been fulfilled." For additional discussion of the messianic expectations in this text, see Loren Stuckenbruck, "Messianic Ideas in the Apocalypse and Related Literature of Early Judaism," in *The Messiah in the Old and New Testaments*, ed. Stanley E. Porter (Grand Rapids: Eerdmans, 2007), 90–113; Gerbern S. Oegema, *Apocalyptic Interpretation of the Bible: Apocalypticism and Biblical Interpretation in Early Judaism, the Apostle Paul, the Historical Jesus, and Their Reception History* (London: T&T Clark International, 2012), 133–42; Torleif Elgvin, *Warrior, King, Servant, Savior: Messianism in the Hebrew Bible and Early Jewish Texts* (Grand Rapids: Eerdmans, 2022), 267–68.

ant Bar Kokhba started dating coins and letters (Year 1, Year 2) to the onset of his movement, even referring to "the liberation of Israel," while there was clearly still a lot that needed to happen.[54] Messianic expectations like these did not emerge out of nowhere but were inspired by biblical texts, notably the story of David himself and the growth imagery of many passages (Jer 33:15 ["in those days I will cause a righteous branch to spring up for David"]; cf. Jer 23:5 ["I will raise up for David a righteous branch"]; Zech 6:12).[55] Particularly influential was Isa 11:1 ("A shoot will come out [יצא] from the stump of Jesse, and a branch shall grow [פרה] from his roots"), which continues into the idealistic vision of the wolf living with the lamb, the end of hostility, and the destruction of Israel's enemies.[56] This was perhaps the most impactful text for messianic speculation in the Second Temple period.

This notion of messianic inauguration, if we may call it that, brings to mind the expectation of a "hidden messiah"—a fascinating tradition that has been underinvestigated by New Testament critics.[57] The recurring view seems to be that a messianic figure exists and lives for some time unknown to his contemporaries—and, in some texts, unknown even to himself—before a great unveiling in which his true identity is manifest to the world. We have an explicit reference to this expectation in the Gospel of John, where the evangelist has invented dialogue for the crowd that is intelligible only if one assumes the currency of the notion of a hidden messiah: "Do the leaders really know that this is the Christ? But we know where this man is from, but when the Christ comes, no one will know where he comes from" (7:26–27).[58] Justin Martyr also preserves something of this tradition

54. They date "the liberation of Israel" to the start of the revolt. The messianic nature of several movements mentioned by Josephus is highly debated, though it is worth noting that several, too, are described as beginning and inaugurating some kind of kingly rule via their early actions; cf., e.g., *Ant.* 17.273 (Simon of Perea "presumed to put on the diadem" and "was declared king" by his followers); 17.278 (Anthronges "dared upon the kingship," "put on the diadem," and "was called king"); *J.W.* 2.434 (Judah the Galilean "returned to Jerusalem in the manner of a king and became leader").

55. See James M. Hamilton Jr., "The Typology of David's Rise to Power: Messianic Patterns in the Book of Samuel," *SBJT* 16 (2012): 4–25.

56. A fact not lost on later interpreters; note y. Ber. 4.3: "all who trust in you will rejoice in the rebuilding of your city and in the restoration of the house of your sanctuary, and in the sprouting of David your servant." See also b. Ber. 29a.

57. For some earlier studies, see Erik Sjöberg, *Der verborgene Menschensohn in den Evangelien* (Lund: Gleerup, 1955), 54–56; Sigmund Mowinckel, *He That Cometh*, trans. G. W. Anderson (Oxford: Blackwell, 1956), 304–8. In Pauline studies, Brant Pitre, Michael P. Barber, and John A. Kincaid, *Paul, a New Covenant Jew: Rethinking Pauline Theology* (Grand Rapids: Eerdmans, 2019), 89, note that the tradition of the "hidden and revealed Messiah" "does not seem to have had as much impact on recent studies of the apocalyptic Paul as one might expect."

58. As also noted by Susan Miller, "'Among You Stands One Whom You Do Not Know'

(as there is no apparent motive for or benefit to blatant invention) when he has Trypho say, "But the Christ, if indeed he has been born, and lives anywhere, is unknown, and does not even know himself and has no power until Elijah comes to anoint him and make him manifest to all" (*Dial* 8.4).[59] The expectation for a messianic "manifestation" or "revealing" appears in numerous other texts that are socially and temporally diffused, including the Septuagint, 1 Enoch, 4 Ezra, 2 Baruch, the targumim, the Pseudo-Clementines, and rabbinic literature and exegesis.[60] We can respect variety and difference here while also admitting that this is likely a wider expectation that predates Christian origins.[61]

(John 1:26): The Use of the Tradition of the Hidden Messiah in John's Gospel," in *The Ways That Often Parted: Essays in Honor of Joel Marcus*, ed. Lori Baron, Jill Hicks-Keeton, and Matthew Thiessen, ECL 24 (Atlanta: SBL Press, 2018), 246–52. Cf. especially 1:26 ("among you stands one whom you do not know"); 7:1–4 ("show yourself to the world!"). See C. K. Barrett, *The Gospel according to St. John*, 2nd ed. (London: SPCK, 1978), 322. The Fourth Evangelist has reworked this tradition in predictable ways, given the realized eschatology elsewhere: Jesus is disclosed to the world as he is "lifted up" on the cross.

59. See also *Dial.* 110.1.

60. Isa 32:1–2 LXX: "A righteous king shall reign . . . and a man shall be hiding his words, and shall be hidden as from rushing water, but shall appear in Zion like a glorious rushing river in a thirsty land." John J. Collins, *The Scepter and the Star: Messianism in Light of the Dead Sea Scrolls*, 2nd ed. (Grand Rapids: Eerdmans, 2010), 204, 211, suggests that Isa 49:1–3 (the servant "hidden away") was influential for this tradition. See 1 En. 46.1–3 (with reference to "all the hidden things" about "that son of man"); 48.6 ("concealed in the presence of the Lord of Spirits"); 62.7 ("hidden to be revealed to the elect at the proper time"). We also find in 62.7–9 that the rulers of the earth see and fall down before the son of man, modeled likely on Isa 49:7, which intrigues in light of the hiddenness of the servant in Isa 49:2. Cf. Pitre, Barber, and Kincaid, *Paul, a New Covenant Jew*, 91. Cf. 4 Ezra 7.28; 12.32; 13.26, 32, 52; 2 Bar. 29.3; 39.7; Tg. Mic. 4.8 (where "and you, Migdal-eder, the hill of the daughter of Zion, unto you it shall come, the former dominion . . . the kingdom" is rewritten as "and you, O messiah of Israel, who have been hidden away from the sins of the congregation of Zion, the kingdom is destined to come to you, and the former dominion shall be restored to the kingdom of the congregation of Jerusalem"); Tg. Eccl. 7.25; Tg. Chr. 3.24. See also Tg. Zech. 3.8 (which rewrites "I bring forth my servant the branch" to "I bring my servant, the messiah, who is to be revealed"); Tg. Zech. 4.7 and 6.12. Cf. Ps.-Clem. Rec. 1.54.8 (for the view that John the Baptist is the concealed messiah), and 1.60.1–2; b. Sanh. 97a ("three things come unexpectedly: the messiah, a found article, and a scorpion"); Midr. Ps. 21.1.

61. Raymond E. Brown, *The Gospel according to John*, AB 29 (Garden City, NY: Doubleday, 1966–1970), 1:53, speaks of a "popular theory." While it could potentially be significant for the arguments adduced here, I remain unsure of what to make of David Daube's interesting contention in *He That Cometh* (London: Council for Christian-Jewish Understanding, 1966), 6–14, rebooting Robert Eisler's earlier argument, "Das letzte Abendmahl," *ZNT* 24 (1925): 161–92, about the hidden messiah and the pre-70 Passover seder. He argues that the piece of unleavened bread hidden in the house, the *afikoman*, derives originally from the Greek ἀφικόμενος, even though the rabbis had forgotten this, where it earlier had symbolized the messianic "one who comes." There

My proposal is that these eschatological views about process and inauguration, and perhaps even the hope for a future unveiling of a hidden messiah (though this is admittedly less clear), illuminate the teaching of Jesus about the kingdom of God and may be how the parousia hope arose in the pre-Easter period.[62] Many interpreters have severed the parousia hope from Jesus because they have assumed that the alternative would either make him too Jewish (so part 2), or too Christian, meaning, too much like the second-century Christian apologists who thought the whole biblical witness unites around the expectation for two advents of the messiah in humiliation and in glory, respectively. If the former has already been challenged as another case study in Christian anti-Judaism, the latter is surely a theological myth whose clarity and tidiness are possible only in hindsight. But it is also an unnecessary narrative that is out of touch with the varieties of Jewish eschatological and messianic thought. To follow the evidence where it has led us so far and locate the origin of the parousia hope in the pre-Easter period in no way requires a suspiciously prescient Jesus who had in mind from the beginning a blueprint of how everything would unfold, including the events of that final Passover in Jerusalem. It is instead to say that Jesus, when he spoke of the drawing near of the kingdom, probably had in mind the inauguration of some kind of eschatological process of fulfillment, albeit with a short fuse, and he saw at the end of that process his own unveiling as Dan 7's son of man. Whether his own death would precede that unveiling—that is, whether he would be spared the time of testing, as he purportedly taught his followers to pray about (Matt 6:13)—may for some time have been an open question for Jesus. It has been written about Paul, "The younger Paul seems confident he will be alive until the parousia, but . . . in his last days Paul realizes that his churches will go on without him."[63] This very

is, we know, an ancient belief that the messiah would appear on the night of Passover. Note Jer 38:7–9 LXX (which adds that the coming of the messiah, restoration of Israel, and new covenant will occur "during the Passover feast"), and also Tg. Onq. on Exod 12:42; cf. Mek. on Exod 12:42; Exod. Rab. 15.1. See also Tg. Lam. 2.22 (where an unspecified "appointed feast" is taken to be Passover, and God proclaims liberty to the people "by the hand of king messiah"). The idea that messiah will appear at Passover was known to Jerome, *Comm. Matt.* on 25:6, who attests to the continuation of this belief in Christian groups awaiting the return of Jesus.

62. This suggestion would corroborate the arguments of others that Jesus hoped to become or one day be recognized as the son of man. Cf. R. H. Fuller, *The Mission and Achievement of Jesus: An Examination of the Presuppositions of New Testament Theology* (London: SCM, 1967), 103 ("not as the one who is already Son of man, but as the one destined to be the Son of man, as the Son of man designate"). See also Volker Hampel, *Menschensohn und historischer Jesus: ein Rätselwort als Schlüssel zum messianischen Selbstverständnis Jesu* (Neukirchen-Vluyn: Neukirchener Verlag, 1990), 164 ("Messias designatus").

63. David B. Capes, Rodney Reeves, and E. Randolph Richards, *Rediscovering Paul: An Introduction to His World, Letters, and Theology* (Downers Grove, IL: InterVarsity Press, 2007),

common suggestion about development in Paul's thought is certainly a reasonable idea (while its veracity is not important to establish here), and we should emphasize that to conclude as much does not mean Paul suddenly changed his former eschatological perspective in a drastic way. It is also not apparent that this development in his thought would have anything to do with conditional eschatology.[64] It would just be that the process was taking longer than initially thought, and Paul concludes he may well succumb before the end to the troubles and afflictions he battled over the course of his career (cf. already 1 Thess 1:6; 3:3).[65] Is it not possible something similar happened to Jesus? This would not be the same as saying that the end for Jesus was conditional and depended on the positive reception of his message but only that God alone knows the final hour.[66] The simultaneous confidence (about imminence) and openness (about not predicting day or hour) we find throughout the tradition suggests that what Mark 13:32 has Jesus say ("concerning that day or hour, no one knows, neither the angels in heaven nor the son, but only the Father") is probably near the historical truth of the matter.[67]

Process and Traditions about Jesus

It is not a mere few isolated logia in the Gospels that support something like this reconstruction of Jesus. There are rather numerous texts at all levels accessible to

255. On development in Paul, see E. P. Sanders, *Paul: The Apostle's Life, Letters, and Thought* (Minneapolis: Fortress, 2015), 429–31, 720–21.

64. At least in Philippians, Paul is not saying he expects death because people are failing to repent and respond to the degree necessary to trigger the end.

65. Sanders, *Paul: Life, Letters, and Thought*, 208: the expectation to still be alive was "one of the aspects of Paul's gospel that changed somewhat with time; with every passing year, more and more believers died, and so Paul had to emphasize resurrection, though he never gave up the expectation that the Lord's return was imminent." See Sanders's summary of Paul's development at 429–31.

66. As Jeremias, *New Testament Theology*, 138, noted concerning the Gethsemane prayer, it appears here that Jesus "considers the possibility that God might bring in his reign even without suffering to precede it."

67. For arguments that this saying is historical in a traditional sense, which I will not seek to justify further here, see T. W. Manson, *The Teaching of Jesus: Studies of Its Form and Content*, 2nd ed. (Cambridge: Cambridge University Press, 1935), 277–78; James D. G. Dunn, *Jesus Remembered* (Grand Rapids: Eerdmans, 2003), 723; Craig S. Keener, *The Historical Jesus of the Gospels* (Grand Rapids: Eerdmans, 2009), 273; Timo Laato, "Der ambivalente Stil und die Eschatologie des Neuen Testaments," *EC* 9 (2018): 100. On the challenges this verse posed for later christological discussion, see the excellent study by Kevin Magidan, "*Christus Nesciens*? Was Christ Ignorant of the Day of Judgment?," in *The Passions of Christ in High-Medieval Thought: An Essay on Christological Development* (Oxford: Oxford University Press, 2007), 39–50.

us that have Jesus speaking as though his activity coincides with the inauguration or beginning of long-awaited eschatological realities. In two sayings, we have Jesus purportedly periodizing history around his own activity vis-à-vis the ministry of John the Baptist, clearly linking the time of "the kingdom of God" to the onset of his work (Luke 7:28 and parr.; Luke 16:16 and parr.).[68] In his reply to John, Jesus speaks as though the signs of the new age foretold by Isaiah have begun to be realized (Q 7:18–23), and he elsewhere evokes the predicted activities of "the anointed" figure in Isa 61.[69] In a similar way, Jesus is said to have announced the presence of the kingdom via his healings and exorcisms (e.g., Q 11:20), pronounced blessed the eyes of those who see what they see (Q 10:23–24), and warned against those who cannot "interpret the signs" of the present times (Q 12:54–56; cf. Mark 4:9, 23; Matt 11:15; 13:43; Luke 14:35).[70] Some have marshaled such material to advocate for a present or realized nature of the kingdom over and against the future, but this is an unfortunate and unnecessary distinction. The above sayings make sense as remarkably bold claims about what has begun in the work of Jesus—what process is underway—assuming there is more to come, including the final consummation.

We see this dynamic clearly in the so-called parables of growth, which made Albert Schweitzer nervous and have received very meager treatment by proponents of an eschatological Jesus ever since his time (as noted in part 1).[71] This

68. This probably has messianic connotations. Note the association between messiah and kingdom in Tg. Onq. and Frg. Tg. on Gen 49:10; Tg. Ps.-J. on Exod 40:9; Num 24:7 LXX and Frg. Tg. on Num 24:7; Tg. 1 Sam. 2.10; Tg. Mic. 4.8. Cf. also the third petition of the Benedictions after the Haftarah, as cited by Chester, *Messiah and Exaltation*, 416: "Make us glad, O Lord our God, with Elijah the prophet, your servant, and with the kingdom of the house of David, your Messiah. May he soon come and make our hearts rejoice." Cf. further Werner Zager, *Gottesherrschaft und Endgericht in der Verkündigung Jesu: Eine Untersuchung zur markinischen Jesusüberlieferung einschließlich der Q-Parallelen*, BZNW 82 (Berlin: de Gruyter, 1996), 119–23; Dunn, *Jesus Remembered*, 451–52.

69. Dale C. Allison Jr., *Constructing Jesus: Memory, Imagination, and History* (Grand Rapids: Baker Books, 2010), 263–66.

70. Pss. Sol. 17.44 ("blessed are those born in those days to see the good fortune of Israel"); 18.6; Sib. Or. 3.371. Cf. Helmut Merklein, *Jesu Botschaft von der Gottesherrschaft: Eine Skizze*, SBS 111 (Stuttgart: Katholisches Bibelwerk, 1983), 66–67; George R. Beasley-Murray, *Jesus and the Kingdom of God* (Grand Rapids: Eerdmans, 1986), 80–85; John P. Meier, *Mentor, Message, and Miracles*, vol. 2 of *A Marginal Jew: Rethinking the Historical Jesus* (New York: Doubleday, 1994), 437 ("Jesus' audience therefore lives in the time of fulfillment of Israel's hopes and prophecies"); Marius Reiser, *Jesus and Judgment: The Eschatological Proclamation in Its Jewish Context*, trans. Linda M. Maloney (Minneapolis: Fortress, 1997), 206–21; Matthias Kreplin, *Das Selbstverständnis Jesu: Hermeneutische und christologische Reflexion—historisch-kritische Analyse*, WUNT 2/141 (Tübingen: Mohr Siebeck, 2001), 212–33.

71. See pp. 52–53 above. And Schweitzer was an improvement from Weiss, *Jesus' Proclamation of the Kingdom of God*, 60–65, who argued the kingdom parables of Matt 13 were inauthen-

includes the parable of the sower (Mark 4:1–9 and parr.; Gos. Thom. 9), the parable of the seed growing secretly (Mark 4:26–29), the parable of the tares (Matt 13:24–30; Gos. Thom. 57), the parable of the mustard seed (Mark 4:30–32 and parr.; Gos. Thom. 20), and the parable of the leaven (Q 13:20–21; Gos. Thom. 96). Schweitzer was right to wrest these parables from nineteenth-century liberal Protestant exegesis where they served as prooftexts for a philosophy of history about development and human progress. But he was wrong to deny that there is any notion of development in these parables. For Schweitzer, the batch of parables share the same, singular point: to contrast a meager beginning with an abundant end—something possible, he thought, only by God's hand, not by human effort. The parables were about supernatural transformation, Schweitzer concluded, about what is to happen when the future kingdom comes.[72] Here we come again upon biblical exegesis that serves as a modern proxy war over differing views on divine and human agency. I do not deny this transformative component, but one has to work unnecessarily hard to argue that these parables of growth are not actually about growth.[73] They all make good sense as representations of either the small ministry of Jesus and its growth over some brief time or the sure and certain expansion of the message about the kingdom and its power.[74] The end result may still be surprising and impossible via human effort alone, so Schweitzer, but these

---

tic in toto and stemmed from the early church's attempt to de-eschatologize the teaching of Jesus. For broader discussion, see Warren S. Kissinger, *The Parables of Jesus: A History of Interpretation and Bibliography* (Metuchen: Scarecrow, 1979); Klyne R. Snodgrass, *Stories with Intent: A Comprehensive Guide to the Parables of Jesus* (Grand Rapids: Eerdmans, 2008), 1–36; Ruben Zimmermann, *Puzzling the Parables of Jesus: Methods of Interpretation* (Minneapolis: Fortress, 2015), 3–56, 57–104.

72. Cf. Albert Schweitzer, *The Quest of the Historical Jesus*, trans. William Montgomery (New York: Macmillan, 1950), 356–57; Schweitzer, *The Mystery of the Kingdom of God: The Secret of Jesus' Messiahship and Passion*, trans. Walter Lowrie (Eugene, OR: Wipf & Stock, 1970), 106–23.

73. So rightly John P. Meier, *Probing the Authenticity of the Parables*, vol. 5 of *A Marginal Jew: Rethinking the Historical Jesus* (New Haven: Yale University Press, 2016), 233, on the parable of the mustard seed (which he thinks is authentic): it is unavoidable that "at least part of the message" is growth or development of the kingdom of God. Note also Cadoux, *Historic Mission of Jesus*, 196, who thought there had been an overreaction to the modern tendency "to discover in the teaching of Jesus a doctrine of ethical and spiritual evolution." He replied, "But after all, growth is growth: and in the case of all these parables, the process culminates in some sort of climax of completeness."

74. See David Flusser, *Jesus*, 3rd ed. (Jerusalem: Hebrew University Magnes Press, 2001), 111; Renate Banschbach Eggen, "Do the Parables Tell Us Something about the Mission of Jesus?," in *The Mission of Jesus*, ed. Samuel Byrskog and Tobias Hägerland, WUNT 2/391 (Tübingen: Mohr Siebeck, 2015), 141–60. On confidence about the future in these parables, see Perrin, *Rediscovering the Teaching of Jesus*, 158–59.

parables make the most sense within the framework of eschatological progress toward consummation as noted above. Indeed, the very image of planting, which Jesus apparently loved, is inherently about starting a process toward the harvest—setting in motion what is to come.[75] It is not a coincidence that many other texts envisage eschatological fulfillment with seed and harvest imagery and to similar effect,[76] with some using "planting" and "growth" language to mark the in-process accomplishment of God's purposes in the world.[77]

I would further wager that this understanding of something started, underway, and growing in Jesus's activity, while also expecting more to come, illuminates

75. Note here 2 Bar. 22.5–6, where Baruch is asked a series of rhetorical questions: "Or he who sows the earth—does he not lose everything unless he reaps its harvest in its own time? Or he who plants a vineyard—does the planter expect to receive fruit from it, unless it grows until its appointed time?"

76. Cf. Shozo Fujita, "The Metaphor of Plant in Jewish Literature of the Intertestamental Period," *JSJ* 7 (1976): 30–45; Stephen C. Carlson, "Eschatological Viviculture in *1 Enoch*, *2 Baruch*, and the Presbyters of Papias," *VC* 71 (2017): 37–58.

77. This, of course, is widespread in biblical literature; see, e.g., Isa 35:1–7; 41:19–20; Jer 31:27–28; 32:41; 41:20; Ezek 17:3–24; Dan 4:10–12, 20–27; etc. But its deployment in the texts nearer Christian origins is particularly intriguing. Cf. 1QS VIII, 5–6 (the community is established as "an everlasting plantation" that in the desert prepares the way of the Lord [ll. 14–15]); 1QH XIV, 14–17 (God "sprouts" a bloom and a "shoot" [the community] that will "grow into the branches of the everlasting plantation so that it covers all the wo[rld] with its shade. . . . All the streams of Eden [will water] its [bra]n[ch]es"); XVI, 5–8 (the "trees of life" are "hidden among all the trees" and are about to "make a shoot [נצר] grow in the everlasting plantation"—this passage may have messianic connotations); CD I, 5–7 (with reference to the founding of the group, framed eschatologically as "he caused a sprout from Israel"); Jub. 1.16–17 ("I shall transplant them as a righteous plant"); 7.34; Pss. Sol. 14.3–4 (though here not eschatologically); 1 En. 10.16 (on "the plant of righteousness and truth" that will "appear" at the end time); 62.8 ("the congregation of the holy ones shall be planted"); 4 Ezra 4.26–32 (in this case negatively with reference to evil "until the time of threshing"); 9.21 (which recycles Ezek 17); 2 Bar. 36.1–37 (the vision of the growing vine—its interpretation that follows declares "the dominion of my Anointed One will be revealed, which is like the fountain and the vine" [39.7]); see also 70.2. Elliott, *Survivors of Israel*, 329, who has also commented on some of these images, suggests that the plant metaphors are "regularly associated with a highly conditional view of the covenant." That is right, but the *kind* of conditionality in view here needs to be defined carefully. There is a type of conditionality present in numerous Jewish texts that draw the line between the righteous and the wicked through, rather than around, Israel. Cf. Tucker S. Ferda, "The Messiah of That Most Mischievous Superstition: Jesus and the Parting of the Ways in the Study of Christian Origins," *EC* 14 (2023): 9–34. This is essentially the premise of there being a final judgment wherein eternal fate, and membership in the covenant community, is dictated by conduct. Such a conditional scenario is different, though, than saying the very arrival of God's day is caused by righteousness or delayed by sinfulness. It would be a stretch to make these metaphors imply such an idea by virtue of their use alone and nothing more in context.

some of the peculiarities of the messianism of the Jesus movement. As already noted, that *some kind* of messianic understanding goes back to Jesus best accounts for Paul's assumptions about Jesus "the Christ" and the scriptural and genealogical curiosity of the earliest Christians, not to mention certain events and sayings in the Gospels themselves.[78] At the same time, critics skeptical of the authenticity of the messianic self-claim of Jesus have rightly stressed various perplexing features of the Gospels on this question, especially Jesus's seeming reticence to publicize his identity and the infrequency of explicit messianic titles in the sayings tradition.[79] The notion of messianic inauguration, however, and perhaps even the idea of a hidden messiah who awaits a dramatic, future unveiling to the world, could in fact be the key that respects and includes the core insights of both perspectives on this debate. The messianic understanding does indeed go back to Jesus, but he expected his messianic unveiling to be a dramatic future event along the lines of the prediction of Dan 7's vision of the son of man coming before the Ancient One. In a sense, then, Jesus was not yet the messiah in terms of his public perception, as that was reserved for the future.[80] To my mind, this scenario is also the most

78. See p. 295 above and literature cited there. See also Strauss, *Life of Jesus*, 284; Craig A. Evans, *Jesus and His Contemporaries: Comparative Studies*, AGJU 25 (Leiden: Brill, 1995), 77–81; Christopher Tuckett, introduction to *The Messianic Secret*, ed. Christopher Tuckett (London: SPCK, 1983), 7–9 (on the fact that messiahship was in no way a corollary of resurrection); John P. Meier, "From Elijah-Like Prophet to Royal Davidic Messiah," in *Jesus: A Colloquium in the Holy Land*, ed. Doris Donnelly (New York: Continuum, 2001), 45–83. Contra John A. T. Robinson, "The Most Primitive Eschatology of All?," *JTS* 7 (1956): 177–89; Ferdinand Hahn, *The Titles of Jesus in Christology*, trans. Harold Knight and George Ogg (London: Lutterworth, 1969), 136–222; Jürgen Becker, *Jesus of Nazareth*, trans. James E. Crouch (Berlin: de Gruyter, 1998), 186–97.

79. See discussion of the relevant issues in Matthias Kreplin, "The Self-Understanding of Jesus," in *Handbook for the Study of the Historical Jesus*, ed. Tom Holmén and Stanley Porter (Leiden: Brill, 2010), 3:2474–76.

80. This is not far from where a few others have ended up. See Alfred Loisy, *The Birth of the Christian Religion and the Origins of the New Testament*, trans. L. P. Jacks (New Hyde Park, NY: University Books, 1962), 78–79 ("Jesus was Messiah in expectation, Messiah presumptive"); Rudolf Otto, *The Kingdom of God and the Son of Man: A Study in the History of Religion*, trans. Floyd V. Filson and Bertram Lee Woolf (Grand Rapids: Zondervan, 1938), 226–43 (at 237 he speaks of Jesus as "the one destined to be the Son of Man" and "the one who must be exalted"); Martin Dibelius, *Jesus* (Philadelphia: Westminster, 1949), 95, 101. Note also Gerd Theissen and Annette Merz, *The Historical Jesus: A Comprehensive Guide*, trans. John Bowden (Minneapolis: Fortress, 1998), 552, which is worth quoting in full:

> Jesus spoke of a future Son of Man who would suddenly be made manifest with the eschatological turning-point. He did not mean anyone else by this. Rather, like Paul in II Cor. 12.1ff. he meant himself. . . . What Paul writes about a past ecstatic experience, Jesus says about a future ecstatic experience: with the dawn of the kingdom of God he is expected to assume

cogent way to make sense of the origin of the messianic secret motif—or motifs—in the Synoptics. Wrede's thesis that the secrecy motif is wholly fictional, inspired by a disjuncture between the messianism of the post-Easter movement and the unmessianic ministry of Jesus, has of course failed to convince many,[81] but so have other attempts to explain the secrecy themes in wholly theological terms from a post-Easter perspective. But if Jesus had messianic pretensions, why keep them under wraps?[82] It may have been partly pragmatic, as others have argued, but also partly inspired by a conviction that he would one day be revealed as the messiah per traditions surveyed above about a messianic unveiling and maybe even the notion of a hidden messiah.[83] Moreover, cross-cultural studies of apocalypticism

---

the role that he attributed to the Son of Man. The turning-point will come unexpectedly and suddenly. With it he too will be changed, like the whole world. Therefore he speaks of this changed man as of a third person, but in so doing is thinking of himself as a changed person. The suddenness and miraculous character of this change is so great that the Son of Man sayings leave a gap here. They say nothing about how the present Son of Man will become the future Son of Man.

81. See already the criticisms by Schweitzer, *Quest of the Historical Jesus*, 330–51, and Johannes Weiss, *Das Urchristentum* (Göttingen: Vandenhoeck & Ruprecht, 1917), 22.

82. Cf. Joseph Klausner, *Jesus of Nazareth: His Life, Times, and Teaching*, trans. Herbert Danby (New York: Macmillan, 1925), 254.

83. Jeremias had an interesting take in an aside in *New Testament Theology*, 267–68, that may be relevant here. He reflects on the fact that some denied the authenticity of Jesus's future predictions about the son of man on the grounds that the kingdom of God proclamation and the son of man sayings stand together but are not "authentically linked" (so the argument goes), and that the linkage came only in the process of compilation after Easter. Jeremias offers another interpretation. Granting some differentiation between the kingdom sayings and the son of man sayings, Jeremias thinks instead that this may reflect something about the historical Jesus: he spoke differently to insiders and outsiders. In particular, he spoke about the coming kingdom to outsiders and the coming son of man to insiders. The Gospels are, of course, notoriously unreliable in terms of the audience of Jesus's utterances, as Jeremias himself notes elsewhere (see *New Testament Theology*, 255–56; Jeremias, *The Parables of Jesus*, trans. S. H. Hooke, 2nd ed. [New York: Scribner's Sons, 1972], 33–42. Cf. also the important and overlooked study by Dale C. Allison Jr., "The Problem of Audience," in *Resurrecting Jesus: The Earliest Christian Tradition and Its Interpreters* [London: T&T Clark, 2005], 27–55). But it is apparent, especially with regard to instructions about discipleship, that Jesus spoke differently to different people. See Tucker S. Ferda, "The Historical Jesus and the Law: The Form of His Activity and the Impact of Social Reputation," *CBQ* 80 (2018): 64–66, 75–77. Moreover, Jeremias's suspicion connects rather easily to a view that some very prominent scholars continue to hold about the betrayal by Judas (assuming that is historical): that for motives we know not, Judas had disclosed the secret known to the inner circle that Jesus had messianic pretensions. For this understanding of Judas's deed, see Schweitzer, *Quest of the Historical Jesus*, 395–97; Benjamin Bacon, "What Did Judas Betray?," *HibJ* 19 (1920–1921): 476–93; E. P. Sanders, *Jesus and Judaism* (Philadelphia: Fortress, 1985), 309; Bart D. Ehrman, *Jesus: Apocalyptic Prophet of the New Millennium* (Oxford: Oxford University

have repeatedly shown that apocalyptic movements often claim to house divinely revealed secrets that are not yet known to the world, but, it is expected, they one day will be (cf. 1 En. 52.2–4).[84] It seems to me that the messianic grammar of early Christians (to use Novenson's language) in talking about Jesus's future "revealing" or "disclosure" as the messiah is too similar to other non-Christian messianic texts to be a mere coincidence.[85]

Death and Process

Now one potential response to this line of argument is that the prospect of the death of Jesus destroys the probability of this reconstruction, since no one else was expecting the death of the messiah. Thus, one might continue, to have Jesus expect a future coming or appearance after death is simply not believable for a figure in first-century Palestine. I would make three points in response to conclude this chapter.

First, and to reiterate a point made above, I am not arguing that Jesus was following a script or blueprint, or that he had everything worked out from the

---

Press, 1999), 218–19 ("What, then, did Judas betray to the authorities? This private teaching of Jesus . . . he called himself the Messiah, the King of Israel").

84. See Jonathan Knight, *Jesus: An Historical and Theological Investigation* (London: T&T Clark, 2004), 138–45. Cf. Markus Bockmuehl, *Revelation and Mystery in Ancient Judaism and Pauline Christianity*, WUNT 2/136 (Tübingen: Mohr Siebeck, 1990), 35–40; Christopher Rowland, *The Open Heaven: A Study of Apocalyptic in Judaism and Early Christianity* (Eugene, OR: Wipf & Stock, 2002), 156–90. For a study of Jesus in this vein, see Leslie A. Baynes, "Jesus the Revealer and the Revealed," in *The Jewish Apocalyptic Tradition and the Shaping of New Testament Thought*, ed. Benjamin E. Reynolds and Loren T. Stuckenbruck (Minneapolis: Fortress, 2017), 15–30.

85. This phrasing is frequent in the targumim; see, e.g., Tg. Ps.-J. on Gen 35:21; Tg. Isa. 53.2; Tg. Jer. 30.21; Tg. Zech. 3.8; 4.7; 6.12; Tg. Cant. 8.1. Cf. also 1 En. 38.2 ("the Righteous One shall appear"); 52.6–9; 69.29 ("that son of man has appeared and has seated himself on the throne of his glory"); 4 Ezra 7.28 ("my son the messiah shall be revealed"), 13.29, 32 ("Behold the days are coming when the Most High will deliver those who are on the earth . . . then my son will be revealed"); 2 Bar. 29.3 ("the Anointed One will begin to be revealed"), 30.1 ("the time of the appearance of the Anointed One"); 39.7 ("the dominion of my Anointed One . . . will be revealed"); b. Sanh. 38a; b. Sukkah 52a ("to the messiah son of David, who is destined to be revealed quickly in our time"). This notion may have influenced the creation of the temptation narrative in the double tradition, whereby Satan thrice tempts Jesus to make a quick and powerful revelation of his messianic identity (Luke 4:1–13 and par.). Note especially in this context Pesiq. Rab. 36 ("at that time when king messiah reveals himself he will come and stand on the roof of the temple"). Could a similar idea undergird the episode about Simon ben Giora recounted by Josephus during the last moments of the Jewish war in Jerusalem? Josephus claims that Simon put on royal (purple) clothes and "appeared out of the ground [ἐκ τῆς γῆς ἀνεφάνη] in the place where the temple had formerly been" (*J.W.* 7.29).

beginning, including his own death. The argument is that Jesus claimed an eschatological process had begun and was underway, and in the future, he expected tribulation but also God's triumph in the resurrection of the dead, the final judgment, and the life thereafter. It may be that, for a time, perhaps for a long time, Jesus thought that he would see that triumph without himself tasting death.[86] It could be.[87] We find in the synoptic presentation the striking fact that parousia

86. Some have argued that Jesus reckoned with the danger of death when in Jerusalem that fateful week. See, e.g., Robert M. Grant, "The Coming of the Kingdom," *JBL* 67 (1948): 297–303; Günther Bornkamm, *Jesus of Nazareth*, trans. Irene and Fraser McLuskey, with James M. Robinson (New York: Harper, 1960), 42; Anton Vögtle, "Jesus von Nazareth," in vol. 1 of *Ökumenische Kirchengeschichte*, ed. Raymund Kottje and Bernd Moller (Munich: Kaiser, 1970), 3–24; Saucy, *Kingdom of God in the Teaching of Jesus*, 336; Joachim Gnilka, *Jesus of Nazareth: Message and History*, trans. Siegfried S. Schatzmann (Peabody, MA: Hendrickson, 1997), 284–87; Craig A. Evans, "Did Jesus Predict His Death and Resurrection?," in *Resurrection*, ed. Stanley E. Porter, Michael A. Hayes, and David Tombs, JSNT 186 (Sheffield: Sheffield Academic, 1999), 86–91 (dates the passion predictions to the final week).

87. Contra Rudolf Bultmann, should we remove death from the picture, it is not suddenly implausible for Jesus to speak still of his coming as the son of man. Bultmann, *Theology of the New Testament*, trans. Kendrick Grobel (New York: Scribner's Sons, 1955), 1:29, framed this as a rhetorical question: "how would Jesus have conceived *the relation of his return as Son of Man to his present historical activity?* He would have had to count upon being removed from the earth and raised to heaven before the final End, the irruption of God's Reign, in order to come from there on the clouds of heaven to perform his real office." He further terms the notion of a translation to heaven a "fantastic idea." For similar views, see Gustaf Dalman, *Die Worte Jesu* (Leipzig: Hinrichs, 1898), 211 ("Ein Gestorbener oder von der Erde Entrückter konnte ja vielleicht so in die Welt wiedereingeführt werden, oder eine niemals auf Erden gewesene Persönlichkeit kam so auf die Erde herab. Dan 7, 13 schien somit von Jesus nicht gelten zu können"); Hermann Werner, *Die psychische Gesundheit Jesu* (Berlin: Runge, 1909), 44; Frederick C. Grant, *The Gospel of the Kingdom* (New York: Macmillan, 1940), 67; Richard H. Hiers, *The Historical Jesus and the Kingdom of God: Present and Future in the Message and Ministry of Jesus* (Gainesville: University of Florida Press, 1973), 45; Joost Holleman, *Resurrection and Parousia: A Traditio-Historical Study of Paul's Eschatology in 1 Corinthians 15*, NovTSup 84 (Leiden: Brill, 1996), 116 ("Jesus *was already present*, and thus it was bizarre, if not impossible, for him to speak about himself as the *coming* Son of Man from heaven"). Bultmann's view needs to be remythologized. See already Oscar Holtzmann, *The Life of Jesus*, trans. J. T. Bealby and Maurice A. Canney (London: Black, 1904), 180, and Schweitzer, *Quest of the Historical Jesus*, 365 (on Jesus expecting "two different conditions: the present, and the future condition into which He is to be transferred at the coming of the new supernatural world"); more recently Theissen and Merz, *Historical Jesus*, 552 ("the turning-point will come unexpectedly and suddenly. With it he too will be changed, like the whole world. Therefore he speaks of this changed man as of a third person, but in so doing is thinking of himself as a changed person"). In addition to eschatological transformation, we have numerous traditions of celestial ascent or being "caught up" to heaven. Cf., e.g., 2 Kgs 2:1–18; Sir 48:9–10 LXX; possibly 4Q471b (though interpretation is particularly difficult); Jub. 4.22; Philo, *QG* 1.86; Philo, *Sacr.* 3.8; Josephus, *Ant.* 4.326; LAB 48.1; T. Levi 2.5–6.2; 1 En. 87.3–4; 89.52; 4 Ezra

predictions are almost all grouped to the middle and later portions of the ministry of Jesus, especially after Peter's confession and Jesus's resolve to travel to Jerusalem. We should place little to no trust at all in the reliability of the chronology of the activity of Jesus as it appears in the Synoptics, to be sure.[88] But this peculiar feature may not be a pure literary creation. It may reflect the historical fact that there was an integral relationship between the prospect of death and the parousia predictions, and that they emerged during his activity at about the same time.

Be that what it may, the key point, as argued above, is that at some point, Jesus must have grappled with the potential of death, and he is remembered as having taught his disciples accordingly in ways that are probably historical in the gist. I leave open the question of how and when the prospect of death dawned on Jesus, since I do not think the sources permit us access to that kind of intimate knowledge that earlier questers often speculated about and even wrote whole books devoted to unraveling.[89]

Moreover, it is striking how quickly historians can forget that when it comes to reconstructing messianic expectations, we are dealing only with fragments. We simply do not know enough to define sharply the edges of messianic speculation—what is and what is not believable.[90] We do know enough to identify variety and difference of opinion, and that sometimes within the same religious group,[91] even if some sectors of scholarship have perhaps overly exaggerated the

6.25–26; 14.8 9; 2 Bar. 76.1–5. Cf. Gerhard Lohfink, *Die Himmelfahrt Jesu: Untersuchungen zu den Himmelfahrts- und Erhöhungstexten bei Lukas* (Munich: Kosel, 1971), 51–79; A. W. Zwiep, *The Ascension of the Messiah in Lukan Christology* (Brill: Leiden, 1997), 36–79; Martha Himmelfarb, "Heavenly Ascent and the Relationship of the Apocalypses and the Hekhalot Literature," and "Revelation and Rapture: The Transformation of the Visionary in the Ascent Apocalypses," in *Between Temple and Torah: Essays on Priests, Scribes, and Visionaries in the Second Temple Period and Beyond*, TSAJ 151 (Tübingen: Mohr Siebeck, 2013), 257–83 and 283–94.

88. Richard Bauckham, *Jesus and the Eyewitnesses: The Gospels as Eyewitness Testimony* (Grand Rapids: Eerdmans, 2006), 243: "That the individual units of the Synoptic Gospels are close to the oral forms in which they previously existed and that in oral transmission they were not necessarily linked together as they are in the Gospels remain, in my opinion, the most significant insights of form criticism and have not been refuted."

89. Scot McKnight, *Jesus and His Death: Historiography, the Historical Jesus, and Atonement Theory* (Waco, TX: Baylor University Press, 2005), 48, asks in the midst of his study "at what point in his life did that [he would die] occur to him?" But he never returns to take up the question in earnest.

90. Aside from being inaccurate, the confident categorical statement by John A. T. Robinson, *Jesus and His Coming: The Emergence of a Doctrine* (New York: Abingdon, 1957), 22, is unjustified: "The Jews did not speak of the Parousia of the Messiah, they did not expect that he would descend with clouds from heaven, and above all they did not expect that he would come back once he had come."

91. So George J. Brooke, "Kingship and Messianism in the Dead Sea Scrolls," in Day, *King and*

fluidity of messianism in the New Testament period. In any case, the key point is this: arguments from silence are especially precarious when so much has been lost.[92] This should make us humble. We do in fact have a messiah who dies in 4 Ezra, and if we did not have 4 Ezra, I doubt that anyone would have been able to predict what we find in this text.[93] As a counterfactual thought experiment, if

---

Messiah in Israel and the Ancient Near East, 455, wrote memorably that "the Scrolls have put the 'mess' into 'messianism.'"

92. Cf. Dieter Georgi, "The Early Church: Internal Jewish Migration or New Religion?," *HTR* 88 (1995): 65: "One can . . . ask whether, in cases where exact Jewish parallels are lacking, the respective phenomenon in the church can be taken as evidence for a variant within Judaism, in the absence of other evidence which may be lost." For reflections on how much has been lost in the second century, which cannot be much different from the first, see Christoph Markschies, "The Canon of the New Testament in Antiquity: Some New Horizons for Future Research," in *Homer, the Bible, and Beyond: Literary and Religious Canons in the Ancient World*, ed. Margaret Finkelberg and Guy G. Stroumsa (Leiden: Brill, 2003), 176 (claims we only have 14 percent of the literature named by extant sources).

93. Michael E. Stone, *Fourth Ezra: A Commentary on the Book of Fourth Ezra*, Hermeneia (Minneapolis: Fortress, 1990), 209, calls the death of the messiah in 4 Ezra "almost unparalleled." In 2 Baruch, we not only have the notion that "the messianic woes . . . precede the Messiah" but that "the misery of the world does not stop the minute the Messiah arrives," so Henze, *Jewish Apocalypticism in Late First Century Israel*, 302. In addition, it is not clear whether the view Justin Martyr attributes to Trypho in *Dial.* 89–90 should be cast aside as mere Christian projection. Trypho says that he agrees with Justin, on the basis of Scripture, that the messiah will experience suffering, but he denies that the messiah will "die such a disgraceful and dishonorable death, cursed by the law" (90.1). This is interesting in light of other texts about eschatological tribulation such as m. Soṭa 9.15, as well as Dan 7:25 (where the holy ones are "worn out" or "afflicted," from בלה). Another potentially important text here is Dan 9:24–26, which mentions "an anointed one" who will be "cut off." In the original context of Daniel, Dan 9:26 may have referred to Onias III (cf. 2 Macc 4:22–28), but in later reception, this could easily be read eschatologically with reference to a still-awaited "anointed one" who will be "cut off." Moreover, the fragmentary 11Q13 II mentions an "anointed one that Daniel spoke of," before breaking off at the end of the line (18), and most critics believe the line that followed must have been either Dan 9:25 or 26 (with its mention of an "anointed one"). We know in other contexts that Dan 9 and its discussion of the seventy weeks was important for calculating the date of the arrival of the messiah. See Roger T. Beckwith, *Calendar and Chronology, Jewish and Christian: Biblical, Intertestamental and Patristic Studies* (Leiden: Brill, 2001), 217–75. All of this deserves more attention by New Testament scholars. Also, for sake of completeness, it is worth mentioning here the Gabriel Revelation and what it might contribute to this conversation, should it be genuine. I am unsure of what to make of this discovery, though some prominent critics have affirmed its authenticity. Israel Knohl, *Messiahs and Resurrection in the Gabriel Revelation* (London: Continuum, 2009), has argued that the inscription attests to the notion of a dying and rising messiah in pre-Christian Judaism, which would, of course, be of major historical significance if true. But there are good reasons to be skeptical of this reading and interpretation. See Collins, *Scepter and the Star*, 166–70; Adela Yarbro Collins, "Response to Israel Knohl, Messiahs and Resurrec-

we imagine that we had all the sources that we currently have minus 4 Ezra, I am sure that many scholars would say that what 4 Ezra claims could not exist because it appears so idiosyncratic in comparison to other sources. But there it is, thanks to the random fact that 4 Ezra has survived. We should recall here Matthew Novenson's observation that "all ancient messiah texts, Jewish or Christian, are the product of the reinterpretation of scriptural oracles in the light of the experience of their respective authors," because this means that some unpredictability is to be expected.[94] To be clear, this is not to speculate in the other direction and say that there was in fact a well-defined understanding of a suffering and dying messiah that influenced Jesus. I have never been convinced that this is the case, despite the arguments to the contrary.[95] My point is this: we hardly know enough to say that potential death in the eschatological tribulation necessarily disqualifies one from having messianic pretensions.[96]

---

tion in 'The Gabriel Revelation,'" in *Hazon Gabriel: New Readings of the Gabriel Revelation*, ed. Matthias Henze (Atlanta: Society of Biblical Literature, 2011), 93–97. Knohl attempts to connect the Gabriel Revelation to the later legend of the messiah ben Joseph. The majority view is that the messiah ben Joseph emerged as a response to the failure of the Bar Kokhba revolt. Cf. Novenson, *Grammar of Messianism*, 179. For another view, see David C. Mitchell, "A Dying and Rising Josephite Messiah in 4Q372," *JSP* 18 (2009): 181–205. Key texts for the messiah ben Joseph include Tg. Ps.-J. on Exod 40:11; Tg. Yer. on Zech 12:10; b. Sukkah 52a–b; Tg. Cant. 4.5; 7.4; Gen. Rab. 75.6; 99.2; Num. Rab. 14.1. William Horbury, *Jewish Messianism and the Cult of Christ* (London: SCM, 1998), 33, has argued, on the basis of Dan 9:26 and Zechariah, that "the notion of a slain messiah is then likely to have been current in the Second-Temple period, partly on the basis of Zechariah, although it seems clearly to have been less prominent than the expectation of a great and glorious king." He has not convinced many.

94. Novenson, *Grammar of Messianism*, 184. Novenson again, "Jewish messianism—of which Christian messianism can be thought of as just an extraordinarily well documented example—always and everywhere involves the interplay of biblical tradition and empirical circumstance" (196); and again, "If what scholars have called 'Christian messianism' is indeed an ingenious, even desperate assimilation of scriptural tradition to the circumstances of a particular messiah's life, then it is not at all something separate from or other than Jewish messianism. On the contrary, it is just an exceptionally well-documented example" (207); and yet again, "all ancient messiah texts, Jewish as well as Christian, find themselves having to manage ideal biblical traditions on the one hand and empirical historical circumstances on the other" (213). See also J. Thomas Hewitt, *Messiah and Scripture*, WUNT 2/522 (Tübingen: Mohr Siebeck, 2020), 75–76.

95. Some have claimed to find the notion of a slain messiah in 4Q285. It is likely, though, that the fragment has the messiah slaying his enemy rather than being slain; so Markus Bockmuehl, "A 'Slain Messiah' in 4Q Serekh Milḥamah (4Q285)?," *TynBul* 43 (1992): 155–69. In any case, the caution of Chester, *Messiah and Exaltation*, 235, is fair: on account of "the tantalizingly fragmentary nature of 4Q285," "the possibility of a Davidic messiah being killed in battle [should not] simply be dismissed." See also Collins, *Scepter and the Star*, 64–67, 141–48.

96. We may be in a similar position with respect to the question of Jesus's predictions of

Help from Heaven

And this leads to my second and third points that will conclude this chapter. The way in which some critics have said that what early Christians claimed about the return of Jesus is novel and without suitable parallel has been greatly exaggerated, and if stated categorically (e.g., that there are no parallels), it is simply false.

In chapter 15, I showed that there are two ways we might contextualize the coming of Jesus apart from the belief of his individual resurrection of the dead: it was simply a way of referring to his return after the resurrection of the dead, or it was indeed conceived as a coming from heaven that coincided with the general

---

the destruction of the temple (cf. Mark 13:2 and parr.; 14:57–58 and Matt 26:60–61; Mark 15:29 and Matt 27:40; John 2:18–22; see also Acts 6:14) and how that relates to his larger eschatological message about the kingdom of God. Most historians affirm the historicity of this prediction—cf. discussion in Klyne R. Snodgrass, "The Temple Incident," in *Key Events in the Life of the Historical Jesus: A Collaborative Exploration of Context and Coherence*, ed. Darrell L. Bock and Robert L. Webb, WUNT 247 (Tübingen: Mohr Siebeck, 2009), 429–80, and Jostein Ådna, "Temple Act," in *Dictionary of Jesus and the Gospels*, ed. Joel B. Green, Jeannine K. Brown, and Nicholas Perrin, 2nd ed. (Downers Grove, IL: InterVarsity Press, 2013), 947–52—while a minority dispute it (notably Paula Fredriksen, *When Christians Were Jews* [New Haven: Yale University Press, 2018], 43–51). But here then is the question, assuming the majority opinion about this prediction is in the right: we have no clear evidence in Second Temple Judaism for the expectation that the temple would be destroyed before or as a part of its eschatological rebuilding (though note the pillars of the old "pulled out" in 1 En. 90.28; cf. also 2 Bar. 32.2–3). Of course, the hope for a new eschatological temple is widely attested (cf. Isa 60:10–14; Ezek 40–43; Tob 13:16–18; 14:5; Jub. 1.15–17; 1QM VII, 4–10; 11Q19 XXIX, 8–10; T. Benj. 9.2; 1 En. 90.28–29; 91.13), but not necessarily its destruction, as noted by many critics over the years. Cf., e.g., already Alfred Edersheim, *The Life and Times of Jesus the Messiah*, 3rd ed. (Grand Rapids: Eerdmans, 1943), 2:433–34; Jeremias, *New Testament Theology*, 125 (the expectation was for "the temple to flourish, not to go under"); Gaston, *No Stone on Another*, 162 ("there is evidence that some groups expected a new temple in the age to come . . . [but] such an expectation is never connected with the idea of the destruction of the old temple"); Sanders, *Jesus and Judaism*, 88–90. *As a question of methodology*, what are we to do about this? Are we to deny the historicity of this prediction on the grounds that there is insufficient evidence in Second Temple Judaism for this particular expectation, or are we to follow what seems most probable about the past on the basis of our main sources, and regard our knowledge of Second Temple Jewish eschatological expectation incomplete and fragmentary with respect to this issue? This is an interesting and instructive parallel to our topic, even while I would contend that we actually do have better parallels for what early Jesus followers were saying about Jesus and the parousia. For some related methodological reflections on Jesus research in general, see Tom Holmén, "An Introduction to the Continuum Approach," in *Jesus from Judaism to Christianity: Continuum Approaches to the Historical Jesus*, ed. Tom Holmén, LNTS 352 (London: Bloomsbury T&T Clark, 2007), 10 ("when . . . a tradition displays an original variation of known Jewish ideas, there often appears in scholarship an especially strong tendency to ascribe without further ado the tradition to early Christians").

resurrection in some way. My discussion below accounts for the ambiguity, but I will start with the primary claim we find in New Testament sources that Jesus will come down from heaven.

Eduard Schweizer wrote, "The idea of a Parousia from heaven is non-existent in Judaism."[97] But Ruben Bühner has more recently asserted nearly the opposite point—"the notion of an eschatological figure of salvation who comes down from heaven is not seldom within the different early Jewish messianic texts."[98] Bühner's assertion is far nearer the truth of the matter than Schweizer's. According to my research, we find a heavenly revealed redeemer figure in at least five texts. While the date of some of these texts remains debated, it is, as noted already, specious to dismiss them summarily as irrelevant to the question at hand. (1) In the first, 11Q13, the date is not an issue (mid-first century BCE),[99] but interpretation is contentious because of the fragmentary nature of the text.[100] What is clear is that the fragment depicts an eschatological agent, Melchizedek, who emerges at "the end of days" (II, 4), who inaugurates an eschatological period of "jubilee" (II, 2–7) that culminates in the forgiveness of sins (II, 8), and he executes "the vengeance of the judgment of God" (II, 13).[101] It is further apparent that the eschatological events initiated by Melchizedek's appearance include the coming of "the messenger of good news" from Isa 52:7 (a figure either identical with [my view] or different from Melchizedek), and this Isaianic personage is connected by the text to an "anointed one about whom Daniel" spoke (II, 18). Unfortunately, the text breaks off at the

97. Eduard Schweizer, "The Son of Man Again," *NTS* 9 (1963): 260. For justification, Schweizer cites Glasson in a footnote. For Glasson's view, see T. Francis Glasson, *The Second Advent: The Origin of the New Testament Doctrine*, 3rd ed. (Eugene, OR: Wipf & Stock, 2009), 13–62. Ulrich B. Müller, "Parusie und Menschensohn," *ZNW* 92 (2001): 42 n. 10, relegates 4 Ezra to a dismissive footnote. See also Nils Alstrup Dahl, *The Crucified Messiah and Other Essays* (Minneapolis: Augsburg, 1974), 142–43.

98. Ruben A. Bühner, *Messianic High Christology: New Testament Variants of Second Temple Judaism* (Waco, TX: Baylor University Press, 2021), 74.

99. Cf. Jimmy J. M. Roberts, "Melchizedek (11Q13 = 11QMelchizedek = 11QMelch)," in *Pesharim, Other Commentaries, and Related Documents*, in vol. 6 of *The Dead Sea Scrolls: Hebrew, Aramaic, and Greek Texts with English Translations*, ed. James H. Charlesworth and Henry W. Rietz (Tübingen: Mohr Siebeck, 2002), 264–73.

100. The major issue dividing interpreters is whether the text refers to a single figure (Melchizedek) or two distinct figures (Melchizedek and another/distinct anointed figure), as already discussed above. Cf. p. 309. As noted there, I favor reading a single figure here. This is because (1) both are described with stock phrases and terms from Isa 61, which suggests they are the same person, and (2) "Melchizedek," meaning "king of righteousness," could suggest a royal and messianic personage (as in Heb 7:2).

101. See Adam S. van der Woude, "Melchisedek als himmlische Erlösergestalt in den neugefundenen eschatologischen Midraschim aus Qumran Höhle XI," *OTS* 14 (1965): 354–73.

point of the Daniel citation, but the most likely candidates are Dan 7:13 or Dan 9:25/26.[102] The exegetical triangulation present in this fragment among Dan 7 or 9, Isa 52 and 61, and Psalms about God's activity clearly parallels exegetical moves we have found in numerous New Testament texts. Since there is no evidence that New Testament authors were actually dependent on 11Q13, these shared exegetical patterns demonstrate the existence of a wider eschatological tradition in Second Temple Judaism.[103]

One's decision about *where* exactly Melchizedek's actions occur is somewhat dependent on one's understanding of the identity of the "anointed one" mentioned in II, 18. All critics agree that Melchizedek is present in the heavenly council, as this assumption has permitted the author to cite Ps 82:1–2 with reference to Melchizedek rather than the God of Israel.[104] So he is clearly a heavenly liberator who rescues persons from the clutches of "Belial" (II, 12–14), and in this capacity, he could be either an angelic or exalted human figure.[105] But does this work involve coming down to earth? That is almost certain if that "anointed one" of II, 18 is in fact Melchizedek, as this figure "proclaims peace" and "speaks to Zion" as in Isa 52 and "comforts" as in Isa 61 (and in Isa 61, of course, those "comforted" are "those who mourn" "in Zion," vv. 2–3).[106] Even should the "anointed one" be distinct from Melchizedek, however, that the text depicts a heavenly manifestation of Melchizedek is probable,[107] since the psalms cited by the text (82:1–2, and likely also 7:8–9) are calls for God to come and execute justice on the earth.

(2) There is a family resemblance between the Melchizedek fragment and what the Similitudes of Enoch have to say about the messianic "son of man." As already noted, discussion about the dating of the Similitudes has in the last twenty years or so undergone a significant transformation, with most critics now arguing that they

102. See Joseph A. Fitzmyer, *Essays on the Semitic Background of the New Testament* (London: Chapman, 1971), 245–67.

103. Cf. P. Sacchi, "Esquisse du Développement du Messianisme Juif à la Lumière du Texte Qumranien 11QMelch," *ZAW* 100 (1988): 202–14; Evans, *Jesus and His Contemporaries*, 118–22.

104. See also 4Q401 frag. 11 lines 1–3.

105. See Collins, *Scepter and the Star*, 181–82, 195; Timo Eskola, *Messiah and the Throne: Jewish Merkabah Mysticism and Early Christian Exaltation Discourse*, WUNT 2/142 (Tübingen: Mohr Siebeck, 2001), 129.

106. Michael Flowers, "The Two Messiahs and Melchizedek in 11QMelchizedek," *JAJ* 7 (2016): 194–227, has argued that the text mentions at least three distinct figures: Melchizedek (an angelic figure), a royal messiah, and a priestly/teaching messiah. Whether Melchizedek is to be connected to the "anointed" of line 18 is an understandable debate, but Flowers is not compelling in his suggestion that we should distinguish further.

107. Cf. Ruben A. Bühner, *Hohe Messianologie: Übermenschliche Aspekte eschatologischer Heilsgestalten im Frühjudentum*, WUNT 2/523 (Tübingen: Mohr Siebeck, 2020), 235–39.

are pre-70 and may even predate the Jesus movement.[108] It seems wise to delay judgment on this and not weigh one's arguments too heavily on the question of date. But the Melchizedek fragment alone shows that some of the exegetical and eschatological traditions contained in 1 Enoch are much older and certainly pre-Christian, especially the notion of a heavenly figure distinct from God who nonetheless enacts God's judgment at the end time (see 61.8–9). We see the involvement of this son of man figure in the second parable that describes the fate of sinners on the day of judgment. The movement of this figure deserves special attention:

> On that day, my Chosen One will sit on the throne of glory, and he will test their works, and their resting places will be innumerable. And their spirits will grow strong within them, when they see my chosen ones and those who appeal to my glorious name. On that day, I shall make my Chosen One dwell among them, and I shall transform heaven and make it a blessing and a light forever; and I shall transform the earth and make it a blessing. And my chosen ones I shall make to dwell on it, but those who commit sin and error will not set foot on it. (1 En. 45.3–5; trans. Nickelsburg and VanderKam)

It is common for some critics to cite the *heavenly* setting of 1 Enoch's son of man to justify the claim that Jesus spoke of "the coming of the son of man" to speak merely of his *heavenly* exaltation. But this important passage, often overlooked in these discussions, challenges such a claim.[109] For the son of man in 1 Enoch does not simply reside in heaven. It is clear that this future prediction "on that day"—future, still, for the perspective of this text's readers—is that the eschatological transformation of the heavens and the earth[110] will coincide with the downward movement of the son of man figure to "dwell" in a renewed earth.[111] The notion of descent to "dwell with/among" is, of course, biblically resonant (cf., e.g.,

108. See p. 316 above.

109. Contra Müller, "Parusie und Menschensohn," 4. See instead Bühner, *Messianic High Christology*, 133–34.

110. See Matthew Black, *The Book of Enoch or 1 Enoch*, SVTP 7 (Leiden: Brill, 1985), 205, on the influence of Isa 65:17 and 66:22 here. See also George W. E. Nickelsburg and James C. VanderKam, *1 Enoch 2*, Hermeneia (Minneapolis: Fortress, 2012), 40, 151: "The setting for this eschatological scenario is a transformed heaven and a transformed earth . . . this passage is the first of two Parables that explicitly express the author's belief that the locus of eschatological blessing will be a transformed earth." See also 1 En. 51.1–5, which mentions resurrection and judgment and renewed life on the earth.

111. So also Bühner, *Hohe Messianologie*, 131 ("die . . . irdische Lokalisierung des Erwählten Menschensohns nicht die Erde in der Form der literarischen Gegenwart meint, sondern eine erneuerte Erde in futurisch-eschatologischer Zeit").

Exod 29:45; Lev 26:11–13; Ezek 37:27; 43:7; Zech 2:10–11; see Jub. 1.26; 11Q19 XXIX, 7–8; Tg. Ps.-J. on Exod 29:45; Tg. Ezek. 37.26–27), where it often refers to God's self. At the end of Revelation, we find a particularly close parallel: the seer describes "a new heaven and a new earth" (21:1) followed by the holy city "coming down out of heaven" (v. 2) where a voice claims, "Behold, the home of God is among mortals. He will dwell with them [σκηνώσει μετ' αὐτῶν]; they will be his peoples, and God himself will be with them" (v. 3). Here the eschatological transformation of the cosmos also coincides with the descent of God "to dwell," although the focus of Rev 21 remains on God. The descent of the son of man in 1 En. 45.3–5 continues to depict a sharing of divine roles and responsibilities between "that son of man" and the "Lord of Spirits" that emerges throughout the Similitudes.[112]

To be sure, 1 En. 45.3–5 is not an afterthought in the Similitudes or an aberration, even while it is true that most of Enoch's descriptions of the son of man figure occur in heaven. There is a futuristic element to 1 Enoch that must be appreciated: many of the descriptions about humans worshiping or paying homage to the son of man *are predicted* as future realities, even if this temporal feature is not consistently maintained.[113] This fact should be paired with the notion that the Danielic figure must remain hidden until the judgment, being before that time known only to the holy and righteous (48.4–7; 62.7).[114] At the outset of the Similitudes, we read (1 En. 38.1–3),

> When the congregation of the righteous appears, the sinners will be judged for their sins, and from the face of the earth they will be driven; and when the Righteous One appears in the presence of the righteous, whose chosen works depend upon the Lord of Spirits, and light appears to the righteous and chosen

112. See Johannes Theisohn, *Der auserwählte Richter* (Göttingen: Vandenhoeck & Ruprecht, 1975), 41–42.

113. See, e.g., 1 En. 46.4–5; 48.5 (a prediction that those who dwell on the earth will fall down and worship before him); 51.3–5; 60.6; 62.9–16; 71.15: "and he said to me, he proclaims unto you peace in the name of the world to come. For from hence has proceeded peace since the creation of the world." Cf. Gabriele Boccaccini, "Protology and Eschatology in the Enochic Traditions," in *Eschatology in Antiquity: Forms and Functions*, ed. Hilary Marlow, Karla Pollmann, and Helen Van Noorden (London: Routledge, 2021), 178–81. The variation could be due to the common belief, as explored by W. D. Davies, *Paul and Rabbinic Judaism: Some Rabbinic Elements in Pauline Theology* (London: SPCK, 1948), 314–20, and others, that since heaven is eternal, in some sense the future already exists in heaven presently.

114. Cf. further 1 En. 46.3 ("he is destined to be victorious"); 46.4–5 ("he will remove kings and mighty ones from their thrones"); 62.6–9 ("On that day, all the kings, governors, and high officials . . . shall fall down before him").

> who dwell on the earth; where (will be) the dwelling place of the sinners, and where (will be) the resting place of those who have denied the Lord of Spirits?[115]

Nickelsburg and VanderKam comment that this introduction "begins by anticipating that moment when God will constitute and make manifest the eschatological community of the righteous," and they call the passage "a poetic oracle that announces a coming epiphany, the great judgement, and its consequences for the sinners and the righteous."[116] A few lines later most likely continue the description (and parallel 45.3–5):

> And it shall come to pass in those days that the children of the elect and the holy ones [will descend] from the high heaven and their seed will become one with the children of the people. (1 En. 39.1)[117]

The actions of these "children of the elect and the holy ones" appear to be a foil to the actions of the angels in the Book of Watchers, even if it remains unclear what it means to say their seed "will become one with the children of the people." Thankfully, that is not important for our purposes. What is important is that we probably have again depicted here a heavenly descent, framed eschatologically ("in those days"), with the specification that "the children of the elect and the holy ones" are also involved. In other words, those who reside in heaven in the time before the eschatological consummation are said to come down to earth around the time that "kings and rulers will perish" and "be delivered into the hands of the righteous and holy ones" (38.5).[118] This also shows that it was possible to believe

115. Translation from Nickelsburg and VanderKam, *1 Enoch 2*, 95.

116. Nickelsburg and VanderKam, *1 Enoch 2*, 97, 95, respectively.

117. Here I follow *OTP* 1:30. Nickelsburg and VanderKam, *1 Enoch 2*, have taken the imperfects as past imperfects, rather than future tenses (see their discussion on 107). But it seems most natural to have these lines continue the future oriented 38.1–6, rather than break suddenly here. Moreover, "the elect/chosen and the holy ones" is not a good description of the angels who had previously sinned. See the same designation at 48.1.

118. This is made clear by other passages. Note 1 En. 39.3–8, wherein Enoch is whisked away to heaven to see what is going on in heaven *before* the end-time events just described in 38.1–39.2. At 39.4–5, in heaven, he "saw other dwelling places of the holy ones and their resting places too. So there my eyes saw their dwelling places with the holy angels and their resting places with the holy ones" where they "interceded and petitioned and prayed on behalf of the children of the people." See also 39.13 ("my eyes saw others who stood before him sleepless [and] blessed [the Lord]"). Also important here is 1 En. 51, which resembles 38.1–39: at the time that the son of man "will sit on my (God's) throne" (v. 3), the earth is renewed (v. 4), and "the earth shall rejoice, and the righteous ones shall dwell upon her and the elect ones shall walk upon her."

that persons who lived before the end of the age could still be expected to participate in or simply witness certain eschatological events—which is to say that being preexistent, or having some kind of heavenly or supernatural nature, is not in itself a prerequisite for this kind of eschatological activity.[119] I will have more to say about this in a moment.

Three other passages from other texts also deserve mention, although they are tantalizingly brief, and it is hard to say much about them other than they appear to hope for a messianic redeemer figure to come from heaven at the end of days.

(3) At the climax of the apocalypse of the twelve calamities in 2 Baruch, there is a transformation of creation: the earth will yield miraculously abundant crops, the hungry will be fed, and "the treasury of manna will come down again from on high" (29.8). This transformation includes the following description:

> And it will be after these [things], when the time of the advent of the Messiah will be fulfilled and when he will have returned in glory, then all who have fallen asleep in hope of him will be rising. At that time, those reservoirs that hold the number of the souls of the righteous will be opened, and they will go out. And the multitude of souls will appear together, in a single gathering, of one mind. (2 Bar. 30.1–2)[120]

As in 1 Enoch, the revelation of the messiah to the world occurs at the time of the transformation of the cosmos. It is probable that the "return" assumes a coming

119. The nature of the son of man figure in 1 Enoch is not clear and highly debated by critics. While some regard him an angelic or heavenly or divine being, others think he is simply human. It is not important for our purposes to take a side on this. I would note, though, that if James C. VanderKam, "Righteous One, Messiah, Chosen One, and Son of Man in 1 Enoch 37–71," in *The Messiah: Developments in Earliest Judaism and Christianity*, ed. James H. Charlesworth (Minneapolis: Fortress, 1992), 176–86, is right in his argument that the final revelation in 1 En 71.14 that Enoch is actually the son of man is original to the text, then it means we are dealing here not with a preexistent heavenly figure but an earthly figure translated to heaven who then at some point comes again "to dwell" (so 45.2–3) with those on the earth. For another view, see Christfried Böttrich, "Konturen des 'Menschensohnes' in äthHen 37–71," in *Gottessohn und Menschensohn: Exegetische Studien zu zwei Paradigmen biblischer Intertextualität*, ed. Dieter Sänger and Knut Backhaus (Neukirchen-Vluyn: Neukirchener, 2004), 53–90. The claim in 1 En. 48.2–3 that the name of this figure was known before time is not necessarily saying the figure actually existed before time and in a way unlike the rest of creation, just that his existence is central to the plan of God and hence known by God before creation. The notion of the name of something being known before creation appears frequently in the targumim to similar effect. The Enochic tradition on this front may develop from reflection on Ps 72:17, as James L. Kugel has argued in *Traditions of the Bible: A Guide to the Bible as It Was at the Start of the Common Era* (Cambridge: Harvard University Press, 1998), 59–60.

120. Translation in Henze, *Jewish Apocalypticism in Late First Century Israel*, 294.

from heaven (30.1), as the description is bracketed by "the treasury of manna coming down again from on high" (29.8), on the one hand, and "the treasuries (of souls) will be opened" (30.2), on the other.[121]

(4) In book 5 of the Sibylline Oracles, dated between 70 and 132 CE, four central oracles contain striking references to a messianic figure who emerges from heaven and resembles what we see in other Jewish texts (5.108; 155–161; 256–259; and 414–433).[122] The first of these, which mentions "a certain king sent from God" (τις θεόθεν βασιλεὺς πεμφθεὶς), does not necessarily mean sent *from heaven*, but this is likely given what follows. In lines 155–161, "a great star" (ἀστὴρ μέγας) "will come from heaven" (ἥξει . . . οὐρανόθεν) and destroy "the sea" and "Babylon" and "the land of Italy"—a description probably inspired by Num 24:17 and Dan 7:1–14.[123] This is to be judgment on the nations for their treatment of the people of

121. Cf. Henze, *Jewish Apocalypticism in Late First Century Israel*, 296 n. 153. Henze suggests that "the language of return implies that the Messiah was absent for a while and now has come back—from heaven to earth, we presume, since his return leads to the rising of the dead" (296). Klaus Koch, "Messias und Menschensohn: Die zweistufige Messianologie der jüngeren Apokalyptik," *Jahrbuch für Biblische Theologie* 8 (1993): 73–102, argues that 2 Baruch has "a two-phase messianism [eine zweistufige Messianologie]."

122. For discussion, see John J. Collins, *The Sibylline Oracles of Egyptian Judaism* (Missoula, MT: Scholars Press, 1974), 87–95; Bühner, *Hohe Messianologie*, 175–89. There is also a passage in book 3 of the Sibylline Oracles, dated by many to the second century BCE, that could be relevant here. In a charged series of anti Roman prophecies, the Sibyl expects "the greatest kingdom of the imperishable king" (βασιλεία μεγίστη ἀθανάτου βασιλῆος) to "appear among people" (ὑπ' ἀνθρώποισι φανεῖται) and divine "wrath" shall fall "upon Latin men" (47–51). And in a later section, we find "then God will send a king from the sun [ἀπ' ἠελίοιο θεὸς πέμψει βασιλῆα] who will stop the entire earth from evil war, killing some, imposing oaths of loyalty on others; and he will not do these things by his private plans but in obedience to the noble teachings of the great God" (652–656). It continues to describe a battle waged by "the kings of the peoples" against Jerusalem and the temple in which God intervenes directly as "fiery swords fall from heaven on the earth" (672–673). Some have argued the "king from the sun" evokes the Egyptian Potter's Oracle. Cf. Gerbern S. Oegema, *The Anointed and His People: Messianic Expectations from Maccabees to Bar Kochba* (Sheffield: Sheffield Academic, 1998), 81–85; Collins, *Scepter and the Star*, 46–49. While this may well be, it is doubtful, contra Oegema and Collins, that the reference is to a Ptolemaic king functioning in a messianic way like Cyrus of Persia. Clear expressions in what follows concerning the restoration of Jerusalem and the temple with allusions to and even verbatim citations of Isa 11's vision of peace (cf. especially 788–795), as well as Isa 2:1–4; Ezek 38:18–23; Zech 14:16–21, suggest instead a Jewish leader and/or messianic figure. Cf. Hans Kippenberg, "Dann wird der Orient herrschen und der Okzident dienen," in *Spiegel und Gleichnis: Festschrift für Jacob Taubes*, ed. Norbert W. Bolz and Wolfgang Hübner (Würzburg: Königshausen & Neumann, 1983), 40–48; Horbury, *Jewish Messianism and the Cult of Christ*, 128.

123. So also Collins, *Sibylline Oracles*, 88, 90–91; Martin Hengel, "Messianische Hoffnung

God in the past (see 5.161). Later we hear of "one prominent man from the sky" (ἀπ' αἰθέρος ἔξοχος ἀνήρ [256]) who emerges at the time of Israel's eschatological vindication, the restoration of Zion, and the transformation of the earth in ways that resemble 1 Enoch as discussed above.[124] The same is true in the last of these oracles in book 5: there "came a blessed man from the expanses of heaven [ἦλθε . . . οὐρανίων νώτων ἀνὴρ μακαρίτης] with a scepter in his hands which God gave him" (414–415) wherein he destroys the wicked and restores Jerusalem and the temple (417–433). These references are too brief to say much about the nature of this figure, but it is not evident, and certainly not stressed anywhere in the text, that this figure comes from heaven because he is angelic or divine (though this may well be); what he is in fact called is "a king" (108) and "a man" (ἀνήρ [256 and 414]). That he is twice called "a man" may be inspired by none other than Dan 7:13's בר אנש/υἱὸς ἀνθρώπου.[125]

(5) And the last text I wish to discuss here is the post-70 apocalypse 4 Ezra. In the famous sixth vision and interpretation in chapter 13, which clearly interacts with Dan 7, Ezra sees "something like the figure of a man" who comes up from "the sea" and "flies with the clouds of heaven" (13.3).[126] Flying "with the clouds of heaven" may not refer literally to a mode of travel, and the interpretation that follows suggests perhaps not (though it is often acknowledged that this is a later interpretation of an originally independent allegory that may have assumed a more literal signification).[127] There are, however, other passages to consider that are sometimes overlooked in this discussion. In the seer's third vision, the very

---

und politischer Radikalismus in der jüdisch-hellenistischen Diaspora: Zur Frage der Voraussetzungen des judischen Aufstands unter Trajan 115–117 n. Chr.," in *Apocalypticism in the Mediterranean World and the Near East*, ed. David Hellholm (Tübingen: Mohr Siebeck, 1983), 675. For Daniel, I would point out (1) the temporal note about "after the fourth year" (cf. Dan 7:25 and 12:7), (2) the mention of the star's "coming," and (3) the "destruction" of Israel's enemies; these are three details that, when appearing collectively and in immediate succession, are highly suggestive.

124. There is a clear Christian interpolation at 257, "who stretched out his hands on the faithful wood," and so we should be cautious with 256 as well. In any case, the basic claim of 256 appears throughout the text in other contexts.

125. It is worth recalling here that 4 Ezra 13.3—"something like the figure of a man came up out of the heart of the sea . . . that man flew with the clouds of heaven"—which clearly rewrites Dan 7:13, uses "man" (*homo*) not "son of man." For Latin text, see A. F. J. Klijn, ed., *Der lateinische Text der Apokalypse des Esra*, TUGAL 131 (Berlin: Akademie-Verlag, 1983). For the suggestion that Paul's use of "man" and "man from heaven" in 1 Cor 15 and Rom 5 relies on Dan 7, see Cullmann, *Christology of the New Testament*, 166–81.

126. See Ulrich B. Müller, *Messias und Menschensohn in jüdischen Apokalypsen und in der Offenbarung des Johannes* (Gütersloh: Gütersloher Verlag, 1972), 107–34.

127. See Stone, *Fourth Ezra*, 382–84, 394–400; Stone, "The Question of the Messiah in 4 Ezra,"

first appearance of the text's starring messianic figure hints at a heavenly revelation: "my son the messiah shall be revealed with those who are with him" (7.28). There seems to be something miraculous about this revealing, given that it stands alongside the "appearance" of the "city which now is not seen" (v. 26) and the "disclosure" of "the land which is now hidden" (v. 27). But the clearest evidence is the detail that the messiah is revealed "with those who are with him." This denotes other figures in heaven with God currently not visible on the earth but apparently expected to return for the time of messianic fulfillment.[128] At 13.52, the Lord says to Ezra, "no one on earth can see my son *or those who are with him except in the time of his day*," and at 14.9, "you [Ezra] will be taken up from among men and henceforth shall live with my Son *and with those who are like you until the times are ended*" (my italics). This clearly refers to return from heaven in the future.[129] It is likely that this messianic figure in 4 Ezra is preexistent (see 13.26), although there has been some dispute about this, and 13.52 and 14.9 show that human figures not regarded as uniquely preexistent could be expected to be revealed from heaven, too, just as we found with those "righteous ones" in the Similitudes above.[130]

The Return of Prophets and Holy Persons

These five texts showcase the creative possibilities of Jewish messianism in the formative period before and just after the destruction of the temple. But there is now a third point to make in response to the view that the expectation for Jesus's return lacks suitable parallels in context. In addition to these texts about a heavenly messiah or redeemer figure, we have widespread traditions about the

in *Judaisms and Their Messiahs at the Turn of the Christian Era*, ed. Jacob Neusner, William S. Green, and Ernest Frerichs (Cambridge: Cambridge University Press, 1987), 213.

128. See Stone, *Fourth Ezra*, 215. Mowinckel, *He That Cometh*, 393, writes with respect to 7:28 that "the Son of Man does not come alone" and that "these [figures] are not necessarily identical with the heavenly community. 1 Enoch distinguishes clearly between a circle of angelic heavenly beings, and a host of elect, righteous ones, who are now in heaven, where they have their blessed abodes near those of the angels, and are with the Elect One."

129. On the assumption here that Ezra will be in heaven for a period of time before returning at the end, see Michael E. Stone, "Coherence and Inconsistency in the Apocalypses: The Case of 'The End' in 4 Ezra," *JBL* 102 (1983): 240; Stone, *Fourth Ezra*, 215. See also Carla Sulzbach, "End Times and Ending Times in 4 Ezra," in Marlow, Pollmann, and Van Noorden, *Eschatology in Antiquity*, 230.

130. J. R. Daniel Kirk, *A Man Attested by God: The Human Jesus of the Synoptic Gospels* (Grand Rapids: Eerdmans, 2016), 156–57, suggests that the figure in 4 Ezra is an "idealized human figure," while also preexistent.

eschatological reappearance (in different ways) of ancient prophets and holy persons. It is surprising that these expectations have not been explored with much depth in debate about the emergence of the parousia hope in Christian origins. The most ancient and most widely attested of these concern the prophet Elijah, who according to 2 Kgs 2:1–12 was caught up to heaven in a chariot of fire and according to the end of Malachi was expected to come back again (ET 4:5–6): "Behold, I will send you the prophet Elijah before the great and terrible day of the Lord comes. He will turn the hearts of parents to their children and the hearts of children to their parents, so that I will not come and strike the land with a curse."[131] This future-coming Elijah may have received a messianic gloss in some circles.[132] But Elijah is a mere one of many.[133] The enigmatic end of Enoch's story (Gen 5:24), which led to the widespread belief that he had been taken up to heaven, led to a similar expectation that he, too, would return at the end of time.[134] In the biblical story of the death of Moses, the mysterious description of his burial (Deut 34:6: "but no one knows his burial place to this day") encouraged some to think that he also had been taken up to heaven, and some reasoned he would come back again like (or even with) Elijah.[135] There is evidence that some expected Jeremiah to

131. For the continuation and elaboration of this expectation, see Sir 48:10; 4 Ezra 6.26–28; 4Q558 1 II, 4; 1 En. 90.31, 37; Sib. Or. 2.187–189; LAB 21; Tg. Ps.-J. on Exod 40:10; Justin Martyr, *Dial.* 8.4; 49.1; b. Sanh. 96b–99a. See also Rev 11:3–13, and discussion in David E. Aune, *Revelation*, WBC 52 (Nashville: Nelson, 1997–1998), 2:592. Cf. in general Markus Öhler, *Elia im Neuen Testament: Untersuchungen zur Bedeutung des alttestamentlichen Propheten im frühen Christentum* (Berlin: de Gruyter, 1997).

132. Important for this view is 4Q521 2 III, 2. See discussion and literature in David M. Miller, "The Messenger, the Lord, and the Coming Judgment in the Reception History of Malachi 3," *NTS* 53 (2001): 8–10.

133. Notice the collective language in 4 Ezra 6.25–26: "those who remain . . . shall see the men who were taken up, who from their birth have not tasted death." See also 7.28 ("my son the messiah will be revealed with those who are with him").

134. Jub. 10.17 (Enoch reports the deeds of each generation on the day of judgment); 1 En. 90.31; 4 Ezra 6.26; Apoc. Dan. 14.1–3; Apoc. El. (C) 4.7. Many patristic commentators regarded the "two witnesses" of Rev 11:1–3 as Enoch and Elijah. Cf. Tertullian, *An.* 50; Hippolytus, *Comm. Dan.* 4.35.3.

135. Cf. Mark 9:2–7 and parr., where Moses and Elijah appear to speak with Jesus. On the connection between the transfiguration story and this tradition, see Joel Marcus, *Mark 8–16: A New Translation with Introduction and Commentary*, AB 27A (New Haven: Yale University Press, 2009), 632–33, 1108–18. According to Aune, *Revelation*, 2:600, most modern commentators take the two witnesses of Rev 11:1–3 to be influenced by expectations about the return of Moses and Elijah. Cf., e.g., Deut. Rab. 3.17 (God says to Moses, "in the time to come when I bring Elijah, the prophet, unto them, the two of you shall come together"). See also Tg. Ps.-J. on Deut 33:21.

make an eschatological curtain call.[136] We find similar traditions about Jeremiah's scribe Baruch,[137] Ezra,[138] and Phinehas.[139] We should probably include Melchizedek here as well. While it is not disputed in 11Q13 that the named Melchizedek is the Melchizedek of Gen 14:17–20, the fragment may assume (as many critics have argued) that Melchizedek appears at "the end of days" because he, too, had been taken up to heaven sometime after the encounter with Abraham.[140]

Of course, the future coming of Elijah, Enoch, and some of these other figures was related to the belief that they had never died.[141] Moreover, in the five texts discussed before that are more likely messianic in nature, none of them appear to coordinate the heavenly coming of their redeemer figure with a prior death. But does the belief in an eschatological return of a prophet, messiah, or anyone else *require* the condition that such a person did not actually die? It does not appear so. There is evidence that the expectation for an eschatological return was *not* limited only to those who had escaped death. One of the more intriguing examples concerns the prophet Jeremiah in the Lives of the Prophets.[142] It is made clear in

136. See discussion below.

137. 2 Bar. 13.3; 25.1; 76.2–4. See also 48.30.

138. 4 Ezra 14.9–10: "You [Ezra] shall be taken up from among men, and henceforth you shall live with my son and with those who are like you, until the times are ended." See Stone, *Fourth Ezra*, 420.

139. See LAB 48.1 ("and afterward you will be lifted up into the place where those who were before you were lifted up, and you will be there until I remember the world. Then I will make you all come, and you will taste what is death"). See also Tg. Ps.-J. on Exod 4:13; 6:18; Deut 30:4. See Robert Hayward, "Phinehas—the Same as Elijah: The Origins of a Rabbinic Tradition," *JJS* 29 (1978): 22–34.

140. The fact that readers do not encounter Melchizedek again in Genesis, coupled with his odd appearance in the throne scene of Ps 110, makes the inference understandable. See Kugel, *Traditions of the Bible*, 276–85. Note the fascination with Melchizedek's odd disappearance from the narrative of Genesis in Heb 7:3 (my italics): "without father, without mother, without genealogy, having neither beginning of days *nor end of life* [μήτε ζωῆς τέλος]." See also 2 En. 71.33 [A]; 72.1 [A and J]. Cf. further discussion in Heinz-Josef Fabry and Ulrich Dahmen, "Melchisedek in Bibel und Qumran," in *Ich werde meinen Bund mit euch niemals brechen! Festschrift für Walter Gross*, ed. Erasmus Gass and Hermann-Josef Stipp (Freiburg: Herder, 2011), 377–98.

141. There is a tradition that Jeremiah never died. See discussion in Origen, *Comm. Jo.* 13.57. Though see below.

142. At the end of the Testament of Zebulon, Zebulon comforts his children before his death by promising that he will one day "rise again in your midst as a leader among your sons, and I shall be glad in the midst of my tribe" (10.2). Cf. Harm W. Hollander and Marinus de Jonge, *The Testaments of the Twelve Patriarchs: A Commentary* (Leiden: Brill, 1985), 275. In LAB 32.15, concerning the song of Deborah, the judge declares that she will cease singing in light of the coming judgments of God but predicts that she will sing again to God in the renewal of creation. Note also the interesting and little-discussed messianic group known as the Dositheans, as explored by Nathan C. Johnson, "Survival of Popular Movements," in *The Next Quest for the Historical Jesus*,

the opening line that the prophet "died in Taphnai of Egypt, having been stoned by the people" (2.1),[143] but that is not the end of his story.[144] Before death, Jeremiah had hid the ark of the covenant with its contents in the desert and "made them to be swallowed up in a rock" (2.9), where he predicted that "in the resurrection the ark will be raised first and will come out of the rock and be placed on Mount Sinai" (2.12).[145] He also prophesied that no one would from that time touch the ark "except Aaron" himself, and no one open the tablets in it "except Moses"—hence claiming that both of these figures, who of course lived centuries before Jeremiah, would return at the end of days (2.14).[146] Cognizant of Jeremiah's own death, the passage ends with this (15): "and God gave this grace to Jeremiah, that he might himself perform [αὐτὸς ποιήσειεν] the completion of this mystery [τὸ τέλος τοῦ μυστηρίου], so that he might become a partner of Moses, and they are together to this day [καὶ ὁμοῦ εἰσιν ἕως σήμερον]." This passage predicts not only the eschatological return of the dead prophet Jeremiah to see the fulfillment of his own prophecy, it expects the eschatological return of Aaron and Moses as well (where it is assumed that Aaron and Moses will resume in the future the kinds of activities they were engaged in during their lifetimes [e.g., Aaron as priest and Moses as lawgiver, 2.14]).[147] Moreover, the text plainly states that both Aaron and

---

ed. James Crossley and Chris Keith (Grand Rapids: Eerdmans, 2024), 541–56, although there are conflicting accounts about what happened to Dositheus or Dusis (some claiming he died and was raised, others that he had never died and was taken up to heaven).

143. For Greek text and verse numbering, I follow Anna Maria Schwemer, *Studien zu den frühjüdischen Prophetenlegenden Vitae prophetarum*, TSAJ (Tübingen: Mohr Siebeck, 1995), 159–61. Translations are my own. In Schwemer's view, text-critical questions about the Jeremiah passage pose "keine besonderen Probleme" (161). See her discussion of v. 15 in particular on 233. Her judgment appears sound.

144. Cf. Christian Wolff, *Jeremia im Frühjudentum und Urchristentum* (Berlin: Akademie-Verlag, 1976), 28–29; Jörg Frey, "The Reception of Jeremiah and the Impact of Jeremianic Traditions in the New Testament: A Survey," in *Jeremiah's Scriptures: Production, Reception, Interaction, and Transformation*, ed. Hindy Najman and Konrad Schmid, JSJSup 173 (Leiden: Brill, 2017), 505–8.

145. For related traditions, see 2 Macc 2:1–8. Also 2 Bar. 6–10; 4 Bar. 3.10–20. On how this tradition may have emerged, see Dale C. Allison Jr., *4 Baruch: Paraleipomena Jeremiou*, CEJL (Berlin: de Gruyter, 2019), 138–39.

146. Schwemer, *Studien zu den frühjüdischen Prophetenlegenden Vitae prophetarum*, 234.

147. It is clear that there are Christian interpolations in Lives of the Prophets, but in the case of the Jeremiah entry, they appear to be fairly obvious intrusions and do not include what is discussed here (in point of fact, to remove them makes the entry flow more smoothly). Aryeh Amihay, "The Stones and the Rock: Jewish and Christian Elements in Vita Jeremiah," *JSP* 32 (2022): 39–56, is right to stress that distinguishing Jewish and Christian elements can be subjective and fall prey to anachronistic and essentialist categories, but his own suggestion that the

Moses, like Jeremiah, had died, naming where they are buried (2.17). The suggestion that Jeremiah is together with Moses "to this day" assumes a continued heavenly existence after death and before the resurrection of the dead, adopting a common belief in Second Temple Judaism that was already discussed above in chapter 15.

The notion that prophets or righteous persons who had died would return for important tasks at the end time can be found elsewhere. In fact, in the Synoptics themselves, the evangelists *assume* such a tradition to serve their own christological agendas. In the preamble to Peter's confession, Mark records three answers to Jesus's question about his identity ("who do people say that I am?"): "they say John the Baptist, and others Elijah, and others that you are one of the prophets" (8:28). These three suggestions hang together and are of one piece. To say "he is John the Baptist" is not merely to say he does things like John or acts in John-like ways (though this is obviously assumed); it is to say he is actually John the Baptist back from the dead, as is plain in the earlier discussion in Mark 6:14–16 (a view that Mark claims was held by "some" and also Herod Antipas himself). In the same way, to say "he is Elijah" is to say he is Elijah *redivivus*, per Mal 3:22 (ET 4:5) and the wider expectation already discussed.[148] To say he is "one of the prophets," then, to continue in the line of the former two identity claims, is not to state that Jesus is of a prophetic type or does prophet-like activities (which, again, is obviously assumed); it is to say he is "one of the prophets" who was formerly known and has returned after a time of absence.[149] Not only does the juxtaposition of "one of the prophets" to "John the Baptist" and "Elijah" favor this interpretation, Mark's

---

text was written in an intentionally ambiguous manner to appeal to both a Jewish and Christian audience at a later time is not compelling. The argument of Schwemer for a Jewish original is strong. See *Studien zu den frühjüdischen Prophetenlegenden Vitae prophetarum*, 25–70. See also Charles Cutler Torrey, *Lives of the Prophets: Greek Text and Translation* (Philadelphia: Society of Biblical Literature, 1946), 6–11 (while I do not necessarily endorse his view of a Hebrew original). The focus on the ark, the commandments, and the primacy of Aaron and Moses have little place in otherwise known Christian eschatological scenarios.

148. Mark, of course, wishes to identify John the Baptist with this expectation (see 1:6; 9:11–13), though how literally the evangelist understood this in the case of John is not clear. For discussion, see Christine E. Joynes, "The Returned Elijah? John the Baptist's Angelic Identity in the Gospel of Mark," *SJT* 58 (2005): 455–67. Note that Luke may imply a more metaphorical fulfillment of this hope in his infancy narrative ("*in the spirit and power of* Elijah" [1:17; my italics]), though this is disputed. Cf. Jaroslav Rindoš, *He of Whom It Is Written: John the Baptist and Elijah in Luke*, ÖBS 38 (New York: Lang, 2010), 231–34.

149. Cf. also Marcus, *Mark 8–16*, 603: "It is not surprising that Jesus should be identified as a great figure of the past returned from the dead, given the widespread ancient Jewish belief that the OT saints and other worthies of bygone eras are alive."

phrasing itself is suggestive—εἷς τῶν προφητῶν—a partitive genitive of a *known* entity ("the prophets").[150] Moreover, Matthew and Luke have clearly understood Mark in this way: Luke rephrases Mark's "one of the prophets" to be "a certain prophet of old" (προφήτης τις τῶν ἀρχαίων [9:19]), which leaves no doubt, and Matthew was compelled to add a fourth to the list—"Jeremiah" (16:14)—which likely corroborates what we found in Lives of the Prophets[151] and was meant by the evangelist literally.[152] To be clear, this discussion assumes nothing about the historicity of this account. While the entire exchange may well be a fiction spun by Mark or a pre-Markan tradent, the point is that the story and its telling presuppose the currency of the belief that dead prophetic figures could return.[153] It is also

150. On "the prophets" as a category elsewhere—even if it remains unclear and was disputed who was in—cf. 2 Macc 15:9; 1QS I, 1–3; CD VII, 15–18; Matt 5:17; 7:12; 11:13 and par.; 22:40 and parr.; 23:37 and par.; Luke 24:44; Rom 3:21; Jas 5:10; Heb 1:1; 4 Macc 18:10; Josephus, *Ag. Ap.* 1.41.

151. So Schwemer, *Studien zu den frühjüdischen Prophetenlegenden Vitae prophetarum*, 235 n. 389: "Mt 16,14 scheint sie selbstverständlich vorauszusetzen." Second Maccabees 15:12–16 does not mention the return of Jeremiah, but he does appear in a dream to Judas Maccabeus alongside the high priest Onias, where it is said he continues to pray for the people and for the holy city before God. So here Jeremiah has a postmortem existence that continues his earthly mission. Note also 5 Ezra 2.18, which is Christian, where Isaiah is mentioned alongside Jeremiah as expected to return in the future. This is intriguing in light of the fact that a belief in Isaiah's martyrdom was common. Cf. Heb 11:37 (which mentions "sawn in two"); Mart. Ascen. Isa. 5.1–16; Justin, *Dial.* 120.5; b. Sanh. 103b. Cf. Anna Maria Schwemer, "Die Zersägung des Propheten Jesaja," in *Martyriumsvorstellungen in Antike und Mittelalter*, ed. Sebastian Fuhrmann and Regina Grundmann, AJEC 80 (Leiden: Brill, 2012), 45–67.

152. See already Cornelius à Lapide, vol. 2 of *The Great Commentary*, trans. Thomas W. Mossman, 4th ed. (Edinburgh: Grant, 1890 [orig. 1681]), 209. Cf. Howard M. Teeple, *The Mosaic Eschatological Prophet* (Philadelphia: Society of Biblical Literature, 1957), 10; Julius Schniewind, *Das Evangelium nach Matthäus*, 11th ed. (Göttingen: Vandenhoeck & Ruprecht, 1964), 187 (on the basis of internal criteria, e.g., what Matthew's text seems to require, which is wise). David R. Law, "Matthew's Enigmatic Reference to Jeremiah in Mt 16,14," in *The Book of Jeremiah and Its Reception*, BETL 128 (Leuven: Leuven University Press, 1997), 280, writes that "by far the most common theory among scholars is that Matthew's insertion of Jeremiah is due to a contemporary belief in Jeremiah as eschatological prophet or messianic forerunner . . . that the Jews of Matthew's day expected the return of Jeremiah." Contrast Michael Knowles, *Jeremiah in Matthew's Gospel: The Rejected-Prophet Motif in Matthean Redaction*, JSNTSup 68 (Sheffield: Sheffield Academic, 1993), 81–95, and Catrin H. Williams, "Jeremiah and His Prophecies in the New Testament," in *The Oxford Handbook of Jeremiah*, ed. Louis Stulman and Edward Silver (Oxford: Oxford University Press, 2021), 523–25, who read the Jeremiah reference in a merely typological or thematical manner, unlike the other figures mentioned in the group.

153. Some have thought that the Damascus Document assumes the beloved Teacher of Righteousness would return after death to resume his role (CD VI, 10–11: "until there arises the one who teaches righteousness at the end of days"). So Peter Schäfer, *The Origins of Jewish Mysticism* (Princeton: Princeton University Press, 2011), 150, on the teacher: "[this is] the founder of the sect who was imagined by his later followers as elevated into heaven and expected to return at

important that the passage groups together figures who had very different ends of life—death ("John"), assumption ("Elijah"), and unclear or undefined ("one of the prophets")—which suggests that more important than *the means* of return was *the fact* of return itself. We recall here the discussion of chapter 15 that identified some ambiguity in the question of whence and whither Jesus might have expected to come that is ultimately of little consequence for my main argument.

There may be further evidence in Mark 13 that early Christians continued to be influenced by expectations of the return of Jesus after death in ways that the evangelist or the evangelist's sources considered problematic and wanted to correct. As widely noted and already discussed, Mark 13 would have been received by Mark's readers as not just predicting the future but commenting on recent past or contemporary events. This is surely the case for Jesus's prediction of the coming of "false christs" and "false prophets" who aim to "lead astray the elect" (Mark 13:6, 21–23 and parr.), as commentators agree.[154] But what is it exactly that Mark's Jesus is predicting? In 13:6, we find, "Many will come in my name, saying 'I am he!'" (πολλοὶ ἐλεύσονται ἐπὶ τῷ ὀνόματί μου λέγοντες ὅτι ἐγώ εἰμι [13:6]). This may be *more* than predicting the coming of messianic claimants; it may be people coming and saying they are *Jesus*.[155] Matthew appears to have received Mark

---

the end of time as the priestly Messiah in order to lead the members of the community into the final battle." For a similar view, see André Dupont-Sommer, *The Essene Writings from Qumran* (Gloucester: Smith, 1973), 131 n. 6, and Joseph M. Baumgarten and Daniel R. Schwartz, *Damascus Document, War Scroll, and Related Documents*, in vol. 2 of *The Dead Sea Scrolls: Hebrew, Aramaic, and Greek Texts with English Translations*, ed. James H. Charlesworth and Henry W. L. Rietz (Tübingen: Mohr Siebeck, 1995), 23 n. 58 (suggesting that this belief of his return explains why the sect refers to the death of the teacher "only by the vague 'gathered'" at CD XIX, 35 and XX, 14). But this is probably a misreading of CD VI, 10–11. See instead Michael Knibb, *The Qumran Community* (Cambridge: Cambridge University Press, 1987), 139–40 (thinks this expected "one who will teach righteousness" is the messiah of Aaron), and John J. Collins, "Teacher and Messiah?," in *The Community of the Renewed Covenant*, ed. Eugene Ulrich and James VanderKam (Notre Dame: University of Notre Dame Press, 1994), 193–210 (perhaps an eschatological high priest); and Johannes Zimmermann, *Messianische Texte aus Qumran: Königliche, priesterliche und prophetische Messiasvorstellungen in den Schriftfunden von Qumran*, WUNT 104 (Tübingen: Mohr Siebeck, 1998), 441–44 (an unspecified eschatological figure, yet "kaum mit dem historischen 'Lehrer der Gerechtigkeit' und Gründer der Gemeinde gleichgesetzt werden" at 443). Knibb, Collins, and Zimmermann are more compelling.

154. Cf., e.g., Adela Yarbro Collins, *Mark: A Commentary*, Hermeneia (Minneapolis: Fortress, 2007), 591–98.

155. For this reading, see Rudolf Pesch, *Naherwartungen: Tradition und Redaktion in Mk 13*, KBANT (Düsseldorf: Patmos Verlag, 1968), 111; Pesch, *Markusevangelium*, part 2, *Commentar zu Kap. 8,27–16,20* (Freiburg: Herder, 1977), 279; Werner H. Kelber, *The Kingdom in Mark* (Philadelphia: Fortress, 1974), 115; Marcus, *Mark 8–16*, 875 ("probably Christians who claim actually to *be* the returning Jesus").

in the former (messianic-claimant) manner (though changes Mark to make the point: λέγοντες· ἐγώ εἰμι *ὁ χριστός* [24:5; my italics]), while Luke preserves Mark's wording more closely and also adds that those who come will say, "the time has drawn near" (ὁ καιρὸς ἤγγικεν [21:8]), that is, they will say things Jesus said (cf. Mark 1:15). One further observation that might support this reading: there are two places in the discourse where Jesus predicts coming deceivers (Mark 13:6 and vv. 21–23, respectively), and while commentators sometimes conflate the two as referring to the same historical referents, this may be unwise, and we should think of them as slightly different phenomena. The latter (vv. 21–23), which specifically mentions ψευδόχριστοι and ψευδοπροφῆται, probably evokes the kinds of figures mentioned by Josephus (see, e.g., *J.W.* 2.259), while v. 6 would instead refer to people claiming to be Jesus himself returned. If this interpretation is on target, two important conclusions follow: (1) it would demonstrate the currency of the belief that important religious persons could return after their death to resume their activities; (2) it would, moreover, support the thesis of part 4 as a whole, since it would indirectly attest to Jesus's own predictions of a soon return, albeit understood, in this case, in a manner that Mark or Mark's sources do *not* approve.

Another book could be written on this line of inquiry, but I will have to end with that. We are, as noted, dealing with fragments, and there remains great variety of belief and expectation in the few that we have. But my objective here is simple, and my conclusion modest: early Christian claims about the future coming of Jesus are not as novel as some have asserted over the years, and there is certainly no reason to deny the prediction to the historical Jesus on the grounds that it would make him a complete outlier in his context.

There are, then, the two scenarios for *das Leben Jesu* and the reasons why I prefer the second about eschatological process. This attempt to ask some big-picture questions about Jesus's activity seeks to integrate to the best we can what we have good reason to think is historical. This approach has also benefited from the insights of more recent methodological discussions. The result is an admittedly "fuzzier" image of Jesus. I have intentionally charted a somewhat different approach in this chapter from what has been typical in historical Jesus research: not arguing for one, singular portrait but weighing the plausibility of two competing scenarios, neither of which can be historical at the same time, but either one, I think, is more likely than an alternative that the origin of the second-coming hope is a post-Easter phenomenon. And that is where I would like to end. With all my skepticism of the Galilean crisis aside, both in my monograph on that topic and in what I have written above, I would happily defend Hase, Keim, and Cadoux over Glasson, Robinson, and Wright when it comes to reconstructing the emergence of the parousia hope in Christian origins.

CONCLUDING THOUGHTS ON PART 4 AND THE STUDY

I opened this book with an anecdote about an undergraduate student in a course on the origins of Christianity. This student had raised her hand to ask why the professor, in discussing the eschatological proclamation of Jesus, had seemingly ignored all of the material in the Gospels that pertains to his future coming. The professor had replied to this by appealing to the supposed consensus of the field that these expectations reflect only the beliefs of the early church after Jesus was gone.

It has taken me 422 pages to get here, but I can now say that the student's question was justified. Beneath the professor's response about "what scholars say" is a complicated story that stretches back centuries, even into Christian polemical and exegetical literature from the Middle Ages. Moreover, detailed arguments about the emergence of this hope after the death of Jesus (especially in the influential studies by T. F. Glasson and James Robinson) are weak, while more recent proponents of an eschatological Jesus do not agree about how this widespread hope emerged, nor have many given the topic the attention it deserves. The time is right to reconsider the whole thing.

It would be tedious at this point to offer a detailed summary of the entirety, but I will attempt here to step back and offer some reflections on the study as a whole and how its various movements fit together. The fundamental methodological premise of the book is that the reconstruction of Jesus as a figure in history must begin with, and eventually circle back to explain the existence of, the only sources about him that we have. Of course, this premise does not mean that every claim early followers of Jesus made must in some way be connected to Jesus's own teaching and behavior, nor does it mean that we will always be able to answer our questions.[1] What this premise means, instead, is that everything requires ar-

1. As I have argued throughout, our sources are theologically biased and self-invested, they mistake Jesus on matters both small and big, and there are questions we simply do not have the evidence to answer. For related reflections here, see Mark Goodacre, "Missing Pieces," in *The Next Quest for the Historical Jesus*, ed. James Crossley and Chris Keith (Grand Rapids: Eerdmans, 2024), 113–27.

gument. All historians start in the same argumentative position, "in front of" the same sources,[2] and they must end in the same place, wherein the overall probability of their reconstructions is judged by the degree to which they make the most historical sense of the most data in context. Nothing gets a free pass. This principle should not be controversial, but it is selectively applied in the study of Christian origins. I hope at least to have demonstrated in these pages that the exegetical and historical questions involved in the topic before us are complex enough and significant enough to deserve more robust engagement and debate than they have heretofore received. Moreover, the implications of one's decisions about the origin of this expectation are potentially far-reaching for our understanding of the eschatology of the early Jesus movement as a whole. For historians sifting through Jesus tradition, it should no longer be possible to strain out the gnat of the future coming of Jesus as something obviously secondary, while swallowing the camel of apocalyptic eschatology in his teaching more generally.

My reconsideration of this topic has involved four distinct moves in four very different parts. Part 1 might be regarded a critical analysis of significant studies in the field that pertain to the future coming of Jesus. While I situated these studies in the historical contexts from which they emerged, the focus of the discussion was accurately summarizing and then critically engaging exegetical positions and historical arguments on their own terms. I prioritized the seminal works of T. F. Glasson and James Robinson, and also influential works on Jesus and eschatology in the scholarship of E. P. Sanders, Paula Fredriksen, and Dale Allison. This discussion created the opportunity to present the rationale for my own approach in subsequent parts of the book: to work backward from the early church to Jesus in terms of time (rather than forward), downward from the broad to the detailed in terms of content (rather than atomistically), and attentive at first to the *claims* of the sources with the material they contain (rather than initially to group material thematically and synchronically).

Part 2 was reception history. Unlike part 1, the objective here was not to evaluate specific arguments about the past in detail but to explain the emergence of social and ideological conditions that made possible the kinds of arguments that we find—including the *lack of* attention and argument in what I have called the consensus of silence. I suggested that long before Glasson and Robinson produced their works, and actually long before Hermann Samuel Reimarus set out to articulate "the goal" of Jesus and his disciples, the parousia hope had become a "painful thorn" in the side of Enlightenment Christianity and was frequently attributed

2. Jens Schröter, *Jesus of Nazareth: Jew from Galilee, Savior of the World*, trans. Wayne Coppins and S. Brian Pounds (Waco, TX: Baylor University Press, 2014), 17.

to the theological imaginations of his earliest followers. My key argument is that the emergence of this view was part of a larger process of policing the boundaries of religious identity and constructing the credibility of Christianity in the early modern Western world, whereby Jesus was distinguished from popular-level eschatology (especially apocalyptic and millenarian movements), and the construct of "Jewish messianism." In terms of the latter, I argued that Christian exegetical and polemical literature from well before the Protestant Reformation had generated a clear "habit of reading" to distance Jesus from a constructed/caricatured "Jewish messianism."[3] When Enlightenment critics connected the construct of "Jewish messianism" to the second advent hope, then, it was only a small step to distance Jesus once again from "Jewish messianism" and attribute the parousia hope to his "Jewish followers."

My focus in these pages was to clarify tendencies in much earlier Jesus research, to be sure, and not necessarily scholarship since Glasson and Robinson's time (though there are exceptions). But I did suggest ways in which reception history has shaped the contours of current discussion, including the emergence of a consensus of silence on this topic. On the one hand, many Christian theologians have certainly not grown any fonder of a literal eschatological scenario in which Christ descends to earth from heaven, and so the tendency to "make of Jesus a modern man" in the mold of recent values and concerns (so Albert Schweitzer's critique) persists.[4] On the other, historians with no interest in the potential theological implications of their work have nevertheless encountered the topic of the second coming as it has been refracted through culture wars that followed the critique of traditional Christian doctrines from critical biblical scholarship. Because of the reception history of the second advent in biblical studies, it has been easy to "leave that to theologians and apologists" and focus instead on other things. This preunderstanding, to use Bultmann's terminology,[5] is no less impacted by the past, and it may unwittingly and ironically permit theological musings about Christian origins to pass for genuine historical reconstruction.

In parts 3 and 4, I started my own reconstruction of Jesus and Christian origins, beginning with the *claims* of early Christians about Jesus and the future in part 3. The approach of these chapters, then, was exegetical. I identified a clear and consistent hope for the return of Jesus in the writings of the apostle Paul, which he

3. On this phrase, see Brenda Schildgen, *Power and Prejudice: The Reception of the Gospel of Mark* (Detroit: Wayne State University Press, 1999), and my discussion above at pp. 10–12.

4. Cited in David Dungan, "Albert Schweitzer's Disillusionment with the Historical Reconstructions of the Life of Jesus," *PSTJ* 29 (1976): 42.

5. See Rudolf Bultmann, "Is Exegesis without Presuppositions Possible?," in *Existence and Faith: Shorter Writings of Rudolf Bultmann* (New York: Meridian, 1960), 289–96.

believed Jesus himself had spoken about. For Paul, this was not a controversial expectation that he had to argue about and defend; he could rather assume it and only discuss it as circumstances required. It was also evident that, for Paul, the return of Jesus was inseparable from his larger expectations about the final judgment and the resurrection of the dead that would bring about a transformed state of life. I then looked in detail at the Synoptic Gospels and the Fourth Gospel, not going immediately to specific passages or even themes but trying instead to grasp at first how these sources construct time and a general understanding of the future. I argue that, although important differences in specific claims and in emphasis are clearly evident, there is nonetheless a shared expectation about Jesus's future coming that is assumed by all of the evangelists and mobilized in different ways. Moreover, in the Synoptics in particular, this future appearance is connected to hopes about the long-awaited day of the Lord from Israel's Scripture, as it was in Paul, and the dream vision of Dan 7 about "one like a son of man." At the end, I briefly expanded the lens to suggest that the expectation for Jesus's future return can be found in nearly every text that made it into the New Testament as well as several others where it was not so much positively advanced but reacted to/against (hence presupposing its prior existence). We are clearly dealing here with not a tangential eschatological belief in the early Jesus movement but a widespread hope that connected groups who otherwise disagreed about significant matters.

Part 4 then offers inferences about the past in light of the work of part 3 and is thus devoted to the task of historical reconstruction.[6] I make my case in several steps, which I will highlight here in slightly more detail, given this is the conclusion to part 4 itself.

1. I argue that the development, subtraction, and even sheer invention that we find in the course of the transmission of eschatological tradition is most often a change *in kind*. What we find is a widely shared future hope that undergoes certain types of changes that do not wholly remake what was present before. Such *Tendenzen* make it doubtful that we might ever recover with confidence the actual words of Jesus, while also taking us back to the very earliest years of the Jesus movement based in Jerusalem.
2. While it is possible that prophetic or charismatic inspiration in the earliest communities is responsible for creating a new future expectation after the death of Jesus, I argue that there is little evidence that prophetic inspiration

6. See Ben F. Meyer, *The Aims of Jesus* (London: SCM, 1979), 76–81, who speaks of interpretation and explanation.

functioned in such a generative way. Moreover, there is counterevidence that suggests memories of Jesus's ministry were *not* so easily blurred with communication by the Spirit after the resurrection experiences. I also contend here that, should it be true that the Jesus tradition was so quickly populated with sayings of the risen Christ, we would have to admit that Jesus material at this early stage was almost completely pervious to fictionalization (given the prominence of claims about Jesus's future coming in Paul's letters and in the Synoptics). Thus, the nature of the sources would really require us to abandon hope of knowing much at all about Jesus's eschatological teaching.

3. I argue next that the intertextuality that informed and filled out the expectation for Jesus's future coming discussed in part 3—particularly Jesus's identity as the son of man from Dan 7, and interest in the coming day of the Lord—is best explained on the grounds that Jesus himself had already used Dan 7 eschatologically and self-referentially, and that he had already spoken of the future with the help of traditions about God's day. We can conclude as much without making specific claims about particular sayings going back to Jesus as written. Moreover, contra one of Glasson's more influential arguments about the second advent, I contend that early Christian interest in theophanic motifs about the day of the Lord do not necessarily presuppose a more exalted κύριος Christology (while they may well have benefited from such beliefs when they arose). Rather, early Christian attempts to link Jesus's activity with the future activity of God in the biblical prophets finds ample parallel in other Second Temple Jewish texts. The "day of the Lord" tradition had already been eschatologized and linked in some cases to God's future kingdom/reign, and the use of passages about God to describe the work of an eschatological redeemer or messianic figure was in fact widespread.
4. Then, against the pervasive assumption that we lack a sufficient *Sitz im Leben Jesu* for the expectation for Jesus's future coming to arise during his own activity, I argue that we do, in fact, have precisely such a setting, if we simply grant that Jesus believed he might die. As I have noted throughout, some proponents of an eschatological Jesus in the Schweitzerian stream of interpretation have not always made clear how their larger understanding of Jesus's eschatological proclamation relates to the prospect of his death. I suggest that there are indeed strong reasons to suppose that Jesus's death in Jerusalem did not catch him by surprise, and we can conclude that while also being skeptical of tracing the many different rationalizations of the cross in the post-Easter period back to Jesus. Moreover, I argue against those who believe that any hint of the expectation of an interim period (e.g., a time in which Jesus is gone and people are still around) sacrifices the eschatological character of the early Christian

movement. I suggest, instead, that my reconstruction actually more accurately describes the sense of eschatological imminence that connects John the Baptist, Jesus, and Paul—imminence *in the sense that* this is likely the last generation, and so urgent response is required. As I have observed throughout, many critics have left "imminence" rather vague and poorly defined (e.g., imminent in what sense?), and we lack evidence for an imminence *more imminent than* the basic idea that the last generation is here.

5. One important way that early Christians reconfigured Jesus (perhaps best termed "memory distortion"),[7] I argue next, is they have him predicting his individual resurrection from the dead after three days. Many have noted over the years that the prediction of the individual resurrection of Jesus is actually never connected directly in our sources to the prediction of Jesus's future coming. I offer my own explanation of that fact: it makes good sense that they are never connected because Jesus had not connected them. For Jesus, I argue, the coming of the son of man is linked to other final events at the end of the age, including the general resurrection of the dead and the final judgment, even if the connection between these things remains for us somewhat cloudy. What early Christians did, then, in believing that Jesus had been raised from the dead individually, is they pulled back into the present the beginning (Paul would say firstfruits) of that general resurrection, thereby creating a more realized eschatological situation. They also put their belief in Jesus's individual resurrection of the dead on his lips in the form of explicit prediction. Recognizing that clarifies a number of interrelated issues in the study of Christian origins.
6. If Jesus had not predicted his individual resurrection after three days, I suggest in chapter 15 that his "coming" was either a way of speaking generally of his return after the general resurrection, or his "coming" was indeed initially regarded as a coming from heaven that would coincide with the general resurrection in some way. While I provide some reasons why I prefer the second of these, the more important point is that either option supports the probability of the basic sequence in Jesus's eschatological expectation that I have argued for: potential death, brief period of absence, "coming" at the consummation of the age. It may also be unwise to systematize and separate these options categorically, and it is, of course, possible that ambiguity on this question was there at the beginning.
7. Last, I return to consider Jesus's activity as a whole on the grounds that attempting to integrate the various claims one makes about Jesus is essential for

7. Cf. Zeba A. Crook, "Collective Memory Distortion and the Quest for the Historical Jesus," *JSHJ* 11 (2013): 53–76.

> any historical reconstruction (making the most sense of the most material). Rather than opt for the traditional route in Jesus research of reconstructing a single scenario about his activity, I argue that the best we can do given the nature of our evidence in this case is to hold up two different and, in some ways, competing scenarios. Despite the fuzziness of this result, my contention is that either one of these is *more probable than* an alternative reconstruction, which would posit the origin of the future coming hope in the post-Easter period. The first scenario is that, somewhat like the old Galilean crisis theory, Jesus had initially hoped for more success than he in fact found. The expectation for the future coming of the son of man, then, was a response to the opposition and rejection that he had faced. The second scenario is that Jesus expected the initiation of an eschatological process before the soon-to-come consummation, including the tribulation and struggle often associated with the so-called messianic woes. Thus, the prospect of suffering and even death, which may well have arisen only later in the ministry, would not require a radical revision of his eschatological expectations. It is this second scenario that I argue is better supported by the sources and makes more sense of early Christian memories of Jesus. Nevertheless, I suggest that we leave both possibilities on the table, my skepticism of the Galilean crisis theory and related views aside.

In the end, my hope is that the four angles of inquiry in the four parts of this book—critical analysis (1), reception history (2), exegesis (3), and historical reconstruction (4)—are mutually reinforcing and ultimately work together to create a more socially informed, literarily sensitive, and accurately constructed history of the second-coming hope in Christian origins. There are, of course, many ways in which the early followers of Jesus saw their own reflection when they peered down into the well of tales about him. But for the topic at the center of this volume, at least, my conclusion is that their appearance was a reflection of his.

Bibliography

Aarde, Andries van. "'On Earth as It Is in Heaven'—Matthew's Eschatology as the Kingdom of the Heavens That Has Come." Pages 35–63 in *Eschatology of the New Testament and Some Related Documents*. Edited by Jan G. van der Watt. WUNT 2/315. Tübingen: Mohr Siebeck, 2011.

Adams, Edward. "The 'Coming of God' Tradition and Its Influence on New Testament Parousia Texts." Pages 1–20 in *Biblical Traditions in Transmission: Essays in Honour of Michael A. Knibb*. Edited by Charlotte Hempel and Judith M. Lieu. JSJSup 111. Leiden: Brill, 2006.

———. "The Coming of the Son of Man in Mark's Gospel." *TynBul* 56 (2005): 39–61.

———. *The Stars Will Fall from Heaven: Cosmic Catastrophe in the New Testament and Its World.* LNTS 347. London: Bloomsbury T&T Clark, 2007.

———. "'Where Is the Promise of His Coming?' The Complaint of the Scoffers in 2 Peter 3:4." *NTS* 51 (2005): 106–22.

Adams, Sean A., and Seth M. Ehorn, eds. *Jewish, Greco-Roman, and Early Christian Uses*. Vol. 1 of *Composite Citations in Antiquity*. LNTS 525. London: Bloomsbury T&T Clark, 2016.

———, eds. *New Testament Uses*. Vol. 2 of *Composite Citations in Antiquity*. LNTS 593. London: Bloomsbury T&T Clark, 2018.

Ådna, Jostein. *Jesu Stellung zum Tempel: Die Tempelaktion und das Tempelwort als Ausdruck seiner messianischen Sendung.* WUNT 2/119. Tübingen: Mohr Siebeck, 2000.

———. "The Messianic Claim of Jesus: An Appreciation and Appraisal of Martin

Hengel's Portrayal of the Historical Jesus." Pages 59–76 in *The Mission of Jesus*. Edited by Samuel Byrskog and Tobias Hägerland. WUNT 2/391. Tübingen: Mohr Siebeck, 2015.

———. "Temple Act." Pages 947–52 in *Dictionary of Jesus and the Gospels*. Edited by Joel B. Green, Jeannine K. Brown, and Nicholas Perrin. 2nd ed. Downers Grove, IL: InterVarsity Press, 2013.

Agbanou, Victor Kossi. *Le discours eschatologique de Matthieu 24–25: Tradition et rédaction*. Paris: Gabalda, 1983.

Albl, Martin C. "Ancient Christian Authors on Jews and Judaism." Pages 15–56 in *The 'New Testament' as a Polemical Tool: Studies in Ancient Christian Anti-Jewish Rhetoric and Beliefs*. Edited by Riemer Roukema and Hagit Amrav. NTOA 118. Göttingen: Vandenhoeck & Ruprecht, 2018.

Alexander, Philip S. "The King Messiah in Rabbinic Judaism." Pages 456–73 in *King and Messiah in Israel and the Ancient Near East*. Edited by John Day. Sheffield: Sheffield Academic, 1998.

Alfonsi, Petrus. *Dialogue against the Jews*. Edited and translated by Irven Michael Resnick. FC Medieval Continuation 8. Washington, DC: Catholic University of America Press, 2006.

Alkier, Stefan. "Intertextuality and the Semiotics of Biblical Texts." Pages 3–21 in *Reading the Bible Intertextually*. Edited by Richard B. Hays, Stefan Alkier, and Leroy A. Huizenga. Waco, TX: Baylor University Press, 2009.

Allison, Dale C., Jr. *4 Baruch: Paraleipomena Jeremiou*. CEJL. Berlin: de Gruyter, 2019.

———. *Constructing Jesus: Memory, Imagination, and History*. Grand Rapids: Baker Books, 2010.

———. "Eldad and Modad." *JSP* 21 (2011): 99–131.

———. *The End of the Ages Has Come: An Early Interpretation of the Passion and Resurrection of Jesus*. Philadelphia: Fortress, 1985.

———. *The Gospel of John and History*. Forthcoming.

———. *The Historical Christ and the Theological Jesus*. Grand Rapids: Eerdmans, 2009.

———. *The Intertextual Jesus: Scripture in Q*. Harrisburg, PA: Trinity International, 2004.

———. "Jesus and the Victory of Apocalyptic." Pages 126–41 in *Jesus and the Restoration of Israel: A Critical Assessment of N. T. Wright's* Jesus and the Victory of God. Edited by Carey C. Newman. Downers Grove, IL: InterVarsity Press, 1999.

———. *Jesus of Nazareth: Millenarian Prophet*. Philadelphia: Fortress, 1998.

———. *The Jesus Tradition in Q*. Valley Forge: Trinity International, 1997.

———. "The Pauline Epistles and the Synoptic Gospels: The Pattern of the Parallels." *NTS* 28 (1982): 1–32.

———. "A Plea for Thoroughgoing Eschatology." *JBL* 113 (1994): 651–56.

———. "Q 12:51–53 and Mark 9:11–13 and the Messianic Woes." Pages 289–310 in *Authenticating the Words of Jesus*. Edited by Bruce Chilton and Craig A. Evans. Leiden: Brill, 2002.

———. *Resurrecting Jesus: The Earliest Christian Tradition and Its Interpreters*. London: T&T Clark, 2005.

———. *The Resurrection of Jesus: Apologetics, Criticism, History*. New York: Bloomsbury T&T Clark, 2021.

———. "The Scriptural Background of a Matthean Legend: Ezekiel 37, Zechariah 14, and Matthew 27." Pages 153–88 in *Life beyond Death in Matthew's Gospel: Religious Metaphor or Bodily Reality?* Edited by Wim Weren, Huub van de Sandt, and Joseph Verheyden. BTS 13. Leuven: Peeters, 2011.

———. *Testament of Abraham*. CEJL. Berlin: de Gruyter, 2003.

Amihay, Aryeh. "The Stones and the Rock: Jewish and Christian Elements in Vita Jeremiah." *JSP* 32 (2022): 39–56.

Ammon, Friedrich von. *Die Fortbildung des Christenthums zur Weltreligion: Eine Ansicht der höheren Dogmatik*. Leipzig: Vogel, 1833.

Anderson, Paul N. "Incidents Dispersed in the Synoptics and Cohering in John: Dodd, Brown, and Johannine Historicity." Pages 176–202 in *Engaging with C. H. Dodd on the Gospel of John: Sixty Years of Tradition and Interpretation*. Edited by Tom Thatcher and Catrin Williams. Cambridge: Cambridge University Press, 2013.

Andrejevs, Olegs. *Apocalypticism in the Synoptic Sayings Source: A Reassessment of Q's Stratigraphy*. WUNT 2/499. Tübingen: Mohr Siebeck, 2019.

———. "The Background of the Term 'Son of Man' in Light of Recent Research." *ExpTim* 130 (2019): 477–84.

Annet, Peter. *The Resurrection of Jesus Considered: In Answer to the Tryal of the Witnesses*. London: the author, 1744.

Aquinas, Thomas. *Catena Aurea: Commentary on the Four Gospels Collected out of the Works of the Fathers*. Translated by John Henry Newman. 4 vols. Southampton: Saint Austin, 1997.

Ariel, Donald T. "Identifying the Mints, Minters and Meanings of the First Jewish Revolt Coins." Pages 373–97 in *The Jewish Revolt against Rome: Interdisciplinary Perspectives*. Edited by Mladen Popović. JSJSup 154. Leiden: Brill, 2011.

Arnal, William. *The Symbolic Jesus: Historical Scholarship, Judaism, and the Construction of Contemporary Identity*. London: Equinox, 2005.

Ashton, John. "Intimations of Apocalyptic: Looking Back and Looking Forward." Pages 3–35 in *John's Gospel and Intimations of Apocalyptic*. Edited by Catrin H. Williams and Christopher Rowland. London: Bloomsbury T&T Clark, 2013.

———. *Understanding the Fourth Gospel*. Oxford: Oxford University Press, 2007.

Attridge, Harold W. "Reflections on Research into Q." *Semeia* 55 (1992): 223–34.

Auler, Samuel. "More Than a Gift: Revisiting Paul's Collection for Jerusalem and the Pilgrimage of Gentiles." *JSPL* 6 (2016): 142–60.

Aune, David E. *Jesus, the Gospel Tradition and Paul in the Context of Jewish and Greco-Roman Antiquity.* WUNT 303. Tübingen: Mohr Siebeck, 2013.

———. *Prophecy in Early Christianity and the Ancient Mediterranean World.* Grand Rapids: Eerdmans, 1983.

———. *Revelation.* WBC 52. 3 vols. Nashville: Nelson, 1997–1998.

———. "The Significance of the Delay of the Parousia for Early Christianity." Pages 87–109 in *Current Issues in Biblical and Patristic Interpretation.* Edited by G. F. Hawthorne. Grand Rapids: Eerdmans, 1975.

Baarlink, Heinrich. *Die Eschatologie der synoptischen Evangelien.* BWANT. Mainz: Kohlhammer, 1986.

Baasland, Ernst. "Fourth Quest? What Did Jesus Really Want?" Pages 31–56 in vol. 1 of *Handbook for the Study of the Historical Jesus.* Edited by Tom Holmén and Stanley Porter. Leiden: Brill, 2010.

Bacon, Benjamin. *The Story of Jesus and the Beginnings of the Church.* New York: Century, 1927.

———. *Studies in Matthew.* London: Constable, 1930.

———. "What Did Judas Betray?" *HibJ* 19 (1920–21): 476–93.

Baird, William. *From C. H. Dodd to Hans Dieter Betz.* Vol. 3 of *History of New Testament Research.* Minneapolis: Fortress, 2013.

———. *From Deism to Tübingen.* Vol. 1 of *History of New Testament Research.* Minneapolis: Fortress, 1992.

Balabanski, Vicky. *Eschatology in the Making: Mark, Matthew, and the Didache.* Cambridge: Cambridge University Press, 1997.

Baldensperger, Wilhelm. *Das Selbstbewusstein Jesu im Lichte der messianischen Hoffnungen seiner Zeit.* Strassburg: Heitz, 1888.

Ball, Bryan W. *A Great Expectation: Eschatological Thought in English Protestantism to 1660.* SHCT 12. Leiden: Brill, 1975.

Bammel, Ernst. "The Farewell Discourse of the Evangelist John and Its Jewish Heritage." *TynBul* 44 (1993): 103–16.

Barber, Michael Patrick. "Did Jesus Anticipate Suffering a Violent Death? The Implications of Memory Research and Dale C. Allison's Methodology." *JSHJ* 18 (2020): 191–219.

Barclay, John M. G. "Believers and the 'Last Judgment' in Paul: Rethinking Grace and Recompense." Pages 195–208 in *Eschatologie—Eschatology: The Sixth Durham-Tübingen Research Symposium; Eschatology in Old Testament, Ancient Judaism and Early Christianity.* Edited by Hans-Joachim Eckstein, Christof Landmesser, and Hermann Lichtenberger. WUNT 272. Tübingen: Mohr Siebeck, 2011.

Barclay, John M. G., and Simon J. Gathercole, eds. *Divine and Human Agency in Paul and His Cultural Environment*. LNTS 335. London: Bloomsbury T&T Clark, 2007.

Barker, J. D. "Day of the Lord." Pages 132–43 in *Dictionary of the Old Testament: Prophets*. Edited by Mark J. Boda and J. Gordon McConville. Downers Grove, IL: InterVarsity Press, 2012.

Barnard, L. W. "Justin Martyr's Eschatology." *VC* 19 (1965): 86–98.

Barnett, S. J. *Idol Temples and Crafty Priests: The Origins of Enlightenment Anticlericalism*. New York: St. Martin's, 1999.

Barrett, C. K. *A Commentary on the First Epistle to the Corinthians*. London: Black, 1971.

———. *Essays on Paul*. Philadelphia: Westminster, 1982.

———. *The Gospel according to St. John*. 2nd ed. London: SPCK, 1978.

———. *The Holy Spirit and the Gospel Tradition*. London: SPCK, 1947.

———. *Jesus and the Gospel Tradition*. London: SPCK, 1967.

Bartsch, Hans-Werner. *Das Auferstehung: Sein historisches und sein theologisches Problem*. TF 41. Hamburg: Reich, 1965.

Basser, Herbert W., with Marsha B. Cohen. *The Gospel of Matthew and Jewish Traditions: A Relevance-Based Commentary*. BRLJ 46. Leiden: Brill, 2015.

Batdorf, Irvin W. "Interpreting Jesus since Bultmann: Selected Paradigms and Their Hermeneutic Matrix." Pages 187–215 in *Society of Biblical Literature 1984 Seminar Papers*. Edited by Kent Harold Richards. SBLSP 23. Chico, CA: Scholars Press, 1985.

Bauckham, Richard. *Jesus and the Eyewitnesses: The Gospels as Eyewitness Testimony*. Grand Rapids: Eerdmans, 2006.

———. *Jude and the Relatives of Jesus in the Early Church*. London: T&T Clark, 2004.

———. "Parousia Parables Again." *NTS* 29 (1983): 129–34.

———. "The Study of Gospel Traditions outside the Canonical Gospels: Problems and Prospects." Pages 369–403 in *The Jesus Tradition outside the Gospels*. Vol. 5 of *Gospel Perspectives*. Sheffield: JSOT Press, 1985.

———. "Synoptic Parousia Parables and the Apocalypse." *NTS* 23 (1977): 162–76.

———. *The Testimony of the Beloved Disciple*. Grand Rapids: Baker Books, 2007.

Baumgarten, Albert I. "Four Stages in the Life of a Millennial Movement." Pages 61–76 in *War in Heaven/Heaven on Earth: Theories of the Apocalyptic*. Edited by Glen S. McGhee and Stephen D. O'Leary. London: Equinox, 2005.

Baumgarten, Joseph M., and Daniel R. Schwartz. *Damascus Document, War Scroll, and Related Documents*. Vol. 2 of *The Dead Sea Scrolls: Hebrew, Aramaic, and Greek Texts with English Translations*. Edited by James H. Charlesworth and Henry W. L. Rietz. Tübingen: Mohr Siebeck, 1995.

Baur, Ferdinand C. *The Church History of the First Three Centuries*. Translated by Allan Menzies. 3rd ed. 2 vols. London: Williams & Norgate, 1878.

———. "Die Bedeutung des Ausdrucks: ὁ υἱὸς τοῦ ἀνθρώπου." *ZWT* 3 (1860): 274–92.

———. *Kritische Untersuchungen über die kanonischen Evangelien.* Tübingen: Dues, 1847.

Bauspiess, Martin. "Die Gegenwart des Heils und das Ende der Zeit: Überlegungen zur lukanischen Eschatologie im Anschluss an Lk 22,66–71 und Apg 7,54–60." Pages 125–48 in *Eschatologie—Eschatology: The Sixth Durham-Tübingen Research Symposium; Eschatology in Old Testament, Ancient Judaism and Early Christianity*. Edited by Hans-Joachim Eckstein, Christof Landmesser, and Hermann Lichtenberger. WUNT 272. Tübingen: Mohr Siebeck, 2011.

Bavinck, Herman. *The Philosophy of Revelation*. New York: Longmans, Green, 1909.

Bayer, Hans F. *Jesus' Predictions of Vindication and Resurrection.* WUNT 2/20. Tübingen: Mohr Siebeck, 1986.

Baynes, Leslie A. "Jesus the Revealer and the Revealed." Pages 15–30 in *The Jewish Apocalyptic Tradition and the Shaping of New Testament Thought.* Edited by Benjamin E. Reynolds and Loren T. Stuckenbruck. Minneapolis: Fortress, 2017.

Beale, G. K. *The Use of Daniel in Jewish Apocalyptic Literature and in the Revelation of St. John.* Eugene, OR: Wipf & Stock, 2010.

Beale, G. K., and D. A. Carson, eds. *Commentary on the New Testament Use of the Old Testament.* Grand Rapids: Baker Books, 2007.

Beare, F. W. "The Synoptic Apocalypse: Matthean Version." Pages 115–33 in *Understanding the Sacred Text: Essays in Honor of Morton S. Enslin.* Edited by John Henry Reumann. Valley Forge: Judson, 1972.

Beasley-Murray, George R. *Jesus and the Kingdom of God.* Grand Rapids: Eerdmans, 1986.

———. *Jesus and the Last Days: An Interpretation of the Olivet Discourse.* Vancouver: Regent College, 1993.

———. *John.* 2nd ed. WBC 36. Nashville: Nelson, 1999.

———. "Resurrection and Parousia of the Son of Man." *TynBul* 42 (1991): 296–309.

Becker, Eve-Marie. *The Birth of Christian History: Memory and Time from Mark to Luke-Acts.* ABRL. New Haven: Yale University Press, 2017.

———. "Eschatology: Pauline and Catholic Epistles." Pages 409–21 in *Eschatology in Antiquity: Forms and Functions*. Edited by Hilary Marlow, Karla Pollmann, and Helen Van Noorden. London: Routledge, 2021.

Becker, Eve-Marie, Helen K. Bond, and Catrin H. Williams, eds. *John's Transformation of Mark.* London: Bloomsbury T&T Clark, 2021.

Becker, Eve-Marie, Troels Engberg-Pedersen, and Mogens Müller, eds. *Mark and Paul: Comparative Essays Part II; For and against Pauline Influence on Mark.* BZNW 199. Berlin: de Gruyter, 2014.

Becker, Jürgen. *Auferstehung der Toten im Urchristentum.* Stuttgart: KBW, 1976.

———. "Das Gottesbild Jesu und die älteste Auslegung von Ostern." Pages 23–47 in

Annäherungen: Zur urchristlichen Theologiegeschichte und zum Umgang mit ihren Quellen. Edited by Ulrich Mell. BZNW 76. Berlin: de Gruyter, 1995.

———. *Die Auferstehung Jesu Christi nach dem Neuen Testament: Ostererfahrung und Osterverständnis im Urchristentum*. Tübingen: Mohr Siebeck, 2007.

———. *Jesus of Nazareth*. Translated by James E. Crouch. Berlin: de Gruyter, 1998.

———. "The Search for Jesus' Special Profile." Pages 57–90 in vol. 1 of *Handbook for the Study of the Historical Jesus*. Edited by Tom Holmén and Stanley Porter. Leiden: Brill, 2010.

Beckwith, Roger T. *Calendar and Chronology, Jewish and Christian: Biblical, Intertestamental and Patristic Studies*. Leiden: Brill, 2001.

Bede. *The Venerable Bede: Commentary on the Acts of the Apostles*. Translated by Lawrence T. Martin. Kalamazoo, MI: Cistercian, 1989.

Beers, Holly. *The Followers of Jesus as the 'Servant': Luke's Model from Isaiah for the Disciples in Luke-Acts*. LNTS 535. London: Bloomsbury T&T Clark, 2015.

Behr, John. *Irenaeus of Lyons: Identifying Christianity*. Oxford: Oxford University Press, 2013.

Bell, Richard H. *The Irrevocable Call of God: An Inquiry into Paul's Theology of Israel*. WUNT 184. Tübingen: Mohr Siebeck, 2005.

Bellinger, William, Jr., and William R. Farmer, eds. *Jesus and the Suffering Servant: Isaiah 53 and Christian Origins*. Eugene, OR: Wipf & Stock, 2009.

Bendemann, Reinhard von. "Das Markusevangelium als Herausforderung für die Theologie." *ZNT* 24 (2021): 23–39.

Bengel, Johann Albrecht. *Gnomon of the New Testament*. 3rd ed. 5 vols. Translated by James Bandinel and Andrew R. Fausset. Edinburgh: T&T Clark, 1858.

———. *Gnomon of the New Testament*. 3rd ed. 4 vols. Translated by James Bandinel. Philadelphia: Smith, English, 1860.

Berger, David. *The Jewish-Christian Debate in the High Middle Ages: A Critical Edition of the Niẓẓaḥon Vetus*. Philadelphia: Jewish Publication Society of America, 1979.

Berger, Klaus. *Die Auferstehung des Propheten und die Erhöhung des Menschensohnes*. Göttingen: Vandenhoeck & Ruprecht, 1976.

Berger, Peter. *The Sacred Canopy: Elements of a Sociological Theory of Religion*. New York: Anchor, 1991.

Bergmann, Claudia D. *Festmahl ohne Ende: Apokalyptische Vorstellungen vom Speisen in der Kommenden Welt im antiken Judentum und ihre biblischen Wurzeln*. BWANT 222. Stuttgart: Kohlhammer, 2019.

Berkouwer, G. C. *The Return of Christ*. Studies in Dogmatics. Grand Rapids: Eerdmans, 1972.

Bermejo Rubio, Fernando. "Calling the Parousia into Question: Doubters and Skeptics in Some Early Christian Texts." *Archiv für Religionsgeschichte* 23 (2022): 173–87.

———. "The Day of the Lord Is Coming: Jesus and the Book of Zechariah." Pages 111–31 in *Jesus and the Scriptures: Problems, Passages and Patterns*. Edited by Tobias Hägerland. LNTS 552. London: Bloomsbury T&T Clark, 2016.

———. "The Fiction of the 'Three Quests': An Argument for Dismantling a Dubious Historiographical Paradigm." *JSHJ* 7 (2009): 211–53.

———. "Was 'Von dem Zwecke Jesu und seiner Jünger' an Innovative Contribution? On Reimarus' Significance in the History of Jesus Research." Pages 261–83 in *From Jesus to Christian Origins: Second Annual Meeting of Bertinoro (1–4 October, 2015)*. Edited by Adriana Destro and Mauro Pesce. Brepols: Turnhout, 2019.

———. "Why Is John the Baptist Used as a Foil for Jesus? Leaps of Faith and Oblique Anti-Judaism in Contemporary Scholarship." *JSHJ* 11 (2013): 170–96.

Bernard, L. W. "Justin Martyr's Eschatology." *VC* 19 (1965): 86–98.

Betz, Hans Dieter. "Eine Episode im Jüngsten Gericht (Mt 7, 21–23)." *ZTK* 78 (1981): 1–30.

Betz, Otto. *Die Menschensohnworte Jesu und die Zukunftserwartung des Paulus (Daniel 7, 13–14)*. ANTJ 6. Frankfurt am Main: Lang, 1985.

Beutel, Albrecht. *Kirchengeschichte im Zeitalter der Aufklarung: Ein Kopendium*. Göttingen: Vandenhoeck & Ruprecht, 2009.

Beutler, Johannes. "Synoptic Jesus Tradition in the Johannine Farewell Discourse." Pages 165–74 in *Jesus in Johannine Tradition*. Edited by Robert T. Fortuna and Tom Thatcher. Louisville: Westminster John Knox, 2001.

Beyschlag, Willibald. *Das Leben Jesu*. 3rd ed. 2 vols. Halle: Strien, 1893.

———. *New Testament Theology, or, Historical Account of the Teaching of Jesus and of Primitive Christianity according to the New Testament Sources*. Translated by Neil Buchanan. 2 vols. Edinburgh: T&T Clark, 1895.

Bibliorum Sacrorum cum Glossa Ordinaria. 6 vols. Venice: Magnam Societatem, 1603.

Bietenhard, Hans. "Der Menschensohn." *ANRW* 25.1:265–350. Part 2, *Principat*, 25.1. Edited by H. Temporini and W. Haase. New York: de Gruyter, 1989.

Bilde, Per. *The Originality of Jesus: A Critical Discussion and a Comparative Attempt*. SANt 1. Göttingen: Vandenhoeck & Ruprecht, 2013.

Billot, Louis. *La Parousie*. Paris: Beauchesne, 1920.

Birch, Jonathan C. P. "Reimarus and the Religious Enlightenment: His Apologetic Project." *ExpTim* 129 (2018): 245–53.

———. "Revolutionary Contexts for the Quest: Jesus in the Rhetoric and Methods of Early Modern Intellectual History." *JSHJ* 17 (2019): 35–80.

———. "The Road to Reimarus: Origins of the Quest of the Historical Jesus." Pages 19–47 in *Holy Land as Homeland?* Edited by Keith W. Whitelam. Social World of Biblical Antiquity 7. Sheffield: Sheffield Phoenix, 2011.

Bird, Michael. *Are You the One Who Is to Come? The Historical Jesus and the Messianic Question*. Grand Rapids: Baker Academic, 2009.

———. "The Crucifixion of Jesus as the Fulfillment of Mark 9:1." *TJ* 24 (2003): 1–11.

———. *Evangelical Theology: A Biblical and Systematic Introduction.* 2nd ed. Grand Rapids: Zondervan Academic, 2020.Black, C. Clifton. "An Oration at Olivet: Some Rhetorical Dimensions of Mark 13." Pages 66–92 in *Persuasive Artistry: Studies in New Testament Rhetoric in Honor of George A. Kennedy.* Edited by Duane F. Watson. JSNTSup 50. Sheffield: Sheffield Academic, 1991.

Bitner, Bradley J. "Unity and Diversity in Emergent Christianity." Pages 74–104 in *Into All the World: Emergent Christianity in Its Jewish and Greco-Roman Context.* Edited by Mark Harding and Alanna Nobbs. Grand Rapids: Eerdmans, 2017.

Black, Mark. "The Messianic Use of Zechariah 9–14 in Matthew, Mark, and the Pre-Markan Tradition." Pages 97–114 in *Scripture and Traditions: Essays on Early Judaism and Christianity in Honor of Carl R. Holladay.* Edited by Patrick Gray and Gail R. O'Day. NovTSup 129. Leiden: Brill, 2008.

Black, Matthew. *The Book of Enoch or 1 Enoch.* SVTP 7. Leiden: Brill, 1985.

———. "The 'Son of Man' in the Teaching of Jesus." *ExpTim* 60 (1948): 32–36.

Blackburn, Barry. Theios Anēr *and the Markan Miracle Traditions: A Critique of the* Theios Anēr *Concept as an Interpretive Background of the Miracle Traditions Used by Mark.* WUNT 2/40. Tübingen: Mohr Siebeck, 1991.

Blank, Josef. *Krisis: Untersuchungen zur johanneischen Christologie und Eschatologie.* Freiburg: Lambertus, 1964.

Blanton, Ward. "Albert Schweitzer's Apocalyptic Jesus and the End of Modernity." Pages 57–78 in *Jesus beyond Nationalism: Constructing the Historical Jesus in a Period of Cultural Complexity.* Edited by Halvor Moxnes, Ward Blanton, and James Crossley. London: Equinox, 2010.

Blondel, Maurice. *"The Letter on Apologetics" and "History and Dogma."* Translated by Alexander Dru and Illtyd Trethowan. Grand Rapids: Eerdmans, 1994.

Blount, Brian K. *Cultural Interpretation: Reorienting New Testament Criticism.* Minneapolis: Fortress, 1995.

Blount, Charles. *The Miscellaneous Works of Charles Blount.* London: s.n., 1695.

Blowers, Paul M. "Origen, the Rabbis, and the Bible: Toward a Picture of Judaism and Christianity in Third-Century Caesarea." Pages 96–116 in *Christianity in Relation to Jews, Greeks, and Romans.* Edited by Everett Ferguson. New York: Garland, 1999.

Boccaccini, Gabriele. "Protology and Eschatology in the Enochic Traditions." Pages 171–83 in *Eschatology in Antiquity: Forms and Functions.* Edited by Hilary Marlow, Karla Pollmann, and Helen Van Noorden. London: Routledge, 2021.

Bock, Darrell L. *Blasphemy and Exaltation in Judaism: The Charge against Jesus in Mark 14:53–65.* Eugene, OR: Wipf & Stock, 2016.

———. "Blasphemy and the Jewish Examination of Jesus." *BBR* 17 (2007): 53–114.

———. *Luke 9:51–24:53.* BECNT. Grand Rapids: Baker Books, 1996.

———. *A Theology of Luke and Acts*. Grand Rapids: Zondervan, 2012.

———. "The Use of Daniel 7 in Jesus' Trial, with Implications for His Self-Understanding." Pages 78–100 in *'Who Is This Son of Man?' The Latest Scholarship on a Puzzling Expression of the Historical Jesus*. Edited by Larry W. Hurtado and Paul L. Owen. LNTS 390. London: Bloomsbury T&T Clark, 2011.

Bock, Darrell L., and James H. Charlesworth, eds. *Parables of Enoch: A Paradigm Shift*. London: Bloomsbury T&T Clark, 2013.

Bockmuehl, Markus. *Revelation and Mystery in Ancient Judaism and Pauline Christianity*. WUNT 2/136. Tübingen: Mohr Siebeck, 1990.

———. "A 'Slain Messiah' in 4Q Serekh Milḥamah (4Q285)?" *TynBul* 43 (1992): 155–69.

Boer, Martinus C. de. *The Defeat of Death: Apocalyptic Eschatology in 1 Corinthians 15 and Romans 5:12–21*. Sheffield: Sheffield Academic, 1988.

———. "Johannine History and Johannine Theology: The Death of Jesus as the Exaltation and the Glorification of the Son of Man." Pages 293–326 in *The Death of Jesus in the Fourth Gospel*. Edited by G. Van Belle. BETL 200. Leuven: Leuven University Press, 2007.

———. "Paul and Apocalyptic Eschatology." Pages 345–83 in *The Origins of Apocalypticism in Judaism and Christianity*. Vol. 1 of *The Encyclopedia of Apocalypticism*. Edited by Bernard McGinn, John J. Collins, and Stephen J. Stein. New York: Continuum, 1998.

Boer, S. de. "Rome, the 'Translatio Imperii' and the Early-Christian Interpretation of Daniel II and VII." *Rivista di Storia e Letteratura Religiosa* 21 (1985): 181–218.

Boismard, M. É. "L'évolution du thème eschatologique dans les traditions Johanniques." *RB* 68 (1961): 514–18.

Bolingbroke, Henry. *The Works of the Late Right Honourable Henry St. John, Lord Viscount Bolingbroke*. 5 vols. London: Mallet, 1754.

Bolt, Peter. *The Cross from a Distance: Atonement in Mark's Gospel*. NSBT 18. Downers Grove, IL: InterVarsity Press, 2004.

———. "Mark 13: An Apocalyptic Precursor to the Passion Narrative." *RTR* 54 (1995): 10–30.

Bond, Helen K. *The First Biography of Jesus: Genre and Meaning in Mark's Gospel*. Grand Rapids: Eerdmans, 2020.

———. *The Historical Jesus: A Guide for the Perplexed*. London: Bloomsbury T&T Clark, 2012.

———. "The Quest for the Historical Jesus: An Appraisal." Pages 337–54 in *The Blackwell Companion to Jesus*. Edited by Delbert Burkett. Malden, MA: Blackwell, 2011.

Borg, Marcus. *Conflict, Holiness and Politics in the Teachings of Jesus*. 2nd ed. Harrisburg, PA: Trinity International, 1998.

———. *Uncovering the Life, Teachings, and Relevance of a Religious Revolutionary*. New York: HarperOne, 2008.

Boring, M. Eugene. *The Continuing Voice of Jesus*. Louisville: Westminster John Knox, 1991.

———. *Mark: A Commentary*. Louisville: Westminster John Knox, 2006.

———. "The Paucity of Sayings in Mark." Pages 371–77 in *SBL 1977 Seminar Papers*. Edited by Paul J. Achtemeier. Missoula, MT: Scholars Press, 1977.

Bornkamm, Günther. "Die Verzögerung der Parusie." Pages 121–25 in *In Memoriam Ernst Lohmeyer*. Edited by Werner Schmauch. Stuttgart: Evangelisches Verlagswerk, 1951.

———. *Jesus of Nazareth*. Translated by Irene and Fraser McLuskey, with James M. Robinson. New York: Harper, 1960.

Borsch, Frederick Houk. *The Christian and Gnostic Son of Man*. SBT 14. London: SCM, 1970.

Bosch, David. *Die Heidenmission in der Zukunftsschau Jesu: Eine Untersuchung zur Eschatologie der synoptischen Evangelien*. Zurich: Zwingli-Verlag, 1959.

Botner, Max. *Jesus Christ as the Son of David in the Gospel of Mark*. SNTSMS 174. Cambridge: Cambridge University Press, 2019.

Böttrich, Christfried. "Konturen des 'Menschensohnes' in äthHen 37–71." Pages 53–90 in *Gottessohn und Menschensohn: Exegetische Studien zu zwei Paradigmen biblischer Intertextualität*. Edited by Dieter Sänger and Knut Backhaus. Neukirchener: Neukirchen-Vluyn, 2004.

Bousset, Wilhelm. *Kyrios Christos: A History of the Belief in Christ*. Nashville: Abingdon, 1970.

Bovon, François. *Lk 1,1–9,50*. Vol. 1 of *Das Evangelium nach Lukas*. EKKNT. Zurich: Benzinger, 1989.

———. *Luke 2: A Commentary on the Gospel of Luke 9:51–19:27*. Translated by Donald S. Deer. Hermeneia. Minneapolis: Fortess, 2002.

———. *Luke 3: A Commentary on the Gospel of Luke 19:28–24:53*. Translated by James E. Crouch. Hermeneia. Minneapolis: Fortess, 2012.

Bowman, John W. "The Background of the Term 'Son of Man.'" *ExpTim* 60 (1948): 283–38.

Boyarin, Daniel. "How Enoch Can Teach Us about Jesus." *EC* 2 (2011): 51–76.

Boyer, Paul. *When Time Shall Be No More: Prophecy Belief in Modern American Culture*. Cambridge: Harvard University Press, 1992.

Bradley, John. *An Impartial View of the Truth of Christianity*. London: Clavel, 1699.

Brakke, David. "Jewish Flesh and Christian Spirit in Athanasius of Alexandria." *JECS* 9 (2001): 453–82.

Brandenburger, Egon. *Markus 13 und die Apokalyptik*. FRLANT 134. Göttingen: Vandenhoeck & Ruprecht, 1984.

Braun, Herbert. *Jesus of Nazareth: The Man and His Time*. Philadelphia: Fortress, 1979.

Breytenbach, Cilliers. "Das Markusevangelium, Psalm 110,1 und 118,22f: Folgetext und Prätext." Pages 197–222 in *The Scriptures in the Gospels*. Edited by Christopher M. Tuckett. Leuven: Leuven University Press, 1997.

———. *The Gospel according to Mark as Episodic Narrative*. NovTSup 182. Leiden: Brill, 2020.

———. "Mark's Future Tense." *EC* 12 (2021): 297–321.

Broadhead, Edwin K. *Naming Jesus: Titular Christology in the Gospel of Mark*. JSNTSup 175. Sheffield: Sheffield Academic, 1999.

Broeck, Roelof van den. "Gnosticism I: Gnostic Religion." Pages 403–16 in *Dictionary of Gnosis and Western Esotericism I*. Edited by Wouter J. Hanegraaf. Leiden: Brill, 2005.

Broer, Ingo. "Redaktionsgeschichtliche Aspekte von Mt. 24:1–28." *NovT* 35 (1993): 209–33.

Brooke, George J. "Kingship and Messianism in the Dead Sea Scrolls." Pages 434–55 in *King and Messiah in Israel and the Ancient Near East*. Edited by John Day. Sheffield: Sheffield Academic, 1998.

Brouwer, Wayne A. "The Chiastic Structure of the Farewell Discourse in the Fourth Gospel, Part I." *BSac* 175 (2018): 195–214.

Brower, Kent. "Mark 9:1: Seeing the Kingdom in Power" *JSNT* 6 (1980): 17–41.

Brown, Alexandra R. "Paul and the Parousia." Pages 47–76 in *The Return of Jesus in Early Christianity*. Peabody, MA: Hendrickson, 2000.

Brown, Colin. *Jesus in European Protestant Thought, 1778–1860*. SHT 1. Durham: Labyrinth, 1985.

Brown, Colin, with Craig A. Evans. *A History of the Quests for the Historical Jesus*. 2 vols. Grand Rapids: Zondervan Academic, 2022.

Brown, Raymond E. *The Birth of the Messiah: A Commentary on the Infancy Narratives in Matthew and Luke*. Garden City, NY: Doubleday, 1977.

———. *The Death of the Messiah*. 2 vols. ABRL. New York: Doubleday, 1994.

———. *The Gospel according to John*. 2 vols. AB 29. Garden City, NY: Doubleday, 1966–1970.

———. "How Much Did Jesus Know?" *CBQ* 29 (1967): 9–39.

———. *An Introduction to New Testament Christology*. New York: Paulist, 1994.

Bruce, F. F. *1 and 2 Thessalonians*. WBC 45. Waco, TX: Word, 1982.

Bucur, Bogdan Gabriel. *Scripture Re-envisioned: Christophanic Exegesis and the Making of a Christian Bible*. Leiden: Brill, 2019.

Buffa, Cristina. "The Magnificat and the Song of Hannah." *RevScRel* 92 (2018): 377–92.

Bühner, Ruben A. "The Contested Character of Divine Messianism: From an Inner-Jewish Debate to an Identity Marker." *EC* 13 (2022): 433–54.

———. *Hohe Messianologie: Übermenschliche Aspekte eschatologischer Heilsgestalten im Frühjudentum*. WUNT 2/523. Tübingen: Mohr Siebeck, 2020.

———. *Messianic High Christology: New Testament Variants of Second Temple Judaism.* Waco, TX: Baylor University Press, 2021.

Bultmann, Rudolf. *History of the Synoptic Tradition.* Translated by John Marsh. 5th ed. Peabody, MA: Hendrickson, 1963.

———. "Is Exegesis without Presuppositions Possible?" Pages 289–96 in *Existence and Faith: Shorter Writings of Rudolf Bultmann.* New York: Meridian, 1960.

———. *Jesus and the Word.* Translated by Louise Pettibone Smith and Erminie Huntress Lantero. New York: Scribner's Sons, 1934.

———. *Jesus Christ and Mythology.* New York: Scribner's Sons, 1958.

———. *The Theology of the New Testament.* Translated by Kendrick Grobel. 2 vols. New York: Scribner's Sons, 1955.

Bundy, Walter. *Our Recovery of Jesus.* Indianapolis: Bobbs-Merrill, 1929.

Burkett, Delbert R. *The Son of Man Debate: A History and Evaluation.* Cambridge: Cambridge University Press, 1999.

———. *The Unity and Plurality of Q.* Vol. 2 of *Rethinking the Gospel Sources.* Atlanta: Society of Biblical Literature, 2009.

Burkitt, F. C. *Church and Gnosis.* Cambridge: Cambridge University Press, 1932.

Burnett, D. Clint. *Christ's Enthronement and Its Greco-Roman Cultural Context.* BZNW 242. Berlin: de Gruyter, 2021.

Byers, Andrew J. "Johannine Readings of the Johannine Gospel: Reception Theology and Practice in John's Epistles." Pages 190–214 in *Gospel Reading and Reception in Early Christian Literature.* Edited by Madison N. Pierce, Andrew J. Byers, and Simon Gathercole. Cambridge: Cambridge University Press, 2022.

Byrne, Brendan. *Paul and the Economy of Salvation: Reading from the Perspective of the Last Judgment.* Grand Rapids: Baker Books, 2021.

Cadbury, Henry J. *The Peril of Modernizing Jesus.* London: SPCK, 1937.

Cadoux, Cecil J. *The Historic Mission of Jesus.* London: Lutterworth, 1941.

Caird, George. *The Language and Imagery of the Bible.* Worcester: Duckworth, 1980.

Callan, Terrance. "Psalm 110:1 and the Origin of the Expectation That Jesus Will Come Again." *CBQ* 44 (1982): 622–36.

Calmet, Augustin. *Dictionnaire historique, critique, chronologique, géographique et littéral de la Bible.* 2 vols. Rev. ed. Paris: Emery, 1730.

Calvin, John. *Commentarius in Harmoniam Evangelicam.* Vol. 45 of *Ioannis Calvini opera quae supersunt omnia.* Edited by Edouard Cunitz, Johann-Wilhelm Baum, and Eduard W. E. Reuss. Brunsvigae: Schwetschke, 1891.

———. *Commentary on a Harmony of the Evangelists.* Translated by William Pringle. 3 vols. Calvin's Commentaries 16–17. Grand Rapids: Baker Books, 2009.

Camery-Hoggatt, Jerry. *Irony in Mark's Gospel: Text and Subtext.* Cambridge: Cambridge University Press, 1992.

Campbell, Douglas A. *The Deliverance of God: An Apocalyptic Rereading of Justification in Paul.* Grand Rapids: Eerdmans, 2009.

Capes, David B., Rodney Reeves, and E. Randolph Richards. *Rediscovering Paul: An Introduction to His World, Letters, and Theology*. Downers Grove, IL: InterVarsity Press, 2007.

Caragounis, Chrys C. *The Son of Man: Vision and Interpretation*. Eugene, OR: Wipf & Stock, 2011.

Carlebach, Elisheva. "Jews, Christians, and the Endtime in Early Modern Germany." *Jewish History* 14 (2000): 331–44.

Carlson, Stephen C. "Eschatological Viviculture in *1 Enoch*, *2 Baruch*, and the Presbyters of Papias." *VC* 71 (2017): 37–58.

Carnazzo, Sebastian A. *Seeing Blood and Water: A Narrative-Critical Study of John 19:34*. Eugene, OR: Pickwick, 2012.

Carroll, John T. "The Parousia of Jesus in Other New Testament Writings." Pages 113–46 in *The Return of Jesus in Early Christianity*. Peabody, MA: Hendrickson, 2000.

———. "The Parousia of Jesus in the Johannine Literature." Pages 78–84 in *The Return of Jesus in Early Christianity*. Peabody, MA: Hendrickson, 2000.

———. *Response to the End of History: Eschatology and Situation in Luke-Acts*. SBLDS 92. Atlanta: Scholars Press, 1988.

Carroll, John T., with Alexandra R. Brown, Claudia J. Setzer, and Jeffrey S. Siker. *The Return of Jesus in Early Christianity*. Peabody, MA: Hendrickson, 2000.

Case, Shirley Jackson. "The Life of Jesus During the Last Quarter-Century." *JR* 5 (1925): 561–75.

Casey, Maurice. *An Aramaic Approach to Q: Sources for the Gospels of Matthew and Luke*. SNTSMS 122. Cambridge: Cambridge University Press, 2002.

———. "Chronology and the Development of Pauline Christology." Pages 124–34 in *Paul and Paulinism: Essays in Honour of C. K. Barrett*. Edited by Morna D. Hooker and S. G. Wilson. London: SPCK, 1982.

———. *Jesus of Nazareth: An Independent Historian's Account of His Life and Teaching*. London: T&T Clark International, 2010.

———. *The Solution to the "Son of Man" Problem*. LNTS 343. London: Bloomsbury T&T Clark, 2007.

———. *The Son of Man: The Interpretation and Influence of Daniel 7*. London: SPCK, 1979.

Catchpole, David. "The Angelic Son of Man in Luke 12:8." *NovT* 24 (1982): 255–65.

Chance, J. Bradley. *Jerusalem, the Temple, and the New Age in Luke-Acts*. Macon, GA: Mercer University Press, 1988.

Chapple, Allan. "The Fantasy of the Frantic Apostle: Paul and the Parousia." *Them* 47 (2022): 288–302.

Charles, R. H. *Eschatology, the Doctrine of a Future Life in Israel, Judaism, and Christianity.* New York: Schocken, 1963.

Charlesworth, James H. "From Messianology to Christian Christology: Some Caveats and Perspectives." Pages 225–64 in *Judaisms and Their Messiahs at the Turn of the Christian Era.* Edited by Jacob Neusner, William S. Green, and Ernest Frerichs. Cambridge: Cambridge University Press, 1987.

———. "Where Does the Concept of Resurrection Appear and How Do We Know That?" Pages 1–21 in *Resurrection: The Origin and Future of a Biblical Doctrine.* New York: T&T Clark, 2006.

Chazan, Robert. *Barcelona and Beyond: The Disputation of 1263 and Its Aftermath.* Berkeley: University of California Press, 1992.

———. *Medieval Stereotypes and Modern Antisemitism.* Berkeley: University of California Press, 1997.

Chazelle, Celia. "Debating the End Times with Bede." *ITQ* 80 (2015): 212–32.

Chester, Andrew. *Messiah and Exaltation: Jewish Messianic and Visionary Traditions and New Testament Christology.* WUNT 207. Tübingen: Mohr Siebeck, 2007.

Chilton, Bruce. *The Glory of Israel.* Sheffield: JSOT Press, 1982.

———. "Implications and Prospects of Jewish Jesus Research: A Review Essay." *JSHJ* 16 (2018): 62–79.

———. "(The) Son of (the) Man, and Jesus." Pages 259–88 in *Authenticating the Words of Jesus.* Edited by Bruce Chilton and Craig A. Evans. Leiden: Brill, 1999.

Chubb, Thomas. *The Posthumous Works of Mr. Thomas Chubb.* 2 vols. London: Baldwin, 1748.

———. *The True Gospel of Jesus Christ Asserted.* London: Cox, 1738.

Clark-Soles, Jaime. "'Will Raise [Whom?] Up on the Last Day': Anthropology as a Feature of Johannine Eschatology." Pages 29–53 in *New Currents through John: A Global Perspective.* Edited by Francisco Lozada Jr. and Tom Thatcher. RBS 54. Atlanta: Society of Biblical Literature, 2006.

Cleves, Maureen. "How Does a Beatle Live?" *London Evening Standard.* March 4, 1966.

Clodd, Edward. *Jesus of Nazareth: Embracing a Sketch of Jewish History to the Time of His Birth.* London: Paul, 1880.

Cohen, Jeremy. *Living Letters of the Law: Ideas of the Jew in Medieval Christianity.* Berkeley: University of California Press, 1999.

Cohn, Norman. *The Pursuit of the Millennium: Revolutionary Millenarians and Mystical Anarchists of the Middle Ages.* Rev. ed. Oxford: Oxford University Press, 1970.

Colani, Timothee. *Jésus-Christ et les croyances messianiques de son temps.* 2nd ed. Strasbourg: Treuttel & Wurtz, 1864.

Collins, Anthony. *Discourse of the Grounds and Reasons of the Christian Religion.* London: Senex, 1724.

Collins, John J. "The Angelic Life." Pages 291–310 in *Metamorphoses: Resurrection, Body and Transformative Practices in Early Christianity*. Edited by Turid Karlsen Seim and Jorunn Økland. Berlin: de Gruyter, 2009.

———. *The Apocalyptic Imagination*. 2nd ed. Grand Rapids: Eerdmans, 1998.

———. *Daniel: A Commentary on the Book of Daniel*. Hermeneia. Minneapolis: Fortress, 1993.

———. *The Scepter and the Star: Messianism in Light of the Dead Sea Scrolls*. 2nd ed. Grand Rapids: Eerdmans, 2010.

———. "The Second Coming." *Chicago Studies* 34 (1995): 262–74.

———. *The Sibylline Oracles of Egyptian Judaism*. Missoula, MT: Scholars Press, 1974.

———. "The Son of God Text from Qumran." Pages 76–82 in *From Jesus to John: Essays on Jesus and New Testament Christology in Honour of Marinus de Jonge*. Edited by Martinus C. De Boer. JSNTSup 84. Sheffield: JSOT Press, 1993.

———. "The Son of Man in Ancient Judaism." Pages 1545–68 in vol. 2 of *Handbook for the Study of the Historical Jesus*. Edited by Tom Holmén and Stanley Porter. Leiden: Brill, 2010.

———. "Teacher and Messiah?" Pages 193–210 in *The Community of the Renewed Covenant*. Edited by Eugene Ulrich and James VanderKam. Notre Dame: University of Notre Dame Press, 1994.

Collins, Raymond F. *First Corinthians*. SP 7. Collegeville, MN: Liturgical Press, 1999.

Colpe, Carsten. "ὁ υἱὸς τοῦ ἀνθρώπου." *TDNT* 8:400–77.

Cone, James. *God of the Oppressed*. Rev. ed. Maryknoll, NY: Orbis Books, 1997.

Cone, Orello. "Jesus' Self-Designation in the Synoptic Gospels." *New World* 2 (1893): 492–518.

Conzelmann, Hans. *1 Corinthians: A Commentary on the First Epistle to the Corinthians*. Translated by James W. Leitch. Hermeneia. Philadelphia: Fortress, 1975.

———. *Die Mitte der Zeit: Studien zur Theologie des Lukas*. 6th ed. Tübingen: Mohr, 1977.

———. *Jesus*. Edited by John Reumann. Translated by J. Raymond Lord. Philadelphia: Fortress, 1973.

———. *An Outline of the Theology of the New Testament*. New York: Harper & Row, 1969.

Cook, Daniel J. "Leibniz on 'Prophets,' Prophecy, and Revelation." *RelS* 45 (2009): 269–87.

Court, John M. *Approaching the Apocalypse: A Short History of Christian Millenarianism*. London: Tauris, 2008.

———. "Paul and the Apocalyptic Pattern." Pages 57–66 in *Paul and Paulinism: Essays in Honour of C. K. Barrett*. Edited by Morna D. Hooker and S. G. Wilson. London: SPCK, 1982.

Cranfield, C. E. B. *A Critical and Exegetical Commentary on the Epistle to the Romans.* 2 vols. Edinburgh: T&T Clark, 1979.

———. *The Gospel according to St. Mark: An Introduction and Commentary.* Cambridge: Cambridge University Press, 1959.

———. "The Resurrection of Jesus Christ." *ExpTim* 101 (1990): 167–72.

———. "Thoughts on New Testament Eschatology." *SJT* 35 (1982): 497–512.

Crawford, Barry. "Near Expectation in the Sayings of Jesus." *JBL* 101 (1982): 225–44.

Crook, Zeba A. "Collective Memory Distortion and the Quest for the Historical Jesus." *JSHJ* 11 (2013): 53–76.

Crossan, John Dominic. *The Historical Jesus: The Life of a Mediterranean Jewish Peasant.* New York: HarperCollins, 1991.

———. *In Parables: The Challenge of the Historical Jesus.* New York: Harper & Row, 1973.

Crossley, James. *Jesus and the Chaos of History: Redirecting the Life of the Historical Jesus.* Oxford: Oxford University Press, 2015.

———. *Jesus in an Age of Neoliberalism: Scholarship, Intellectuals and Ideology.* London: Equinox, 2012.

———. "A 'Very Jewish' Jesus: Perpetuating the Myth of Superiority." *JSHJ* 11 (2013): 109–29.

———. "Chartism and Forgotten Quests." Pages 201–21 in *The Next Quest for the Historical Jesus.* Edited by James Crossley and Chris Keith. Grand Rapids: Eerdmans, 2024.

Crossley, James, and Robert J. Myles. *Jesus: A Life in Class Conflict.* Winchester: Zero, 2023.

Cullmann, Oscar. *The Christology of the New Testament.* Rev. ed. Translated by Shirley C. Guthrie and Charles A. M. Hall. Philadelphia: Westminster, 1963.

———. "Die Hoffnung der Kirche auf die Wiederkunft Christi nach dem Neuen Testament" (1944). Pages 378–402 in *Vorträge und Aufsätze 1925–1962.* Edited by K. Fröhlich. Tübingen: Mohr Siebeck, 1966.

———. *Peter: Disciple-Apostle-Martyr.* Translated by Floyd V. Filson. Philadelphia: Westminster, 1953.

Culpepper, R. Alan. "Realized Eschatology in the Experience of the Johannine Community." Pages 253–76 in *The Resurrection of Jesus in the Gospel of John.* Edited by Craig R. Koester and R. Bieringer. WUNT 222. Tübingen: Mohr Siebeck, 2008.

Dahl, Nils Alstrup. *The Crucified Messiah and Other Essays.* Minneapolis: Augsburg, 1974.

———. "The Problem of the Historical Jesus." Pages 81–111 in *Jesus the Christ: The Historical Origins of Christological Doctrine.* Edited by Donald A. Juel. Minneapolis: Fortress, 1991.

Daley, Brian E. *The Hope of the Early Church: A Handbook of Patristic Eschatology*. Cambridge: Cambridge University Press, 1991.

Dalman, Gustaf. *Die Worte Jesu*. Leipzig: Hinrichs, 1898.

Daniélou, Jean. *The Theology of Jewish Christianity*. London: Darton, Longman & Todd, 1964.

Danker, F. W. *Jesus and the New Age: A Commentary on Luke's Gospel*. Philadelphia: Fortress, 1988.

Darby, John Nelson. "Lectures on the Second Coming of Christ." Pages 313–512 in vol. 11 of *The Collected Writings of J. N. Darby*. Edited by William Kelly. 2nd ed. 34 vols. London: Morrish, n.d.

Daube, David. *He That Cometh*. London: Council for Christian-Jewish Understanding, 1966.

Davies, J. G. "The Genesis of Belief in an Imminent Parousia." *JTS* 14 (1963): 104–7.

Davies, J. P. *Paul among the Apocalypses? An Evaluation of the 'Apocalyptic Paul' in the Context of Jewish and Christian Apocalyptic Literature*. LNTS 562. London: Bloomsbury T&T Clark, 2016.

Davies, W. D. *Paul and Rabbinic Judaism: Some Rabbinic Elements in Pauline Theology*. London: SPCK, 1948.

Davies, W. D., and Dale C. Allison Jr. *A Critical and Exegetical Commentary on the Gospel according to Saint Matthew*. 3 vols. ICC. Edinburgh: T&T Clark, 1988–1997.

Dawes, Gregory. *The Historical Jesus Question: The Challenge of History to Religious Authority*. Louisville: Westminster John Knox, 2001.

Day, Adam W. *Jesus, the Isaianic Servant: Quotations and Allusions in the Gospel of John*. Piscataway, NJ: Gorgias, 2018.

DeConick, April. "Reading the Gospel of Thomas as a Repository of Early Christian Communal Memory." Pages 207–20 in *Memory, Tradition, and Text: Uses of the Past in Early Christianity*. Edited by Alan Kirk and Tom Thatcher. SemeiaSt 52. Atlanta: Society of Biblical Literature, 2005.

Deissmann, Adolf. *Licht vom Osten: Das Neue Testament und die neuentdeckten Texte der hellenistisch-römischen Welt*. Tübingen: Mohr, 1923.

De La Torre, Miguel. *Embracing Hopelessness*. Minneapolis: Fortress, 2017.

Delling, Gerhard. "ἡμέρα." *TDNT* 2:947–53.

Dettwiler, Andreas. *Die Gegenwart des Erhöhten: Eine exegetische Studie zu den johanneischen Abschiedsreden (Joh 13,31–16,33) unter besonderer Berücksichtigung ihres Relecture-Charakters*. FRLANT. Göttingen: Vandenhoeck & Ruprecht, 1995.

Deutsch, Yaacov. *Judaism in Christian Eyes: Ethnographic Descriptions of Jews and Judaism in Early Modern Europe*. Oxford: Oxford University Press, 2012.

Dewey, Arthur J. *Inventing the Passion: How the Death of Jesus Was Remembered*. Salem: Polebridge, 2017.

Dewey, John. *How We Think*. Boston: Heath, 1910.

Dibelius, Martin. *Jesus*. Philadelphia: Westminster, 1949.

Dienstag, Jacob I. "Maimonides in English Christian Thought and Scholarship: An Alphabetical Survey." *Hebrew Studies* 26 (1985): 249–99.

Dillard, Annie. "The Book of Luke." Pages 263–78 in *The Annie Dillard Reader*. New York: HarperCollins, 1994.

———. *Living by Fiction*. New York: Harper & Row, 1988.

Dixon, Sarah Underwood. "The End of the Temple or the End of the World? First Century Eschatology in the Gospels of Mark and Matthew." Pages 371–82 in *Eschatology in Antiquity: Forms and Functions*. Edited by Hilary Marlow, Karla Pollmann, and Helen Van Noorden. London: Routledge, 2021.

Dobschütz, Ernst von. *The Eschatology of the Gospels*. London: Hodder & Stoughton, 1910.

Dodd, C. H. *According to the Scriptures*. London: Nisbet, 1952.

———. *The Apostolic Preaching and Its Developments*. New York: Harper, 1960.

———. *The Founder of Christianity*. London: Collins, 1971.

———. *Historical Tradition in the Fourth Gospel*. Cambridge: Cambridge University Press, 1963.

———. *More New Testament Studies*. Manchester: Manchester University Press, 1969.

———. *New Testament Studies*. Manchester: Manchester University Press, 1953.

———. *The Parables of the Kingdom*. Rev. ed. New York: Scribner's Sons, 1961.

Doerfler, Maria. "Ambrose's Jews: The Creation of Judaism and Heterodox Christianity in Ambrose of Milan's *Expositio evangelii secundum Lucam*." *CH* 80 (2011): 749–72.

Donfried, Karl Paul. "The Kingdom of God in Paul." Pages 175–90 in *The Kingdom of God in 20th-Century Interpretation*. Edited by Wendell Willis. Peabody, MA: Hendrickson, 1987.

Doole, J. Andrew. "Did Paul Really Think He Wasn't Going to Die? Paul, the Parousia, and the First Person Plural in 1 Thess 4:13–18." *NovT* 62 (2020): 44–59.

Downing, F. Gerald. "Feasible Researches in Historical Jesus Tradition: A Critical Response to Chris Keith." *JSNT* 40 (2017): 51–61.

Droysen, Johann Gustav. *Outline of the Principles of History*. Translated by E. Benjamin Andrews. New York: Fertig, 1893.

Dulk, Matthijs den. *Between Jews and Heretics: Reconfiguring Justin Martyr's Dialogue with Trypho*. RSECW. New York: Routledge, 2018.

Dunbar, David. "The Delay of the Parousia in Hippolytus." *VC* 37 (1983): 313–27.

Duncan, George. *Jesus, Son of Man*. New York: Macmillan, 1949.

Dungan, David. "Albert Schweitzer's Disillusionment with the Historical Reconstructions of the Life of Jesus." *PSTJ* 29 (1976): 27–48.

Dunn, James D. G. *Jesus Remembered*. Grand Rapids: Eerdmans, 2003.

———. "John the Baptist's Use of Scripture." Pages 42–54 in *The Gospels and the Scriptures of Israel*. Edited by Craig A. Evans and W. Richard Stegner. Sheffield: JSOT Press, 1994.

———. *A New Perspective on Jesus: What the Quest for the Historical Jesus Missed*. Grand Rapids: Baker Books, 2005.

———. *The Oral Gospel Tradition*. Grand Rapids: Eerdmans, 2013.

———. *Romans*. 2 vols. WBC 38. Nashville: Nelson, 1988.

———. *The Theology of Paul the Apostle*. Grand Rapids: Eerdmans, 1998.

Dupont, Jacques. "'Assis à la droite de Dieu': L'interprétation du Ps 110, 1 dans le Nouveau Testament." Pages 340–422 in *Resurrexit: Actes du Symposium international sur la résurrection de Jésus*. Edited by Édouard Dhanis, Barnabas M. Ahern, and Giuseppe Ghiberti. Vatican City: Libreria Editrice Vaticana, 1974.

Dupont-Sommer, André. *The Essene Writings from Qumran*. Gloucester: Smith, 1973.

Eastman, Susan. "Israel and the Mercy of God: A Re-reading of Galatians 6.16 and Romans 9–11." *NTS* 56 (2010): 367–95.

Eck, Ernest van. "Eschatology and Kingdom in Mark." Pages 64–91 in *Eschatology of the New Testament and Some Related Documents*. Edited by Jan G. van der Watt. WUNT 2/315. Tübingen: Mohr Siebeck, 2011.

Edersheim, Alfred. *The Life and Times of Jesus the Messiah*. 2 vols. 3rd ed. Grand Rapids: Eerdmans, 1943.

Edsall, Benjamin A. "This Is Not the End: The Present Age and the Eschaton in Mark's Narrative." *CBQ* 80 (2018): 429–47.

Eggen, Renate Banschbach. "Do the Parables Tell Us Something about the Mission of Jesus?" Pages 141–60 in *The Mission of Jesus*. Edited by Samuel Byrskog and Tobias Hägerland. WUNT 2/391. Tübingen: Mohr Siebeck, 2015.

Ehrman, Bart D. *Heaven and Hell: A History of the Afterlife*. New York: Simon & Schuster, 2020.

———. *Jesus: Apocalyptic Prophet of the New Millennium*. Oxford: Oxford University Press, 1999.

Eisler, Robert. "Das letzte Abendmahl." *ZNT* 24 (1925): 161–92.

Eisner, Elliott. *The Educational Imagination: On the Design and Evaluation of School Programs*. New York: Macmillan, 1979.

Eklund, Rebekah. "Jesus of Nazareth." Pages 139–60 in *The State of New Testament Studies: A Survey of Recent Research*. Edited by Scot McKnight and Nijay K. Gupta. Grand Rapids: Baker Books, 2019.

Elgvin, Torleif. *Warrior, King, Servant, Savior: Messianism in the Hebrew Bible and Early Jewish Texts*. Grand Rapids: Eerdmans, 2022.

Elledge, C. D. "Resurrection of the Dead: Exploring Our Earliest Evidence Today." Pages

22–52 in *Resurrection: The Origin and Future of a Biblical Doctrine*. New York: T&T Clark, 2006.

———. *Resurrection of the Dead in Early Judaism: 200 BCE–CE 200*. Oxford: Oxford University Press, 2017.

Elliott, Mark A. *The Survivors of Israel: A Reconsideration of the Theology of Pre-Christian Judaism*. Grand Rapids: Eerdmans, 2000.

Ellis, Earle E. *Christ and the Future in New Testament History*. NovTSup 97. Leiden: Brill, 2000.

———. "The Role of the Christian Prophet in Acts." Pages 55–67 in *Apostolic History and the Gospel*. Edited by W. Ward Gasque and Ralph P. Martin. Grand Rapids: Eerdmans, 1970.

Ellwood, Thomas. *Sacred History, or, The Historical Part of the Holy Scriptures of the New Testament: Gathered out from the Other Parts Thereof, and Digested (as Near as Well Could Be) into Due Method, with Respect to the Order of Time and Place*. 2nd ed. London: Sowle, 1719.

Emmerson, Richard K. "The Advent Hope in the Middle Ages." Pages 96–114 in *The Advent Hope in Scripture and History*. Edited by V. Norskon Olsen. Washington, DC: Review & Herald, 1987.

Erdman, Charles R. "The Coming of Christ." Pages 87–99 in vol. 11 of *The Fundamentals: A Testimony to the Truth*. Chicago: Testimony, 1910–1915.

Erlemann, Kurt. *Naherwartung und Parusieverzögerung im Neuen Testament: Ein Beitrag zur Frage religiöser Zeiterfahrung*. Tübingen: Francke, 1995.

Eskola, Timo. *Messiah and the Throne: Jewish Merkabah Mysticism and Early Christian Exaltation Discourse*. WUNT 2/142. Tübingen: Mohr Siebeck, 2001.

———. "Paul et le Judaïsme du Second Temple: La sotériologie de Paul avant et après E. P. Sanders." *RSR* 90 (2002): 377–98.

Evans, Craig A. "Daniel in the New Testament: Visions of God's Kingdom." Pages 490–527 in vol. 2 of *The Book of Daniel: Composition and Reception*. Edited by John J. Collins and Peter W. Flint. Leiden: Brill, 2002.

———. "Did Jesus Predict His Death and Resurrection?" Pages 82–97 in *Resurrection*. Edited by Stanley E. Porter, Michael A. Hayes, and David Tombs. JSNTSup 186. Sheffield: Sheffield Academic, 1999.

———. "Inaugurating the Kingdom of God and Defeating the Kingdom of Satan." *BBR* 15 (2005): 49–75.

———. "Isaiah 53 in the Letters of Peter, Paul, Hebrews, and John." Pages 145–70 in *The Gospel according to Isaiah 53*. Edited by Darrell L. Bock and Mitch Glaser. Grand Rapids: Kregel, 2012.

———. *Jesus and His Contemporaries: Comparative Studies*. AGJU 25. Leiden: Brill, 1995.

———. *Mark 8:27–16:20*. WBC 34B. Nashville: Nelson, 2001.

———. "Prophet, Sage, Healer, Messiah, and Martyr: Types and Identities of Jesus."

Pages 1217–43 in vol. 2 of *Handbook for the Study of the Historical Jesus*. Edited by Tom Holmén and Stanley Porter. Leiden: Brill, 2010.

———. "Sitting on the Twelve Thrones of Israel: Scripture and Politics in Luke 22:24–30." Pages 455–80 in *Jesus in Context: Temple, Purity, and Restoration*. Edited by Bruce Chilton and Craig A. Evans. AGJU 39. Leiden: Brill, 1997.

———. "The Twelve Thrones of Israel: Scripture and Politics in Luke 22:24–30." Pages 154–70 in *Luke and Scripture*. Edited by Craig A. Evans and James A. Sanders. Minneapolis: Augsburg, 1993.

Eve, Eric. *Behind the Gospels: Understanding the Oral Tradition*. Minneapolis: Fortress, 2014.

Evelyn, John. *The History of the Three Late Famous Imposters*. London: Herringman, 1669.

Everson, A. Joseph. "The Days of Yahweh." *JBL* 93 (1974): 329–37.

Fabry, Heinz-Josef, and Ulrich Dahmen. "Melchisedek in Bibel und Qumran." Pages 377–98 in *Ich werde meinen Bund mit euch niemals brechen! Festschrift für Walter Gross*. Edited by Erasmus Gass and Hermann-Josef Stipp. Freiburg: Herder, 2011.

Fagal, Harold E. "The Advent Hope in the New Testament." Pages 46–64 in *The Advent Hope in Scripture and History*. Edited by V. Norskon Olsen. Washington, DC: Review & Herald, 1987.

Fee, Gordon D. *The First and Second Letters to the Thessalonians*. NICNT. Grand Rapids: Eerdmans, 2009.

———. *The First Epistle to the Corinthians*. Rev. ed. NICNT. Grand Rapids: Eerdmans, 2014.

Ferda, Tucker S. "Doubling Down: Zechariah's Oracle, Judah's Blessing, and the Triumphal Entry in Matthew." *JTS* 71 (2020): 1–27.

———. "The Enlightenment, Deism, and the 'Painful Thorn' of the Parousia Expectation." Paper presented at the Annual Meeting of the Society of Biblical Literature (History of Interpretation section). Atlanta, November 21, 2015.

———. "The Galilean Crisis and Jesus Research Past and Present: A Response to Paula Fredriksen, Sarah Rollens, and Jens Schröter." *JSHJ* 20 (2022): 127–43.

———. "God of the Nations: Daniel, Satan, and the Temptation of Jesus in Luke." *ZNW* 110 (2019): 1–20.

———. "The Historical Jesus and the Law: The Form of His Activity and the Impact of Social Reputation." *CBQ* 80 (2018): 62–80.

———. "The Historicity of Confusion: Jesus, John the Baptist, and the Construction of Public Identity." *JBL* 139 (2020): 747–67.

———. *Jesus, the Gospels, and the Galilean Crisis*. LNTS 601. London: Bloomsbury T&T Clark, 2019.

———. "John the Baptist, Isaiah 40, and the Ingathering of the Exiles." *JSHJ* 10 (2012): 154–88.

———. "Matthew's Titulus and Psalm 2's King on Mount Zion." *JBL* 133 (2014): 561–81.

———. "The Messiah of That Most Mischievous Superstition: Jesus and the Parting of the Ways in the Study of Christian Origins." *EC* 14 (2023): 9–34.

———. "Naming the Messiah: A Contribution to the 4Q246 'Son of God' Debate." *DSD* 21 (2014): 150–75.

———. "The Origin of the Second Advent Reconsidered." Paper presented at the Annual Meeting of the Eastern Great Lakes Biblical Society (New Testament section). Perrysville, OH, March 12, 2015.

———. "Reason to Weep: Isaiah 52 and the Subtext of Luke's Triumphal Entry." *JTS* 66 (2015): 28–60.

———. Review of *Jesus' Twofold Teaching about the Kingdom of God*, by Barry D. Smith. *JSHJ* 14 (2016): 274–76.

———. "The Soldiers' Inscription and the Angel's Word: The Significance of 'Jesus' in Matthew's *Titulus*." *NovT* 55 (2013): 221–31.

Festinger, Leon, Henry W. Riecken, and Stanley Schachter. *When Prophecy Fails*. New York: Harper & Row, 1964.

Finney, Mark T. *Resurrection, Hell and the Afterlife: Body and Soul in Antiquity, Judaism and Early Christianity*. New York: Routledge, 2016.

Fischer, Ulrich. *Eschatologie und Jenseitserwartung im hellenistischen Diasporajudentum*. Berlin: de Gruyter, 1978.

Fish, Stanley. *Is There a Text in This Class? The Authority of Interpretive Communities*. Cambridge: Harvard University Press, 1980.

Fitzmyer, Joseph A. *Essays on the Semitic Background of the New Testament*. London: Chapman, 1971.

———. *First Corinthians: A New Translation with Introduction and Commentary*. AB 32. New Haven: Yale University Press, 2008.

———. *The Gospel according to Luke X–XXIV*. AB 28A. Garden City, NY: Doubleday, 1985.

———. *To Advance the Gospel: New Testament Studies*. 2nd ed. Grand Rapids: Eerdmans, 1998.

———. *A Wandering Aramean: Collected Aramaic Essays*. Vol. 1 of *The Semitic Background of the New Testament*. Missoula, MT: Scholars Press, 1979.

Fleddermann, Harry T. *Q: A Reconstruction and Commentary*. BTS 1. Leuven: Peeters, 2005.

Fletcher-Louis, Crispin H. T. *Luke-Acts: Angels, Christology and Soteriology*. WUNT 2/94. Tübingen: Mohr Siebeck, 1997.

Fleury, Claude. *An Historical Account of the Manners and Behaviour of the Christians.* 2nd ed. London: Midwinter & Leigh, 1703.

Flew, R. Newton. *Jesus and His Church: A Study of the Idea of the Ecclesia in the New Testament.* London: Epworth, 1960.

Flint, Peter W. "The Daniel Tradition at Qumran." Pages 41–60 in *Eschatology, Messianism, and the Dead Sea Scrolls.* Edited by Craig A. Evans and Peter W. Flint. Grand Rapids: Eerdmans, 1997.

Flowers, Michael. "The Two Messiahs and Melchizedek in 11QMelchizedek." *JAJ* 7 (2016): 194–227.

Flusser, David. *Jesus.* 3rd ed. Jerusalem: Hebrew University Magnes Press, 2001.

———. "Jewish Messianism Reflected in the Early Church." Pages 258–88 in *Sages and Literature.* Vol. 2 of *Judaism of the Second Temple Period.* Edited by David Flusser and Azzan Yadin. Grand Rapids: Eerdmans, 2009.

———. "Resurrection and Angels in Rabbinic Judaism, Early Christianity, and Qumran." Pages 568–72 in *The Dead Sea Scrolls Fifty Years after Their Discovery.* Edited by Lawrence H. Schiffmann, Emanuel Tov, James C. VanderKam, and Galen Marquis. Jerusalem: Israel Exploration Society, 2000.

Formesyn, R. E. C. "Was There a Pronominal Connection for the Bar Nasha Self-Designation?" *NovT* 8 (1967): 1–35.

Foster, Paul. "The Eschatology of the Gospel of Matthew." Pages 77–103 in *"To Recover What Has Been Lost": Essays on Eschatology, Intertextuality, and Reception History in Honor of Dale C. Allison Jr.* Edited by Tucker S. Ferda, Daniel Frayer-Griggs, and Nathan C. Johnson. NovTSup 183. Leiden: Brill, 2021.

———. "Paul and Matthew: Two Strands of the Early Jesus Movement with Little Sign of Connection." Pages 86–114 in *Paul and the Gospels: Christologies, Conflicts and Convergences.* Edited by Michael F. Bird and Joel Willitts. LNTS 411. London: Bloomsbury T&T Clark, 2011.

———. "Who Wrote 2 Thessalonians? A Fresh Look at an Old Problem." *JSNT* 35 (2012): 150–75.

Fowl, Stephen. "The Use of Scripture in Philippians." Pages 163–84 in *Paul and Scripture: Extending the Conversation.* Edited by Christopher D. Stanley. ECL 9. Atlanta: Society of Biblical Literature, 2012.

France, R. T. *The Gospel of Matthew.* NICNT. Grand Rapids: Eerdmans, 2007.

———. *Jesus and the Old Testament: His Application of Old Testament Passages to Himself and His Mission.* Downers Grove, IL: InterVarsity Press, 1971.

———. *Mark: A Commentary on the Greek Text.* NIGTC. Grand Rapids: Eerdmans, 2002.

Frankel, Steven. "The Invention of Liberal Theology: Spinoza's Theological-Political Analysis of Moses and Jesus." *Review of Politics* 63 (2001): 287–315.

Frayer-Griggs, Daniel. "The Johannine Reception of a Matthean Legend." Paper presented at the Annual Meeting of the Society of Biblical Literature. San Antonio, November 20, 2023.

———. *Saved through Fire: The Fiery Ordeal in New Testament Eschatology.* Eugene, OR: Pickwick, 2016.

Fredriksen, Paula. "*Al Tirah* ('Fear Not!'): Jewish Apocalyptic Eschatology, from Schweitzer to Allison, and After." Pages 15–38 in *"To Recover What Has Been Lost": Essays on Eschatology, Intertextuality, and Reception History in Honor of Dale C. Allison Jr.* Edited by Tucker S. Ferda, Daniel Frayer-Griggs, and Nathan C. Johnson. NovTSup 183. Leiden: Brill, 2021.

———. "Apocalypse and Redemption in Early Christianity: From John of Patmos to Augustine of Hippo." *VC* 45 (1991): 151–83.

———. *From Jesus to Christ: The Origins of the New Testament Images of Christ.* 2nd ed. New Haven: Yale University Press, 2000.

———. *Jesus of Nazareth, King of the Jews: A Jewish Life and the Emergence of Christianity.* New York: Knopf, 1999.

———. "*Jesus, the Gospels, and the Galilean Crisis*, by Tucker Ferda." *JSHJ* 20 (2022): 117–26.

———. "*Secundum Carnem*: History and Israel in the Theology of St. Augustine." Pages 26–41 in *The Limits of Ancient Christianity: Essays on Late Antique Thought and Culture in Honor of R. A. Markus.* Edited by William E. Klingshirn and Mark Vessey. Ann Arbor: University of Michigan Press, 1999.

———. *When Christians Were Jews.* New Haven: Yale University Press, 2018.

Fredriksen, Paula, and Oded Irshai. "Christian Anti-Judaism: Polemics and Policies." Pages 977–1034 in *Late Roman-Rabbinic Period.* Vol. 4 of *The Cambridge History of Judaism.* Edited by Steven T. Katz. Cambridge: Cambridge University Press, 2006.

Frey, Jörg. "Continuity and Discontinuity between 'Jesus' and 'Christ': The Possibilities of an Implicit Christology." *RCT* 36 (2011): 69–98.

———. *Die johanneische Eschatologie: Das johanneische Zeitverständnis.* WUNT 110. Tübingen: Mohr Siebeck, 1998.

———. *Die johanneische Eschatologie: Die eschatologische Verkündigung in den johanneischen Texten.* WUNT 117. Tübingen: Mohr Siebeck, 2000.

———. *Die johanneische Eschatologie: Ihre Probleme im Spiegel der Forschung seit Reimarus.* WUNT 96. Tübingen: Mohr Siebeck, 1997.

———. "Die 'theologia crucifixi' des Johannesevangeliums." Pages 485–554 in *Die Herrlichkeit des Gekreuzigten: Studien zu den Johanneischen Schriften.* Edited by Juliane Schlegel. WUNT 307. Tübingen: Mohr Siebeck, 2013.

———. "Eschatology in the Gospel of John and in the Johannine Epistles." Pages 396–408 in *Eschatology in Antiquity: Forms and Functions.* Edited by Hilary Marlow, Karla Pollmann, and Helen Van Noorden. London: Routledge, 2021.

———. "Eschatology in the Johannine Circle." Pages 47–82 in *Theology and Christology in the Fourth Gospel: Essays by the Members of the SNTS Johannine Writings Seminar*. Edited by Gilbert van Belle, Jan G. van der Watt, and Petrus J. Maritz. BETL 184. Leuven: Leuven University Press, 2005.

———. "New Testament Eschatology—an Introduction: Classical Issues, Disputed Themes, and Current Perspectives." Pages 3–34 in *Eschatology of the New Testament and Some Related Documents*. Edited by Jan G. van der Watt. WUNT 2/315. Tübingen: Mohr Siebeck, 2011.

———. "The Reception of Jeremiah and the Impact of Jeremianic Traditions in the New Testament: A Survey." Pages 499–522 in *Jeremiah's Scriptures: Production, Reception, Interaction, and Transformation*. Edited by Hindy Najman and Konrad Schmid. JSJSup 173. Leiden: Brill, 2017.

———. *Theology and History in the Fourth Gospel: Tradition and Narration*. Waco, TX: Baylor University Press, 2018.

Friedman, Jerome. "The Myth of Jewish Antiquity: New Christians and Christian-Hebraica in Early Modern Europe." Pages 35–66 in *Jewish Christians and Christian Jews: From the Renaissance to the Enlightenment*. Edited by Richard H. Popkin and Gordon M. Weiner. IAHI 138. Dordrecht: Kluwer, 1994.

Frisch, Alexandria. *The Danielic Discourse on Empire in Second Temple Literature*. JSJSup 176. Leiden: Brill, 2016.

Froitzheim, Franzjosef. *Christologie und Eschatologie bei Paulus*. Würzburg: Echter, 1979.

Fujita, Shozo. "The Metaphor of Plant in Jewish Literature of the Intertestamental Period." *JSJ* 7 (1976): 30–45.

Fuller, R. H. *The Mission and Achievement of Jesus: An Examination of the Presuppositions of New Testament Theology*. London: SCM, 1967.

Funk, Robert. *Honest to Jesus: Jesus for a New Millennium*. San Francisco: HarperSanFrancisco, 1996.

Funk, Robert, Roy W. Hoover, and the Jesus Seminar. *The Five Gospels: The Search for the Authentic Words of Jesus*. New York: Macmillan, 1993.

Fusco, Vittorio. "Problems of Structure in Luke's Eschatological Discourse." Pages 72–92 in *Luke and Acts*. Edited by Gerald O'Collins and Gilberto Marconi. New York: Paulist, 1991.

Gadamer, Hans-Georg. *Truth and Method*. 2nd ed. New York: Crossroad, 1989.

Gager, John G. *Kingdom and Community: The Social World of Early Christianity*. Englewood Cliffs, NJ: Prentice Hall, 1975.

———. *The Origins of Antisemitism: Attitudes toward Judaism in Pagan and Christian Antiquity*. Oxford: Oxford University Press, 1985.

Gaon, Saadia. *The Book of Beliefs and Opinions*. Translated by Samuel Rosenblatt. New Haven: Yale University Press, 1976.

Garber, David G., Jr. "Biblical Prophecy and Popular Fantasy and Science Fiction." Pages 183–200 in *The Oxford Handbook of the Bible and American Popular Culture*. Edited by Dan W. Clanton Jr. and Terry R. Clark. Oxford: Oxford University Press, 2021.

Garland, David E. *1 Corinthians*. BECNT. Grand Rapids: Baker Books, 2003.

Garrett, Susan R. *The Demise of the Devil*. Minneapolis: Fortress, 1989.

Gaston, Lloyd. *No Stone on Another: Studies in the Significance of the Fall of Jerusalem in the Synoptic Gospels*. NovTSup 23. Leiden: Brill, 1970.

Gathercole, Simon. *The Composition of the Gospel of Thomas: Original Language and Influence*. SNTSMS 151. Cambridge: Cambridge University Press, 2012.

———. *The Gospel and the Gospels*. Grand Rapids: Eerdmans, 2022.

———. "The Son of Man in Mark's Gospel." *ExpTim* 115 (2004): 366–72.

Gaventa, Beverly Roberts. "The Eschatology of Luke-Acts Revisited." *Enc* 43 (1982): 27–42.

Gawlick, Günter. "Der Deismus als Grundzug der Religionsphilosophie der Aufklärung." Pages 15–43 in *Hermann Samuel Reimarus (1694–1768): Ein bekannter Unbekannter der Aufklärung in Hamburg*. Göttingen: Vandenhoeck & Ruprecht, 1973.

Gay, Peter. *The Enlightenment: An Interpretation*. London: Weidenfeld & Nicolson, 1967.

Geddert, Timothy J. *Watchwords: Mark 13 in Markan Eschatology*. JSNTSup 26. Sheffield: Sheffield Academic, 1989.

Geertz, Clifford. *The Interpretation of Cultures*. New York: Basic, 1973.

Geldenhuys, Norval. *Commentary on the Gospel of Luke*. London: Marshall, Morgan & Scott, 1950.

Georgi, Dieter. "The Early Church: Internal Jewish Migration or New Religion?" *HTR* 88 (1995): 35–68.

———. "The Interest in Life of Jesus Theology as a Paradigm for the Social History of Biblical Criticism." *HTR* 85 (1992): 51–83.

———. "Rudolf Bultmann's *Theology of the New Testament* Revisited." Pages 75–87 in *Bultmann, Retrospect and Prospect: The Centenary Symposium at Wellesley*. HTS 35. Philadelphia: Fortress, 1985.

Gerdmar, Anders. *Roots of Theological Anti-Semitism: German Biblical Interpretation and the Jews, from Herder and Semler to Kittel and Bultmann*. SJHC 20. Leiden: Brill, 2009.

Gerhardsson, Birger. *Memory and Manuscript: Oral Tradition and Written Transmission in Rabbinic Judaism and Early Christianity*. Translated by Eric J. Sharpe. Lund: Gleerup, 1961.

Giesen, Heinz. "Mk 9,1—ein Wort Jesu über die nahe Parusie." *TTZ* 92 (1983): 134–48.

———. "Naherwartung des Paulus in 1 Thess 4, 13–18?" *SNTU* 10 (1985): 123–50.

Gill, John. *Gill's Commentary*. 6 vols. Grand Rapids: Baker Books, 1980.

Gillman, John. "A Thematic Comparison: 1 Cor 15:50–57 and 2 Cor 5:1–5." *JBL* 107 (1988): 439–54.

Gire, Pierre. "L'idée du Christ chez Spinoza." *Théophilyon* 18 (2013): 345–57.

Glasson, T. Francis. *Jesus and the End of the World*. Edinburgh: St. Andrews, 1980.

———. "Schweitzer's Influence: Blessing or Bane?" *JTS* 28 (1977): 289–302.

———. *The Second Advent: The Origin of the New Testament Doctrine*. 3rd ed. Eugene, OR: Wipf & Stock, 2009.

———. "The Second Advent—25 Years Later." *ExpTim* 82 (1971): 307–9.

———. "Theophany and Parousia." *NTS* 34 (1988): 259–70.

Gnilka, Joachim. *Das Evangelium nach Markus*. 2 vols. Benziger: Neukirchener Verlag, 1978–1979.

———. *Jesus of Nazareth: Message and History*. Translated by Siegfried S. Schatzmann. Peabody, MA: Hendrickson, 1997.

———. "Wie urteilte Jesus über seinen Tod?" Pages 13–50 in *Der Tod Jesu*. Edited by Johannes Beutler and Karl Kertelge. QD 74. Freiburg: Herder, 1976.

Goff, Matthew. "The Mystery of God's Wisdom, the Parousia of a Messiah, and Visions of Heavenly Paradise." Pages 175–92 in *The Jewish Apocalyptic Tradition and the Shaping of New Testament Thought*. Edited by Benjamin E. Reynolds and Loren T. Stuckenbruck. Minneapolis: Fortress, 2017.

Goldingay, John. *Daniel*. WBC 30. Dallas: Word, 1989.

Goodacre, Mark. *The Case against Q: Studies in Markan Priority and the Synoptic Problem*. Harrisburg, PA: Trinity, 2002.

———. "Missing Pieces." Pages 113–27 in *The Next Quest for the Historical Jesus*. Edited by James Crossley and Chris Keith. Grand Rapids: Eerdmans, 2024.

———. "The Orthodox Redaction of Mark: How Matthew Rescued Mark's Reputation." Pages 319–36 in *"To Recover What Has Been Lost": Essays on Eschatology, Intertextuality, and Reception History in Honor of Dale C. Allison Jr*. Edited by Tucker S. Ferda, Daniel Frayer-Griggs, and Nathan C. Johnson. NovTSup 183. Leiden: Brill, 2021.

———. *Thomas and the Gospels: The Case for Thomas's Familiarity with the Synoptics*. Grand Rapids: Eerdmans, 2012.

Goodrich, John K. "Until the Fullness of the Gentiles Comes In: A Critical Review of Recent Scholarship on the Salvation of 'All Israel' (Romans 11:26)." *JSPL* 6 (2016): 5–32.

Goppelt, Leonhard. *Jesu Wirken in seiner theologischen Bedeutung*. Göttingen: Vandenhoeck & Ruprecht, 1976.

Grabbe, Lester L. "'Son of Man': Its Origin and Meaning in Second Temple Judaism." Pages 169–98 in *Enoch and the Synoptic Gospels: Reminiscences, Allusions, Intertextuality*. Edited by Loren T. Stuckenbruck and Gabriele Boccaccini. EJL 44. Atlanta: SBL Press, 2016.

Grant, Frederick C. *The Gospel of the Kingdom*. New York: Macmillan, 1940.

Grant, Robert M. "The Coming of the Kingdom." *JBL* 67 (1948): 297–303.
———. *The Earliest Lives of Jesus*. London: SPCK, 1961.
———. *Gnosticism and Early Christianity*. New York: Columbia University Press, 1959.
Grass, Hans. "Zur Frage der Wiederkunft Christi." Pages 136–47 in *Altes Testament und christliche Verkündigung: Festschrift für Antonius H. J. Gunneweg zum 65. Geburtstag*. Edited by Antonius H. J. Gunneweg, Manfred Oeming, and Axel Graupner. Köln: Kohlhammer, 1987.
Grässer, Erich. *Das Problem der Parusieverzögerung in den synoptischen Evangelien und in der Apostelgeschichte*. 3rd ed. Berlin: de Gruyter, 1977.
Gray, Patrick. *Paul as a Problem in History and Culture: The Apostle and His Critics through the Centuries*. Grand Rapids: Baker Books, 2016.
Green, Joel B. *The Theology of the Gospel of Luke*. Cambridge: Cambridge University Press, 1991.
Green, William Scott. "Messiah in Judaism: Rethinking the Question." Pages 1–13 in *Judaisms and Their Messiahs at the Turn of the Christian Era*. Edited by Jacob Neusner, William Scott Green, and Ernest S. Frerichs. Cambridge: Cambridge University Press, 1987.
Greeven, Heinrich. "Kirche und Parusie Christi." *KD* 10 (1964): 113–35.
Gregg, Brian Han. *The Historical Jesus and the Final Judgment Sayings in Q*. WUNT 2/207. Tübingen: Mohr Siebeck, 2006.
Gregory, Andrew F., and C. Kavin Rowe, eds. *Rethinking the Unity and Reception of Luke and Acts*. Columbia: University of South Carolina Press, 2010.
Grelot, Pierre. "Les Versions grecques de Daniel." *Bib* 47 (1966): 383–91.
Gribben, Crawford. *Evangelical Millennialism in the Trans-Atlantic World, 1500–2000*. New York: Palgrave Macmillan, 2011.
Grindheim, Sigurd. *God's Equal: What Can We Know about Jesus' Self-Understanding in the Synoptic Gospels?* LNTS 446. London: T&T Clark International, 2011.
Grotius, Hugo. *The Truth of the Christian Religion, with Jean Le Clerc's Notes and Additions*. Translated by John Clarke. Edited by Maria Rosa Antognazza. Indianapolis: Liberty Fund, 2012.
Guelich, Robert A. *Mark 1–8:26*. WBC 34A. Dallas: Word, 1982.
Guignebert, Charles. *Jesus*. Translated by S. H. Hooke. New York: Knopf, 1935.
Gundry, Robert H. *Mark: A Commentary on His Apology for the Cross*. Grand Rapids: Eerdmans, 1993.
———. *Matthew: A Commentary on His Handbook for a Mixed Church under Persecution*. Grand Rapids: Eerdmans, 1994.
Gurtner, Daniel M. "Danielic Influence at the Intersection of Matthew and the Dead Sea Scrolls." Pages 27–54 in *Matthew within Judaism: Israel and the Nations in*

the First Gospel. Edited by Anders Runesson and Daniel M. Gurtner. ECL 27. Atlanta: SBL Press, 2020.

Guttenberger, Gundrun. "Zur Hermeneutik des Markusevangeliums." *ZNT* 47 (2021): 107–26.

Haacker, K. B. "Der Geist und das Reich im Lukanischen Werk: Konkurrenz oder Konvergenz zwischen Pneumatologie und Eschatologie?" *NTS* 59 (2013): 325–45.

Hadorn, Wilhelm. *Zukunft und Hoffnung: Grundzüge einer Lehre von der christlichen Hoffnung*. Gütersloh: Bertelsmann, 1914.

Haenchen, Ernst. *A Commentary on the Gospel of John: Chapters 1–6*. Hermeneia. Translated by Robert W. Funk. Philadelphia: Fortress, 1984.

Hägerland, Tobias. "The Future of Criteria in Historical Jesus Research." *JSHJ* 13 (2015): 1–23.

———. "Jesus and the Scriptures—Problems of Authentication and Interpretation." Pages 3–32 in *Jesus and the Scriptures: Problems, Passages and Patterns*. Edited by Tobias Hägerland. LNTS 552. London: Bloomsbury T&T Clark, 2016.

———. "The Role of the Disciples in the Prophetic Mission of Jesus." Pages 177–202 in *The Mission of Jesus*. Edited by Samuel Byrskog and Tobias Hägerland. WUNT 2/391. Tübingen: Mohr Siebeck, 2015.

Hagner, Donald. *Matthew*. 2 vols. WBC 33. Dallas: Word, 1993–1995.

Hahn, Ferdinand. "Die Rede von der Parusie des Menschensohnes Markus 13." Pages 240–66 in *Jesus der Menschensohn*. Edited by Rudolf Pesch and Rudolf Schnackenburg. Freiburg: Herder, 1975.

———. *The Titles of Jesus in Christology*. Translated by Harold Knight and George Ogg. London: Lutterworth, 1969.

Hailperin, Herman. *Rashi and the Christian Scholars*. Pittsburgh: University of Pittsburgh Press, 1963.

Hamilton, James M., Jr. "The Typology of David's Rise to Power: Messianic Patterns in the Book of Samuel." *SBJT* 16 (2012): 4–25.

Hampel, Volker. "Ihr werdet mit den Städten Israels nicht zu Ende kommen." *TZ* 45 (1989): 1–31.

———. *Menschensohn und historischer Jesus: Ein Rätselwort als Schlüssel zum messianischen Selbstverständnis Jesu*. Neukirchen-Vluyn: Neukirchener Verlag, 1990.

Hanna, William. *The Life of Christ*. New York: Carter, 1883.

Hannah, Darrell D. "The Elect Son of Man in the Parables of Enoch." Pages 130–58 in *'Who Is This Son of Man?' The Latest Scholarship on a Puzzling Expression of the Historical Jesus*. Edited by Larry W. Hurtado and Paul L. Owen. LNTS 390. London: Bloomsbury T&T Clark, 2011.

Harder, Günther. "Das eschatologische Geschichtsbild der sogenannten kleinen Apokalypse Markus 13." *ThViat* 4 (1952): 71–107.

Harding, Mark. "Apocalypticism in the Pastoral Epistles." Pages 259–76 in *The Jewish*

Apocalyptic Tradition and the Shaping of New Testament Thought. Edited by Benjamin E. Reynolds and Loren T. Stuckenbruck. Minneapolis: Fortress, 2017.

Harnack, Adolf von. "Die Verklärungsgeschichte Jesu, der Bericht des Paulus (I. Kor 15,3ff) und die beiden Christusvisionen des Petrus." Pages 89–117 in *Zur neutestamentlichen Überlieferung von der Auferstehung Jesu*. Edited by Paul Hoffmann. Darmstadt: Wissenschaftliche Buchgesellschaft, 1988.

Harriman, K. R. "A Synthetic Proposal about the Corinthian Resurrection Deniers." *NovT* 62 (2020): 190–200.

Harrington, Daniel J. "Afterlife Expectations in Pseudo-Philo, 4 Ezra, and 2 Baruch, and Their Implications for the New Testament." Pages 21–34 in *Resurrection in the New Testament: Festschrift for J. Lambrecht*. Edited by Reimund Bieringer. Leuven: Leuven University Press, 2002.

———. *The Gospel of Matthew*. SP 1. Collegeville, MN: Liturgical Press, 1991.

Harris, Mark. "The Comings and Goings of the Son of Man: Is Matthew's Risen Jesus 'Present' or 'Absent'?" *BibInt* 22 (2014): 51–70.

Harris, Murray J. "2 Corinthians 5:1–10: Watershed in Paul's Eschatology?" *TynBul* 22 (1971): 32–57.

Hartman, Lars. *Prophecy Interpreted: The Formation of Some Jewish Apocalyptic Texts and of the Eschatological Discourse Mark 13 Par.* Lund: Gleerup, 1966.

Harvey, Anthony E. *Jesus and the Constraints of History*. Philadelphia: Westminster, 1982.

Hatina, Thomas R. "The Focus of Mark 13:24–27: The Parousia, or the Destruction of the Temple?" *BBR* 6 (1996): 43–66.

Haufe, Günter. "Reich Gottes bei Paulus und in der Jesustradition." *NTS* 31 (1985): 467–72.

Hawthorne, Martin, and Ralph P. Martin. *Philippians*. Rev. ed. WBC 43. Grand Rapids: Zondervan Academic, 2015.

Hay, David M. *Glory at the Right Hand: Psalm 110 in Early Christianity.* Nashville: Abingdon, 1973.

Hayes, John H. "The Resurrection as Enthronement in the Earliest Church Christology." *Int* 22 (1968): 333–45.

Hays, Christopher M., with Brandon Gallaher, Richard J. Ounsworth, Julia S. Konstantinovsky, and C. A. Stine. *When the Son of Man Didn't Come: A Constructive Proposal on the Delay of the Parousia*. Minneapolis: Fortress, 2016.

Hays, Richard B. *The Conversion of the Imagination: Paul as Interpreter of Israel's Scripture*. Grand Rapids: Eerdmans, 2005.

———. *Echoes of Scripture in the Gospels*. Waco, TX: Baylor University Press, 2016.

———. *Echoes of Scripture in the Letters of Paul*. New Haven: Yale University Press, 1989.

———. *The Moral Vision of the New Testament: Community, Cross, New Creation*. San Francisco: HarperSanFrancisco, 1996.

Hayward, Robert. "Phinehas—the Same as Elijah: The Origins of a Rabbinic Tradition." *JJS* 29 (1978): 22–34.

Hegel, G. W. F. *Three Essays, 1793–1795: The Tübingen Essay, Berne Fragments, the Life of Jesus*. Edited and translated by Peter Fuss and John Dobbins. Notre Dame: University of Notre Dame Press, 1984.

Heil, John Paul. "Final Parables in the Eschatological Discourse in Matthew 24–25." Pages 177–209 in *Matthew's Parables: Audience-Oriented Perspectives*. Edited by Warren Carter and John Paul Heil. Washington, DC: Catholic Biblical Association of America, 1998.

Heil, Uta. "Theologische Interpretation von 1 Kor 15, 23–28." *ZNW* 84 (1993): 27–35.

Hengel, Martin. "Abba, Maranatha, Hosanna und die Anfänge der Christologie." Pages 496–534 in *Studien zur Christologie*. Vol. 4 of *Kleine Schriften*. Edited by Claus-Jürgen Thornton. WUNT 201. Tübingen: Mohr Siebeck, 2006.

———. "Messianische Hoffnung und politischer Radikalismus in der jüdisch-hellenistischen Diaspora: Zur Frage der Voraussetzungen des judischen Aufstands unter Trajan 115–117 n. Chr." Pages 655–86 in *Apocalypticism in the Mediterranean World and the Near East*. Edited by David Hellholm. Tübingen: Mohr Siebeck, 1983.

———. *Studies in Early Christology*. Edinburgh: T&T Clark, 1995.

Hengel, Martin, and Anna Maria Schwemer. *Der Messianische Anspruch Jesu und die Anfänge der Christologie*. WUNT 138. Tübingen: Mohr Siebeck, 2001.

Henneken, B. *Verkündigung und Prophetie im Ersten Thessalonicherbrief*. SBS 29. Stuttgart: Katholisches Bibelwerk, 1969.

Henry, Matthew. *Commentary on the Whole Bible*. Edited by Leslie F. Church. Grand Rapids: Zondervan, 1960.

Henze, Matthias. *Jewish Apocalypticism in Late First Century Israel: Reading Second Baruch in Context*. TSAJ 142. Tübingen: Mohr Siebeck, 2011.

———. "Torah and Eschatology in the Syriac Apocalypse of Baruch." Pages 201–15 in *The Significance of Sinai: Traditions about Sinai and Divine Revelation in Judaism and Christianity*. Edited by George Brooke, Hindy Najman, and Loren Stuckenbruck. TBN 12. Leiden: Brill, 2008.

Herbert, Edward. *De Veritate*. London: Routledge, 1992.

Herder, Johann. *Vom Erlöser der Menschen nach unsern drei ersten Evangelien*. Riga: Hartknoch, 1796.

Herzog, W. R. *Prophet and Teacher: An Introduction to the Historical Jesus*. Louisville: Westminster John Knox, 2005.

Heschel, Susannah. *Abraham Geiger and the Jewish Jesus*. Chicago: University of Chicago Press, 1998.

———. *The Aryan Jesus: Christian Theologians and the Bible in Nazi Germany*. Princeton: Princeton University Press, 2008.

Hess, Johann Jakob. *Lebensgeschichte Jesu*. 3 vols. Zurich: Drell, Fußli, 1822.

Hewitt, J. Thomas. *Messiah and Scripture*. WUNT 2/522. Tübingen: Mohr Siebeck, 2020.

Hicks-Keeton, Jill. "Already/Not Yet: Eschatological Tension in the Book of Tobit." *JBL* 132 (2013): 97–117.

Hiers, Richard H. "The Day of the Lord," *ABD* 2:82–83.

———. *The Historical Jesus and the Kingdom of God: Present and Future in the Message and Ministry of Jesus*. Gainesville: University of Florida Press, 1973.

———. *Jesus and the Future: Unresolved Questions for Understanding and Faith*. Atlanta: John Knox, 1981.

Hill, Charles E. "Paul's Understanding of Christ's Kingdom in 1 Corinthians 15:20–28." *NovT* 30 (1988): 297–320.

———. *Regnum Caelorum: Patterns of Millennial Thought in Early Christianity*. 2nd ed. Grand Rapids: Eerdmans, 2001.

Hillerbrand, Hans J. "The Decline and Fall of the True Christian Church: The English Deist View." *ZRGG* 60 (2008): 97–110.

Himmelfarb, Martha. *Between Temple and Torah: Essays on Priests, Scribes, and Visionaries in the Second Temple Period and Beyond*. TSAJ 151. Tübingen: Mohr Siebeck, 2013.

Hochschild, Ralph. "Eschatologischer Prophet oder 'Non-Eschatological Jesus'? Wissenschaftssoziologische Überlegungen zur Rezeption von Johannes Weiß: 'Die Predigt Jesu vom Reiche Gottes.'" Pages 411–28 in *Jesus—Gestalt und Gestaltungen: Rezeptionen des Galiläers in Wissenschaft, Kirke und Gesellschaft; Festschrift fur Gerd Theißen zum 70. Geburtstag*. Edited by Petra von Gemünden, David G. Horrell, and Max Küchler. NTOA 100. Göttingen: Vandenhoeck & Ruprecht, 2013.

Hoffmann, Jean G. H. *Les vies de Jésus et le Jésus de l'histoire: Étude de la valeur historique des vies de Jésus de langue française, non catholiques, d'Ernest Renan à Charles Guignebert*. Paris: Prostant apud Messageries Évangéliques, 1947.

Hoffmann, Paul. "Der Menschensohn in Lukas 12:8." *NTS* 44 (1998): 357–79.

———. *Studien zur Theologie der Logienquelle*. 3rd ed. Münster: Aschendorff, 1982.

Hoffmann, R. Joseph, ed. and trans. *Porphyry's* Against the Christians*: The Literary Remains*. Amherst: Prometheus Books, 1994.

Hogan, Karina. "The Apocalyptic Eschatology of Romans: Creation, Judgment, Resurrection, and Glory." Pages 155–74 in *The Jewish Apocalyptic Tradition and the Shaping of New Testament Thought*. Edited by Benjamin E. Reynolds and Loren T. Stuckenbruck. Minneapolis: Fortress, 2017.

Hogeterp, Albert. *Expectations of the End*. STDJ 83. Leiden: Brill, 2009.

Holbach, Paul Tiry d'. *Ecce Homo! or, A Critical Inquiry into the History of Jesus Christ*. 2nd ed. London: Eaton, 1813.

Holladay, Carl R. *Acts: A Commentary*. NTL. Louisville: Westminster John Knox, 2016.

Hollander, Harm W., and Marinus de Jonge. *The Testaments of the Twelve Patriarchs: A Commentary*. Leiden: Brill, 1985.

Holleman, Joost. *Resurrection and Parousia: A Traditio-Historical Study of Paul's Eschatology in 1 Corinthians 15*. NovTSup 84. Leiden: Brill, 1996.

Holmén, Tom. "Authenticity Criteria." Pages 43–54 in *Encyclopedia of the Historical Jesus*. Edited by Craig A. Evans. New York: Routledge, 2008.

———. "An Introduction to the Continuum Approach." Pages 1–16 in *Jesus from Judaism to Christianity: Continuum Approaches to the Historical Jesus*. Edited by Tom Holmén. LNTS 352. London: T&T Clark, 2007.

———. "Seven Theses on the So-Called Criteria of Authenticity of Historical Jesus Research." *RCT* 33 (2008): 343–76.

Holtz, Traugott. "Paul and the Oral Gospel Tradition." Pages 380–93 in *Jesus in the Oral Gospel Tradition*. Edited by Henry Wansbrough. JSNTSup 64. Sheffield: Sheffield Academic, 1991.

Holtzmann, H. J. *Sammlung Theologischer Lehrbücher: Neutestamentliche Theologie*. Freiburg: Mohr, 1897.

Holtzmann, Oscar. *The Life of Jesus*. Translated by J. T. Bealby and Maurice A. Canney. London: Black, 1904.

Hooker, Morna. "Foreword: Forty Years On." Pages xii–xvii in *Jesus, Criteria, and the Demise of Authenticity*. Edited by Chris Keith and Anthony Le Donne. London: T&T Clark, 2012.

———. *Jesus and the Servant*. London: SPCK, 1959.

———. "On Using the Wrong Tool." *Theology* 75 (1972): 570–81.

———. "Philippians 2:6–11." Pages 151–64 in *Jesus und Paulus: Festschrift für W. G. Kümmel*. Edited by E. E. Ellis and Erich Grässer. Göttingen: Vandenhoeck & Ruprecht, 1975.

———. *The Son of Man in Mark*. London: SPCK, 1967.

Horbury, William. *Jewish Messianism and the Cult of Christ*. London: SCM, 1998.

———. *Jews and Christians: In Contact and Controversy*. Edinburgh: T&T Clark, 2006.

———. "The Messianic Associations of 'The Son of Man.'" *JTS* 36 (1985): 34–55.

———. *Messianism among Jews and Christians: Biblical and Historical Studies*. 2nd ed. London: Bloomsbury T&T Clark, 2016.

———. "The New Testament and Rabbinic Study: An Historical Sketch." Pages 1–40 in *The New Testament and Rabbinic Literature*. Edited by R. Bieringer. Leiden: Brill, 2010.

Horsley, Richard. *The Prophet Jesus and the Renewal of Israel: Moving beyond a Divisionary Debate*. Grand Rapids: Eerdmans, 2012.

———. *You Shall Not Bow Down and Serve Them: The Political Economic Projects of Jesus and Paul*. Eugene, OR: Cascade, 2021.

Howes, Llewellyn. *Judging Q and Saving Jesus: Q's Contribution to the Wisdom-Apocalypticism Debate in Historical Jesus Studies.* Durbanville: AOSIS, 2015.

Hull, John. *Saint Peters Prophesie of These Last Daies: Discovering the Iniquity of the Time, and Atheisme of the Age.* London: Paules, 1610.

Hultgren, Arland J. *The Parables of Jesus: A Commentary.* Grand Rapids: Eerdmans, 2000.

Hume, David. "Of Superstition and Enthusiasm." Pages 144–49 in vol. 3 of *The Philosophical Works of David Hume.* Edited by T. H. Green and T. H. Grose. 4 vols. London: Longmans, Green, 1875.

Hurtado, Larry. "Interactive Diversity: A Proposed Model of Christian Origins." *JTS* 64 (2013): 445–62.

———. *One God, One Lord: Early Christian Devotion and Ancient Jewish Monotheism.* 3rd ed. London: Bloomsbury T&T Clark, 2015.

Ingolfsland, Dennis. "Kloppenborg's Stratification of Q and Its Significance for Historical Jesus Studies." *JETS* 46 (2003): 217–32.

Instone-Brewer, David. "The Eighteen Benedictions and the Minim before 70 CE." *JTS* 54 (2003): 25–44.

Israel, Jonathan I. *Radical Enlightenment: Philosophy and the Making of Modernity 1650–1750.* Oxford: Oxford University Press, 2001.

Jacob, Margaret C. "The Enlightenment Critique of Christianity." Pages 265–82 in *Enlightenment, Reawakening and Revolution 1660–1815.* Vol. 7 of *The Cambridge History of Christianity.* Edited by Stewart J. Brown and Timothy Tackett. Cambridge: Cambridge University Press, 2006.

Jacobsen, Anders-Christian. "Eschatology in Origen from Alexandria." Pages 435–46 in *Eschatology in Antiquity: Forms and Functions.* Edited by Hilary Marlow, Karla Pollmann, and Helen Van Noorden. London: Routledge, 2021.

Jacobson, Arland D. "The Literary Unity of Q." *JBL* 101 (1982): 365–89.

Jason, Mark A. *Repentance at Qumran: The Penitential Framework of Religious Experience in the Dead Sea Scrolls.* Minneapolis: Fortress, 2015.

Jefferson, Thomas. *The Jefferson Bible: With the Annotated Commentaries on Religion of Thomas Jefferson.* Edited by O. I. A. Roche. New York: Potter, 1964.

Jennings, Mark. "The Fourth Gospel's Reversal of Mark in John 13:31–14:3." *Bib* 94 (2013): 210–36.

Jeremias, Joachim. "Die Drei-Tage-Worte der Evangelien." Pages 221–30 in *Tradition und Glaube: Das Frühe Christentum in seiner Umwelt; Festschrift für Karl Georg Kuhn.* Edited by Gert Jeremias, Heinz Wolfgang Kuhn, and Hartmut Stegemann. Göttingen: Vandenhoeck & Ruprecht, 1971.

———. *The Eucharistic Words of Jesus.* 3rd ed. London: SCM, 1966.

———. "Flesh and Blood Cannot Inherit the Kingdom of God." *NTS* 2 (1955–1956): 151–59.

———. *New Testament Theology: The Proclamation of Jesus*. Translated by John Bowden. New York: Scribner's Sons, 1971.

———. *The Parables of Jesus*. Translated by S. H. Hooke. 2nd ed. New York: Scribner's Sons, 1972.

———. *Unknown Sayings of Jesus*. Translated by R. H. Fuller. 2nd ed. London: SPCK, 1964.

Jewett, Robert. *Romans: A Commentary*. Hermeneia. Minneapolis: Fortress, 2007.

Jipp, Joshua W. *The Messianic Theology of the New Testament*. Grand Rapids: Eerdmans, 2020.

Joest, Wilfried. "Die Kirche und die Parusie Jesu Christi." Pages 536–50 in vol. 1 of *Gott in Welt: Festgabe für Karl Rahner*. Edited by Johannes Baptist Metz, Walter Kern, Adolf Darlapp, and Herbert Vorgrimler. 2 vols. Freiburg: Herder, 1964.

Johnson, Luke Timothy. *The Real Jesus: The Misguided Quest for the Historical Jesus and the Truth of the Traditional Gospels*. San Francisco: HarperSanFrancisco, 1996.

Johnson, Nathan C. "Survival of Popular Movements." Pages 541–56 in *The Next Quest for the Historical Jesus*. Edited by James Crossley and Chris Keith. Grand Rapids: Eerdmans, 2024.

Johnston, George. "'Kingdom of God' Sayings in Paul's Letters." Pages 143–56 in *From Jesus to Paul: Studies in Honour of Francis Wright Beare*. Edited by Peter Richardson and John C. Hurd. Waterloo, ON: Wilfrid Laurier University Press, 1984.

Jonge, Henk Jan de. "Les Origines Historique de l'Attente du Retour de Jesus." *ETR* 74 (1999): 491–504.

———. "The Sayings on Confessing and Denying Jesus in Q 12:8–9 and Mark 8:38." Pages 105–21 in *Sayings of Jesus: Canonical and Non-canonical*. Edited by William L. Petersen. NovTSup 89. Leiden: Brill, 1997.

Jonge, Marinus de. *God's Final Envoy: Early Christology and Jesus' Own View of His Mission*. Grand Rapids: Eerdmans, 1998.

———. *Jesus, the Servant Messiah*. New Haven: Yale University Press, 1991.

———. *Jewish Eschatology, Early Christian Christology, and the Testaments of the Twelve Patriarchs*. NovTSup 63. Leiden: Brill, 1991.

Joynes, Christine E. "The Returned Elijah? John the Baptist's Angelic Identity in the Gospel of Mark." *SJT* 58 (2005): 455–67.

Juel, Donald H. *Messianic Exegesis: Christological Interpretation of the Old Testament in Early Christianity*. Philadelphia: Fortress, 1988.

Justnes, Årstein. *The Time of Salvation: An Analysis of 4QApocryphon of Daniel ar (4Q246), 4QMessianic Apocalypse (4Q521 2), and 4QTime of Righteousness (4Q215a)*. Frankfurt: Lang, 2009.

Juza, Ryan P. "One of the Days of the Son of Man: A Reconsideration of Luke 17:22." *JBL* 135 (2016): 575–95.

Kammler, H.-C. *Christologie und Eschatologie: Joh 5, 17–30 als Schlüsseltext johanneischer Theologie*. WUNT 126. Tübingen: Mohr Siebeck, 2000.

Kant, Immanuel. *Religion within the Limits of Reason Alone*. Translated by Theodore M. Greene and Hoyt H. Hudson. New York: Harper, 1960.

Käsemann, Ernst. "Das Problem des Historischen Jesus." *ZTK* 51 (1954): 125–53.

———. "Die Anfänge christlicher Theologie." *ZTK* 57 (1960): 162–85.

———. *New Testament Questions of Today*. London: SCM, 1969.

Katz, David S. *God's Last Words: Reading the English Bible from the Reformation to Fundamentalism*. New Haven: Yale University Press, 2004.

Kazen, Thomas. "The Coming Son of Man Revisited." *JSHJ* 5 (2007): 155–74.

———. *Scripture, Interpretation, or Authority? Motives and Arguments in Jesus' Halakic Conflicts*. WUNT 320. Tübingen: Mohr Siebeck, 2014.

Keener, Craig S. *Acts*. NCBC. Cambridge: Cambridge University Press, 2020.

———. *Christobiography: Memory, History, and the Reliability of the Gospels*. Grand Rapids: Eerdmans, 2019.

———. *The Gospel of John: A Commentary*. 2 vols. Peabody, MA: Hendricksen, 2003.

———. *The Historical Jesus of the Gospels*. Grand Rapids: Eerdmans, 2009.

Keim, Theodor. *The History of Jesus of Nazara, Freely Investigated in Its Connection with the National Life of Israel, and Related in Detail*. Translated by Arthur Ransom. 2nd ed. 6 vols. London: Williams & Norgate, 1876–1883.

Keith, Chris. *The Gospel as Manuscript: An Early History of the Jesus Tradition as Material Artifact*. Oxford: Oxford University Press, 2020.

———. "The Indebtedness of the Criteria Approach to Form Criticism and Recent Attempts to Rehabilitate the Search for an Authentic Jesus." Pages 25–48 in *Jesus, Criteria, and the Demise of Authenticity*. Edited by Chris Keith and Anthony Le Donne. London: T&T Clark, 2012.

———. "The Narratives of the Gospels and the Historical Jesus: Current Debates, Prior Debates and the Goal of Historical Jesus Research." *JSNT* 38 (2016): 426–55.

Kelber, Werner H. *The Kingdom in Mark*. Philadelphia: Fortress, 1974.

Kellermann, Ulrich. *Auferstehung in den Himmel: 2 Makk 7 und die Auferstehung der Martyrer*. SBS 95. Stuttgart: Katholisches Bibelwerk, 1978.

Keown, Mark. "An Imminent Parousia and Christian Mission: Did the New Testament Writers Really Expect Jesus' Return?" Pages 242–63 in *Christian Origins and the Establishment of the Early Jesus Movement*. Edited by Stanley E. Porter and Andrew W. Pitts. TENTS 12. Leiden: Brill, 2018.

Kidner, Derek. *Psalms 73–150*. Downers Grove, IL: InterVarsity Press, 2014.

Kiel, Micah D. "The Open Horizon of Mark 13." *JBL* 136 (2017): 145–62.

Kilgallen, John J. "Jesus' First Trial: Messiah and Son of God (Luke 22,66–71)." *Bib* 80 (1999): 401–14.

Kim, Seyoon. "The Jesus Tradition in 1 Thess 4.13–5.11." *NTS* 48 (2002): 225–42.

———. "Paul as an Eschatological Herald." Pages 9–24 in *Paul as Missionary: Identity, Activity, Theology, and Practice*. Edited by Trevor J. Burke and Brian S. Rosner. LNTS 420. London: Bloomsbury T&T Clark, 2011.

———. *"The Son of Man" as the Son of God*. WUNT 30. Tübingen: Mohr Siebeck, 1983.

Kim, Yoonjong. *The Divine-Human Relationship in Romans 1–8 in the Light of Interdependence Theory*. LNTS 635. London: Bloomsbury T&T Clark, 2020.

Kim, Young Ho. *Die Parusie bei Lukas: Eine literarisch-exegetische Untersuchung zu den Parusieaussagen im lukanischen Doppelwerk*. BZNW 217. Berlin: de Gruyter, 2016.

Kimelman, Reuven. "The Messiah of the Amidah: A Study in Comparative Messianism." *JBL* 116 (1997): 313–24.

Kimondo, Stephen S. *The Gospel of Mark and the Roman-Jewish War of 66–70 CE: Jesus' Story as a Contrast to the Events of the War*. Eugene, OR: Pickwick, 2018.

Kinman, Brent. "Parousia, Jesus' 'A-Triumphal' Entry, and the Fate of Jerusalem (Luke 19:28–44)." *JBL* 118 (1999): 279–94.

Kippenberg, Hans. "Dann wird der Orient herrschen und der Okzident Dienen." Pages 40–48 in *Spiegel und Gleichnis: Festschrift für Jacob Taubes*. Edited by Norbert W. Bolz and Wolfgang Hübner. Würzburg: Königshausen & Neumann, 1983.

Kirk, Alan, and Tom Thatcher, eds. *Memory, Tradition, and Text: Uses of the Past in Early Christianity*. SemeiaSt 52. Atlanta: Society of Biblical Literature, 2005.

Kirk, David R. "Heaven Opened: Intertextuality and Meaning in John 1:51." *TynBul* 63 (2012): 237–56.

Kirk, J. R. Daniel. *A Man Attested by God: The Human Jesus of the Synoptic Gospels*. Grand Rapids: Eerdmans, 2016.

———. "Why Does the Deliverer Come ἐκ Σιών (Romans 11.26)?" *JSNT* 33 (2010): 81–99.

Kissinger, Warren S. *The Lives of Jesus: A History and Bibliography*. New York: Garland, 1985.

———. *The Parables of Jesus: A History of Interpretation and Bibliography*. Metuchen: Scarecrow, 1979.

Klancher, Nancy. "A Genealogy for Reception History." *BibInt* 21 (2013): 99–129.

Klassen, Walter. *Living at the End of the Ages: Apocalyptic Expectation in the Radical Reformation*. Lanham, MD: University Press of America, 1992.

Klausner, Joseph. *Jesus of Nazareth: His Life, Times, and Teaching*. Translated by Herbert Danby. London: Allen & Unwin, 1925.

———. *The Messianic Idea in Israel: From Its Beginning to the Completion of the Mishnah*. 3rd ed. Translated by W. F. Stinespring. New York: Macmillan, 1955.

Klepper, Deena Copeland. *The Insight of Unbelievers: Nicholas of Lyra and Christian*

Reading of Jewish Text in the Later Middle Ages. Philadelphia: University of Pennsylvania Press, 2007.

Klijn, A. F. J., ed. *Der lateinische Text der Apokalypse des Esra*. TUGAL 131. Berlin: Akademie-Verlag, 1983.

Kloppenborg, John S. "As One Unknown, without a Name? Co-opting the Apocalyptic Jesus." Pages 1–23 in *Apocalypticism, Anti-Semitism and the Historical Jesus: Subtexts in Criticism*. Edited by John S. Kloppenborg with John W. Marshall. London: T&T Clark International, 2006.

———. "'Evocatio Deorum' and the Date of Mark." *JBL* 124 (2005): 419–50.

Kloppenborg, John S. *Excavating Q: The History and Setting of the Sayings Gospel*. Minneapolis: Fortress, 2000.

———. *The Formation of Q: Trajectories in Ancient Wisdom Collections*. 2nd ed. Minneapolis: Fortress, 2007.

———. "On Dispensing with Q? Goodacre on the Relation of Luke to Matthew." *NTS* 49 (2003): 210–36.

———. "The Sayings Gospel Q and the Quest of the Historical Jesus." *HTR* 89 (1996): 307–44.

———. "Symbolic Eschatology and the Apocalypticism of Q." Pages 157–78 in *Synoptic Problems*. Edited by John S. Kloppenborg. WUNT 329. Tübingen: Mohr Siebeck, 2014.

Knibb, Michael. *The Qumran Community*. Cambridge: Cambridge University Press, 1987.

Knight, Jonathan. *Jesus: An Historical and Theological Investigation*. London: T&T Clark, 2004.

Knohl, Israel. *Messiahs and Resurrection in the Gabriel Revelation*. London: Continuum, 2009.

Knowles, Michael. *Jeremiah in Matthew's Gospel: The Rejected-Prophet Motif in Matthean Redaction*. JSNTSup 68. Sheffield: Sheffield Academic, 1993.

Knox, W. L. *St. Paul*. New York: Appleton, 1932.

Koch, Dietrich-Alex. "Inhaltliche Gliederung und geographischer Aufriss im Markusevangelium." *NTS* 29 (1983): 145–66.

Koch, Klaus. *Das Buch Daniel*. EdF 144. Darmstadt: Wissenschaftliche Buchgesellschaft, 1980.

———. "Messias und Menschensohn: Die zweistufige Messianologie der jüngeren Apokalyptik." *Jahrbuch für Biblische Theologie* 8 (1993): 73–102.

———. *The Rediscovery of Apocalyptic: A Polemical Work on a Neglected Area of Biblical Studies and Its Damaging Effects on Theology and Philosophy*. Naperville, IL: Allenson, 1972.

Koester, Helmut. *Ancient Christian Gospels*. Philadelphia: Trinity International, 1990.

———. "GNOMAI DIAPHOROI: The Origin and Nature of Diversification in the

History of Early Christianity." Pages 114–57 in *Trajectories through Early Christianity*. Edited by Helmut Koester and James Robinson. Eugene, OR: Wipf & Stock, 2006.

Konradt, Matthias. *Israel, Church, and the Gentiles in the Gospel of Matthew*. Waco, TX: Baylor University Press, 2014.

Korn, Manfred. *Die Geschichte Jesu in veränderter Zeit: Studien zur bleibenden Bedeutung Jesu im lukanischen Doppelwerk*. WUNT 51. Tübingen: Mohr Siebeck, 1993.

Kosch, Daniel. "Die Gottesherrschaft erreicht das Jetzt: Eine Annäherung an Mk 1,15 und Lk 11,2 par Mt 6,10." *BK* 62 (2007): 85–88.

Köstenberger, Andreas J. *John*. BECNT. Grand Rapids: Baker Books, 2004.

Kraeling, Carl H. *John the Baptist*. New York: Scribner's Sons, 1951.

Kraynak, Robert P. "The Idea of the Messiah in the Theology of Thomas Hobbes." *JPSR* 4 (1992): 115–37.

Kreitzer, Larry J. *Jesus and God in Paul's Eschatology*. JSNTSup 19. London: Bloomsbury Academic, 2015.

Kreplin, Matthias. *Das Selbstverständnis Jesu: Hermeneutische und christologische Reflexion—historisch-kritische Analyse*. WUNT 2/141. Tübingen: Mohr Siebeck, 2001.

———. "The Self-Understanding of Jesus." Pages 2473–2516 in vol. 3 of *Handbook for the Study of the Historical Jesus*. Edited by Tom Holmén and Stanley Porter. Leiden: Brill, 2010.

Krewson, William L. *Jerome and the Jews: Innovative Supersessionism*. Eugene, OR: Wipf & Stock, 2017.

Kubis, Adam. *The Book of Zechariah in the Gospel of John*. EBib 64. Paris: Gabalda, 2012.

Kucicki, Janusz. *Eschatology of the Thessalonian Correspondence: A Comparative Study of 1 Thess 4,13–5,11 and 2 Thess 2,1–12 to the Dead Sea Scrolls and the Old Testament Pseudepigrapha*. Bern: Lang, 2014.

———. *The Function of the Speeches in the Acts of the Apostles: A Key to Interpretation of Luke's Use of Speeches in Acts*. Leiden: Brill, 2018.

Kugel, James. "The Jubilees Apocalypse." *DSD* 3 (1994): 322–37.

———. *Traditions of the Bible: A Guide to the Bible as It Was at the Start of the Common Era*. Cambridge: Harvard University Press, 1998.

Kuhn, Karl A. "The 'One like a Son of Man' Becomes the 'Son of God.'" *CBQ* 69 (2008): 22–42.

Kümmel, Werner Georg. *The New Testament: The History of the Investigation of Its Problems*. Translated by S. McLean Gilmour and Howard C. Kee. Nashville: Abingdon, 1972.

———. *Promise and Fulfillment: The Eschatological Message of Jesus*. Translated by Dorothea M. Barton. 2nd ed. London: SCM, 1961.

Künzi, Martin. *Das Naherwartungslogion Markus 9,1 par: Geschichte seiner Auslegung.* Tübingen: Mohr Siebeck, 1977.

Kwaak, H. van der. "Die Klage über Jerusalem (Matth. xxiii. 37–39)." *NovT* 8 (1966): 156–70.

Kwon, Yon-Gyong. *Eschatology in Galatians.* WUNT 183. Tübingen: Mohr Siebeck, 2004.

Kyle, Richard. *The Last Days Are Here Again: A History of the End Times.* Grand Rapids: Baker Books, 1998.

Laato, Timo. "Der ambivalente Stil und die Eschatologie des Neuen Testaments." *EC* 9 (2018): 83–106.

Lamb, William R. S., ed. and trans. *The* Catena in Marcum*: A Byzantine Anthology of Early Commentary on Mark.* Leiden: Brill, 2012.

Lambrecht, Jan. *Die Redaktion der Markus-Apokalypse: Literarische Analyse und Strukturuntersuchung.* Rome: Päpstliches Bibelinstitut, 1967.

———. "The Line of Thought in Matthew 24:1–35." *ETL* 84 (2008): 519–28.

———. "Naherwartung in Luke?" *ETL* 87 (2011): 425–31.

———. *Pauline Studies.* BETL 115. Leuven: Leuven University Press, 1994.

Landa, Paul J. "The Advent Hope in Early Christianity." Pages 65–95 in *The Advent Hope in Scripture and History.* Edited by V. Norskon Olsen. Washington, DC: Review & Herald, 1987.

Landmesser, Christof. "Die Entwicklung der paulinischen Theologie und die Frage nach der Eschatologie." Pages 173–94 in *Eschatologie—Eschatology: The Sixth Durham-Tübingen Research Symposium; Eschatology in Old Testament, Ancient Judaism and Early Christianity.* Edited by Hans-Joachim Eckstein, Christof Landmesser, and Hermann Lichtenberger. WUNT 272. Tübingen: Mohr Siebeck, 2011.

———. "Parusieverzögerung und die Gegenwart der Glaubenden: Zur Hermeneutik von Ambiguität und Ambivalenz der christlichen Existenz in der Theologie des Paulus." *EC* 9 (2018): 107–30.

Lang, F. G. "Kompositionsanalyse des Markusevangeliums." *ZTK* 74 (1977): 1–24.

Lapide, Cornelius à. *The Great Commentary.* 4th ed. 6 vols. Translated by Thomas W. Mossman. Edinburgh: Grant, 1890.

Larsen, Kevin W. "The Structure of Mark's Gospel: Current Proposals." *CurBR* 3 (2004): 140–60.

Larsen, Matthew D. C. *Gospels before the Book.* Oxford: Oxford University Press, 2018.

Laudan, Larry. *Progress and Its Problems: Towards a Theory of Scientific Growth.* Berkeley: University of California Press, 1977.

Laursen, John Christian. "Bayle's Anti-millenarianism: The Dangers of Those Who Claim to Know the Future." Pages 95–106 in *Continental Millenarians: Protestants, Catholics, Heretics.* Vol. 4 of *Millenarianism and Messianism in Early*

Modern European Culture. Edited by John Christian Laursen and Richard H. Popkin. IAHI 176. Dordrecht: Kluwer, 2001.

Law, David R. "Matthew's Enigmatic Reference to Jeremiah in Mt 16,14." Pages 280–86 in *The Book of Jeremiah and Its Reception*. BETL 128. Leuven: Leuven University Press, 1997.

Law, Edmund. *Considerations on the State of the World with Regard to the Theory of Religion*. Cambridge: Bentham, 1745.

Lawson, John. *The Biblical Theology of St. Irenaeus*. London: Epworth, 1948.

Le Donne, Anthony. "The Criterion of Coherence: Its Development, Inevitability, and Historiographical Limitations." Pages 95–114 in *Jesus, Criteria, and the Demise of Authenticity*. Edited by Chris Keith and Anthony Le Donne. London: T&T Clark, 2012.

———. *The Historiographical Jesus: Memory, Typology, and the Son of David*. Waco, TX: Baylor University Press, 2009.

———. "The Problem of Selectivity in Memory Research: A Response to Zeba Crook." *JSHJ* 11 (2013): 77–97.

———. "The Quest for the Historical Jesus: A Revisionist History through the Lens of Jewish-Christian Relations." *JSHJ* 10 (2012): 63–86.

———. "Remapping Schweitzer's Quest through Jewish-Christian Polemic, Apology, and Dialogue." Pages 111–28 in *Soundings in the Religion of Jesus: Perspectives and Methods in Jewish and Christian Scholarship*. Edited by Bruce Chilton, Anthony Le Donne, and Jacob Neusner. Minneapolis: Fortress, 2012.

Lee, Aquila H. I. *From Messiah to Preexistent Son: Jesus' Self-Consciousness and Early Christian Exegesis of Messianic Psalms*. WUNT 2/192. Tübingen: Mohr Siebeck, 2005.

Lee, Yongbom. "Dominical Shame Tradition in Paul: An Allusion to Jesus' Use of Shame Language from the Book of Daniel." Pages 234–45 in *Searching the Scriptures: Studies in Context and Intertextuality*. Edited by Craig A. Evans and Jeremiah J. Johnson. LNTS 543. London: Bloomsbury T&T Clark, 2015.

Legapsi, Michael C. *The Death of Scripture and the Rise of Biblical Studies*. Oxford: Oxford University Press, 2010.

Leim, Joshua E. "In the Glory of His Father: Intertextuality and the Apocalyptic Son of Man in the Gospel of Mark." *JTS* 7 (2013): 213–22.

Leivestad, Ragnar. "Exit the Apocalyptic Son of Man." *NTS* 18 (1972): 243–67.

Léon-Dufour, Xavier. *The Gospels and the Jesus of History*. Edited and translated by John McHugh. New York: Desclee, 1968.

Leroy, Herbert. *Rätsel und Missverständnis: Ein Beitrag zur Formgeschichte des Johannesevangeliums*. Bonn: Hanstein, 1968.

Leslie, Charles. *A Short and Easy Method with the Jews: Wherein the Certainty of the Christian Religion Is Demonstrated*. Rev. ed. London: Goakman, 1812.

Levey, Samson H. *The Messiah: An Aramaic Interpretation*. Cincinnati: Hebrew Union College, 1974.

Levine, Amy-Jill. "Bearing False Witness: Common Errors Made about Early Judaism." Pages 759–62 in *The Jewish Annotated New Testament*. Edited by Amy-Jill Levine and Marc Z. Brettler. 2nd ed. Oxford: Oxford University Press, 2017.

———. Introduction to *The Historical Jesus in Context*, 1–39. Edited by Amy-Jill Levine, Dale C. Allison Jr., and John Dominic Crossan. Princeton: Princeton University Press, 2006.

———. *The Misunderstood Jew: The Church and the Scandal of the Jewish Jesus*. San Francisco: HarperSanFrancisco, 2006.

Lieu, Judith M. *Marcion and the Making of a Heretic: God and Scripture in the Second Century*. Cambridge: Cambridge University Press, 2015.

Liew, Tat-siong Benny. *Politics of Parousia: Reading Mark Inter(con)textually*. BibInt 42. Leiden: Brill, 1999.

Lightfoot, John. *The Whole Works of Rev. John Lightfoot. D.D.* Edited and translated by John Rogers Pitman. 13 vols. London: Dove, 1825.

Lincoln, Andrew T. *Paradise Now and Not Yet: Studies on the Role of the Heavenly Dimension in Paul's Thought with Special Reference to His Eschatology*. SNTSMS 43. Cambridge: Cambridge University Press, 1991.

Lindars, Barnabas. "Re-enter the Apocalyptic Son of Man." *NTS* 22 (1975): 52–72.

Lindemann, Andreas. *Die Aufhebung der Zeit: Geschichtsverständnis und Eschatologie im Epheserbrief*. SNT 12. Gütersloh: Mohn, 1975.

———. "Kommentare zum Markusevangelium 2000–2017." *TRu* 83 (2018): 217–73.

Loader, William R. G. "Christ at the Right Hand: Ps. XC.1 in the New Testament." *NTS* 24 (1978): 199–217.

———. *Jesus in John's Gospel: Structure and Issues in Johannine Christology*. Grand Rapids: Eerdmans, 2017.

Locke, John. *The Reasonableness of Christianity*. Edited by I. T. Ramsey. London: Black, 1958.

Lohfink, Gerhard. *Die Himmelfahrt Jesu: Untersuchungen zu den Himmelfahrts- und Erhöhungstexten bei Lukas*. Munich: Kosel, 1971.

Lohmeyer, Ernst. "*Syn Christō*." Pages 218–57 in *Festgabe für Adolf Deissmann zum 60. Geburtstag*. Edited by Karl Ludwig Schmidt. Tübingen: Mohr, 1927.

Loisy, Alfred. *The Birth of the Christian Religion and the Origins of the New Testament*. Translated by L. P. Jacks. New Hyde Park, NY: University Books, 1962.

Long, Philip J. *Jesus the Bridegroom: The Origin of the Eschatological Feast as a Wedding Banquet in the Synoptic Gospels*. Eugene, OR: Pickwick, 2013.

Longenecker, Richard. *Galatians*. WBC 41. Dallas: Word, 1990.

Love, Christopher. *The Penitent Pardoned*. London: Rothwell, 1657.

Luckensmeyer, David. *The Eschatology of First Thessalonians*. NTOA 71. Göttingen: Vandenhoeck & Ruprecht, 2009.

Lüdemann, Gerd. *Jesus after Two Thousand Years: What He Really Said and Did.* Amherst: Prometheus, 2001.

———. *Paulus, der Heidenapostel.* Göttingen: Vandenhoeck & Ruprecht, 1983.

Ludlow, Jared. "Death and the Afterlife in *2 Baruch*." Pages 116–23 in *Interpreting 4 Ezra and 2 Baruch: International Studies*. Edited by Gabriele Boccaccini and Jason M. Zurawski. LSTS. London: Bloomsbury T&T Clark, 2014.

Lundsteen, August Christen. *Hermann Samuel Reimarus und die Anfänge der Leben-Jesu Forschung.* Copenhagen: Olsen, 1939.

Lundström, Gösta. *The Kingdom of God in the Teaching of Jesus: A History of Interpretation from the Last Decades of the Nineteenth Century to the Present Day.* Translated by Joan Bulman. Richmond: John Knox, 1963.

Luther, Martin. *About the Jews and Their Lies, 1543*. In *Christian Life in the World*. Pages 441–608 in vol. 5 of *The Annotated Luther*. Edited by Hans J. Hillerbrand. Minneapolis: Fortress, 2017.

Luz, Ulrich. *Das Geschichtsverständnis des Paulus*. München: Kaiser, 1968.

———. *Exegetische Aufsätze*. WUNT 357. Tübingen: Mohr Siebeck, 2016.

———. "Looking at Q through the Eyes of Matthew." Pages 571–90 in *New Studies in the Synoptic Problem: Essays in Honour of Christopher M. Tuckett*. Edited by Paul Foster. BETL 239. Leuven: Peeters, 2011.

———. *Matthew: A Commentary*. Translated by James E. Crouch. 3 vols. Hermeneia. Minneapolis: Fortress, 2005–2007.

Macaskill, Grant. "Apocalypse and the Gospel of Mark." Pages 53–78 in *The Jewish Apocalyptic Tradition and the Shaping of New Testament Thought*. Edited by Benjamin E. Reynolds and Loren T. Stuckenbruck. Minneapolis: Fortress, 2017.

Mack, Burton. *The Lost Gospel: The Book of Q and Christian Origins*. San Francisco: HarperSanFrancisco, 1993.

Maddox, Robert. "The Functions of the Son of Man according to the Synoptic Gospels." *NTS* 15 (1968): 45–74.

Mader, Heidrun E. "Narratives Gestalten paulinischer Theologoumena? Paulus und Markus im Vergleich." *ZNT* 24 (2021): 41–58.

Magidan, Kevin. *The Passions of Christ in High-Medieval Thought: An Essay on Christological Development.* Oxford: Oxford University Press, 2007.

Malherbe, Abraham J. *The Letters to the Thessalonians: A New Translation with Introduction and Commentary.* AB 32B. New York: Doubleday, 2000.

Manseau, Peter. *The Jefferson Bible: A Biography*. Princeton: Princeton University Press, 2020.

Manson, T. W. "Is It Possible to Write a Life of Christ?" *ExpTim* 53 (1942): 248–51.

———. "The Son of Man in Daniel, Enoch, and the Gospels." *BJRL* 32 (1950): 171–93.

———. *Studies in the Gospels and Epistles*. Philadelphia: Westminster, 1962.

———. *The Teaching of Jesus: Studies of Its Form and Content*. 2nd ed. Cambridge: Cambridge University Press, 1935.

Manuel, Frank E. "Israel and the Enlightenment." *Daedalus* 111 (1982): 33–52.

Marcovich, Miroslav, ed. *Iustini Martyris Dialogus cum Tryphone*. PTS 47. Berlin: de Gruyter, 1997.

Marcus, Joel. "The Beelzebul Controversy and the Eschatologies of Jesus." Pages 247–78 in *Authenticating the Activities of Jesus*. Edited by Bruce Chilton and Craig A. Evans. Leiden: Brill, 2002.

———. "Birkat Ha-Minim Revisited." *NTS* 55 (2009): 523–51.

———. "Crucifixion as Parodic Exaltation." *JBL* 125 (2006): 73–87.

———. *John the Baptist in History and Theology*. Columbia: University of South Carolina Press, 2018.

———. *Mark 1–8: A New Translation with Introduction and Commentary*. AB 27. New Haven: Yale University Press, 2000.

———. *Mark 8–16: A New Translation with Introduction and Commentary*. AB 27A. New Haven: Yale University Press, 2009.

———. "Mark—Interpreter of Paul." *NTS* 46 (2000): 473–87.

———. "Son of Man as Son of Adam." *RB* 110 (2003): 38–61.

———. "'The Time Has Been Fulfilled!' (Mark 1.15)." Pages 49–68 in *Apocalyptic and the New Testament: Essays in Honor of J. Louis Martyn*. Edited by Joel Marcus and Marion L. Soards. London: Bloomsbury Academic, 2015.

———. *The Way of the Lord*. Louisville: Westminster John Knox, 1992.

Marguerat, Daniel. "Pourquoi s'intéresser à la Source? Histoire de la recherche et questions ouvertes." Pages 19–49 in *La source des paroles de Jésus (Q): Aux origins du christianisme*. Edited by Andreas Dettwiler and Daniel Marguerat. Paris: Labor et Fides, 2008.

Markschies, Christoph. "The Canon of the New Testament in Antiquity: Some New Horizons for Future Research." Pages 175–94 in *Homer, the Bible, and Beyond: Literary and Religious Canons in the Ancient World*. Edited by Margaret Finkelberg and Guy G. Stroumsa. Leiden: Brill, 2003.

Marsh, Clive. "Quests of the Historical Jesus in New Historicist Perspective." *BibInt* 5 (1997): 403–37.

Martin, Dale. "Jesus in Jerusalem: Armed and Not Dangerous." *JSNT* 37 (2014): 3–24.

Martínez, García. "Messianische Erwartungen in den Qumranschriften." *Jahrbuch für Biblische Theologie* 9 (1993): 171–208.

Martini, Raymundi. *Pugio Fidei adversus Mauros et Judaeos*. Leipzig: Lanckisi, 1687.

März, C. P. "Das Gleichnis vom Dieb." Pages 633–48 in vol. 1 of *The Four Gospels, 1992:*

Festschrift Frans Neirynck. Edited by F. van Segbroeck, C. M. Tuckett, G. Van Belle, and J. Verheyden. 3 vols. Leuven: Leuven University Press, 1992.

Massey, Brandon. "The Radical Historical Jesus in Chicago: History from Below and New Directions in the History of the Quest." Paper presented at the Annual Meeting of the Society of Biblical Literature (Historical Jesus section). San Antonio, November 21, 2023.

Maston, Jason. *Divine and Human Agency in Second Temple Judaism and Paul: A Comparative Study*. WUNT 2/297. Tübingen: Mohr Siebeck, 2010.

Matera, Frank J. *New Testament Christology*. Louisville: Westminster John Knox, 1999.

Mbuvi, Andrew M. *African Biblical Studies: Unmasking Embedded Racism and Colonialism in Biblical Studies*. London: Bloomsbury T&T Clark, 2023.

McArthur, Harvey K. *The Quest through the Centuries: The Search for the Historical Jesus*. Philadelphia: Fortress, 1966.

McCown, Chester Charlton. *The Search for the Real Jesus: A Century of Historical Study*. New York: Scribner's Sons, 1940.

McDermott, J. M. "Luke xii, 8–9: Stone of Scandal." *RB* 84 (1977): 523–37.

McGinn, Bernard. *Visions of the End: Apocalyptic Traditions in the Middle Ages*. New York: Columbia, 1979.

McGrath, Alister E. *Christian Theology: An Introduction*. 3rd ed. Oxford: Blackwell, 2001.

———. *The Making of Modern German Christology: From the Enlightenment to Pannenberg*. Oxford: Blackwell, 1986.

McGrath, James F. "Obedient unto Death: Philippians 2:8, Gethsemane, and the Historical Jesus." *JSHJ* 14 (2016): 223–40.

McKnight, Scot. *Jesus and His Death: Historiography, the Historical Jesus, and Atonement Theory*. Waco, TX: Baylor University Press, 2005.

———. *A New Vision for Israel: The Teachings of Jesus in National Context*. Grand Rapids: Eerdmans, 1999.

McLay, R. Timothy. "Daniel (Old Greek and Theodotion)." Pages 544–54 in *The T&T Clark Companion to the Septuagint*. Edited by James K. Aitken. London: Bloomsbury T&T Clark, 2015.

McNicol, Allan J. *Jesus' Directions for the Future: A Source and Redaction-History Study of the Use of the Eschatological Traditions in Paul and in the Synoptic Accounts of Jesus' Last Eschatological Discourse*. Macon, GA: Mercer University Press, 1996.

Mearns, Chris. "The Son of Man: Trajectory and Eschatological Development." *ExpTim* 97 (1985): 8–12.

Meier, John P. "From Elijah-Like Prophet to Royal Davidic Messiah." Pages 45–83 in *Jesus: A Colloquium in the Holy Land*. Edited by Doris Donnelly. New York: Continuum, 2001.

———. *A Marginal Jew: Rethinking the Historical Jesus*. 5 vols. New York: Doubleday, 1991–2016.

Méndez, Hugo. "Mixed Metaphors: Resolving the Eschatological Headache of John 5." *JBL* 137 (2018): 711–32.

Merklein, Helmut. "Der Theologe als Prophet: Zur Funktion prophetischen Redens im theologischen Diskurs des Paulus." *NTS* 38 (1992): 402–29.

———. *Jesu Botschaft von der Gottesherrschaft: Eine Skizze*. SBS 111. Stuttgart: Katholisches Bibelwerk, 1983.

———. *Studien zu Jesus und Paulus*. WUNT 43. Tübingen: Mohr Siebeck, 1987.

Merx, Adalbert. *Das Evangelium Matthäus*. Berlin: Reimer, 1902.

Meyer, Ben F. *The Aims of Jesus*. London: SCM, 1979.

———. *Christus Faber: The Master Builder and the House of God*. Allison Park, PA: Pickwick, 1992.

———. "Did Paul's View of the Resurrection of the Dead Undergo Development?" *TS* 47 (1986): 363–87.

Meyer, H. A. W. *Kritisch exegetisches Handbuch über das Evangelium des Matthäus*. Göttingen: Vandenhoeck & Ruprecht, 1864.

Michaelis, Wilhelm. *Der Herr verzieht nicht die Verheißung: Die Aussagen Jesu über die Nähe des Jüngsten Tages*. Bern: Buchhandlung der Evangelischen Gesellschaft, 1942.

Michaels, J. Ramsey. *The Gospel of John*. NICNT. Grand Rapids: Eerdmans, 2010.

Michel, Otto. *Paulus und seine Bibel*. Darmstadt: Wissenschaftliche Buchgesellschaft, 1972.

Mihalios, Stefanos. *The Danielic Eschatological Hour in the Johannine Literature*. LNTS 436. New York: T&T Clark, 2011.

Milhoc, Vasile. "How Did the Church Fathers Understand the History of Jesus?" Pages 115–52 in *Gospel Images of Jesus Christ in Church Tradition and Biblical Scholarship*. Edited by Christos Karakolis, Karl-Wilhelm Niebuhr, and Sviatoslav Rogalsky. WUNT 288. Tübingen: Mohr Siebeck, 2012.

Miller, David M. "The Messenger, the Lord, and the Coming Judgment in the Reception History of Malachi 3." *NTS* 53 (2001): 1–17.

Miller, Robert J., ed. *The Apocalyptic Jesus: A Debate*. Santa Rosa, CA: Polebridge, 2001.

———. "Theological Stakes in the Apocalyptic Jesus Debate." Pages 111–21 in *Apocalypticism, Anti-Semitism and the Historical Jesus: Subtexts in Criticism*. Edited by John S. Kloppenborg with John W. Marshall. London: T&T Clark International, 2006.

Miller, Susan. "'Among You Stands One Whom You Do Not Know' (John 1:26): The Use of the Tradition of the Hidden Messiah in John's Gospel." Pages 243–64 in *The Ways That Often Parted: Essays in Honor of Joel Marcus*. Edited by Lori Baron, Jill Hicks-Keeton, and Matthew Thiessen. ECL 24. Atlanta: SBL Press, 2018.

Mills, Mary E. *Human Agents of Cosmic Power in Hellenistic Judaism and the Synoptic Tradition*. JSNTSup 41. Sheffield: JSOT Press, 1990.

Minear, Paul. *Christian Hope and the Second Coming*. Philadelphia: Westminster, 1954.

Mitchel, Patrick. "New Testament Eschatologies." Pages 224–52 in *The State of New Testament Studies: A Survey of Recent Research*. Edited by Scot McKnight and Nijay K. Gupta. Grand Rapids: Baker Books, 2019.

Mitchell, David C. "A Dying and Rising Josephite Messiah in 4Q372." *JSP* 18 (2009): 181–205.

Miura, Yuzuru. *David in Luke-Acts: His Portrayal in the Light of Early Judaism*. WUNT 2/232. Tübingen: Mohr Siebeck, 2007.

Modica, Joseph B. "Jesus as Glutton and Drunkard." Pages 50–75 in *Who Do My Opponents Say That I Am? An Investigation of the Accusations against the Historical Jesus*. Edited by Scot McKnight and Joseph B. Modica. London: T&T Clark, 2008.

Moller, Hilde Brekke. *The Vermes Quest: The Significance of Geza Vermes for Jesus Research*. LNTS 576. London: Bloomsbury T&T Clark, 2017.

Moloney, Francis J. *The Johannine Son of Man*. 2nd ed. Eugene, OR: Wipf & Stock, 2007.

Moloney, Raymond. "Approaches to Christ's Knowledge in the Patristic Era." Pages 37–66 in *Studies in Patristic Christology*. Edited by Thomas Finan and Vincent Twomey. Portland: Four Courts, 1998.

Montgomery, James A. *A Critical and Exegetical Commentary on the Book of Daniel*. ICC. Edinburgh: T&T Clark, 1964.

Moo, Douglas J. *The Old Testament in the Gospel Passion Narrative*. Sheffield: Almond, 1983.

Moore, Arthur L. *The Parousia in the New Testament*. NovTSup 13. Leiden: Brill, 1966.

Moore, George Foot. "Christian Writers on Judaism." *HTR* 14 (1921): 197–254.

Morelli, Enrico. "Why Did Early Believers in Jesus Write Apocalypses?" *ZAC* 20 (2016): 63–83.

Morgan, Thomas. *The Moral Philosopher: In a Dialogue between Philalethes a Christian Deist, and Theophanes a Christian Jew*. London: s.n., 1737.

Morris, Leon. *The Gospel according to John*. Rev. ed. NICNT. Grand Rapids: Eerdmans, 1995.

Moss, Candida R., and Joel S. Baden. "1 Thessalonians 4.13–18 in Rabbinic Perspective." *NTS* 58 (2012): 1–16.

Motyer, Stephen. *Come, Lord Jesus! A Biblical Theology of the Second Coming of Christ*. London: Apollos, 2016.

Moule, C. F. D. "The Influence of Circumstances on the Use of Eschatological Terms." *JTS* 15 (1964): 1–15.

———. *The Origin of Christology*. Cambridge: Cambridge University Press, 1977.

———. "Reconsideration of the Context of Maranatha." *NTS* 6 (1960): 307–10.

———. "'The Son of Man': Some of the Facts." *NTS* 31 (1995): 277–79.

Mowinckel, Sigmund. *He That Cometh*. Translated by G. W. Anderson. Oxford: Blackwell, 1956.

———. *Psalmenstudien*. Amsterdam: Schippers, 1961.

Moxnes, Halvor. "From Unique Personality to Charismatic Movement: 100 Years of Shifting Paradigms in Historical Jesus Research." Pages 187–200 in *Religion in Late Modernity: Essays in Honor of Pål Repstad*. Edited by Inger Furseth and Paul Leer-Salvesen. Trondheim: Tapir, 2007.

———. *Jesus and the Rise of Nationalism: A New Quest for the Nineteenth Century Historical Jesus*. London: Tauris, 2012.

———. "Jesus the Jew: Dilemmas of Interpretation." Pages 83–103 in *Fair Play: Diversity and Conflicts in Early Christianity; Essays in Honour of Heikki Räisänen*. Edited by Ismo Dunderberg, Christopher Tuckett, and Kari Syreeni. Leiden: Brill, 2002.

Moxnes, Halvor, Ward Blanton, and James Crossley, eds. *Jesus beyond Nationalism: Constructing the Historical Jesus in a Period of Cultural Complexity*. London: Equinox, 2010.

Mühling, Markus. *T&T Clark Handbook of Christian Eschatology*. Translated by Jennifer Adams-Maßmann and David Andrew Gilland. London: Bloomsbury, 2015.

Muirhead, Lewis A. *The Eschatology of Jesus, or, The Kingdom Come and Coming: A Brief Study of Our Lord's Apocalyptic Language in the Synoptic Gospels*. London: Melrose, 1904.

Müller, Karlheinz. "Der Menschensohn im Danielzyklus." Pages 37–80 in *Jesus und der Menschensohn: Festschrift A. Vögtle*. Edited by Rudolf Pesch and Rudolf Schnackenburg. Freiburg: Herder, 1975.

Müller, Mogens. *Der Ausdruck "Menschensohn" in den Evangelien: Voraussetzungen und Bedeutung*. Leiden: Brill, 1984.

Müller, Mogens, and Heike Omerzu, eds. *Gospel Interpretation and the Q-Hypothesis*. LNTS 573. London: Bloomsbury T&T Clark, 2018.

Müller, Peter. "Zwischen dem Gekommenden und dem Kommenden: Intertextuelle Aspekte der Menschensohnaussagen im Markusevangelium." Pages 130–57 in *Gottessohn und Menschensohn: Exegetische Studien zu zwei Paradigmen biblischer Intertextualität*. Edited by Dieter Sänger. Neukirchen-Vluyn: Neukirchener, 2004.

Müller, Ulrich B. "Auferweckt und erhöht: Zur Genese des Osterglaubens." *NTS* (2008): 201–20.

———. *Messias und Menschensohn in jüdischen Apokalypsen und in der Offenbarung des Johannes*. Gütersloh: Gütersloher Verlag, 1972.

———. "Parusie und Menschensohn." *ZNW* 92 (2001): 1–19.

———. "Zur Rezeption Gesetzes-Kritischer Jesusüberlieferung im Frühen Christentum." *NTS* 27 (1981): 158–85.

Mussner, Franz. "Die Idee der Apokatastasis in der Apostelgeschichte." Pages 293–306 in *Lex Tua Veritas: Festschrift für Hubert Junker zur Vollendung des siebzigsten*

Lebensjahres am 8. August 1961. Edited by Heinrich Gross and Franz Mussner. Trier: Paulinus, 1961.

———. *Was lehrt Jesus über das Ende der Welt?* Rev. ed. Freiburg: Herder, 1987.

Myles, Robert J. "The Fetish for a Subversive Jesus." *JSHJ* 14 (2016): 52–70.

Myllykoski, Matti. "'Christian Jews' and 'Jewish Christians': The Jewish Origins of Christianity in English Literature from Elizabeth I to Toland's *Nazarenus*." Pages 3–44 in *The Rediscovery of Jewish Christianity: From Toland to Baur*. Edited by F. Stanley Jones. SBLHBS 5. Atlanta: Society of Biblical Literature, 2012.

Nardoni, Enrique. "A Redactional Interpretation of Mark 9:1." *CBQ* 43 (1981): 365–84.

Neander, August. *Das Leben Jesu Christi: In seinem geschichtlichen Zusammenhange und seiner geschichtlichen Entwickelung Dargestellt*. Hamburg: Perthes, 1837.

Neirynck, Frans. "Paul and the Sayings of Jesus." Pages 267–321 in *L'Apôtre Paul: Personnalité, style et conception du ministère*. Edited by A. Vanhoye. SETL 73. Leuven: Leuven University Press, 1986.

Nel, Marius. "'Son of Man' in the Gospel of Mark." *IDS* 51 (2017): 1–9.

———. "What Is 'the Sign of the Son of Man in Heaven' (Mt 24:30)." *IDS* 49 (2015): 1–9.

Nepper-Christensen, P. "Das verborgene Herrenwort: Eine Untersuchung über 1. Thess. 4,13–18." *ST* 19 (1965): 136–54.

Neugebauer, Johannes. *Die eschatologischen Aussagen in den johanneischen Abschiedsreden: Eine Untersuchung zu Johannes 13–17*. BWZT 140. Stuttgart: Kohlhammer, 1995.

Neusner, Jacob. *Messiah in Context: Israel's History and Destiny in Formative Judaism*. Minneapolis: Fortress, 1984.

———. Preface. Pages ix–xiv in *Judaisms and Their Messiahs at the Turn of the Christian Era*. Edited by Jacob Neusner, William S. Green, and Ernest Frerichs. Cambridge: Cambridge University Press, 1987.

Neville, David J. *A Peaceable Hope: Contesting Violent Eschatology in New Testament Narratives*. Grand Rapids: Baker Academic, 2013.

Newman, Hillel. "Jerome's Judaizers." *JECS* 9 (2001): 421–52.

Neyrey, Jerome H. *The Passion according to Luke: A Redaction Study of Luke's Soteriology*. New York: Paulist, 1985.

Nickelsburg, George W. E. "Response: Context, Text, and Social Setting of the Apocalypse of Weeks." Pages 234–41 in *Enoch and Qumran Origins: New Light on a Forgotten Connection*. Edited by Gabriele Boccaccini. Grand Rapids: Eerdmans, 2005.

———. "Son of Man." *ABD* 6:137–50.

Nickelsburg, George W. E., and James C. Vanderkam. *1 Enoch: A New Translation*. Minneapolis: Fortress, 2004.

———. *1 Enoch 2*. Hermeneia. Minneapolis: Fortress, 2012.

Nicklas, Tobias. "Gnostic 'Eschatologies.'" Pages 601–28 in *Eschatology of the New Testament and Some Related Documents*. Edited by Jan G. van der Watt. WUNT 2/315. Tübingen: Mohr Siebeck, 2011.

Nielsen, Anders E. *Until It Is Fulfilled: Lukan Eschatology according to Luke 22 and Acts 20*. WUNT 2/126. Tübingen: Mohr Siebeck, 2000.

Noack, Bent. "Current and Backwater in the Epistle to the Romans." *ST* 19 (1965): 155–66.

Nolland, John. *The Gospel of Matthew: A Commentary on the Greek Text*. NIGTC. Grand Rapids: Eerdmans, 2005.

———. "The Gospel Prohibition of Divorce: Tradition History and Meaning." *JSNT* 17 (1995): 19–35.

———. *Luke 18:35–24:53*. WBC 35C. Dallas: Word, 1993.

———. "'The Times of the Nations' and a Prophetic Pattern in Luke 21." Pages 133–47 in *The Gospel of Luke*. Vol. 3 of *Biblical Interpretation in Early Christian Gospels*. Edited by Thomas R. Hatina. LNTS 376. London: T&T Clark International, 2006.

North, Wendy E. S. *What John Knew and What John Wrote: A Study in John and the Synoptics*. Minneapolis: Fortress, 2020.

Novakovic, Lidija. *Raised from the Dead according to Scripture: The Role of Israel's Scripture in the Early Christian Interpretations of Jesus' Resurrection*. Jewish and Christian Texts in Contexts and Related Studies Series. London: Bloomsbury, 2012.

———. *Resurrection: A Guide for the Perplexed*. London: Bloomsbury T&T Clark, 2016.

Novenson, Matthew V. *Christ among the Messiahs: Christ Language in Paul and Messiah Language in Ancient Judaism*. Oxford: Oxford University Press, 2012.

———. *The Grammar of Messianism: An Ancient Jewish Political Idiom and Its Users*. Oxford: Oxford University Press, 2017.

Numbers, Ronald L., and Jonathan M. Butler, eds. *The Disappointed: Millerism and Millenarianism in the Nineteenth Century*. Bloomington: Indiana University Press, 1987.

Numbers, Ronald L., and Janet S. Numbers. "Millerism and Madness: A Study of 'Religious Insanity' in Nineteenth-Century America." Pages 92–118 in *The Disappointed: Millerism and Millenarianism in the Nineteenth Century*. Edited by Ronald L. Numbers and Jonathan M. Butler. Bloomington: Indiana University Press, 1987.

Nützel, Johannes M. "Zum Schicksal der eschatologischen Propheten." *BZ* 20 (1976): 59–94.

Oakes, Peter. "Remapping the Universe: Paul and the Emperor in 1 Thessalonians and Philippians." *JSNT* 27 (2005): 301–22.

Oakman, Douglas E. *The Political Aims of Jesus*. Minneapolis: Fortress, 2012.

O'Donnell, Tim. "Complementary Eschatologies in John 5:19–30." *CBQ* 70 (2008): 750–65.

Odo of Tournai. *A Disputation with the Jew, Leo, concerning the Advent of Christ, the Son of God*. Translated by Iren M. Resnick. Philadelphia: University of Pennsylvania Press, 1994.

Oegema, Gerbern S. *The Anointed and His People: Messianic Expectations from Maccabees to Bar Kochba*. Sheffield: Sheffield Academic, 1998.

———. *Apocalyptic Interpretation of the Bible: Apocalypticism and Biblical Interpretation in Early Judaism, the Apostle Paul, the Historical Jesus, and Their Reception History*. London: T&T Clark International, 2012.

———. "Jesus' Use and Interpretation of Scripture: What Was 'Scripture' to Jesus and How Did Such Texts Influence Him?" Pages 802–26 in *Jesus Research: New Methodologies and Perceptions*. Edited by James H. Charlesworth. Grand Rapids: Eerdmans, 2007.

Oepke, Albrecht. "παρουσία, κτλ." *TDNT* 5:858–71.

Öhler, Markus. *Elia im Neuen Testament: Untersuchungen zur Bedeutung des alttestamentlichen Propheten im frühen Christentum*. Berlin: de Gruyter, 1997.

———. "The Expectation of Elijah and the Presence of the Kingdom of God." *JBL* 118 (1999): 461–76.

Oliver, Isaac W. *Luke's Jewish Eschatology: The National Restoration of Israel in Luke-Acts*. Oxford: Oxford University Press, 2021.

Oort, Johannes van. "The End Is Now: Augustine on History and Eschatology." *HvTSt* 68 (2012): 1–7.

Orchard, Bernard. "St. Paul and the Book of Daniel." *Bib* 20 (1939): 172–79.

Origen. *The Commentary of Origen on the Gospel of Matthew*. Translated by Ronald E. Heine. 2 vols. OECT. Oxford: Oxford University Press, 2018.

Orr, John. *English Deism: Its Roots and Its Fruits*. Grand Rapids: Eerdmans, 1934.

Otto, Rudolf. *The Kingdom of God and the Son of Man: A Study in the History of Religion*. Translated by Floyd V. Filson and Bertram Lee Woolf. Grand Rapids: Zondervan, 1938.

———. *Life and Ministry of Jesus: According to the Historical Critical Method, Being a Course of Lectures*. Translated by H. J. Whitby. 3rd ed. Chicago: Open Court, 1908.

Owen, Paul. "Problems with Casey's 'Solution.'" Pages 28–49 in *'Who Is This Son of Man?' The Latest Scholarship on a Puzzling Expression of the Historical Jesus*. Edited by Larry W. Hurtado and Paul L. Owen. LNTS 390. London: Bloomsbury T&T Clark, 2011.

Paget, James Carleton. "Anti-Judaism and Early Christian Identity." *ZAC* (1997): 195–225.

———. "Quests for the Historical Jesus." Pages 138–55 in *The Cambridge Companion to Jesus*. Edited by Markus Bockmuehl. Cambridge: Cambridge University Press, 2001.

———. "Some Observations on the Delay of the Parousia in the Historiography of Its Discussion." *EC* 9 (2018): 9–36.

Pahl, Michael W. *Discerning the 'Word of the Lord': The 'Word of the Lord' in 1 Thessalonians 4:15*. LNTS 389. London: Bloomsbury T&T Clark, 2009.

Paine, Thomas. *The Age of Reason, Being an Investigation of the True and Fabulous Theology.* Paris: s.n., 1794.

Pals, Daniel L. *The Victorian "Lives" of Jesus*. San Antonio: Trinity University Press, 1982.

Palu, Ma'afu. *Jesus and Time: An Interpretation of Mark 1.15*. LNTS 468. London: Bloomsbury T&T Clark, 2012.

Parsenios, George. *Departure and Consolation: The Johanine Farewell Discourses in Light of Greco-Roman Literature*. NovTSup 117. Leiden: Brill, 2005.

Patai, Raphael. *The Messiah Texts*. Detroit: Wayne State University Press, 1979.

Pate, C. M., and D. W. Kennard. *Deliverance Now and Not Yet: The New Testament and the Great Tribulation*. StBibLit 54. New York: Lang, 2003.

Patterson, Stephen J. *The God of Jesus: The Historical Jesus and the Search for Meaning*. Harrisburg, PA: Trinity International, 1998.

Paulus, Heinrich. *Philologisch-kritischer und historischer Commentar über die drey ersten Evangelien*. 2nd ed. Lübeck: Bohn, 1804.

Peel, Malcolm L. "Gnostic Eschatology and the New Testament." *NovT* 12 (1970): 141–65.

Penley, Paul T. *The Common Tradition behind Synoptic Sayings of Judgment and John's Apocalypse*. LNTS 424. London: T&T Clark International, 2010.

Pérez i Díaz, Mar. *Mark, a Pauline Theologian: A Re-reading of the Traditions of Jesus in the Light of Paul's Theology.* WUNT 2/251. Tübingen: Mohr Siebeck, 2020.

Perkins, Pheme. "The Resurrection of Jesus." Pages 2409–32 in vol. 3 of *Handbook for the Study of the Historical Jesus*. Edited by Tom Holmén and Stanley Porter. Leiden: Brill, 2010.

Perriman, Andrew C. "Paul and the Parousia: 1 Corinthians 15:50–57 and 2 Corinthians 5:1–5." *NTS* 35 (1989): 512–21.

Perrin, Norman. *The Kingdom of God in the Teaching of Jesus*. Philadelphia: Westminster, 1963.

———. "Mark 14.62: The End Product of a Christian Pesher Tradition?" *NTS* 12 (1965): 150–55.

———. *A Modern Pilgrimage in New Testament Christology.* Philadelphia: Fortress, 1974.

———. *Rediscovering the Teaching of Jesus*. New York: Harper & Row, 1967.

Pesch, Rudolf. *Das Abendmahl und Jesu Todesverständnis*. Freiburg: Herder, 1978.

———. *Das Markusevangelium*. Part 2, *Commentar zu Kap. 8,27–16,20*. Freiburg: Herder, 1977.

———. *Naherwartungen: Tradition und Redaktion in Mk 13*. KBANT. Düsseldorf: Patmos Verlag, 1968.

———. *Simon Petrus: Geschichte und geschichtliche Bedeutung des ersten Jüngers Jesu Christi.* Stuttgart: Hiersemann, 1980.

———. "Zur Entstehung des Glaubens an die Auferstehung Jesu." *TQ* 153 (1973): 201–28.

———. "Zur Entstehung des Glaubens an die Auferstehung Jesu: Ein neuer Versuch." *FZPhTh* 30 (1983): 73–98.

Peterson, Jeffrey. "The Extent of Christian Theological Diversity." *ResQ* 47 (2005): 1–12.

Peter the Venerable. *Against the Inveterate Obduracy of the Jews.* Edited and translated by Irven M. Resnick. FC Medieval Continuation 16. Washington, DC: Catholic University of America Press, 2013.

Pfleiderer, Otto. *Paulinism: A Contribution to the History of Primitive Christian Theology.* Translated by Edward Peters. 2 vols. London: Williams & Norgate, 1877.

Piotrowski, Nicholas G. *Matthew's David at the End of Exile: A Socio-rhetorical Study of Scriptural Quotations.* NovTSup 170. Leiden: Brill, 2016.

Pippin, Tina. "The Rapture in American Imagination." Pages 262–75 in *The Oxford Handbook of the Bible and American Popular Culture.* Edited by Dan W. Clanton Jr. and Terry R. Clark. Oxford: Oxford University Press, 2021.

Pitre, Brant. "From Reimarus to Allison: The Quest for Jesus and the Christological 'Thunderbolt' (Matt 11:25–27 // Luke 10:21–22)." Pages 373–404 in *"To Recover What Has Been Lost": Essays on Eschatology, Intertextuality, and Reception History in Honor of Dale C. Allison Jr.* Edited by Tucker S. Ferda, Daniel Frayer-Griggs, and Nathan C. Johnson. NovTSup 183. Leiden: Brill, 2021.

———. *Jesus and the Last Supper.* Grand Rapids: Eerdmans, 2015.

———. *Jesus, the Tribulation, and the End of the Exile: Restoration Eschatology and the Origin of the Atonement.* WUNT 204. Tübingen: Mohr Siebeck; Grand Rapids: Baker Books, 2005.

Pitre, Brant, Michael P. Barber, and John A. Kincaid. *Paul, a New Covenant Jew: Rethinking Pauline Theology.* Grand Rapids: Eerdmans, 2019.

Plevnik, Joseph. *Paul and the Parousia: An Exegetical and Theological Investigation.* Eugene, OR: Wipf & Stock, 2014.

———. "Son of Man Seated at the Right Hand of God: Luke 22,69 in Lucan Christology." *Bib* 72 (1991): 331–47.

———. *What Are They Saying about Paul and the End Time?* New York: Paulist, 2009.

Pokorny, Petr. "Die Eschatologie des Thomasevangeliums." *ZAC* 13 (2009): 48–54.

Polag, Athanasius. *Die Christologie der Logienquelle.* WMANT 45. Neukirchen-Vluyn: Neukirchener Verlag, 1977.

Poole, Matthew. *A Commentary on the Holy Bible.* McLean: MacDonald, 1962.

Popa, Romeo. "Parusieverzögerung und Generationenkonflikt im Zweiten Petrusbrief." *BZ* 61 (2017): 161–81.

Popkin, Richard. "Jewish-Christian Relations in the Sixteenth and Seventeenth Centuries: The Conception of the Messiah." *Jewish History* 6 (1992): 163–77.

———. "Jewish Messianism and Christian Millenarianism." Pages 67–90 in *Culture and Politics from Puritanism to the Enlightenment*. Edited by Perez Zagorin. Berkeley: University of California Press, 1980.

———. "Three English Tellings of the Sabbatai Zevi Story." *Jewish History* 8 (1994): 43–54.

Pratscher, Wolfgang. "Die Parusieerwartung im 2. Klemensbrief." Pages 91–108 in *Apokalyptik als Herausforderung neutestamentlicher Theologie*. Edited by Michael Becker and Markus Öhler. WUNT 2/214. Tübingen: Mohr Siebeck, 2006.

Pressense, Edmond de. *Jesus Christus: Seine Zeit, sein Leben und sein Werk*. Halle: Waisenhauses, 1866.

Priest, Robert D. "Reading, Writing, and Religion in Nineteenth-Century France: The Popular Reception of Renan's Life of Jesus." *Journal of Modern History* 86 (2014): 258–94.

Pseudo-Cyprian. *Adversus Judaeos* (*Gegen die Judenchristen*). Edited and translated by Dirk van Damme. Freiburg: Universitätsverlag, 1969.

Pseudo-Gregory. *Pseudo-Gregory of Nyssa: Testimonies against the Jews*. Edited and translated by Martin C. Albl. Atlanta: Society of Biblical Literature, 2004.

The Rachovian Catechism, with Notes and Illustrations, Translated from the Latin. Translated by Thomas Rees. London: Longman, 1818.

Rad, Gerhard von. "The Origin of the Day of Yahweh." *JSS* 4 (1959): 97–108.

Rahner, Johanna. "Vergegenwärtigende Erinnerung: Die Abschiedsreden, der Geist Paraklet und die Retrospektive des Johannesevangeliums." *ZNW* 91 (2000): 72–90.

Räisänen, Heikki. "Did Paul Expect an Earthly Kingdom?" Pages 2–20 in *Paul, Luke and the Graeco-Roman World*. Edited by Alf Christophersen. JSNTSup 217. Sheffield: Sheffield Academic, 2002.

Rand, Jan A. du. "Depicting Eschatology in the Gospel of John." Pages 535–66 in *Eschatology of the New Testament and Some Related Documents*. Edited by Jan G. van der Watt. WUNT 2/315. Tübingen: Mohr Siebeck, 2011.

Ratzinger, Joseph. *Eschatology: Death and Eternal Life*. Translated by Michael Waldstein. 2nd ed. Washington, DC: Catholic University of America Press, 2007.

Rau, Eckhard. *Jesus, Freund von Zöllnern und Sündern: Eine methodenkritische Untersuchung*. Stuttgart: Kohlhammer, 2000.

Rau, Eckhard, and Silke Petersen. *Perspektiven des Lebens Jesu: Plädoyer für die Anknüpfung an eine schwierige Forschungstradition*. Stuttgart: Kohlhammer, 2013.

Ravens, David. *Luke and the Restoration of Israel*. JSNTSup 119. Sheffield: Sheffield Academic, 1995.

Reed, Annette Yoshiko. "Messianism between Judaism and Christianity." Pages 23–62 in *Rethinking the Messianic Idea in Judaism*. Edited by Michael L. Morgan and Steven Weitzman. Bloomington: Indiana University Press, 2015.

Reed, Annette Yoshiko, and Adam H. Becker. "Traditional Models and New Directions." Pages 1–34 in *The Ways That Never Parted*. Edited by Annette Yoshiko Reed and Adam H. Becker. TSAJ 95. Tübingen: Mohr Siebeck, 2003.

Rehm, Bernhard, and Georg Strecker, eds. *Die Pseudoklementinen*. 2 vols. GCS. Berlin: Akademie-Verlag, 1965.

Reimarus, Hermann Samuel. *Reimarus: Fragments*. Edited by Charles H. Talbert. Translated by Ralph S. Fraser. Chico, CA: Scholars Press, 1985.

Reinhard, F. V. *Plan of the Founder of Christianity*. Translated by Oliver A. Taylor from the 5th German ed. New York: Carvill, 1831.

Reiser, Marius. *Jesus and Judgment: The Eschatological Proclamation in Its Jewish Context*. Translated by Linda M. Maloney. Minneapolis: Fortress, 1997.

Renan, Ernest. *The Life of Jesus*. Translator s.n. New York: Modern Library, 1927.

Rensburg, Fika J. van. "The Eschatology of 1 Peter—Hope and Vindication for Visiting Resident Strangers." Pages 472–92 in *Eschatology of the New Testament and Some Related Documents*. Edited by Jan G. van der Watt. WUNT 2/315. Tübingen: Mohr Siebeck, 2011.

Repschinski, Boris. "Re-imagining the Presence of God: The Temple and the Messiah in the Gospel of Matthew." *ABR* 54 (2006): 37–49.

Resnick, Irven M. "Odo of Tournai and the Dehumanization of Medieval Jews: A Reexamination." *JQR* 98 (2008): 471–84.

Reumann, John. "'Lives of Jesus' during the Great Quest of the Historical Jesus." *IJT* 23 (1974): 33–59.

Reventlow, Henning Graf. *The Authority of the Bible and the Rise of the Modern World*. Translated by John Bowden. Philadelphia: Fortress, 1985.

———. "Das Arsenal der Bibelkritik des Reimarus: Die Auslegung der Bibel, insbesondere des Alten Testaments, bei den englischen Deisten." Pages 44–65 in *Hermann Samuel Reimarus (1694–1768): Ein "bekannter Unbekannter" der Aufklärung in Hamburg*. Göttingen: Vandenhoeck & Ruprecht, 1973.

———. *From the Enlightenment to the Twentieth Century*. Vol. 4 of *History of Biblical Interpretation*. Translated by Leo G. Perdue. Atlanta: Society of Biblical Literature, 2010.

Réville, Albert. *Jésus de Nazareth*. 2 vols. Paris: Fischbacher, 1897.

Reynolds, Benjamin E. *The Apocalyptic Son of Man in the Gospel of John*. WUNT 249. Tübingen: Mohr Siebeck, 2008.

Reynolds, Benjamin E., and Loren T. Stuckenbruck, eds. *The Jewish Apocalyptic Tradition and the Shaping of New Testament Thought*. Minneapolis: Fortress, 2017.

Rhoads, David, Joanna Dewey, and Donald Michie. *Mark as Story: An Introduction to the Narrative of a Gospel*. 3rd ed. Minneapolis: Fortress, 2012.

Richter, Amy E. *Enoch and the Gospel of Matthew*. Eugene, OR: Pickwick, 2012.

Ricoeur, Paul. "History and Rhetoric." *Diogenes* 168 (1994): 7–24.

Riesner, Rainer. *Die Frühzeit des Apostels Paulus: Studien zur Chronologie, Missionsstrategie und Theologie*. Tübingen: Mohr Siebeck, 1994.

———. "From the Messianic Teacher to the Gospels of Jesus Christ." Pages 405–46 in vol. 1 of *Handbook for the Study of the Historical Jesus*. Edited by Tom Holmén and Stanley Porter. Leiden: Brill, 2010.

———. *Jesus als Lehrer: Eine Untersuchung zum Ursprung der Evangelien—Überlieferung*. WUNT 2/7. Tübingen: Mohr Siebeck, 1984.

———. "Vom Messias Jesus zum christlichen Bekenntnis: Jüdische Voraussetzungen und judenchristliche Überlieferungen." *TBei* 32 (2001): 373–92.

Rigaux, Béda. *Saint Paul: Les Épitres aux Thessaloniciens*. EB. Paris: Gabalda, 1956.

Rindoš, Jaroslav. *He of Whom It Is Written: John the Baptist and Elijah in Luke*. ÖBS 38. New York: Lang, 2010.

Rissi, Mathias. "Die Erscheinung Christi nach Off. 19:11–16." *TZ* 21 (1965): 81–95.

Ritschl, Albrecht. *Die christliche Lehre von der Rechtfertigung und Versöhnung*. 3 vols. Hildescheim: Olms, 1978.

Rivkin, Ellis. "The Meaning of the Messiah in Jewish Thought." *USQR* 26 (1971): 383–406.

Roberts, Jimmy J. M. "Melchizedek (11Q13 = 11QMelchizedek = 11QMelch)." Pages 264–73 in *Pesharim, Other Commentaries, and Related Documents*. Vol. 6 of *The Dead Sea Scrolls: Hebrew, Aramaic, and Greek Texts with English Translations*. Edited by James H. Charlesworth and Henry W. Rietz. Tübingen: Mohr Siebeck, 2002.

Robinson, James M. "The Critical Edition of Q and the Study of Jesus." Pages 27–52 in *The Sayings Source Q and the Historical Jesus*. Edited by Andreas Lindemann. BETL 158. Leuven: Leuven University Press; Sterling: Peeters, 2001.

———. "The Legacy of Albert Schweitzer's Quest of the Historical Jesus." Pages 246–55 in *Reverence for Life: the Ethics of Albert Schweitzer for the Twenty-First Century*. Edited by Marvin Meyer and Kurt Bergel. Syracuse: Syracuse University Press, 2002.

———. *A New Quest of the Historical Jesus and Other Essays*. Philadelphia: Fortress, 1983.

Robinson, John A. T. *In the End, God: A Study of the Christian Doctrine of the Last Things*. London: Clarke, 1950.

———. *Jesus and His Coming: The Emergence of a Doctrine*. New York: Abingdon, 1957.

———. "The Most Primitive Eschatology of All?" *JTS* 7 (1956): 177–89.

Rodríguez, Rafael. *Structuring Early Christian Memory: Jesus in Tradition, Performance, and Text*. LNTS 407. London: T&T Clark, 2010.

———. "Your Will Be Done: Remembering Jesus' Submission to the Father." Pages 294–318 in *"To Recover What Has Been Lost": Essays on Eschatology, Intertextuality, and Reception History in Honor of Dale C. Allison Jr.* Edited by Tucker S. Ferda, Daniel Frayer-Griggs, and Nathan C. Johnson. NovTSup 183. Leiden: Brill, 2021.

Rogerson, John W. *W. M. L. de Wette: Founder of Modern Biblical Criticism; An Intellectual Biography.* JSOTSup 126. Sheffield: JSOT Press, 1992.

Roth, Dieter. *The Parables in Q.* LNTS 582. London: Bloomsbury T&T Clark, 2018.

Roukema, Riemer. "Origen, the Jews, and the New Testament." Pages 241–54 in *The 'New Testament' as a Polemical Tool: Studies in Ancient Christian Anti-Jewish Rhetoric and Beliefs*. Edited by Riemer Roukema and Hagit Amrav. NTOA 118. Göttingen: Vandenhoeck & Ruprecht, 2018.

Rowland, Christopher. *Christian Origins: An Account of the Setting and Character of the Most Important Messianic Sect of Judaism.* London: SPCK, 1985.

———. "John 1:51, Jewish Apocalyptic and Targumic Tradition." *NTS* 30 (1984): 498–507.

———. *The Open Heaven: A Study of Apocalyptic in Judaism and Early Christianity.* Eugene, OR: Wipf & Stock, 2002.

———. "Paul as Apocalyptist." Pages 131–54 in *The Jewish Apocalyptic Tradition and the Shaping of New Testament Thought.* Edited by Benjamin E. Reynolds and Loren T. Stuckenbruck. Minneapolis: Fortress, 2017.

Rowlands, Jonathan. *The Metaphysics of Historical Jesus Research: A Prolegomenon to a Future Quest for the Historical Jesus.* New York: Routledge, 2023.

Rudd, Anthony. *Kierkegaard and the Limits of the Ethical.* Oxford: Clarendon, 1993.

Rudman, Dominic. "Authority and Right of Disposal in Luke 4.6." *NTS* 50 (2004): 77–87.

Runesson, Anders. *Divine Wrath and Salvation in Matthew: The Narrative World of the First Gospel.* Minneapolis: Fortress, 2016.

Russell, J. Stuart. *The Parousia: A Critical Inquiry into the New Testament Doctrine of Our Lord's Second Coming.* Grand Rapids: Baker Books, 1982.

Rutgers, Victor. *Making Myths: Jews in Early Christian Identity Formation.* Leuven: Peeters, 2009.

Sacchi, P. "Esquisse du Développement du Messianisme Juif à la Lumière du Texte Qumranien 11QMelch." *ZAW* 100 (1988): 202–14.

Salvatorelli, Luigi. "From Locke to Reitzenstein: The Historical Investigation of the Origins of Christianity." *HTR* 22 (1929): 263–369.

Sand, Alexander. "Die Gemeinde zwischen 'jenen Tagen Jesu' und 'dem Tag des Gerichts': Zum Geschichtsverständnis des Matthäusevangeliums." *TTZ* 99 (1990): 49–71.

Sanders, E. P. *The Historical Figure of Jesus.* London: Penguin Books, 1993.

———. *Jesus and Judaism.* Philadelphia: Fortress, 1985.

———. *Paul and Palestinian Judaism.* Minneapolis: Fortress, 1977.

———. *Paul: The Apostle's Life, Letters, and Thought.* Minneapolis: Fortress, 2015.

Sanders, Jack T. "The Criterion of Coherence and the Randomness of Charisma: Poring through some Aporias in the Jesus Tradition." *NTS* 44 (1998): 1–25.

Sandmel, Samuel. "Parallelomania." *JBL* 81 (1962): 1–13.

Sapp, David A. "The LXX, 1QIsa, and MT Versions of Isaiah 53 and the Christian Doctrine of Atonement." Pages 170–92 in *Jesus and the Suffering Servant: Isaiah 53 and Christian Origins*. Edited by William Bellinger Jr. and William R. Farmer. Eugene, OR: Wipf & Stock, 2009.

Sasse, Markus. *Der Menschensohn im Evangelium nach Johannes.* Tübingen: Francke, 2000.

Satō, Migaku. *Q und Prophetie: Studien zur Gattungs- und Traditionsgeschichte der Quelle Q.* WUNT 29. Tübingen: Mohr Siebeck, 1988.

———. "Wisdom Statements in the Sphere of Prophecy." Pages 139–58 in *The Gospel behind the Gospels: Current Studies in Q*. Edited by Ronald A. Piper. NovTSup 75. Leiden: Brill, 1995.

Saucy, Mark. *The Kingdom of God in the Teaching of Jesus.* Dallas: Word, 1997.

Schaberg, Jane. "Daniel 7.12 and the New Testament Passion-Resurrection Predictions." *NTS* 31 (1985): 208–22.

———. "Mark 14:62: Early Christian Merkabah Imagery?" Pages 69–94 in *Apocalyptic and the New Testament: Essays in Honor of J. Louis Martyn*. Edited by Joel Marcus and Marion L. Soards. JSNTSup 24. Sheffield: JSOT Press, 1989.

Schäfer, Peter. "Diversity and Interaction: Messiahs in Early Judaism." Pages 15–35 in *Towards the Millennium: Messianic Expectations from the Bible to Waco*. Edited by Peter Schäfer and Mark R. Cohen. SHR 77. Leiden: Brill, 1998.

———. *The Origins of Jewish Mysticism*. Princeton: Princeton University Press, 2011.

———. *Two Gods in Heaven: Jewish Concepts of God in Antiquity.* Princeton: Princeton University Press, 2020.

Schaff, Philip. *The Creeds of Christendom*. 3 vols. Grand Rapids: Baker Books, 1969.

Schenkel, Daniel. *Das Charakterbild Jesu*. 3rd ed. Wiesbaden: Kreidel, 1864.

Schiffman, Lawrence H. *The Eschatological Community of the Dead Sea Scrolls*. SBLMS 38. Atlanta: Scholars Press, 1989.

———. *Qumran and Jerusalem: Studies in the Dead Sea Scrolls and the History of Judaism.* Grand Rapids: Eerdmans, 2010.

Schildgen, Brenda. *Power and Prejudice: The Reception of the Gospel of Mark*. Detroit: Wayne State University Press, 1999.

Schlosser, Jacques. *Le règne de Dieu dans les dits de Jesus*. 2 vols. Paris: Gabalda, 1980.

Schmidt, Karl Ludwig. "Die Stellung der Evangelien in der allgemeinen Literaturegeschichte." Pages 55–76 in *ΕΥΧΑΡΙΣΤΗΡΙΟΝ: Studien zur Religion und Literatur des Alten und Neuen Testaments*. Edited by Emil Balla and Hans Schmidt. Göttingen: Vandenhoeck & Ruprecht, 1923.

Schmidt, Nathaniel. "The 'Son of Man' in the Book of Daniel." *JBL* 19 (1900): 22–28.

Schmidt, Thomas C., and Nick Nicholas. *Hippolytus of Rome: Commentary on Daniel and "Chronicon."* GSECP 67. Piscataway, NJ: Gorgias, 2017.

Schnackenburg, Rudolf. *God's Rule and Kingdom*. Montreal: Palm, 1963.

Schnelle, Udo. *Das Evangelium nach Johannes*. THKNT 4. Leipzig: Evangelische Verlagsanstalt, 1998.

———. "Johannes 16 im Rahmen der Abschiedsreden." Pages 425–46 in *Studies in the Gospel of John and Its Christology: Festschrift Gilbert van Belle*. Edited by Joseph Verheyden. Walpole: Peeters, 2014.

Schniewind, Julius. *Das Evangelium nach Matthäus*. 11th ed. Göttingen: Vandenhoeck & Ruprecht, 1964.

Schnutenhaus, Frank. "Das Kommen und Erscheinen Gottes im Alten Testament." *ZAW* 76 (1964): 1–22.

Schoepflin, Rennie B. "Apocalypticism in an Age of Science." Pages 427–41 in *Apocalypticism in the Modern Period and the Contemporary Age*. Vol. 3 of *The Encyclopedia of Apocalypticism*. Edited by Stephen J. Stein. New York: Continuum, 1998.

Schoettgen, Christian Heinrich. *Horae Hebraicae et Talmudicae, in quibus adnotationes criticae et exegeticae, in Sacram Scripturam, praecipue in Novum Testamentum, ex fontibus Hebraicis et Talmudicis desumptae, exhibentur.* Hamburg: Langenhemii, 1733.

Scholem, Gershom. *Sabbatai Sevi: The Mystical Messiah*. Translated by R. J. Zwi Werblowsky. Princeton: Princeton University Press, 1973.

Schrage, Wolfgang. "Das messianische Zwischenreich bei Paulus." Pages 343–54 in *Eschatologie und Schöpfung: Festschrift für Erich Grässer*. Edited by Martin Evang, Helmut Merklein, and Michael Wolter. BZNW 89. Berlin: de Gruyter, 1997.

Schreiber, Stefan. "Paulus im 'Zwischenzustand': Phil 1.23 und die Ambivalenz des Sterbens als Provokation." *NTS* 49 (2003): 336–59.

Schröter, Jens. "B.IV.1. Das Evangelium nach Thomas." Pages 483–526 in *Antike christliche Apokryphen in deutscher Übersetzung, 1.1–2, Evangelien und Verwandtes*. Edited by Christoph Markschies and Jens Schröter. Tübingen: Mohr Siebeck, 2012.

———. *Das Abendmahl: Frühchristliche Deutungen und Impulse für die Gegenwart.* SBS 210. Stuttgart: Katholisches Bibelwerk, 2006.

———. *Jesus of Nazareth: Jew from Galilee, Savior of the World*. Translated by Wayne Coppins and S. Brian Pounds. Waco, TX: Baylor University Press, 2014.

Schröter, Jens, and Christine Jacobi, eds. *The Jesus Handbook*. Translated by Robert L. Brawley. Grand Rapids: Eerdmans, 2022.

Schultz, Brian. "Jesus as Archelaus in the Parable of the Pounds (Lk. 19:11–27)." *NovT* 49 (2007): 105–27.

Schulz, Siegfried. *Q: Die Spruchquelle der Evangelisten*. Zurich: Theologischer Verlag, 1972.

Schürmann, Heinz. "Beobachtungen zum Menschensohn-Titel in der Redequelle." Pages 124–47 in *Jesus und der Menschensohn: Festschrift A. Vögtle*. Edited by Rudolf Pesch and Rudolf Schnackenburg. Freiburg: Herder, 1975.

———. *Gottes Reich, Jesu Geschick: Jesu ureigener Tod im Licht seiner Basileia-Verkündigung*. Freiburg: Herder, 1983.

———. *Jesus, Gestalt und Geheimnis: Gesammelte Beiträge*, ed. Klaus Scholtissek. Paderborn: Bonifatius, 1994.

Schwartz, Hillel. "The Eschatology of Everyday Things." Pages 171–80 in *The Millenarian Turn: Millenarian Contexts of Science, Politics, and Everyday Anglo-American Life in the Seventeenth and Eighteenth Centuries*. Vol. 3 of *Millenarianism and Messianism in Early Modern European Culture*. Edited by James E. Force and Richard H. Popkin. IAHI 175. Dordrecht: Kluwer, 2001.

———. *Knaves, Fools, Madmen, and That Subtle Effluvium: A Study of the Opposition to the French Prophets in England, 1706–1710*. Gainesville: University of Florida Press, 1978.

Schwartzkopff, Paul. *Die Weissagungen Jesu Christi von seinem Tode, seiner Auferstehung und Wiederkunft und ihre Erfüllung*. Göttingen: Vandenhoeck & Ruprecht, 1895.

Schweitzer, Albert. *The Mystery of the Kingdom of God: The Secret of Jesus' Messiahship and Passion*. Translated by Walter Lowrie. Eugene, OR: Wipf & Stock, 1970.

———. *The Mysticism of Paul the Apostle*. Translated by William Montgomery. New York: Holt, 1931.

———. *The Quest of the Historical Jesus*. Translated by William Montgomery. New York: Macmillan, 1955.

Schweizer, Eduard. "Der Menschensohn." *ZNW* 50 (1959): 185–209.

———. *Jesus*. Translated by David E. Green. Atlanta: John Knox, 1971.

———. "The Son of Man Again." *NTS* 9 (1963): 256–61.

Schwemer, Anna Maria. "Die Zersägung des Propheten Jesaja." Pages 45–67 in *Martyriumsvorstellungen in Antike und Mittelalter*. Edited by Sebastian Fuhrmann and Regina Grundmann. AJEC 80. Leiden: Brill, 2012.

———. *Studien zu den frühjüdischen Prophetenlegenden Vitae Prophetarum*. TSAJ. Tübingen: Mohr Siebeck, 1995.

Scott, Bernard Brandon. "How Did We Get Here?" Pages 47–64 in *Jesus Reconsidered: Scholarship in the Public Eye*. Edited by Bernard Brandon Scott. Santa Rosa, CA: Polebridge, 2007.

Scott, James M. "Philo and the Restoration of Israel." Pages 553–75 in *Society of Biblical Literature 1995 Seminar Papers*. SBLSP 34. Atlanta: Scholars Press, 1995.

Seeley, John. *Ecce Homo: A Survey of the Life and Work of Jesus Christ*. Boston: Roberts Brothers, 1867.

Seeskin, Kenneth. "Maimonides and the Idea of a Deflationary Messiah." Pages 93–107 in *Rethinking the Messianic Idea in Judaism*. Edited by Michael L. Morgan and Steven Weitzman. Bloomington: Indiana University Press, 2015.

Segal, Alan F. *Life after Death: A History of the Afterlife in Western Religion*. New York: Doubleday, 2004.

Sellin, Gerhard. *Der Streit um die Auferstehung der Toten: Eine religionsgeschichtliche und exegetische Untersuchung von 1 Korinther 15*. FRLANT 138. Göttingen: Vandenhoeck & Ruprecht, 1986.

Semler, J. S. *Beantwortung der Fragmente eines Ungenannten, inbesonders vom Zweck Jesu und seiner Jünger*. Rev. ed. Halle: Erziehungsinstitut, 1780.

Sevenster, Jan Nicolass. "Some Remarks on the GYMNOS in II Cor. V 3." Pages 202–14 in *Studia Paulina: In honorem Johannis de Zwaan Septuagenarii*. Edited by Jan Nicolass Sevenster and W. C. van Unnik. Haarlem: Bohn, 1953.

Sheinfeld, Shayna. "Scenes from the End of the World in American Popular Culture." Pages 201–18 in *The Oxford Handbook of the Bible and American Popular Culture*. Edited by Dan W. Clanton Jr. and Terry R. Clark. Oxford: Oxford University Press, 2021.

Sheppard, Beth M. *The Craft of History and the Study of the New Testament*. Atlanta: Society of Biblical Literature, 2012.

Sherwood, Yvonne. "'Not with a Bang but a Whimper': Shrunken Eschatologies of the Twentieth Century and the Bible." Pages 94–116 in *Apocalyptic in History and Tradition*. Edited by Christopher Rowland and John Barton. JSPSup 43. Sheffield: Sheffield Academic, 2002.

Shively, Elizabeth E. "The Eclipse of the Markan Narrative: On the (Re)cognition of a Coherent Story and Implications for Genre." *EC* 12 (2021): 369–87.

Shogren, G. S. *1 and 2 Thessalonians*. Grand Rapids: Zondervan, 2012.

Sibbes, Richard. *The Bride's Longing*. London: Purslow, 1638.

Sievers, Joseph. "Josephus and the Afterlife." Pages 20–34 in *Understanding Josephus: Seven Perspectives*. Edited by Steve Mason. Sheffield: Sheffield Academic, 1998.

Sigvartsen, Jan A. *Afterlife and Resurrection Beliefs in the Pseudepigrapha*. London: Bloomsbury T&T Clark, 2019.

Sim, David C. *Apocalyptic Eschatology in the Gospel of Matthew*. SNTSMS 88. Cambridge: Cambridge University Press, 1996.

———. *The Gospel of Matthew and Christian Judaism: The History and Social Setting of the Matthean Community*. SNTW. Edinburgh: T&T Clark, 1998.

———. "Life after Death? The Question of Immediate Life after Death in the Dead Sea Scrolls and in the Gospel of Matthew." Pages 329–46 in *Matthew within Judaism: Israel and the Nations in the First Gospel*. Edited by Anders Runesson and Daniel M. Gurtner. ECL 27. Atlanta: SBL Press, 2020.

Simon, Marcel. *Verus Israel: A Study of the Relations between Christians and Jews in the Roman Empire (113–425)*. Translated by H. McKeating. Oxford: Oxford University Press, 1986.

———. *Verus Israel: Étude sur les relations entre chrétiens et juifs dans l'empire romain (135–425)*. Paris: Boccard, 1964.

Sjöberg, Erik. "בן אדם und בר אנש im Hebräischen und Aramäischen." *AcOr* 21 (1950): 57–65, 91–107.

———. *Der verborgene Menschensohn in den Evangelien*. Lund: Gleerup, 1955.

Smalley, Stephen S. "The Delay of the Parousia." *JBL* 83 (1963): 41–54.

Smith, Abraham. "First Letter to the Thessalonians." *NIB* 11.

Smith, Barry D. *Jesus' Twofold Teaching about the Kingdom of God*. Sheffield: Sheffield Phoenix, 2009.

———. *The Meaning of Jesus' Death: Reviewing the New Testament's Interpretations*. London: Bloomsbury T&T Clark, 2017.

Smith, David. *The Days of His Flesh: The Earthly Life of Our Lord and Saviour Jesus Christ*. London: Hodder & Stoughton, 1906.

Smith, Mark S. *The Early History of God: Yahweh and the Other Deities in Ancient Israel*. 2nd ed. Grand Rapids: Eerdmans, 2002.

Smith, Murray. "The Lord Jesus and His Coming in the Didache." Pages 363–407 in *The Didache: A Missing Piece of the Puzzle in Early Christianity*. Edited by Jonathan A. Draper and Clayton N. Jefford. ECL 14. Atlanta: SBL Press, 2015.

Smith, Murray, and Ian J. Vaillancourt. "Enthroned and Coming to Reign: Jesus' Eschatological Use of Psalm 110:1 in Mark 14:62." *JBL* 141 (2022): 513–31.

Snodgrass, Klyne R. *Stories with Intent: A Comprehensive Guide to the Parables of Jesus*. Grand Rapids: Eerdmans, 2008.

———. "The Temple Incident." Pages 429–80 in *Key Events in the Life of the Historical Jesus: A Collaborative Exploration of Context and Coherence*. Edited by Darrell L. Bock and Robert L. Webb. WUNT 247. Tübingen: Mohr Siebeck, 2009.

Soards, Marion L. *The Speeches in Acts: Their Content, Context, and Concerns*. Louisville: Westminster John Knox, 1994.

Spinoza, Baruch. *Tractatus theologico-politicus*. Translated by Samuel Shirley. Leiden: Brill, 1989.

Stanley, Christopher D. "'The Redeemer Will Come ἐκ Σιών': Romans 11.26–27 Revisited." Pages 118–42 in *Paul and the Scriptures of Israel*. Edited by Craig A. Evans and James A. Sanders. London: Bloomsbury, 2015.

Stanton, Graham N. *The Gospels and Jesus*. 2nd ed. Oxford: Oxford University Press, 2002.

Stanton, Vincent Henry. *The Jewish and the Christian Messiah*. Edinburgh: T&T Clark, 1886.

Steck, Odil H. *Israel und das gewaltsame Geschick der Propheten*. WMANT 23. Neukirchen-Vluyn: Neukirchener, 1967.

Stein, Robert H. *Jesus, the Temple, and the Coming Son of Man: A Commentary on Mark 13*. Downers Grove, IL: InterVarsity Press, 2014.

———. *Mark*. BECNT. Grand Rapids: Baker Books, 2008.

Steinmetz, David. "Uncovering a Second Narrative: Detective Fiction and the Construction of Historical Method." Pages 54–65 in *The Art of Reading Scripture*. Edited by Ellen F. Davis and Richard B. Hays. Grand Rapids: Eerdmans, 2003.

Stemberger, Günter. "Die Messiasfrage in den christlich-jüdischen Disputationen des Mittelalters." *Jahrbuch für Biblische Theologie* 9 (1993): 239–20.

Stendahl, Krister. "Quis et Unde? An Analysis of Mt 1–2." Pages 94–105 in *Judentum Urchristentum Kirche: Festschrift für Joachim Jeremias*. Edited by Walther Eltester. Berlin: Töpelmann, 1960.

Stettler, Christian. *Das letzte Gericht: Studien zur Endgerichtserwartung von den Schriftpropheten bis Jesus*. WUNT 2/299. Tübingen: Mohr Siebeck, 2011.

Steyn, Gert J. "The Eschatology of Hebrews—As Understood within a Cultic Setting." Pages 429–50 in *Eschatology of the New Testament and Some Related Documents*. Edited by Jan G. van der Watt. WUNT 2/315. Tübingen: Mohr Siebeck, 2011.

Stock, Brian. *The Implications of Literacy: Written Language and Models of Interpretation in the Eleventh and Twelfth Centuries*. Princeton: Princeton University Press, 1983.

Stone, Michael E. "Coherence and Inconsistency in the Apocalypses: The Case of 'The End' in 4 Ezra." *JBL* 102 (1983): 229–43.

———. *Fourth Ezra: A Commentary on the Book of Fourth Ezra*. Hermeneia. Minneapolis: Fortress, 1990.

———. "The Question of the Messiah in 4 Ezra." Pages 209–24 in *Judaisms and Their Messiahs at the Turn of the Christian Era*. Edited by Jacob Neusner, William S. Green, and Ernest Frerichs. Cambridge: Cambridge University Press, 1987.

Strauss, David Friedrich. *The Life of Jesus Critically Examined*. Translated by George Eliot. 4th ed. London: Sonnenschein, 1902.

———. *A New Life of Jesus*. Translator s.n. 2 vols. London: Williams & Norgate, 1865.

Strecker, Georg. *Theology of the New Testament*. Translated by M. Eugene Boring. Louisville: Westminster John Knox, 2000.

Striker, Jeffrey S. "The Parousia of Jesus in Second- and Third-Century Christianity." Pages 147–68 in *The Return of Jesus in Early Christianity*. Peabody, MA: Hendrickson, 2000.

Stuckenbruck, Loren T. "Messianic Ideas in the Apocalypse and Related Literature of Early Judaism." Pages 90–113 in *The Messiah in the Old and New Testaments*. Edited by Stanley E. Porter. Grand Rapids: Eerdmans, 2007.

Stuckenbruck, Loren T., Stephen C. Barton, and Benjamin G. Wold, eds. *Memory in the Bible and Antiquity*. WUNT 212. Tübingen: Mohr Siebeck, 2007.

Stuckenbruck, Loren T., and Gabriele Boccaccini, eds. *Enoch and the Synoptic Gospels: Reminiscences, Allusions, Intertextuality*. EJL 44. Atlanta: SBL Press, 2016.

Stuhlmacher, Peter. "Die Stellung Jesu und des Paulus zu Jerusalem: Versuch einer Erinnerung." *ZNW* 86 (1989): 140–56.

———. *Grundlegung von Jesus zu Paulus*. Vol. 1 of *Biblische Theologie des Neuen Testaments*. Göttingen: Vandenhoeck & Ruprecht, 1992.

Such, W. A. *The Abomination of Desolation in the Gospel of Mark: Its Historical Reference in Mark 13:14 and Its Impact in the Gospel.* Lanham, MD: University Press of America, 1999.

Sulzbach, Carla. "End Times and Ending Times in 4 Ezra." Pages 222–34 in *Eschatology in Antiquity: Forms and Functions*. Edited by Hilary Marlow, Karla Pollmann, and Helen Van Noorden. London: Routledge, 2021.

Sutcliffe, Adam. *Judaism and Enlightenment*. New York: Cambridge University Press, 2003.

Syreeni, Kari. *Becoming John: The Making of a Passion Gospel.* LNTS 590. London: Bloomsbury T&T Clark, 2018.

Syrén, Roger. *The Blessings in the Targums: A Study on the Targumic Interpretations of Genesis 49 and Deuteronomy 33.* Åbo: Åbo Akademi, 1986.

Talbert, Charles H. *Literary Patterns, Theological Themes, and the Genre of Luke-Acts.* Missoula, MT: Scholars Press, 1975.

———. "2 Peter and the Delay of the Parousia." *VC* 20 (1966): 137–45.

Talmon, Shemaryahu. "Waiting for the Messiah: The Spiritual Universe of the Qumran Covenanters." Pages 111–37 in *Judaisms and Their Messiahs at the Turn of the Christian Era*. Edited by Jacob Neusner, William S. Green, and Ernest S. Frerichs. Cambridge: Cambridge University Press, 1987.

Tan, Kim Huat. *The Zion Traditions and the Aims of Jesus*. SNTSMS 91. Cambridge: Cambridge University Press, 1997.

Taylor, Barbara Brown. "Expecting the Second Coming: Don't Say When." *ChrCent* 121 (2004): 34–35, 37–38.

Taylor, Jeremy. *The Life of Our Blessed Saviour Jesus Christ.* Somerset: Patton, 1818.

Taylor, Vincent. *Life and Ministry of Jesus*. New York: Abingdon, 1955.

———. "The Son of Man Sayings Relating to the Parousia." *ExpTim* 58 (1946–47): 12–15.

Teeple, Howard M. *The Mosaic Eschatological Prophet*. Philadelphia: Society of Biblical Literature, 1957.

Telford, William R. "Major Trends and Interpretive Issues in the Study of Jesus." Pages 33–74 in *Studying the Historical Jesus: Evaluations of the State of Current Research*. Edited by Bruce Chilton and Craig A. Evans. Leiden: Brill, 1994.

———. *The Theology of the Gospel of Mark*. Cambridge: Cambridge University Press, 1999.

Thackeray, Henry St. John. *The Relation of Saint Paul to Contemporary Jewish Thought*. London: Macmillan, 1900.

Thate, Michael J. *Remembrance of Things Past? Albert Schweitzer, the Anxiety of Influence, and the Untidy Jesus of Markan Memory*. WUNT 2/351. Tübingen: Mohr Siebeck, 2013.

Theisohn, Johannes. *Der auserwählte Richter*. Göttingen: Vandenhoeck & Ruprecht, 1975.

Theissen, Gerd, and Annette Merz. *The Historical Jesus: A Comprehensive Guide*. Translated by John Bowden. Minneapolis: Fortress, 1998.

Theissen, Gerd, and Dagmar Winter. *Die Kriterienfrage in der Jesusforschung: Vom Differenzkriterium zum Plausibilitätskriterium*. Göttingen: Vandenhoeck & Ruprecht, 1997.

———. *The Quest for the Plausible Jesus: The Question of Criteria*. Louisville: Westminster John Knox, 2002.

Theobald, Michael. "'Ihr habt die Blasphemie gehört!' (Mk 14:64): Warum der Hohe Rat in Jerusalem auf den Tod Jesu hinwirkte." *NovT* 58 (2016): 233–58.

Thiselton, Anthony C. *The First Epistle to the Corinthians: A Commentary on the Greek Text*. NIGTC. Grand Rapids: Eerdmans, 2000.

———. "The Parousia in Modern Theology: Some Questions and Comments." *TynBul* 27 (1976): 27–53.

Thrall, Margaret E. *A Critical and Exegetical Commentary on the Second Epistle to the Corinthians*. 2 vols. ICC. Edinburgh: T&T Clark, 1994.

Tilly, Michael. *Johannes der Täufer und die Biographie der Propheten: Die synoptische Täuferüberlieferung und das jüdische Prophetenbild zur Zeit des Täufers*. BZANT 7. Stuttgart: Kohlhammer, 1994.

Tindal, Matthew. *Christianity as Old as the Creation, or, The Gospel, a Republication of the Religion of Nature*. London: s.n., 1730.

Titius, Arthur. *Lehre Jesu vom Reiche Gottes*. Vol. 1 of *Die neutestamentliche Lehre von der Seligkeit und ihre Bedeutung für die Gegenwart*. Freiburg: Mohr, 1895.

Tödt, H. E. *The Son of Man in Synoptic Tradition*. Translated by D. M. Barton. Philadelphia: Westminster, 1965.

Toit, David S. du. *Der abwesende Herr: Strategien im Markusevangelium zur Bewältigung der Abwesenheit des Auferstandenen*. WMANT 111. Neukirchen-Vluyn: Neukirchener Verlag, 2006.

———. "Die Danielrezeption in Markus 13." Pages 55–78 in *Die Geschichte der Daniel-Auslegung in Judentum, Christentum und Islam: Studien zur Kommentierung des Danielbuches in Literatur und Kunst*. Edited by Katharina Bracht and David S. du Toit. BZAW 371. Berlin: de Gruyter, 2007.

———. "Prolepsis als Prophetie: Zur christologischen Funktion narrativer Anachronie im Markusevangelium." *WD* 26 (2001): 165–89.

Toland, John. *Nazarenus, or, Jewish, Gentile, and Mahometan Christianity*. London: Brown, Roberts, Brotherson, 1718.

Tomson, Peter. "Paul as a Recipient and Teacher of Tradition." Pages 393–410 in *Studies on Jews and Christians in the First and Second Centuries*. WUNT 418. Tübingen: Mohr Siebeck, 2019.

Torrey, Charles Cutler. *Lives of the Prophets: Greek Text and Translation*. Philadelphia: Society of Biblical Literature, 1946.

Travis, Stephen H. "Wrath of God." *ABD* 6:996–98.

Triebel, Johannes. "Das koranische Evangelium: Kritische Anmerkungen zur koranischen Darstellung der Person und Botschaft Jesu." *TBei* 38 (2007): 269–82.

Trotter, Christine. "Consolatory Rhetoric in 1 Thessalonians 4:9–12." Paper presented at the Annual Meeting of the Eastern Great Lakes Biblical Society, March 18, 2022.

Trumbower, Jeffrey A. "The Role of Malachi in the Career of John the Baptist." Pages 28–41 in *The Gospels and the Scriptures of Israel*. Edited by Craig A. Evans and W. Richard Stegner. Sheffield: JSOT Press, 1994.

Tuckett, Christopher. "Francis Watson, Q and 'L/M.'" Pages 115–38 in *Gospel Interpretation and the Q-Hypothesis*. Edited by Mogens Müller and Heike Omerzu. LNTS 573. London: Bloomsbury T&T Clark, 2018.

———. *From the Sayings to the Gospels*. WUNT 328. Tübingen: Mohr Siebeck, 2014.

———. Introduction to *The Messianic Secret*, 1–28. Edited by Christopher Tuckett. London: SPCK, 1983.

———. *Q and the History of Early Christianity: Studies on Q*. London: T&T Clark, 2004.

Turner, David L. *Israel's Last Prophet: Jesus and the Jewish Leaders in Matthew 23*. Minneapolis: Fortress, 2015.

———. *Matthew*. BECNT. Grand Rapids: Baker Books, 2008.

Tyson, Joseph B. "Jesus and Herod Antipas." *JBL* 79 (1960): 239–46.

Vaage, Leif E. "The Son of Man Sayings in Q: Stratigraphical Location and Significance." *Semeia* 55 (1991): 103–29.

Vander Hart, Mark D. "The Transition of the Old Testament Day of the Lord into the New Testament Day of the Lord Jesus Christ." *Mid-America Journal of Theology* 9 (1993): 3–25.

VanderKam, James C. *Jubilees: A Commentary*. 2 vols. Hermeneia. Minneapolis: Fortress, 2018.

———. "Messianism and Apocalypticism." Pages 193–228 in *The Origins of Apocalypticism in Judaism and Christianity*. Vol. 1 of *The Encyclopedia of Apocalypticism*. Edited by Bernard McGinn, John J. Collins, and Stephen J. Stein. New York: Continuum, 1998.

———. "Righteous One, Messiah, Chosen One, and Son of Man in 1 Enoch 37–71." Pages 169–91 in *The Messiah: Developments in Earliest Judaism and Christianity*. Edited by James H. Charlesworth. Minneapolis: Fortress, 1992.

———. "Studies in the Apocalypse of Weeks (1 Enoch 93:1–10; 91:11–17)." *CBQ* 46 (1984): 511–23.

Vena, Osvaldo D. *The Parousia and Its Rereadings: The Development of the Eschatological Consciousness in the Writings of the New Testament*. SBT 27. New York: Lang, 2001.

Verheyden, Joseph. "Describing the Parousia: The Cosmic Phenomena in Mark 13, 24–25." Pages 525–50 in *The Scriptures in the Gospels*. Edited by Christopher M. Tuckett. Leuven: Leuven University Press, 1997.

Vermes, Geza. *Jesus the Jew: A Historian's Reading of the Gospels*. London: Collins, 1973.

———. "The Jewish Jesus Movement." Pages 1–26 in *Partings: How Judaism and Christianity Became Two*. Edited by Hershel Shanks. Washington, DC: Biblical Archaeological Society, 2013.

———. *The Resurrection: History and Myth*. New York: Doubleday, 2008.

Vielhauer, Philipp. *Aufsätze zum Neuen Testament*. TB 31. Munich: Kaiser, 1965.

Vincent, Thomas. *Christ's Sudden and Certain Appearance to Judgment*. Morgan: Soli Deo Gloria, 1996.

Viviano, Benedict T. "Eschatology in the Quest for the Historical Jesus." Pages 73–90 in *The Oxford Handbook of Eschatology*. Edited by Jerry L. Walls. Oxford: Oxford University Press, 2008.

Vogel, C. J. de. "Reflexions on Philippians i.23–24." *NovT* 19 (1977): 262–74.

Vögtle, Anton. "Exegetische Erwägungen über das Wissen und Selbstbewusstein Jesu." Pages 608–67 in vol. 1 of *Gott in Welt: Festgabe für Karl Rahner*. Edited by Johannes Baptist Metz, Walter Kern, Adolf Darlapp, and Herbert Vorgrimler. Freiburg: Herder, 1964.

———. "Jesus von Nazareth." Pages 3–24 in vol. 1 of *Ökumenische Kirchengeschichte*. Edited by Raymund Kottje and Bernd Moller. Munich: Kaiser, 1970.

Volkmar, Gustav. *Jesus Nazarenus und die erste christliche Zeit*. Zurich: Schmidt, 1882.

Vollenweider, Samuel. "Auferstehung als Verwandlung: Die paulinische Eschatologie von 1 Kor 15 im Vergleich mit der syrischen Baruchapokalypse (2 Bar)." Pages 463–90 in *Anthropologie und Ethik im Frühjudentum und im Neuen Testament*. Edited by Matthias Konradt and Esther Schläpfer. WUNT 322. Tübingen: Mohr Siebeck, 2014.

Voltaire. *Mélanges*. Paris: Gallimard, 1961.

———. "Messie." Pages 177–95 in *Dictionnaire philosophique* in vol. 41 of *Oeuvres complètes de Voltaire*. Paris: Werdet & Lequien, 1827.

Waddell, James A. *The Messiah: A Comparative Study of the Enochic Son of Man and the Pauline Kyrios*. London: T&T Clark International, 2011.

Waetjen, Herman C. *The Origin and Destiny of Humanness: An Interpretation of the Gospel according to Matthew.* Corte Madera: Omega, 1976.

Wagner, J. Ross. *Heralds of the Good News: Isaiah and Paul 'in Concert' in the Letter to the Romans.* NovTSup 101. Leiden: Brill, 2002.

Wahlde, Urban C. von. "C. H. Dodd, the Historical Jesus, and Realized Eschatology." Pages 149–62 in *Engaging with C. H. Dodd on the Gospel of John: Sixty Years of Tradition and Interpretation.* Edited by Tom Thatcher and Catrin Williams. Cambridge: Cambridge University Press, 2013.

Walker, Peter. *Jesus and the Holy City: New Testament Perspectives on Jerusalem.* Grand Rapids: Eerdmans, 1996.

Wallace, James Buchanan. "Benefactor and Paradigm: Viewing Jesus' Ascension in Luke-Acts through Greco-Roman Ascension Traditions." Pages 83–110 in *Ascent into Heaven in Luke-Acts: New Explorations of Luke's Narrative Hinge.* Edited by David K. Bryan and David W. Pao. Minneapolis: Fortress, 2016.

Walls, Jerry L. Introduction to *The Oxford Handbook of Eschatology*, 73–90. Edited by Jerry L. Walls. Oxford: Oxford University Press, 2007.

Walter, Nikolaus. "Hellenistische Eschatologie bei Paulus? Zu 2 Kor 5, 1–10." *TQ* 176 (1996): 53–64.

———. "Paulus und die urchristliche Jesustradition." *NTS* 31 (1985): 498–522.

Walton, Steve. "The End: What and When? Eschatology in Luke-Acts." Pages 383–95 in *Eschatology in Antiquity: Forms and Functions.* Edited by Hilary Marlow, Karla Pollmann, and Helen Van Noorden. London: Routledge, 2021.

Wasserman, Emma. "Gentile Gods at the Eschaton: A Reconsideration of Paul's 'Principalities and Powers' in 1 Cor. 15." *JBL* 136 (2017): 727–46.

Watson, Francis. "Eschatology and the Twentieth Century." Pages 331–47 in *Eschatologie—Eschatology: The Sixth Durham-Tübingen Research Symposium; Eschatology in Old Testament, Ancient Judaism and Early Christianity.* Edited by Hans-Joachim Eckstein, Christof Landmesser, and Hermann Lichtenberger. WUNT 272. Tübingen: Mohr Siebeck, 2011.

———. *Gospel Writing: A Canonical Perspective.* Grand Rapids: Eerdmans, 2013.

———. "'I Received from the Lord . . .': Paul, Jesus, and the Last Supper." Pages 103–24 in *Jesus and Paul Reconnected: Fresh Pathways into an Old Debate.* Edited by Todd D. Still. Grand Rapids: Eerdmans, 2007.

———. *Paul and the Hermeneutics of Faith.* 2nd ed. London: Bloomsbury T&T Clark, 2016.

———. "Seven Theses on the Synoptic Problem, in Disagreement with Christopher Tuckett." Pages 115–38 in *Gospel Interpretation and the Q-Hypothesis.* Edited by Mogens Müller and Heike Omerzu. LNTS 573. London: Bloomsbury T&T Clark, 2018.

Watt, Jan van der. "Eschatology in John—a Continuous Process of Realizing Events."

Pages 109–40 in *Eschatology of the New Testament and Some Related Documents*. Edited by Jan G. van der Watt. WUNT 2/315. Tübingen: Mohr Siebeck, 2011.

Watts, Rikki E. *Isaiah's New Exodus and Mark*. Grand Rapids: Baker Books, 2000.

Weaver, Walter P. *The Historical Jesus in the Twentieth Century: 1900–50*. Harrisburg, PA: Trinity International, 1999.

Webb, Robert L. "The Historical Enterprise and Historical Jesus Research." Pages 9–93 in *Key Events in the Life of the Historical Jesus: A Collaborative Exploration of Context and Coherence*. Edited by Darrell L. Bock and Robert L. Webb. WUNT 247. Tübingen: Mohr Siebeck, 2009.

———. *John the Baptizer and Prophet: A Sociohistorical Study*. JSNTSup 62. Sheffield: JSOT Press, 1991.

Wedderburn, Alexander J. M. *Jesus and the Historians*. WUNT 269. Tübingen: Mohr Siebeck, 2010.

Weiffenbach, Wilhelm. *Die Wiederkunftsgedanke Jesu*. Leipzig: Druck, 1873.

Weiss, Bernard. *The Life of Christ*. Translated by John Walter Hope. 3 vols. Clark's Foreign Theological Library 14–16. Edinburgh: T&T Clark, 1883.

Weiss, Johannes. *Das Urchristentum*. Göttingen: Vandenhoeck & Ruprecht, 1917.

———. *Jesus' Proclamation of the Kingdom of God*. Translated by Richard H. Hiers and David Larrimore Holland. Philadelphia: Fortress, 1971.

Weisse, Hermann. *Die evangelische Geschichte, kritisch und philosophisch bearbeit*. Leipzig: Breitkopf & Hartel, 1838.

Weizsäcker, Carl. *Untersuchungen über die evangelische Geschichte: Ihre Quellen und den Gang ihrer Entwicklung*. 2nd ed. Tübingen: Mohr, 1901.

Welch, Claude. *1799–1870*. Vol. 1 of *Protestant Thought in the Nineteenth Century*. New Haven: Yale University Press, 1972.

———. *1870–1914*. Vol. 2 of *Protestant Thought in the Nineteenth Century*. New Haven: Yale University Press, 1985.

Wellhausen, Julius. *Einleitung in die drei ersten Evangelien*. 2nd ed. Berlin: Reimer, 1911.

———. *Evangelienkommentare*. Berlin: de Gruyter, 1987.

Wells, Kyle B. *Grace and Agency in Paul and Second Temple Judaism*. NovTSup 157. Leiden: Brill, 2015.

Wendebourg, Nicola. *Der Tag des Herrn: Zur Gerichtserwartung im Neuen Testament auf ihrem alttestamentlichen und frühjüdischen Hintergrund*. WMANT 96. Neukirchen-Vluyn: Neukirchener, 2003.

Wendt, Hans Hinrich. *Der Inhalt der Lehre Jesu*. Göttingen: Vandenhoeck & Ruprecht, 1890.

Wenham, David. "The Kingdom of God and Daniel." *ExpTim* 98 (1987): 132–34.

———. *Paul: Follower of Jesus or Founder of Christianity?* Grand Rapids: Eerdmans, 1995.

Werner, Hermann. *Die psychische Gesundheit Jesu*. Berlin: Runge, 1909.

Werner, Martin. *Die Entstehung des christlichen Dogmas*. Bern: Haupt, 1954.

———. *The Formation of Christian Dogma: An Historical Study of Its Problem*. Translated by S. G. F. Brandon. New York: Harper, 1957.

Wernle, Paul. *Jesus*. Tübingen: Mohr, 1916.

Wette, W. M. L. de. *Lehrbuch der christliche Dogmatik in ihrer historischen Entwicklung dargestellt*. Berlin: Realschulbuchhandlung, 1813.

White, Joel. "Anti-imperial Subtexts in Paul: An Attempt at Building a Firmer Foundation." *Bib* 90 (2009): 305–33.

Whiteley, D. E. H. *The Theology of St. Paul*. Philadelphia: Fortress, 1966.

Wieland, Konstantin. *Hat Jesus geirrt? Ein Lösungsversuch zur Parusiefrage*. Dillingen: Keller, 1910.

Wilken, Robert L. "Early Christian Chiliasm, Jewish Messianism, and the Idea of the Holy Land." *HTR* 79 (1986): 298–307.

Williams, Catrin H. "Faith, Eternal Life, and the Spirit in the Gospel of John." Pages 347–62 in *The Oxford Handbook of Johannine Studies*. Edited by Judith M. Lieu and Martinus C. de Boer. Oxford: Oxford University Press, 2018.

———. "Isaiah in John's Gospel." Pages 101–16 in *Isaiah in the New Testament*. Edited by Steve Moyise and Maarten J. J. Menken. London: T&T Clark, 2005.

———. "Jeremiah and His Prophecies in the New Testament." Pages 520–38 in *The Oxford Handbook of Jeremiah*. Edited by Louis Stulman and Edward Silver. Oxford: Oxford University Press, 2021.

Williams, George Huntson. *The Radical Reformation*. Philadelphia: Westminster, 1962.

Williams, Jarvis. *Maccabean Martyr Traditions in Paul's Theology of Atonement: Did Martyr Theology Shape Paul's Conception of Jesus' Death?* Eugene, OR: Wipf & Stock, 2010.

Williams, Michael A. *Rethinking "Gnosticism": An Argument for Dismantling a Dubious Category*. Princeton: Princeton University Press, 1996.

Williams, P. J. "Expressing Definiteness in Aramaic: A Response to Casey's Theory concerning the Son of Man Sayings." Pages 61–77 in *'Who Is This Son of Man?' The Latest Scholarship on a Puzzling Expression of the Historical Jesus*. Edited by Larry W. Hurtado and Paul L. Owen. LNTS 390. London: Bloomsbury T&T Clark, 2011.

Wilson, Alistair I. *When Will These Things Happen? A Study of Jesus as Judge in Matthew 21–25*. Eugene, OR: Wipf & Stock, 2004.

Wilson, S. G. "Lukan Eschatology." *NTS* 16 (1970): 330–47.

Winter, Dagmar. "The Dissimilar Jesus: Anti-Semitism, Protestantism, Hero-Worship, and Dialectical Theology." Pages 129–42 in *Soundings in the Religion of Jesus:*

Perspectives and Methods in Jewish and Christian Scholarship. Edited by Bruce Chilton, Anthony Le Donne, and Jacob Neusner. Minneapolis: Fortress, 2012.

Witherington, Ben, III. *Jesus, Paul, and the End of the World*. Downers Grove, IL: InterVarsity Press, 1992.

Wold, Benjamin. "Apocalyptic Thought in the Epistles of Colossians and Ephesians." Pages 219–32 in *The Jewish Apocalyptic Tradition and the Shaping of New Testament Thought*. Edited by Benjamin E. Reynolds and Loren T. Stuckenbruck. Minneapolis: Fortress, 2017.

Wolfe, Judith. "The Eschatological Turn in German Philosophy." *Modern Theology* 35 (2019): 55–70.

Wolff, Christian. *Jeremia im Frühjudentum und Urchristentum*. Berlin: Akademie-Verlag, 1976.

Wolff, Hans Walter. *Jesaja 53 im Urchristentum*. Berlin: Evangelische Verlagsanstalt, 1950.

Wolter, Michael. "Das Evangelium." Pages 337–42 in *Paulus Handbuch*. Edited by Friedrich W. Horn. Tübingen: Mohr Siebeck, 2013.

———. "Eschatology in the Gospel according to Luke." Pages in 91–108 in *Eschatology of the New Testament and Some Related Documents*. Edited by Jan G. van der Watt. WUNT 2/315. Tübingen: Mohr Siebeck, 2011.

———. *Paulus: Ein Grundriss seiner Theologie*. Göttingen: Vandenhoeck & Ruprecht, 2021.

———. *Theologie und Ethos im frühen Christentum: Studien zu Jesus, Paulus und Lukas*. Tübingen: Mohr Siebeck, 2009.

Wood, A. Skevington. "The Eschatology of Irenaeus." *EvQ* 40 (1968): 30–41.

Woolston, Thomas. *A Second Supplement to the Moderator between an Infidel and an Apostate*. London: the author, 1725.

———. *A Third Discourse on the Miracles of Our Saviour*. London: the author, 1728.

Woude, Adam S. van der. "Melchisedek als himmlische Erlösergestalt in den neugefundenen eschatologischen Midraschim aus Qumran Höhle XI." *OTS* 14 (1965): 354–73.

Wright, N. T. *The Climax of the Covenant: Christ and the Law in Pauline Theology*. Minneapolis: Fortress, 1993.

———. *History and Eschatology: Jesus and the Promise of Natural Theology*. Waco, TX: Baylor University Press, 2019.

———. "Hope Deferred? Against the Dogma of Delay." *EC* 9 (2018): 37–82.

———. *Jesus and the Victory of God*. Minneapolis: Fortress, 1996.

———. "Jesus, Quest for the Historical." *ABD* 3:796–802.

———. *The New Testament and the People of God*. Minneapolis: Fortress, 1992.

———. *Paul and the Faithfulness of God*. Minneapolis: Fortress, 2013.

———. *The Resurrection of the Son of God*. Minneapolis: Fortress, 2003.

———. *Surprised by Hope: Rethinking Heaven, the Resurrection, and the Mission of the Church*. New York: HarperOne, 2008.

———. *Who Was Jesus?* Grand Rapids: Eerdmans, 1992.

Yarbro Collins, Adela. "Apocalypticism and Christian Origins." Pages 326–39 in *The Oxford Handbook of Apocalyptic Literature*. Edited by John J. Collins. Oxford: Oxford University Press, 2014.

———. "Apocalypticism and New Testament Theology." Pages 31–50 in *The Nature of New Testament Theology*. Edited by Christopher Rowland and Christopher Tuckett. Malden, MA: Blackwell, 2006.

———. "Daniel 7 and the Historical Jesus." Pages 187–94 in *Of Scribes and Scrolls*. Edited by Harold W. Attridge, John J. Collins, and Thomas H. Tobin. Lanham, MD: University Press of America, 1990.

———. *Mark: A Commentary*. Hermeneia. Minneapolis: Fortress, 2007.

———. "Response to Israel Knohl, Messiahs and Resurrection in 'The Gabriel Revelation.'" Pages 93–97 in *Hazon Gabriel: New Readings of the Gabriel Revelation*. Edited by Matthias Henze. Atlanta: Society of Biblical Literature, 2011.

Yarbro Collins, Adela, and John J. Collins. *King and Messiah as Son of God: Divine, Human, and Angelic Messianic Figures in Biblical and Related Literature*. Grand Rapids: Eerdmans, 2008.

Yieh, John Yueh-Han. *One Teacher: Jesus' Teaching Role in Matthew's Gospel Report*. BZNW 124. Berlin: de Gruyter, 2004.

Zacharias, H. Daniel. *Matthew's Presentation of the Son of David: Davidic Tradition and Typology in the Gospel of Matthew*. London: Bloomsbury T&T Clark, 2017.

Zager, Werner. *Gottesherrschaft und Endgericht in der Verkündigung Jesu: Eine Untersuchung zur markinischen Jesusüberlieferung einschließlich der Q-Parallelen*. BZNW 82. Berlin: de Gruyter, 1996.

Zimmermann, Johannes. *Messianische Texte aus Qumran: Königliche, priesterliche und prophetische Messiasvorstellungen in den Schriftfunden von Qumran*. WUNT 104. Tübingen: Mohr Siebeck, 1998.

———. "Observations on 4Q246—the 'Son of God.'" Pages 175–90 in *Qumran-Messianism: Studies on the Messianic Expectations in the Dead Sea Scrolls*. Edited by James H. Charlesworth, Hermann Lichtenberger, and Gerbern S. Oegema. Tübingen: Mohr Siebeck, 1998.

Zimmermann, Ruben. "Eschatology and Time in the Gospel of John." Pages 292–310 in *The Oxford Handbook of Johannine Studies*. Edited by Judith M. Lieu and Martinus C. de Boer. Oxford: Oxford University Press, 2018.

———. *Puzzling the Parables of Jesus: Methods of Interpretation*. Minneapolis: Fortress, 2015.

Zizioulas, John D. *Being as Communion: Studies in Personhood in the Church.* Crestwood, NY: St. Vladimir's Seminary Press, 1985.

Zoccali, Christopher. "'And So All Israel Will Be Saved': Competing Interpretations of Romans 11.26 in Pauline Scholarship." *JSNT* 30 (2008): 289–318.

Zugmann, Michael. *Missionspredigt in nuce: Studien zu 1 Thess 1,9b–10.* Linz: Wagner, 2012.

Zwiep, A. W. *The Ascension of the Messiah in Lukan Christology.* Leiden: Brill, 1997.

Index of Subjects

Index of Scripture and Other Ancient Sources